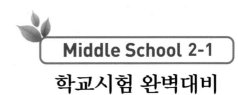

Middle School 2-1
학교시험 완벽대비

1학기 전과정
적중"100plus⁺

영어 기출문제집

중2
미래 | 최연희

Best Collection

구성과 특징

교과서의 주요 학습 내용을 중심으로 학습 영역별 특성에 맞춰 단계별로 다양한 학습 기회를 제공하여
단원별 학습능력 평가는 물론 중간 및 기말고사 시험 등에 완벽하게 대비할 수 있도록 내용을 구성

Words & Expressions

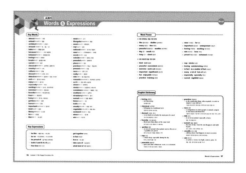

Step1 Key Words 단원별 핵심 단어 설명 및 풀이
Key Expression 단원별 핵심 숙어 및 관용어 설명
Word Power 반대 또는 비슷한 뜻 단어 배우기
English Dictionary 영어로 배우는 영어 단어

Step2 실력평가 단원별 수시평가 대비 주관식, 객관식 문제풀이

Step3 서술형 대비 학업성취도 및 수행능력평가 대비 서술형 문제풀이

Conversation

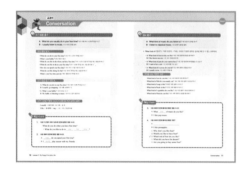

Step1 핵심 의사소통 소통에 필요한 주요 표현 방법 요약
핵심 Check 기본적인 표현 방법 및 활용능력 확인

Step2 대화문 익히기 교과서 대화문 심층 분석 및 확인

Step3 교과서 확인학습 빈칸 채우기를 통한 문장 완성 능력 확인

Step4 기본평가 시험대비 기초 학습 능력 평가

Step5 실력평가 단원별 수시평가 대비 주관식, 객관식 문제풀이

Step6 서술형 대비 학업성취도 및 수행능력평가 대비 서술형 문제풀이

Grammar

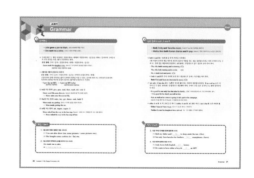

Step1 주요 문법 단원별 주요 문법 사항과 예문을 알기 쉽게 설명
핵심 Check 기본 문법사항에 대한 이해 여부 확인

Step2 기본평가 시험대비 기초 학습 능력 평가

Step3 실력평가 단원별 수시평가 대비 주관식, 객관식 문제풀이

Step4 서술형 대비 학업성취도 및 수행능력평가 대비 서술형 문제풀이

Reading

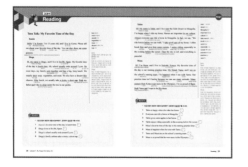

Step1 구문 분석 단원별로 제시된 문장에 대한 구문별 분석과 내용 설명
확인문제 문장에 대한 기본적인 이해와 인지능력 확인

Step2 확인학습A 빈칸 채우기를 통한 문장 완성 능력 확인

Step3 확인학습B 제시된 우리말을 영어로 완성하여 작문 능력 키우기

Step4 실력평가 단원별 수시평가 대비 주관식, 객관식 문제풀이

Step5 서술형 대비 학업성취도 및 수행능력평가 대비 서술형 문제풀이
교과서 구석구석 교과서에 나오는 기타 문장까지 완벽 학습

Composition

|영역별 핵심문제|

단어 및 어휘, 대화문, 문법, 독해 등 각 영역별 기출문제의 출제 유형을 분석하여 실전에 대비하고 연습할 수 있도록 문제를 배열

|단원별 예상문제|

기출문제를 분석한 후 새로운 시험 출제 경향을 더하여 새롭게 출제될 수 있는 문제를 포함하여 시험에 완벽하게 대비할 수 있도록 준비

|서술형 실전 및 창의사고력 문제|

학교 시험에서 점차 늘어나는 서술형 시험에 집중 대비하고 고득점을 취득하는데 만전을 기하기 위한 학습 코너

|단원별 모의고사|

영역별, 단계별 학습을 모두 마친 후 실전 연습을 위한 모의고사

교과서 파헤치기

- 단어Test1~3 영어 단어 우리말 쓰기, 우리말을 영어 단어로 쓰기, 영영풀이에 해당하는 단어와 우리말 쓰기
- 대화문Test1~2 대화문 빈칸 완성 및 전체 대화문 쓰기
- 본문Test1~5 빈칸 완성, 우리말 쓰기, 문장 배열연습, 영어 작문하기 복습 등 단계별 반복 학습을 통해 교과서 지문에 대한 완벽한 습득
- 구석구석지문Test1~2 지문 빈칸 완성 및 전문 영어로 쓰기

Lesson 1

Great Things about Yourself

🎤 의사소통 기능

- 능력 표현하기
  I'm good at jumping rope.
- 확신 표현하기
  I'm sure it's going to rain soon.

🎤 언어 형식

- 주격 관계대명사
  - She told me about her coworkers **who** had special talents.
  - She rides a super scooter **which[that]** can fly.
- 때를 나타내는 접속사
  - **While** I was walking home, I saw a woman on a scooter.
  - **After** I got home, I began to write a new graphic novel.

교과서

Words & Expressions

Key Words

- **activity** [æktívəti] 몡 활동
- **actually** [ǽktʃuəli] 뮈 실제로, 정말로
- **adventurous** [ædvéntʃərəs] 헹 모험성이 강한, 모험을 즐기는
- **awesome** [ɔ́ːsəm] 헹 경탄할 만한, 엄청난
- **bake** [beik] 동 (빵을) 굽다
- **become** [bikʌ́m] 동 ~이 되다
- **cafeteria** [kæfətíəriə] 몡 카페테리아, 구내식당
- **cartoon** [kaːrtúːn] 몡 만화, 만화 영화
- **cartoonist** [kaːrtúːnist] 몡 만화가
- **character** [kǽriktər] 몡 성격, 등장인물
- **cheerfully** [tʃíərfəli] 뮈 기분 좋게, 쾌활하게
- **cloudy** [kláudi] 헹 흐린, 구름이 잔뜩 낀
- **cookbook** [kúkbùk] 몡 요리책
- **coworker** [kóuwə̀ːrkər] 몡 함께 일하는 사람, 동료
- **danger** [déindʒər] 몡 위험
- **decide** [disáid] 동 결정하다, 결심하다
- **drawing** [drɔ́ːiŋ] 몡 그림, 데생
- **enough** [inʌ́f] 뮈 ~에 필요한 정도로, ~할 만큼 (충분히)
- **fun** [fʌn] 몡 재미 헹 재미있는, 즐거운
- **funny** [fʌ́ni] 헹 우스운, 웃기는
- **graphic novel** 만화 소설
- **hit** [hit] 동 때리다, 치다 몡 인기 작품, 히트
- **husband** [hʌ́zbənd] 몡 남편
- **janitor** [dʒǽnitər] 몡 문지기, 수위
- **joke** [dʒouk] 몡 우스개, 농담
- **jump rope** 줄넘기를 하다
- **listener** [lísnər] 몡 듣는 사람, 청자
- **model** [mádl] 동 모델로 하다 몡 모델, 모형

- **nervous** [nɔ́ːrvəs] 헹 불안해[초조해/두려워] 하는
- **novel** [návəl] 몡 소설
- **once** [wʌns] 뮈 한 번, 언젠가
- **outside** [áutsáid] 뮈 밖에(서)
- **pause** [pɔːz] 몡 (말이나 행동 등의) 멈춤
- **per** [pər] 전 각[매] ~에 대하여, ~당[마다]
- **practice** [prǽktis] 동 연습하다
- **president** [prézədənt] 몡 대통령, 회장
- **push-up** [pʌ́ʃʌ̀p] 몡 엎드려 팔굽혀펴기
- **ranger** [réindʒər] 몡 공원[삼림] 관리원
- **real** [ríːəl] 헹 진정한, 진짜의
- **recycle** [riːsáikl] 동 재활용[재생]하다
- **role model** 역할 모델, 모범이 되는 사람
- **scooter** [skúːtər] 몡 스쿠터(소형 오토바이)
- **skill** [skil] 몡 기량, 기술
- **skip stones** 물수제비뜨다
- **someone** [sʌ́mwʌn] 대 어떤 사람, 누군가
- **speaker** [spíːkər] 몡 연사, 말[이야기]하는 사람
- **speech** [spiːtʃ] 몡 연설, 담화
- **super** [súːpər] 헹 대단한, 굉장히 좋은
- **superhero** [sjúːpərhìərou] 몡 슈퍼히어로
- **sure** [ʃuər] 헹 확신하는, 확실히 아는
- **talent** [tǽlənt] 몡 재능, 탤런트
- **tooth** [tuːθ] 몡 이, 치아, 이빨
- **travel** [trǽvəl] 동 여행하다
- **unique** [juːníːk] 헹 유일무이한, 독특한
- **vote** [vout] 동 투표하다
- **wrong** [rɔ́ːŋ] 헹 틀린, 잘못된

Key Expressions

- **at last** 마침내, 드디어
- **be afraid of** ~을 두려워하다
- **be good at** ~을 잘하다
- **be good for** ~에 좋다
- **do a good job** (~을) 잘하다
- **fall asleep** 잠들다
- **give away** 거저 주다, 나누어 주다
- **Guess what?** 있잖아, 알겠니?, 맞혀 봐!

- **I guess so.** 그렇다고 생각한다.
- **make one's day** ~을 행복하게 만들다
- **out of** ~으로, ~에 의해
- **say hello to** ~에게 안부 전하다
- **such as** ~와 같은
- **take a look at** ~을 보다
- **watch out** 조심하다
- **Why don't you ~?** ~하지 그래?

Word Power

※ 동사에 -er, -or, -ist를 붙여서 행위자를 나타내는 단어

- □ speak (말하다) → speaker (연사)
- □ listen (듣다) → listener (듣는 사람)
- □ write (쓰다) → writer (작가)
- □ paint (그리다) → painter (화가)
- □ invent (발명하다) → inventor (발명가)
- □ act (연기하다) → actor (배우)

- □ direct (감독하다) → director (감독)
- □ visit (방문하다) → visitor (방문객)
- □ art (예술, 미술) → artist (예술가, 미술가)
- □ science (과학) → scientist (과학자)
- □ cartoon (만화) → cartoonist (만화가)
- □ novel (소설) → novelist (소설가)

English Dictionary

□ **attend** 참석하다
→ to be present at a meeting or event
회의나 행사에 참석하다

□ **cartoonist** 만화가
→ a person whose job is to draw cartoons for newspapers and magazines
신문과 잡지의 만화를 그리는 일을 하는 사람

□ **cafeteria** 카페테리아, 구내식당
→ a restaurant where you choose your food from a counter and take it to your table after paying for it
당신이 카운터에서 음식을 선택하고 그것에 대해 지불한 후에 테이블로 가져가는 레스토랑

□ **coworker** 함께 일하는 사람, 동료
→ the people you work with, especially people on the same job or project as you
당신이 함께 일하는 사람들, 특히 당신과 같은 일이나 프로젝트를 하는 사람들

□ **janitor** 문지기, 수위
→ a person whose job is to look after a building
직업이 건물을 관리하는 사람

□ **joke** 농담, 우스개
→ something that is said or done to make you laugh, for example a funny story
예를 들면 우스운 이야기처럼 당신을 웃게 하기 위해 말하거나 행해진 것

□ **nervous** 불안해[초조해] 하는
→ frightened or worried about something that is happening or might happen
일어나고 있거나 또는 일어날 수 있는 일에 대해 두려워하거나 걱정하는

□ **novel** 소설
→ a long written story about imaginary people and events
상상의 사람들과 사건에 대해 쓴 긴 이야기

□ **pause** (말이나 행동 등의) 멈춤
→ a short period when you stop doing something before continuing
무언가를 계속하기 전에 하는 것을 멈추는 짧은 시간

□ **recycle** 재활용[재생]하다
→ to process things that have already been used, such as bottles or sheets of paper so that they can be used again
병이나 종이와 같이 이미 사용된 것을 다시 사용될 수 있도록 처리하다

□ **scooter** 스쿠터(소형 오토바이)
→ a small light motorcycle which has a low seat
좌석이 낮은 작고 가벼운 오토바이

□ **speech** 연설, 담화
→ the ability to speak or the act of speaking
말하는 능력 또는 말하는 행위

□ **speaker** 연사, 말[이야기]하는 사람
→ a person who is making a speech or giving a talk
연설을 하거나 이야기를 하는 사람

□ **second** (시간 단위인) 초
→ one of the sixty parts that a minute is divided into
1분이 나뉘어진 60개의 부분 중의 하나

□ **tooth** 이, 이빨
→ the hard white object in your mouth, which you use for biting and chewing
당신이 물고 씹는 데 사용하는 당신의 입안에 있는 딱딱한 하얀 물체

01 다음 중 단어의 성격이 <u>다른</u> 하나는?

① writer   ② scooter

③ speaker   ④ painter

⑤ listener

 중요

02 다음 빈칸에 알맞은 말이 바르게 짝지어진 것은?

> • He was standing in front _____ me in the line.
>
> • Eating too many snacks is not good _____ your health.

① of – at   ② of – for

③ at – in   ④ at – with

⑤ to – over

중요

03 다음 영영풀이에 해당하는 단어로 알맞은 것은?

> to go from one place to another, often to a place that is far away

① stay   ② spend

③ carry   ④ travel

⑤ dwell

서답형

04 다음 짝지어진 단어의 관계가 같도록 빈칸에 알맞은 말을 쓰시오.

> boy : girl = husband : _____

05 다음 우리말에 맞게 빈칸에 알맞은 것은?

> 그들은 서로 인사한다.
> ➡ They say hello _____ each other.

① to   ② of

③ at   ④ for

⑤ with

서답형

06 다음 영영풀이에 해당하는 단어를 쓰시오.

> the possibility that someone may be harmed or killed

➡ _____

서답형

07 다음 우리말에 맞게 빈칸에 알맞은 말을 쓰시오.

> 나는 무엇을 입을 것인지 결정할 수가 없어.
> ➡ I can't _____ what to wear.

08 다음 빈칸에 공통으로 알맞은 것은?

> • The man is afraid _____ the mouse.
> • There is a lot _____ water in the bottle.

① in   ② of

③ up   ④ about

⑤ at

01 다음 짝지어진 두 단어의 관계가 같도록 빈칸에 알맞은 말을 쓰시오.

(1) listen : listener = act : _____

(2) art : artist = cartoon : _____

(3) invent : _____ = write : writer

02 다음 우리말에 맞게 빈칸에 알맞은 말을 쓰시오.

(1) 바이러스들은 독감과 같은 질병을 일으킨다.
➡ Viruses cause diseases _____ _____ the flu.

(2) 나는 Erica가 잘할 거라고 믿는다.
➡ I think that Erica will _____ _____ _____ _____.

(3) 제가 가서 그 집을 한 번 보면 어떻겠습니까?
➡ Why don't I just go take _____ _____ _____ the house?

03 다음 빈칸에 들어갈 알맞은 말을 〈보기〉에서 골라 쓰시오.

┌─ 보기 ─┐
per   give   fun   unique

(1) We had a lot of _____ at Sarah's party.

(2) He will _____ an important speech tomorrow.

(3) That will be 50 dollars _____ day.

(4) Everyone's fingerprints are _____.

04 다음 괄호 안의 단어를 문맥에 맞게 고쳐 쓰시오.

(1) The next night was dark and _____. (cloud)

(2) She felt _____ on her wedding day. (nerve)

(3) Some robots do _____ jobs for humans. (danger)

05 다음 빈칸에 알맞은 말을 〈보기〉에서 골라 쓰시오.

┌─ 보기 ─┐
fall asleep   good for
give away   good at

(1) Tom is _____ singing.

(2) Milk is _____ your health.

(3) I think he will _____ food to hungry people.

(4) He used to _____ after drinking a glass of beer.

06 다음 영영풀이에 해당하는 단어를 주어진 철자로 시작하여 쓰시오.

(1) h_____ : the man a woman is married to

(2) d_____ : to choose to do something, usually after you have thought carefully about the other possibilities

교과서
Conversation

1 능력 표현하기

> **A** What are you good at? 넌 무엇을 잘하니?
> **B** I'm good at skipping stones. 나는 물수제비뜨기를 잘해.

■ be good at은 '~을 잘하다, ~에 능숙하다'라는 의미로 at 뒤에는 명사 혹은 동사에 -ing를 붙인 동명사가 온다. be good at 대신 조동사 can을 쓸 수도 있다.

- I am good at playing basketball. 나는 농구를 잘해.
  = I can play basketball well.

■ be not good at ~은 어떤 일을 할 능력이 없는 것을 표현할 때 사용하는 표현이다. be poor at이나 조동사 can't[cannot]를 쓸 수도 있다.

- I'm not good at playing chess. 나는 체스를 잘 못해.
  = I'm poor at playing chess.
  = I can't play chess well.

■ 상대방의 능력 여부를 묻는 표현으로 'how+to부정사'의 구문을 쓰기도 하며 '~하는 법'의 뜻이다.

- Do you know how to ride a bike? 너는 자전거를 탈 줄 아니?
  = Can you ride a bike?

- A: Do you know how to grow these plants? 이 식물들을 어떻게 키우는지 아세요?
  B: No, I don't. 아니요.

핵심 Check

1. 다음 우리말과 일치하도록 빈칸에 알맞은 말을 쓰시오.

   (1) **A:** I'm making gimbap. (난 김밥을 만들고 있어.)

   B: Wow! You're _____ _____ making gimbap. (와! 너 김밥 잘 만드는구나.)

   (2) **A:** Can you show me _____ _____ use computers?

   (컴퓨터 사용하는 법을 내게 알려 줄래?)

   B: I'm sorry. I'm _____ _____ using computers. (미안해. 난 컴퓨터 사용이 서툴러.)

   (3) **A:** Do you know _____ _____ _____? (너는 수영할 줄 아니?)

   B: No, I don't know. (아니, 몰라.)

2 **확신 표현하기**

> **A** It's so cloudy. 날씨가 아주 흐려.
>
> **B** I'm sure it's going to rain soon. 곧 비가 올 것이 틀림없어.

■ I'm sure ~.는 '나는 ~을 확신한다.'라는 의미로, 어떤 일이나 상황에 대해 확신하고 있음을 나타낼 때 사용하는 표현이다.

비슷한 표현

- It's certain that he is ill. 그가 아픈 것이 확실해.
- Certainly[Surely], Ann will succeed. 분명히 Ann은 성공할 거야.
- It's obvious that she is an actress. 그녀가 배우인 것은 명백해.
- There's no question about that. 그것에 대해서는 의심할 것이 없어.

■ 상대방이 확신하고 있는지의 여부를 물을 때는 Are you sure?로 물으며, 확신하고 있으면 Yes, I'm sure.로, 확신하고 있지 않으면 No, I'm not sure.로 답할 수 있다.

- A: What am I doing? 내가 무엇을 하고 있게?
  B: I think you're cleaning the window. 나는 네가 창문을 닦고 있다고 생각해.
  A: Are you sure? 확실해?
  B: Yes. I'm sure that you're cleaning the window. 응. 나는 네가 창문을 닦고 있다고 확신해.

비슷한 표현

- Are you certain? 확실하니?
- Are you serious? 정말이니?

- A: What am I doing? 내가 무엇을 하고 있게?
  B: I think you're singing a song. 나는 네가 노래를 부르고 있다고 생각해.
  A: Are you sure? 확실해?
  B: Yes, I'm sure. / No, I'm not sure. 응. 확실해. / 아니, 확실하지 않아.

핵심 Check

2. 다음 우리말과 일치하도록 빈칸에 알맞은 말을 쓰시오.

(1) **A:** I hope my mom will get better. (우리 엄마 건강이 좋아지시면 좋겠어.)

　B: Don't worry. I _____ _____ your mom will get better.

　(걱정하지 마. 틀림없이 너의 엄마 건강이 좋아지실 거야.)

(2) **A:** _____ you _____ that he'll win the game? (그가 그 게임에 이길 거라고 확신하니?)

　B: Yes, I am. (응. 그래.)

Listen & Speak 1 A-1

B: ❶What are you doing, Nami?

G: ❷I'm making a smart phone case out of my old jeans.

B: Wow! ❸You're good at recycling old things.

G: Thanks. I like recycling. ❹It's fun, and it's also good for our Earth.

B: 나미야, 뭐 하고 있니?

G: 오래된 청바지로 스마트폰 케이스를 만들고 있어.

B: 와! 너 오래된 것들을 재활용하는 것을 잘하는구나.

B: 고마워. 나는 재활용하는 것을 좋아해. 그것은 재미있고, 우리의 지구에도 좋아.

❶ 의문사로 시작되는 진행형 의문문: '의문사+be동사+주어+-ing ∼?'의 구문을 취한다.

❷ out of: ∼으로

❸ be good at+동명사: ∼을 잘하다

❹ It은 인칭대명사로 앞에 나오는 recycling을 받는다. be good for: ∼에 좋다

Check(√) True or False

(1) The boy is good at recycling old things. T ☐ F ☐

(2) Recycling is good for our Earth. T ☐ F ☐

 Listen & Speak 2 A-1

B: Hi, Cindy. ❶Is something wrong?

G: ❷I have to give a speech in front of the whole school. I'm so nervous.

B: Don't worry. You're a very good speaker. ❸I'm sure you'll do a good job.

G: Thanks, Minho. I feel much better now.

B: 안녕, Cindy. 무슨 일 있니?

G: 학교 전체 학생들 앞에서 연설을 해야 해. 아주 긴장이 돼.

B: 걱정하지 마. 넌 말을 아주 잘하잖아. 분명히 잘할 거야.

G: 고마워, 민호야. 이제 기분이 훨씬 좋아졌어.

❶ 상대방이 기분이 좋지 않아 보일 때 묻는 표현으로 What's the matter (with you)?로 바꿔 쓸 수 있다.

❷ have to: ∼해야 한다 / give a speech: 연설하다 / in front of: ∼ 앞에서

❸ I'm sure (that) ∼.: 나는 ∼을 확신해. / do a good job: 잘하다

Check(√) True or False

(3) The girl doesn't look so nervous. T ☐ F ☐

(4) The girl speaks very well. T ☐ F ☐

 Listen & Speak 2 A-2

G: Tomorrow is my mom's birthday. ❶What should I do for her?

B: ❷Why don't you bake a cake for her? You're good at baking.

G: That's a good idea. ❸I hope my mom will like my cake.

B: I'm sure your mom will love it.

G: 내일은 우리 엄마의 생일이야. 내가 그녀를 위해 무엇을 해야 할까?

B: 너의 엄마를 위해 케이크를 굽는 건 어때? 넌 빵을 잘 굽잖아.

G: 좋은 생각이야. 엄마가 내 케이크를 좋아하셨으면 좋겠다.

B: 너의 엄마는 분명히 아주 좋아하실 거야.

❶ should: ∼해야 한다

❷ Why don't you ∼?: ∼하지 그래?(제안을 나타내는 표현) / bake a cake: 케이크를 굽다

❸ I hope (that) ∼.: 나는 ∼하기를 바란다.

Check(√) True or False

(5) Tomorrow is the girl's mother's birthday. T ☐ F ☐

(6) The boy is good at baking. T ☐ F ☐

Listen & Speak 1 A-2

B: Hello, everyone. I'm Kim Yujin. ❶I want to be your class president. ❷I'm a good listener and always try to help others. ❸I'm also good at planning fun school activities. ❹I'll work hard for our class, so please vote for me. ❺Thank you for listening!

❶ want to: ～하기를 원하다
❷ I'm a good listener = I'm good at listening / try to: ～하기 위해 애쓰다 / others = other people
❸ fun: 재미있는
❹ so: 그래서, 그러니까 / vote for: ～에 찬성하는 투표를 하다
❺ Thank you for -ing: ～해 주어서 감사합니다

Communicate: A. Listen and Answer

Yuri: What are you doing, Jaden?
Jaden: ❶I'm drawing cartoons.
Yuri: Really? ❷Can I take a look at them?
Jaden: ❸No, not yet.
Yuri: ❹Why not? ❺You can show me a few, can't you?
Jaden: ❻Well, I guess so.
Yuri: (pause) Ha, ha, ha! Awesome! I like your cartoons. You're really good at drawing.
Jaden: ❼Do you think so? ❽I want to be a cartoonist, but I don't think my drawing skills are good enough.
Yuri: Your cartoons are really funny, and you have unique characters. I'm sure you'll be a great cartoonist.
Jaden: Thank you, Yuri. ❾You just made my day.

❶ be동사+-ing: 현재진행형
❷ take a look at: ～을 보다
❸ No, not yet.=No, you cannot take a look at them yet.
❹ Why not?=Why can't I take a look at them?
❺ a few=a few cartoons / can't you?: 그렇지 않니?(확인을 위한 부가의문문)
❻ I guess so.=I guess I can show you a few.
❼ Do you think so?=Do you think that I'm good at drawing?
❽ want to: ～하기를 원하다 / are good enough: enough는 부사로 형용사를 수식할 때는 그 뒤에 위치한다.
❾ make one's day: ～을 행복하게 만들다

Communicate: B. Make Your Own Dialogue

A: ❶Why don't you join our musical theater club? ❷You're good at singing.
B: ❸Well, I'd like to, but I don't think I'm good at acting or dancing.
A: Don't worry. We can teach you. ❹I'm sure you'll learn fast. Just join us.
B: O.K. I'll think about it.

❶ Why don't you ～?: ～하는 게 어때?(상대방에게 제안을 하는 표현) ❷ be good at+동명사: ～을 잘하다 ❸ I'd like to = I'd like to join your musical theater club ❹ I'm sure (that) ～.: 나는 ～을 확신한다.

Progress Check 1

B: What are you doing?
G: ❶I'm making pizza for dinner.
B: Wow! ❷You're really good at cooking!
G: Thanks.

❶ for dinner: 저녁 식사를 위해
❷ You're really good at cooking!=You can cook really well!

Progress Check 2

B: ❶Is something wrong?
G: ❷I have to give a speech in English. ❸I'm so nervous.
B: Don't worry. ❹Practice your speech in front of your family. ❺I'm sure you'll do a good job.
G: Thank you. ❻I'll try.

❶ Is something wrong? = What's the matter (with you)? ❷ give a speech in English: 영어로 연설을 하다 ❸ nervous: 불안해 하는, 초조해 하는 ❹ 동사원형으로 시작하는 명령문 ❺ I'm sure (that) ～.: 나는 ～을 확신해. ❻ I'll try.: 그렇게 해볼게.

Progress Check 3

W: ❶Everybody is good at something. ❷Some people are good at drawing. ❸Other people are good at singing. ❹What are you good at?

❶ everybody는 부정대명사로 단수동사로 받는다.
❷, ❸ Some people ～. Other people ...: 어떤 사람들은 ～한다. 또 어떤 사람들은 …한다
❹ 의문대명사 What이 전치사 at의 목적어이다.

● 다음 우리말과 일치하도록 빈칸에 알맞은 말을 쓰시오.

Listen & Speak 1 A. Listen and Check

1. **B:** _____ are you _____, Nami?

   G: I'm _____ a smart phone case _____ of my old jeans.

   B: Wow! You're _____ at _____ old things.

   G: Thanks. I like _____. It's _____, and it's also _____ for our Earth.

2. **B:** Hello, _____. I'm Kim Yujin. I want to _____ your class _____. I'm a good _____ and always _____ to help others. I'm also _____ at planning _____ school activities. I'll _____ hard for our _____, so please _____ for me. Thank you for _____!

해석

1. B: 나미야, 뭐 하고 있니?
   G: 오래된 청바지로 스마트폰 케이스를 만들고 있어.
   B: 와! 너 오래된 것들을 재활용하는 것을 잘하는구나.
   G: 고마워. 나는 재활용하는 것을 좋아해. 그것은 재미있고, 우리의 지구에도 좋아.

2. B: 여러분, 안녕하세요. 저는 김유진입니다. 저는 여러분의 반 학급회장이 되고 싶습니다. 저는 남의 말을 잘 경청하고 항상 다른 사람들을 도우려고 노력합니다. 저는 재미있는 학교 활동 계획도 잘합니다. 저는 우리 반을 위해 열심히 일하겠으니 저에게 투표해 주세요. 들어주셔서 감사합니다!

Listen & Speak 2 A. Listen and Check

1. **B:** _____, Cindy. Is something _____?

   G: I _____ to give a speech in _____ of the whole school. I'm so _____.

   B: Don't _____. You're a very good _____. I'm _____ you'll do a good _____.

   G: _____, Minho. I feel much _____ now.

2. **G:** Tomorrow is my mom's _____. What _____ I do for her?

   B: Why _____ you bake a cake _____ her? You're _____ at baking.

   G: That's a good _____. I _____ my mom will _____ my cake.

   B: I'm _____ your mom will _____ it.

1. B: 안녕, Cindy. 무슨 일 있니?
   G: 난 학교 전체 학생 앞에서 연설을 해야 해. 아주 긴장이 돼.
   B: 걱정하지 마. 너는 말을 아주 잘하잖아. 분명히 잘할 거야.
   G: 고마워, 민호야. 이제 기분이 훨씬 좋아졌어.

2. G: 내일은 우리 엄마의 생일이야. 내가 엄마를 위해 무엇을 해야 할까?
   B: 너의 엄마를 위해 케이크를 굽는 건 어때? 넌 빵을 잘 굽잖아.
   G: 좋은 생각이야. 엄마가 내 케이크를 좋아하셨으면 좋겠다.
   B: 너의 엄마는 분명히 아주 좋아하실 거야.

Communicate A. Listen and Answer

1. **Yuri:** _____ are you _____, Jaden?

   Jaden: I'm drawing _____.

   Yuri: Really? _____ I take a _____ at them?

   Jaden: No, not _____.

   Yuri: Why _____? You can _____ me a few, _____ you?

   Jaden: Well, I _____ so.

   Yuri: (*pause*) Ha, ha, ha! Awesome! I like your _____. You're really _____ at _____.

   Jaden: Do you think _____? I want to _____ a cartoonist, but I don't _____ my drawing skills are good _____.

   Yuri: Your cartoons are really _____, and you have _____ characters. I'm _____ you'll be a great _____.

   Jaden: _____ you, Yuri. You just made my _____.

2. **A:** Why _____ you join our _____ theater club? You're good at _____.

   B: Well, I'd _____ to, but I don't _____ I'm _____ at acting or dancing.

   A: Don't _____. We can _____ you. I'm _____ you'll learn fast. Just _____ us.

   B: O.K. I'll _____ about it.

Progress Check

1. **B:** What are you _____?

   G: I'm _____ pizza for dinner.

   B: Wow! You're _____ good _____ cooking!

   G: Thanks.

2. **B:** Is something _____?

   G: I have to _____ a speech _____ English. I'm so _____.

   B: Don't _____. _____ your speech in _____ of your family. I'm _____ you'll do a good _____.

   G: Thank you. I'll _____.

3. **W:** Everybody is good at _____. _____ people are good _____ drawing. _____ people are _____ at singing. _____ are you good at?

해석

1. 유리: 너 뭐 하고 있니, Jaden?
   Jaden: 만화를 그리고 있어.
   유리: 정말? 내가 그것들을 봐도 되니?
   Jaden: 아니, 아직은 아니야.
   유리: 왜 안 되는데? 몇 개 보여줄 수 있지, 안 그래?
   Jaden: 음, 그럴 수 있지.
   유리: (멈춤) 하, 하, 하! 대단해! 너의 만화가 마음에 들어. 넌 그림을 정말 잘 그리는구나.
   Jaden: 그렇게 생각하니? 나는 만화가가 되고 싶지만, 내 그림 그리는 기술이 충분히 능숙하지 않다고 생각해.
   유리: 네 만화들은 정말 재미있고, 독특한 캐릭터를 가지고 있어. 나는 네가 훌륭한 만화가가 될 거라고 확신해.
   Jaden: 고마워, 유리야. 넌 날 행복하게 해줬어.

2. A: 우리 뮤지컬 연극 동아리에 가입하는 게 어때? 노래를 잘하는구나.
   B: 음, 그러고 싶지만, 연기나 춤을 잘 못해.
   A: 걱정하지 마. 우리가 가르쳐 줄 수 있어. 나는 네가 빨리 배울 거라고 확신해. 그냥 우리와 함께 해.
   B: 좋아. 생각해 볼게.

1. B: 너 뭐 하고 있니?
   G: 저녁으로 피자를 만들고 있어.
   B: 와! 넌 요리를 정말 잘하는구나!
   G: 고마워.

2. B: 무슨 문제 있어?
   G: 영어로 연설을 해야 해. 아주 긴장이 돼.
   B: 걱정하지 마. 가족 앞에서 연설을 연습해 봐. 넌 분명히 잘할 거야.
   G: 고마워. 그렇게 해볼게.

3. W: 모든 사람은 잘하는 것이 있습니다. 어떤 사람들은 그림을 잘 그립니다. 또 어떤 사람들은 노래를 잘 부릅니다. 당신은 무엇을 잘합니까?

01 다음 대화의 빈칸에 들어갈 말로 알맞은 것은?

> A: Are you _____ at skiing?
> B: No, I'm not. But I can skate very well.

① bad   ② good   ③ well
④ fine   ⑤ better

02 다음 두 문장이 공통으로 의도하는 것은?

> • I'm sure that you're cleaning the window.
> • Surely, Ann is playing the piano.

① 확신하기   ② 허락하기
③ 변명하기   ④ 충고하기
⑤ 사과하기

03 다음 두 문장의 뜻이 같도록 빈칸에 알맞은 것은?

> Peter can play musical instruments well.
> = Peter _____ playing musical instruments.

① is well with   ② is better to
③ is good at   ④ is as well as
⑤ is good for

» musical instrument 악기

04 다음 대화의 빈칸에 알맞은 것은? (2개)

> A: What am I doing?
> B: I think you're singing a song.
> A: _____
> B: Yes. I'm sure that you're singing a song.

① Are you sure?   ② Are you right?
③ Are you certain?   ④ Are you wrong?
⑤ Are you satisfied?

01 다음 대화를 의미가 통하도록 알맞게 배열한 것은?

> (A) Wow! You're good at recycling old things.
> (B) What are you doing, Nami?
> (C) I'm making a smart phone case out of my old jeans.
> (D) Thanks. I like recycling. It's fun, and it's also good for our Earth.

① (A) – (D) – (B) – (C)
② (B) – (C) – (A) – (D)
③ (C) – (D) – (B) – (A)
④ (D) – (B) – (C) – (A)
⑤ (D) – (C) – (B) – (A)

02 다음 문장과 바꾸어 쓸 수 있는 말은?

> Do you know how to use this machine?

① Are you using this machine?
② Why do you use this machine?
③ Can you use this machine?
④ May I use this machine?
⑤ Did you use this machine?

서답형
03 다음 우리말에 맞도록 빈칸에 알맞은 말을 쓰시오.

> 너는 그것이 네 개의 다리를 가지고 있다고 확신하니?
> ➡ Are you _____ that it has four legs?

서답형
04 다음 대화의 밑줄 친 말을 주어진 표현을 이용하여 영작하시오.

> A: Can you play the guitar?
> B: No, 나는 기타를 잘 못 쳐. (be good at)

➡ _____

05 다음 〈보기〉의 문장과 의미가 같은 것은?

> ┤ 보기 ├
> I'm sure that he is alive.

① I think that he is alive.
② I don't know if he is alive.
③ I know where he lives.
④ It's certain that he is alive.
⑤ I've heard that he is alive.

06 다음 짝지어진 대화 중 어색한 것은?

① A: Can you fly?
　 B: Sure. I am good at flying.
② A: Are you sure that Jake is honest?
　 B: Of course. He never lies.
③ A: Sally drinks ten glasses of milk every day.
　 B: That's surprising!
④ A: You play the violin so beautifully!
　 B: I don't know how to play the violin.
⑤ A: Did you paint this?
　 B: Yes, I am good at painting.

[07~11] 다음 담화문을 읽고, 물음에 답하시오.

> B: Hello, everyone. I'm Kim Yujin. I want @to be your class president. ⓑI'm a good listener and always try to help others. I'm also good ⓒ planning fun school activities. I'll work hard for our class, so please vote for me. Thank you for ⓓlisten!

07 위 담화문의 밑줄 친 @와 용법이 같은 것은?

① He has made a promise to help me.
② You are foolish to believe the rumor.
③ They sent some people to live on the planet.
④ We decided to go fishing in the river.
⑤ I awoke to find myself lying on the floor.

서답형
08 위 담화문의 밑줄 친 ⓑ와 같은 뜻이 되도록 다음 문장의 빈칸에 알맞은 말을 쓰시오.

> I _____ to others _____

중요
09 위 담화문의 빈칸 ⓒ에 알맞은 것은?

① to   ② at
③ of   ④ for
⑤ with

서답형
10 위 담화문의 밑줄 친 ⓓ를 알맞은 형으로 고치시오.

➡ _____

11 위 담화문의 내용으로 알 수 없는 것은?

① 김유진은 반 학급회장이 되기를 원한다.
② 김유진은 남의 말을 잘 듣는다.
③ 김유진은 남을 돕기 위해 애쓴다.
④ 김유진은 공부를 열심히 한다.
⑤ 김유진은 자신을 반 학급회장으로 뽑아 달라고 말하고 있다.

[12~14] 다음 대화를 읽고, 물음에 답하시오.

> B: Hi, Cindy. @Is something wrong?
> G: I have to _ⓑ_ a speech in front of the whole school. I'm so nervous.
> B: Don't worry. You're a very good speaker. ⓒI'm sure you'll do a good job.
> G: Thanks, Minho. I feel much better now.

서답형
12 위 대화의 밑줄 친 @와 같은 뜻이 되도록 다음 문장의 빈칸에 알맞은 말을 쓰시오.

> What's the _____ _____ you?

중요
13 위 대화의 빈칸 ⓑ에 알맞지 <u>않은</u> 것은?

① give   ② make
③ take   ④ deliver
⑤ bring

서답형
14 위 대화의 밑줄 친 ⓒ를 우리말로 옮기시오.

➡ _____

01 다음 괄호 안에 주어진 단어를 이용하여 우리말을 영어로 옮기시오.

(1) 그는 중국어를 잘한다. (good)

➡ _____

(2) 나는 방에 두 명의 소년이 있다고 확신해.
(sure, there)

➡ _____

(3) 너 쿠키를 어떻게 만드는 줄 아니?
(how, make, cookies)

➡ _____

02 다음 대화의 밑줄 친 우리말을 영어로 옮기시오.

A: Do you know how to make gimbap?
B: 나 요리 잘 못해.

➡ _____

03 다음 대화를 의미가 통하도록 알맞게 배열하시오.

(A) Thanks.
(B) What are you doing?
(C) Wow! You're really good at cooking!
(D) I'm making pizza for dinner.

➡ _____

04 다음 우리말과 일치하도록 괄호 안에 주어진 단어를 사용하여 문장을 완성하시오.

A: Are you sure?
B: Yes. 나는 그가 시험에 합격할 거라고 확신해.
(sure, that, exam)

➡ _____

[05~07] 다음 대화를 읽고, 물음에 답하시오.

G: Tomorrow is my mom's birthday. What should I do for her?
B: ⓐWhy don't you bake a cake for her? You're good ⓑ_____ baking.
G: ⓒThat's a good idea. I hope my mom will like my cake.
B: I'm sure your mom will love it.

05 위 대화의 밑줄 친 ⓐ를 다음과 같이 바꿔 쓸 때 빈칸에 알맞은 말을 쓰시오.

How _____ _____ a cake for her?

06 위 대화의 빈칸 ⓑ에 알맞은 전치사를 쓰시오.

➡ _____

07 위 대화의 밑줄 친 ⓒ가 가리키는 것을 우리말로 쓰시오.

➡ _____

Grammar

1 주격 관계대명사

> • She told me about her coworkers **who** had special talents.
> 그녀는 내게 특별한 재능을 가지고 있는 자기 동료들에 대해 말했다.
>
> • This is the book **which** changed my view of life. 이것은 나의 인생관을 변화시킨 책이다.
>
> • Hold the door open for someone **that** is behind you.
> 여러분 뒤에 있는 사람을 위하여 문을 열어 두세요.

■ 관계대명사는 선행사인 명사를 대신하는 일종의 대명사이면서 이 대명사가 이끄는 절을 접속시킨다는 점에서 「접속사+대명사」의 기능을 동시에 갖는다. 관계대명사가 이끄는 관계사절에 의하여 수식받는 명사·대명사를 선행사라 하며 이때 관계사절은 선행사인 명사를 수식하므로 형용사절이다. 관계대명사는 선행사에 따라 which, who, that 등을 쓴다.

선행사	주격	소유격	목적격
사람	who	whose	whom / who
사물	which	whose / of which	which
사람, 동물, 사물	that	-	that

■ 주격 관계대명사는 관계대명사가 주어의 역할을 하는 경우에 쓰이며, 뒤따르는 동사는 선행사의 수에 일치시킨다.
   • The boy **who** is wearing a blue shirt is my little brother. 파란색 셔츠를 입고 있는 소년은 내 남동생이다.
   • This is a restaurant **which** is famous for pizza. 이것은 피자로 유명한 식당이다.

■ **주격 관계대명사 who, which, that**: 관계대명사가 이끄는 문장에서 주어 역할을 한다. 사람을 설명할 때는 「사람+who+동사」의 형태이고, 사물이나 동물을 설명할 때는 「사물[동물]+which+동사」의 형태이다. that은 사람, 사물, 동물에 모두 쓰인다.
   • Mrs. Parker is a teacher **who[that]** is from Canada. Parker 씨는 캐나다에서 오신 선생님이다.
   • Look at the robots **that[which]** are playing soccer. 축구를 하고 있는 로봇들을 봐.

cf. 선행사 앞에 all, every, no, any, the same, the only, the+최상급/서수 등이 올 경우, 보통 that을 사용한다.
   • Jake is the only student **that** can speak Korean. Jake는 한국어를 말할 수 있는 유일한 학생이다.

핵심 Check

1. 다음 괄호 안에서 알맞은 것을 고르시오.
   (1) Do you know the lady (who / which) is sitting on the bench?
   (2) This is the smart phone (who / which) was made in Korea.
   (3) The man (who / which) I met on the street is Mina's father.
   (4) This is a novel (who / which) was written in easy English.
   (5) Mr. White is a teacher (who / which) teaches English.

② 때를 나타내는 접속사

> • **While** I was walking home, I saw a woman on a scooter.
> 나는 집에 걸어가는 동안 스쿠터를 탄 여인을 보았다.
>
> • **After** I got home, I began to write a new graphic novel.
> 나는 집에 도착한 후에 새로운 만화 소설을 쓰기 시작했다.
>
> • You should come back **before** it gets dark. 너는 어두워지기 전에 돌아와야 한다.

■ while

while은 '~하는 동안'의 뜻으로 뒤에는 상태를 나타내는 동사나 진행형이 올 때가 많다. while이 이끄는 부사절은 주절의 앞이나 뒤 어느 쪽에도 올 수 있다.

• **While** I'm out, be careful of the wolf. 내가 없는 동안 늑대를 조심하렴.
• I often sing **while** I'm taking a shower. 나는 샤워를 하는 동안 종종 노래를 부른다.

■ when

when은 '~할 때'의 뜻으로 while과 비슷한 의미를 나타낸다. when이 이끄는 부사절도 주절의 앞이나 뒤 어느 쪽에도 올 수 있다.

• It was snowing **when** I got up. 내가 일어났을 때 눈이 오고 있었다.
• **When** my aunt was young, she was rich. 나의 이모는 젊었을 때 부자였다.

■ before, after

before와 after는 때를 나타내는 접속사로 문장의 순서를 바꿔 같은 의미를 나타내기도 한다.

A before B: B하기 전에 A를 하다 (A가 먼저 → B가 나중)
A after B: B한 후에 A를 하다 (B가 먼저 → A가 나중)

• I eat breakfast **before** I go to school. 나는 학교에 가기 전에 아침밥을 먹는다.
• **After** I washed the dishes, I watched TV. 나는 설거지를 한 후에 텔레비전을 보았다.
• I washed my hands **before** I had dinner. 나는 저녁을 먹기 전에 손을 씻었다.
• I had dinner **after** I washed my hands. 나는 손을 씻은 후에 저녁을 먹었다.

■ 전치사로 쓰이는 before, after

• Take a bath **before** you go to bed. [접속사] 잠자리에 들기 전에 목욕을 해라.
  = Take a bath **before** going to bed. [전치사]
• I went to bed **after** I took a bath [접속사] 나는 목욕을 한 후에 잠자리에 들었다.
  = I went to bed **after** taking a bath. [전치사]

핵심 Check

2. 다음 괄호 안에서 알맞은 것을 고르시오.

(1) A man visited Ms. White (if / while) she was out.

(2) I'm going to go to the party (before / after) I put on this pretty dress.

(3) (Before / After) he goes to bed, he brushes his teeth.

01 다음 두 문장을 한 문장으로 만들 때 빈칸에 알맞은 말을 쓰시오. (that은 쓸 수 없음.)

stage 무대
necklace 목걸이

(1) I know the girl. She is dancing on the stage.

➡ I know the girl _____ is dancing on the stage.

(2) This is the necklace. I got it from Mike.

➡ This is the necklace _____ I got from Mike.

(3) My uncle lives in a house. It has a beautiful garden.

➡ My uncle lives in a house _____ has a beautiful garden.

(4) The boy is wearing a blue shirt. He is my little brother.

➡ The boy _____ is wearing a blue shirt is my little brother.

(5) Turkey is a country. It has many interesting things.

➡ Turkey is a country _____ has many interesting things.

02 다음 우리말과 일치하도록 빈칸에 알맞은 말을 쓰시오.

hurt 다치다
free 한가한
enter ~에 들어가다

(1) 나는 어제 축구를 하는 동안 다쳤다.

➡ I hurt myself _____ I was playing soccer yesterday.

(2) Jenny는 한가할 때 책을 읽는다.

➡ Jenny reads books _____ she has free time.

(3) Kirk는 숙제를 마친 후 네게 전화할 거야.

➡ Kirk will call you _____ he finishes his homework.

(4) 나는 방에 들어가기 전에 신발을 벗는다.

➡ I take off my shoes _____ I enter the room.

03 다음 괄호 안에서 알맞은 것을 고르시오.

water 물을 주다
flow 흐르다

(1) Look at the girl (who / which) is watering a flower.

(2) Those are the dolls (who / which) were made by my grandmother.

(3) I have a friend (which / who) lives in China.

(4) Kathy is the girl (that / which) is playing curling.

(5) The Thames is the river (who / which) flows through London.

01 다음 빈칸에 들어갈 말이 바르게 짝지어진 것은?

> • I was late _____ the bus broke down.
> • You can go swimming _____ I'm having lunch.

① when – if ② when – as
③ if – because ④ because – though
⑤ because – while

02 중요 다음 대화의 빈칸 ⓐ, ⓑ에 들어갈 말이 순서대로 짝지어진 것은?

> A: Do you know the girl ___ⓐ___ is sitting next to Mr. Brown?
> B: Yes. She is Kevin's sister. Her hobby is ___ⓑ___ pretty dolls.

① who – collecting ② whom – collecting
③ which – to collect ④ whose – collecting
⑤ whose – to collect

03 다음 두 문장이 같은 뜻이 되도록 빈칸에 알맞은 것은?

> Somebody knocked on the door before I finished the shower.
> = I finished the shower _____ somebody knocked on the door.

① before ② while
③ because ④ until
⑤ after

04 서답형 다음 밑줄 친 부분을 어법상 바르게 고쳐 쓰시오.

(1) He's the boy <u>which</u> broke the window.

　➡ _____

(2) This is the biggest dog <u>whom</u> I have ever seen.

　➡ _____

05 중요 다음 밑줄 친 ①~⑤ 중 어법상 어색한 것은?

> You ①should ②come here ③before ④it ⑤will get dark.

①　　②　　③　　④　　⑤

[06~07] 다음 문장의 빈칸에 알맞은 것을 고르시오.

06
> Do you know the man _____ is running after a dog?

① how ② who
③ whom ④ which
⑤ whose

07
> This is the building _____ was built in 1790.

① who ② how
③ what ④ which
⑤ where

08 다음 중 빈칸에 while[While]이 들어가기에 적절한 문장은?

① _____ you do your homework, you can play.
② The girl plays the guitar _____ she is lonely.
③ _____ it rains tomorrow, we will stay home.
④ _____ it was very warm, she didn't take off her coat.
⑤ Would you clean my room _____ I'm out?

09 다음 빈칸에 알맞은 말이 순서대로 짝지어진 것은?

• Susan is the girl _____ will go to Europe with me.
• The dolls _____ are on the sofa are my sister's.

① who – which   ② whom – that
③ which – who   ④ which – which
⑤ whose – that

10 다음 중 밑줄 친 부분의 쓰임이 나머지와 <u>다른</u> 것은?

① Some people have long hair <u>while</u> others have short hair.
② <u>While</u> I was sleeping, I heard some strange sounds.
③ You can use my computer <u>while</u> I am out.
④ <u>While</u> I was in Rome, I visited some museums.
⑤ I was very happy <u>while</u> I was playing baseball.

11 다음 빈칸에 공통으로 알맞은 것은?

• My dad bought me a bag _____ was black.
• She would like to have a job _____ uses her talents.

① what   ② who
③ whom   ④ where
⑤ which

12 다음 두 문장의 의미가 같도록 빈칸에 알맞은 것은? (2개)

The bus goes to the station. It comes every fifteen minutes.
= The bus _____ goes to the station comes every fifteen minutes.

① who   ② that
③ what   ④ which
⑤ where

13 다음 우리말을 영어로 바르게 옮긴 것은?

내가 코트를 입는 동안 내 가방을 들고 있어 줘.

① Please hold my bag during I put on my coat.
② Please hold my bag if I put off my coat.
③ Please hold my bag though I put on my coat.
④ Please hold my bag while I put off my coat.
⑤ Please hold my bag while I put on my coat.

14 다음 문장에서 어법상 어색한 부분을 찾아 바르게 고쳐 쓰시오.

> Look at the boy and his dog which are running in the park.

_____ ➡ _____

15 다음 빈칸에 공통으로 알맞은 것은?

> • The flower died _____ I was away on a trip.
> • Mr. White likes golf, _____ his wife likes tennis.

① as ② while
③ when ④ since
⑤ whether

16 다음 〈보기〉의 밑줄 친 부분과 쓰임이 같은 것은?

> ─┤ 보기 ├─
> I know a man that works in a famous restaurant.

① They can't go that far.
② I'm afraid that he will not come.
③ The climate of Korea is similar to that of Germany.
④ There is a cat that is sleeping on the bench.
⑤ It was really nice weather that day.

17 다음 문장에서 어법상 어색한 부분을 바르게 고쳐서 문장을 다시 쓰시오.

> I will ask him about it when he will come home.

➡ _____

18 다음 중 밑줄 친 부분의 쓰임이 나머지 넷과 다른 것은?

① I'll call you after I arrive.
② She takes a walk after breakfast.
③ After I called my mom, I went to bed.
④ Tim and I always play tennis after school is over.
⑤ Apply this lotion on your body after you take a shower.

19 다음 중 어법상 어색한 것은?

① Do you know the boy which is running in the park?
② The woman is the only person that loves me.
③ Look at the trees which stand in front of the house.
④ We remember the typhoon that hit the island last year.
⑤ The girl who danced with you is my sister.

20 다음 중 밑줄 친 부분의 쓰임이 〈보기〉와 다른 것은? (2개)

> ─┤ 보기 ├─
> Frank plays computer games when he's not busy.

① I don't know when he will come.
② It was snowing when I got up.
③ Monday is the day when I wash clothes.
④ I cook for my father when my mother is out.
⑤ He was watching television when I called him.

01 다음 두 문장을 한 문장으로 만들 때 빈칸에 알맞은 말을 쓰시오.

> The cat has a long tail. It is lying over there.
> ➡ The cat _____ is lying over there has a long tail.

02 다음 문장에서 먼저 일어난 일을 밑줄로 표시하시오.

(1) I went shopping before he called me.
(2) After I had dinner, I read a book.
(3) They closed the door after it started to rain.
(4) Before he crosses the street, he looks around.

03 다음 빈칸에 공통으로 알맞은 말을 쓰시오.

> • Hajun has some photos _____ I took.
> • I know the woman _____ is playing the violin.

04 다음 문장에서 어법상 어색한 부분을 바르게 고쳐 문장을 다시 쓰시오.

> I will call you when I will arrive.
> ➡ _____

05 다음 두 문장을 괄호 안의 관계대명사를 이용하여 한 문장으로 바꿔 쓰시오.

(1) The young lady is sitting on the bench. She is our music teacher. (who)
   ➡ _____
   _____

(2) We found a dog. It was running toward us. (which)
   ➡ _____

(3) This is the firefighter. He saved the baby from the burning building. (that)
   ➡ _____
   _____

(4) This is the only story. It is interesting to read. (that)
   ➡ _____

06 다음 빈칸에 알맞은 말을 〈보기〉에서 골라 쓰시오. (문장의 앞에 오는 경우 대문자로 쓰시오.)

> ┤ 보기 ├
> when   while   after   before

(1) You must wash your hands _____ you eat.
(2) What do you usually do _____ you have free time?
(3) Mary and I always play tennis _____ school is over.
(4) We slept _____ they were working.

07 다음 두 문장을 관계대명사를 사용하여 한 문장으로 만드시오.

(1) I know the woman. She is standing by the car.

➡ _____

_____

(2) Did you see the car? It has only two doors.

➡ _____

_____

(3) This is a restaurant. The restaurant is famous for its spaghetti.

➡ _____

(4) The lady is my English teacher. She lives next door.

➡ _____

_____

08 다음 우리말과 일치하도록 주어진 단어를 바르게 배열하시오.

우리가 저녁을 먹는 동안, 엄마는 전화로 통화를 했다.
(dinner / having / we / while / are)

➡ _____, my mother talked on the phone.

09 다음 우리말을 영어로 바꾸어 쓸 때 빈칸에 각각 알맞은 말을 쓰시오.

어제 발생한 교통사고는 끔찍했다.
➡ The traffic accident _____ happened yesterday _____ terrible.

10 다음 주어진 문장을 괄호 안의 지시에 따라 바꿔 쓰시오.

After they finished dinner, they washed the dishes. (before를 사용하여)

➡ _____

_____

_____

11 다음 문장에서 어법상 어색한 부분을 찾아 바르게 고쳐 쓰시오.

Could you hold the line before my mom is taking off her shoes?

_____ ➡ _____

12 다음 주어진 단어를 이용하여 우리말을 영어로 옮기시오.

나는 야구를 좋아하는 의사를 알고 있다.
(know)

➡ _____

13 다음 우리말을 괄호 안의 단어를 이용하여 영어로 쓰시오.

그들은 그녀가 그곳에 도착한 후에 파티를 했다.
(have a party, arrive)

➡ _____

_____

Reading

Lunch Lady Begins

My name is Hojin, and I like to make graphic novels. While I was
walking home from school last week, I saw a woman on a scooter. She
looked really cool, and her scooter was very unique.

"Are you going home, Hojin?" she said to me suddenly.

"Yes, but do I know you?" I asked.

"Of course," she answered. "I see you at the school cafeteria every
day."

Surprisingly, she was one of the cafeteria workers at school.

"Amazing! She looks so different outside the school," I thought. "I
should write a graphic novel about her."

After I got home, I began to write a new graphic novel, *Lunch Lady
Begins*. In it, Lunch Lady is a superhero. She rides a super scooter
that can fly. She saves people from danger around the world. She
also makes 100 cookies per second and gives them away to hungry
children.

---

graphic 그래픽[도표]의

novel 소설

scooter 스쿠터(소형 오토바이)

unique 유일무이한, 독특한

surprisingly 놀랍게도

amazing 놀라운

different 다른

outside ~ 밖에서

superhero 슈퍼히어로

ride 타다

save 구하다

danger 위험

per ~당[마다]

give away 거저 주다

hungry 배가 고픈

확인문제

● 다음 문장이 본문의 내용과 일치하면 T, 일치하지 않으면 F를 쓰시오.

1 Hojin likes to write romantic novels. ☐

2 The woman on a scooter works at the school cafeteria. ☐

3 Hojin never saw the woman at the school cafeteria. ☐

4 *Lunch Lady Begins* is Hojin's graphic novel. ☐

5 Lunch Lady rides a super scooter that can fly. ☐

A few days later, I showed my graphic novel to my friends.
며칠 후에 = showed my friends my graphic novel

"Awesome! I love this superhero. She's so cool," said all my friends.
awe(경외감)+some(형용사 어미)

"Guess what? I modeled her on Ms. Lee, one of our cafeteria
있잖아 동격 관계

workers," I told them.

I showed my book to Ms. Lee. She loved it, too. She also told me
= showed Ms. Lee my book = my book

about her coworkers who had special talents. Ms. Park, another
주격 관계대명사 또 다른, 또 하나의

cafeteria worker, won a dancing contest. Mr. Kim, the janitor at our
win의 과거형 win—won—won 동격 관계

school, was once an adventurous park ranger.
한때, 예전에 adventure(모험)+ous(형용사 어미)

"I'd like to write superhero stories about them. Do you think they'll
= would like to: ~하고 싶다

like that?" I asked Ms. Lee.
그들에 대한 슈퍼히어로 이야기를 쓰는 것

"Of course they will," she said cheerfully. "Let's go and say hello to
~하자 ~에게 인사하다

our new superhero friends."

awesome	경탄할 만한, 엄청난
cool	멋진
guess	추측하다
worker	근로자, 직공
coworker	함께 일하는 사람, 동료
special	특별한
talent	재능, 탤런트
janitor	문지기, 수위
adventurous	모험성이 강한, 모험을 즐기는
ranger	공원[삼림] 관리원[경비 대원]
cheerfully	기분 좋게, 쾌활하게

확인문제

● 다음 문장이 본문의 내용과 일치하면 T, 일치하지 않으면 F를 쓰시오.

1 Hojin showed his graphic novel to his friends. ☐

2 Some of Hojin's friends didn't like his novel. ☐

3 Ms. Lee didn't read Hojin's novel. ☐

4 Ms. Lee's coworkers had special talents. ☐

5 Ms. Park once won a dancing contest. ☐

6 Hojin wrote a new superhero story about Ms. Lee's coworkers. ☐

● 우리말을 참고하여 빈칸에 알맞은 말을 쓰시오.

1 My _____ is Hojin, and I _____ to make graphic _____.

2 _____ I was walking _____ from school last week, I saw a _____ on a scooter.

3 She _____ really cool, and her scooter was very _____.

4 "Are you _____ home, Hojin?" she said to me _____.

5 "Yes, _____ do I know you?" I _____.

6 "Of _____," she answered.

7 "I _____ you at the school cafeteria _____ day."

8 _____, she was one of the cafeteria _____ at school.

9 "Amazing! She looks so _____ outside the school," I _____.

10 "I _____ write a graphic novel _____ her."

11 _____ I got home, I _____ to write a new graphic novel, *Lunch Lady Begins*.

12 In it, Lunch Lady is a _____.

13 She _____ a super scooter _____ can fly.

14 She _____ people from _____ around the world.

15 She _____ makes 100 cookies _____ second and gives them away to _____ children.

---

1 내 이름은 호진이고, 만화 소설 쓰는 것을 좋아한다.

2 지난주에 나는 학교에서 집으로 걸어가던 중에 스쿠터에 탄 여자를 보았다.

3 그녀는 정말 멋져 보였고 그녀의 스쿠터는 매우 독특했다.

4 "호진아, 너 집에 가는 중이니?" 그녀가 갑자기 나에게 말했다.

5 "네, 그런데 저를 아시나요?" 나는 물었다.

6 "물론이지."라고 그녀가 대답했다.

7 "난 매일 학교 식당에서 너를 본단다."

8 놀랍게도, 그녀는 학교 식당 직원 중 한 명이었다.

9 "놀라워! 그녀는 학교 밖에서는 아주 달라 보여."라고 나는 생각했다.

10 "그녀에 대한 만화 소설을 써야 겠다."

11 집에 도착한 후, 나는 〈런치 레이디 탄생하다〉라는 새로운 만화 소설을 쓰기 시작했다.

12 그 소설에서 런치 레이디는 슈퍼히어로이다.

13 그녀는 날 수 있는 슈퍼 스쿠터를 탄다.

14 그녀는 전 세계의 위험에 빠진 사람들을 구한다.

15 그녀는 또한 1초에 100개의 쿠키를 만들어 배고픈 아이들에게 나누어 준다.

16 A few days _____, I showed my _____ novel to my friends.

17 "Awesome! I love this _____. She's so _____," said all my friends.

18 "Guess _____? I modeled her _____ Ms. Lee, one of our cafeteria _____," I told them.

19 I _____ my book _____ Ms. Lee.

20 She _____ it, too.

21 She _____ told me about her coworkers _____ had special _____.

22 Ms. Park, _____ cafeteria worker, won a _____ contest.

23 Mr. Kim, the _____ at our school, was _____ an adventurous park _____.

24 "I'd _____ to write superhero _____ about them. Do you _____ they'll like that?" I _____ Ms. Lee.

25 "Of _____ they will," she said _____.

26 "Let's _____ and say _____ to our new _____ friends."

16 며칠 후에 나는 나의 만화 소설을 친구들에게 보여 주었다.

17 "멋져! 나는 이 슈퍼히어로가 너무 좋아. 그녀는 아주 멋져."라고 내 모든 친구들이 말했다.

18 "있잖아. 나는 그녀를 우리 식당 직원 중 한 명인 이 여사를 모델로 했어."라고 나는 친구들에게 말했다.

19 나는 이 여사에게 내 책을 보여 주었다.

20 그녀도 그것을 아주 좋아했다.

21 그녀는 또한 나에게 특별한 재능을 가진 그녀의 동료들에 대해 말해 주었다.

22 또 다른 식당 직원인 박 여사는 댄스 경연대회에서 우승했다.

23 우리 학교의 관리인인 김 선생님은 한때 모험적인 공원 관리원이었다.

24 "저는 그들에 대한 슈퍼히어로 이야기를 쓰고 싶어요. 그분들이 그걸 좋아할 것 같아요?" 나는 이 여사한테 물어보았다.

25 "물론 그럴 거야."라고 그녀가 기분 좋게 말했다.

26 "가서 우리의 새 슈퍼히어로로 친구들에게 인사하자."

● 우리말을 참고하여 본문을 영작하시오.

1 내 이름은 호진이고, 만화 소설 쓰는 것을 좋아한다.

➡ _____

2 지난주에 학교에서 집으로 걸어가던 중에 스쿠터에 탄 여자를 보았다.

➡ _____

3 그녀는 정말 멋져 보였고 그녀의 스쿠터는 매우 독특했다.

➡ _____

4 "호진아, 너 집에 가는 중이니?" 그녀가 갑자기 나에게 말했다.

➡ _____

5 "네, 그런데 저를 아시나요?" 나는 물었다.

➡ _____

6 "물론이지," 그녀가 대답했다.

➡ _____

7 "난 매일 학교 식당에서 너를 본단다."

➡ _____

8 놀랍게도, 그녀는 학교 식당 직원 중 한 명이었다.

➡ _____

9 "놀라워! 그녀는 학교 밖에서는 아주 달라 보여."라고 나는 생각했다.

➡ _____

10 "그녀에 대한 만화 소설을 써야겠다."

➡ _____

11 집에 도착한 후, 나는 〈런치 레이디 탄생하다〉라는 새로운 만화 소설을 쓰기 시작했다.

➡ _____

12 그 소설에서 런치 레이디는 슈퍼히어로이다.

➡ _____

13 그녀는 날 수 있는 슈퍼 스쿠터를 탄다.

➡ _____

14 그녀는 전 세계의 위험에 빠진 사람들을 구한다.

➡ _____

15 그녀는 또한 1초에 100개의 쿠키를 만들어 배고픈 아이들에게 나누어 준다.

➡ _____

16 며칠 후에 나는 나의 만화 소설을 친구들에게 보여 주었다.

➡ _____

17 "멋져! 나는 이 슈퍼히어로가 너무 좋아. 그녀는 아주 멋져."라고 내 모든 친구들이 말했다.

➡ _____

18 "있잖아, 나는 그녀를 우리 식당 직원 중 한 명인 이 여사를 모델로 했어."라고 나는 친구들에게 말했다.

➡ _____

19 나는 이 여사에게 내 책을 보여 주었다.

➡ _____

20 그녀도 그것을 아주 좋아했다.

➡ _____

21 그녀는 또한 나에게 특별한 재능을 가진 그녀의 동료들에 대해 말해 주었다.

➡ _____

22 또 다른 식당 직원인 박 여사는 댄스 경연대회에서 우승했다.

➡ _____

23 우리 학교의 관리인인 김 선생님은 한때 모험적인 공원 관리원이었다.

➡ _____

24 "저는 그들에 대한 슈퍼히어로 이야기를 쓰고 싶어요. 그분들이 그걸 좋아할 것 같아요?"
나는 이 여사한테 물어보았다.

➡ _____

25 "물론 그럴 거야."라고 그녀가 기분 좋게 말했다.

➡ _____

26 "가서 우리의 새 슈퍼히어로로 친구들에게 인사하자."

➡ _____

[01~05] 다음 글을 읽고, 물음에 답하시오.

My name is Hojin, and I like to make graphic novels. (①) ___ⓐ___ I was walking home from school last week, I saw a woman on a scooter. (②)

"Are you going home, Hojin?" she said to me ⓑsudden. (③)

"Yes, but do I know you?" I asked. (④)

"Of course," she answered. "ⓒI see you at the school cafeteria every day." (⑤)

Surprisingly, she was one of the cafeteria workers at school.

01 위 글의 ①~⑤ 중 다음 주어진 문장이 들어갈 알맞은 곳은?

> She looked really cool, and her scooter was very unique.

①   ②   ③   ④   ⑤

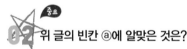

02 위 글의 빈칸 ⓐ에 알맞은 것은?

① If   ② After
③ While   ④ Before
⑤ Though

서답형

03 위 글의 밑줄 친 ⓑ를 알맞은 형으로 고치시오.

➡ _____

서답형

04 위 글의 밑줄 친 ⓒ를 우리말로 옮기시오.

➡ _____

05 위 글의 내용으로 보아 대답할 수 없는 질문은?

① What does Hojin like to do?
② When did Hojin see a woman on a scooter?
③ Where does Hojin lives?
④ Does the woman know Hojin?
⑤ What does the woman do?

[06~10] 다음 글을 읽고, 물음에 답하시오.

Surprisingly, the woman was one of the cafeteria workers at school.

"Amazing! She looks so ___ⓐ___ outside the school," I thought. "I should write a graphic novel about her."

___ⓑ___ I got home, I began to write a new graphic novel, *Lunch Lady Begins*. In it Lunch Lady is a superhero. She rides a super scooter that can fly. She saves people from ___ⓒ___ around the world. She also makes 100 cookies ⓓper second and gives them away to hungry children.   * I=Hojin

06 위 글의 빈칸 ⓐ에 알맞은 것은?

① same   ② happy
③ busy   ④ different
⑤ pleased

07 위 글의 빈칸 ⓑ에 알맞은 것은?

① Because   ② If
③ Before   ④ While
⑤ After

서답형

08 위 글의 빈칸 ⓒ에 다음 정의에 해당하는 단어를 주어진 글자로 시작하여 쓰시오.

> the possibility of something happening that will injure, harm, or kill someone

➡ d_____

중요

09 위 글의 밑줄 친 ⓓ와 바꿔 쓸 수 있는 것은?

① a　　　　　　② an
③ the　　　　　④ that
⑤ some

10 위 글의 내용과 일치하지 <u>않는</u> 것은?

① The woman worked at the school cafeteria.
② Hojin didn't see the woman before.
③ Hojin wanted to write a graphic novel about her.
④ Lunch Lady rides a super scooter that can fly.
⑤ Lunch Lady saves people from danger around the world.

[11~14] 다음 글을 읽고, 물음에 답하시오.

A few days ⓐlate, I showed my graphic novel ___ⓑ___ my friends.

"Awesome! I love this superhero. She's so cool," said all my friends.

"___ⓒ___ what? I modeled her on Ms. Lee, one of our cafeteria workers," I told them.

* I=Hojin

서답형

11 위 글의 밑줄 친 ⓐ를 알맞은 형으로 바꿔 쓰시오.

➡ _____

12 위 글의 빈칸 ⓑ에 알맞은 것은?

① at　　　　　　② of
③ to　　　　　　④ for
⑤ with

13 위 글의 빈칸 ⓒ에 알맞은 것은?

① Say　　　　　② Tell
③ Think　　　　④ Guess
⑤ Believe

서답형

14 Whom did Hojin model her on? Answer in English.

➡ _____
_____

[15~19] 다음 글을 읽고, 물음에 답하시오.

I showed my book to Ms. Lee. She loved it, too. She also told me about her coworkers ⓐwho had special talents. Ms. Park, ___ⓑ___ cafeteria worker, won a dancing contest. Mr. Kim, the janitor at our school, was once an ⓒadventure park ranger.

"I'd like to write superhero stories about them. Do you think they'll like ⓓthat?" I asked Ms. Lee.

"Of course they will," she said cheerfully. "Let's go and say hello to our new superhero friends."

* I=Hojin

15 위 글의 밑줄 친 ⓐ 대신 쓸 수 있는 것은?

① whom　　　　② whose
③ that　　　　④ what
⑤ which

16 위 글의 빈칸 ⓑ에 알맞은 것은?

① any　　　　② some
③ other　　　　④ another
⑤ the other

서답형
17 위 글의 밑줄 친 ⓒ를 알맞은 형으로 고치시오.

➡ _____

서답형
18 위 글의 밑줄 친 ⓓ가 가리키는 것을 우리말로 쓰시오.

➡ _____

19 위 글의 내용으로 보아 대답할 수 없는 질문은?

① What did Hojin show to Ms. Lee?
② Whom did Ms. Lee tell Hojin about?
③ What does Mr. Kim do for a living?
④ When did Ms. Park win a dancing contest?
⑤ Why do Ms. Lee and Hojin go to their superhero friends?

[20~23] 다음 글을 읽고, 물음에 답하시오.

My aunt is my ___ⓐ___ . She is smart, strong, and adventurous. In her 30s, she traveled to 70 different countries. ___ⓑ___ she was traveling, she made friends from all over the world. I want to be someone ⓒwho is not afraid of trying new things just ⓓlike her.

서답형
20 위 글의 빈칸 ⓐ에 다음 정의에 해당하는 말을 주어진 철자로 시작하여 쓰시오.

someone you admire and try to imitate

➡ r_____ m_____

21 위 글의 빈칸 ⓑ에 알맞은 것은?

① As　　　　② If
③ After　　　　④ Since
⑤ While

서답형
22 위 글의 밑줄 친 ⓒ 대신 쓸 수 있는 것을 쓰시오.

➡ _____

23 위 글의 밑줄 친 ⓓ와 용법이 같은 것은?

① Do you like their new house?
② I've never seen a pretty cat like his cat.
③ I didn't like to watch TV.
④ At weekends I like to sleep late.
⑤ We'd like you to come and visit us.

[24~27] 다음 글을 읽고, 물음에 답하시오.

Julia Child was a person ____ⓐ____ found her real ____ⓑ____ in her 30s. At age 36, she moved to Paris with her husband. She ____ⓒ____ a famous cooking school there. While she was studying, she decided ⓓto write a cookbook. That book became a big hit.

24 위 글의 빈칸 ⓐ에 알맞은 것은? (2개)

① who   ② whose
③ that   ④ what
⑤ which

25 위 글의 빈칸 ⓑ에 다음 정의에 해당하는 단어를 주어진 글자로 시작하여 쓰시오.

> the natural ability to do something well

➡ t_____

26 위 글의 빈칸 ⓒ에 알맞은 것은?

① went   ② visited
③ stayed   ④ attended
⑤ studied

27 위 글의 밑줄 친 ⓓ와 같은 용법으로 쓰인 것은?

① I need a baseball cap to wear.
② We hoped to find the hidden treasure.
③ Were you glad to hear the news?
④ I went to a shopping mall to buy gloves.
⑤ Is there anything to eat in the fridge?

[28~31] 다음 글을 읽고, 물음에 답하시오.

My name is Hojin, and I like ①making graphic novels. ②While I was walking home from school last week, I saw a woman ____ⓑ____ a scooter. She looked really ③coolly, and her scooter was very unique.

"Are you going home, Hojin?" she said ④to me suddenly.

"Yes, ____ⓒ____ do I know you?" I asked.

"Of course," she answered. "I see you ⑤at the school cafeteria every day."

28 위 글의 밑줄 친 ①~⑤ 중 어법상 어색한 것은?

①   ②   ③   ④   ⑤

29 위 글의 빈칸 ⓑ에 알맞은 것은?

① by   ② on
③ in   ④ at
⑤ over

서답형

30 위 글의 빈칸 ⓒ에 알맞은 접속사를 쓰시오.

➡ _____

31 위 글의 내용으로 보아 알 수 없는 것은?

① 호진이는 만화 소설 쓰기를 좋아한다.
② 호진이는 지난주에 스쿠터를 탄 여인을 보았다.
③ 그 여인의 스쿠터는 아주 독특했다.
④ 그 여인은 호진이를 알아보았다.
⑤ 그 여인은 학교 식당에서 근무하고 있다.

[01~06] 다음 글을 읽고, 물음에 답하시오.

ⓐSurprising, she was one of the cafeteria workers at school.

"Amazing! She looks so ___ⓑ___ outside the school," I thought. "I should write a graphic novel about her."

After I got home, I began to write a new graphic novel, *Lunch Lady Begins*. In it Lunch Lady is a superhero. She rides a super scooter ⓒthat can fly. She saves people ___ⓓ___ danger around the world. She also makes 100 cookies per second and gives ⓔthem away to hungry children.

01 위 글의 밑줄 친 ⓐ를 알맞은 형으로 고치시오.

➡ _____

02 위 글의 빈칸 ⓑ에 same의 반의어를 쓰시오.

➡ _____

03 위 글의 밑줄 친 ⓒ 대신 쓸 수 있는 관계대명사를 쓰시오.

➡ _____

04 위 글의 빈칸 ⓓ에 알맞은 전치사를 쓰시오.

➡ _____

05 위 글의 밑줄 친 ⓔ가 가리키는 것을 영어로 쓰시오.

➡ _____

06 How many cookies does Lunch Lady make per second? Answer in Korean.

➡ _____

[07~09] 다음 글을 읽고, 물음에 답하시오.

A few days later, I showed my graphic novel ___ⓐ___ my friends.

"Awesome! I love this ___ⓑ___. She's so cool," said all my friends.

"Guess what? ⓒI modeled her on Ms. Lee, one of our cafeteria workers," I told them.

07 위 글의 빈칸 ⓐ에 알맞은 전치사를 쓰시오.

➡ _____

08 위 글의 빈칸 ⓑ에 다음 정의에 해당하는 단어를 주어진 글자로 시작하여 쓰시오.

> a character in a cartoon or film who has special powers and fights against evil

➡ s_____

09 위 글의 밑줄 친 ⓒ를 우리말로 옮기시오.

➡ _____

[10~15] 다음 글을 읽고, 물음에 답하시오.

ⓐI showed Ms. Lee my book. She loved it, too. She also told me about her coworkers ⓑwho had special talents. ⓒMs. Park, other cafeteria worker, won a dancing contest. Mr. Kim, the janitor at our school, was once an adventurous park ranger.

"I'd like to write superhero stories about ⓓthem. Do you think they'll like that?" I asked Ms. Lee.

"Of course they will," she said ⓔcheerful. "Let's go and say hello to our new superhero friends."

10 위 글의 밑줄 친 ⓐ와 같은 뜻이 되도록 빈칸에 알맞은 말을 쓰시오.

I showed my book _____ Ms. Lee.

11 위 글의 밑줄 친 ⓑ 대신 쓸 수 있는 관계대명사를 쓰시오.

➡ _____

12 위 글의 밑줄 친 ⓒ에서 어법상 어색한 것을 고치시오.

_____ ➡ _____

13 위 글의 밑줄 친 ⓓ가 가리키는 것을 우리말로 구체적으로 쓰시오.

➡ _____

14 위 글의 밑줄 친 ⓔ를 알맞은 형으로 고치시오.

➡ _____

15 Was Ms. Park good at dancing? Answer in English.

➡ _____

[16~19] 다음 글을 읽고, 물음에 답하시오.

My aunt is my role model. She is smart, strong, and ⓐadventure. In her 30s, she traveled to 70 different countries. ⓑWhile she was traveling, she made a friend from all over the world. I want to be someone _____ⓒ_____ is not afraid _____ⓓ_____ trying new things just like her.

16 위 글의 밑줄 친 ⓐ를 알맞은 형으로 고치시오.

➡ _____

17 위 글의 밑줄 친 ⓑ에서 어법상 어색한 것을 고치시오.

_____ ➡ _____

18 위 글의 빈칸 ⓒ에 알맞은 관계대명사를 쓰시오.

➡ _____

19 위 글의 빈칸 ⓓ에 알맞은 전치사를 쓰시오.

➡ _____

해석

Listen & Speak 1-B

A: I'm good at jumping rope.
   be good at+동명사: ~을 잘하다

B: Suji is good at jumping rope. I'm good at playing the guitar.

C: Suji is good at jumping rope. Hansu is good at playing the guitar. I'm
                                                                    현재진행형
baking cookies.

구문해설 • be good at: ~을 잘하다 • jump rope: 줄넘기를 하다 • bake: 굽다 • cookie: 쿠키

A: 저는 줄넘기를 잘해요.

B: 수지는 줄넘기를 잘해요. 저는 기타를 잘 칩니다.

C: 수지는 줄넘기를 잘해요. 한수는 기타를 잘 칩니다. 저는 쿠키를 굽고 있어요.

Language Arts

Two boys are studying in a library. There is a fire. The boys can't get out.
          현재진행형   ~이 있다
Lunch Lady flies on her scooter and saves them.
                                         = the boys

구문해설 • fire: 불, 화재 • get out: 나가다 • save: 구하다

두 소년이 도서관에서 공부하고 있다. 불이 났다. 그 소년들은 나갈 수 없다. Lunch Lady는 스쿠터를 타고 날아와서 그들을 구한다.

Write

My aunt is my role model. She is smart, strong, and adventurous. In her 30s,
                                                              in one's 30s: 30대에
she traveled to 70 different countries. While she was traveling, she made
                                         접 ~하는 동안   친구를 사귀다
friends from all over the world. I want to be someone who is not afraid of
              전 세계에서   주격 관계대명사(=that)   ~을 두려워하다
trying new things just like her.
                        전 ~처럼

구문해설 • role model: 롤 모델 • adventurous: 모험심이 강한 • travel: 여행하다 • different: 다른
• try: 시도하다

나의 이모는 내 롤 모델이다. 그녀는 똑똑하고, 강하고, 모험심이 강하다. 30대 때, 그녀는 70개국을 여행했다. 여행을 하는 동안, 그녀는 전 세계의 친구들을 사귀었다. 나는 그녀처럼 새로운 것을 시도하는 것을 두려워하지 않는 사람이 되고 싶다.

Culture Project - Share

Julia Child was a person who found her real talent in her 30s. At age 36, she
                          주격 관계대명사 who(=that)   36살에
moved to Paris with her husband. She attends a famous cooking school there.
          ~와 함께   = in Paris
While she was studying, she decided to write a cookbook. That book became
접 ~하는 동안   decide to부정사: ~하기로 결정하다
a big hit.

구문해설 • person: 사람 • real: 진정한 • talent: 재능 • move: 이사하다 • husband: 남편
• attend: ~에 다니다 • famous: 유명한 • cookbook: 요리책 • hit: 히트

Julia Child는 30대에 그녀의 진정한 재능을 발견한 사람이었다. 36살 때, 그녀는 남편과 함께 파리로 이사를 했다. 그녀는 그곳에서 유명한 요리 학교에 다닌다. 그녀는 공부하는 동안 요리책을 쓰기로 결심했다. 그 책은 큰 인기를 끌었다.

Words & Expressions

01 다음 중 짝지어진 단어의 관계가 나머지와 다른 것은?

① write – writer ② listen – listener

③ paint – painter ④ cook – cooker

⑤ speak – speaker

02 다음 빈칸에 들어갈 말로 적절하지 않은 것은?

- He is going to _____ a wedding.
- It is _____ with occasional showers.
- She felt _____ on her wedding day.
- Aluminum cans are very easy to _____.

① cloudy ② attend

③ repair ④ recycle

⑤ nervous

03 다음 짝지어진 두 단어의 관계가 같도록 빈칸에 주어진 글자로 시작하여 쓰시오.

cheap : expensive = right : w_____

04 다음 빈칸에 들어갈 말이 바르게 짝지어진 것은?

- Are you afraid _____ spiders?
- Exercise is good _____ the health.

① in – on ② on – off

③ of – for ④ for – after

⑤ from – for

05 다음 영영풀이에 해당하는 단어는?

to be present at a meeting or event

① join ② observe

③ share ④ visit

⑤ attend

06 다음 문장의 빈칸에 알맞은 것은?

Let me _____ a look at the map.

① take ② make

③ let ④ get

⑤ bring

07 다음 우리말에 맞게 빈칸에 알맞은 말을 쓰시오.

이 집은 우리가 살 수 있을 만큼 크지가 않다.
➡ This house isn't big _____ for us to live in.

Conversation

08 다음 대화의 빈칸에 알맞은 것은?

A: Can you jump high?
B: Yes, I can. I am _____ at jumping.

① poor ② good

③ well ④ bad

⑤ pretty

[09~14] 다음 대화를 읽고, 물음에 답하시오.

> Yuri: What are you doing, Jaden?
> Jaden: I'm drawing cartoons.
> Yuri: Really? Can I take a look at them?
> Jaden: ⓐNo, not yet.
> Yuri: ___ⓑ___ not? You can show me a few, can't you?
> Jaden: Well, I guess so.
> Yuri: (*pause*) Ha, ha, ha! Awesome! I like your cartoons. You're really good ___ⓒ___ drawing.
> Jaden: Do you think so? I want to be a cartoonist, ___ⓓ___ I don't think my drawing skills are good enough.
> Yuri: Your cartoons are really funny, and you have unique characters. ⓔI'm sure you'll be a great cartoonist.
> Jaden: Thank you, Yuri. You just made my day.

09 위 대화의 밑줄 친 ⓐ를 생략되지 <u>않은</u> 문장으로 바꾸시오.

➡ _____

10 위 대화의 빈칸 ⓑ에 알맞은 것은?

① Why   ② How
③ What   ④ Who
⑤ Where

11 위 대화의 빈칸 ⓒ에 알맞은 것은?

① to   ② in
③ at   ④ for
⑤ with

12 위 대화의 빈칸 ⓓ에 알맞은 것은?

① so   ② or
③ and   ④ but
⑤ for

13 위 대화의 밑줄 친 ⓔ와 같은 뜻이 되도록 다음 문장의 빈칸에 알맞은 말을 쓰시오.

> _____ is _____ that you'll be a great cartoonist.

14 위 대화의 내용으로 보아 대답할 수 <u>없는</u> 질문은?

① What is Jaden doing?
② Why does Yuri want to look at Jaden's cartoons?
③ Does Jaden draw well?
④ Does Yuri like Jaden's cartoons?
⑤ What does Jaden hope to be?

15 다음 대화의 밑줄 친 부분의 의도로 알맞은 것은?

> A: Are you good at cooking?
> B: Yes, I know how to make cookies and sandwiches.

① 열거하기   ② 선호 표현하기
③ 의견 표현하기   ④ 능력 표현하기
⑤ 걱정 표현하기

16 다음 우리말에 맞도록 빈칸에 알맞은 말을 쓰시오.

> 너는 내가 그 영화를 좋아할 것이라고 확신하니?
> ➡ Are you _____ that I'll like that movie?

Grammar

[17~18] 다음 문장의 빈칸에 알맞은 것을 고르시오.

17

> Susan is the girl _____ comes from New Zealand.

① who   ② what
③ whom   ④ which
⑤ whose

18

> Please be quiet _____ I'm talking to your teacher.

① and   ② so
③ unless   ④ while
⑤ after

19 다음 빈칸에 공통으로 알맞은 것은?

> • Look at the bird _____ is standing with one leg.
> • Mike, _____ food do you like better, pizza or hamburgers?

① who   ② which
③ that   ④ where
⑤ what

20 다음 우리말과 뜻이 같도록 괄호 안의 어구들을 바르게 배열하시오.

> 그는 저녁 식사를 마친 후, 양치질을 했다.
> (his teeth, his dinner, he, he, after, finished, brushed).

➡ _____

21 다음 중 어법상 어색한 것은?

① He is the only man that can solve the problems.
② Korea is a country which exports cars all over the world.
③ I have a dog which has long ears.
④ There is a man at the door who wants to see you.
⑤ The men who is in front of the house are my friends.

22 다음 중 밑줄 친 부분의 쓰임이 나머지와 다른 것은?

① He went there <u>before</u> they arrived.
② I got up <u>before</u> the alarm clock rang.
③ I have to finish this work <u>before</u> seven o'clock.
④ They helped her <u>before</u> she asked for help.
⑤ <u>Before</u> you go out, make sure to turn off the light.

23 다음 중 밑줄 친 that의 쓰임이 나머지 넷과 다른 하나는?

① The park <u>that</u> is near my house is good.
② I think <u>that</u> golf is more interesting than tennis.
③ I know a man <u>that</u> works in a famous restaurant.
④ I live in an apartment <u>that</u> has no heating system.
⑤ We'll go to a restaurant <u>that</u> has a children's menu.

24 다음 문장의 빈칸에 알맞지 <u>않은</u> 것은?

> Everybody stopped to see _____ that were playing together.

① the boy   ② the tigers
③ the children   ④ a cat and a dog
⑤ a man and a monkey

25 다음 중 어법상 <u>어색한</u> 것은?

① Ann and I always play tennis after school is over.
② While I was sleeping, he made breakfast for me.
③ If you don't hurry, you will be late for the movie.
④ You can use my car while I'm studying.
⑤ Jenny arrived at the station after the train leaves.

26 다음 두 문장을 한 문장으로 바꿔 쓰시오.

> • What is the name of the tallest boy?
> • He just came in.

➡ _____

_____

27 다음 문장에서 어법상 옳지 <u>않은</u> 부분을 바르게 고쳐 쓰시오.

> Clean up that mess before your father will see it.

_____ ➡ _____

Reading

[28~31] 다음 글을 읽고, 물음에 답하시오.

> ___ⓐ___ I got home, I began to write a new graphic novel, *Lunch Lady Begins*. In ⓑit Lunch Lady is a superhero. She rides a super scooter that can fly. ⓒ그녀는 전 세계에서 사람들을 위험으로부터 구한다. She also makes 100 cookies per second and gives them ___ⓓ___ to hungry children.

28 위 글의 빈칸 ⓐ에 알맞은 것은?

① If   ② After
③ While   ④ Since
⑤ Before

29 위 글의 밑줄 친 ⓑ가 가리키는 것을 영어로 쓰시오.

➡ _____

30 위 글의 밑줄 친 ⓒ의 우리말을 괄호 안에 주어진 단어를 이용하여 영어로 옮기시오.

> (save, from, danger, around)

➡ _____

31 위 글의 빈칸 ⓓ에 알맞은 것은?

① up   ② on
③ from   ④ off
⑤ away

[32~37] 다음 글을 읽고, 물음에 답하시오.

A few days ___ⓐ___, I showed my graphic novel to my friends.

"Awesome! I love this superhero. She's so cool," said all my friends.

"Guess ___ⓑ___? I modeled her on Ms. Lee, one of our cafeteria ⓒwork," I told them.

I showed my book to Ms. Lee. She loved it, too. She also told me about her coworkers ⓓthat had special talents. Ms. Park, another cafeteria worker, won a dancing contest. Mr. Kim, the janitor at our school, was once an adventurous park ___ⓔ___.

"I'd like to write superhero stories about them. Do you think they'll like that?" I asked Ms. Lee.

"Of course they will," she said cheerfully. "Let's go and say hello ___ⓕ___ our new superhero friends."

32 위 글의 빈칸 ⓐ에 알맞은 것은?

① late
② early
③ earlier
④ later
⑤ latter

33 위 글의 빈칸 ⓑ에 알맞은 것은?

① this
② that
③ what
④ who
⑤ which

34 위 글의 밑줄 친 ⓒ를 알맞은 어형으로 바꿔 쓰시오.

➡ _____

35 위 글의 밑줄 친 ⓓ 대신 쓸 수 있는 관계대명사를 쓰시오.

➡ _____

36 위 글의 빈칸 ⓔ에 다음 정의에 해당하는 단어를 쓰시오.

> a person whose job is to look after a forest or large park

➡ _____

37 위 글의 빈칸 ⓕ에 알맞은 전치사를 쓰시오.

➡ _____

[38~39] 다음 글을 읽고, 물음에 답하시오.

Two boys are studying in a library. ⓐThere is a fire. The boys can't get ___ⓑ___. Lunch Lady flies on her scooter and saves them.

38 위 글의 밑줄 친 ⓐ와 같은 뜻이 되도록 다음 문장의 빈칸에 알맞은 말을 쓰시오.

> A fire breaks _____.

39 위 글의 빈칸 ⓑ에 알맞은 것은?

① in
② of
③ into
④ out
⑤ from

단원별 예상문제

출제율 90%

01 다음 중 짝지어진 단어의 관계가 <u>다른</u> 것은?

① right : wrong ② long : short
③ different : same ④ funny : interesting
⑤ dangerous : safe

출제율 100%

02 다음 빈칸에 공통으로 알맞은 것은?

- I made this doll out _____ an old dress.
- The bus stops right in front _____ our house.

① in ② of
③ from ④ with
⑤ onto

출제율 95%

03 다음 짝지어진 두 단어의 관계가 같도록 빈칸에 알맞은 말을 쓰시오.

cloud : cloudy = rain : _____

출제율 90%

04 다음 중 영영풀이가 <u>잘못된</u> 것은?

① awesome: very impressive and often frightening
② superhero: a character in a cartoon or film who has special powers and fights against evil
③ role model: someone you admire and try to imitate
④ adventurous: willing to take risks and to try new methods
⑤ poem: a long written story about imaginary people and events

출제율 90%

05 다음 우리말에 맞게 빈칸에 알맞은 말을 쓰시오.

나는 그가 그의 우산을 선뜻 내놓을 것이라고는 기대하지 않았다.
➡ I didn't expect that he would give _____ his umbrella.

출제율 100%

06 다음 대화의 밑줄 친 부분의 의도로 알맞은 것은?

A: What am I doing?
B: I think you're watering the flowers.
A: <u>Are you sure?</u>
B: Yes. I'm sure that you're watering the flowers.

① 설득하기 ② 제안하기
③ 의견 묻기 ④ 확신 여부 묻기
⑤ 충고 청하기

출제율 95%

07 다음 중 짝지어진 대화가 <u>어색한</u> 것은?

① A: Is he good at solving puzzles?
  B: Yes, he is.
② A: Are you certain that she'll win the race?
  B: Sure.
③ A: Will you teach me how to play baduk?
  B: Let me see. OK, I will.
④ A: When did he win first prize?
  B: He won it last year.
⑤ A: Are you sure that you locked the door?
  B: Yes, I'm sure. I'll go and check.

[08~11] 다음 대화를 읽고, 물음에 답하시오.

> Yuri: What are you doing, Jaden?
>
> Jaden: I'm drawing cartoons.
>
> Yuri: Really? Can I ⓐtake a look at them?
>
> Jaden: No, not yet.
>
> Yuri: ⓑWhy not? You can show me a few, can't you?
>
> Jaden: Well, I guess so.
>
> Yuri: (*pause*) Ha, ha, ha! Awesome! I like your cartoons. You're really good at drawing.
>
> Jaden: Do you think ⓒso? I want to be a cartoonist, but I don't think my drawing skills are good enough.
>
> Yuri: Your cartoons are really funny, and you have unique characters. I'm sure you'll be a great cartoonist.
>
> Jaden: Thank you, Yuri. ⓓYou just made my day.

출제율 90%

08 위 대화의 밑줄 친 ⓐ 대신 쓸 수 있는 것은?

① do
② get
③ make
④ have
⑤ join

출제율 100%

09 위 대화의 밑줄 친 ⓑ를 생략하지 <u>않은</u> 문장으로 바꿔 쓰시오.

➡ _____

출제율 95%

10 위 대화의 밑줄 친 ⓒ가 가리키는 것을 영어로 쓰시오.

➡ _____

출제율 95%

11 위 대화의 밑줄 친 ⓓ를 우리말로 옮기시오.

➡ _____

출제율 100%

12 다음 두 문장을 한 문장으로 연결할 때 빈칸에 알맞은 것은?

> There is a girl. She is sitting on the bench.
> ➡ There is a girl _____ is sitting on the bench.

① who
② what
③ whom
④ which
⑤ whose

출제율 95%

13 다음 문장의 빈칸에 알맞은 것은?

> _____ they are sleeping, somebody knocked on the door.

① Before
② After
③ While
④ If
⑤ Unless

출제율 90%

14 다음 문장에서 어법상 어색한 것을 찾아 바르게 고치시오.

> A man who is dressed like Santa Claus gave presents to children.

_____ ➡ _____

출제율 100%

15 다음 두 문장의 의미가 일치하도록 빈칸에 알맞은 말을 쓰시오

> He gave me this book after he read it.
> = He read this book _____ he gave it to me.

16 다음 빈칸에 알맞은 말이 순서대로 짝지어진 것은? 출제율 90%

- I like pizza _____ has lots of cheese.
- The people _____ work in the office are very friendly.

① who – whom
② which – who
③ who – which
④ whom – which
⑤ which – whom

[17~18] 다음 밑줄 친 부분의 쓰임이 다른 하나를 고르시오.

17 출제율 95%
① Please tell me which is your notebook?
② Can you see the bird which is flying over there?
③ Look at the castle which stands on the hill.
④ I will give him the vase which is very expensive.
⑤ This is the dictionary which gives me the meaning of words.

18 출제율 95%
① While you were out, your sister cleaned your room.
② Some are tall while others are short.
③ He turned on the music while he worked.
④ Work hard while you are young.
⑤ Frank finished the work while I was sleeping.

19 다음 밑줄 친 부분 중 어법상 어색한 것은? 출제율 100%
① I need a chair which is made of wood.
② The closet that they are carrying looks heavy.
③ Do you know the woman who is playing curling?
④ Jenny is the famous singer who appeared on TV last night.
⑤ Jane likes a man whom is tall and humorous.

[20~22] 다음 글을 읽고, 물음에 답하시오.

(①) My aunt is my role model. (②) In her 30s, she traveled to 70 different countries. (③) While she was traveling, she _____ ⓐ friends from all over the world. (④) ⓑI want to be someone who is not afraid of try new things just like her. (⑤)

20 위 글의 ①~⑤ 중 다음 주어진 문장이 들어갈 알맞은 곳은? 출제율 95%

She is smart, strong, and adventurous.

①   ②   ③   ④   ⑤

21 위 글의 빈칸 ⓐ에 알맞은 것은? 출제율 100%
① did   ② got
③ made   ④ took
⑤ became

22 위 글의 밑줄 친 ⓑ에서 어법상 어색한 것을 고치시오. 출제율 95%

_____ ➡ _____

[23~27] 다음 글을 읽고, 물음에 답하시오.

My name is Hojin, and I like to make graphic novels. ⓐWhile I am walking home from school last week, I saw a woman on a scooter. ⓑShe looked really cool, and her scooter was very unique.

"Are you going home, Hojin?" she said to me _____ⓒ_____.

"Yes, but do I know you?" I asked.

"Of course," she answered. "I see you at the school cafeteria every day."

Surprisingly, she was one of the cafeteria workers at school.

"ⓓAmaze! She looks so different outside the school," I thought. "I should write a graphic novel about her."

23 위 글의 밑줄 친 ⓐ에서 어법상 어색한 것을 고치시오.

_____ ➡ _____

24 위 글의 밑줄 친 ⓑ와 같은 문형으로 쓰인 것은?

① The candy tastes sweet.
② The song made me sad.
③ There are some apples in the basket.
④ She made us some cookies.
⑤ My father planted some trees.

25 위 글의 빈칸 ⓒ에 다음 정의에 해당하는 단어를 주어진 글 자로 시작하여 쓰시오.

quickly and unexpectedly

➡ s_____

26 위 글의 밑줄 친 ⓓ를 알맞은 어형으로 고치시오.

➡ _____

27 위 글의 내용과 일치하지 <u>않는</u> 것은?

① Hojin likes to make graphic novels.
② Hojin saw a woman on a scooter last week.
③ Hojin recognized the woman immediately.
④ The woman sees Hojin at the school cafeteria every day.
⑤ Hojin wanted to write a graphic novel about the woman.

[28~29] 다음 글을 읽고, 물음에 답하시오.

Julia Child was a person who found her real talent in her 30s. _____ⓐ_____ age 36, she moved to Paris with her husband. She attended a famous cooking school there. While she was studying, she decided to write a cookbook. That book _____ⓑ_____ a big hit.

28 위 글의 빈칸 ⓐ에 알맞은 것은?

① In   ② On
③ For   ④ At
⑤ From

29 위 글의 빈칸 ⓑ에 알맞은 것은?

① did   ② got
③ came   ④ took
⑤ became

서술형 실전문제

[01~03] 다음 대화를 읽고, 물음에 답하시오.

> B: ⓐ<u>Is something wrong?</u>
> G: I have to give a speech in English. I'm so ⓑ<u>nerve</u>.
> B: Don't worry. Practice your speech in front of your family. ⓒ<u>I'm sure you'll do a good job.</u>
> G: Thank you. I'll try.

01 위 대화의 밑줄 친 부분과 바꿔 쓸 수 있는 표현을 두 가지 쓰시오.

➡ _____

_____

_____

02 위 대화의 밑줄 친 ⓑ를 알맞은 형으로 고치시오.

➡ _____

03 위 대화의 밑줄 친 ⓒ를 우리말로 옮기시오.

➡ _____

04 다음 대화의 순서를 바르게 배열하시오.

> (A) I'm sure your mom will love it.
> (B) Tomorrow is my mom's birthday. What should I do for her?
> (C) Why don't you bake a cake for her? You're good at baking.
> (D) That's a good idea. I hope my mom will like my cake.

➡ _____

05 다음 두 문장을 관계대명사를 써서 한 문장으로 나타내시오.

(1) Dad cooks me a fried egg. It is my favorite.

➡ _____

(2) I have an uncle. He is a math teacher.

➡ _____

(3) She has a bird. It speaks English.

➡ _____

06 다음 〈조건〉에 맞게 괄호 안의 단어를 이용하여 우리말을 영어로 옮기시오.

> ┤ 조건 ├
> 1. 주어진 단어를 모두 이용할 것.
> 2. 필요시 관사를 붙이거나 단어를 추가하고 동사의 어형 변화를 할 것.
> 3. 종속절이 주절의 뒤에 위치할 것.
> 4. 대·소문자 및 구두점에 유의할 것.

(1) Kathy는 목욕한 뒤에 잠자리에 들었다.
(go, bed, take, bath)

➡ _____

(2) Smith 씨는 네가 외출한 동안 너를 보러 오셨다.
(come, see, be out)

➡ _____

(3) 너는 어두워지기 전에 돌아와야 한다.
(should, back, get dark)

➡ _____

[11~14] 다음 글을 읽고, 물음에 답하시오.

07 다음 문장에서 어법상 <u>어색한</u> 것을 찾아 바르게 고치시오.

(1) The animals that is in cages are not happy.

_____ ➡ _____

(2) Where is the letter who came from Cathy this morning?

_____ ➡ _____

(3) The boy and the dog who fell into the river were saved.

_____ ➡ _____

[08~10] 다음 글을 읽고, 물음에 답하시오.

My aunt is my role model. She is smart, ___ⓐ___, and adventurous. In her 30s, she traveled to 70 ___ⓑ___ countries. While she was traveling, she made friends from all over the world. ⓒI want to be someone who is not afraid of trying new things just like her.

08 위 글의 빈칸 ⓐ에 weak의 반의어를 쓰시오.

➡ _____

09 위 글의 빈칸 ⓑ에 다음 정의에 해당하는 단어를 주어진 글자로 시작하여 쓰시오.

not like each other in one or more ways

➡ d_____

10 위 글의 밑줄 친 ⓒ를 우리말로 옮기시오.

➡ _____
_____

Julia Child was a person ___ⓐ___ found her real talent in her 30s. At ___ⓑ___ 36, she moved to Paris with her husband. ⓒShe attended at a famous cooking school there. While she was studying, she decided ⓓ (to write, writing) a cookbook. That book became a big hit.

11 위 글의 빈칸 ⓐ에 알맞은 관계대명사를 쓰시오.

➡ _____

12 위 글의 빈칸 ⓑ에 다음 정의에 해당하는 단어를 쓰시오.

the number of years that you have lived

➡ _____

13 위 글의 밑줄 친 ⓒ를 어법상 <u>어색한</u> 것을 고쳐 다시 쓰시오.

➡ _____

14 위 글의 괄호 ⓓ에서 알맞은 것을 고르시오.

➡ _____

01 다음 주어진 단어를 활용하여 예시와 같이 쓰시오.

Teacher	teach, students, school	ex) A teacher is someone who teaches students at a school.
Waiter	serve, food, restaurant	(1)
Zookeeper	look after, animals, zoo	(2)
Dessert	sweet food, serve, after a meal	(3)

(1) _____

(2) _____

(3) _____

02 다음 〈보기〉처럼 두 문장을 괄호 안에 주어진 접속사를 사용하여 하나의 문장으로 바꿔 쓰시오.

> ┤ 보기 ├
>
> Kirk was in Paris. / He fell in love with a girl. (while)
> ➡ While Kirk was in Paris, he fell in love with a girl. / Kirk fell in love with a girl while he was in Paris.

(1) I leave this town. / I'm going to visit my friend. (before)

➡ _____

_____

(2) I bought the PS4. / I saw the advertisement on TV. (after)

➡ _____

_____

(3) The rain will stop. / You go out. (before)

➡ _____

(4) Please hold my bag. / I put on my coat. (while)

➡ _____

_____

(5) We eat something. / We're going to see a movie. (after)

➡ _____

_____

(6) I came home. My sister was watching TV. (when)

➡ _____

_____

(7) You go out. / You have to finish this. (before)

➡ _____

단원별 모의고사

01 다음 영영풀이에 해당하는 단어로 알맞은 것은?

> to choose to do something, usually after you have thought carefully about the other possibilities

① decide
② advise
③ share
④ select
⑤ mention

02 다음 중 우리말 뜻이 잘못된 것은?

① fall asleep: 잠들다
② do a good job: 잘하다
③ in front of: ~ 앞에(서)
④ be good for: ~을 잘하다
⑤ be afraid of: ~을 두려워하다

03 다음 빈칸에 알맞은 말이 바르게 짝지어진 것은?

> • My uncle cleans his car _____ a week.
> • They're on sale today, only 99 cents _____ pound.

① one – per
② one – a
③ way – per
④ once – per
⑤ once – the

04 다음 짝지어진 두 단어의 관계가 같도록 빈칸에 알맞은 말을 쓰시오.

> art : artist = cartoon : _____

05 다음 빈칸에 공통으로 들어갈 말을 쓰시오.

> • Let me take a look _____ the map.
> • Jack is good _____ singing and dancing.

➡ _____

[06~07] 다음 담화문을 읽고, 물음에 답하시오.

> W: ⓐEverybody are good at something. Some people are good at drawing. _ⓑ_ people are good at singing. What are you good at?

06 위 담화문의 밑줄 친 ⓐ에서 어법상 어색한 것을 고쳐 다시 쓰시오.

➡ _____

07 위 담화문의 빈칸 ⓑ에 알맞은 것은?

① Another
② Other
③ Others
④ The other
⑤ The others

[08~11] 다음 대화를 읽고, 물음에 답하시오.

> B: Hi, Cindy. ⓐIs something wrong?
> G: I have to give a speech in front of the whole school. I'm so _ⓑ_.
> B: Don't worry. ⓒYou're a very good speaker. I'm _ⓓ_ you'll do a good job.
> G: Thanks, Minho. I feel much better now.

08 위 대화의 밑줄 친 ⓐ와 같은 뜻이 되도록 빈칸에 알맞은 말을 쓰시오.

➡ What's the _____ with you?

09 위 대화의 흐름상 빈칸 ⓑ에 알맞은 것은?

① tired   ② busy
③ nervous   ④ free
⑤ excited

10 위 대화의 밑줄 친 ⓒ와 같은 뜻이 되도록 빈칸에 알맞은 말을 쓰시오.

➡ You _____ very _____.

11 위 대화의 빈칸 ⓓ에 알맞은 것은? (2개)

① well   ② right
③ sure   ④ good
⑤ certain

12 다음 빈칸에 알맞은 말이 순서대로 바르게 짝지어진 것은?

• Jenny is the famous singer _____ appeared on TV last night.
• I bought a chair _____ was made of wood.

① who – which   ② whom – that
③ which – who   ④ which – which
⑤ whose – that

13 다음 문장에서 틀린 것을 고치시오.

I have three books that tells us about China.

_____ ➡ _____

14 다음 문장의 빈칸에 문맥상 알맞은 것은?

While you are jogging, _____.

① you get up late
② they may get a toothache
③ you won't get cold
④ watch out for dogs
⑤ he may be tired yesterday

15 다음 중 밑줄 친 부분의 쓰임이 나머지와 다른 것은?

① I want to know who she is.
② This is the boy who came from Africa.
③ The man who is in the room is my cousin.
④ Do you know the man who is wearing a blue jumper?
⑤ The teacher likes the students who ask many questions.

16 다음 문장의 빈칸에 공통으로 알맞은 것을 쓰시오.

• I've never seen such a horrible movie _____.
• He raised his hand _____ the teacher called his name.

17 다음 두 문장을 한 문장으로 연결할 때 빈칸에 알맞은 것은?

> There is a boy. He is riding a bike.
> ➡There is a boy _____ is riding a bike.

① how   ② who
③ whom   ④ which
⑤ whose

18 다음 중 어법상 알맞지 <u>않은</u> 문장은?

① There's a house which has two chimneys.
② Can you see a boy who is running along the river?
③ I visited a town that is famous as a hot spring resort.
④ Mark is the cook who was on TV last night.
⑤ The man who is sitting on the box have a problem.

19 다음 두 문장의 뜻이 같도록 빈칸에 알맞은 말을 쓰시오.

> After the sun rises, she gets up.
> = _____ she gets up, the sun rises.

[20~21] 다음 글을 읽고, 물음에 답하시오.

> I'm good ___ⓐ___ making spaghetti and doing push-ups. I'm also good ___ⓑ___ telling funny jokes. I play badminton, and ⓒ<u>I have long beautiful hairs.</u> Who am I?

20 위 글의 빈칸 ⓐ와 ⓑ에 공통으로 알맞은 것은?

① to   ② on
③ at   ④ for
⑤ with

21 위 글의 밑줄 친 ⓒ에서 어법상 어색한 것을 고치시오.

➡ _____ ➡ _____

[22~24] 다음 글을 읽고, 물음에 답하시오.

> (①) After I got home, I began to write a new graphic novel, *Lunch Lady Begins.* (②) She rides a super scooter that can fly. (③) She saves people from danger around the world. (④) She also makes 100 cookies per ___ⓐ___ and gives them away to hungry children. (⑤)

22 위 글의 ①~⑤ 중 다음 주어진 문장이 들어갈 알맞은 곳은?

> In it, Lunch Lady is a superhero.

①   ②   ③   ④   ⑤

23 위 글의 빈칸 ⓐ에 다음 정의에 해당하는 단어를 쓰시오.

> one of the sixty parts that a minute is divided into

➡ _____

24 위 글의 내용으로 보아 대답할 수 없는 질문은?

① When did the writer begin to write a new graphic novel?
② What does Lunch Lady ride?
③ Why is Lunch Lady a superhero?
④ How does Lunch Lady save people from danger?
⑤ To whom does Lunch Lady give away cookies?

[25~27] 다음 글을 읽고, 물음에 답하시오.

> ⓐI showed my book to Ms. Lee. She loved it, ①too. She also told me ②about her coworkers who had special talents. Ms. Park, ③other cafeteria worker, won a dancing contest. Mr. Kim, the janitor ④at our school, was ⑤once an adventurous park ranger.

25 위 글의 밑줄 친 ①~⑤ 중 어법상 어색한 것은?

①   ②   ③   ④   ⑤

26 위 글의 밑줄 친 ⓐ와 문형이 같은 것은?

① Jane sent me a birthday card.
② The man is strong.
③ There are many books in the library.
④ The news made her glad.
⑤ My grandfather planted some trees last year.

27 What does Mr. Kim do for a living? Answer in English.

➡ _____

[28~30] 다음 글을 읽고, 물음에 답하시오.

> My name is Hojin, and I like to make graphic novels. ____ⓐ____ I was walking home from school last week, I saw a woman on a scooter. ⓑShe looked really cool, and her scooter was very unique.
>
> "Are you going home, Hojin?" she said to me suddenly.
>
> "Yes, but do I know you?" I asked.
>
> "Of course," she answered. "I see you at the school cafeteria every day."

28 위 글의 빈칸 ⓐ에 알맞은 것은?

① If   ② After
③ Before   ④ Since
⑤ While

29 위 글의 밑줄 친 ⓑ를 우리말로 옮기시오.

➡ _____

30 위 글의 내용과 일치하지 않는 것은?

① 호진이는 만화 소설 쓰기를 좋아한다.
② 호진이는 지난주에 한 여인을 만났다.
③ 그 여인의 스쿠터는 아주 독특했다.
④ 그 여인은 호진이를 알고 있었다.
⑤ 호진이는 그 여인을 학교 식당에서 매일 보았다.

Lesson 2

Where Do People Live?

 의사소통 기능

- 의향 묻고 답하기
  A: What kind of house do you want to live in?
  B: I want to live in a cave house.

- 위치 묻고 답하기
  A: Where can I find men's hats?
  B: You can find them on the first floor.

 언어 형식

- 현재완료
  People **have built** wooden houses for a long time.

- each
  Each house **is** big enough for a whole village.

교과서

Words & Expressions

Key Words

- **airplane-shaped** 〔형〕 비행기 모양의
- **avoid** [əvɔ́id] 〔동〕 방지하다, 막다, 피하다
- **become** [bikʌ́m] 〔동〕 ~이 되다
- **build** [bild] 〔동〕 짓다, 건설[건축]하다
- **cafeteria** [kæfətíəriə] 〔명〕 카페테리아, 구내식당
- **cave** [keiv] 〔명〕 동굴
- **century** [séntʃəri] 〔명〕 100년, 세기
- **collector** [kəléktər] 〔명〕 수집가, 징수원
- **cone** [koun] 〔명〕 원뿔, 원뿔형 물체
- **cover** [kʌ́vər] 〔동〕 씌우다, 가리다, 덮다
- **decide** [disáid] 〔동〕 결정하다, 결심하다
- **design** [dizáin] 〔명〕 디자인, 설계 〔동〕 디자인하다
- **dining room** 식당
- **else** [els] 〔부〕 또[그 밖의] 다른, 다른
- **enemy** [énəmi] 〔명〕 적
- **enough** [inʌ́f] 〔부〕 ~에 필요한 정도로, ~할 만큼 (충분히)
- **entrance** [éntrəns] 〔명〕 입구, 문
- **fifth** [fifθ] 〔형〕 다섯 번째의, 제5의
- **fine dust** 미세먼지
- **floor** [flɔːr] 〔명〕 마루, 바닥, (건물의) 층
- **forest** [fɔ́ːrist] 〔명〕 숲, 삼림
- **fresh** [freʃ] 〔형〕 신선한
- **gate** [geit] 〔명〕 문, 정문
- **goat** [gout] 〔명〕 염소
- **grass** [græs] 〔명〕 풀, 잔디
- **guesthouse** [gesthɑus] 〔명〕 게스트하우스
- **guide** [gaid] 〔명〕 안내[가이드], 관광 안내 책자
- **harmony** [hɑ́ːrməni] 〔명〕 조화, 화합
- **information** [infərméiʃən] 〔명〕 정보
- **jeans** [dʒiːnz] 〔명〕 바지, 면[청]바지
- **kind** [kaind] 〔명〕 종류

- **lovely** [lʌ́vli] 〔형〕 사랑스러운, 아름다운
- **low** [lou] 〔형〕 낮은
- **mall** [mɔːl] 〔명〕 쇼핑몰, 쇼핑 센터
- **meal** [miːl] 〔명〕 식사, 끼니
- **nature** [néitʃər] 〔명〕 자연
- **ocean** [óuʃən] 〔명〕 대양, 바다
- **part** [pɑːrt] 〔명〕 부분
- **pay** [pei] 〔동〕 지불하다, 내다
- **piano-shaped** 〔형〕 피아노 모양의
- **plant** [plænt] 〔명〕 식물, 초목
- **practice** [prǽktis] 〔동〕 연습하다
- **protect** [prətékt] 〔동〕 보호하다, 지키다
- **restroom** [réstruːm] 〔명〕 화장실, 세면실
- **round** [raund] 〔형〕 둥근, 동그란 〔전〕 ~을 돌아
- **shaped** [ʃeipt] 〔형〕 ~의 모양[형태]의
- **since** [sins] 〔전〕 ~부터[이후]
- **sometimes** [sʌ́mtàimz] 〔부〕 때때로, 가끔
- **southern** [sʌ́ðərn] 〔형〕 남쪽[남부]에 위치한
- **stone** [stoun] 〔명〕 돌
- **storage** [stɔ́ːridʒ] 〔명〕 저장, 보관
- **story** [stɔ́ːri] 〔명〕 (건물의) 층
- **tax** [tæks] 〔명〕 세금
- **thousand** [θáuzənd] 〔명〕 1, 000, 천 〔형〕 수천의
- **tour** [tuər] 〔명〕 여행, 관광
- **unique** [juːníːk] 〔형〕 유일무이한, 독특한
- **view** [vjuː] 〔명〕 경관, 전망
- **village** [víidʒ] 〔명〕 마을, 마을 사람들
- **welcome** [wélkəm] 〔동〕 맞이하다, 환영하다 〔형〕 환영받는
- **wind** [wind] 〔명〕 바람
- **without** [wiðáut] 〔전〕 ~ 없이, ~을 사용하지 않고
- **wooden** [wúdn] 〔형〕 나무로 된, 목재의

Key Expressions

- **be afraid of** ~을 두려워하다
- **be good at** ~을 잘하다
- **Excuse me.** (모르는 사람의 관심을 끌려고 할 때) 실례합니다.
- **give it a try** 시도하다, 한번 해 보다
- **in harmony with** ~와 조화를 이루어
- **kind of** 약간, 어느 정도
- **look at** ~을 보다

- **look for** ~을 찾다
- **next to** ~ 옆에
- **out of** ~의 안에서 밖으로, ~의 밖으로
- **pile up** 쌓아 올리다
- **take down** (구조물을 해체하여) 치우다
- **upside down** 거꾸로, 뒤집혀
- **watch out for** ~을 조심하다

58   Lesson 2. Where Do People Live?

Word Power

※ 기수와 서수

- one → first
- two → second
- three → third
- four → fourth
- five → fifth
- six → sixth
- seven → seventh

- eight → eighth
- nine → ninth
- ten → tenth
- eleven → eleventh
- twelve → twelfth
- nineteen → nineteenth
- twenty → twentieth

- thirty → thirtieth
- forty → fortieth
- eighty → eightieth
- ninety → ninetieth
- hundred → hundredth
- thousand → thousandth
- million → millionth

English Dictionary

- **avoid** 방지하다, 막다, 피하다
  → to take action in order to prevent something unpleasant from happening
  불쾌한 일이 일어나지 않도록 조치를 취하다

- **cave** 동굴
  → a large hole in the side of a cliff or hill, or one that is under the ground
  절벽이나 언덕의 측면에 있는 큰 구멍 또는 땅 밑에 있는 큰 구멍

- **cafeteria** 카페테리아, 구내식당
  → a restaurant where you choose your food from a counter and take it to your table after paying for it
  당신이 카운터에서 음식을 선택하고 그것에 대해 지불한 후에 테이블로 가져가는 레스토랑

- **century** 100년, 세기
  → a period of a hundred years that is used when stating a date
  날짜를 말할 때 사용되는 100년의 기간

- **collector** 징수원
  → someone whose job is to collect taxes or debts etc.
  세금이나 부채 등을 징수하는 사람

- **enemy** 적
  → someone who hates you or wants to harm you
  당신을 싫어하거나 해치고 싶어 하는 사람

- **forest** 숲, 삼림
  → a large area where trees grow close together
  나무들이 서로 가까이 자라는 넓은 지역

- **guesthouse** 게스트하우스
  → a private home or boarding house offering accommodation to travellers
  여행자에게 숙박을 제공하는 개인 주택 또는 기숙사

- **information** 정보
  → facts about someone or something
  어떤 사람 또는 어떤 것에 관한 사실들

- **plant** 식물, 초목, 나무
  → a living thing that grows in the earth and has a stem, leaves, and roots, especially one that is smaller than a tree or bush
  땅에서 자라고 줄기, 잎, 뿌리를 가진 생물, 특히 나무나 덤불보다 작은 생물

- **protect**: 보호하다, 지키다
  → to prevent someone or something from being harmed or damaged
  누군가 또는 무언가가 다치거나 손상되지 않도록 막다

- **restroom** 화장실, 세면실
  → a room with a toilet for customers to use
  손님이 사용하기 위한 변기가 있는 방

- **tax** 세금
  → an amount of money that you have to pay to the government so that you can use public services
  공공 서비스를 이용하기 위해 당신이 정부에 지불해야 하는 금액

- **thousand** 1,000, 천
  → the number 1,000
  1,000이라는 수

- **wind** 바람
  → a current of air that is moving across the earth's surface
  지구 표면을 가로질러 움직이는 공기의 흐름

- **wooden** 나무로 된, 목재의
  → made of wood
  나무로 만들어진

01 다음 중 나머지 넷을 대표할 수 있는 단어는?

① goat ② animal
③ bear ④ rabbit
⑤ giraffe

02 다음 빈칸에 알맞은 말이 바르게 짝지어진 것은?

> • I think the dog is kind _____ strange.
> • Henry was looking _____ his shoes.

① of – at ② of – for
③ at – in ④ at – with
⑤ to – over

03 다음 영영풀이에 해당하는 단어로 알맞은 것은?

> the way into a place, for example a door or gate

① hall ② yard
③ lobby ④ entrance
⑤ bridge

서답형
04 다음 짝지어진 단어의 관계가 같도록 빈칸에 알맞은 말을 쓰시오.

> cheap : expensive = low : _____

05 다음 우리말에 맞게 빈칸에 알맞은 것은?

> 천천히 물병을 거꾸로 뒤집어라.
> ➡ Slowly turn the jar upside _____.

① up ② on
③ down ④ from
⑤ along

서답형
06 다음 영영풀이에 해당하는 단어를 쓰시오.

> casual trousers that are usually made of strong blue cotton cloth called denim

➡ _____

서답형
07 다음 우리말에 맞게 빈칸에 알맞은 말을 쓰시오.

> 마른 풀에 불이 붙었다.
> ➡ The dry _____ caught fire.

08 다음 빈칸에 공통으로 알맞은 것은?

> • He took some coins out _____ his pocket.
> • We had a lot _____ fun at the party.

① in ② of
③ up ④ about
⑤ at

01 다음 짝지어진 두 단어의 관계가 같도록 빈칸에 알맞은 말을 쓰시오.

(1) one : first = two : _____
(2) four : fourth = five : _____
(3) nine : _____ = seven : seventh

02 다음 우리말에 맞게 빈칸에 알맞은 말을 쓰시오.

(1) 전통 가옥들은 자연과 조화를 이루고 있다.
➡ Traditional houses are _____ _____ _____ nature.
(2) 우리는 서로 바로 옆에 앉았다.
➡ We sat _____ _____ each other.
(3) 너의 앨범을 봐도 될까?
➡ May I _____ _____ your album?

03 다음 빈칸에 들어갈 알맞은 말을 〈보기〉에서 골라 쓰시오.

┌─── 보기 ───┐
build   entrance   avoid   protect

(1) I left early to _____ the rush hour.
(2) He wanted to _____ his own house.
(3) Parents have the right to _____ their children.
(4) I'll meet you at the main _____ .

04 다음 괄호 안의 단어를 문맥에 맞게 고쳐 쓰시오.

(1) Kathy looked particularly _____ that night. (love)
(2) The river falls into the _____ sea. (south)
(3) I found a _____ box in the room. (wood)

05 다음 빈칸에 알맞은 말을 〈보기〉에서 골라 쓰시오.

┌─── 보기 ───┐
take down   look for   pile up   good at

(1) Nancy is _____ dancing.
(2) We have to _____ a tent.
(3) You had better _____ your dog at the park.
(4) Work is starting to _____ .

06 다음 영영풀이에 해당하는 단어를 주어진 철자로 시작하여 쓰시오.

(1) c_____ : someone whose job is to collect taxes or debts etc.
(2) e_____ : someone who hates you or wants to harm you

Conversation

1 의향 묻고 답하기

> **A** What kind of house do you want to live in? 너는 어떤 종류의 집에서 살고 싶니?
> **B** I want to live in a cave house. 나는 동굴 집에서 살고 싶어.

- want to ~는 '~하고 싶다'의 뜻으로 상대방의 의향을 묻거나 대답할 때 쓰는 표현이다.

  - A: What kind of movie do you want to see? 너는 어떤 종류의 영화를 보고 싶니?
    B: I want to see a horror movie. 나는 공포 영화를 보고 싶어.

  - A: What do you want to read? 너는 무엇을 읽고 싶니?
    B: I want to read this book. 나는 이 책을 읽고 싶어.

- what 대신 where, when 등의 의문사를 사용해 상대방이 원하는 것을 물을 수 있다.

  - A: Where do you want to go? 너는 어디에 가고 싶니?
    B: I want to go to the zoo. 나는 동물원에 가고 싶어.

  - A: When do you want to go to the movies? 너는 언제 영화 보러 가고 싶니?
    B: I want to go to the movies tomorrow. 나는 내일 영화 보러 가고 싶어.

- Do you want to ~?는 '너는 ~하고 싶니?'의 뜻으로 상대방이 특정한 일을 하고 싶은지 물을 때 쓰인다.

  - A: Do you want to buy this hat? 너는 이 모자를 사고 싶니?
    B: Sure, I do. 물론, 사고 싶어.

- 무엇이 되고 싶은지 장래 희망을 물을 때는 What do you want to be in the future? / What would you like[do you want] to be when you grow up? 등의 표현을 사용한다. 이에 대한 응답으로 되고 싶은 것에 대해 말할 때는 I want to be ~ / I would like to be ~ 등의 표현을 사용한다.

  - A: What do you want to be in the future? 너는 미래에 무엇이 되고 싶니?
    B: I want to be an animal doctor. 나는 수의사가 되고 싶어.

핵심 Check

1. 다음 우리말과 일치하도록 빈칸에 알맞은 말을 쓰시오.

   (1) **A:** What _____ of house do you _____ to live in? (너는 어떤 종류의 집에서 살고 싶니?)

   B: I want _____ _____ in a tree house. (나는 나무 위의 집에서 살고 싶어.)

   (2) **A:** _____ do you want to _____ in the future? (너는 미래에 무엇이 되고 싶니?)

   B: I _____ _____ be a computer programmer. (나는 컴퓨터 프로그래머가 되고 싶어.)

2 위치 묻고 답하기

> **A** Where can I find men's hats? 남성용 모자는 어디에 있어요?
> **B** You can find them on the first floor. 1층에서 찾을 수 있어요.

■ Where can I find ~?는 '~은 어디에 있습니까?'라는 뜻으로 위치를 묻는 표현이다.

- A: Where can I find the nurse's office? 양호실은 어디에 있니?
  B: It's between teachers' office and the art room. 교무실과 미술실 사이에 있어.

■ Where can I find ~? 대신 Where is ~?를 써서 위치를 물을 수 있다.

- A: Where is the Eiffel Tower? 에펠탑은 어디에 있니?
  B: It's in Paris. 파리에 있어.

장소를 묻는 여러 가지 표현

- Where can I find ~?
- Where is ~?
- Can you tell me where ~ is[are]?
- Do you know where ~ is[are]?

■ 장소를 말할 때는 「It's in+장소.(그것은 ~에 있다.)」의 표현을 이용할 수 있다.

- A: Where is Chinatown? 차이나타운은 어디에 있니?
  B: It's in Incheon. 인천에 있어.

핵심 Check

2. 다음 우리말과 일치하도록 빈칸에 알맞은 말을 쓰시오.

(1) **A:** _____ can I _____ the restroom? (화장실은 어디 있습니까?)

   B: It's _____ to the elevator. (엘리베이터 옆에 있어요.)

(2) **A:** _____ is the bus stop? (버스 정류장은 어디에 있니?)

   B: It's _____ the bank. (은행 뒤에 있어.)

(3) **A:** _____ is the Haeundae Beach? (해운대는 어디에 있니?)

   B: It's _____ Busan. (부산에 있어.)

(4) **A:** Can you _____ me _____ the bus stop is? (버스 정류장은 어디에 있는지 알려주시겠어요?)

   B: It's in _____ of the bank. (은행 앞에 있습니다.)

Listen & Speak 1 A-1

B: Hey, ❶look at this house in the picture. ❷It looks like a big shoe!

G: Oh, it's very unique, ❸but I don't want to live in a shoe.

B: ❹What kind of house do you want to live in?

G: Well, I want to live in an airplane-shaped house.

B: 어이, 이 사진 속의 집을 봐. 그것은 큰 신발처럼 보여!
G: 오, 아주 독특하긴 하지만, 난 신발 속에서 살고 싶지 않아.
B: 넌 어떤 종류의 집에서 살고 싶니?
G: 음, 나는 비행기 모양의 집에서 살고 싶어.

❶ 동사원형으로 시작하는 명령문이다.
❷ look like: ~처럼 보이다
❸ want to: ~하기를 원하다
❹ What kind of ~?: 어떤 종류의 ~?

Check(√) True or False

(1) The house in the picture looks like a big shoe.　　　　T ☐ F ☐

(2) The girl doesn't want to live in an airplane-shaped house.　　　T ☐ F ☐

Listen & Speak 1 A-2

M: ❶Excuse me, is there a restaurant in this mall?

W: Yes. What kind of food would you like?

M: ❷I'd like Chinese food.

W: There is a great restaurant on the fifth floor.

M: Thank you.

M: 실례합니다. 이 쇼핑몰에 식당이 있나요?
W: 네. 어떤 음식을 드시겠어요?
M: 중국 음식을 먹고 싶어요.
W: 5층에 멋진 식당이 있어요.
M: 감사합니다.

❶ Excuse me: 죄송합니다(모르는 사람에게 말을 걸 때 쓰는 관용적인 표현)
❷ I'd like = I want

Check(√) True or False

(3) There is a Korean restaurant in this mall.　　　　T ☐ F ☐

(4) The man likes Chinese food.　　　　T ☐ F ☐

Progress Check 2

W: Excuse me, where can I find women's shoes?

M: ❶You can find them on the second floor. ❷They're next to the elevator.

W: Thank you.

M: ❸You're welcome.

W: 실례합니다. 여자 신발은 어디에 있어요?
M: 2층에서 찾을 수 있어요. 엘리베이터 옆에 있어요.
W: 감사합니다.
M: 천만에요.

❶ them = women's shoes / on the second floor: 2층에
❷ next to: ~ 옆에
❸ You're welcome.: 감사에 대한 응답으로 Don't mention it., Not at all. 등도 같은 뜻으로 쓰인다.

Check(√) True or False

(5) The woman wants to buy women's shoes.　　　　T ☐ F ☐

(6) The woman can find women's shoes on the first floor.　　　T ☐ F ☐

Listen & Speak 2 A-2

W: ❶Can I help you?

M: ❷I'm looking for watches. ❸Where can I find them?

W: ❹They're on the third floor, next to the restroom.

M: Thank you.

---

❶ Can I help you?: 도와드릴까요?(=May I help you? / What can I do for you?)

❷ look for: ~을 찾다

❸ them = watches

❹ on the third floor: 3층에

Work Together - Act

A: What kind of house do you want to build?

B: ❶I want to build a two-story house that looks like a boat.

A: ❷Where is the kitchen?

B: ❸It's on the second floor.

---

❶ that은 주격 관계대명사로 which로 바꿔 쓸 수 있다.

❷ Where is ~?: ~은 어디에 있니?

❸ It's = It is(이때의 is는 '있다'의 뜻임)

Communicate: A. Listen and Answer

Woman: ❶Welcome to Jeonju Hanok Guesthouse. ❷May I help you?

Man: Yes, ❸I'd like a room for two nights.

Woman: Well, what kind of room would you like?

Man: ❹Do you have a room with a garden view? You have a lovely garden.

Woman: Yes, we do. ❺Every room in our house has a garden view, but there are no beds in the rooms.

Man: ❻Do I have to sleep on the floor?

Woman: Yes, you do.

Man: O.K. ❼I'll give it a try. Where can I have breakfast?

Woman: You can have breakfast in the dining room, next to the kitchen.

Man: ❽I see.

Woman: O.K. You're in the Nabi room. ❾Here's your key.

Man: Thank you.

---

❶ Welcome to ~: ~에 오신 것을 환영합니다

❷ May I help you?: 도와 드릴까요?(= Can I help you?/ What can I do for you?)

❸ I'd like = I would like = I want

❹ a room with a garden view: 정원이 보이는 방

❺ 주어에 every가 있을 때는 단수동사로 받는다.

❻ Do I have to sleep ~? = Must I sleep ~?

❼ I'll give it a try.: 한번 시도해 볼게요.

❽ I see.: 알겠습니다.

❾ Here's ~ = Here is ~: 여기에 ~이 있다

Progress Check 1

B: Hey, ❶look at this unique house in the picture. It's upside down.

G: ❷Oh, it looks interesting, but I think it's kind of strange.

B: What kind of house do you want to live in?

G: ❸I like music, so I want to live in a piano-shaped house.

---

❶ in the picture: 사진에 있는(house를 수식하는 형용사구)

❷ kind of: 좀, 약간

❸ so: 그래서

Progress Check 3

W: Excuse me, where can I find men's hats?

M: ❶You can find them on the second floor. ❷They're next to the elevator.

W: Thank you.

M: You're welcome.

---

❶ them = men's hats / on the second floor: 2층에

❷ They=Men's hats

● 다음 우리말과 일치하도록 빈칸에 알맞은 말을 쓰시오.

Listen & Speak 1 A. Listen and Check

1. B: Hey, _____ at this house _____ the picture. It looks _____ a big shoe!

   G: Oh, it's very _____, but I don't _____ _____ live in a shoe.

   B: What _____ of house do you want to _____ in?

   G: Well, I want _____ live in an airplane-shaped _____.

2. M: _____ me, is _____ a restaurant in this _____?

   W: Yes. What _____ of food _____ you like?

   M: I'd _____ Chinese food.

   W: _____ is a great restaurant _____ the fifth floor.

   M: _____ you.

Listen & Speak 2 A. Listen and Write

1. W: _____ me, where can I _____ women's shoes?

   M: You _____ find them on the _____ floor. They're _____ to the elevator.

   W: Thank _____.

   M: You're _____.

2. W: Can I _____ you?

   M: I'm looking _____ watches. Where _____ I find them?

   W: They're _____ the third floor, _____ to the restroom.

   M: Thank you.

Communicate A. Listen and Answer

Woman: _____ to Jeonju Hanok Guesthouse. _____ I help you?

Man: Yes, I'd _____ a room _____ two nights.

Woman: Well, what _____ of room would you _____?

Man: Do you have a room _____ a garden _____? You have a lovely _____.

Woman: Yes, we _____. Every _____ in our house has a garden _____, but there are _____ beds in the rooms.

Man: Do I _____ to sleep on the _____?

해석

1. B: 어이, 이 사진 속의 집을 봐. 그것은 큰 신발처럼 보여!
   G: 오, 아주 독특하긴 하지만, 난 신발 속에서 살고 싶지 않아.
   B: 넌 어떤 종류의 집에서 살고 싶니?
   G: 음, 나는 비행기 모양의 집에서 살고 싶어.

2. M: 실례합니다, 이 쇼핑몰에 식당이 있나요?
   W: 네. 어떤 음식을 드시겠어요?
   M: 중국 음식을 먹고 싶어요.
   W: 5층에 멋진 식당이 있어요.
   M: 감사합니다.

1. W: 실례합니다, 여자 신발은 어디에 있어요?
   M: 2층에서 찾을 수 있어요. 엘리베이터 옆에 있어요.
   W: 감사합니다.
   M: 천만에요.

2. W: 뭘 도와드릴까요?
   M: 시계를 찾고 있어요. 어디에서 찾을 수 있습니까?
   W: 3층에, 화장실 옆에 있어요.
   M: 감사합니다.

W: 전주 한옥 게스트하우스에 오신 걸 환영합니다. 무엇을 도와드릴까요?
M: 네, 이틀 밤 묵을 방을 원해요.
W: 음, 어떤 방을 원하세요?
M: 정원이 보이는 방이 있어요? 정원이 아름답군요.
W: 네, 그렇습니다. 우리 집 모든 방에서는 정원이 보입니다. 하지만 방에는 침대가 없어요.
M: 바닥에서 자야 합니까?

Woman: Yes, you _____.

Man: O.K. I'll _____ it a _____. _____ can I _____ breakfast?

Woman: You _____ have breakfast in the _____ room, next _____ the kitchen.

Man: I _____.

Woman: O.K. You're _____ the Nabi room. _____ your key.

Man: _____ you.

W: 네, 그렇습니다.
M: 알았습니다. 한번 시도해 볼게요. 아침 식사는 어디서 해요?
W: 아침 식사는 부엌 옆에 있는 식당에서 할 수 있어요.
M: 알겠습니다.
W: 좋아요, 나비 방에 들어가세요. 여기 당신의 열쇠가 있습니다.
M: 고맙습니다.

Progress Check

1. **B:** Hey, look _____ this unique house _____ the picture. It's upside _____.

   G: Oh, it _____ interesting, _____ I think it's _____ of strange.

   B: What _____ of house do you _____ to live in?

   G: I like music, _____ I want to _____ in a piano-shaped house.

2. **W:** _____ me, where can I _____ women's jeans?

   M: You can _____ them on the _____ floor. They're _____ to the elevator.

   W: _____ you.

   M: You're _____.

3. **M:** Excuse me, _____ can I find men's _____?

   W: You _____ find them on the second _____. They're next _____ the elevator.

   M: Thank _____.

   W: You're _____.

1. B: 이봐, 사진 속의 이 독특한 집을 봐. 집이 거꾸로 있어.
   G: 아, 재미있어 보이지만, 좀 이상한 것 같아.
   B: 넌 어떤 집에서 살고 싶니?
   G: 나는 음악을 좋아해서 피아노 모양의 집에서 살고 싶어.
2. W: 실례합니다. 여자 청바지는 어디에 있나요?
   M: 2층에서 찾을 수 있어요. 엘리베이터 옆에 있어요.
   W: 감사합니다.
   M: 천만에요.
3. M: 실례합니다. 남성용 모자는 어디에 있나요?
   W: 2층에서 찾을 수 있어요. 엘리베이터 옆에 있어요.
   M: 감사합니다.
   W: 천만에요.

Work -Act

A: _____ kind of house do you want to _____?

B: I want _____ build a two-story house _____ looks _____ a boat.

A: _____ is the kitchen?

B: It's on the _____ floor.

A: 넌 어떤 집을 짓고 싶어?
B: 보트처럼 생긴 2층짜리 집을 짓고 싶어.
A: 부엌이 어디 있어?
B: 2층에 있어.

01 다음 대화의 빈칸에 알맞은 말을 쓰시오.

> **A:** What kind of house do you _____ to live in?
> **B:** I _____ to live in a cave house.

cave 동굴

02 다음 대화의 밑줄 친 부분과 바꿔 쓸 수 있는 것은? (2개)

> **A:** Excuse me. I'm looking for shoes. <u>Where can I find them?</u>
> **B:** They're on the first floor.
> **A:** Thank you very much.

Excuse me.: 죄송합니다.
look for: ~을 찾다

① Where are they?　　② How may I help you?
③ Where can I buy them?　　④ Where do I need to go?
⑤ What do you want to have?

03 다음 대화의 밑줄 친 부분의 의도로 알맞은 것은?

> **A:** <u>What kind of house do you want to live in?</u>
> **B:** I want to live in a piano-shaped house.

① 의향 묻기　　② 주의하기
③ 요청하기　　④ 제안하기
⑤ 계획 묻기

04 다음 대화의 빈칸에 알맞은 것은?

> **A:** Excuse me. Where can I find women's clothes?
> **B:** _____
> **A:** Oh, I see. Thanks.

① You're welcome.　　② You can't miss it.
③ It's on the first floor.　　④ They're on the second floor.
⑤ I'm looking for them, too.

01 다음 대화를 의미가 통하도록 알맞게 배열한 것은?

(A) What kind of house do you want to live in?
(B) Hey, look at this house in the picture. It looks like a big shoe!
(C) Oh, it's very unique, but I don't want to live in a shoe.
(D) Well, I want to live in an airplane-shaped house.

① (A) – (D) – (B) – (C)
② (B) – (C) – (A) – (D)
③ (C) – (D) – (B) – (A)
④ (D) – (B) – (C) – (A)
⑤ (D) – (C) – (B) – (A)

02 다음 의도하는 바가 나머지 넷과 <u>다른</u> 하나는?

① Where can I find it?
② How can I go there?
③ How do I get there?
④ How may I help you?
⑤ Can you tell me where it is?

서답형
[03~04] 다음 대화의 빈칸에 알맞은 말을 쓰시오.

03
A: _____ can I find men's clothes?
B: They're on the second floor.
A: Oh, I see. Thanks.

04
A: Do you want to go on a picnic on Sunday?
B: Sure. I _____.

05 다음 대화의 밑줄 친 부분의 의도로 알맞은 것은?

A: Excuse me. <u>Do you know where I can find ball pens?</u>
B: Yes. They are on shelf A in aisle 1.

① 요청하기　　　　② 의도 묻기
③ 위치 묻기　　　　④ 능력 여부 묻기
⑤ 관심 사항 묻기

06 다음 중 짝지어진 대화가 <u>어색한</u> 것은?

① A: Where can I find women's clothes?
　 B: They're on the first floor.
② A: How can I get to the bookstore?
　 B: Go straight two blocks and turn left.
③ A: Where can I find socks?
　 B: They are on shelf C in aisle 1.
④ A: Where is the Statue of Liberty?
　 B: It's in New York.
⑤ A: Do you know where I can find the library?
　 B: Yes, that's right.

[07~11] 다음 대화를 읽고, 물음에 답하시오.

> Woman: Welcome to Jeonju Hanok Guesthouse.
> ⓐMay I help you?
> Man: Yes, I'd like a room for two nights.
> Woman: Well, what kind of room would you like?
> Man: Do you have a room ⓑwith a garden view? You have a lovely garden.
> Woman: Yes, we do. Every room in our house has a garden view, but there are no beds in the rooms.
> Man: Do I have to sleep on the floor?
> Woman: Yes, you do.
> Man: O.K. I'll ___ⓒ___ it a try. Where can I have breakfast?
> Woman: You can have breakfast in the dining room, next to the kitchen.
> Man: ⓓI see.
> Woman: O.K. You're in the Nabi room. Here's your key.
> Man: Thank you.

서답형

07 위 대화의 밑줄 친 ⓐ와 같은 뜻이 되도록 바꿔 쓸 때 빈칸에 알맞은 말을 쓰시오.

> _____ _____ I do for you?

08 위 대화의 밑줄 친 ⓑ와 같은 의미로 쓰인 것은?

① I often play with my classmates.
② Lucy is the girl with long hair.
③ Don't write with a pencil.
④ Do you agree with him?
⑤ Ben was pleased with the present.

서답형

09 위 대화의 빈칸 ⓒ에 알맞은 말을 쓰시오.

➡ _____

서답형

10 위 대화의 밑줄 친 ⓓ를 우리말로 옮기시오.

➡ _____

11 위 대화의 내용과 일치하지 않는 것은?

① 남자는 이틀 밤을 묵기를 원한다.
② 남자는 정원을 볼 수 있는 방을 원한다.
③ 남자는 침대에서 자는 것에 익숙하다.
④ 남자는 침대가 있는 방을 원한다.
⑤ 남자는 식당에서 아침식사를 할 것이다.

[12~13] 다음 대화를 읽고, 물음에 답하시오.

> B: Hey, look ___ⓐ___ this house in the picture. It looks like a big shoe!
> G: Oh, it's very unique, ___ⓑ___ I don't want to live in a shoe.
> B: What kind of house do you want to live in?
> G: Well, I want to live in an airplane-shaped house.

서답형

12 위 대화의 빈칸 ⓐ에 알맞은 전치사를 쓰시오.

➡ _____

중요

13 위 대화의 빈칸 ⓑ에 알맞은 것은?

① but   ② so
③ or   ④ for
⑤ and

01 다음 대화의 밑줄 친 우리말에 맞도록 주어진 단어를 이용하여 완성하시오.

> A: Where can I find computers?
> B: 그것들은 4층에 있다. (floor)
> A: Oh, I see. Thanks.

➡ _____

02 다음 대화의 괄호 안의 단어들을 바르게 배열하시오.

> A: (to / of / do / you / have / kind / what / pet / want)
> B: I want to have a rabbit.

➡ _____

[03~04] 다음 대화를 의미가 통하도록 알맞게 배열하시오.

03
> (A) You're welcome.
> (B) Thank you.
> (C) Excuse me, where can I find women's shoes?
> (D) You can find them on the second floor. They're next to the elevator.

➡ _____

04
> (A) Where is the kitchen?
> (B) What kind of house do you want to build?
> (C) It's on the second floor.
> (D) I want to build a two-story house that looks like a boat.

➡ _____

[05~08] 다음 대화를 읽고, 물음에 답하시오.

> M: ___ⓐ___ me, is there a restaurant in this mall?
> W: Yes. What ___ⓑ___ of food would you like?
> M: I'd like Chinese food.
> W: There is a great restaurant on the ⓒfive floor.
> M: Thank you.
> W: ⓓYou're welcome.

05 위 대화의 빈칸 ⓐ에 알맞은 것은?

① Guess   ② Forgive
③ Believe   ④ Pardon
⑤ Excuse

06 위 대화의 빈칸 ⓑ에 알맞은 말을 쓰시오.

➡ _____

07 위 대화의 밑줄 친 ⓒ를 알맞은 어형으로 고치시오.

➡ _____

08 위 대화의 밑줄 친 ⓓ와 같은 뜻이 되도록 다음 문장의 빈칸에 알맞은 말을 쓰시오.

> Don't _____ it.

Grammar

① 현재완료

> • People **have built** wooden houses for a long time. 사람들은 오랫동안 나무로 집을 지었다.
> • **Have** you ever **seen** a goat on the roof of a house?
>   당신은 집 지붕 위에 있는 염소를 본 적이 있나요?

■ **현재완료의 형태**
'have[has]+과거분사'의 형태를 취한다.

 • It **has been** such a long time. 정말 오랜만이다.
 • I **have had** many different jobs. 나는 많은 다양한 직업을 가져왔다.
cf. yesterday, two days ago, last Sunday 등과 같이 특정한 과거 시점을 나타내는 표현이 오면 현재
    완료시제로 쓰지 않고 과거시제로 써야 한다.
 • I **read** the book yesterday.   (○) 나는 어제 그 책을 읽었다.
   I have read the book yesterday. (✕)

■ **현재완료의 용법**
현재완료는 경험, 계속, 완료, 결과의 용법이 있다.

분류	용법	예문
경험	• 과거부터 현재까지의 경험 • before, ever, never, often 등과 쓰임	I **have** never **been** to Rome. 나는 로마에 가 본 적이 없다.
계속	• 과거의 일이 지금까지 계속됨 • 'since+특정 시점', 'for+기간' 등과 쓰임	I **have known** him since I was a little child. 나는 어릴 때부터 그를 알아 왔다.
완료	• 과거에 시작된 일이 이제 막 완료됨 • just, already, yet 등과 쓰임	He **has** just **finished** his homework. 그는 방금 숙제를 끝냈다.
결과	• 과거의 일이 현재의 결과를 가져옴 • '~해서 (지금) …하다'의 의미임	They **have gone** to Madrid. 그들은 마드리드에 가고 없다.

■ **현재완료의 부정문**
have[has]와 과거분사 사이에 not을 넣는다.

 • He **has not written** the letter yet. 그는 아직 그 편지를 쓰지 않았다.

■ **현재완료의 의문문**
'Have[Has]+주어+과거분사 ~?'의 형태를 취한다.

 • **Have** you ever **seen** a lion? 너는 사자를 본 적이 있니?

핵심 Check

1. 다음 괄호 안에서 알맞은 것을 고르시오.

   (1) Ann has just (did / done) her homework.

   (2) They (have / has) not (ate / eaten) the pizza.

   (3) He (lived, has lived) in this town since he was seven.

   (4) I have known her (for / since) three years.

2 each

- **Each** house **is** big enough for a whole village. 각 집은 마을 전체가 살 만큼 크다.
- **Each** person **has** different strengths. 각 사람은 각기 다른 강점을 가지고 있다.
- **Each** of the girls **has** her own desk. 소녀들 각각은 그녀 자신의 책상을 가지고 있다.

■ each가 형용사로 쓰일 때는 '각각의'라는 의미로, 전체를 구성하는 하나하나의 개별적인 것을 가리킨다. 「each+단수 명사+단수 동사」의 형태로 쓴다.

 • **Each** artist **has** his own character. 예술가는 각자 자신의 특성을 지니고 있다.

■ each가 대명사로 쓰일 때는 '각각, 각자'라는 의미로, 단수로 취급한다. 「each of+복수 명사+단수 동사」의 형태로 '~의 각각'이라는 의미를 나타낼 수 있다.

 • **Each** of them **has** different interests. 그들은 각자 다른 흥미를 갖고 있다.

■ each가 부사로 쓰일 때는 '각각, 하나에'의 의미로 사용된다.

 • I gave them two dollars **each**. 나는 그들에게 각각 2달러씩 주었다.

■ each other는 '서로'의 뜻으로 관용적으로 쓰인다.

 • You should help **each other**. 너희들은 서로 도와야 한다.

■ every는 '모든'의 뜻으로 형용사로만 쓰인다. each와 마찬가지로 뒤에 오는 명사는 단수형이 된다.

 • **Every** student **knows** him. 모든 학생이 그를 알고 있다.

■ both는 '둘 다'의 뜻으로 형용사와 대명사로 쓰인다. both가 형용사로 쓰일 때는 뒤에 복수 명사가 오고 복수 동사로 받는다.

 • **Both** teams **have** to get two points. [형용사] 두 팀 다 2점을 얻어야 한다.

 • **Both** of them **are** kind. [대명사] 그들은 둘 다 친절하다.

핵심 Check

2. 다음 괄호 안에서 알맞은 것을 고르시오.

 (1) Each of the boys (have / has) a bike.

 (2) Each student (is / are) carrying a lunch box.

 (3) All of us help (each / every) other.

 (4) I always get up early every (day / days).

 (5) Both of us (is / are) Korean tourists.

01 다음 괄호 안에서 알맞은 것을 고르시오.

(1) Jane (was / has been) busy since last week.

(2) How often have you (gone / been) to the United States?

(3) He (has finished / finished) reading two hours ago.

(4) He (has just finished / just finishes) his homework.

(5) We (arrived / have arrived) here yesterday.

(6) When (have you reached / did you reach) here?

reach 도착하다

02 다음 괄호 안에서 알맞은 것을 고르시오.

(1) Each of the girls (do / does) her best.

(2) Each student (have / has) his own desk.

(3) There are some trees on each (side / sides) of the street.

(4) Each of the (student / students) is doing his homework.

(5) Every (boy / boys) was kind to me.

(6) Both her parents (is / are) teachers.

do one's best 최선을 다하다
own 자신의
side 쪽, 편

03 다음 괄호 안에 주어진 단어를 어법상 알맞은 형태로 바꾸어 문장을 완성하시오.

(1) He (be) sick in bed since last Friday.

⇒ _____

(2) How long (you know) Miss Smith?

⇒ _____

(3) (you ever read) Christmas Carol?

⇒ _____

(4) My father (not read) the newspaper yet.

⇒ _____

sick 아픈
newspaper 신문

01 다음 두 문장을 한 문장으로 만들 때 빈칸에 알맞은 것은?

> I moved here two years ago. I still live here.
> ➡ I _____ here for two years.

① live   ② lived
③ will live   ④ am living
⑤ have lived

[02~03] 다음 문장의 빈칸에 알맞은 것을 고르시오.

02

> Each of the girls _____ willing to join the game.

① am   ② are
③ was   ④ were
⑤ being

03

> Ted is hungry, because he _____ nothing since this morning.

① eat   ② eats
③ ate   ④ has eaten
⑤ had eaten

서답형

[04~05] 다음 빈칸에 공통으로 알맞은 말을 쓰시오

04

> • _____ room is furnished with a table and chairs.
> • _____ of my friends bought me a present for my birthday.

05

> • Sorry to _____ kept you waiting. I _____ been to the station.
> • We _____ known each other since our childhood.

06 다음 중 밑줄 친 부분의 쓰임이 나머지 넷과 다른 것은?

① They got two cookies <u>each</u>.
② He had a bottle in <u>each</u> hand.
③ <u>Each</u> ticket costs 20 dollars.
④ <u>Each</u> boy has his own cell phone.
⑤ Bake the bread for five minutes on <u>each</u> side.

07 다음 문장의 빈칸에 알맞지 <u>않은</u> 것은?

> They have been to England _____.

① once   ② twice
③ before   ④ never
⑤ many times

08 다음 문장의 빈칸에 알맞은 것은?

> The two girls smiled at _____.

① another   ② other
③ the other   ④ each other
⑤ one the other

09 다음 괄호 안에 주어진 단어를 어법상 바르게 쓴 것은?

> I know some good restaurants here because I (live) in this town for five years.

① live
② lived
③ is living
④ have lived
⑤ had lived

10 다음 각 문장의 빈칸에 들어갈 수 <u>없는</u> 것은? (대 · 소문자 무시)

> • I enjoyed _____ minute of the party.
> • _____ the brothers are dead.
> • _____ the eggs in the box were broken.
> • She cut the cake into pieces and gave one to _____ of them.

① each
② both
③ all
④ some
⑤ every

서답형
11 다음 빈칸에 알맞은 말을 쓰시오.

> My mother has gone shopping. She is _____ here.

12 다음 문장의 빈칸에 알맞은 것은?

> The teacher gave two books to _____ boy.

① all
② each
③ other
④ each of
⑤ all of

서답형
13 다음 두 문장의 의미가 같도록 빈칸에 알맞은 말을 쓰시오.

> We have been married for ten years.
> = Ten years have passed _____ we got married.

중요
14 다음 빈칸에 알맞은 말이 바르게 짝지어진 것은?

> This year's School Sports Day was held on the school playing field. ___ⓐ___ class showed its best teamwork, and ___ⓑ___ the students had great fun.

① All − all
② All − each
③ Each − every
④ Each − all
⑤ Each of − each

15 다음 대화의 빈칸에 알맞은 것은?

> A: Have you ever heard the news?
> B: No, I _____ the news.

① heard
② have not heard
③ was not heard
④ did not heard
⑤ had not heard

서답형
16 다음 우리말을 영어로 옮길 때 빈칸에 알맞은 말을 쓰시오.

> 이 반의 각 학생은 영어를 매우 잘한다.
> ➡ _____ _____ in this class _____ English vey well.

17 다음 중 밑줄 친 부분의 쓰임이 나머지 넷과 <u>다른</u> 것은?

① <u>Each</u> man has his own taste.
② <u>Each</u> of them loves the other.
③ <u>Each</u> country has its own custom.
④ The elevator stopped at <u>each</u> floor.
⑤ The poem has 12 lines with 20 letters in <u>each</u> line.

[18~19] 다음 중 어법상 어색한 것을 고르시오.

18 ① I have had a fever since last Friday.
② Two years have passed since I came here.
③ We have known each other for many years.
④ He has been seventy years old when he died.
⑤ It has been a long time since I saw you.

19 ① He gave money to each of his sons.
② Each of us has his or her opinion.
③ Each of these plans have their merits and demerits.
④ The teacher shook hands with each of his pupils.
⑤ Each of his friends is going camping this summer.

서답형
20 다음 대화의 빈칸에 알맞은 말을 쓰시오.

A: How long has she been absent from school?
B: She _____ _____ _____ from school since this Wednesday.

서답형
21 다음 빈칸에 공통으로 알맞은 말을 쓰시오.

• Have you done your homework _____?
• She hasn't come home _____.

22 다음 중 밑줄 친 부분의 쓰임이 바르지 <u>않은</u> 것은?

① <u>All the rooms are</u> full today.
② <u>Every student</u> passed the test.
③ <u>Each of us have</u> a responsibility for our own health.
④ <u>Each year</u> thousands of people fall ill with flu.
⑤ We've known <u>each other</u> for ten years.

23 다음 중 밑줄 친 부분의 쓰임이 나머지 넷과 <u>다른</u> 하나는?

① I <u>have seen</u> the movie before.
② My uncle <u>has</u> never <u>lived</u> in China before.
③ How many times <u>have</u> they <u>been</u> to England?
④ Mr. Smith <u>has gone</u> to Berlin on business.
⑤ Paul and Marie <u>have been</u> to America once.

01 다음 우리말을 참조하여 문장을 완성하시오.

(1) 그들은 이미 콘서트를 시작했다.
➡ They _____ already _____ the concert.

(2) 그는 아직 런던에서 돌아오지 않았다.
➡ He _____ _____ _____ from London yet.

(3) 죄송하지만, 그녀는 회의에 가고 없습니다.
➡ I'm sorry, but she _____ _____ _____ a meeting.

02 다음 빈칸에 알맞은 말을 〈보기〉에서 골라 쓰시오.

┌─ 보기 ┐
both   all   each   every
└────────────────┘

(1) They sell oranges 5 cents _____.

(2) _____ of my parents look happy.

(3) _____ the chairs are broken.

(4) Please tell me about the meaning of _____ of the words.

(5) Not _____ student passed the exam.

03 다음 문장에서 어법상 어색한 것을 찾아 바르게 고쳐 쓰시오.

(1) She has gone to Bangladesh last Friday.
_____ ➡ _____

(2) My father hasn't left Seoul already.
_____ ➡ _____

04 다음 빈칸에 공통으로 알맞은 말을 쓰시오.

┌──────────────────────┐
│ • _____ student has to answer the question. │
│ • They have known _____ other for a long time. │
└──────────────────────┘

05 다음 문장에서 어법상 어색한 것을 찾아 바르게 고쳐 쓰시오.

(1) I didn't see him since then.
_____ ➡ _____

(2) The weather is good for ten days.
_____ ➡ _____

06 다음 주어진 단어를 바르게 배열하여 문장을 완성하시오.

(1) (Italy / many / he / to / been / times / has)
➡ _____

(2) (very / days / I / busy / these / been / have)
➡ _____

(3) (have / Paris / before / I / visited / never)
➡ _____

07 다음 〈보기〉에서 알맞은 말을 골라 빈칸에 쓰시오.

┌─── 보기 ───┐
all each both every some any
└─────────────┘

(1) Kirk lost _____ his money.

(2) Jenny enjoyed _____ minute of the party.

(3) They don't eat _____ meat.

(4) Tim cut the apple into pieces and gave one to _____ of us.

(5) Linda borrowed _____ money from him.

(6) Frank pulled the rope with _____ hands.

08 다음 문장에서 어법상 <u>어색한</u> 부분을 바르게 고쳐 문장을 다시 쓰시오.

(1) I have gone to London four years ago.

➡ _____

(2) When have you seen a white lion?

➡ _____

(3) I have often played with her when I was a child.

➡ _____

(4) He has been ill in bed last month.

➡ _____

09 다음 문장에서 어법상 <u>어색한</u> 부분을 고쳐 문장을 다시 쓰시오.

(1) Each of us have to finish our project.

➡ _____

(2) There were four book on the table. Each book was in a different color.

➡ _____
_____

(3) Every drivers should be careful.

➡ _____

10 다음 주어진 단어를 이용하여 우리말을 영어로 옮기시오.

(1) 그는 1970년 이래로 뉴욕에서 살았다.
(live, since)

➡ _____

(2) 너는 이 이야기를 벌써 다 읽었니?
(finish, this, story, yet)

➡ _____

(3) 나는 그 영화를 한 번 본 적이 있다.
(see, once)

➡ _____

11 다음 우리말과 일치하도록 문장을 완성하시오.

┌─────────────────────────────┐
각각의 학생은 자신의 최선을 다해야 한다.
➡ _____ student _____ to do his or her best.
└─────────────────────────────┘

Roofs Around the World

Grass Roofs

Have you ever seen a goat on the roof of a house? In Norway, we
can see animals on roofs. Norway has large forests. In harmony with
nature, people have built wooden houses for a long time. To build
strong and warm houses, they cover their roofs with grass. The grass
roofs protect them from the long cold winters and strong winds.
Sometimes, trees or plants grow out of the grass roofs, and some
animals enjoy their meals there.

Cone-shaped Roofs

A roof is an essential part of a house, but long ago some people built
roofs only to take them down easily. Centuries ago in southern Italy,
people who had a house without a roof paid lower taxes.

---

goat 염소
animal 동물, 짐승
forest 숲, 삼림
harmony 조화
nature 자연
build 짓다, 건설하다
wooden 나무의, 목재의
cover A with B B로 A를 덮다
protect A from B B로부터 A를 보호하다
sometimes 때때로
plant 식물, 초목
grow 자라다, 성장하다
grass 풀, 잔디
meal 음식
cone-shaped 원뿔 모양의
essential 필수적인, 본질적인
part 부분
take down 철거하다
easily 쉽게
century 세기, 100년
southern 남부의, 남쪽의
pay 지불하다
low 낮은
tax 세금

 확인문제

● 다음 문장이 본문의 내용과 일치하면 T, 일치하지 않으면 F를 쓰시오.

1 In Norway, you can see a goat on the roof of a house. ☐

2 People have built stone houses in Norway for a long time. ☐

3 Some animals sometimes enjoy their meals on the grass roofs. ☐

4 A roof is an essential part of a house. ☐

5 In southern Italy, people who had a house with a roof paid lower taxes centuries
   ago. ☐

To avoid high taxes on their houses, some people built cone-shaped
목적을 나타내는 부사적 용법의 to부정사   build의 과거형 build—built—built
roofs by piling up stones. When tax collectors came to the town,
        by+동명사   때를 나타내는 접속사
people took their roofs down quickly. After the tax collectors left, they
        '타동사+목적어(명사)+부사'의 이어동사   접 ~한 후에
piled up the stones again.

Big Round Roofs

From the sky in a part of southern China, you can see round roofs
                sky를 수식하는 형용사구   일반 사람을 나타내는 you
that look like big doughnuts. They are the roofs of the big round houses
= which ~처럼 보이다   = The round roofs   = the big round houses
of the Hakka people. They have lived in houses like these for about a
                    계속적 용법의 현재완료   ~와 같은
thousand years to protect themselves from enemies. The houses have
                        재귀 용법의 재귀대명사
only one gate without any windows on the first floor. Each house is big
                    1층에는 창문이 하나도 없이
enough for a whole village. It usually has four stories. It has kitchens
사+enough+for: ~을 위해 충분히 ...한   빈도부사: 일반동사 앞에 위치
on the first floor, storage rooms on the second floor, and living rooms
        one의 서수   two의 서수
and bedrooms on the third and fourth floors.
                    three의 서수   four+-th

avoid 피하다
cone-shaped 원뿔 모양의
pile up 쌓다
stone 돌
collector 징수원, 수집가
take down 철거하다
quickly 빨리
round 둥근
sky 하늘
doughnut 도넛
about 약
thousand 천, 1,000
enemy 적
gate 문, 대문
without ~이 없는
each 각각의; 각각
enough 충분히
whole 전체의
village 마을, 마을 사람들
story 층
kitchen 부엌
storage 저장
living room 거실

 **확인문제**

● 다음 문장이 본문의 내용과 일치하면 T, 일치하지 <u>않으면</u> F를 쓰시오.

1 In southern Italy, some people built cone-shaped roofs. ☐

2 When tax collectors came to the town, people built roofs by piling up stones. ☐

3 People can see round roofs that look like big doughnuts in a part of southern China. ☐

4 The Hakka people have lived in the big round houses for about a hundred years. ☐

5 The houses have only one gate without any windows on the first floor. ☐

● 우리말을 참고하여 빈칸에 알맞은 말을 쓰시오.

1 _____ you ever _____ a goat on the _____ of a house?

2 In Norway, we can _____ animals _____ roofs.

3 Norway has large _____.

4 In _____ with nature, people have _____ wooden houses _____ a long time.

5 To _____ strong and warm houses, they _____ their roofs _____ grass.

6 The grass roofs _____ them _____ the long cold winters and _____ winds.

7 Sometimes, trees or plants _____ out of the grass roofs, and _____ animals enjoy their _____ there.

8 A roof is an essential _____ of a house, but long _____ some people built roofs _____ to take them down easily.

9 _____ ago in southern Italy, people _____ had a house without a roof _____ lower taxes.

10 To _____ high taxes on their houses, _____ people built cone-shaped roofs by _____ up stones.

1 여러분은 집의 지붕 위에 있는 염소를 본 적이 있는가?

2 노르웨이에서, 우리는 지붕 위에 있는 동물들을 볼 수 있다.

3 노르웨이는 큰 숲을 가지고 있다.

4 자연과 조화를 이루면서, 사람들은 오랫동안 나무로 집을 지었다.

5 강하고 따뜻한 집을 만들기 위해, 그들은 지붕을 잔디로 덮는다.

6 잔디 지붕은 길고 추운 겨울과 강한 바람으로부터 그들을 보호한다.

7 때때로, 나무나 식물들이 잔디 지붕에서 자라며, 어떤 동물들은 거기서 식사를 즐긴다.

8 지붕은 집의 필수적인 부분이지만, 오래 전에 어떤 사람들은 오직 지붕을 쉽게 철거하기 위해 지었다.

9 수세기 전 남부 이탈리아에서는 지붕 없는 집을 가진 사람들이 더 적은 세금을 냈다.

10 그들의 집에 부과되는 높은 세금을 피하기 위해, 어떤 사람들은 돌을 쌓아 올려 원뿔 모양의 지붕을 만들었다.

11 _____ tax collectors came to the _____, people _____ their roofs _____ quickly.

12 _____ the tax collectors left, they _____ up the _____ again.

13 From the _____ in a part of _____ China, you can see _____ roofs that look _____ big doughnuts.

14 They are the _____ of the big round houses of the Hakka _____.

15 They _____ lived in houses like these for _____ a thousand years to protect _____ from enemies.

16 The houses have _____ one gate _____ any windows on the first floor.

17 Each house _____ big enough for a _____ village.

18 It _____ has four stories.

19 It has kitchens on the _____ floor, storage rooms on the _____ floor, and _____ rooms and bedrooms on the third and _____ floors.

11 세금 징수원들이 마을에 오면, 사람들은 재빨리 지붕을 철거했다.

12 세금 징수원들이 떠난 후 그들은 다시 돌을 쌓아 올렸다.

13 중국 남부의 일부 지역의 하늘에서 보면, 여러분은 큰 도넛처럼 생긴 둥근 지붕들을 볼 수 있다.

14 그것들은 하카족의 크고 둥근 집들의 지붕이다.

15 그들은 적으로부터 스스로를 보호하기 위해 약 천 년 동안 이런 집에서 살아왔다.

16 그 집들에는 1층에 창문이 하나도 없고 문이 하나만 있다.

17 각각의 집은 전체 마을이 들어갈 만큼 크다.

18 그 집은 보통 4개의 층을 가지고 있다.

19 1층에는 주방, 2층에는 창고, 3층과 4층에는 거실과 침실이 있다.

● 우리말을 참고하여 본문을 영작하시오.

1 여러분은 집의 지붕 위에 있는 염소를 본 적이 있는가?

➡ _____

2 노르웨이에서, 우리는 지붕 위에 있는 동물들을 볼 수 있다.

➡ _____

3 노르웨이는 큰 숲을 가지고 있다.

➡ _____

4 자연과 조화를 이루면서, 사람들은 오랫동안 나무로 집을 지었다.

➡ _____

5 강하고 따뜻한 집을 만들기 위해, 그들은 지붕을 잔디로 덮는다.

➡ _____

6 잔디 지붕은 길고 추운 겨울과 강한 바람으로부터 그들을 보호한다.

➡ _____

7 때때로, 나무나 식물들이 잔디 지붕에서 자라며, 어떤 동물들은 거기서 식사를 즐긴다.

➡ _____

8 지붕은 집의 필수적인 부분이지만, 오래 전에 어떤 사람들은 오직 지붕을 쉽게 철거하기 위해 지었다.

➡ _____

9 수세기 전 남부 이탈리아에서는 지붕 없는 집을 가진 사람들이 더 적은 세금을 냈다.

➡ _____

10 그들의 집에 부과되는 높은 세금을 피하기 위해, 어떤 사람들은 돌을 쌓아 올려 원뿔 모양의 지붕을 만들었다.

➡ _____

11 세금 징수원들이 마을에 오면, 사람들은 재빨리 지붕을 철거했다.

➡ _____

12 세금 징수원들이 떠난 후 그들은 다시 돌을 쌓아 올렸다.

➡ _____

13 중국 남부의 일부 지역의 하늘에서 보면, 여러분은 큰 도넛처럼 생긴 둥근 지붕들을 볼 수 있다.

➡ _____

14 그것들은 하카족의 크고 둥근 집들의 지붕이다.

➡ _____

15 그들은 적으로부터 스스로를 보호하기 위해 약 천 년 동안 이런 집에서 살아왔다.

➡ _____

16 그 집들에는 1층에 창문이 하나도 없고 문이 하나만 있다.

➡ _____

17 각각의 집은 전체 마을이 들어갈 만큼 크다.

➡ _____

18 그 집은 보통 4개의 층을 가지고 있다.

➡ _____

19 1층에는 주방, 2층에는 창고, 3층과 4층에는 거실과 침실이 있다.

➡ _____
_____

[01~05] 다음 글을 읽고, 물음에 답하시오.

(①) Have you ever seen a goat on the roof of a house? (②) Norway has large forests. (③) In harmony ⓐ nature, people have built ⓑwood houses for a long time. (④) ⓒTo build strong and warm houses, they cover their roofs ⓓ grass. (⑤)

01 위 글의 ①~⑤ 중 다음 주어진 문장이 들어갈 알맞은 곳은?

In Norway, we can see animals on roofs.

①　　②　　③　　④　　⑤

02 위 글의 빈칸 ⓐ와 ⓓ에 공통으로 알맞은 것은?

① of
② to
③ with
④ from
⑤ along

서답형

03 위 글의 밑줄 친 ⓑ를 알맞은 형으로 고치시오.

➡ _____

04 위 글의 밑줄 친 ⓒ와 같은 용법으로 쓰인 것은?

① I have a baseball cap to wear.
② Love is to trust each other.
③ To live without air is impossible.
④ I went to a shopping mall to buy clothes.
⑤ I have some homework to do today.

05 위 글의 내용으로 보아 알 수 없는 것은?

① 노르웨이의 집들의 지붕 위에는 염소가 올라간다.
② 노르웨이는 큰 숲들이 있다.
③ 노르웨이 사람들은 오랫동안 나무로 된 집을 지어 왔다.
④ 노르웨이 사람들은 강하고 따뜻한 집을 짓기를 원한다.
⑤ 노르웨이 사람들은 지붕을 잔디로 덮는다.

[06~07] 다음 글을 읽고, 물음에 답하시오.

The grass roofs protect them ⓐ the long cold winters and strong winds. Sometimes, trees or plants grow out of the grass roofs, and some animals enjoy their meals ⓑthere.

06 위 글의 빈칸 ⓐ에 알맞은 것은?

① of
② to
③ over
④ from
⑤ with

서답형

07 위 글의 밑줄 친 ⓑ가 구체적으로 가리키는 것을 우리말로 쓰시오.

➡ _____

[08~12] 다음 글을 읽고, 물음에 답하시오.

A roof is an essential part of a house, ____ⓐ____ long ago some people built roofs only to take them ____ⓑ____ easily. Centuries ago in ⓒsouth Italy, people ⓓwho had a house without a roof ⓔpay lower taxes.

08 위 글의 빈칸 ⓐ에 알맞은 것은?

① and   ② or
③ so   ④ for
⑤ but

09 위 글의 빈칸 ⓑ에 알맞은 것은?

① up   ② on
③ off   ④ down
⑤ with

서답형

10 위 글의 밑줄 친 ⓒ를 알맞은 형으로 고쳐 쓰시오.

➡ _____

11 위 글의 밑줄 친 ⓓ 대신 쓸 수 있는 것은?

① why   ② that
③ what   ④ which
⑤ whose

서답형

12 위 글의 밑줄 친 ⓔ를 알맞은 형으로 고쳐 쓰시오.

➡ _____

[13~17] 다음 글을 읽고, 물음에 답하시오.

To ____ⓐ____ high taxes on their houses, some people built cone-shaped roofs by ⓑpile up stones. ____ⓒ____ tax collectors came to the town, people took their roofs down quickly. ____ⓓ____ the tax collectors left, they piled up the stones again.

13 위 글의 빈칸 ⓐ에 알맞은 것은?

① avoid   ② pay
③ give   ④ lend
⑤ follow

서답형

14 위 글의 밑줄 친 ⓑ를 알맞은 형으로 고치시오.

➡ _____

15 위 글의 빈칸 ⓒ에 알맞은 것은?

① If   ② Since
③ While   ④ When
⑤ Though

16 위 글의 빈칸 ⓓ에 알맞은 것은?

① During   ② Though
③ After   ④ While
⑤ Before

서답형

17 위 글의 내용과 일치하도록 다음 문장의 빈칸에 알맞은 말을 쓰시오.

세금을 많이 내지 않기 위해 어떤 사람들은 _____. 그리고 세금 징수원이 마을에 왔을 때 _____.

[18~20] 다음 글을 읽고, 물음에 답하시오.

From the ⓐ in a part of southern China, you can see round roofs ⓑthat look like big doughnuts. They are the roofs of the big round houses of the Hakka people. They ⓒhave lived in houses like these for about a thousand years to protect themselves from enemies.

서답형

18 위 글의 빈칸 ⓐ에 다음 정의에 해당하는 말을 주어진 글자로 시작하여 쓰시오.

the space around the earth which you can see when you stand outside and look upwards

➡ _____

서답형

19 위 글의 밑줄 친 ⓑ와 바꿔 쓸 수 있는 관계대명사를 쓰시오.

➡ _____

중요

20 위 글의 밑줄 친 ⓒ와 같은 용법으로 쓰인 것은?

① I have known her for ten years.
② I have seen a bear in the mountain.
③ Nancy has already had lunch.
④ He has been to Rome three times.
⑤ The man has lost his money, so he couldn't buy the hat.

[21~24] 다음 글을 읽고, 물음에 답하시오.

The houses have only one gate without ⓐ windows on the first floor. ⓑEach house are big enough for a whole village. It usually has four stories. It has ⓒ on the first floor, storage rooms on the second floor, and living rooms and bedrooms on the third and fourth floors.

중요

21 위 글의 빈칸 ⓐ에 알맞은 것은?

① no   ② any
③ some   ④ few
⑤ little

서답형

22 위 글의 밑줄 친 ⓑ에서 어법상 어색한 것을 고치시오.

_____ ➡ _____

서답형

23 위 글의 빈칸 ⓒ에 다음 정의에 해당하는 단어를 쓰시오. 필요하면 어형 변화를 하시오.

a room that is used for cooking and for household jobs such as washing dishes

➡ _____

24 위 글의 내용으로 보아 대답할 수 없는 질문은?

① How many gates do the house have?
② How many windows are there on the first floor of the house?
③ How many stories does the house usually have?
④ What is on the second floor?
⑤ How many bedrooms are there on the fourth floor?

[25~29] 다음 글을 읽고, 물음에 답하시오.

Have you ever ⓐ<u>see</u> a goat on the roof of a house? (①) In Norway, we can see animals on roofs. (②) Norway has large forests. (③) In harmony with nature, people ⓑ<u>have built</u> wooden houses for a long time. (④) To build strong and warm houses, they cover their roofs ___ⓒ___ grass. (⑤) Sometimes, trees or plants grow out of the grass roofs, and some animals enjoy their meals there.

25 위 글의 ①~⑤ 중 다음 주어진 문장이 들어갈 알맞은 곳은?

The grass roofs protect them from the long cold winters and strong winds.

①   ②   ③   ④   ⑤

서답형
26 위 글의 밑줄 친 ⓐ를 알맞은 어형으로 고치시오.

➡ _____

27 위 글의 밑줄 친 ⓑ와 용법이 같은 것은? (2개)

① I <u>have been</u> in this country since last month.
② Yumi <u>has seen</u> this movies many times.
③ Mike <u>has</u> just <u>cleaned</u> his room.
④ Lisa <u>has had</u> this cat for ten years.
⑤ She <u>has gone</u> to Europe for her summer holidays.

서답형
28 위 글의 빈칸 ⓒ에 알맞은 전치사를 쓰시오.

➡ _____

29 위 글의 내용으로 보아 알 수 <u>없는</u> 것은?

① In Norway, we can see a goat on the roof of a house.
② There are large forests in Norway.
③ People have built wooden houses for a long time in Norway.
④ People in Norway want to build strong and warm houses.
⑤ Some animals live on the roofs of houses.

[30~32] 다음 글을 읽고, 물음에 답하시오.

A roof is an essential part of a house, but ① <u>long ago</u> some people built roofs only ②<u>to take them down</u> ③<u>easily</u>. ④<u>Centuries before</u> in ⓐ<u>south Italy</u>, ⓑ<u>people who had a house without a roof</u> paid ⑤<u>lower taxes</u>.

30 위 글의 밑줄 친 ①~⑤ 중 어법상 어색한 것은?

①   ②   ③   ④   ⑤

서답형
31 위 글의 밑줄 친 ⓐ를 알맞은 어형으로 고치시오.

➡ _____

32 위 글의 밑줄 친 ⓑ와 같은 뜻이 되도록 바꿔 쓸 때 빈칸에 알맞은 말이 바르게 짝지어진 것은? (2개)

people who had a house _____ has _____ roof

① that / no   ② that / any
③ that / some   ④ which / no
⑤ which / some

[01~05] 다음 글을 읽고, 물음에 답하시오.

ⓐ(To avoid, Avoiding) high taxes on their houses, some people built cone-shaped roofs ____ⓑ____ piling up stones. ⓒWhen tax collectors came to the town, people took their roofs ____ⓓ____ quickly. ⓔAfter the tax collectors left, they piled up the stones again.

01 위 글의 괄호 ⓐ에서 알맞은 것을 고르시오.

➡ _____

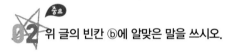 위 글의 빈칸 ⓑ에 알맞은 말을 쓰시오.

➡ _____

03 위 글의 밑줄 친 ⓒ 대신 쓸 수 있는 접속사를 쓰시오.

➡ _____

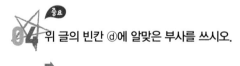 위 글의 빈칸 ⓓ에 알맞은 부사를 쓰시오.

➡ _____

05 위 글의 밑줄 친 ⓔ를 우리말로 옮기시오.

➡ _____

[06~09] 다음 글을 읽고, 물음에 답하시오.

From the sky in a part of southern China, you can see round roofs ⓐthat look like big ____ⓑ____. They are the roofs of the big round houses of the Hakka people. They ⓒ(lived, have lived) in houses like these for about a thousand years to protect ⓓthem from enemies.

06 위 글의 밑줄 친 ⓐ 대신 쓸 수 있는 관계대명사를 쓰시오.

➡ _____

07 위 글의 빈칸 ⓑ에 다음 정의에 해당하는 단어를 쓰시오. (필요하면 어형을 바꾸시오.)

a bread-like cake made from sweet dough that has been cooked in hot fat

➡ _____

08 위 글의 괄호 ⓒ에서 알맞은 것을 고르시오.

➡ _____

09 위 글의 밑줄 친 ⓓ를 알맞은 어형으로 고치시오.

➡ _____

[10~14] 다음 글을 읽고, 물음에 답하시오.

The houses have only one gate ⓐwithout any windows on the first floor. Each house is big enough ____ⓑ____ a whole village. ⓒIt usually has four stories. It has kitchens on the first floor, storage rooms on the second floor, and living rooms and bedrooms on the ⓓthree and fourth floors.

10 위 글의 밑줄 친 ⓐ를 우리말로 옮기시오.

➡ _____

11 위 글의 빈칸 ⓑ에 알맞은 전치사를 쓰시오.

➡ _____

12 위 글의 밑줄 친 ⓒ가 가리키는 것을 영어로 쓰시오.

➡ _____

13 위 글의 밑줄 친 ⓓ를 알맞은 어형으로 고치시오.

➡ _____

14 Where are storage rooms? Answer in English.

➡ _____

[15~19] 다음 글을 읽고, 물음에 답하시오.

Sejong National Library is ____ⓐ____ Sejong, Korea. ⓑIt is a four-stories building that looks like an open book. It has about 400 thousand books on the first and second floors and a large cafeteria on the top floor. It opened in 2013. ⓒ(Since, For) then, many people have visited this unique building.

15 위 글의 빈칸 ⓐ에 알맞은 전치사를 쓰시오.

➡ _____

16 위 글의 밑줄 친 ⓑ에서 어법상 어색한 것을 고치시오.

_____ ➡ _____

17 위 글의 괄호 ⓒ에서 알맞은 것을 고르시오.

➡ _____

18 How many books are there in Sejong National Library? Answer in English.

➡ _____

19 When did Sejong National Library open? Answer in English.

➡ _____

해석

Link

I can't open windows <u>because of</u> the fine dust these days. <u>How about making a</u>
~ 때문에 　　　　　　　　　　　　　　　~하는 것이 어때?
small garden on the roof?

구문해설 · **fine dust:** 미세 먼지 　· **these days:** 요즘

나는 요즘 미세먼지 때문에 창
문을 열 수가 없어요. 지붕에
작은 정원을 만드는 것은 어떨
까요?

Fine dust <u>has been</u> a big problem in the spring. We designed a roof <u>that</u> has a
현재완료 　　　　　　　　　　　　　　　　　　　　　　관계대명사 주격
small garden <u>with</u> trees and <u>many other plants</u>. This garden will give us fresh
~이 있는 　　　　　many other+복수명사
air.

구문해설 · **problem:** 문제 　· **design:** 설계하다 　· **plant:** 식물

봄에는 미세먼지가 큰 문제가
되어 왔다. 우리는 나무와 다
른 많은 식물들이 있는 작은
정원을 가진 지붕을 설계했다.
이 정원은 우리에게 신선한 공
기를 줄 것이다.

Write

Sejong National Library is in Sejong, Korea. <u>It</u> is a four-story building <u>that</u>
= Sejong National Library 　　주격 관계대명사
<u>looks like</u> an open book. It has about 400 thousand books on the first and
~처럼 보이다
second floors and a large cafeteria on the top floor. It opened <u>in 2013</u>. Since
in + 연도
then, many people <u>have visited</u> this unique building.
계속 용법의 현재완료

구문해설 · **national:** 국립의 　· **story:** (건물의) 층 　· **open:** 펼쳐 놓은 　· **floor:** (건물의) 층
· **unique:** 독특한

국립 세종 도서관은 한국의 세
종시에 있다. 그것은 펴놓은
책처럼 보이는 4층 건물이다. 1
층과 2층에는 약 40만 권의 책
이 있고, 맨 위층에는 큰 구내
식당이 있다. 그것은 2013년에
문을 열었다. 그 이후로, 많은
사람들이 이 독특한 건물을 방
문했다.

Culture Project

In Granada, Spain, some people <u>have lived</u> in cave houses <u>for a long time.</u>
in + 도시 　　　　　　　　　　현재완료의 계속 용법 　　　　　　　오랫동안
The weather in this place is very hot in the summer and cold in the winter. <u>It's</u>
날씨를 나타내는 비인칭 주어 it
<u>not</u> too cold <u>or</u> hot in cave houses.
not A or B: A도 B도 아닌

구문해설 · **cave:** 동굴 　· **weather:** 날씨 　· **hot:** 더운 　· **cold:** 추운

스페인의 그라나다에서는, 몇
몇 사람들이 오랫동안 동굴 집
에서 살아왔다. 이곳의 날씨는
여름에는 매우 덥고 겨울에는
춥다. 동굴 집은 너무 춥거나
덥지도 않다.

영역별 핵심문제

01 다음 중 짝지어진 단어의 관계가 나머지와 다른 것은? (2개)

① slow – slowly ② love – lovely
③ kind – kindly ④ friend – friendly
⑤ quick – quickly

02 다음 빈칸에 들어갈 말로 적절하지 않은 것은?

> • I'd like a room with a _____.
> • He was at the door to _____ us.
> • He found the place _____ difficulty.
> • What _____ did he say?

① else   ② without
③ other   ④ view
⑤ welcome

03 다음 짝지어진 두 단어의 관계가 같도록 빈칸에 알맞은 말을 쓰시오.

> warm : cool = high : _____

04 다음 문장의 빈칸에 알맞은 것은?

> Vegetables are good _____ the health.

① in   ② on
③ to   ④ for
⑤ with

05 다음 영영풀이에 해당하는 단어는?

> a large area where trees grow close together

① zoo   ② park
③ jungle   ④ garden
⑤ forest

06 다음 문장의 빈칸에 공통으로 들어갈 말을 쓰시오.

> • What _____ of movies do you like?
> • That made me feel _____ of stupid.

07 다음 우리말에 맞게 빈칸에 알맞은 말을 쓰시오.

> 나는 보통 이런 종류의 기계를 다루지는 않지만, 한번 해 보기는 하겠다.
> ➡ I don't usually work with these kinds of machines but I'll _____ it _____ _____.

08 다음 대화의 빈칸에 알맞은 말을 쓰시오.

> A: _____ can I find men's shirts?
> B: They're on the second floor.
> A: Oh, I see. Thanks.
> B: No problem.

[09~15] 다음 대화를 읽고, 물음에 답하시오.

Woman: Welcome ____ⓐ____ Jeonju Hanok Guesthouse. ____ⓑ____ I help you?

Man: Yes, I'd like a room for two nights.

Woman: Well, what kind of room would you like?

Man: Do you have a room with a garden view? You have a ⓒlove garden.

Woman: Yes, we do. ⓓEvery room in our house have a garden view, ____ⓔ____ there are no beds in the rooms.

Man: Do I have to sleep on the floor?

Woman: Yes, you do.

Man: O.K. ⓕI'll give it a try. Where can I have breakfast?

Woman: You can have breakfast in the dining room, next to the kitchen.

Man: I see.

Woman: O.K. You're in the Nabi room. Here's your key.

Man: Thank you.

09 위 대화의 빈칸 ⓐ에 알맞은 말을 쓰시오.

➡ _____

10 위 대화의 빈칸 ⓑ에 알맞은 것은? (2개)

① May   ② Will

③ Must   ④ Can

⑤ Should

11 위 대화의 밑줄 친 ⓒ를 알맞은 어형으로 고치시오.

➡ _____

12 위 대화의 밑줄 친 ⓓ에서 어법상 어색한 것을 고치시오.

_____ ➡ _____

13 위 대화의 빈칸 ⓔ에 알맞은 것은?

① so   ② or

③ and   ④ but

⑤ for

14 위 대화의 밑줄 친 ⓕ를 우리말로 옮기시오.

➡ _____

15 위 대화의 내용으로 보아 대답할 수 없는 질문은?

① Where is the man now?

② How many nights is the man going to stay?

③ What room does the man want?

④ Why are there no beds in the rooms?

⑤ Where can the man have breakfast?

16 다음 대화의 빈칸에 알맞은 것은?

> **A:** _____
>
> **B:** Yes. I'm looking for smart phones.
>
> **A:** They're near the escalator.

① May I help you?

② What should I do?

③ Where can I find them?

④ What are you looking for?

⑤ Where can I take an escalator?

17 다음 문장의 빈칸에 알맞은 것은?

> I _____ never seen such a beautiful mountain.

① be   ② did
③ have   ④ was
⑤ must

18 다음 문장의 빈칸에 알맞은 말이 바르게 짝지어진 것은?

> • Each of the children _____ a toy car.
> • Some of these books _____ interesting, but others are not.

① has – is   ② has – be
③ have – is   ④ has – are
⑤ have – are

19 다음 괄호 안에 주어진 단어를 어법상 바르게 쓴 것은?

> Jack (want) this video game since last year.

① want   ② wants
③ wanted   ④ has wanted
⑤ is wanting

20 다음 괄호 안에서 알맞은 말을 고르시오.

> A: How's Janet? Do you see her often?
> B: She's good. We call (each other / each others) regularly.

21 다음 중 어법상 어색한 것은?

① He has been sick in bed for a week.
② How long have you stayed in America?
③ I have climbed that mountain last week.
④ You have already walked 100 kilometers.
⑤ I have never been to America.

22 다음 중 빈칸에 들어갈 말이 다른 하나는? (대·소문자 무시)

① These cups were five dollars _____.
② _____ ticket costs 20 dollars.
③ When the children arrive, give _____ of them a balloon.
④ _____ student came forward to receive a medal.
⑤ Almost _____ window was broken.

23 다음 문장과 뜻이 가장 가까운 것은?

> Jack's father has gone to Rome.

① Jack's father is going to Rome.
② Jack's father went to Rome.
③ Jack's father went to Rome but he is here now.
④ Jack's father went to Rome and he isn't here now.
⑤ Jack's father went to Rome and he has just come back.

24 다음 〈보기〉의 밑줄 친 부분과 같은 용법으로 사용된 것은?

> ┌─ 보기 ─
> Nancy <u>has read</u> the novel three times.
> └─

① I <u>have lived</u> here since last year.
② Ted <u>has seen</u> a panda before.
③ My mother <u>has finished</u> washing the dishes already.
④ Jack <u>has wanted</u> to have a cat for a long time.
⑤ Mrs. Brown <u>has lost</u> her purse somewhere.

25 다음 중 어법상 어색한 것은?

① Each weekend, they work at home.
② Each member has to pay a membership fee.
③ Each the students received a special gift.
④ We each wanted the bedroom with the TV.
⑤ Each of the buildings is surrounded by tall trees.

26 다음 중 밑줄 친 부분의 쓰임이 올바르지 <u>않은</u> 것은?

① He <u>has gone</u> to Madrid ten years ago.
② Kate <u>has lived</u> in Seoul for five years.
③ Mike <u>has been</u> sick in hospital since last Monday.
④ She <u>has</u> never <u>seen</u> such a beautiful lake.
⑤ How often <u>have</u> you <u>been</u> to Paris?

27 다음 밑줄 친 부분을 어법상 바르게 고쳐 쓰시오.

> <u>Each their opinions</u> has both good points and bad points.

➡ _____

Reading

[28~32] 다음 글을 읽고, 물음에 답하시오.

ⓐHave you ever seen a goat on the roof of a house? In Norway, we can see animals on roofs. ⓑNorway has large forests. In harmony with nature, people have built wooden houses for a long time. To build strong and warm houses, they cover their roofs ⓒ____ grass. The grass roofs ⓓ____ them from the long cold winters and strong winds. Sometimes, trees or plants grow out of the grass roofs, and some animals enjoy their meals there.

28 위 글의 밑줄 친 ⓐ와 같은 용법으로 쓰인 것은?

① I <u>have been</u> in Japan since last month.
② Kirk <u>has seen</u> a panda before.
③ My father <u>has</u> already <u>eaten</u> breakfast.
④ He <u>has wanted</u> to be a painter for a long time.
⑤ She <u>has lost</u> her smartphone somewhere.

29 위 글의 밑줄 친 ⓑ와 같은 뜻이 되도록 다음 문장의 빈칸에 알맞은 말을 쓰시오.

> _____ large forests in Norway.

30 위 글의 빈칸 ⓒ에 알맞은 것은?

① of   ② in
③ at   ④ with
⑤ from

31 위 글의 빈칸 ⓓ에 다음 정의에 해당하는 단어를 쓰시오.

> to prevent someone or something from being harmed or damaged

➡ _____

32 위 글의 내용으로 보아 알 수 <u>없는</u> 것은?

① 노르웨이에서는 집 지붕 위에 동물들이 올라가기도 한다.
② 노르웨이 사람들은 오랫동안 목조 가옥을 지어 왔다.
③ 노르웨이 사람들은 잔디로 지붕을 덮는다.
④ 노르웨이의 겨울은 길고 바람이 강하게 분다.
⑤ 노르웨이에서는 동물들이 보통 집 지붕 위에서 사료를 먹는다.

[33~36] 다음 글을 읽고, 물음에 답하시오.

In Granada, Spain, some people have lived in cave houses ⓐ a long time. ⓑThe weather in this place is very hot in the summer and cold in the winter. It's not too cold ⓒ hot in cave houses.

33 위 글의 빈칸 ⓐ에 알맞은 것은?

① in ② to
③ with ④ for
⑤ since

34 위 글의 밑줄 친 ⓑ를 우리말로 옮기시오.

➡ _____

35 위 글의 빈칸 ⓒ에 알맞은 것은?

① or ② so
③ and ④ but
⑤ for

36 스페인의 그라나다에서 사람들이 동굴 집에서 사는 이유를 우리말로 간단히 쓰시오.

➡ _____

[37~38] 다음 글을 읽고, 물음에 답하시오.

Sejong National Library is in Sejong, Korea. It is a four-story building that looks ⓐ an open book. It has ⓑabout 400 thousand books on the first and second floors and a large cafeteria on the top floor. It opened in 2013. Since then, many people have visited this unique building.

37 위 글의 빈칸 ⓐ에 알맞은 말을 쓰시오.

➡ _____

38 위 글의 밑줄 친 ⓑ와 같은 의미로 쓰인 것은?

① I know nothing about her.
② He studies about two hours a day.
③ Books were thrown about the room.
④ I want an easy book about wild birds.
⑤ The girls walked about in the park.

출제율 95%

01 다음 중 짝지어진 단어의 관계가 나머지 넷과 <u>다른</u> 것은?

① wrong : right   ② high : low

③ enemy : friend   ④ near : close

⑤ entrance : exit

출제율 95%

02 다음 빈칸에 공통으로 알맞은 것은?

> • I was fond _____ sports when I was young.
> • The prisoner hopes to get out _____ jail within a few months.

① in   ② of

③ from   ④ with

⑤ onto

출제율 90%

03 다음 짝지어진 두 단어의 관계가 같도록 빈칸에 알맞은 말을 쓰시오.

> one : first = three : _____

출제율 100%

04 다음 중 영영풀이가 <u>잘못된</u> 것은?

① wooden: made of wood

② sometimes: on some occasions rather than all the time

③ restroom: a room with a toilet for customers to use

④ dress: casual trousers that are usually made of strong blue cotton cloth called denim

⑤ meal: an occasion when people sit down and eat, usually at a regular time

출제율 85%

05 다음 우리말에 맞게 빈칸에 알맞은 말을 쓰시오.

> 박쥐에게 거꾸로 매달리는 것은 지극히 정상입니다.
> ➡ To bats hanging _____ _____ is perfectly normal.

출제율 95%

06 다음 대화의 의도로 알맞은 것은?

> A: Excuse me. <u>Where can I find children's toys?</u>
> B: You can find them on the sixth floor.
> A: Thank you very much.
> B: You're welcome.

① 요청하기   ② 충고하기

③ 제안하기   ④ 위치 묻기

⑤ 상품 광고하기

출제율 90%

07 다음 대화의 빈칸에 알맞지 <u>않은</u> 것은?

> A: What do you want to be in the future?
> B: _____

① I haven't decided yet.

② I'm going to have tea.

③ Well, I'm not sure. How about you?

④ I want to be a reporter like my dad.

⑤ Well, I have several jobs in my mind.

출제율 90%

08 다음 중 짝지어진 대화가 <u>어색한</u> 것은?

① A: What kind of food would you like?
B: I'd like Chinese food.

② A: What kind of house do you want to live in?
B: Well, I want to live in an airplane-shaped house.

③ A: Do you want to see the baseball game?
B: Yes, I do.

④ A: What do you want to do on your birthday?
B: Yes, I want to go to Fun Park.

⑤ A: I'm looking for the cheese. Where can I find it?
B: It's in aisle B.

[09~11] 다음 대화를 읽고, 물음에 답하시오.

A: _____ ⓐ _____ men's clothes.
B: You can find them at Men's Day.
A: Where is that?
B: ⓑ <u>그것은 2층에 있어요.</u>
A: Thank you.
B: ⓒ<u>No problem.</u>

출제율 95%

09 위 대화의 빈칸 ⓐ에 알맞은 것은?

① I'm wondering   ② I'm checking
③ I'm looking for   ④ I'm waiting for
⑤ I'm looking around

출제율 100%

10 위 대화의 밑줄 친 ⓑ를 영어로 바르게 옮긴 것은?

① There are two floors.
② It's on the two floor.
③ It's on the second floor.
④ It's over the second floor.
⑤ Here is the second floor.

출제율 90%

11 위 대화의 밑줄 친 ⓒ 대신 쓸 수 <u>없는</u> 것은? (2개)

① You're welcome.
② You're right.
③ That's fine with me.
④ That's all right.
⑤ Don't mention it.

출제율 95%

12 다음 문장의 빈칸에 알맞지 <u>않은</u> 것은?

Frank has been to London _____.

① once   ② twice
③ never   ④ before
⑤ many times

출제율 90%

13 다음 문장의 빈칸에 알맞은 말이 바르게 짝지어진 것은?

• Each person _____ to finish the project by tomorrow.
• I think all of the children _____ hungry now.

① has – be   ② has – is
③ have – is   ④ have – are
⑤ has – are

14 다음 밑줄 친 단어의 올바른 형태를 쓰시오.

출제율 90%

> Jane <u>lived</u> in England since she was ten years old.

➡ _____

15 다음 두 문장의 의미가 일치하도록 빈칸에 알맞은 말을 쓰시오

출제율 85%

> He gave me this book after he read it.
> = He read this book _____ he gave it to me.

16 다음 각 문장의 빈칸에 들어갈 수 <u>없는</u> 것은? (대·소문자 무시)

출제율 95%

> · She has a flower in _____ hand.
> · _____ of us want to see the movie.
> · _____ of the milk was spilled.
> · _____ word in this dictionary is important

① all   ② both   ③ each
④ any   ⑤ every

17 다음 〈보기〉 문장과 뜻이 가장 가까운 것은?

출제율 95%

> ── 보기 ──
> Tom has lost his watch.

① Tom lost his watch.
② Tom lost his watch and he forgot it.
③ Tom lost his watch, but he found it.
④ Tom lost his watch, and he hasn't found it yet.
⑤ Tom lost his watch, so he is going to buy a new one.

18 다음 중 어법상 <u>어색한</u> 문장은?

출제율 100%

① Each of the girls has her own bed.
② Every player has to do his best.
③ Both of them looks very tired.
④ You can have all the cake.
⑤ All the boys are playing baseball at the park.

19 다음 밑줄 친 부분의 쓰임이 나머지 넷과 <u>다른</u> 하나는?

출제율 85%

① Lily <u>has seen</u> the movie before.
② My grandfather <u>has</u> never <u>visited</u> Seoul.
③ Mr. Lincoln <u>has gone</u> to Berlin on business.
④ How many times <u>have</u> they <u>been</u> to China?
⑤ They <u>have been</u> to Italy three times.

[20~24] 다음 글을 읽고, 물음에 답하시오.

> A roof is an essential part of a house, _____ⓐ_____ long ago some people built roofs only to take them down ⓑ<u>easy</u>. Centuries ago in southern Italy, people who had a house without a roof paid _____ⓒ_____ taxes. To avoid high taxes on their houses, some people built cone-shaped roofs _____ⓓ_____ piling up stones. When tax collectors came to the town, people took their roofs down quickly. After the tax collectors left, they piled up the stones again.

20 위 글의 빈칸 ⓐ에 알맞은 것은?

출제율 95%

① but   ② or
③ so   ④ and
⑤ for

✏️ 출제율 100%
21 위 글의 밑줄 친 ⓑ를 알맞은 형으로 고치시오.

➡ _____

✏️ 출제율 95%
22 위 글의 빈칸 ⓒ에 알맞은 것은?

① much　　② less
③ lower　　④ more
⑤ higher

✏️ 출제율 95%
23 위 글의 빈칸 ⓓ에 알맞은 것은?

① to　　② by
③ in　　④ with
⑤ from

✏️ 출제율 90%
24 위 글의 내용과 일치하도록 다음 물음에 대하여 우리말로 간단히 쓰시오.

(1) 세금 징수원들이 마을에 왔을 때 사람들이 한 일
➡ _____

(2) 세금 징수원들이 마을에 떠났을 때 사람들이 한 일
➡ _____

[25~29] 다음 글을 읽고, 물음에 답하시오.

_____ⓐ_____ the sky in a part of southern China, you can see round roofs ____ⓑ____ look like big doughnuts. ⓒThey are the roofs of the big round houses of the Hakka people. They ____ⓓ____ in houses like these for about a thousand years to protect ⓔthem from enemies.

✏️ 출제율 90%
25 위 글의 빈칸 ⓐ에 알맞은 것은?

① In　　② On
③ From　　④ Over
⑤ Along

✏️ 출제율 100%
26 위 글의 빈칸 ⓑ에 알맞은 것은? (2개)

① who　　② what
③ whose　　④ that
⑤ which

✏️ 출제율 90%
27 위 글의 밑줄 친 ⓒ가 가리키는 것을 우리말로 쓰시오.

➡ _____

✏️ 출제율 90%
28 위 글의 빈칸 ⓓ에 알맞은 것은?

① live　　② lived
③ are living　　④ have lived
⑤ had lived

✏️ 출제율 90%
29 위 글의 밑줄 친 ⓔ를 알맞은 어형으로 고치시오.

➡ _____

[01~03] 다음 대화를 읽고, 물음에 답하시오.

M: _____ⓐ_____ me, is there a restaurant in this mall?

W: Yes. _____ⓑ_____ kind of food would you like?

M: I'd like Chinese food.

W: There is a great restaurant on the fifth floor.

M: Thank you.

W: ⓒYou're welcome.

01 위 대화의 빈칸 ⓑ에 알맞은 말을 쓰시오.

➡ _____

02 위 대화의 빈칸 ⓐ에 알맞은 말을 쓰시오.

➡ _____

03 위 대화의 밑줄 친 ⓒ와 같은 뜻이 되도록 빈칸에 알맞은 말을 쓰시오.

No _____ .

04 다음 대화의 순서를 바르게 배열하시오.

(A) Thank you.

(B) You're welcome.

(C) Excuse me, where can I find women's jeans?

(D) You can find them on the second floor. They're next to the elevator.

➡ _____

05 다음 〈보기〉와 같이 현재완료 시제를 이용해 두 문장을 한 문장으로 쓰시오.

┤ 보기 ├
Jane moved to Tokyo ten years ago. She still lives there.

➡ Jane has lived in Tokyo for ten years.

(1) Peter moved to Peking in 2010. He still lives in Peking.

➡ _____

(2) Tom went to hospital a week ago. He is still in hospital.

➡ _____

(3) My mother went shopping. She is not here.

➡ _____

06 다음 〈조건〉에 맞게 괄호 안의 단어를 이용하여 우리말을 영어로 옮기시오.

┤ 조건 ├
1. 주어진 단어를 모두 이용할 것.
2. 필요시 관사를 붙이거나 단어를 추가하고 동사의 어형변화를 할 것.
3. 대·소문자 및 구두점에 유의할 것.

(1) 나는 런던에 머무는 동안 매일 아침을 먹었다.
(eat, each, during, stay, in)

➡ _____

(2) 문의 양쪽에 나무가 있다.
(there, on, both, side, gate)

➡ _____

(3) 그에게는 매일 매일이 똑같이 여겨진다.
(every, seem, same, to)

➡ _____

07 다음 문장에서 어법상 어색한 것을 찾아 바르게 고치시오.

(1) He has been to Spain last year.

_____ ➡ _____

(2) When have you seen Kathy's little brother?

_____ ➡ _____

(3) I have often played the piano when I was a child.

_____ ➡ _____

[08~11] 다음 글을 읽고, 물음에 답하시오.

The houses have only one ⓐ_____ without any windows on the first floor. ⓑEach houses is big enough for a whole village. It usually has four stories. It has kitchens on the first floor, storage rooms on the second floor, and living rooms and bedrooms on the third and ⓒfour floors.

08 위 글의 빈칸 ⓐ에 다음 정의에 해당하는 단어를 쓰시오.

> a structure like a door which is used at the entrance to a field, a garden, or the grounds of a building

➡ _____

09 위 글의 밑줄 친 ⓑ에서 어법상 어색한 것을 고치시오.

_____ ➡ _____

10 위 글의 밑줄 친 ⓒ를 알맞은 어형으로 고치시오.

➡ _____

11 Where are kitchens? Answer in English.

➡ _____

[12~15] 다음 글을 읽고, 물음에 답하시오.

Sejong National Library is ⓐ_____ Sejong, Korea. It is a four-story building ⓑ_____ looks like an open book. It has about 400 thousand books on the first and second floors and a large ⓒ_____ on the top floor. It opened in 2013, ⓓSince then, many people visited this unique building.

12 위 글의 빈칸 ⓐ에 알맞은 전치사를 쓰시오.

➡ _____

13 위 글의 빈칸 ⓑ에 알맞은 관계대명사를 쓰시오.

➡ _____

14 위 글의 빈칸 ⓒ에 다음 정의에 해당하는 단어를 쓰시오.

> a restaurant where you choose your food from a counter and take it to your table after paying for it

➡ _____

15 위 글의 밑줄 친 ⓓ에서 어법상 어색한 것을 고치시오.

_____ ➡ _____

01 다음 빈칸에 알맞은 말을 넣어 대화를 완성하시오.

(1) A: What do you want to do this weekend?

B: _____

A: Let's go to the movies this Saturday.

B: OK.

(2) A: Do you want to play chess?

B: _____

A: Let's play chess after supper.

B: All right.

02 다음 대화의 밑줄 친 표현과 바꾸어 쓸 수 있는 것을 2개 쓰시오.

A: I'm looking for shoes. <u>Where can I find them?</u>

B: They're on the first floor.

➡ _____

03 다음 (A), (B), (C)에 주어진 단어를 이용하여 4개의 문장을 만드시오.

(A)	(B)	(C)
each	friends of mine	has a TV
each of	the films	are very kind
every	student	has passed the exam
all	room	was very wonderful

(1) _____

(2) _____

(3) _____

(4) _____

단원별 모의고사

01 다음 중 우리말 뜻이 <u>잘못된</u> 것은?

① next to: ~ 옆에
② kind of: 약간, 어느 정도
③ in harmony with: ~와 조화를 이루어
④ take down: ~을 운반하다
⑤ give it a try: 시도하다, 한번 해보다

02 다음 영영풀이에 해당하는 단어로 알맞은 것은?

> a living thing that grows in the earth and has a stem, leaves, and roots

① garden　　② plant　　③ flower
④ grass　　⑤ animal

03 다음 빈칸에 알맞은 말이 바르게 짝지어진 것은?

> • Her office is on the second _____ .
> • Ask somebody _____ to help you.

① hall – else　　② floor – other
③ hall – other　　④ floor – else
⑤ story – other

04 다음 짝지어진 두 단어의 관계가 같도록 빈칸에 알맞은 말을 쓰시오.

> paint : painter = collect : _____

05 다음 빈칸에 공통으로 들어갈 말을 쓰시오.

> • Let's pile _____ stones here.
> • We walked _____ to the sixth floor.

➡ _____

06 다음 대화를 의미가 통하도록 알맞게 배열한 것은?

> (A) What kind of house do you want to live in?
> (B) I like music, so I want to live in a piano-shaped house.
> (C) Oh, it looks interesting, but I think it's kind of strange.
> (D) Hey, look at this unique house in the picture. It's upside down.

① (A) – (D) – (B) – (C)
② (B) – (C) – (A) – (D)
③ (C) – (D) – (B) – (A)
④ (D) – (B) – (C) – (A)
⑤ (D) – (C) – (A) – (B)

07 다음 중 짝지어진 대화가 <u>어색한</u> 것은?

① A: I'm looking for a hat store.
　 B: You can go to Lucy's Hats.
② A: How do I get to the bank?
　 B: Go straight one block and turn right.
③ A: Is there a bookshop near here?
　 B: Yes, there's one across from the post office.
④ A: How may I help you?
　 B: I'm looking for women's clothes.
⑤ A: I'm looking for women's shoes.
　 B: How do I get there?

08 다음 대화의 빈칸에 공통으로 알맞은 말을 쓰시오.

> A: Where can I _____ children's toys?
> B: You can _____ them on the sixth floor.

➡ _____

[09~13] 다음 대화를 읽고, 물음에 답하시오.

> Woman: Welcome to Jeonju Hanok Guesthouse. @May I help you?
>
> Man: Yes, I'd like a room for two nights.
>
> Woman: Well, what kind of room would you like?
>
> Man: ⓑDo you have a room with a garden view? You have a lovely garden.
>
> Woman: Yes, we do. Every room in our house has a garden view, ⓒbut there are no beds in the rooms.
>
> Man: Do I have to sleep on the floor?
>
> Woman: Yes, you do.
>
> Man: O.K. I'll give it a try. Where can I have breakfast?
>
> Woman: You can have breakfast in the dining room, next ___ⓓ___ the kitchen.
>
> Man: I see.
>
> Woman: O.K. You're in the Nabi room. Here's your key.
>
> Man: Thank you.

09 위 대화의 밑줄 친 @ 대신 쓸 수 없는 것은? (2개)

① Can I help you?
② Should I help you?
③ Why do I help you?
④ What can I do for you?
⑤ How may I help you?

10 위 대화의 밑줄 친 ⓑ를 우리말로 옮기시오.

➡ _____

11 위 대화의 밑줄 친 ⓒ와 같은 뜻이 되도록 빈칸에 알맞은 말을 쓰시오.

➡ but the rooms _____ _____ beds.

12 위 대화의 빈칸 ⓓ에 알맞은 것은?

① to   ② at
③ in   ④ on
⑤ from

13 위 대화의 내용과 일치하지 <u>않는</u> 것은?

① The man is in Jeonju Hanok Guesthouse now.
② The man wants a room for two nights.
③ There is a lovely garden in the guesthouse.
④ The man often sleeps on the floor.
⑤ The man will have breakfast in the dining room.

14 다음 괄호 안에 주어진 단어를 어법상 바르게 쓴 것은?

> He left home at six and (not return) yet.

① doesn't return
② wasn't returned
③ didn't return
④ hasn't returned
⑤ hadn't returned

15 다음 문장의 빈칸에 알맞은 것은? (2개)

> The teacher gave a ball pen to _____ student.

① all   ② each
③ other   ④ each of
⑤ every

16 다음 문장 중 어법상 어색한 것은?

① I've gone to Paris five years ago.
② Jack has practiced the piano since last year.
③ Ann has been sick in bed for two weeks.
④ I have never seen such a wonderful movie.
⑤ Has your teacher ever been to Europe?

17 다음 문장 중 어법상 어색한 것은?

① All the boys were kind to Ann.
② Every boy likes baseball.
③ Each of them have a ticket for the concert.
④ There is a tree on each side of the gate.
⑤ They have known each other for twenty years.

18 다음 두 문장의 뜻이 같도록 빈칸에 알맞은 말을 쓰시오.

> I _____ _____ my car key.
> = I lost my car key. I don't have it now.

19 다음 우리말과 일치하도록 주어진 어구를 바르게 배열하여 문장을 완성하시오.

> 보트 안의 모든 사람은 팀으로 함께 일해야 한다.
> (the boat / together / has to / a team / in / work / everyone / as)

➡ _____
    _____

20 다음 빈칸에 알맞은 것은?

> Frank _____ never seen such a cute cat.

① be   ② did
③ has   ④ was
⑤ must

[21~23] 다음 글을 읽고, 물음에 답하시오.

> Fine dust has been a big problem _ⓐ_ the spring. We designed a roof that has a small garden ⓑwith trees and many other plants. ⓒ This garden will give us fresh air.

21 위 글의 빈칸 ⓐ에 알맞은 것은?

① to   ② at
③ in   ④ on
⑤ from

22 위 글의 밑줄 친 ⓑ와 같은 의미로 쓰인 것은?

① I'm pleased with your present.
② Who is the man with the beard?
③ Wash it with soap and water.
④ Bill went for a walk with his dog.
⑤ Frank was in bed with the flu.

23 위 글의 밑줄 친 ⓒ와 같은 뜻이 되도록 다음 문장의 빈칸에 알맞은 말을 쓰시오.

➡ This garden will give fresh air _____ us.

27 위 글의 빈칸 ⓒ에 알맞은 것은?

① high   ② low

③ little   ④ much

⑤ least

[24~27] 다음 글을 읽고, 물음에 답하시오.

(①) A roof is an essential part of a house, ⓐbut long ago some people have built roofs only to take them down easily. (②) Centuries ago in southern Italy, people who had a house ⓑ(with, without) a roof paid lower taxes. (③) To avoid ___ⓒ___ taxes on their houses, some people built cone-shaped roofs by piling up stones. (④) After the tax collectors left, they piled up the stones again. (⑤)

[28~30] 다음 글을 읽고, 물음에 답하시오.

Have you ever seen a goat on the roof of a house? In Norway, we can see animals on roofs. Norway has large forests. In harmony ___ⓐ___ nature, people ⓑ(build) wooden houses for a long time. To build strong and warm houses, they cover their roofs ___ⓒ___ grass. The grass roofs protect them from the long cold winters and strong winds. Sometimes, trees or plants grow out of the grass roofs, and some animals enjoy their meals ⓓthere.

24 위 글의 ①~⑤ 중 다음 주어진 문장이 들어갈 알맞은 곳은?

When tax collectors came to the town, people took their roofs down quickly.

①   ②   ③   ④   ⑤

28 위 글의 빈칸 ⓐ와 ⓒ에 공통으로 알맞은 것은?

① on   ② in

③ with   ④ to

⑤ from

25 위 글의 밑줄 친 ⓐ에서 어법상 어색한 것을 고치시오.

_____ ➡ _____

29 위 글의 괄호 ⓑ의 단어를 알맞은 형태로 쓰시오.

➡ _____

26 위 글의 괄호 ⓑ에서 알맞은 것을 고르시오.

➡ _____

30 위 글의 밑줄 친 ⓓ가 가리키는 것을 전치사 on을 사용하여 쓰시오.

➡ _____

Lesson 3

My Travel, My Way

🎙 의사소통 기능

- 경험 묻고 답하기
  A: Have you ever eaten pancakes?
  B: Yes, I have.

- 날씨 묻고 답하기
  A: How's the weather in London in March?
  B: It's rainy and cool.

🎙 언어 형식

- to부정사의 형용사적 용법
  A B&B is a popular place **to stay** in England.

- 가주어 it
  It was just amazing **to see** the ring of huge stones.

교과서 Words & Expressions

Key Words

- **actually** [ǽktʃuəli] 튀 실제로, 정말로
- **admire** [ædmáiər] 동 존경하다, 감탄하며 바라보다
- **amazing** [əméiziŋ] 형 놀라운
- **anything** [éniθiŋ] 대 무엇, 아무것, 무엇이든
- **appear** [əpíər] 동 나타나다, 출연하다
- **around** [əráund] 전 ~ 둘레에, ~ 주위에, ~을 돌아
- **avatar** [ǽvətɑːr] 명 화신, 아바타
- **become** [bikʌ́m] 동 ~(해)지다, ~이 되다
- **bungee jumping** 번지 점프
- **capture** [kǽptʃər] 동 잡다, 포착하다, 담아내다
- **chance** [tʃæns] 명 가능성, 기회
- **check** [tʃek] 동 살피다, 점검하다
- **cloudy** [kláudi] 형 흐린, 구름이 잔뜩 낀
- **college** [kálidʒ] 명 대학, 전문학교
- **create** [kriéit] 동 창조[창작/창출]하다
- **decide** [disáid] 동 결정하다, 결심하다
- **diary** [dáiəri] 명 수첩, 일기
- **different** [dífərənt] 형 다른
- **drawing** [drɔ́ːiŋ] 명 그림, 소묘, 데생
- **drive** [draiv] 동 (차량을) 몰다, 운전하다
- **during** [djúəriŋ] 전 ~ 동안[내내], (~하는) 중에
- **earth** [əːrθ] 명 지구, 땅
- **else** [els] 튀 또 다른, 다른
- **enough** [inʌ́f] 형 필요한 만큼의, 충분한
- **expect** [ikspékt] 동 예상[기대]하다
- **ever** [évər] 튀 언제든, 한번이라도
- **famous** [féiməs] 형 유명한
- **field trip** 견학 여행, 현장 학습
- **finally** [fáinəli] 튀 마침내
- **food** [fuːd] 명 식량, 음식
- **forecast** [fɔ́rkæst] 명 예측, 예보

- **foreign** [fɔ́ːrən] 형 외국의
- **freezing** [fríːziŋ] 형 꽁꽁 얼게[너무나] 추운
- **graduate** [grǽdʒuət] 동 졸업하다
- **guess** [ges] 동 추측하다, 짐작하다
- **huge** [hjuːdʒ] 형 큰, 거대한
- **indoors** [indɔ́ːrz] 튀 실내에, 집안에
- **invite** [inváit] 동 초대하다, 초청하다
- **island** [áilənd] 명 섬
- **journal** [dʒɔ́ːnl] 명 일기
- **market** [máːrkit] 명 시장
- **moment** [móumənt] 명 잠깐, 잠시, 순간
- **mostly** [móustli] 튀 주로, 대개
- **mystery** [místəri] 명 수수께끼, 미스터리
- **object** [ɑ́bdʒikt] 명 물건, 물체
- **pack** [pæk] 동 (짐을) 싸다[꾸리다/챙기다]
- **perfect** [pə́ːrfikt] 형 완전한
- **plate** [pleit] 명 접시, 그릇
- **portrait** [pɔ́ːrtrit] 명 초상화
- **relax** [rilǽks] 동 휴식을 취하다
- **remain** [riméin] 동 남다, 남아 있다
- **scary** [skɛ́əri] 형 무서운, 겁나는
- **seafood** [siːfud] 명 해산물
- **simple** [símpl] 형 간단한, 단순한
- **touch** [tʌtʃ] 동 만지다, 건드리다
- **travel** [trǽvəl] 명 여행 동 여행하다
- **trip** [trip] 명 여행
- **turtle** [tə́ːtl] 명 거북, 바다거북
- **university** [jùːnəvə́ːrsəti] 명 대학교
- **vacation** [veikéiʃən] 명 방학, 휴가
- **weather** [wéðər] 명 날씨
- **windy** [wíndi] 형 바람이 많이 부는

Key Expressions

- **a few** 소수의, 약간의
- **a little** 좀, 약간; 약간의
- **a lot of** 많은
- **at last** 마침내
- **be full of** ~으로 가득 차다
- **get into** ~에 들어가다, ~에 타다

- **get to** ~에 도착하다
- **right now** 지금, 당장
- **set foot at[in]** ~에 발을 들여놓다
- **show up** 나타나다
- **stay[keep] indoors** 집안에 머물러 있다
- **such as** ~와 같은

Word Power

※ 날씨를 나타내는 단어

□ **hot** (더운) → **cold** (추운)

□ **warm** (따뜻한) → **cool** (서늘한)

□ **fine** (맑은, 비가 안 오는)

□ **mild** (온화한, 포근한)

※ 다음은 명사에 -y가 붙어 날씨를 나타내는 형용사가 되는 단어들이다. -y를 붙일 때 철자가 변하는 것이 있으므로 주의해야 한다.

□ **sun** (해, 태양) → **sunny** (화창한)

□ **rain** (비) → **rainy** (비가 오는)

□ **snow** (눈) → **snowy** (눈이 오는)

□ **cloud** (구름) → **cloudy** (구름이 낀, 흐린)

□ **wind** (바람) → **windy** (바람이 부는)

□ **fog** (안개) → **foggy** (안개가 낀)

English Dictionary

□ **admire** 존경하다
→ to like and respect someone or something very much
누군가 또는 무언가를 매우 좋아하고 존중하다

□ **amazing** 놀라운
→ very surprising and making you feel pleasure, approval, or wonder
매우 놀랍고 당신을 기쁨, 승인, 또는 놀라움을 느끼게 만드는

□ **beach** 해변, 바닷가
→ an area of sand or stones beside the sea
바다 옆에 모래나 돌이 있는 지역

□ **chance** 가능성
→ the possibility that something will happen
무슨 일이 일어날 가능성

□ **create** 창조[창작/창출]하다
→ to cause something to happen or exist
어떤 일이 발생하거나 존재하게 하다

□ **decide** 결정하다, 결심하다
→ to choose to do something, usually after you have thought carefully about the other possibilities
보통 당신이 다른 가능성에 대해 신중하게 고려한 후에, 무언가를 하기로 선택하다

□ **drawing** 그림, 소묘, 데생
→ a picture made with a pencil or pen
연필이나 펜으로 그린 그림

□ **drive** (차량을) 몰다, 운전하다
→ to operate a car or other vehicle and control its movement and direction
자동차나 다른 차량을 조작하여 그 움직임과 방향을 제어하다

□ **food** 식량, 음식
→ what people and animals eat
사람과 동물이 먹는 것

□ **invite** 초대하다, 초청하다
→ to ask someone to come to something such as a party
어떤 사람에게 파티와 같은 것에 와 달라고 청하다

□ **island** 섬
→ a piece of land that is completely surrounded by water
물에 완전히 둘러싸인 땅

□ **market** 시장
→ a place where goods are bought and sold, usually outdoors
보통 옥외에서 물건을 사고파는 장소

□ **mystery** 수수께끼, 미스터리
→ something that is not understood or known about
이해되거나 알려지지 않은 어떤 것

□ **pack** (짐을) 싸다[꾸리다/챙기다]
→ to put clothes and other things into a bag, because you are leaving a place
당신이 어떤 곳을 떠나기 때문에 옷이나 다른 것들을 가방에 넣다

□ **relax** 휴식을 취하다
→ to spend time resting or doing something enjoyable especially after you have been doing work
특히 일이 끝난 후 쉬거나 즐거운 일을 하면서 시간을 보내다

□ **strange** 이상한, 낯선
→ unusual or unexpected, and making you feel slightly nervous or afraid
이상하거나 예상치 못한, 그리고 당신을 약간 긴장시키거나 두려워하게 만드는

□ **travel** 여행하다
→ to go from one place to another, often to a place that is far away
한 장소에서 다른 곳, 종종 멀리 떨어진 곳으로 가다

01 다음 중 짝지어진 단어의 성격이 <u>다른</u> 하나는?

① wind – windy   ② health – healthy
③ snow – snowy   ④ fog – foggy
⑤ sun – sunny

02 다음 빈칸에 알맞은 말이 바르게 짝지어진 것은?

• Ann has a lot _____ friends here.
• I put on my seat belt as soon as I get _____ the car.

① into – at   ② of – into
③ on – in   ④ out – with
⑤ off – over

03 다음 영영풀이에 해당하는 단어로 알맞은 것은?

a place where goods are bought and sold, usually outdoors

① mart   ② area
③ field   ④ market
⑤ factory

서답형

04 다음 짝지어진 단어의 관계가 같도록 빈칸에 알맞은 말을 쓰시오.

advise : advice = decide : _____

05 다음 우리말에 맞게 빈칸에 알맞은 것은?

나는 그의 사진을 몇 장 가지고 있다.
➡ I have _____ pictures of him.

① few   ② little
③ a few   ④ a little
⑤ a lot

서답형

06 다음 영영풀이에 해당하는 단어를 주어진 철자로 시작하여 쓰시오.

the possibility that something will happen

➡ c_____

서답형

07 다음 우리말에 맞게 빈칸에 알맞은 말을 쓰시오.

내가 창문을 잠갔는지 가서 확인해 봐.
➡ Go and _____ that I've locked the windows.

08 다음 빈칸에 공통으로 알맞은 것은?

• The parking lot is full _____ snow.
• I can't think _____ her name at the moment.

① in   ② of
③ up   ④ about
⑤ at

01 다음 짝지어진 두 단어의 관계가 같도록 빈칸에 알맞은 말을 쓰시오.

(1) wind : windy = snow : _____

(2) hot : cold = warm : _____

(3) teach : teacher = create : _____

02 다음 우리말에 맞게 빈칸에 알맞은 말을 쓰시오.

(1) 마침내 여름방학이 왔다.
➡ Summer vacation has come _____ _____.

(2) Jane은 중국어를 좀 한다.
➡ Jane speaks Chinese _____ _____.

(3) 더 이상 나는 집안에 머물지 않아도 될 것이다.
➡ I won't have to _____ _____ any more.

03 다음 빈칸에 들어갈 알맞은 말을 〈보기〉에서 골라 쓰시오.

┌─ 보기 ─┐
pack mostly different anything
└─────────┘

(1) Would you like _____ else?

(2) The sauce is _____ cream.

(3) Did you _____ the camera?

(4) They are sold in many _____ colours.

04 다음 괄호 안의 단어를 문맥에 맞게 고쳐 쓰시오.

(1) It's not _____ raining now. (actual)

(2) That's _____, isn't it? (amaze)

(3) A _____ young woman is living next door. (mystery)

05 다음 빈칸에 알맞은 말을 〈보기〉에서 골라 쓰시오.

┌─ 보기 ─┐
get to   right now
is full of catch a cold
└─────────┘

(1) I'm coming down _____.

(2) We will _____ London at eight.

(3) The room _____ children.

(4) If you _____, you will cough a lot.

06 다음 영영풀이에 해당하는 단어를 주어진 철자로 시작하여 쓰시오.

(1) a_____ : to like and respect someone or something very much

(2) d_____ : a picture made with a pencil or pen

(3) f_____ : what people and animals eat

Conversation

① 경험 묻고 답하기

> **A** Have you ever eaten pancakes? 넌 팬케이크를 먹어 본 적이 있니?
>
> **B** Yes, I have. 응, 있어.

■ **경험 묻기**

'~해 본 적이 있나요?'라고 과거부터 현재까지의 상대방의 경험을 물을 때는 「Have you (ever)+과거분사 ~?」 형태인 현재완료 의문문으로 물을 수 있다.

■ **경험에 대한 물음에 대답하기**

경험이 있으면 Yes, I have. / Yes, I have+과거분사. 등으로 한다.
경험이 없으면 No, I haven't. / No, I have never+과거분사 / Not yet. 등으로 한다.

- A: Have you ever seen a bear? 너는 곰을 본 적이 있니?
  B: Yes, I have. / No, I haven't. 응, 본 적이 있어. / 아니, 본 적이 없어.

cf. '~에 가본 적 있니?'라고 묻는 표현은 Have you ever gone to ~?가 아니라 Have you ever been to ~?임에 주의한다.

- have been to: ~에 가본 적이 있다(경험) / ~에 갔다왔다(완료)
- have gone to: ~에 가버렸다(결과)

■ 경험을 나타낼 때는 다음과 같은 부사(구)를 함께 쓰는 경우가 많다. ever(지금까지), never(~한 적 없는), before(이전에), once(한 번), twice(두 번), 「숫자+times(~번, ~차례)」, many times(여러 번), often(자주)

- She has made fried rice many times. 그녀는 볶음밥을 여러 번 만든 적이 있다.

핵심 Check

1. 다음 우리말과 일치하도록 빈칸에 알맞은 말을 쓰시오.

   (1) **A:** _____ you ever _____ *Les Miserables*? (너 '레미제라블' 읽어 봤니?)

   B: Yes, I _____. (응, 있어.)

   (2) **A:** _____ you _____ this food? (너는 이 음식을 먹어 봤니?)

   B: No, I _____. (아니, 나는 못 먹어 봤어.)

2 날씨 묻고 답하기

> **A** How's the weather in London in March? 3월에 런던 날씨는 어떠니?
>
> **B** It's rainy and cool. 비가 오고 시원해.

■ **날씨 묻기**

오늘 날씨가 어떤지 물을 때는 What's the weather like today?, 혹은 How's the weather today?라고 한다. 특정 지역의 날씨를 물을 때는 What's the weather like in+지역명? 혹은 How's the weather in+지역명?으로 나타낸다.

비슷한 표현

• What's today's forecast? 오늘 일기 예보가 어떻습니까?

■ **날씨 말하기**

날씨에 대해 말할 때에는 비인칭 주어 it을 사용해 It's ~라고 한다. 날씨에 따라서 fine, sunny, warm, cool, hot, cold, cloudy, snowy, rainy 등의 표현을 사용한다.

• A: What's the weather like today? 오늘 날씨는 어떠니?
  B: It's rainy / sunny / hot / cold / cloudy / snowy.

cf. 현재진행형을 사용하여 '비가[눈이] 오는 중'이라고 말할 때는 「It's 동사원형+-ing.」라고 말한다. 또한 「It's+형용사.」 형태를 사용하여 말할 수도 있다.

• A: What's the weather like outside? 바깥 날씨 어떠니?
  B: It's raining. / It's rainy. 비가 내리고 있어.

cf. it은 날씨, 온도, 명암, 날짜 등을 말할 때 쓰는 주어로 인칭을 나타내는 주어가 아니기 때문에 비인칭 주어라고 한다.

▶ **핵심 Check**

2. 다음 우리말과 일치하도록 빈칸에 알맞은 말을 쓰시오.

(1) **A**: _____ is the _____ in Cleveland? (클리브랜드의 날씨는 어때?)

   B: It's _____ and cold this time of year. (이맘때는 눈이 오고 추워.)

(2) **A**: _____ the weather _____ today? (오늘 날씨는 어떠니?)

   B: It's _____ and sunny. (덥고 화창해.)

(3) **A**: _____ the weather? (날씨가 어때?)

   B: It's _____ a lot. Let's stay at home. (비가 많이 와. 집에 있도록 하자.)

Listen & Speak 1 A-1

G: ❶Have you ever tried Indian food?

B: ❷Yes, I have, but I've only tried Indian curry.

G: ❸How was it?

B: ❹It was really hot, but I loved it.

G: 너 인도 음식을 먹어 본 적이 있니?
B: 응, 있어, 하지만 인도 카레만 먹어 봤어.
G: 어땠어?
B: 정말 매웠지만, 아주 좋았어.

❶ 경험을 나타내는 현재완료는 경험을 묻는 표현으로 사용된다.
❷ I have 다음에는 tried Indian food이 생략되었다.
❸ It은 Indian curry를 가리킨다.
❹ hot은 '뜨거운'이라는 뜻 외에 '매운'이라는 뜻이 있다.

Check(√) True or False

(1) The girl wants to eat Indian food.　　　　T ☐ F ☐

(2) The boy has only tried Indian curry.　　　T ☐ F ☐

Listen & Speak 1 A-2

G: ❶Bill, have you ever gone bungee jumping?

B: ❷No, I haven't. ❸How about you, Katie?

G: ❹When I visited New Zealand, I tried bungee jumping once.

B: ❺Wasn't it scary?

G: No, I liked it. I want to do it again.

G: Bill, 번지 점프하러 가 본 적 있니?
B: 아니, 없어. Katie, 넌 어때?
G: 뉴질랜드를 방문했을 때, 번지 점프를 한 번 해봤어.
B: 무섭지 않았어?
G: 아니, 좋았어. 또 하고 싶어.

❶ go bungee jumping: 번지 점프하러 가다
❷ I haven't = I haven't gone bungee jumping
❸ How about you?: 너는 어때?
❹ once: 한 번
❺ 부정의문문으로 Was it not scary?로 바꿔 쓸 수 있다.

Check(√) True or False

(3) Bill has ever gone bungee jumping.　　　T ☐ F ☐

(4) Katie did bungee jumping once.　　　　　T ☐ F ☐

Listen & Speak 2 A-1

B: ❶Mom, how's the weather today? Do I need an umbrella?

W: ❷It's quite cloudy outside. I'll check the weather forecast.

B: Thank you, Mom.

W: ❸Well, it's not going to rain today.

B: Good! Then, I don't need an umbrella today.

B: 엄마, 오늘 날씨 어때요? 우산이 필요한가요?
W: 바깥 날씨가 아주 흐려. 일기 예보를 확인해 볼게.
B: 고마워요, 엄마.
W: 음, 오늘은 비가 안 올 거야.
B: 좋아요! 그럼, 오늘은 우산이 필요 없어요.

❶ how's = how is
❷ It은 날씨를 나타내는 비인칭 주어로 우리말로 옮기지 않는다.
❸ be going to는 가까운 미래를 나타내는 어구이다.

Check(√) True or False

(5) It's quite cloudy outside now.　　　　　T ☐ F ☐

(6) The boy needs an umbrella today.　　　　T ☐ F ☐

Listen and Speak 2 A-2

W: Good morning, and ❶welcome to the weather forecast. ❷It's sunny outside, but we're expecting some rain in the afternoon. ❸Don't leave home without your umbrella. That's the weather forecast for today. Have a nice day.

❶ welcome to ~: ~에 오신 걸 환영하다 / weather forecast: 일기 예보
❷ It: 날씨를 나타내는 비인칭 주어 / expect: 예상하다
❸ Don't + 동사원형 ~: ~하지 마라

Communicate: A. Listen and Answer

Suho: ❶Anna, have you been to Australia before?
Anna: ❷Yes, I have. Actually, I lived in Sydney for a year.
Suho: Great! ❸How's the weather there in April? I'm going to visit Sydney on vacation next week.
Anna: ❹April is a great time to visit Sydney. In April, it's autumn in Australia.
Suho: Good. ❺I'm planning to spend some time on the beach and relax in the sun.
Anna: ❻Well, it often rains in April, but you may have some sunny days.
Suho: I'll take my hat and pack an umbrella, too.
Anna: ❼That's a good idea. Have a great time.

❶ Have you been to ~?: ~에 가 본 적이 있니?
❷ have = have been to Australia
❸ How's the weather there in April? = What's the weather like there in April?
❹ to visit Sydney는 time을 수식하는 형용사적 용법의 to부정사이다.
❺ be planning to: ~할 계획이다
❻ often은 빈도부사로 일반동사 앞에 위치한다.
❼ That은 지시대명사로 앞 문장의 내용을 받는다.

Communicate B. Make Your Own Dialogue

A: ❶Have you been to any special places in Korea?
B: Yes, I have. ❷I went to Ulleungdo last summer with my family.
A: How was the weather there?
B: ❸It was mostly sunny, but the weather changed often.

❶ have been to: ~에 다녀오다
❷ last summer: 지난 여름에
❸ It은 날씨를 나타내는 비인칭 주어이다. mostly: 주로, 대개

Progress Check 1

G: ❶Have you ever ridden a horse?
B: Yes, I have. How about you?
G: ❷No, I haven't. ❸How was it?
B: It was fun, but it was a little scary, too.

❶ ride – rode – ridden
❷ I haven't=I haven't ridden a horse
❸ it은 인칭대명사로 말을 탄 것을 가리킨다.

Progress Check 2

B: Mom, how's the weather today?
W: ❶It's quite cloudy outside. ❷I'll check the weather forecast.
B: Thanks, Mom.
W: ❸Well, it's going to rain in the afternoon.

❶ quite: 아주 / cloudy: 흐린, 구름이 많은
❷ the weather forecast: 일기 예보
❸ be going to: ~할 것이다

Progress Check 3

M: ❶Good evening, and welcome to the weather forecast. ❷It's raining right now, but we're expecting a sunny day tomorrow. ❸Don't leave home tomorrow without your hat.

❶ welcome to ~: ~에 오신 것을 환영합니다
❷ 현재진행형 문장이다. right now: 지금, 당장
❸ leave home: 집을 떠나다 / without: ~이 없이, ~을 사용하지 않고

● 다음 우리말과 일치하도록 빈칸에 알맞은 말을 쓰시오.

Listen & Speak 1 A. Listen and Check

1. **G:** _____ you ever _____ Indian food?

   B: Yes, I _____, but I've only _____ Indian curry.

   G: _____ was it?

   B: It was really hot, _____ I loved it.

2. **G:** Bill, have you _____ gone bungee _____?

   B: No, I _____. How _____ you, Katie?

   G: _____ I visited New Zealand, I _____ bungee jumping once.

   B: _____ it scary?

   G: No, I _____ it. I _____ to do it again.

Listen & Speak 2 A. Listen and Answer

1. **B:** Mom, how's the _____ today? Do I _____ an umbrella?

   W: It's quite cloudy _____. I'll _____ the weather forecast.

   B: Thank you, Mom.

   W: Well, it's not _____ to rain today.

   B: Good! Then, I _____ need an umbrella today.

2. **W:** _____ morning, and _____ to the weather _____. It's _____ outside, _____ we're expecting some _____ in the afternoon. Don't leave _____ without your umbrella. That's the weather _____ for today. _____ a nice day.

해석

1. **G:** 너 인도 음식을 먹어 본 적 있니?
   B: 응, 있어, 하지만 인도 카레만 먹어 봤어.
   G: 어땠어?
   B: 정말 매웠지만, 아주 좋았어.

2. **G:** Bill, 번지 점프하러 가 본 적 있니?
   B: 아니, 없어. Katie, 넌 어때?
   G: 뉴질랜드를 방문했을 때, 번지 점프를 한 번 해봤어.
   B: 무섭지 않았어?
   G: 아니, 좋았어. 또 하고 싶어.

1. **B:** 엄마, 오늘 날씨 어때요? 우산이 필요한가요?
   W: 바깥 날씨가 아주 흐려. 일기예보를 확인해 볼게.
   B: 고마워요, 엄마.
   W: 음, 오늘은 비가 안 올 거야.
   B: 좋아요! 그럼, 오늘은 우산이 필요 없어요.

2. **W:** 좋은 아침입니다. 일기예보에 오신 것을 환영합니다. 밖은 화창하지만 오후에는 약간의 비가 예상됩니다. 우산 없이 집을 나서지 마세요. 오늘의 일기예보입니다. 좋은 하루 되세요.

Communicate A~B

A. **Suho** Anna, have you _____ to Australia _____?

   Anna: Yes, I _____. Actually, I _____ in Sydney _____ a year.

   Suho: Great! How's the _____ there in April? I'm _____ to visit Sydney on _____ next week.

   Anna: April is a great _____ to _____ Sydney. In April, it's _____ in Australia.

   Suho: Good. I'm _____ to spend some time on the beach and _____ in the sun.

   Anna: Well, it _____ rains in April, but you _____ have some sunny days.

   Suho: I'll _____ my hat and _____ an umbrella, too.

   Anna: That's a good _____. Have a _____ time.

B. **A:** Have you _____ to any special _____ in Korea?

   B: Yes, I _____. I went to Ulleungdo _____ summer with my family.

   A: _____ was the _____ there?

   B: It was _____ sunny, but the weather _____ often.

Progress Check

1. **G:** Have you ever _____ a horse?

   B: Yes, I _____. How _____ you?

   G: No, I _____. How _____ it?

   B: It was _____, but it was a _____ scary, too.

2. **B:** Mom, how's the _____ today?

   W: It's _____ cloudy outside. I'll _____ the weather forecast.

   B: _____, Mom.

   W: Well, it's _____ to rain in the afternoon.

3. **M:** _____ evening, and _____ to the weather forecast. It's _____ right now, _____ we're expecting a _____ day tomorrow. Don't _____ home tomorrow _____ your hat.

01 다음 두 문장의 의미가 같도록 빈칸에 알맞은 말을 쓰시오.

> How's the weather today?
> = _____ the weather _____ today?

02 다음 대화의 밑줄 친 우리말에 해당하는 것은?

> A: Jina, I'm going to Vietnam with my family this winter.
> B: Wow. That sounds like fun.
> A: 너 전에 그곳에 가 본 적 있니?
> B: No, I haven't.

① Did you be there before?
② Had you been there before?
③ Have you been there before?
④ Have you gone there before?
⑤ When did you get there before?

03 다음 대화의 빈칸에 알맞지 <u>않은</u> 것은?

> A: What's the weather like outside?
> B: _____

① It's snowing.   ② It's very cold.
③ It's really cloudy.   ④ It will be very hot.
⑤ It's raining outside.

04 다음 대화의 빈칸에 알맞은 것은?

> A: Have you eaten this food?
> B: No, _____.

① I don't   ② I didn't
③ I haven't   ④ I hadn't
⑤ I loved it

01 다음 대화의 빈칸에 알맞은 것은?

> A: What's the weather like outside?
> B: _____

① It's fall.
② It's windy.
③ It's too cold to drink.
④ I like rainy days.
⑤ I dislike cold weather.

서답형

02 다음 대화의 빈칸에 알맞은 말을 쓰시오.

> A: _____ you _____ tried gimchi, Ann?
> B: Yes, I _____. It was very tasty.

03 다음 대화를 의미가 통하도록 알맞게 배열한 것은?

> (A) Well, it's going to rain in the afternoon.
> (B) Thanks, Mom.
> (C) Mom, how's the weather today?
> (D) It's quite cloudy outside. I'll check the weather forecast.

① (A) – (D) – (B) – (C)
② (B) – (C) – (D) – (A)
③ (C) – (D) – (B) – (A)
④ (D) – (B) – (C) – (A)
⑤ (D) – (C) – (B) – (A)

04 다음 대화의 빈칸에 가장 알맞은 것은?

> A: Have you seen the movie, *Avatar*, Sue?
> B: No, I haven't. _____
> A: Yes, it's my favorite movie.

① Do you?　　　② Will you?
③ Had you?　　　④ Have you?
⑤ What do you want to see?

05 다음 대화의 빈칸에 알맞은 것은?

> A: How's the weather today?
> B: _____
> A: Really? I should wear my sunglasses then. Thanks.

① It's sunny and hot.
② I don't like sunny days.
③ It's cloudy and windy.
④ It looks like rain soon.
⑤ We have good weather in the fall.

[06~09] 다음 대화를 읽고, 물음에 답하시오.

> G: Bill, ___ⓐ___ you ever gone bungee jumping?
> B: No, I haven't. ___ⓑ___ about you, Katie?
> G: ⓒWhen I visited New Zealand, I tried bungee jumping once.
> B: Wasn't ⓓit scary?
> G: No, I liked it. I want to do it again.

06 위 대화의 빈칸 ⓐ에 알맞은 것은?

① do　　　　② did
③ were　　　④ had
⑤ have

07 위 대화의 빈칸 ⓑ에 알맞은 것은? (2개)

① Why   ② How

③ Who   ④ Which

⑤ What

서답형

08 위 대화의 밑줄 친 ⓒ를 우리말로 옮기시오.

➡ _____

서답형

09 위 대화의 밑줄 친 ⓓ가 가리키는 것을 영어로 쓰시오.

➡ _____

[10~14] 다음 대화를 읽고, 물음에 답하시오.

Suho: Anna, have you _____ⓐ_____ to Australia before?

Anna: Yes, I have. ⓑActual, I lived in Sydney for a year.

Suho: Great! ⓒHow's the weather there in April? I'm going to visit Sydney on vacation next week.

Anna: April is a great time to visit Sydney. In April, it's autumn in Australia.

Suho: Good. I'm planning to spend some time on the beach and _____ⓓ_____ in the sun.

Anna: Well, it often rains in April, but you may have some sunny days.

Suho: I'll take my hat and pack an umbrella, too.

Anna: That's a good idea. Have a great time.

10 위 대화의 빈칸 ⓐ에 알맞은 것은?

① were   ② go

③ be   ④ been

⑤ gone

서답형

11 위 대화의 밑줄 친 ⓑ를 알맞은 어형으로 고치시오.

➡ _____

중요

12 위 대화의 밑줄 친 ⓒ와 같은 뜻이 되도록 다음 문장의 빈칸에 알맞은 말을 쓰시오.

_____ the weather _____ there in April?

서답형

13 위 대화의 빈칸 ⓓ에 다음 영영풀이에 해당하는 단어를 쓰시오.

to spend time resting or doing something enjoyable especially after you have been doing work

➡ _____

14 위 대화를 읽고, 답할 수 없는 질문은?

① When did Ann go to Australia?

② Where did Ann live in Australia?

③ When will Suho visit Australia?

④ How is the weather in Sydney in April?

⑤ What will Suho take?

[01~02] 다음 대화의 빈칸에 알맞은 말을 쓰시오.

01
> A: What's the weather _____ today?
> B: _____ is warm and sunny.

02
> A: _____ you ever slept in a tent?
> B: No, I _____.

03 다음 대화를 의미가 통하도록 알맞게 배열하시오.

> (A) It was really hot, but I loved it.
> (B) Have you ever tried Indian food?
> (C) Yes, I have, but I've only tried Indian curry.
> (D) How was it?

➡ _____

[04~06] 다음 대화를 읽고, 물음에 답하시오.

> B: Mom, how's the ⓐ _____ today? Do I need an umbrella?
> W: It's quite ⓑcloud outside. I'll check the weather ⓒ _____ .
> B: Thank you, Mom.
> W: Well, it's not going to rain today.
> B: Good! Then, I don't need an umbrella today.

04 위 대화의 빈칸 ⓐ에 알맞은 말을 쓰시오.

➡ _____

05 위 대화의 밑줄 친 ⓑ를 알맞은 어형으로 고치시오.

➡ _____

06 위 대화의 빈칸 ⓒ에 다음 정의에 해당하는 단어를 쓰시오.

> a statement of what is expected to happen in the future, especially in relation to a particular event or situation

➡ _____

[07~09] 다음 담화문을 읽고, 물음에 답하시오.

> W: Good morning, and _____ⓐ to the weather forecast. It's ⓑsun outside, but we're expecting some rain in the afternoon. Don't leave home without your umbrella. That's the weather forecast for today. Have a nice day.

07 위 담화문의 빈칸 ⓐ에 알맞은 말을 쓰시오.

➡ _____

08 위 담화문의 밑줄 친 ⓑ를 알맞은 어형으로 고치시오.

➡ _____

09 What's the weather like in the afternoon? Answer in Korean.

➡ _____

Grammar

교과서

① to부정사의 형용사적 용법

- A B&B is a popular place **to stay** in England. B&B는 영국에서 머무는 곳으로 인기가 있다.
- They need something **to drink**. 그들은 마실 것이 필요하다.
- I have a lot of homework **to do** tonight. 나는 오늘밤 해야 할 숙제가 많다.

■ to부정사의 형용사적 용법은 명사나 대명사 뒤에서 '~하는, ~할'의 뜻으로 쓰인다. 이 때 앞의 명사는 to부정사의 주어 또는 목적어 역할을 한다.

- I have no money **to give** you. [목적어] 나는 너에게 줄 돈이 없다.
  = I have no money that I can give you.

- He had no friends **to help** him. [주어] 그는 자기를 도와줄 친구가 하나도 없었다.
  = He had no friends who would help him.

■ to부정사의 수식을 받는 명사가 전치사의 목적어일 경우, to부정사 뒤에 전치사가 온다.

- Ann has elderly parents **to look** after. Ann은 돌보아야 할 나이 드신 부모가 있다.
- I want a small room **to live** in by myself. 나는 혼자 살 작은 방을 원한다.

■ -thing으로 끝나는 부정대명사는 「-thing+(형용사+)to부정사」의 어순을 따른다.

- I want something cold **to drink**. 나는 차가운 마실 것을 원한다.
- You feel that you have nothing **to wear**. 너는 입을 것이 아무것도 없다고 느낀다.

핵심 Check

1. 다음 괄호 안에서 알맞은 것을 고르시오.

   (1) It's time (go / to go) to school.

   (2) Jack has a lot of friends (helping / to help).

   (3) Give me a pen (to write / to write with).

   (4) Would you like something (to cold drink / cold to drink)?

❷ 가주어 it

> • **It** was just amazing **to see** the ring of huge stones.
> 거대한 돌들의 고리를 보는 것은 아주 놀라웠다.
>
> • **It** is easy **to bake** cookies. 쿠키를 굽는 것은 쉽다.
>
> • **It** will be nice **to become** a musician. 음악가가 되는 것은 멋질 거야.

■ 가주어 it

to부정사구가 문장 안에서 주어로 쓰일 경우, to부정사구를 문장의 뒤로 보내고 그 자리에 it을 쓴다. 이 때의 it은 아무런 의미가 없는 주어로 '가주어'라고 하고, to부정사구를 '진주어'라고 한다.

• **To master** English in a month is impossible. 영어를 한 달 동안에 습득하는 것은 불가능하다.

→ **It** is impossible **to master** English in a month.
　　가주어　　　　　　　진주어

cf. to부정사 이외에도 진주어로 명사절이 쓰일 때가 있다. 이때 명사절을 이끄는 접속사는 보통 that이 쓰인다.

• It is a bad habit **that** people read in bed. 침대에서 독서하는 것은 나쁜 버릇이다.

■ to부정사의 의미상의 주어

to부정사의 의미상의 주어가 문장의 주어와 일치하지 않는 경우, 일반적으로 「for+목적격」의 형태로 진주어 앞에 쓴다. kind, foolish, wise, honest, polite 등과 같이 사람의 성격을 나타내는 형용사가 보어로 쓰이면 의미상의 주어로 「of+목적격」의 형태를 쓴다.

• **It** is natural **for** your parents **to get** angry. 너희 부모님이 화를 내시는 것은 당연한 것이다.

• **It** is very kind **of** you **to help** me. 나를 도와주다니 넌 참 친절하다.

핵심 Check

2. 다음 괄호 안에서 알맞은 것을 고르시오.

(1) It is hard (understanding / to understand) his words.

(2) (It / That) is interesting to watch basketball games.

(3) It is good for your health (to exercise / exercise) every day.

(4) It is honest (for / of) you to say so.

(5) It is not easy (for / of) us to learn foreign languages.

Grammar 시험대비 기본평가

01 다음 괄호 안에서 알맞은 것을 고르시오.

> travel 여행하다
> solve 풀다

(1) There are many places (visit / to visit) in Jeju.

(2) Do you have anything (to do / doing) this evening?

(3) (It / That) is fun to travel to some countries in Asia.

(4) It is very kind (of / for) you to help me.

(5) It is hard (of / for) me to solve this problem.

02 다음 밑줄 친 부분을 바르게 고쳐 쓰시오.

> exercise 운동하다
> impossible 불가능한
> save 구하다

(1) It's difficult <u>exercise</u> every day.

➡ _____

(2) It is impossible <u>finish</u> this work in an hour.

➡ _____

(3) <u>That</u> is very important to learn a foreign language.

➡ _____

(4) It was brave <u>for</u> him to save the child.

➡ _____

(5) It was easy <u>of</u> me to answer all the questions.

➡ _____

03 다음 우리말과 일치하도록 빈칸에 알맞은 말을 쓰시오.

> schedule 일정
> country 나라

(1) 우리는 일정을 바꿀 시간이 없다.

➡ We have no time _____ _____ the schedule.

(2) 그는 우리나라를 방문한 최초의 미국인이었다.

➡ He was the first American _____ _____ our country.

(3) 나는 기차에서 읽을 책을 가져가고 싶다.

➡ I want to bring a book _____ _____ on the train.

[01~02] 다음 문장의 빈칸에 알맞은 것을 고르시오.

01

It is good for the health _____ early.

① get up　　　② got up
③ to get up　　④ to getting up
⑤ to be getting up

02 중요

Do you have anything _____?

① read　　　② reads
③ reading　　④ to read
⑤ to be reading

03 다음 중 밑줄 친 부분의 쓰임이 나머지 넷과 다른 것은?

① He is always the first to come.
② He has nothing to write with.
③ He went to England to study English.
④ There are a lot of things for him to do.
⑤ He was looking for an apartment to live in.

04 서답형 다음 두 문장의 뜻이 같도록 빈칸에 알맞은 말을 쓰시오.

I have a lot of letters _____ _____.
= I have a lot of letters that I should write.

05 서답형 다음 두 문장의 뜻이 같도록 빈칸에 알맞은 말을 쓰시오

To change the schedule is very difficult.

➡ _____ is very difficult _____ change the schedule.

06 다음 우리말과 같도록 할 때, 빈칸에 알맞은 말이 바르게 짝지어진 것은?

자전거를 탈 때는 헬멧을 쓰는 것이 안전하다.
➡ _____ is safe _____ a helmet when you ride a bike.

① It － to wear　　② This － wear
③ It － wears　　④ It － wear
⑤ That － to wear

07 다음 중 밑줄 친 부분의 쓰임이 〈보기〉와 같은 것은?

보기
I have lots of books to read by next month.

① Jina has no chair to sit on.
② My hobby is to listen to music.
③ She is glad to get a letter from Tony.
④ He wants to play baseball after school.
⑤ I went to the market to buy some eggs.

서답형

08 다음 우리말과 일치하도록 주어진 단어를 바르게 배열하여 문장을 완성하시오.

> 너 뭐 좀 먹을래?
> (anything / you / want / do / eat / to)

➡ _____

_____

중요

09 다음 중 어법상 어색한 문장은?

① It's almost time to go to bed.
② It's time to get aboard a plane.
③ It is time to eat dinner.
④ It's time for the children to going to bed.
⑤ It's time for my dad to buy a new car.

중요

10 다음 중 밑줄 친 it의 쓰임이 나머지 넷과 다른 하나는?

① It's important to be kind to others.
② Is it fun to play computer games?
③ It is not surprising for him to say so.
④ It's hard to believe, but it's a flower.
⑤ It's not easy to understand other cultures.

서답형

11 다음 괄호 안에 주어진 말을 사용하여 우리말을 영작하시오.

> 그 기계를 고치는 것은 어렵다.
> (it / difficult / fix / machine)

➡ _____

중요

12 다음 빈칸에 알맞은 말이 바르게 짝지어진 것은?

> • It is very kind _____ you to say so.
> • It is natural _____ a baby to cry.

① of – of   ② of – for
③ for – for   ④ for – of
⑤ for – with

13 다음 빈칸에 공통으로 알맞은 것은?

> • It was honest _____ you to tell the truth.
> • It is wise _____ her to make such a decision.

① of   ② for
③ with   ④ at
⑤ upon

서답형

14 다음 빈칸에 공통으로 알맞은 말을 쓰시오.

> • You don't have _____ worry about it.
> • I have no reason _____ be angry at you.

중요

15 다음 빈칸에 들어갈 동사의 형태로 적절한 것은?

> It's necessary _____ on time.

① to be   ② is
③ be   ④ are
⑤ will be

16 다음 문장의 빈칸에 to를 쓸 수 <u>없는</u> 것은?

① It is natural for your mom _____ get angry.

② She hopes _____ visit her uncle.

③ He is kind enough _____ help us.

④ It is easy _____ speak English.

⑤ She made me _____ wash the dishes.

17 다음 문장에서 어법상 어색한 부분을 바르게 고쳐 쓰시오.

> I need a chair to sit.

_____ ➡ _____

18 다음 중 밑줄 친 부분의 쓰임이 바르지 <u>않은</u> 것은?

① There is no bench <u>to sit on</u>.

② I have no money <u>to give</u> you.

③ Judy has a lot of friends <u>to talk</u>.

④ She doesn't have a house <u>to live in</u>.

⑤ Do you have a pen <u>to write with</u>?

19 다음 중 밑줄 친 부분의 쓰임이 나머지 넷과 <u>다른</u> 것은?

① <u>It</u> will soon be a new year.

② Is <u>it</u> easy to use this camera?

③ <u>It</u> is a lot of fun to ski in winter.

④ <u>It</u> isn't difficult to use the computer.

⑤ <u>It</u> is interesting to read English books.

20 다음 중 밑줄 친 to부정사의 쓰임이 <u>다른</u> 하나는?

① It is important <u>to try</u> your best.

② My dream is <u>to be</u> a singer.

③ I want a house <u>to live</u> in.

④ I decided <u>to study</u> Spanish.

⑤ It is very kind of you <u>to help</u> me.

21 다음 주어진 어구를 이용하여 〈보기〉와 같이 문장을 쓰시오.

> ┤ 보기 ├
>
> (boring / watch news on TV)
>
> ➡ It is boring to watch news on TV.

> (pleasant / listen to music)
>
> ➡ _____

22 다음 빈칸에 들어갈 말이 바르게 짝지어진 것은?

> • It's time for our children _____ to bed.
>
> • You don't have _____ an umbrella with you.

① go – take   ② to go – taken

③ going – taking   ④ going – to take

⑤ to go – to take

23 다음 문장에서 어법상 어색한 부분을 찾아 바르게 고쳐 쓰시오.

> It is necessary for you going there as soon as possible.

_____ ➡ _____

01 다음 두 문장의 뜻이 같도록 빈칸에 알맞은 말을 쓰시오.

> To cook French food is difficult.
> ➡ _____ is difficult _____ cook French food.

02 다음 빈칸에 공통으로 알맞은 말을 쓰시오.

> • Mike had no time _____ do his homework.
> • I'm going to buy some paper _____ write on.

03 다음 주어진 단어를 바르게 배열하여 문장을 완성하시오.

(1) (bake / is / cookies / to / it / easy)

➡ _____

(2) (a magazine / on / he / read / the train / bought / to)

➡ _____

04 다음 밑줄 친 단어를 알맞은 형태로 고쳐 쓰시오.

> It is strange for her <u>receive</u> fan letters.

➡ _____

05 다음 괄호 안에 주어진 말을 사용하여 우리말을 영작하시오. (가주어 – 진주어 구문을 사용할 것.)

(1) 주말마다 그를 방문하는 것은 쉽지 않았다.
(visit, easy, every)

➡ _____

(2) 다른 나라에서 사는 것은 재미있는 경험이다.
(it, exciting, live, another)

➡ _____

06 다음 괄호 안에 주어진 어구를 이용하여 우리말을 영어로 옮기시오.

(1) 그녀는 가수가 되려는 강한 욕망을 갖고 있다.
(strong desire, be, singer)

➡ _____

(2) 나는 이 문제를 해결하기 위해 모든 노력을 할 것이다. (every effort, solve)

➡ _____

(3) 우리는 이야기할 것이 있었다.
(something, talk about)

➡ _____

(4) 나는 쓸 종이를 한 장 원한다.
(want, write)

➡ _____

(5) 제게 뜨거운 마실 것을 좀 주십시오.
(please, something, drink)

➡ _____

07 중요 다음 빈칸에 알맞은 말을 〈보기〉에서 골라 쓰시오. (중복해서 사용할 수 없음.)

┌─ 보기 ────────────────┐
  to   on   with   it
└──────────────────────┘

(1) _____ is hard to follow good advice.

(2) Do you have anything to write _____?

(3) I need a knife to cut the rope _____.

(4) I have a lot of things _____ do today.

08 중요 다음 문장에서 어법상 어색한 것을 찾아 바르게 고쳐 쓰시오.

(1) He doesn't have time play with his friends.

_____ ➡ _____

(2) It is important of you to study hard.

_____ ➡ _____

[09~10] 다음 우리말을 참고하여 문장을 완성하시오.

09
┌──────────────────────────┐
이 도시에는 방문해야 할 장소가 많이 있다.
➡ There are many places _____
_____ in this city.
└──────────────────────────┘

10
┌──────────────────────────┐
너는 공부를 열심히 하는 것이 중요하다.
➡ It is important _____ _____ to study hard.
└──────────────────────────┘

11 중요 다음 두 문장의 뜻이 같도록 빈칸에 알맞은 말을 쓰시오.

┌──────────────────────────────┐
To learn to ride a bike was not difficult.
➡ _____ was not difficult _____ _____ to ride a bike.
└──────────────────────────────┘

12 다음 빈칸에 공통으로 알맞은 말을 쓰시오.

┌──────────────────────────────┐
• It's time for my brother _____ come home.
• You don't have _____ water the flowers.
└──────────────────────────────┘

13 중요 다음 문장에서 어법상 어색한 것을 찾아 바르게 고쳐 쓰시오.

(1) It was stupid for you to believe the rumor.

_____ ➡ _____

(2) It isn't necessary of you to come here today.

_____ ➡ _____

14 고난이도 다음 주어진 단어를 이용하여 우리말을 영어로 옮기시오.

┌──────────────────────────────┐
그곳은 24시간 동안 많은 물건들을 파는 장소이다.
(it's / a place / to sell / things)
└──────────────────────────────┘

➡ _____

Reading

My Special Travel Journal

Hi, I am Lucy Hunter, and I live in London. Last week, my family went on a vacation for three days. During our trip, I made simple drawings in my journal. That was a great way to capture all the special moments.

August 5

At last, we set foot at Stonehenge, one of the most mysterious places on Earth. After a two-hour drive from our home in London, we finally got to Stonehenge. It was just amazing to see the ring of huge stones. How did those huge stones get there thousands of years ago? What were they for? I guess Stonehenge will remain a mystery for a long time.

Lucy's Drawing Tips

Don't try to make perfect drawing. A few colors will be enough.

August 6

In the morning, we walked around the Cotswolds. It started to rain in the afternoon, so we decided to stay indoors at our B&B. A B&B is a popular place to stay in England. It feels more like a home than a hotel.

---

go on a vacation 휴가를 가다
during ~ 중에
simple 간단한, 단순한
journal 일기
capture 담아내다, 포착하다
special 특별한
moment 순간
set 놓다, 두다
mysterious 신비스러운
amazing 놀라운
ring 반지, 고리
huge 거대한, 큰
thousands of 수천의
guess 추측하다, 생각하다
remain 남아 있다
mystery 미스터리, 신비
tip 충고
perfect 완전한
enough 충분한
decide 결정하다
feel like ~처럼 느껴지다

확인문제

● 다음 문장이 본문의 내용과 일치하면 T, 일치하지 않으면 F를 쓰시오.

1 Lucy's family went on a vacation last week. ☐

2 Lucy wrote interesting poems in her journal. ☐

3 Lucy's family went to Stonehenge. ☐

4 Stonehenge was an old temple. ☐

5 Lucy's family stayed indoors at their B&B on August 6. ☐

The owner invited us for afternoon tea today. The dining table was full of cookies, cake, bread, and cheese. While I was busy eating, Mom was admiring the beautiful cups and plates. I ate too much, so I couldn't eat anything for dinner.

Lucy's Drawing Tips

It is O.K to draw everyday objects like cups and plates in your journal.

August 7

Our last stop was Oxford. We first visited Christ Church College. It has become a world famous place to visit since it appeared in the *Harry Potter* movies. In the movies, Harry and everyone else eat dinner at the Hall of Christ Church. We also saw portraits of famous people who graduated from the college. When we were outside the building. I walked to the famous olive tree and touched it. "Because I touched this tree," I said, "I will get into Oxford University!" Then, my brother said to me with a smile, "I can't wait to see your portrait on the wall."

Lucy's Drawing Tips

Create your own avatar. Your drawing journal will become much more interesting.

owner 주인

invite 초대하다

be full of ~으로 가득 차다

while ~하는 동안

be busy –ing ~하느라 바쁘다

admire 감탄하며 바라보다

plate 접시

everyday 매일의, 일상적인,

object 사물

become ~이 되다

appear 나타나다, 출연하다

else 또 다른, 다른

portrait 초상화

graduate 졸업하다

college 대학

touch 만지다, 대다

smile 미소, 웃음

확인문제

● 다음 문장이 본문의 내용과 일치하면 T, 일치하지 않으면 F를 쓰시오.

1 Lucy's mom wanted to buy the beautiful cups and plates. ☐

2 Lucy's family visited Christ Church College. ☐

3 Christ Church College appeared in the *Harry Potter* movies. ☐

4 Lucy didn't touch the famous olive tree. ☐

● 우리말을 참고하여 빈칸에 알맞은 말을 쓰시오.

1 Hi, I am Lucy Hunter, and I _____ in London.

2 Last _____, my family went on a _____ for three days.

3 During our _____, I made simple drawings in my _____.

4 That was a great _____ to capture all the _____ moments.

5 At last, we _____ foot at Stonehenge, one of the most _____ places on _____.

6 After a two-hour _____ from our home in London, we _____ got to Stonehenge.

7 It was just _____ to see the _____ of huge stones.

8 How did those huge _____ get there _____ of years ago?

9 What were they _____?

10 I _____ Stonehenge will remain a _____ for a long time.

11 Don't try to make a _____ drawing.

12 A few _____ will be enough.

13 _____ the morning, we walked _____ the Cotswolds.

14 It _____ to rain in the afternoon, _____ we decided to stay indoors at our B&B.

15 A B&B is a _____ place to _____ in England.

1 안녕, 나는 Lucy Hunter이고 런던에 살아요.

2 지난주에 우리 가족은 3일 동안 휴가를 갔습니다.

3 여행 중에 나는 일기에 간단한 그림을 그렸어요.

4 그것은 모든 특별한 순간을 포착하는 훌륭한 방법이었어요.

5 마침내, 우리는 지구에서 가장 불가사의한 장소 중 하나인 스톤헨지에 발을 디뎠다.

6 런던에 있는 집에서 차로 두 시간을 달려서 우리는 마침내 스톤헨지에 도착했다.

7 원형으로 둘러서 있는 거대한 돌들을 보는 것은 정말 놀라웠다.

8 어떻게 그 거대한 돌들이 수천 년 전에 그곳에 도착했을까?

9 그것들은 무엇을 위한 것이었을까?

10 스톤헨지는 오랫동안 미스터리로 남을 것 같다.

11 완벽한 그림을 그리려고 하지 마세요.

12 몇 가지 색깔이면 충분할 것입니다.

13 아침에 우리는 코츠월드 언덕을 돌아다녔다.

14 오후에 비가 오기 시작해서, 우리는 B&B의 실내에서 머물기로 결정했다.

15 B&B는 영국에서 체류하는 곳으로 인기가 있다.

16 It feels more _____ a home than a hotel.

17 The owner _____ us for afternoon tea today.

18 The dining table was _____ of cookies, cake, bread, _____ cheese.

19 While I was _____ eating, Mom was _____ the beautiful cups and plates.

20 I ate too _____, so I couldn't eat _____ for dinner.

21 It is O.K. to _____ everyday objects _____ cups and plates in your journal.

22 Our last _____ was Oxford.

23 We first _____ Christ Church College.

24 It has _____ a world famous place to visit _____ it appeared in the *Harry Potter* movies.

25 In the _____, Harry and everyone _____ eat _____ at the Hall of Christ Church.

26 We _____ saw portraits of famous people _____ graduated from the college.

27 _____ we were _____ the building, I _____ to the famous olive tree and touched it.

28 "Because I _____ this tree," I said, "I will _____ into Oxford University!"

29 Then, my brother _____ to me with a _____, "I can't wait to see your _____ on the wall."

30 _____ your own avatar.

31 Your drawing _____ will become _____ more interesting.

16 그것은 호텔이라기보다는 집처럼 느껴진다.

17 주인은 오늘 오후의 다과회에 우리를 초대했다.

18 식탁에는 쿠키, 케이크, 빵, 그리고 치즈가 가득했다.

19 내가 먹느라고 바쁠 때, 엄마는 아름다운 컵과 접시를 감탄하며 바라보고 계셨다.

20 나는 너무 많이 먹어서 저녁으로 아무것도 먹을 수 없었다.

21 당신의 일기에 컵과 접시 같은 일상적인 물건들을 그려도 괜찮습니다.

22 우리가 마지막으로 머문 곳은 옥스퍼드였다.

23 우리는 먼저 Christ Church College를 방문했다.

24 이곳은 해리포터 영화에 등장한 이후 방문해야 할 세계적으로 유명한 장소가 되었다.

25 영화에서 Harry와 다른 모든 사람들이 Christ Church의 회관에서 저녁을 먹는다.

26 우리는 또한 그 대학을 졸업한 유명한 사람들의 초상화를 보았다.

27 우리가 건물 밖으로 나왔을 때, 나는 유명한 올리브 나무로 걸어가서 그것을 만졌다.

28 "이 나무를 만졌기 때문에, 난 옥스퍼드 대학교에 들어갈 거야!"라고 말했다.

29 그러자 오빠가 웃으면서 "벽에 걸린 네 초상화가 빨리 보고 싶어."라고 내게 말했다.

30 여러분 자신의 아바타를 만드세요.

31 그림일기가 훨씬 더 재미있을 거예요.

• 우리말을 참고하여 본문을 영작하시오.

1 안녕, 나는 Lucy Hunter이고 런던에 살아요.

➡ _____

2 지난주에 우리 가족은 3일 동안 휴가를 갔습니다.

➡ _____

3 여행 중에 나는 일기에 간단한 그림을 그렸어요.

➡ _____

4 그것은 모든 특별한 순간을 포착하는 훌륭한 방법이었어요.

➡ _____

5 마침내, 우리는 지구에서 가장 불가사의한 장소 중 하나인 스톤헨지에 발을 디뎠다.

➡ _____

6 런던에 있는 집에서 차로 두 시간을 달려서 우리는 마침내 스톤헨지에 도착했다.

➡ _____

7 원형으로 둘러서 있는 거대한 돌들을 보는 것은 정말 놀라웠다.

➡ _____

8 어떻게 그 거대한 돌들이 수천 년 전에 그곳에 도착했을까?

➡ _____

9 그것들은 무엇을 위한 것이었을까?

➡ _____

10 완벽한 그림을 그리려고 하지 마세요.

➡ _____

11 몇 가지 색깔이면 충분할 것입니다.

➡ _____

12 스톤헨지는 오랫동안 미스터리로 남을 것 같다.

➡ _____

13 아침에 우리는 코츠월드 언덕을 돌아다녔다.

➡ _____

14 오후에 비가 오기 시작해서, 우리는 B&B의 실내에서 머물기로 결정했다.

➡ _____

15 B&B는 영국에서 체류하는 곳으로 인기가 있다.

➡ _____

16 그것은 호텔이라기보다는 집처럼 느껴진다.

➡ _____

17 주인은 오늘 오후의 다과회에 우리를 초대했다.

➡ _____

18 식탁에는 쿠키, 케이크, 빵, 그리고 치즈가 가득했다.

➡ _____

19 내가 먹느라 바쁠 때, 엄마는 아름다운 컵과 접시를 감탄하며 바라보고 계셨다.

➡ _____

20 나는 너무 많이 먹어서 저녁으로 아무것도 먹을 수 없었다.

➡ _____

21 당신의 일기에 컵과 접시 같은 일상적인 물건들을 그려도 괜찮습니다.

➡ _____

22 우리가 마지막으로 머문 곳은 옥스퍼드였다.

➡ _____

23 우리는 먼저 Christ Church College를 방문했다.

➡ _____

24 이곳은 해리포터 영화에 등장한 이후 방문해야 할 세계적으로 유명한 장소가 되었다.

➡ _____

25 영화에서 Harry와 다른 모든 사람들이 Christ Church의 회관에서 저녁을 먹는다.

➡ _____

26 우리는 또한 그 대학을 졸업한 유명한 사람들의 초상화를 보았다.

➡ _____

27 우리가 건물 밖으로 나왔을 때, 나는 유명한 올리브 나무로 걸어가서 그것을 만졌다.

➡ _____

28 "이 나무를 만졌기 때문에, 난 옥스퍼드 대학교에 들어갈 거야!"라고 말했다.

➡ _____

29 그러자 오빠가 웃으면서 "벽에 걸린 네 초상화가 빨리 보고 싶어."라고 말했다.

➡ _____

30 여러분 자신의 아바타를 만드세요.

➡ _____

31 그림일기가 훨씬 더 재미있을 거예요.

➡ _____

[01~04] 다음 글을 읽고, 물음에 답하시오.

Hi, I am Lucy Hunter, and I live in London. Last week, my family went ___ⓐ___ a vacation ___ⓑ___ three days. ___ⓒ___ our trip, I made simple drawings in my journal. ⓓThat was a great way to capture all the special moments.

01 위 글의 빈칸 ⓐ에 알맞은 것은?

① on   ② to
③ at   ④ by
⑤ for

02 위 글의 빈칸 ⓑ와 ⓒ에 알맞은 말이 바르게 짝지어진 것은?

① on – During   ② in – During
③ on – While   ④ for – During
⑤ for – While

서답형

03 위 글의 밑줄 친 ⓓThat이 가리키는 것을 우리말로 쓰시오.

➡ _____

서답형

04 일기에 간단한 그림을 그리는 것의 장점을 우리말로 간단히 쓰시오.

➡ _____

[05~09] 다음 글을 읽고, 물음에 답하시오.

At last, we set foot at Stonehenge, one of the most mysterious places on Earth. (①) After a two-hour drive from our home in London, we finally got ___ⓐ___ Stonehenge. (②) It was just amazing to see the ring of huge stones. (③) What were they for? (④) I guess Stonehenge will remain a ___ⓑ___ for a long time. (⑤)
Lucy's Drawing Tips
Don't try to make a perfect drawing. ___ⓒ___ colors will be enough.

05 위 글의 ①~⑤ 중 주어진 문장이 들어갈 알맞은 곳은?

How did those huge stones get there thousands of years ago?

①   ②   ③   ④   ⑤

06 위 글의 빈칸 ⓐ에 알맞은 것은?

① at   ② to
③ on   ④ for
⑤ over

서답형

07 위 글의 빈칸 ⓑ에 다음 정의에 해당하는 단어를 주어진 철자로 시작하여 쓰시오.

something that is not understood or known about

➡ m_____

08 위 글의 빈칸 ⓒ에 알맞은 것은?

① Few   ② A few

③ Much   ④ Many

⑤ A little

09 위 글의 내용으로 보아 대답할 수 없는 질문은?

① Where did they go?

② Is Stonehenge a mysterious place?

③ How long did it take them to get to Stonehenge from their home?

④ What were the ring of huge stones for?

⑤ What is Lucy's drawing tip?

[10~15] 다음 글을 읽고, 물음에 답하시오.

(①) In the morning, we walked around the Cotswolds. (②) ⓐIt started to rain in the afternoon, so we decided to stay indoors at our B&B. A B&B is a popular place to stay in England. (③) The owner invited us for afternoon tea today. (④) The dining table was full ___ⓑ___ cookies, cake, bread, and cheese. (⑤) ___ⓒ___ I was busy eating, Mom was admiring the beautiful cups and plates. ⓓI ate too much, so I couldn't eat anything for dinner.   I = Lucy

10 위 글의 ①~⑤ 중 주어진 문장이 들어갈 알맞은 곳은?

> It feels more like a home than a hotel.

①   ②   ③   ④   ⑤

11 위 글의 밑줄 친 ⓐ와 같은 용법으로 쓰이지 않은 것은?

① It's ten past twelve.

② It was raining this morning.

③ It is very dark in the room.

④ It's two miles to the beach from here.

⑤ It is in Mike's house.

12 위 글의 빈칸 ⓑ에 알맞은 것은?

① in   ② of

③ off   ④ with

⑤ from

13 위 글의 빈칸 ⓒ에 알맞은 것은?

① If   ② During

③ Since   ④ While

⑤ Though

서답형

14 위 글의 밑줄 친 ⓓ와 같은 뜻이 되도록 다음 문장의 빈칸에 알맞은 말을 쓰시오.

> I couldn't eat anything _____ I ate too much.

15 위 글의 내용으로 보아 대답할 수 없는 질문은?

① Where did they walk?

② When did it begin to rain?

③ Where did they stay?

④ Why did the owner invite them for afternoon tea?

⑤ What was Lucy's mother admiring?

[16~20] 다음 글을 읽고, 물음에 답하시오.

(①) Our last stop was Oxford. (②) We first visited Christ Church College. (③) ⓐ It has become a world famous place to visit _____ ⓑ it appeared in the *Harry Potter* movies. (④) ⓒWe also saw portraits of famous people who graduated the college. (⑤)

16 위 글의 ①~⑤ 중 주어진 문장이 들어갈 알맞은 곳은?

In the movies, Harry and everyone else eat dinner at the Hall of Christ Church.

①   ②   ③   ④   ⑤

서답형

17 위 글의 밑줄 친 ⓐ가 가리키는 것을 영어로 쓰시오.

➡ _____

중요

18 위 글의 빈칸 ⓑ에 알맞은 것은?

① when   ② as
③ if   ④ while
⑤ since

서답형

19 위 글의 밑줄 친 ⓒ를 어법상 <u>어색한</u> 것을 고쳐 다시 쓰시오.

➡ _____
_____

20 위 글의 내용에서 언급되지 <u>않은</u> 것은?

① 우리가 마지막으로 들른 곳은 옥스퍼드였다.
② 우리는 Christ Church College를 방문했다.
③ Christ Church College는 영국에서 가장 인기 있는 관광지 중의 하나이다.
④ Christ Church College에서 Harry Potter 영화를 촬영했다.
⑤ Christ Church College에서 이 학교를 졸업한 유명 인사들의 초상화를 볼 수 있다.

[21~24] 다음 글을 읽고, 물음에 답하시오.

_____ ⓐ we were outside the building, I walked to the _____ ⓑ olive tree and touched it. "Because I touched this tree," I said, "I will get into Oxford University!" Then, my brother said to me with a smile, "I can't wait to see your portrait on the wall."

Lucy's Drawing Tips
Create your own avatar. Your drawing journal will become ⓒ*much more interesting.*

I = Lucy

21 위 글의 빈칸 ⓐ에 알맞은 것은?

① When   ② Though
③ If   ④ Because
⑤ Since

서답형

22 위 글의 빈칸 ⓑ에 다음 정의에 해당하는 말을 쓰시오.

very well known

➡ _____

23 위 글의 밑줄 친 ⓒ와 바꿔 쓸 수 없는 것은? (2개)

① many ② even
③ very ④ far
⑤ a lot

24 위 글의 내용과 일치하지 <u>않는</u> 것은?

① Lucy went out of the building.
② Lucy touched the olive tree.
③ Lucy wants to enter Oxford University.
④ Lucy's brother can see her portrait on the wall.
⑤ Lucy advises us to create our own avatar.

[25~30] 다음 글을 읽고, 물음에 답하시오.

Last winter, I went to Laos with my family. (①) We visited ⓐa lot of beautiful temples and went to the night ⓑ_____ in Vientiane. (②) We also enjoyed their ⓒtradition food. (③) ⓓIt was a lot of fun to try new things in a foreign country. (④) I hope I will have a chance to visit Laos again. (⑤)

I = Minsu

25 위 글의 ①~⑤ 중 주어진 문장이 들어갈 알맞은 곳은?

Then, we moved to Vang Vieng and went river tubing.

① ② ③ ④ ⑤

26 위 글의 밑줄 친 ⓐ와 바꿔 쓸 수 있는 것은?

① few ② many
③ much ④ a few
⑤ little

27 위 글의 빈칸 ⓑ에 다음 정의에 해당하는 단어를 쓰시오.

a place where goods are bought and sold, usually outdoors

➡ _____

28 위 글의 밑줄 친 ⓒ를 알맞은 어형으로 고치시오.

➡ _____

29 위 글의 밑줄 친 ⓓ가 가리키는 것을 우리말로 쓰시오.

➡ _____

30 위 글의 내용으로 보아 대답할 수 <u>없는</u> 질문은?

① Who did Minsu go to Laos with?
② Why did Minsu visit temples?
③ What did Minsu do at Vang Vieng?
④ What food did Minsu enjoy?
⑤ What does Minsu hope to do?

[01~05] 다음 글을 읽고, 물음에 답하시오.

August 5

At last, we set ____ⓐ____ at Stonehenge, one of the most mysterious places on Earth. ____ⓑ____ a two-hour drive from our home in London, we finally got to Stonehenge. It was just ⓒ(amazed, amazing) to see the ring of huge stones. How did those huge stones get ⓓthere thousands of years ago? What were they for? I guess Stonehenge will remain a mystery for a long time.

Lucy's Drawing Tips
Don't try to make a perfect drawing. A few colors will be enough.

01 위 글의 빈칸 ⓐ에 다음 정의에 해당하는 단어를 쓰시오.

> the part of your body that is at the ends of your legs, and that you stand on

➡ _____

02 위 글의 빈칸 ⓑ에 알맞은 전치사를 쓰시오.

➡ _____

03 위 글의 괄호 ⓒ에서 알맞은 것을 고르시오.

➡ _____

04 위 글의 밑줄 친 ⓓ가 가리키는 것을 영어로 쓰시오.

➡ _____

05 What is Lucy's drawing tip? Answer in Korean.

➡ _____

[06~08] 다음 글을 읽고, 물음에 답하시오.

Hi, I am Lucy Hunter, and I live in London. Last week, my family went ____ⓐ____ a vacation for three days. ⓑ(For, During) our trip, I made simple drawings in my journal. ⓒThat was a great way to capture the all special moments.

06 위 글의 빈칸 ⓐ에 알맞은 전치사를 쓰시오.

➡ _____

07 위 글의 괄호 ⓑ에서 알맞은 것을 고르시오.

➡ _____

08 위 글의 밑줄 친 ⓒ에서 어법상 어색한 것을 고쳐 다시 쓰시오.

➡ _____

[09~15] 다음 글을 읽고, 물음에 답하시오.

August 6

In the morning, we walked around the Cotswolds. It started to rain in the afternoon, so we decided ⓐ(staying, to stay) indoors at our B&B. A B&B is a popular place to stay in England. It feels more _____ⓑ_____ a home than a hotel. The ⓒown invited us for afternoon tea today. ⓓThe dining table was full of cookies, cake, bread, and cheese. While I was busy eating, Mom was admiring the beautiful cups and plates. I ate too much, ⓔso I couldn't eat nothing for dinner.

Lucy's Drawing Tips
ⓕIt is O.K. to draw everyday objects like cups and plates in your journal.

09 위 글의 괄호 ⓐ에서 알맞은 것을 고르시오.

➡ _____

10 위 글의 빈칸 ⓑ에 알맞은 말을 쓰시오.

➡ _____

11 위 글의 밑줄 친 ⓒ를 알맞은 어형으로 고치시오.

➡ _____

12 위 글의 밑줄 친 ⓓ와 같은 뜻이 되도록 다음 문장의 빈칸에 알맞은 말을 쓰시오.

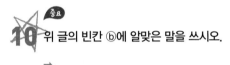

The dining table was filled _____ cookies, cake, bread, and cheese.

13 위 글의 밑줄 친 ⓔ에서 어법상 어색한 것을 고치시오.

_____ ➡ _____

14 위 글의 밑줄 친 ⓕ를 우리말로 옮기시오.

➡ _____
_____

15 What was Lucy's mom doing when she was busy eating? Answer in English.

➡ _____

[16~18] 다음 글을 읽고, 물음에 답하시오.

We went on a field trip _____ⓐ_____ Namhae last month. ⓑIt was just amazing to see so many beautiful islands. We also visited Namhae German Village. We'll never ⓒ(forget, remember) that trip.

16 위 글의 빈칸 ⓐ에 알맞은 말을 쓰시오.

➡ _____

17 위 글의 밑줄 친 ⓑ가 가리키는 내용을 우리말로 쓰시오.

➡ _____

18 위 글의 괄호 ⓒ에서 알맞은 것을 고르시오.

➡ _____

Link - Share

We went on a field trip to Namhae last month. It was just amazing to see so
　　　　~로 현장 학습을 갔다　　　　지난달　　가주어　　　　　　진주어
many beautiful islands. We also visited Namhae German Village. We'll never
　　　　　　　　　　　　　　　　　　　　　　빈도부사는 일반동사 앞에 위치한다.
forget that trip.

구문해설 · amazing: 놀라운　· island: 섬　· village: 마을　· trip: 여행

우리는 지난달에 남해로 현장 학습을 갔다. 그토록 아름다운 많은 섬들을 보는 것은 아주 놀라웠다. 우리는 남해 독일 마을도 방문했다. 우리는 그 여행을 절대 잊지 못할 것이다.

Write

Last winter, I went to Laos with my family. We visited a lot of beautiful
　　　　　　　　　　　　　　~와 함께　　　　　　　　많은(=lots of. many)
temples and went to the night market in Vientiane. Then, we moved to Vang
　　　　　　　　　야시장
Vieng and went river tubing. We also enjoyed their traditional food. It was a
　　　　　　　　　　　　　　　　　　　　　　　　　　　가주어　= much
lot of fun to try new things in a foreign country. I hope I will have a chance to
진주어　　　　　　　　　　　　　　　　to부정사의 형용사적 용법(~할)
visit Laos again.

구문해설 · temple: 사원, 절　· traditional: 전통적인, 전통의　· foreign: 외국의　· country: 나라
· chance: 기회

지난 겨울, 나는 가족과 함께 라오스에 갔다. 우리는 아름다운 절들을 많이 방문했고 Vientiane의 야시장에 갔다. 그리고 나서, 우리는 Vang Vieng으로 옮겨서 강에 튜브를 타러 갔다. 우리는 또한 그들의 전통 음식을 즐겼다. 외국에서 새로운 것을 시도하는 것은 매우 재미있었다. 나는 라오스를 다시 방문할 기회가 있기를 바란다.

Culture Project

September 15, 1835

We finally arrived on this island. There are many animals to study here.
　　　　　　　　　　　　　　　　There are + 복수 명사 ~: ~가 있다　to부정사의 형용사적 용법(~할)
Today, I saw some strange turtles. It was amazing to watch them.
　　　　　　　　　　　　　　　가주어　　　　　진주어　= some strange turtles

구문해설 · finally: 마침내　· arrive: 도착하다　· strange: 이상한　· amazing: 놀라운

1835년 9월 15일
우리는 마침내 이 섬에 도착했다. 여기는 조사할 동물들이 많다. 오늘, 나는 몇몇 이상한 거북들을 보았다. 그들을 보는 것은 놀라웠다.

영역별 핵심문제

Words & Expressions

01 다음 중 짝지어진 단어의 관계가 나머지 넷과 <u>다른</u> 것은?

① final – finally ② slow – slowly
③ kind – kindly ④ friend – friendly
⑤ actual – actually

02 다음 빈칸에 들어갈 말로 적절하지 <u>않은</u> 것은?

> • Did you _____ hear anything like that?
> • Is there _____ room for me?
> • What _____ did he say?
> • Do you really _____ me to believe you?

① else ② ever
③ appear ④ expect
⑤ enough

03 다음 짝지어진 두 단어의 관계가 같도록 빈칸에 알맞은 말을 쓰시오.

> cold : hot = same : _____

04 다음 빈칸에 들어갈 말이 바르게 짝지어진 것은?

> • This is the line to get _____ the theater.
> • Watch _____! There's a car coming!

① in – on ② to – off
③ into – out ④ to – after
⑤ into – for

05 다음 영영풀이에 해당하는 단어는?

> a piece of land that is completely surrounded by water

① ground ② ocean
③ garden ④ earth
⑤ island

06 다음 문장의 밑줄 친 부분과 바꿔 쓸 수 있는 것은?

> <u>At last</u>, the guests began to arrive.

① Usually ② Finally
③ Actually ④ Extremely
⑤ Especially

07 다음 우리말에 맞게 빈칸에 알맞은 말을 쓰시오.

> 그의 나이를 추측해 볼 수 있겠니?
> ➡ Can you _____ his age?

Conversation

08 다음 중 의도하는 바가 나머지 넷과 <u>다른</u> 하나는?

① Have you seen the movie before?
② Have you had my spaghetti before?
③ Has our teacher gone home?
④ Have you ever been to China?
⑤ How many times have you been to the park?

[09~10] 다음 대화의 빈칸에 알맞은 것을 고르시오.

09

> A: _____
>
> B: It's raining.

① Do you like summer?

② Is it sunny today?

③ What's the weather like outside?

④ Do you like the windy weather?

⑤ Can you see the blue sky?

10

> A: Have you ever tried Italian food?
>
> B: _____ It was very tasty.

① Yes, I do.　　② Yes, I have.

③ No, I don't.　　④ No, I haven't.

⑤ Yes, I did.

11 다음 대화의 순서를 바르게 배열하시오.

> (A) No, I haven't. How was it?
>
> (B) Have you ever ridden a horse?
>
> (C) Yes, I have. How about you?
>
> (D) It was fun, but it was a little scary, too.

➡ _____

12 다음 빈칸에 들어갈 말로 적절하지 <u>않은</u> 것은?

> A: How's the weather over there in London?
>
> B: It's rainy. How about Seoul?
>
> A: _____

① It's raining, too.

② It's sunny and warm.

③ It's windy and cloudy.

④ It's a beautiful city.

⑤ It's snowy and cold.

[13~16] 다음 대화를 읽고, 물음에 답하시오.

> B: Mom, ⓐhow's the weather today? Do I need an umbrella? (①)
>
> W: It's quite cloudy outside. (②)
>
> B: Thank you, Mom. (③)
>
> W: Well, ⓑit's not going to rain today. (④)
>
> B: Good! Then, I don't need an umbrella today. (⑤)

13 위 대화의 ①~⑤ 중 다음 주어진 문장이 들어갈 알맞은 곳은?

> I'll check the weather forecast.

①　　②　　③　　④　　⑤

14 위 대화의 밑줄 친 ⓐ와 바꿔 쓸 수 있는 것은?

① what's the weather today?

② what is it today?

③ how is it today?

④ what's the weather like today?

⑤ how's the weather like today?

15 위 대화의 밑줄 친 ⓑ와 같은 뜻이 되도록 다음 문장의 빈칸에 알맞은 말을 쓰시오.

> it _____ rain today

16 Does the boy need an umbrella? Answer in English.

➡ _____

[17~18] 다음 문장의 빈칸에 알맞은 것을 고르시오.

17
> It is very dangerous _____ climb the mountain.

① to ② in
③ of ④ for
⑤ with

18
> Do you have anything _____ tomorrow?

① do ② did
③ doing ④ to do
⑤ to doing

19 다음 빈칸에 공통으로 알맞은 것은?

> • It was stupid _____ you to believe him.
> • It is clever _____ him to solve the problem.

① at ② of
③ for ④ from
⑤ with

20 다음 대화의 빈칸에 알맞은 말을 쓰시오.

> A: I think _____ _____ difficult to find the things I want to buy.
> B: You know, they have information desks.

21 다음 중 어법상 어색한 것은?

① Jane kept her promise to enter a university.
② Kathy wants someone to travel with.
③ Mike wants interesting something to read.
④ Linda doesn't have a pen to write with.
⑤ She was the first woman to land on the moon.

22 다음 중 밑줄 친 부분의 쓰임이 〈보기〉와 다른 것은?

> ┤ 보기 ├
> Jake has a lot of homework to do today.

① I need somebody to talk to.
② Frank must be crazy to quit his job.
③ I don't have time to chat with you.
④ She couldn't find any chairs to sit on.
⑤ Do you know the way to get to City Hall?

23 다음 중 밑줄 친 부분의 쓰임이 나머지 넷과 다른 것은?

① It is necessary for you to study hard.
② It is too cold to go swimming in the lake.
③ It's good to try to solve the problem.
④ It is difficult for us to achieve the goal.
⑤ It is dangerous to walk alone at midnight.

24 다음 문장에서 어법상 <u>어색한</u> 부분을 바르게 고쳐 쓰시오.

> Kirk needs a ball pen to write.

➡ _____ ➡ _____

25 다음 우리말을 영어로 바르게 옮긴 것은?

> 냉장고에는 먹을 음식이 많이 있다.

① There are a lot of food to eat in the refrigerator.
② There are a lot of food eating in the refrigerator.
③ There is a lot of food eating in the refrigerator.
④ There is a lot of foods to eat in the refrigerator.
⑤ There is a lot of food to eat in the refrigerator.

26 다음 단어를 바르게 배열하여 문장을 완성하시오.

> anything / myself / to make / slimmer / look

➡ I will do _____.

27 다음 두 문장이 같은 뜻이 되도록 빈칸에 알맞은 말을 쓰시오.

> To finish this work is very important.
> = _____ is very important _____ finish this work.

Reading

[28~31] 다음 글을 읽고, 물음에 답하시오.

> Last winter, I went to Laos with my family. (①) We visited ⓐ<u>a lot of</u> beautiful temples and went to the night market in Vientiane. (②) Then, we moved to Vang Vieng and went river tubing. (③) We also enjoyed their traditional food. (④) I hope I will have a chance ⓑ<u>visit</u> Laos again. (⑤)   I=Minsu

28 위 글의 ①~⑤ 중 다음 주어진 문장이 들어갈 알맞은 곳은?

> It was a lot of fun to try new things in a foreign country.

①   ②   ③   ④   ⑤

29 위 글의 밑줄 친 ⓐ 대신 쓸 수 있는 것은? (2개)

① many   ② few
③ much   ④ a little
⑤ lots of

30 위 글의 밑줄 친 ⓑ를 알맞은 형태로 고치시오.

➡ _____

31 위 글의 내용으로 보아 알 수 <u>없는</u> 것은?

① Minsu went to Laos last winter.
② Minsu's family visited beautiful temples.
③ Minsu did shopping at the night market in Vientiane.
④ Minsu's family went to Vang Vieng.
⑤ Minsu wishes to visit Laos again.

[32~37] 다음 글을 읽고, 물음에 답하시오.

August 7

Our last stop was Oxford. We first visited Christ Church College. It ___ⓐ___ a world famous place to visit since it appeared in the *Harry Potter* movies. In the movies, Harry and everyone else ⓑ<u>eat</u> dinner at the Hall of Christ Church. We also saw portraits of famous people ___ⓒ___ graduated from the college. When we were outside the building, I walked to the famous olive tree and touched it. "ⓓ<u>Because</u> I touched this tree," I said, "I will get into Oxford University!" Then, my brother said to me with a smile, "I can't wait to see your portrait on the wall."

Lucy's Drawing Tips
Create your own avatar. Your drawing journal will become ⓔ<u>much</u> *more interesting.*

32 위 글의 빈칸 ⓐ에 알맞은 것은?

① becomes
② became
③ is becoming
④ has become
⑤ had become

33 위 글의 밑줄 친 ⓑ 대신 쓸 수 있는 말을 쓰시오.

➡ _____

34 위 글의 빈칸 ⓒ에 알맞은 것은? (2개)

① whom
② who
③ that
④ what
⑤ which

35 위 글의 밑줄 친 ⓓ 대신 쓸 수 있는 것은?

① As
② If
③ When
④ Though
⑤ While

36 위 글의 밑줄 친 ⓔ 대신 쓸 수 없는 것은? (2개)

① far
② very
③ even
④ many
⑤ a lot

37 위 글의 내용으로 보아 대답할 수 없는 질문은?

① What was their last stop?
② Why is Christ Church College famous?
③ Who graduated from Christ Church College?
④ What did Lucy do when she was outside the building?
⑤ What did Lucy's brother say to her?

[38~39] 다음 글을 읽고, 물음에 답하시오.

September 15, 1835

We ⓐ<u>final</u> arrived on this island. There are many animals to study here. Today, I saw some strange turtles. ⓑ<u>It</u> was amazing to watch them.

38 위 글의 밑줄 친 ⓐ를 알맞은 형으로 고치시오.

➡ _____

39 위 글의 밑줄 친 ⓑ가 가리키는 것을 우리말로 쓰시오.

➡ _____

01 출제율 90%

다음 중 짝지어진 단어의 관계가 나머지 넷과 <u>다른</u> 것은?

① warm : cool
② different : same
③ remember : forget
④ huge : large
⑤ indoors : outdoors

02 출제율 95%

다음 두 문장이 같은 뜻이 되도록 빈칸에 알맞은 것은?

> A bus appeared around the corner.
> = A bus showed _____ around the corner.

① in
② up
③ out
④ off
⑤ onto

03 출제율 90%

다음 짝지어진 두 단어의 관계가 같도록 빈칸에 알맞은 말을 쓰시오.

> create : _____ = decide : decision

04 출제율 85%

다음 우리말에 맞게 빈칸에 알맞은 말을 쓰시오.

> 다른 누군가에게 도와 달라고 부탁해 봐.
> ➡ Ask somebody _____ to help you.

05 출제율 95%

다음 중 영영풀이가 <u>잘못된</u> 것은?

① earth: the planet on which we live
② invite: to ask someone to come to something such as a party
③ relax: to feel more calm and less worried or tense
④ travel: to go from one place to another, often to a place that is far away
⑤ carry: to put clothes and other things into a bag, because you are leaving a place

06 출제율 100%

다음 빈칸에 알맞은 것을 <u>모두</u> 고르시오.

> A: _____
> B: It's snowing.
> A: Really? I should wear my snow boots. Thanks.

① How's the weather today?
② What weather do you like today?
③ What's the snowy weather today?
④ What's the weather like today?
⑤ What does the cloud look like?

07 출제율 95%

다음 대화의 빈칸에 알맞은 것은?

> A: _____
> B: No, I haven't, but I've heard of it many times.

① How often have you been to Namsan?
② Did you go to Namsan?
③ When did you go to Namsan?
④ Have you ever been to Namsan?
⑤ How many times did you visit Namsan?

Suho: Anna, have you ⓐbe to Australia before?

Anna: Yes, I have. Actually, I lived in Sydney for a year.

Suho: Great! How's the weather there in April? I'm going to visit Sydney on vacation next week.

Anna: April is a great time to visit Sydney. In April, it's autumn in Australia.

Suho: Good. ⓑI'm planning to spend some time on the beach and relax in the sun.

Anna: Well, it often rains in April, but you may have some sunny days.

Suho: I'll take my hat and pack an umbrella, too.

Anna: That's a good idea. Have a great time.

출제율 100%

08 위 대화의 밑줄 친 ⓐ를 알맞은 어형으로 고치시오.

➡ _____

출제율 90%

09 위 대화의 밑줄 친 ⓑ를 우리말로 옮기시오.

➡ _____

_____

출제율 95%

10 위 대화의 내용과 일치하지 않는 것은?

① Anna는 호주를 방문한 적이 있다.

② Anna는 시드니에서 1년간 산 적이 있다.

③ 수호는 다음 주에 시드니를 방문할 예정이다.

④ 4월에 호주의 날씨는 가을이다.

⑤ 4월의 시드니 날씨는 대체로 화창하다.

출제율 90%

11 다음 문장에서 어법상 어색한 부분을 바르게 고쳐 쓰시오.

Mary needs some paper to write.

_____ ➡ _____

출제율 95%

12 다음 빈칸에 알맞은 말이 바르게 짝지어진 것은?

- It was wise _____ you to agree to the proposal.
- It is impossible _____ us to win the game.

① of – of
② of – for
③ for – for
④ for – of
⑤ for – with

출제율 100%

13 다음 빈칸에 들어갈 동사의 형태로 적절한 것은?

It's necessary for you _____ the piano every day.

① practice
② practiced
③ practicing
④ to practice
⑤ to practicing

출제율 95%

14 다음 두 문장이 같은 뜻이 되도록 빈칸에 알맞은 말을 쓰시오.

To solve this puzzle is very difficult.

➡ _____ is very difficult _____ solve this puzzle.

15 다음 중 〈보기〉의 밑줄 친 It과 쓰임이 같은 것은? (출제율 95%)

> ┤ 보기 ├
> It is very important to check the weather forecast every day.

① It is freezing here.
② It is not my lost puppy.
③ It was built by them.
④ It rained a lot yesterday morning.
⑤ It is fun to play soccer with my friends.

16 다음 중 어법상 어색한 문장은? (출제율 90%)

① I need a chair to sit.
② Columbus was the first man to discover the American Continent.
③ We have no house to live in.
④ He has a wish to become a pilot.
⑤ She forgot to bring something to write with.

17 다음 우리말을 영어로 바르게 옮긴 것은? (출제율 85%)

> 로마에는 방문할 장소가 많이 있다.

① There is many places visit in Rome.
② There are visiting many places in Rome.
③ There are many places visiting in Rome.
④ There are to visit many places in Rome.
⑤ There are many places to visit in Rome.

18 다음 중 밑줄 친 부분의 쓰임이 나머지 넷과 다른 하나는? (출제율 95%)

① He drove very quickly to get there on time.
② Katherine is coming to Seoul to visit us.
③ I'm going to the park to walk my dogs.
④ There's nothing to be afraid of any more.
⑤ I went to the post office to send the parcel.

[19~20] 다음 글을 읽고, 물음에 답하시오.

> Hi, I am Lucy Hunter, and I live in London. Last week, my family went on a vacation ⓐ_____ three days. During our trip, I made simple drawings in my journal. That was a great way ⓑto capture all the special moments.

19 위 글의 빈칸 ⓐ에 알맞은 것은? (출제율 100%)

① in   ② for
③ to   ④ at
⑤ during

20 위 글의 밑줄 친 ⓑ와 같은 용법으로 쓰인 것은? (출제율 90%)

① We wished to reach the North Pole.
② He made a promise to come again.
③ He was excited to see the scenery.
④ The boy grew up to be a poet.
⑤ We decided to go fishing in the river.

[21~26] 다음 글을 읽고, 물음에 답하시오.

August 5

ⓐAt last, we set foot at Stonehenge, one of the most mysterious places on Earth. After a two-hour drive from our home in London, we finally ⓑgot to Stonehenge. It was just amazing to see the ring of huge stones. ⓒ<u>How did those huge stones get there thousand of years ago?</u> What were they for? I guess Stonehenge will ___ⓓ___ a mystery for a long time.

Lucy's Drawing Tips
Don't try ⓔ*(making, to make) a perfect drawing. A few colors will be enough.*

출제율 95%

21 위 글의 밑줄 친 ⓐ 대신 쓸 수 있는 것은?

① In fact   ② In contrast
③ As a fact   ④ As a result
⑤ In the long run

출제율 100%

22 위 글의 밑줄 친 ⓑ 대신 쓸 수 있는 것은?

① arrived   ② reached
③ received   ④ appeared
⑤ happened

출제율 85%

23 위 글의 밑줄 친 ⓒ에서 어법상 어색한 것을 고치시오.

_____ ➡ _____

출제율 90%

24 위 글의 빈칸 ⓓ에 알맞은 것은?

① seem   ② look
③ remain   ④ appear
⑤ belong

출제율 95%

25 위 글의 괄호 ⓔ에서 알맞은 것을 고르시오

➡ _____

출제율 85%

26 위 글의 내용으로 보아 알 수 <u>없는</u> 것은? (2개)

① 스톤헨지는 세계에서 가장 신비한 곳들 중의 하나다.
② 런던의 집에서 스톤헨지까지 가는 데는 자동차로 두 시간 걸렸다.
③ 스톤헨지에서 거대한 돌들의 고리를 보았다.
④ Lucy는 그 거대한 돌들의 용도를 알았다.
⑤ 머지않아 스톤헨지의 미스터리가 풀릴 것이다.

[27~29] 다음 글을 읽고, 물음에 답하시오.

We went on a field trip to Namhae last month. ⓐ<u>It was just amazing to see so many beautiful islands.</u> We also visited Namhae German Village. We'll never forget that trip.

출제율 95%

27 위 글의 밑줄 친 ⓐ를 우리말로 옮기시오.

➡ _____

출제율 90%

28 When did they go to Namhae? Answer in English.

➡ _____

[01~03] 다음 대화를 읽고, 물음에 답하시오.

> W: ⓐHave you gone to any special places in Korea?
> M: Yes, I have. I went to Ulleungdo last summer with my family.
> W: ⓑHow was the weather there?
> M: It was mostly sunny, ___ⓒ___ the weather changed often.

01 위 대화의 밑줄 친 ⓐ에서 어법상 어색한 것을 고치시오.

_____ ➡ _____

02 위 대화의 밑줄 친 ⓑ와 같은 뜻이 되도록 다음 문장의 빈칸에 알맞은 말을 쓰시오.

| _____ was the weather _____ there? |

03 위 대화의 빈칸 ⓒ에 알맞은 접속사를 쓰시오.

➡ _____

04 다음 대화의 순서를 바르게 배열하시오.

> (A) Mom, how's the weather today?
> (B) Thanks, Mom.
> (C) It's quite cloudy outside. I'll check the weather forecast.
> (D) Well, it's going to rain in the afternoon.

➡ _____

05 다음 우리말의 의미에 맞도록 주어진 어구를 이용하여 영작하시오.

(1) 매일 일기를 쓰는 것은 쉽지 않다.
  (it, easy, keep, every)
  ➡ _____

(2) 나는 내 남동생이 찍는 사진들을 좋아한다.
  (photographs, which, takes)
  ➡ _____
  _____

06 다음 〈조건〉에 맞게 괄호 안의 단어를 이용하여 우리말을 영어로 옮기시오.

> ┤ 조건 ├
> 1. 주어진 단어를 모두 이용할 것.
> 2. 필요시 관사를 붙이거나 단어를 추가할 것.
> 3. It으로 시작할 것.
> 4. 대·소문자 및 구두점에 유의할 것.

(1) 내가 자동차를 주차하기는 어렵다.
  (difficult, me, park, car)
  ➡ _____

(2) 헬멧을 쓰고 자전거를 타는 것이 안전하다.
  (safe, ride, bike, with, helmet)
  ➡ _____

(3) 다른 나라에서 사는 것은 흥미진진한 경험이다.
  (exciting, experience, live, another, country)
  ➡ _____
  _____

07 다음 하루 일과표를 보고 빈칸에 알맞은 내용을 완성하시오.

8:00 a.m.	school
12:10 p.m.	lunch
5:00 p.m.	playground
6:30 p.m.	homework

(1) It's 8 a.m. It's time _____ .

(2) It's 12:10 p.m. It's time _____ .

(3) It's 5 p.m. It's time _____ .

(4) It's 6:30 p.m. It's time _____ .

[08~12] 다음 글을 읽고, 물음에 답하시오.

August 6

In the morning, we walked around the Cotswolds. ⓐIt started to rain in the afternoon, so we decided to stay indoors at our B&B. A B&B is a popular place to stay in England. ⓑIt feels more like a home than a hotel. The owner invited us for afternoon tea today. The dining table was full _____ⓒ_____ cookies, cake, bread, and cheese. While I was busy eating, Mom was admiring the beautiful cups and plates. I ate too much, so I couldn't eat ⓓ(something, anything) for dinner.

08 위 글의 밑줄 친 ⓐ와 같은 뜻이 되도록 빈칸에 알맞은 말을 쓰시오.

> We decided to stay indoors at our B&B _____ it started to rain in the afternoon.

09 위 글의 밑줄 친 ⓑ가 가리키는 것을 영어로 쓰시오.

➡ _____

10 위 글의 빈칸 ⓒ에 알맞은 전치사를 쓰시오.

➡ _____

11 위 글의 괄호 ⓓ에서 알맞은 것을 고르시오.

➡ _____

12 What did they do in the morning? Answer in English.

➡ _____

[13~15] 다음 글을 읽고, 물음에 답하시오.

Last winter, I went to Laos with my family. We visited ⓐa lot of beautiful temples and went to the night market in Vientiane. Then, we moved to Vang Vieng and went river tubing. We also enjoyed their traditional food. It was a lot of fun to try new things in a foreign country. ⓑI hope I will have a chance to visit Laos again.

13 위 글의 밑줄 친 ⓐ를 한 단어로 바꿔 쓰시오.

➡ _____

14 위 글의 밑줄 친 ⓑ를 우리말로 옮기시오.

➡ _____

15 Who did the writer go to Laos with? Answer in English.

➡ _____

01 다음 주어진 상황에 맞게 〈to부정사〉와 괄호 안의 단어를 이용하여 〈보기〉처럼 문장을 완성하시오.

> ═ 보기 ═
>
> I'm hungry. I need some food to eat. (eat)

(1) I'm very thirsty. _____ (drink)

(2) There's no chair here. _____ (sit)

(3) Tony feels lonely. _____ (talk)

02 다음 어구들을 연결하여 〈보기〉와 같이 한 문장으로 쓰시오.

• impossible	• him	• to visit	• his hometown
• kind	• foreigners	• to watch	• Korean
• difficult	• us	• to agree	• the work on time
• stupid	• her	• to finish	• the poor
• possible	• you	• to help	• to the proposal
• necessary	• me	• to learn	• the game

> ═ 보기 ═
>
> It is impossible for him to visit his hometown.

(1) _____

(2) _____

(3) _____

(4) _____

(5) _____

03 다음 Jessica의 이번 주 일정표를 보고, 내용에 맞도록 문장을 완성하시오.

Mon.	Tue.	Wed.	Thu.	Fri.
movie / watch	a piano lesson / take	a baseball game / watch	a piano lesson / take	four comic books / read

(1) Jessica has _____ _____ _____ _____ this Monday.

(2) Jessica has _____ _____ _____ _____ _____ on TV this Wednesday.

(3) Jessica has _____ _____ _____ _____ _____ on Tuesday and Thurday.

(4) Jessica has _____ _____ _____ _____ _____ on Friday.

단원별 모의고사

01 다음 영영풀이에 해당하는 단어로 알맞은 것은?

> to cause something to happen or exist

① make ② repair ③ fix
④ create ⑤ prepare

02 다음 중 우리말 뜻이 <u>잘못된</u> 것은?

① at last: 마침내
② a little: 좀, 약간; 약간의
③ right now: 잠시
④ a lot of: 많은
⑤ set foot at: ~에 발을 디디다

03 다음 빈칸에 공통으로 알맞은 것은?

> • The bathtub was full _____ hot water.
> • Tom is fond _____ Kathy.

① at ② to ③ for
④ of ⑤ with

04 다음 짝지어진 두 단어의 관계가 같도록 빈칸에 알맞은 말을 쓰시오.

> arrive : arrival = decide : _____

05 다음 빈칸에 공통으로 들어갈 말을 쓰시오.

> • Mary didn't show _____ for the meeting yesterday.
> • I'm planning to clean _____ the park with my dad.

[06~08] 다음 대화의 빈칸에 알맞은 것을 고르시오.

06
> A: Have you ever caught a big fish?
> B: _____ I wish to catch it someday.

① Yes, I have.
② No, I haven't.
③ I caught a big fish.
④ Yes, my uncle caught a big fish.
⑤ I caught it and put it back.

07
> A: _____
> B: No, I haven't.

① Do you have a sister?
② Does he live with his grandparents?
③ Have you ever seen a bear?
④ Which country have you travelled?
⑤ Are you happy with the new class?

08
> A: What's the weather like there?
> B: _____

① I like hot summer.
② I got a bad cold.
③ I enjoy skiing here.
④ I should wear a coat.
⑤ It's cold and sometimes it snows a lot.

[09~10] 다음 대화를 읽고, 물음에 답하시오.

G: Bill, have you ever gone bungee jumping?
B: No, I haven't. ___ⓐ___ about you, Katie?
G: When I visited New Zealand, I tried bungee jumping once.
B: Wasn't it scary?
G: No, I liked it. I want to do it again.

09 위 대화의 빈칸 ⓐ에 알맞은 것은? (2개)

① How   ② Who
③ What   ④ Why
⑤ Which

10 위 대화의 내용으로 보아 알 수 <u>없는</u> 것은?

① Bill은 번지 점프를 해 본 적이 없다.
② Katie는 뉴질랜드를 방문한 적이 있다.
③ Katie는 번지 점프를 해 본 적이 있다.
④ Bill은 두려워서 번지 점프를 시도해 보지 않았다.
⑤ Katie는 다시 번지 점프를 하기를 원한다.

[11~13] 다음 문장의 빈칸에 알맞은 것을 고르시오.

11

My brother has many things _____ tonight.

① do   ② does
③ doing   ④ to do
⑤ to be doing

12

Kate is looking for a friend to travel _____.

① at   ② in   ③ with
④ on   ⑤ for

13

Alice and Ken are going to enter Berkeley. They need a dormitory _____.

① live   ② to live
③ to live in   ④ to live with
⑤ to living

14 다음 빈칸에 주어진 단어의 알맞은 형태를 쓰시오.

Is it possible _____ the project by tomorrow? (finish)

15 다음 밑줄 친 부분의 쓰임이 〈보기〉와 같은 것은?

┌─── 보기 ───┐
I have nothing special to eat in my bag.

① She packed her bag <u>to go</u> home.
② I was happy <u>to find</u> my cell phone.
③ The man needs someone <u>to look</u> after his cat.
④ <u>To eat</u> breakfast is good for your brain.
⑤ We went to the school store <u>to buy</u> some snacks.

[16~17] 다음 중 어법상 알맞지 <u>않은</u> 문장을 고르시오.

16 ① The man needs a piece of paper to write on.
② Amy has no house to live in.
③ There's nothing to worry about.
④ Give me a pen to write with.
⑤ You seem to have important something to tell me.

17 ① It's hard to climb the tree.
② It's great fun skate on ice.
③ It's fun to watch a baseball game.
④ It's important for us to study English.
⑤ It's interesting to take a trip to strange lands.

18 다음 괄호 안의 단어 형태가 바르게 짝지어진 것은?

> • I have something (tell) you.
> • Do you have anything (read)?

① tell – read
② tell – to read
③ to tell – read
④ telling – read
⑤ to tell – to read

19 다음 밑줄 친 ⓐ, ⓑ를 어법상 올바른 형태로 쓰시오.

> I think shopping on the Internet is good.
> It's easy ⓐfind the things I want to buy.
> It's also easy ⓑfind good prices.

ⓐ ＿＿＿＿＿＿＿＿ ⓑ ＿＿＿＿＿＿＿＿

[20~23] 다음 글을 읽고, 물음에 답하시오.

> Our ①last stop was Oxford. We ②first visited Christ Church College. It has become a world famous place to visit ＿ⓐ＿ it appeared in the *Harry Potter* movies. In the movies, Harry and everyone ③other eat dinner ④at the Hall of Christ Church. We ⑤also saw portraits of famous people ＿ⓑ＿ graduated from the college.

20 위 글의 밑줄 친 ①~⑤ 중 어법상 어색한 것은?

① ② ③ ④ ⑤

21 위 글의 빈칸 ⓐ에 알맞은 것은?

① for ② when
③ during ④ since
⑤ while

22 위 글의 빈칸 ⓑ에 알맞은 것은?

① who ② that
③ what ④ whom
⑤ which

23 위 글의 내용으로 보아 알 수 <u>없는</u> 것은?

① 우리가 마지막으로 들른 곳은 옥스퍼드였다.
② 우리는 Christ Church College를 방문했다.
③ Christ Church College는 Harry Potter 영화에 나왔다.
④ Harry Potter는 Christ Church College의 학생이다.
⑤ 우리는 Christ Church College를 졸업한 유명한 사람들의 초상화를 보았다.

[24~27] 다음 글을 읽고, 물음에 답하시오.

_____ⓐ_____ we were outside the building, I walked to the famous olive tree and touched it. "_____ⓑ_____ I touched this tree," I said, "I will get into Oxford University!" Then, my brother said to me with a smile, "I can't wait to see your _____ⓒ_____ on the wall."

Lucy's Drawing Tips
Create your own avatar. Your drawing journal will become _____ⓓ_____ more interesting.

24 위 글의 빈칸 ⓐ와 ⓑ에 알맞은 말이 바르게 짝지어진 것은?

① If – Because
② As – Though
③ When – Because
④ Since – Because
⑤ When – While

25 위 글의 빈칸 ⓒ에 다음 정의에 해당하는 단어를 쓰시오.

a painting, drawing, or photograph of a particular person

➡ _____

26 위 글의 빈칸 ⓓ에 알맞지 <u>않은</u> 것은?

① very
② far
③ even
④ much
⑤ a lot

27 Why is the olive tree famous? Answer in Korean.

➡ _____

[28~30] 다음 글을 읽고, 물음에 답하시오.

Last winter, I went to Laos with my family. (①) We visited <u>a lot of</u> beautiful temples and went to the night market in Vientiane. (②) We also enjoyed their traditional food. (③) It was a lot of fun to try new things in a foreign country. (④) I hope I will have a chance to visit Laos again. (⑤)

I=Minsu

28 위 글의 ①~⑤ 중 다음 주어진 문장이 들어갈 알맞은 곳은?

Then, we moved to Vang Vieng and went river tubing.

①　　　　②　　　　③　　　　④　　　　⑤

29 위 글의 밑줄 친 부분을 한 단어로 쓰시오.

➡ _____

30 위 글의 내용으로 보아 대답할 수 <u>없는</u> 질문은?

① Where did Minsu go last winter?
② Where did Minsu go in Vientiane?
③ Was it a lot of fun to try new things in a foreign country?
④ What was their traditional food?
⑤ Does Minsu wish to visit Laos again?

Lesson 4

Giving a Hand

🎤 의사소통 기능

- 도움 요청하기
  Can you do me a favor?
- 감사하기
  Thank you for sharing your umbrella with me.

🎤 언어 형식

- 목적격 관계대명사
  He was the person **who[whom]** Kenneth respected the most in the world.
- so ~ that ... 구문
  He was **so** happy **that** he jumped for joy.

교과서
Words & Expressions

Key Words

- **activity** [æktívəti] 몡 활동
- **actually** [ǽktʃuəli] 閉 실제로, 정말로
- **always** [ɔ́ːlweiz] 閉 항상, 언제나
- **bath** [bæθ] 몡 목욕, 욕조
- **believe** [bilíːv] 동 믿다, 생각하다
- **board** [bɔːrd] 몡 판자, 널
- **build** [bild] 동 (건물을) 짓다, 건설[건축]하다
- **childhood** [tʃáildhùd] 몡 어린 시절
- **clean** [kliːn] 혱 깨끗한 동 닦다, 청소하다
- **close** [klouz] 혱 가까운, 친한
- **comfortable** [kʌ́mfərtəbl] 혱 편한, 편안한
- **condition** [kəndíʃən] 몡 상태
- **create** [kriéit] 동 창조[창작]하다, 만들어 내다
- **daughter** [dɔ́ːtər] 몡 딸, 여식
- **disease** [dizíːz] 몡 질병, 병
- **driver** [dráivər] 몡 운전자, 운전기사
- **error** [érər] 몡 실수, 오류
- **favor** [féivər] 몡 호의, 친절
- **fix** [fiks] 동 고정시키다, 수리하다
- **generation** [dʒènəréiʃən] 몡 세대, 대
- **gift** [gift] 몡 선물, 재능
- **happiness** [hǽpinis] 몡 행복, 만족, 기쁨
- **heavy** [hévi] 혱 무거운 (↔ light)
- **heel** [hiːl] 몡 발뒤꿈치, 뒤꿈치
- **homeless** [hóumlis] 혱 노숙자의
- **invention** [invénʃən] 몡 발명, 발명품
- **inventor** [invéntər] 몡 발명가, 창안자
- **joy** [dʒɔi] 몡 기쁨, 환희
- **just** [dʒʌst] 閉 그저, 단지, 방금
- **local** [lóukəl] 혱 (특정) 지역의, 현지의

- **lucky** [lʌ́ki] 혱 운이 좋은, 행운의
- **material** [mətíəriəl] 몡 (물건의) 재료
- **nothing** [nʌ́θiŋ] 때 아무것도[단 하나도] (~ 아니다)
- **perfect** [pə́ːrfikt] 혱 완전한, 완벽한
- **person** [pə́ːrsn] 몡 사람, 개인
- **plant** [plænt] 몡 식물, 초목
- **pleasure** [pléʒər] 몡 기쁨, 즐거움
- **pressure** [préʃər] 몡 압력, 압박
- **project** [prɑ́dʒekt] 몡 프로젝트, 과제
- **proud** [praud] 혱 자랑스러워하는, 자랑스러운
- **purpose** [pə́ːrpəs] 몡 목적
- **respect** [rispékt] 동 존경하다 몡 존경
- **safety** [séifti] 몡 안전, 안전성
- **sensor** [sénsər] 몡 센서, 감지기
- **share** [ʃɛər] 동 함께 쓰다, 공유하다
- **shock** [ʃɑk] 몡 충격 동 쇼크[충격]를 주다
- **shopping** [ʃɑ́piŋ] 몡 쇼핑
- **signal** [sígnəl] 몡 신호
- **still** [stil] 閉 아직(도), 여전히
- **succeed** [səksíːd] 동 성공하다 (↔ fail)
- **support** [səpɔ́ːrt] 동 지지하다, 지원하다
- **trial** [tráiəl] 몡 시험, 실험
- **truly** [trúːli] 閉 정말로, 진심으로
- **trusty** [trʌ́sti] 혱 신뢰할 수 있는
- **understand** [ʌ̀ndərstǽnd] 동 이해하다, 알아듣다
- **until** [əntíl] 접 ~할 때까지 전 ~까지
- **volunteer** [vὰləntíər] 몡 자원 봉사자
- **wander** [wɑ́ndər] 동 거닐다, 돌아다니다, 헤매다
- **worry** [wə́ːri] 동 걱정하다, 걱정[불안]하게 만들다
- **worse** [wəːrs] 혱 더 나쁜, 더 심한 閉 더 심하게

Key Expressions

- **at first** 처음에는
- **be thankful for** ~에 대해 감사히 여기다
- **cheer up** 힘을 불러일으키다, ~을 격려하다
- **come over to** ~에 오다
- **come up with** (해답 등을) 찾아내다[내놓다]
- **feel like -ing** ~하고 싶다
- **for[with] joy** 기뻐서

- **give up** 포기하다
- **grow up** 성장하다, 자라다
- **keep an eye on** ~을 계속 지켜보다
- **look for** ~을 찾다
- **take care of** ~을 돌보다, 뒷바라지하다
- **thank A for B** A에게 B에 대해 감사하다
- **wander off** 여기저기 쏘다니다

162 Lesson 4. Giving a Hand

Word Power

※ 별개의 단어를 쓰는 남성명사와 여성명사

□ **son**(아들) – **daughter**(딸)

□ **king**(왕) – **queen**(여왕)

□ **husband**(남편) – **wife**(아내)

□ **nephew**(조카) – **niece**(조카딸)

□ **boy**(소년) – **girl**(소녀)

□ **uncle**(삼촌) – **aunt**(숙모)

□ **bull**(황소) – **cow**(암소)

□ **dad**(아빠) – **mom**(엄마)

□ **rooster**(수탉) – **hen**(암탉)

English Dictionary

□ **always** 항상, 언제나
→ at all times 항상

□ **believe** 믿다
→ to accept or regard something as true
원가를 사실로 받아들이거나 간주하다

□ **build** (건물을) 짓다, 건설[건축]하다
→ to make something by joining things together
사물들을 함께 결합해서 어떤 것을 만들다

□ **childhood** 어린 시절
→ the period of a person's life when they are a child
어떤 사람이 아이이던 시절

□ **comfortable** 편한, 편안한
→ making you feel physically relaxed when you use something
당신이 무언가를 사용할 때 신체적으로 편안함을 느끼게 만드는

□ **create** 창조하다, 만들어 내다
→ cause something to happen or exist
어떤 것이 발생하거나 존재하게 하다

□ **driver** 운전자, 운전기사
→ the person who is driving a vehicle
차를 운전하는 사람

□ **gift** 선물
→ something that you give someone as a present
당신이 누군가에게 선물로 주는 것

□ **heavy** 무거운
→ weighing a lot
무게가 많이 나가는

□ **heel** 발뒤꿈치, 뒤꿈치
→ the back part of your foot, just below your ankle
발목 바로 아래에 있는 발의 뒷부분

□ **inventor** 발명가
→ a person who has invented something, or whose job is to invent things
무언가를 발명했거나, 무언가를 발명하는 것이 직업인 사람

□ **joy** 기쁨, 환희
→ a feeling of great happiness 대단한 행복감

□ **perfect** 완전한, 완벽한
→ as good as something could possibly be
어떤 것이 가능할 수 있을 만큼 좋은

□ **plant** 식물, 초목
→ a living thing that grows in the earth and has a stem, leaves, and roots, especially one that is smaller than a tree or bush
땅에서 자라고 줄기, 잎, 뿌리를 가진 생물, 특히 나무나 덤불보다 작은 생물

□ **pressure** 압력, 압박
→ force that you produce when you press hard on something
어떤 것을 세게 누를 때 당신이 만들어 내는 힘

□ **project** 프로젝트, 과제
→ a task or problem in school that requires careful work over a long period of time
학교에서 장기간에 걸쳐 주의 깊은 연구가 필요한 임무 또는 문제

□ **safety** 안전
→ the state of being safe from harm or danger
해로움 또는 위험으로부터 안전한 상태

□ **support** 지지하다, 후원하다
→ to agree with someone, and perhaps help them because you want them to succeed
다른 사람의 의견에 동의하고, 어쩌면 그들이 성공하기를 원하기 때문에 그들을 돕다

□ **worry** 걱정하다
→ to keep thinking about problems that you have or about unpleasant things that might happen
당신이 가지고 있는 문제나 일어날지도 모르는 불쾌한 것들에 대해 계속 생각하다

01 다음 중 나머지 넷을 대표할 수 있는 단어는?

① corn
② plant
③ carrot
④ rose
⑤ flower

02 다음 빈칸에 알맞은 말이 바르게 짝지어진 것은?

> • _____ first she didn't seem to notice me.
> • We should be thankful _____ our parents.

① To – with
② For – at
③ At – to
④ At – for
⑤ For – with

03 다음 영영풀이에 해당하는 단어로 알맞은 것은?

> to walk around a place in a casual way, often without intending to go in any particular direction

① jump
② move
③ wander
④ travel
⑤ wonder

04 다음 짝지어진 두 단어의 관계가 같도록 빈칸에 알맞은 말을 쓰시오.

> low : high = light : _____

05 다음 우리말에 맞게 빈칸에 알맞은 것은?

> 그들은 일자리를 찾고 있다.
> ➡ They are looking _____ work.

① at
② for
③ down
④ to
⑤ with

서답형
06 다음 영영풀이에 해당하는 단어를 쓰시오.

> to cause something to happen or exist

➡ _____

서답형
07 다음 우리말에 맞게 빈칸에 알맞은 말을 쓰시오.

> 비가 그칠 때까지 기다리자.
> ➡ Let's wait _____ the rain stops.

08 다음 빈칸에 공통으로 알맞은 것은?

> • She grew _____ in Boston.
> • She doesn't give _____ easily.

① in
② of
③ up
④ about
⑤ at

01 다음 짝지어진 두 단어의 관계가 같도록 빈칸에 알맞은 말을 쓰시오.

(1) boy : girl = son : _____
(2) safe : safety = active : _____

02 다음 우리말에 맞게 빈칸에 알맞은 말을 쓰시오.

(1) 기뻐서 내 가슴이 터질 지경이야.
  ➡ My heart will burst _____ _____.
(2) 여름에 영국에 오지 그러니?
  ➡ Why don't you _____ _____ _____ England in the summer?
(3) 나는 Mary에게 편지를 써서 그 선물에 대해 감사의 뜻을 전해야 한다.
  ➡ I must write and _____ Mary _____ the present.

03 다음 빈칸에 들어갈 알맞은 말을 〈보기〉에서 골라 쓰시오.

┌─ 보기 ─────────────────────┐
  build   someone   share
      still   understand
└─────────────────────────────┘

(1) Do you _____ live at the same address?
(2) He wanted to _____ his own house.
(3) Can you _____ French?
(4) There's _____ at the door.
(5) Sue will _____ a house with three other students.

04 다음 괄호 안의 단어를 문맥에 맞게 고쳐 쓰시오.

(1) These new shoes are not very _____. (comfort)
(2) You are the reason for my _____. (happy)
(3) He used magic to _____ a thunderstorm. (creator)

05 다음 빈칸에 알맞은 말을 〈보기〉에서 골라 쓰시오. 필요하면 대문자로 쓰시오.

┌─ 보기 ─────────────────────┐
  cheer up   at first
  keep an eye on   come up with
└─────────────────────────────┘

(1) _____, I was very interested in acting.
(2) _____! You'll do better next time.
(3) I'll try to _____ some ideas to solve the problem.
(4) _____ my suitcase while I buy a ticket.

06 다음 영영풀이에 해당하는 단어를 주어진 철자로 시작하여 쓰시오.

(1) g_____ : something that you give someone as a present
(2) d_____ : the person who is driving a vehicle

Conversation
교과서

A Can you do me a favor? 부탁 좀 해도 될까?
B Of course. / Sorry, I can't. 물론이지. / 미안하지만, 그럴 수 없어.

도움을 요청하는 다양한 표현들

• Can you do me a favor? / Could you please help me? / Can you give me a hand? /
May I ask you a favor? / Can you help me? / Help me, please. / Can I ask you to do something?

• Can you help me move my bag? 내 가방을 옮기는 것을 도와줄 수 있니?

• Could you open the door? 문을 좀 열어 주시겠어요?

• Would you bring me a cup of water? 물 한 잔 가져다주시겠어요?

도움 요청을 부탁받았을 때 대답하기

승낙: Sure. / Okay. / No problem. / Of course, I can. / Why not?

거절: I'm sorry, I can't. / Sorry, but I'm busy. / I'm afraid I can't.

• A: Can you do me a favor? 부탁 하나 해도 되니?
  B: Sure. Go ahead. 물론이지. 어서 말해.
  A: I have a headache. Please buy some medicine for me. 머리가 아파. 약 좀 사 줘

• A: Can you do me a favor? 부탁 좀 해도 될까?
  B: Sure. What is it? 물론이지. 뭔데?

• A: Can you help me wash the dog right now? 지금 개를 씻기는 것을 도와줄래?
  B: I'm afraid I can't. I'm busy now. 유감스럽지만, 안 될 것 같아. 난 지금 바쁘거든.

핵심 Check

1. 다음 우리말과 일치하도록 빈칸에 알맞은 말을 쓰시오.

(1) A: Can you _____ me a _____? (부탁 좀 해도 될까?)

    B: Sure. _____ is it? (물론이야. 뭔데?)

(2) A: Can you _____ _____ make lunch right now?

    (지금 내가 점심 만들고 있는 것 좀 도와줄 수 있어?)

    B: Of _____. (물론이지.)

(3) A: Can you _____ _____ _____ my key? (내 열쇠 찾는 것을 도와줄 수 있니?)

    B: Sorry, I _____. I have to go out now. (미안하지만 안 돼. 나는 지금 나가야 돼.)

② 감사하기

> **A** Thank you for inviting me tonight. 오늘 밤 저를 초대해 주셔서 감사합니다.
> **B** My pleasure. 별말씀을요.

■ 상대방에게 감사를 표현할 때에는 'Thank you for+명사/동명사'의 형태로 나타내며, '~해 주셔서 감사하다'의 의미로 사용된다. for 뒤에는 무엇에 대해 감사한지를 명시해 주면 되며, 동명사나 명사가 온다는 것에 유의한다. 감사 표현에 대한 응답으로는 You're welcome. / No problem. / Not at all. / My pleasure. / Don't mention it. 등을 사용한다.

- A: Thank you for painting the wall. 벽을 페인트칠해 줘서 고맙습니다.
  B: No problem. 별말씀을요.
  A: You're very kind. 매우 친절하시군요.

감사를 나타내는 다른 표현

- Thanks a million. 대단히 감사합니다.
- I cannot thank you enough. 어떻게 감사 인사를 드려야 할지 모르겠네요.
- I really appreciate it. 정말 감사합니다.
- I'm very grateful. 정말 고맙습니다.

핵심 Check

2. 다음 우리말과 일치하도록 빈칸에 알맞은 말을 쓰시오.

(1) **A:** _____ you for taking care of the children. (아이들을 돌봐 줘서 고맙습니다.)

　　B: My _____. (별말씀을요.)

(2) **A:** Please call me if you need any help. (도움이 필요하면 전화해요.)

　　B: I'm very _____. (정말 고맙습니다.)

　　A: Not _____ _____. (천만에요.)

(3) **A:** I can ride you to that restaurant. (그 식당까지 태워 드릴게요.)

　　B: I really _____ your kindness. (친절을 베풀어 주셔서 감사합니다.)

　　A: No _____. (천만에요.)

Listen & Speak 1 A-1

G: ❶Mark, can you do me a favor?

B: Sure. What is it?

G: ❷My family is going on vacation for a week. ❸Can you come to our house and water the plants?

B: Yes, I can.

G: Mark, 부탁 하나 들어줄래?
B: 물론이지. 부탁할게 무엇이지?
G: 우리 가족은 일주일 동안 휴가를 갈 거야. 우리 집에 와서 식물들에게 물을 줄 수 있니?
B: 응, 할 수 있어.

❶ do me a favor: 나의 부탁을 들어주다
❷ go on vacation: 휴가를 가다
❸ water the plants: 식물들에게 물을 주다

Check(√) True or False

(1) The girl's family will go on vacation for a week.   T ☐ F ☐

(2) The boy can't water the plants.   T ☐ F ☐

Listen & Speak 1 A-2

G: Kevin, can you do me a favor?

B: O.K. What is it?

G: ❶Can you help me with my science project this afternoon?

B: ❷Sorry, but I can't. I have to visit my grandma with my mom.

G: Kevin, 부탁 하나 들어줄래?
B: 좋아. 뭔데?
G: 오늘 오후에 내 과학 프로젝트 좀 도와줄래?
B: 미안하지만 안 돼. 엄마랑 할머니 댁에 가야 해.

❶ help me with ~: 내가 ~하는 것을 돕다
❷ Sorry, but I can't.: 거절할 때 쓰는 표현

Check(√) True or False

(3) The girl wants to do her science project by herself.   T ☐ F ☐

(4) The boy must visit his grandma.   T ☐ F ☐

Listen & Speak 2 A-2

G: ❶What are you doing this weekend, Eric?

B: Nothing special. ❷I'll just stay home and watch TV.

G: Great! ❸I'm having a birthday party this weekend. Can you come?

B: Sure. Thank you for inviting me.

G: Eric, 이번 주말에 뭐 할 거니?
B: 특별한 건 없어. 그냥 집에 있으면서 TV를 볼 거야.
G: 좋아! 이번 주말에 생일 파티를 할 거야. 올 수 있니?
B: 물론이지. 초대해 줘서 고마워.

❶ What are you doing ~?: 현재진행형이 미래를 나타내는 경우이다.
❷ stay home: 집에 머물다
❸ have a birthday party: 생일 파티를 열다

Check(√) True or False

(5) Eric will watch TV at home this weekend.   T ☐ F ☐

(6) The girl won't invite Eric.   T ☐ F ☐

Communicate: A. Listen and Answer

Jaden: Can you do me a favor, Yuri?

Yuri: Sure. What is it, Jaden?

Jaden: ❶Can we go shopping together for a baseball cap for a girl?

Yuri: Yes, of course. ❷Who is it for?

Jaden: ❸It's for my little sister Kate.

Yuri: ❹Oh, are you getting her a birthday gift?

Jaden: ❺No, her birthday isn't until October.

Yuri: Then, why are you getting a baseball cap for her?

Jaden: ❻She broke her leg while she was riding her bike last week. ❼I just want to cheer her up.

Yuri: ❽Oh, I see. I can go this Friday afternoon.

Jaden: ❾That sounds perfect. Thank you.

❶ go shopping: 쇼핑하러 가다
❷ Who is it for? = Whom is it for?
❸ It's for ~.: 그것은 ~을 위한 것이다.
❹ get her a birthday gift: 그녀에게 생일 선물을 사 주다
❺ isn't until ~: ~까지는 아니다
❻ She broke her leg: 그녀의 다리가 부러졌다
❼ cheer her up: 그녀를 격려하다
❽ Oh, I see.: 아, 알겠어.
❾ That sounds perfect.: 그거 아주 좋구나.

Progress Check 1

G: Andrew, can you do me a favor?

B: O.K. What is it?

G: ❶My family is going to go to Jejudo this weekend. ❷Can you take care of my cat during the weekend?

B: Sure. ❸Don't worry about her, and enjoy your trip.

❶ is going to go = will go
❷ take care of: ~을 돌보다 / during: ~ 중에
❸ worry about: ~에 대해 걱정하다 / her = your dog

Progress Check 2

G: Hello, Mr. Smith. ❶We haven't had a chance to thank you for being our teacher. Every morning, you welcome us in the classroom. ❷ You always teach us important and interesting things. ❸We're lucky to have you, and we're proud to be your students.

❶ haven't had: 계속을 나타내는 현재완료 / to thank: a chance를 수식하는 형용사적 용법의 to부정사 / thank you for -ing(동명사): ~인 것에 대하여 당신에게 감사하다
❷ always: 빈도부사로 일반동사의 앞에 위치한다.
❸ be lucky to ~: ~해서 행운이다 / be proud to ~: ~해서 자랑스럽다

Progress Check 3

G: ❶Do you have any special plans this weekend?

B: No, I'm just going to stay home.

G: ❷Oh, then can you come over to my house for dinner?

❶ any: (의문문에서) 어떤, 무슨
❷ come over to: ~에 오다 / for dinner: 저녁을 먹으러

Listen & Speak 1-3

A: Can you do me a favor?

B: Sure. What is it?

A: ❶Can you move this table with me? It's too heavy.

B: Sure. ❷No problem.

A: ❸Thank you for helping me.

❶ move this table: 이 식탁을 옮기다
❷ No problem.: 문제없어., 걱정 마.
❸ Thank A for B: B에 대하여 A에게 감사하다

● 다음 우리말과 일치하도록 빈칸에 알맞은 말을 쓰시오.

Listen & Speak 1 A. Listen and Check

1. **G:** Mark, can you _____ me a _____?

   B: Sure. _____ is it?

   G: My _____ is going on _____ for a week. Can you _____ to our house and _____ the plants?

   B: Yes, I _____.

2. **G:** Kevin, _____ you do me a _____?

   B: O.K. What is _____?

   G: Can you _____ me _____ my science _____ this afternoon?

   B: _____, but I _____. I _____ to visit my grandma with my mom.

Listen & Speak 2 A. Listen and Check

1. **G:** _____, Mom! Hi, Dad! As you _____, today is my 15th _____. I _____ had a chance _____ thank you for _____ my parents. You've truly _____ my friends _____ my teachers. Thank you for _____ me and always _____ to understand me. I'm really _____ to be your _____.

2. **G:** What are you _____ this _____, Eric?

   B: Nothing _____. I'll just _____ home and _____ TV.

   G: Great! I'm _____ a birthday _____ this weekend. Can you come?

   B: Sure. Thank you for _____ me.

Listen & Speak 1-B

A: Can you do me a _____?

B: Sure. _____ is it?

A: Can you _____ this table _____ me? It's too _____.

B: Sure. No _____.

A: _____ you for _____ me.

해석

1. G: Mark, 부탁 하나 들어줄래?
   B: 물론이지. 부탁할게 무엇이지?
   G: 우리 가족은 일주일 동안 휴가를 갈 거야. 우리 집에 와서 식물들에게 물을 줄 수 있니?
   B: 응, 할 수 있어.

2. G: Kevin, 부탁 하나 들어줄래?
   B: 좋아. 뭔데?
   G: 오늘 오후에 내 과학 프로젝트 좀 도와줄래?
   B: 미안하지만 안 돼. 엄마랑 할머니 댁에 가야 해.

1. G: 안녕, 엄마! 안녕, 아빠! 엄마, 아빠도 아시다시피, 오늘은 제 15번째 생일이에요. 제 부모님이 되어주신 것에 대해 감사할 기회가 없었어요. 두 분께서는 정말 제 친구이자 선생님이셨어요. 저를 지지해 주시고 항상 저를 이해하려고 노력해 주셔서 감사해요. 저는 두 분의 딸이 되어서 정말 자랑스러워요.

2. G: Eric, 이번 주말에 뭐 할 거니?
   B: 특별한 건 없어. 그냥 집에 있으면서 TV를 볼 거야.
   G: 좋아! 이번 주말에 생일 파티를 할 거야. 올 수 있니?
   B: 물론이지. 초대해 줘서 고마워.

A: 부탁 하나 들어줄래?
B: 그래. 뭔데?
A: 이 테이블 좀 옮겨줄래? 너무 무거워.
B: 물론이지. 문제없어.
A: 도와줘서 고마워.

Communicate A. Listen and Answer

Jaden: _____ you _____ me a favor, Yuri?

Yuri: Sure. _____ is it, Jaden?

Jaden: Can we go _____ together _____ a baseball cap for a girl?

Yuri: Yes, of _____. Who is it _____?

Jaden: It's _____ my little sister Kate.

Yuri: Oh, are you _____ her a birthday _____?

Jaden: No, her birthday isn't _____ October.

Yuri: Then, _____ are you getting a baseball _____ for her?

Jaden: She _____ her leg _____ she was riding her bike _____ week. I _____ want to _____ her up.

Yuri: Oh, I _____. I can _____ this Friday afternoon.

Jaden: That sounds _____. Thank you.

Progress Check

1. G: Andrew, can you _____ me a _____?

   B: O.K. What is _____?

   G: My family is _____ to go to Jejudo _____ weekend. Can you take _____ of my cat _____ the weekend?

   B: Sure. Don't _____ about her. And _____ your trip.

2. G: _____, Mr. Smith. We _____ had a chance to thank you for _____ our teacher. _____ morning, you _____ us in the classroom. You always _____ us important and interesting _____. We're _____ to have you, and we're _____ to be your _____.

3. G: Do you have _____ special _____ this weekend?

   B: No, I'm _____ going to _____ home.

   G: Oh, _____ can you come _____ to my house for _____?

해석

Jaden: 유리야, 부탁 하나 들어줄래?
유리: 물론이지. 뭐야, Jaden?
Jaden: 우리 같이 여자용 야구 모자 사러 쇼핑갈 수 있을까?
유리: 응, 물론이지. 누구 주려고?
Jaden: 내 여동생 Kate에게 줄 거야.
유리: 아, 너 그 애에게 생일 선물을 사 주려고 하는 거야?
Jaden: 아니, 그 애의 생일은 10월이 되어야 해.
유리: 그렇다면, 왜 야구 모자를 사 주려고 하는 거야?
Jaden: 그 애는 지난주에 자전거를 타다가 다리가 부러졌어. 난 그저 그 애를 격려하고 싶어
유리: 아, 그렇구나. 이번 주 금요일 오후에 갈 수 있어.
Jaden: 그거 아주 좋아. 고마워.

1. G: Andrew, 부탁 하나 들어줄래?
   B: 좋아. 뭔데?
   G: 우리 가족은 이번 주말에 제주도에 갈 거야. 주말에 내 고양이 좀 봐줄래?
   B: 물론이지. 고양이 걱정은 하지 말고, 여행을 즐겨.

2. G: 안녕하세요, Smith 선생님. 우리의 선생님이 되어주신 것에 대해 감사할 기회가 없었습니다. 매일 아침, 선생님은 교실에서 우리를 맞이하십니다. 선생님은 항상 우리에게 중요하고 흥미로운 것들을 가르쳐주십니다. 우리는 선생님이 계셔서 행운이고, 선생님의 학생이라는 것이 자랑스럽습니다.

3. G: 이번 주말에 무슨 특별한 계획 있니?
   B: 아니, 그냥 집에 있을 거야.
   G: 아, 그럼 우리 집에 저녁 먹으러 올 수 있어?

01 다음 중 의도하는 바가 나머지 넷과 <u>다른</u> 것은?

① Can I ask you a favor?
② Can you do me a favor?
③ Can you help me, please?
④ What can I do for you?
⑤ Could you give me a hand?

invite 초대하다

02 다음 대화의 밑줄 친 부분과 바꿔 쓸 수 있는 것은?

> A: Thank you for inviting me tonight.
> B: <u>My pleasure.</u>

① Sure.　　　　　② Not at all.
③ I don't know.　　④ Of course.
⑤ I'm sorry I can't.

03 다음 대화의 빈칸에 알맞은 말은?

> A: Can you do me a _____?
> B: Sure. What is it?

① favor　　　② help　　　③ work
④ share　　　⑤ pleasure

04 다음 대화의 밑줄 친 말과 바꾸어 쓸 수 있는 것은?

> A: I came here to help you with your homework.
> B: <u>I appreciate your help.</u>

① Thank you.　　　② You're welcome.
③ That's right.　　④ You're right.
⑤ My pleasure.

172　Lesson 4. Giving a Hand

01 다음 대화를 의미가 통하도록 알맞게 배열한 것은?

(A) Can you help me with my science project this afternoon?
(B) Kevin, can you do me a favor?
(C) O.K. What is it?
(D) Sorry, but I can't. I have to visit my grandma with my mom.

① (A) – (D) – (B) – (C)
② (B) – (C) – (A) – (D)
③ (C) – (D) – (B) – (A)
④ (D) – (B) – (C) – (A)
⑤ (D) – (C) – (B) – (A)

02 다음 대화의 빈칸에 알맞은 것은?

A: Happy birthday! This is for you.
B: Oh, thank you for your present.
A: _____

① Go ahead.   ② Thanks a lot.
③ Okay.   ④ It's my pleasure.
⑤ I'm very grateful.

서답형

03 다음 대화의 빈칸에 알맞은 말을 쓰시오.

A: I can ride you to the bus station.
B: I really _____ your kindness.
A: No _____.

서답형

04 다음 우리말과 같도록 빈칸에 알맞은 말을 쓰시오.

이 상자들을 날라 주셔서 감사해요.
➡ _____ you _____ carrying these boxes.

05 다음 밑줄 친 말과 바꾸어 쓸 수 있는 것은?

A: <u>Can you give me a hand?</u>
B: Sure. What is it?

① Show me your hand.
② I am left-handed.
③ Please hand me that book.
④ Can you help me?
⑤ Put your right hand up.

06 다음 중 짝지어진 대화가 <u>어색한</u> 것은?

① A: May I ask you a favor?
   B: No problem. What is it?
② A: Can you turn down TV?
   B: You're welcome.
③ A: Help me, please.
   B: Okay. What's the matter?
④ A: Can you help me?
   B: Of course.
⑤ A: Can you help me with something?
   B: Sure. What is it?

[07~11] 다음 대화를 읽고, 물음에 답하시오.

Jaden: ⓐCan you do me a favor, Yuri?

Yuri: Sure. What is it, Jaden?

Jaden: Can we go ⓑshop together for a baseball cap for a girl?

Yuri: Yes, of course. Who is it for?

Jaden: It's for my little sister Kate.

Yuri: Oh, are you getting her a birthday gift?

Jaden: No, her birthday isn't until October.

Yuri: Then, ___ⓒ___ are you getting a baseball cap for her?

Jaden: She broke her leg while she was riding her bike last week. I just want to cheer her ___ⓓ___.

Yuri: Oh, I see. I can go this Friday afternoon.

Jaden: That sounds perfect. Thank you.

서답형

07 위 대화의 밑줄 친 ⓐ와 같은 뜻이 되도록 다음 빈칸에 알맞은 말을 쓰시오.

Can you _____ me a _____, Yuri?

서답형

08 위 대화의 밑줄 친 ⓑ를 알맞은 어형으로 고치시오.

➡ _____

09 위 대화의 빈칸 ⓒ에 알맞은 것은?

① why　　② when　　③ how
④ what　　⑤ where

10 위 대화의 빈칸 ⓓ에 알맞은 것은?

① on　　② to　　③ up
④ for　　⑤ over

11 위 대화의 내용과 일치하지 않는 것은?

① Jaden은 유리에게 도움을 청한다.
② Jaden은 여동생의 생일 선물을 사기를 원한다.
③ Jaden의 여동생 생일은 10월이다.
④ Jaden의 여동생은 다리가 부러졌다.
⑤ 유리는 Jaden과 함께 모자를 사러 갈 것이다.

[12~14] 다음 대화를 읽고, 물음에 답하시오.

G: What are you doing this weekend, Eric?

B: ⓐ특별히 할 일은 없어. I'll just stay home and watch TV.

G: Great! I'm having a birthday party this weekend. Can you come?

B: Sure. Thank you ___ⓑ___ inviting me.

G: You're ___ⓒ___.

서답형

12 위 대화의 밑줄 친 ⓐ와 같은 뜻이 되도록 다음 문장의 빈칸에 알맞은 말을 쓰시오.

_____ special.

중요

13 위 대화의 빈칸 ⓑ에 알맞은 것은?

① to　　　　　② at
③ in　　　　　④ for
⑤ with

서답형

14 위 대화의 빈칸 ⓒ에 알맞은 말을 쓰시오.

➡ _____

01 다음 우리말과 같도록 빈칸에 알맞은 말을 쓰시오.

우리의 프로젝트를 도와 주셔서 감사해요.
➡ Thank you _____ _____ with our project.

[02~03] 다음 대화의 빈칸에 알맞은 말을 쓰시오.

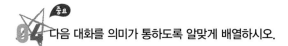

02

A: Can you give me a _____?
B: Sure. What is it?

03

A: Can you _____ me a favor?
B: Sure. Go _____.
A: I have a headache. Please buy some medicine _____ me.

04 다음 대화를 의미가 통하도록 알맞게 배열하시오.

(A) I have no special plans. Why?
(B) Sure. Thank you for inviting me.
(C) I'm going to have my birthday party. Would you like to come?
(D) Sora, what are you going to do this Friday?

➡ _____

[05~08] 다음 담화문을 읽고, 물음에 답하시오.

G: Hi, Mom! Hi, Dad! As you know, today is my 15th birthday. I ⓐ(have / haven't) had a chance to thank you for being my parents. You've truly been my friends and my teachers. Thank you for supporting me and always ⓑtry to understand me. ⓒI'm really proud to be your daughter.

05 위 글의 괄호 ⓐ에서 알맞은 말을 골라 쓰시오.

➡ _____

06 위 글에서 다음 정의에 해당하는 단어를 찾아 쓰시오.

a suitable time or situation when you have the opportunity to do someting

➡ _____

07 위 글의 밑줄 친 ⓑ를 알맞은 어형으로 고치시오.

➡ _____

08 위 글의 밑줄 친 ⓒ를 우리말로 옮기시오.

➡ _____

Grammar
교과서

① 목적격 관계대명사

> - He was the person (**who/whom/that**) Kenneth respected the most in the world.
>   그는 Kenneth가 세상에서 가장 존경하는 사람이었다.
>
> - There were many things (**that/which**) Kenneth had to do.
>   Kenneth가 해야 할 많은 일들이 있었다.
>
> - The snack (**that/which**) I ate at night was Hawaiian pizza.
>   내가 밤에 먹은 간식은 하와이안 피자였다.

■ 관계대명사는 선행사와 뒤에 이어지는 문장을 연결해 주는 역할을 하며, 문장 내에서의 역할에 따라 주격, 목적격, 소유격으로 나뉜다.

	사람	사물/동물	사람/사물/동물
주격	who	which	that
목적격	who(m)	which	that

■ 목적격 관계대명사는 선행사가 뒤에 이어지는 문장(관계대명사절)에서 목적어 역할을 할 때 쓰며, 생략할 수 있다. 선행사가 사람이면 who(m) 또는 that을, 사물이나 동물이면 which 또는 that을 쓴다. 일반적으로 선행사가 사람일 때 whom보다는 who를 더 많이 쓴다.

- Ann was the person. I met her on the way home.
  → Ann was the person **who[whom, that]** I met on the way home.
  Ann은 내가 집에 오는 길에 만난 사람이었다.

■ 선행사가 최상급이거나 서수, -thing으로 끝나는 경우, 또는 the very, the only가 선행사를 수식하는 경우에는 whom이나 which 대신 that을 쓸 때가 많다.

- This is the biggest dog **that** I have ever seen. 이것은 지금까지 내가 본 가장 큰 개다.

■ 관계대명사가 전치사의 목적어로 쓰일 때는 who(m)이나 which 대신 that을 전치사와 함께 사용할 수 없다.

- The bed in **which** I slept was comfortable. (○) 내가 잔 침대는 편안했다.
  The bed in that I slept was comfortable.   (×)

핵심 Check

1. 다음 괄호 안에서 알맞은 것을 고르시오.

(1) I know the doctor (which / that) everyone likes.

(2) That is the very problem (that / what) I wanted to solve.

(3) The man to (whom / that) you spoke is my homeroom teacher.

(4) This is the book (who / which) I read yesterday.

(5) Police found the knife with (which / that) the man killed her.

2 so ... that ~

- He was **so** happy **that** he jumped for joy. 그는 아주 행복해 기뻐서 펄쩍 뛰었다.
- He wandered off at night **so** often **that** someone had to keep an eye on him.
그는 밤에 아주 종종 여기저기 쏘다녔기 때문에 누군가가 그를 지켜보아야만 했다.
- Shirley became **so** busy **that** she began to use her father's garage as her office. Shirley는 아주 바빠져서 아버지의 차고를 사무실로 사용하기 시작했다.

■ 'so+형용사+that절'의 구문은 '너무 ~해서 …하다'의 의미로 결과를 나타내는 구문이다. so 다음에는 원인에 해당하는 형용사나 부사가 오고, that절에는 결과를 나타내는 절이 온다. 이유를 나타내는 접속사 because나 결과를 나타내는 접속사를 이용해서 문장을 바꿔 쓸 수도 있다.
  - Nick woke up **so** late **that** he missed the bus. Nick은 너무 늦게 일어나서 버스를 놓쳤다.
    = Nick missed the bus because[as] he woke up too late.
    = Nick woke up too late, so he missed the bus.
  - My grandma is **so** wise **that** everyone respects her.
    나의 할머니는 아주 현명하셔서 모든 사람들이 그녀를 존경한다.
    = Everyone respects my grandma because[as] she is so wise.
    = My grandma is very wise, so everyone respects her.

■ '너무 ~해서 …할 수 없다'의 의미를 나타낼 경우에는 'so ~ that … can't' 구문을 이용한다. 이 구문은 'too ~ to부정사' 구문으로 바꿔 쓸 수 있다.
  - I am **so** tired **that** I **can't** do it right now. 나는 너무 피곤해서 지금 바로 그 일을 할 수 없다.
    = I am **too** tired **to** do it right now.

■ '형용사/부사+enough to+동사원형'은 '…할 만큼 충분히 ~한/하게'의 뜻을 나타내며, 'so+형용사/부사+that+주어+can+동사원형'의 형태로 바꿔 쓸 수 있다.
  - He is rich **enough to** buy the house. 그는 그 집을 살 만큼 충분히 부유하다.
    = He is **so** rich **that** he can buy the house.

핵심 Check

2. 다음 괄호 안에서 알맞은 것을 고르시오.
  (1) She got up early _____ _____ catch the first train.
  (2) Sam was _____ strong _____ he could move the rock.
  (3) I am _____ busy with my homework _____ play computer games.
  (4) The girl is _____ young _____ she can't ride a bike.
  (5) This book is _____ difficult for me _____ read.

01 다음 괄호 안에서 알맞은 것을 고르시오.

heavy 무거운
carry 나르다, 가지고 가다

(1) The bags are (so / very) heavy that I can't carry them.

(2) Emma is (too / so) young to go to school.

(3) This is the boy (whom / which) I play basketball with every weekend.

(4) I am reading the letter (whom / which) you gave me yesterday.

02 다음 두 문장이 의미가 같도록 빈칸에 알맞은 말을 쓰시오.

(1) She got up early enough to catch the first train.

➙ She got up _____ early _____ she _____ catch the first train.

(2) He is too poor to buy the house.

➙ He is _____ _____ that he _____ buy the house.

(3) My grandma is so old that she cannot run fast.

➙ My grandma is _____ old _____ run fast.

03 다음 빈칸에 알맞은 말을 〈보기〉에서 골라 쓰시오. (한 단어를 중복해서 쓸 수 없음.)

┌─┤ 보기 ├─────────────────────────────┐

　　　　that　　which　　whom　　who

└───────────────────────────────────┘

(1) Look at the boy _____ is watering a flower.

(2) You are the only friend with _____ I can talk.

(3) I need a knife with _____ I can cut the rope.

(4) Money is the only thing _____ he wants.

01 다음 문장의 빈칸에 알맞은 것은?

> The gentleman _____ I met yesterday was a teacher.

① which
② who
③ at which
④ with who
⑤ with that

02 다음 빈칸에 들어갈 말이 바르게 짝지어진 것은?

> The box was _____ heavy that I _____ move it by myself.

① so – couldn't
② too – couldn't
③ so – could
④ enough – could
⑤ such – could

03 다음 두 문장이 같은 뜻이 되도록 빈칸에 알맞은 말을 쓰시오.

> The library is too far for me to go to on foot.
> = The library is _____ far that I _____ go there on foot.

04 다음 문장에서 어법상 어색한 곳을 찾아 바르게 고쳐 쓰시오.

(1) He is an engineer which my father knows very well.

_____ ➡ _____

(2) The village in that I live is very small.

_____ ➡ _____

05 다음 빈칸에 들어갈 말이 바르게 짝지어진 것은?

> We have to go now. We are _____ busy _____ wait for her.

① so – that
② so – to
③ enough – to
④ as – too
⑤ too – to

[06~07] 다음 중 어법상 어색한 것을 고르시오.

06 ① This is the pen I lost yesterday.
② I will give you everything that you need.
③ I forgot to bring the homework which I did yesterday.
④ The music which we listened is by Mozart.
⑤ The car which I bought last month already has engine problems.

07 ① You are too young to drive a car.
② I ran fast enough to catch the bus.
③ My father is too busy to play with me.
④ She was too strong that she could carry the boxes.
⑤ My sister is so tall that she can play basketball well.

08 다음 밑줄 친 부분을 바르게 고쳐 쓰시오.

> Dami is very tired that she can't do her homework.

➡ _____

09 다음 두 문장에서 생략된 것이 바르게 짝지어진 것은?

> • He ate the food everyone hated.
> • The tree I cut yesterday was very big.

① who – who
② who – that
③ that – who
④ who – which
⑤ that – which

서답형

10 다음 빈칸에 공통으로 알맞은 말을 쓰시오.

> • The building _____ I visited yesterday is a museum.
> • The man _____ everyone knows well built his house for himself.

11 다음 빈칸에 공통으로 알맞은 것은?

> • I got up early _____ that I could catch the train.
> • The ice cream is _____ cold that I can't eat it.

① so
② as
③ too
④ never
⑤ rarely

서답형

12 다음 우리말과 일치하도록 주어진 단어를 바르게 배열하시오.

> 그 남자는 자기가 갖고 있는 모든 돈을 내게 주었다.
> (he / gave / had / the / man / me / money / all / that / the)

➡ _____

13 다음 우리말을 영어로 바르게 옮긴 것은?

> 음식이 너무 짜서 나는 그것을 먹을 수 없었다.

① The food was too salty that I could eat it.
② The food was so salty that I couldn't eat.
③ I couldn't eat it so that the food was salty.
④ The food was salty enough for me to eat.
⑤ The food was so salty that I couldn't eat it.

14 다음 중 밑줄 친 부분의 쓰임이 옳은 것은?

① The man which I met yesterday will call me this afternoon.
② I can give you the textbook what I bought last week.
③ The rumor who Jeff told me was very interesting.
④ This is the pen with which he wrote the novel.
⑤ Thanks to the textbooks whom you gave me, I could pass the exam.

15 다음 주어진 문장과 의미가 같은 것은?

> It was too hot for him to go out.

① It was not so hot for him to go out.
② It was so hot, but he went out.
③ It was so hot that he couldn't go out.
④ It was hot enough for him to go out.
⑤ It was so hot that he wanted to go out.

서답형

16 다음 두 문장이 같은 뜻이 되도록 빈칸에 알맞은 말을 쓰시오.

> These books are so heavy that I can't carry them.
> = These books are _____ heavy for me _____ _____.

서답형

17 다음 문장에서 어법상 어색한 부분을 찾아 바르게 고쳐 쓰시오.

(1) The girl which I like will leave this town.

_____ ➡ _____

(2) The knife with which I cut these apples were very sharp.

_____ ➡ _____

18 다음 밑줄 친 부분 중 생략할 수 없는 것은?

① This is the piano which Mozart played.
② The boy who is throwing a ball is my brother.
③ Rome is the place that I really want to visit again.
④ These are the gifts which she gave me on my birthday.
⑤ I'm going to return the book that I borrowed last week.

19 다음 중 어법상 올바른 문장을 모두 고른 것은?

> ⓐ This book is so easy that I can read it.
> ⓑ My sister is enough old to ride a bike.
> ⓒ This problem is so difficult that I can't solve.
> ⓓ The bag was too expensive for her to buy.
> ⓔ Jane was so hungry that she had some cake.

① ⓐ, ⓒ, ⓔ   ② ⓐ, ⓑ
③ ⓐ, ⓓ, ⓔ   ④ ⓐ, ⓑ, ⓒ, ⓓ
⑤ ⓐ, ⓑ, ⓒ, ⓔ

중요

20 다음 중 밑줄 친 that의 쓰임이 나머지와 다른 하나는?

① It is true <u>that</u> we were a little late.
② This is a bag <u>that</u> I bought yesterday.
③ This is the hotel <u>that</u> I stayed at last time.
④ Do you know the boy <u>that</u> I met yesterday?
⑤ This is the tree <u>that</u> I planted five years ago.

21 다음 중 우리말을 알맞게 옮긴 것은? (2개)

> 나는 너무 화가 나서 말을 하지 못했다.

① I was too angry to speak.
② I was too angry not to speak.
③ I was so angry that I can't speak.
④ I was so angry that I could speak.
⑤ I was so angry that I couldn't speak.

01 다음 두 문장을 관계대명사를 써서 한 문장으로 바꿔 쓰시오.

(1) I know the man. You are looking for the man.

➡ _____

_____

(2) This is the bag. I got it from Nancy.

➡ _____

_____

(3) He is the boy. I meet him at the bus stop every morning.

➡ _____

_____

02 다음 빈칸에 알맞은 말을 〈보기〉에서 골라 쓰시오.

┌─ 보기 ─┐
too   so   enough   that
└──────┘

(1) He was _____ kind that he helped me.

(2) Mike is wise _____ to control himself.

(3) My father was _____ sleepy to drive.

(4) This English book is so easy _____ I can read it.

03 다음 빈칸에 공통으로 알맞은 말을 쓰시오.

┌─────────────────────────┐
│ • This is the hat _____ Ann bought │
│   yesterday.   │
│ • I know the girl _____ is playing the │
│   drums.   │
└─────────────────────────┘

04 다음 문장에서 어법상 틀린 부분을 찾아 바르게 고쳐 쓰시오.

(1) The test was too difficult that I failed it.

_____ ➡ _____

(2) The bag is too heavy for me to carry it.

_____ ➡ _____

(3) It's enough warm for the children to play outside.

_____ ➡ _____

(4) Nick woke up so late what he missed the bus.

_____ ➡ _____

05 다음 우리말과 같은 뜻이 되도록 빈칸에 알맞은 말을 쓰시오.

┌─────────────────────────┐
│ 그가 너무 빨리 말을 해서 우리는 알아들을 수 없 │
│ 었다.   │
│ ➡ He spoke _____ fast _____ we │
│   couldn't understand him.   │
└─────────────────────────┘

06 다음 주어진 문장을 어법에 맞게 고쳐 쓰시오.

(1) I bought my sister a blouse who was made in France.

➡ _____

_____

(2) Do you know the boy whom I met him on the street yesterday?

➡ _____

_____

(3) This is the city that are famous for its beautiful buildings.

➡ _____

_____

07 다음 우리말과 일치하도록 빈칸에 알맞은 말을 쓰시오.

(1) 이 문제는 너무 어려워서 내가 풀 수 없다.
➡ This problem is ＿＿＿＿ difficult
＿＿＿＿ I ＿＿＿＿ solve it.

(2) 그녀는 다행히도 그 화재를 모면했다.
➡ She was ＿＿＿＿ ＿＿＿＿ ＿＿＿＿
escape the fire.

08 다음 주어진 어구들을 바르게 배열하시오.

(1) (easy / the question / everyone / that / the answer / knows / so / is).

➡ ＿＿＿＿＿＿＿＿＿＿＿＿＿＿＿
＿＿＿＿＿＿＿＿＿＿＿＿＿＿＿

(2) (right now / I / tired / I / can't / it / do / am / so / that).

➡ ＿＿＿＿＿＿＿＿＿＿＿＿＿＿＿

09 다음 두 문장의 의미가 같도록 빈칸에 알맞은 말을 쓰시오.

(1) This book is too difficult for me ＿＿＿＿ read.
➡ This book is ＿＿＿＿ difficult ＿＿＿＿
I ＿＿＿＿ read it.

(2) The wind was strong ＿＿＿＿ to blow down trees.
➡ The wind was ＿＿＿＿ strong that it
＿＿＿＿ ＿＿＿＿ down trees.

(3) Dad walked ＿＿＿＿ fast that I ＿＿＿＿
catch up with him.
➡ Dad walked ＿＿＿＿ fast for me
＿＿＿＿ catch up with.

10 다음 두 문장을 관계대명사를 이용하여 한 문장으로 쓰시오.

(1) The girl saw a man and his dog. They looked very tired.

➡ ＿＿＿＿＿＿＿＿＿＿＿＿＿＿＿
＿＿＿＿＿＿＿＿＿＿＿＿＿＿＿

(2) John is the best player in this town. I played tennis with him yesterday.

➡ ＿＿＿＿＿＿＿＿＿＿＿＿＿＿＿
＿＿＿＿＿＿＿＿＿＿＿＿＿＿＿

(3) This bike is my treasure. My father bought it for me last year.

➡ ＿＿＿＿＿＿＿＿＿＿＿＿＿＿＿
＿＿＿＿＿＿＿＿＿＿＿＿＿＿＿

(4) My sister ate the only ice cream. My mother bought it for me.

➡ ＿＿＿＿＿＿＿＿＿＿＿＿＿＿＿
＿＿＿＿＿＿＿＿＿＿＿＿＿＿＿

(5) The house was in Incheon. We lived in it two years ago.

➡ ＿＿＿＿＿＿＿＿＿＿＿＿＿＿＿
＿＿＿＿＿＿＿＿＿＿＿＿＿＿＿

11 다음 우리말과 일치하도록 빈칸에 알맞은 말을 쓰시오.

(1) 이 아이가 내 남동생이 지난밤에 만난 소년이다.
➡ This is the boy ＿＿＿＿ my brother
met last night.

(2) 이것이 나의 부모님이 사 주신 자전거이다.
➡ This is the bike ＿＿＿＿ my parents
bought for me.

Socks for Grandpa

Kenneth Shinozuka grew up in a big happy family of three
               _{grow의 과거형}
generations. Since he was little, he has always been very close to his
          _{~한 이래로}   _{계속을 나타내는 현재완료}
grandfather. He was Kenneth's first friend, his trusty driver, and his
                                            _{trust의 형용사형}
cook. He also taught him many life lessons. He was the person who
               _{간접목적어}   _{직접목적어}   _{관계대명사 목적격}
Kenneth respected the most in the world.
               _{much의 최상급}

When Kenneth was four, his grandfather went out for a walk one
 _{~이었을 때–때를 나타내는 접속사}   _{산책하러 나갔다}
day and got lost. He had Alzheimer's disease. Everyone in Kenneth's
      _{lose의 과거형}   _{모든 사람 – 부정대명사}
family was in shock. His condition became worse over the next 10
                             _{bad의 비교급}
years. He wandered off at night so often that someone had to keep an
                 _{so ~ that … 구문: 너무 ~해서 …하다}   _{~해야 했다}   _{~을 감시하다}
eye on him all night long. One night, Kenneth's grandfather got out
                                           _{~에서 나왔다}
of bed, and Kenneth saw it. At that moment, he said to himself, "Why
                  _{그 순간에}   _{혼잣말을 했다}   _{내가 ~하는 게 어떨까}
don't I put pressure sensors on the heels of his socks?"

---

grow up 자라다, 성장하다

generation 대, 세대

close 가까운, 친한

trusty 신뢰할 수 있는

lesson 교훈

respect 존경하다

get lost 길을 잃다

disease 병

shock 충격

condition 상태

worse 더 나쁜

wander off 여기저기 돌아다니다

all night long 밤새

moment 순간

pressure 압력

censor 센서, 감지기

heel 발뒤꿈치, 뒤꿈치

 확인문제

● 다음 문장이 본문의 내용과 일치하면 T, 일치하지 <u>않으면</u> F를 쓰시오.

1   Kenneth Shinozuka had a small family. ☐

2   Kenneth Shinozuka and his grandfather were very close. ☐

3   Kenneth Shinozuka respected his grandfather. ☐

4   Kenneth Shinozuka and his grandfather often took a walk at night. ☐

5   Kenneth Shinozuka's grandfather got ill. ☐

There were many things that Kenneth had to do. He first had to
= which: 관계대명사 목적격
create a pressure sensor and then find a way to send a signal to his
그리고 나서   to부정사의 형용사적 용법
smart phone. Kenneth also tried many different materials to make
시도해 보았다   to부정사의 목적을 나타내는 부사적 용법
comfortable socks for his elderly grandfather.

When he felt like giving up, he thought about his grandfather's safety.
feel like+-ing: ~하고 싶은 생각이 들다   safe의 명사형
After much trial and error, he finally succeeded in making his device.
~을 만드는 데 성공했다
When it first worked, he was so happy that he jumped for joy. He could
work: 작동하다   기뻐서
not believe that his invention actually worked. For his grandfather,
명사절을 이끄는 접속사
Kenneth is the best inventor in the world. For Kenneth, his grandfather
good의 최상급
is still his best friend.
아직도, 여전히

create 창조하다, 만들어 내다
signal 신호
material 재료
comfortable 편한, 편안한
elderly 연로한
give up 포기하다
safety 안전
trial and error 시행착오
succeed 성공하다
device 장치, 도구
actually 사실
inventor 발명가
still 여전히

확인문제

● 다음 문장이 본문의 내용과 일치하면 T, 일치하지 않으면 F를 쓰시오.

1 Kenneth created a pressure sensor. ☐

2 Kenneth bought comfortable socks for his grandfather. ☐

3 Kenneth gave up making things for his grandfather. ☐

4 Kenneth created his device at last. ☐

5 Kenneth is famous for his invention. ☐

● 우리말을 참고하여 빈칸에 알맞은 말을 쓰시오.

1 Kenneth Shinozuka grew _____ in a big happy _____ of three generations.

2 _____ he was little, he has always _____ very close to his grandfather.

3 He was Kenneth's first _____, his trusty _____, and his _____.

4 He also _____ him many life _____.

5 He was the person _____ Kenneth respected the _____ in the world.

6 _____ Kenneth was four, his grandfather _____ out for a walk one day and _____ lost.

7 He had Alzheimer's _____.

8 _____ in Kenneth's family was in _____.

9 His condition _____ worse _____ the next 10 years.

10 He wandered _____ at night so often _____ someone had to keep an eye on him _____ night long.

11 One night, Kenneth's grandfather _____ out of bed, and Kenneth _____ it.

12 At that _____, he said to _____, "Why _____ I put pressure sensors on the _____ of his socks?"

1 Kenneth Shinozuka는 3대의 행복한 대가족에서 자랐다.

2 그는 어렸을 때부터 항상 할아버지와 매우 친했다.

3 그는 Kenneth의 첫 친구이자, 신뢰할 수 있는 운전기사이자, 요리사였다.

4 그는 또한 그에게 많은 인생 교훈을 가르쳐 주었다.

5 그는 Kenneth가 세상에서 가장 존경하는 사람이었다.

6 Kenneth가 네 살이었을 때, 그의 할아버지는 어느 날 산책을 나갔다가 길을 잃었다.

7 그는 알츠하이머병에 걸렸다.

8 Kenneth의 가족 모두는 충격에 빠졌다.

9 그의 상태는 10년 동안 더 악화되었다.

10 그는 자주 밤에 여기저기 돌아다니기 때문에 누군가가 그를 밤새 감시해야 했다.

11 어느 날 밤, Kenneth의 할아버지가 침대에서 일어났는데, Kenneth가 그것을 보았다.

12 그 순간, 그는 혼잣말을 했다. "내가 할아버지의 양말 뒤꿈치에 압력 감지기를 설치하는 게 어떨까?"

13 There were many things _____ Kenneth had to _____.

14 He first had to _____ a pressure sensor and _____ find a way to send a _____ to his smart phone.

15 Kenneth also _____ many different _____ to make comfortable _____ for his elderly grandfather.

16 When he felt _____ giving up, he thought about his grandfather's _____.

17 _____ much trial and error, he finally _____ in making his device.

18 When it first _____, he was so happy _____ he jumped for _____.

19 He could not _____ that his invention _____ worked.

20 _____ his grandfather, Kenneth is the best _____ in the world.

21 For Kenneth, his grandfather is still his best _____.

13 Kenneth가 해야 할 많은 일들이 있었다.

14 그는 처음에 압력 감지기를 만들고 나서 그의 스마트폰으로 신호를 보낼 방법을 찾아야 했다.

15 Kenneth는 또한 그의 연로한 할아버지에게 편안한 양말을 만들어 주기 위해 많은 다양한 재료들을 가지고 만들어 보았다.

16 그는 포기하고 싶은 생각이 들 때 할아버지의 안전에 대해 생각했다.

17 많은 시행착오 끝에 그는 마침내 자신의 장치를 만드는 데 성공했다.

18 그것이 처음 작동했을 때, 그는 너무 행복해 기뻐서 펄쩍 뛰었다.

19 그는 자신의 발명품이 실제로 작동했다는 것을 믿을 수 없었다.

20 그의 할아버지에게 Kenneth는 세계 최고의 발명가이다.

21 Kenneth에게 그의 할아버지는 여전히 그의 가장 친한 친구이다.

● 우리말을 참고하여 본문을 영작하시오.

1 Kenneth Shinozuka는 3대의 행복한 대가족에서 자랐다.

➡ _____

2 그는 어렸을 때부터 항상 할아버지와 매우 친했다.

➡ _____

3 그는 Kenneth의 첫 친구이자, 신뢰할 수 있는 운전기사이자, 요리사였다.

➡ _____

4 그는 또한 그에게 많은 인생 교훈을 가르쳐 주었다.

➡ _____

5 그는 Kenneth가 세상에서 가장 존경하는 사람이었다.

➡ _____

6 Kenneth가 네 살이었을 때, 그의 할아버지는 어느 날 산책을 나갔다가 길을 잃었다.

➡ _____

7 그는 알츠하이머병에 걸렸다.

➡ _____

8 Kenneth의 가족 모두는 충격에 빠졌다.

➡ _____

9 그의 상태는 10년 동안 더 악화되었다.

➡ _____

10 그는 자주 밤에 여기저기 돌아다니기 때문에 누군가가 그를 밤새 감시해야 했다.

➡ _____

11 어느 날 밤, Kenneth의 할아버지가 침대에서 일어났는데, Kenneth가 그것을 보았다.

➡ _____

12 그 순간, 그는 혼잣말을 했다. "내가 할아버지의 양말 뒤꿈치에 압력 감지기를 설치하는 게 어떨까?"

➡ _____

13 Kenneth가 해야 할 많은 일들이 있었다.

➡ _____

14 그는 처음에 압력 감지기를 만들고 나서 그의 스마트폰으로 신호를 보낼 방법을 찾아야 했다.

➡ _____

15 Kenneth는 또한 그의 연로한 할아버지에게 편안한 양말을 만들어 주기 위해 많은 다양한 재료들을 가지고 만들어 보았다.

➡ _____

16 그는 포기하고 싶은 생각이 들 때 할아버지의 안전에 대해 생각했다.

➡ _____

17 많은 시행착오 끝에 그는 마침내 자신의 장치를 만드는 데 성공했다.

➡ _____

18 그것이 처음 작동했을 때, 그는 너무 행복해 기뻐서 펄쩍 뛰었다.

➡ _____

19 그는 자신의 발명품이 실제로 작동했다는 것을 믿을 수 없었다.

➡ _____

20 그의 할아버지에게 Kenneth는 세계 최고의 발명가이다.

➡ _____

21 Kenneth에게 그의 할아버지는 여전히 그의 가장 친한 친구이다.

➡ _____

[01~05] 다음 글을 읽고, 물음에 답하시오.

(①) Kenneth Shinozuka grew up in a big happy family of three generations. (②) _____ ⓐ he was little, he has always been very close to his grandfather. (③) He was Kenneth's first friend, his trusty ⓑdrive, and his cook. (④) He was the person _____ ⓒ Kenneth respected the most in the world. (⑤)

01 위 글의 ①~⑤ 중 다음 주어진 문장이 들어갈 알맞은 곳은?

He also taught him many life lessons.

①   ②   ③   ④   ⑤

02 위 글의 빈칸 ⓐ에 알맞은 것은?

① If   ② For
③ Since   ④ When
⑤ After

서답형
03 위 글의 밑줄 친 ⓑ를 알맞은 형으로 고치시오.

➡ _____

04 위 글의 빈칸 ⓒ에 알맞은 것은? (3개)

① who   ② whom
③ which   ④ whose
⑤ that

05 위 글의 내용으로 보아 알 수 없는 것은?

① Kenneth의 가족은 대가족이다.
② Kenneth는 할아버지와 아주 친하게 지내 왔다.
③ Kenneth의 할아버지는 운전을 잘하였다.
④ Kenneth의 할아버지는 Kenneth에게 음식을 요리해 주었다.
⑤ Kenneth는 할아버지를 세상에서 가장 존경했다.

[06~10] 다음 글을 읽고, 물음에 답하시오.

When Kenneth was four, his grandfather went out for a walk one day and got ⓐlose. ①He had Alzheimer's disease. Everyone in Kenneth's family was in shock. ②His condition became worse over the next 10 years. ③He wandered off at night _____ ⓑ often that someone had to keep an eye on ④him all night long. One night, Kenneth's grandfather got out of bed, and Kenneth saw ⓒit. At that moment, ⑤he said to himself, "Why don't I put pressure sensors on the heels of his socks?"

06 위 글의 밑줄 친 ①~⑤ 중 가리키는 대상이 <u>다른</u> 것은?

①   ②   ③   ④   ⑤

서답형
07 위 글의 밑줄 친 ⓐ를 알맞은 형으로 고치시오.

➡ _____

08 위 글의 빈칸 ⓑ에 알맞은 것은?

① too

② so

③ very

④ such

⑤ also

09 위 글의 밑줄 친 ⓒ가 가리키는 것을 우리말로 쓰시오.

➡ _____

10 Kenneth의 할아버지에 관해 위 글의 내용과 일치하지 않는 것은?

① 길을 잃은 적이 있다.

② 알츠하이머병에 걸렸다.

③ 밤에 돌아다녔다.

④ Kenneth를 보살펴 주었다.

⑤ 10년간 건강이 악화되었다.

[11~13] 다음 글을 읽고, 물음에 답하시오.

There were many things ⓐthat Kenneth had to do. He first had to create a pressure sensor and then find a way ⓑto send a signal to his smart phone. Kenneth also tried many different materials to make ⓒcomfort socks for his elderly grandfather.

11 위 글의 밑줄 친 ⓐ와 바꿔 쓸 수 있는 것은?

① who

② how

③ what

④ when

⑤ which

12 위 글의 밑줄 친 ⓑ와 용법이 같은 것은?

① We wished to reach the North Pole.

② I was sad to hear the music.

③ Please give me something to drink.

④ Kate wanted to go to Paris again.

⑤ He must study hard to pass the math exam.

13 위 글의 밑줄 친 ⓒ를 알맞은 형으로 바꿔 쓰시오.

➡ _____

[14~18] 다음 글을 읽고, 물음에 답하시오.

When he felt like giving ___ⓐ___, he thought about his grandfather's safety. (①) After much ⓑtry and error, he finally succeeded in making his device. (②) When it first worked, he was so happy that he jumped ⓒfor joy. (③) For his grandfather, Kenneth is the best inventor in the world. (④) For Kenneth, his grandfather is still his best friend. (⑤)

14 위 글의 ①~⑤ 중 다음 주어진 문장이 들어갈 알맞은 곳은?

He could not believe that his invention actually worked.

①　　　②　　　③　　　④　　　⑤

15 위 글의 빈칸 ⓐ에 알맞은 것은?

① up

② on

③ to

④ over

⑤ with

서답형

16 위 글의 밑줄 친 ⓑ를 알맞은 형으로 고치시오.

➡ _____

17 위 글의 밑줄 친 ⓒ 대신 쓸 수 있는 것은?

① at   ② in
③ over   ④ with
⑤ from

서답형

18 Kenneth가 장비를 만드는 것을 포기하지 않은 이유를 우리말로 쓰시오.

➡ _____

[19~22] 다음 글을 읽고, 물음에 답하시오.

Kenneth Shinozuka grew ___ⓐ___ in a big happy family of three generations. Since he was little, he has always ⓑbe very close to his grandfather. He was Kenneth's first friend, his trusty driver, and his cook. ⓒHe also taught him many life lessons. He was the person ⓓwho Kenneth respected the most in the world.

중요

19 위 글의 빈칸 ⓐ에 알맞은 것은?

① on   ② up
③ to   ④ over
⑤ into

서답형

20 위 글의 밑줄 친 ⓑ를 알맞은 형으로 고치시오.

➡ _____

서답형

21 위 글의 밑줄 친 ⓒ를 우리말로 옮기시오.

➡ _____

중요

22 위 글의 밑줄 친 ⓓ 대신 쓸 수 있는 것은? (2개)

① that   ② whom
③ what   ④ whose
⑤ which

[23~25] 다음 글을 읽고, 물음에 답하시오.

___ⓐ___ Kenneth was four, his grandfather went out for a walk one day and ___ⓑ___ lost. He had Alzheimer's ___ⓒ___. Everyone in Kenneth's family was in shock. His condition became worse over the next 10 years.

23 위 글의 빈칸 ⓐ에 알맞은 것은?

① When   ② If
③ Because   ④ Though
⑤ While

중요

24 위 글의 빈칸 ⓑ에 알맞은 것은?

① made   ② fell
③ got   ④ turned
⑤ became

서답형

25 위 글의 빈칸 ⓒ에 다음 정의에 해당하는 단어를 쓰시오.

> an illness which affects people, animals, or plants, for example one which is caused by bacteria or infection

➡ _____

[26~29] 다음 글을 읽고, 물음에 답하시오.

> He wandered off ___ⓐ___ night so often that someone had to keep an eye on him all night long. ⓑOne night, Kenneth's grandfather got out of bed, and Kenneth saw it. ⓒAt that moment, he said to him, " ___ⓓ___ don't I put pressure sensors on the heels of his socks?"

26 위 글의 빈칸 ⓐ에 알맞은 것은?

① at　　　　　② in
③ on　　　　　④ to
⑤ from

서답형

27 위 글의 밑줄 친 ⓑ를 우리말로 옮기시오.

➡ _____

_____

서답형

28 위 글의 밑줄 친 ⓒ에서 어법상 어색한 것을 고치시오.

_____ ➡ _____

29 위 글의 빈칸 ⓓ에 알맞은 것은?

① How　　　　② Why
③ What　　　　④ When
⑤ Which

[30~32] 다음 글을 읽고, 물음에 답하시오.

> There ①were many things ___ⓐ___ Kenneth had to do. He ②first had to create a pressure sensor and then find a way to send a signal ③to his smart phone. Kenneth ④also tried many different materials ⓑto make comfortable socks ⑤to his elderly grandfather.

30 위 글의 밑줄 친 ①~⑤ 중 어법상 어색한 것은?

①　　　②　　　③　　　④　　　⑤

중요

31 위 글의 빈칸 ⓐ에 알맞은 것은? (2개)

① who　　　　② that
③ whom　　　④ which
⑤ what

32 위 글의 밑줄 친 ⓑ와 용법이 같은 것은?

① My hope is to work as a doctor in Africa.
② It's time to go to bed now.
③ My job is to report the news.
④ The boys hoped to win the baseball game.
⑤ Kate went to a bookstore to buy a book.

[01~06] 다음 글을 읽고, 물음에 답하시오.

When he felt like ⓐgive up, he thought about his grandfather's ___ⓑ___ . After much trial and error, he finally succeeded ___ⓒ___ making his device. When it first worked, ⓓhe was so happy that he jumped for joy. He could not believe that his invention actually worked. For his grandfather, Kenneth is the best ⓔinvent in the world. For Kenneth, his grandfather is still his best friend.

01 위 글의 밑줄 친 ⓐ를 알맞은 형으로 고치시오.

➡ _____

02 위 글의 빈칸 ⓑ에 다음 정의에 해당하는 말을 쓰시오.

the state of being safe from harm or danger

➡ _____

03 위 글의 빈칸 ⓒ에 알맞은 말을 쓰시오.

➡ _____

04 위 글의 밑줄 친 ⓓ와 같은 뜻이 되도록 다음 문장의 빈칸에 알맞은 말을 쓰시오.

he jumped for joy _____ he was very happy.

05 위 글의 밑줄 친 ⓔ를 알맞은 형으로 고치시오.

➡ _____

06 Why was Kenneth happy? Answer in English.

➡ _____

[07~09] 다음 글을 읽고, 물음에 답하시오.

Do you want to help children? Join our Child Care Project in Laos. You'll teach local children. You'll also build a school for them. The work is ⓐ(so, too) hard that you'll want to go home at first, but you'll find ⓑhappy in helping these children.

07 위 글의 괄호 ⓐ에서 알맞은 것을 고르시오.

➡ _____

08 위 글의 밑줄 친 ⓑ를 알맞은 형으로 고치시오.

➡ _____

09 라오스의 Child Care Project가 하고 있는 일 두 가지를 우리말로 쓰시오.

① _____
② _____

[10~14] 다음 글을 읽고, 물음에 답하시오.

Hello, I am Kim Doha, and I would like to join your volunteer project. One day, I saw some poor dogs ___ⓐ___ TV. ⓑThey looked so sad that I wanted to help them. I like dogs, and there are many things ⓒthat I can do for them. I can walk the dogs, give them a bath, and play with them. I am the person who you are looking ___ⓓ___!

10 위 글의 밑줄 친 ⓐ에 알맞은 말을 쓰시오.

➡ _____

11 위 글의 밑줄 친 ⓑ와 같은 뜻이 되도록 다음 문장의 빈칸에 알맞은 말을 쓰시오.

> They looked very sad, _____ I wanted to help them.

12 위 글의 밑줄 친 ⓒ와 바꿔 쓸 수 있는 것을 쓰시오.

➡ _____

13 위 글의 빈칸 ⓓ에 알맞은 말을 쓰시오.

➡ _____

14 What can Kim Doha do for dogs? Answer in Korean.

➡ _____
_____

[15~19] 다음 글을 읽고, 물음에 답하시오.

Kenneth Shinozuka grew ___ⓐ___ in a big happy family of three generations. ⓑSince he was little, he is always been very close to his grandfather. ⓒHe was Kenneth's first friend, his trusty driver, and his cook. ⓓHe also taught him many life lessons. He was the person who Kenneth respected the most in the world.

15 위 글의 빈칸 ⓐ에 알맞은 부사를 쓰시오.

➡ _____

16 위 글의 밑줄 친 ⓑ에서 어법상 어색한 것을 고치시오.

_____ ➡ _____

17 위 글의 밑줄 친 ⓒ에서 Kenneth의 할아버지가 Kenneth에게 한 일 두 가지를 우리말로 쓰시오.

① _____
② _____

18 위 글의 밑줄 친 ⓓ와 같은 뜻이 되도록 다음 문장의 빈칸에 알맞은 말을 쓰시오.

> He also taught many life lessons _____ him.

19 Who did Kenneth respect the most in the world? Answer in English.

➡ _____

해석

Link - Share

I'd like to talk about the volunteer work that we're planning to do for the
관계대명사 목적격(=which)   ~할 계획이다

elderly people in our city. We came up with three activities. One of them is to
                            ~을 생각해 냈다   ~ 중 하나 = three activities

make patbingsu for them and eat it together.
                = the elderly people = patbingsu

구문해설 • volunteer work: 자원봉사 • elderly: 연세가 드신; 어르신들 • acticity: 활동
• together: 함께

나는 우리가 우리 도시의 노인들을 위해 계획하고 있는 자원봉사에 대해 이야기하고 싶다. 우리는 세 가지 활동을 생각해 냈다. 그 중 하나는 그들을 위해 팥빙수를 만들어 함께 먹는 것이다.

Write - Write

Hello, I am Kim Doha, and I would like to join your volunteer project. One
                            would like to+동사원형: ~하고 싶다   어느 날

day, I saw some poor dogs on TV. They looked so sad that I wanted to help
                            텔레비전에서   so ~ that … 구문: 너무 ~해서 …하다

them. I like dogs, and there are many things that I can do for them. I can walk
= some poor dogs   there are + 복수명사: ~이 있다   관계대명사 목적격(=which)

the dogs, give them a bath, and play with them. I am the person who you are
        = give a bath to them   관계대명사 목적격(=that)

looking for!
look for: ~을 찾다

구문해설 • poor: 불쌍한 • sad: 슬픈 • walk: 산책시키다 • bath: 목욕 • person: 사람

안녕, 나는 김도하야, 그리고 나는 너의 자원봉사 프로젝트에 참가하고 싶어. 어느 날, 나는 TV에서 몇 마리의 불쌍한 개들을 보았어. 그들은 너무 슬퍼 보여서 나는 그들을 돕고 싶었어. 나는 개를 좋아하고, 그들을 위해 내가 할 수 있는 많은 것들이 있어. 나는 개들을 산책시키고, 목욕시키고 그들과 함께 놀 수 있어. 네가 찾는 사람이 바로 나야!

Culture Project

Do you want to help children? Join our Child Care Project in Laos. You'll
                            동사원형 ~: ~해라   in + 국가명

teach local children. You'll also build a school for them. The work is so hard
                                            = local children

that you'll want to go home at first, but you'll find happiness in helping these
so ~ that … 구문: 너무 ~해서 …하다   처음에   전치사 in+동명사

children.

구문해설 • care: 보호 • local: 지역의, 현지의 • build: 짓다, 건설하다 • hard: 어려운, 힘든
• happiness: 행복

여러분은 아이들을 돕고 싶나요? 라오스에 있는 우리의 아동 보호 프로젝트에 참여하십시오. 여러분은 지역 아이들을 가르칠 겁니다. 여러분은 또한 그들을 위해 학교를 지을 겁니다. 일이 너무 힘들어 처음에는 집에 가고 싶지만, 이 아이들을 돕는 데서 행복을 찾을 수 있을 겁니다.

01 다음 중 짝지어진 두 단어의 관계가 나머지 넷과 다른 것은?

① true – truly　　② real – really

③ slow – slowly　　④ love – lovely

⑤ actual – actually

02 다음 빈칸에 들어갈 말로 적절하지 않은 것은?

- It's raining _____ than ever.
- He was at the door to _____ us.
- I don't _____ what he's saying.
- The _____ time is 10:50 in the morning.

① local　　　　② understand

③ still　　　　④ worse

⑤ welcome

03 다음 짝지어진 두 단어의 관계가 같도록 빈칸에 알맞은 말을 쓰시오.

warm : cool = light : _____

04 다음 문장의 빈칸에 알맞은 것은?

Kate, take this boy and keep an eye _____ him.

① in　　　　　② on

③ to　　　　　④ for

⑤ with

05 다음 영영풀이에 해당하는 단어는?

to agree with someone, and perhaps help them because you want them to succeed

① advise　　　② fail

③ praise　　　④ share

⑤ support

06 다음 문장의 빈칸에 공통으로 들어갈 말을 쓰시오.

- Andy grew _____ in Paris.
- I hope you can come _____ with a better idea than this.

07 다음 우리말에 맞게 빈칸에 알맞은 말을 쓰시오.

그것은 단지 시행착오의 과정일 뿐이다.
➡ It's just a process of _____ and _____.

08 다음 대화의 빈칸에 알맞지 않은 것은?

A: Can you do me a favor?
B: _____

① Sure.　　　　　② Of course.

③ Sorry, I can't.　　④ I'm afraid I can't.

⑤ I cannot thank too much.

[09~13] 다음 대화를 읽고, 물음에 답하시오.

Jaden: Can you ____ⓐ____ me a favor, Yuri?

Yuri: Sure. What is it, Jaden?

Jaden: Can we go shopping together for a baseball cap for a girl?

Yuri: Yes, of course. Who is it for?

Jaden: It's for my little sister Kate.

Yuri: Oh, are you getting her a birthday gift? (①)

Jaden: No, her birthday isn't ____ⓑ____ October. (②)

Yuri: ⓒThen, why are you getting a baseball cap to her? (③)

Jaden: She broke her leg while she was riding her bike last week. (④)

Yuri: Oh, I see. I can go this Friday afternoon. (⑤)

Jaden: That sounds perfect. Thank you.

09 위 대화의 ①~⑤ 중 다음 주어진 문장이 들어갈 알맞은 곳은?

> I just want to cheer her up.

①   ②   ③   ④   ⑤

10 위 대화의 빈칸 ⓐ에 알맞은 것은?

① do   ② help
③ give   ④ make
⑤ take

11 위 대화의 빈칸 ⓑ에 알맞은 것은?

① on   ② to
③ as   ④ when
⑤ until

12 위 대화의 밑줄 친 ⓒ에서 어법상 어색한 것을 고치시오.

_____ ➡ _____

13 위 대화의 내용으로 보아 대답할 수 없는 질문은?

① What does Jaden want to buy?
② Will Yuri help Jaden buy a baseball cap?
③ Who is Kate?
④ When is Kate's birthday?
⑤ Why did Kate break her leg?

14 다음 대화의 빈칸에 알맞은 것은?

> A: Thank you for helping me with my homework.
>
> B: _____

① Yes, I got it.
② That's great.
③ No problem.
④ You're right.
⑤ I appreciate your help.

Grammar

15 다음 문장의 빈칸에 알맞은 것은?

> I lost the ring _____ my best friend Yujin gave me.

① who   ② how
③ what   ④ which
⑤ where

16 다음 빈칸에 알맞은 말이 바르게 짝지어진 것은?

> Vicky was _____ tired _____ she went to bed early last night.

① so – as
② so – that
③ as – to
④ too – to
⑤ such – to

17 다음 두 문장을 한 문장으로 만들 때 빈칸에 알맞은 말을 쓰시오.

> You are the only friend. I can look to you for advice.
> = You are the only friend to _____ I can look for advice.

18 다음 문장의 빈칸에 알맞은 것은?

> The man was brave enough to save the boy from the fire.
> = The man was _____ brave that he _____ the boy from the fire.

① such – save
② so – save
③ too – saved
④ as – saved
⑤ so – could save

[19~20] 다음 중 어법상 어색한 것을 고르시오.

19 ① The woman with whom I went there is my aunt.
② The man with whom she is talking is Mr. Allen.
③ I have no friends with whom I can talk about it.
④ The people whom I work are all very kind.
⑤ Those whom he lived with respected him.

20 ① My brother is old enough to drive a car.
② I didn't have enough money to buy the sneakers.
③ The policeman was enough fast to catch the pickpocket.
④ I like the doll that Ann gave to me the other day.
⑤ The girl whom you are looking at is my cousin.

21 다음 〈보기〉의 밑줄 친 부분과 쓰임이 다른 하나는?

> ┤ 보기 ├
> Do you know the boy that you saw at the library?

① Meryl Streep is a famous actress that I like a lot.
② He is the smartest boy that I've ever met.
③ The tomato pasta that we ate for lunch was a little spicy.
④ I thought that I had to finish my homework.
⑤ The pants that I'm wearing are very comfortable.

22 다음 문장을 같은 뜻으로 바꿔 쓴 것은?

> My dad is very sick, so he can't go to work.

① My dad is so sick not to go to work.
② My dad is too sick not to go to work.
③ My dad is so sick that he can't go to work.
④ My dad is such sick that he can't go to work.
⑤ My dad is very sick that he can't go to work.

23 다음 밑줄 친 부분의 쓰임이 바르지 <u>않은</u> 것은?

① I know the girl <u>whom</u> you met at the store.
② The woman <u>whom</u> we saw on the street is a famous singer.
③ This is the house in <u>that</u> she was born.
④ Do you know the doctor <u>who</u> I visited last night?
⑤ I cannot find the watch <u>which</u> I bought last week.

Reading

[24~28] 다음 글을 읽고, 물음에 답하시오.

When Kenneth was four, his grandfather went out ____ⓐ____ a walk one day and got lost. He had Alzheimer's disease. ⓑ<u>Everyone in Kenneth's family were in shock.</u> His condition became worse over the next 10 years. He wandered off at night so often that someone had to keep an eye ____ⓒ____ him all night long. One night, Kenneth's grandfather got out of bed, and Kenneth saw it. At that moment, he said to himself, "____ⓓ____ don't I put pressure sensors on the heels of his socks?"

24 위 글의 빈칸 ⓐ에 알맞은 것은?

① to   ② in
③ at   ④ for
⑤ along

25 위 글의 밑줄 친 ⓑ에서 어법상 어색한 것을 고치시오.

_____ ➡ _____

26 위 글의 빈칸 ⓒ에 알맞은 것은?

① at   ② on
③ to   ④ in
⑤ with

27 위 글의 빈칸 ⓓ에 알맞은 것은?

① Why   ② How
③ When   ④ What
⑤ Which

28 위 글의 내용으로 보아 대답할 수 <u>없는</u> 질문은?

① How old was Kenneth when his grandfather got lost?
② What disease did Kenneth's grandfather have?
③ Did Kenneth's grandfather get well?
④ What did Kenneth see one night?
⑤ Did Kenneth put pressure sensors on the heels of his grandfather's socks?

[29~32] 다음 글을 읽고, 물음에 답하시오.

I'd like to talk about the volunteer work ⓐ<u>that</u> we're planning to do for the elderly people in our city. We came ____ⓑ____ with three activities. One of them is to make *patbingsu* ____ⓒ____ them and eat it together.

29 위 글의 밑줄 친 ⓐ와 바꿔 쓸 수 있는 것은?

① who ② whom ③ what
④ whose ⑤ which

30 위 글의 빈칸 ⓑ에 알맞은 것은?

① on ② to ③ in
④ up ⑤ over

31 위 글의 빈칸 ⓒ에 알맞은 것은?

① of ② to ③ for
④ at ⑤ over

32 What is one of three activities? Answer in Korean.

➡ _____

[33~37] 다음 글을 읽고, 물음에 답하시오.

Hello, I am Kim Doha, and I would like to join your ___ⓐ___ project. (①) One day, I saw some poor dogs on TV. (②) ⓑThey looked so sad that I wanted to help them. (③) I can walk the dogs, give them a bath, and play with them. (④) I am the person ⓒwho you are looking for! (⑤)

33 위 대화의 ①~⑤ 중 다음 주어진 문장이 들어갈 알맞은 곳은?

I like dogs, and there are many things that I can do for them.

① ② ③ ④ ⑤

34 위 글의 빈칸 ⓐ에 다음 정의에 해당하는 단어를 쓰시오.

someone who does work without being paid for it, because they want to do it

➡ _____

35 위 글의 밑줄 친 ⓑ와 같은 뜻이 되도록 다음 문장의 빈칸에 알맞은 말을 쓰시오.

They looked very sad, _____ I wanted to help them.

36 위 글의 밑줄 친 ⓒ와 바꿔 쓸 수 있는 것은? (2개)

① whom ② what
③ whose ④ that
⑤ which

37 위 글의 내용으로 보아 대답할 수 없는 질문은?

① What is the writer's name?
② What is Kim Doha's hobby?
③ What did Kim Doha see on TV?
④ How did the dogs look?
⑤ What can Kim Doha do for dogs?

01 출제율 95%

다음 중 짝지어진 단어의 관계가 나머지 넷과 <u>다른</u> 것은?

① wrong : right   ② heavy : light
③ clean : dirty   ④ near : close
⑤ succeed : fail

02 출제율 100%

다음 빈칸에 공통으로 알맞은 것은?

> • Mike is looking _____ his hat.
> • You should be thankful _____ your health.

① at   ② for
③ to   ④ with
⑤ from

03 출제율 90%

다음 중 영영풀이가 <u>잘못된</u> 것은?

① safety: the state of being safe from harm or danger
② always: at all times
③ praise: to agree with someone, and perhaps help them because you want them to succeed
④ inventor: a person who has invented something, or whose job is to invent things
⑤ heel: the back part of your foot, just below your ankle

04 출제율 90%

다음 짝지어진 두 단어의 관계가 같도록 빈칸에 알맞은 말을 쓰시오.

> son : daughter = king : _____

05 출제율 95%

다음 우리말에 맞게 빈칸에 알맞은 말을 쓰시오.

> 낮 동안에 날씨가 더 나빠졌다.
> ➡ The weather got _____ during the day.

06 출제율 90%

다음 대화의 밑줄 친 부분의 의도로 알맞은 것은?

> A: <u>Thank you for taking care of the children.</u>
> B: My pleasure.
> A: You're very kind.

① 제안하기   ② 동의하기
③ 초대하기   ④ 감사하기
⑤ 화남 표현하기

07 출제율 100%

다음 대화의 빈칸에 알맞은 것은?

> A: Can you return this book for me?
> B: _____

① It's a very famous story.
② Sorry, but I'm busy now.
③ No, I will return it for you.
④ It's very kind of you to help me.
⑤ Where should we meet tomorrow?

08 다음 중 짝지어진 대화가 <u>어색한</u> 것은?

① A: Can you do me a favor?
　 B: Sure. What is it?

② A: Can you help me do my homework?
　 B: I'm afraid I can't. I'm busy now.

③ A: Thank you for cleaning the refrigerator.
　 B: My pleasure.

④ A: Thank you for making cookies.
　 B: I'm sorry I can't.

⑤ A: Could you open the door?
　 B: No problem.

[09~11] 다음 대화를 읽고, 물음에 답하시오.

G: Andrew, can you do me a ___ⓐ___ ?
B: O.K. What is it?
G: My family is going to go to Jejudo this ___ⓑ___ . Can you ⓒtake care of my cat during the weekend?
B: Sure. Don't worry about her. And enjoy your trip.

09 위 대화의 빈칸 ⓐ에 알맞은 말을 쓰시오.

➡ _____

10 위 대화의 빈칸 ⓑ에 다음 정의에 해당하는 단어를 쓰시오.

> Saturday and Sunday

➡ _____

11 위 대화의 밑줄 친 ⓒ와 바꿔 쓸 수 있는 것은?

① wait for　　　② look for
③ look after　　④ watch out
⑤ watch on

12 다음 빈칸에 공통으로 알맞은 말은?

> • I like the doll _____ my mom made.
> • Do you know the man _____ Jane wants to meet?

① how　　　② who
③ whom　　④ which
⑤ that

13 다음 빈칸에 알맞은 말이 바르게 짝지어진 것은?

> 그녀의 노래들은 너무 좋아서 나는 마치 꿈속에 있는 것 같다.
> ➡ Her songs are _____ nice _____ I feel like I'm in dream.

① so － as　　　② as － as
③ so － that　　④ such － as
⑤ such － that

14 다음 문장에서 어법상 <u>어색한</u> 부분을 찾아 고치시오.

> When you read, you will often find words you don't know them.

_____ ➡ _____

15 다음 문장에서 어법상 어색한 부분을 찾아 바르게 고쳐 쓰시오

> The cookie was too hard that Shirley almost broke her tooth.

_____ ➡ _____

16 다음 우리말과 일치하도록 괄호 안에 주어진 어구를 배열하시오.

> 이것은 내가 Paul에게 빌렸던 책이다.
> (the book / which / this is / I / from Paul / borrowed)

➡ _____

17 다음 중 밑줄 친 관계대명사가 잘못 쓰인 것은?

① Jack needs a car which he can drive.
② I need a man that can speak English.
③ I know the girl which you are looking for.
④ This is the book which I bought two days ago.
⑤ They saw the old man and his cat that were running in the park.

18 다음 우리말을 참고하여 빈칸에 알맞은 말을 쓰시오.

> 시험이 너무 어려워서 그는 잘 보지 못했다.
> = The test was _____ difficult _____ he didn't do well.

19 다음 문장의 밑줄 친 부분 중 생략할 수 없는 것은?

① This is the story that Kevin wrote.
② The dress which she is wearing is pink.
③ This is the table which his father made.
④ The man whom I saw yesterday was Mr. Brown.
⑤ The man who lives in Seoul will come tomorrow.

[20~23] 다음 글을 읽고, 물음에 답하시오.

> (①) Join our Child Care Project in Laos. You'll teach local children. (②) You'll also build a school for them. (③) The work is so hard that you'll want to go home ____ⓐ____ first. (④) But you'll find happiness in ⓑhelp these children. (⑤)

20 위 글의 ①~⑤ 중 다음 주어진 문장이 들어갈 알맞은 곳은?

> Do you want to help children?

①   ②   ③   ④   ⑤

21 위 글의 빈칸 ⓐ에 알맞은 것은?

① to   ② in
③ at   ④ on
⑤ for

22 위 글의 밑줄 친 ⓑ를 알맞은 형으로 고치시오.

➡ _____

23 출제율 100%
라오스에서 행해지는 Child Care Project의 목적이 무엇인지 우리말로 간단히 쓰시오.

➡ _____

[24~27] 다음 글을 읽고, 물음에 답하시오.

ⓐThere were many things Kenneth had to do. He first had to create a pressure sensor and then find a way ___ⓑ___ a signal to his smart phone. Kenneth also tried many different materials to make comfortable socks ___ⓒ___ his elderly grandfather.

24 출제율 90%
위 글의 밑줄 친 ⓐ를 생략된 관계대명사를 보충하여 다시 쓰시오.

➡ _____
_____

25 출제율 95%
위 글의 빈칸 ⓑ에 알맞은 것은?

① send   ② sending
③ for send   ④ to send
⑤ to sending

26 출제율 90%
위 글의 빈칸 ⓒ에 알맞은 것은?

① at   ② of
③ for   ④ to
⑤ with

27 출제율 85%
What did Kenneth do to make comfortable socks? Answer in Korean.

➡ _____

[28~31] 다음 글을 읽고, 물음에 답하시오.

When he felt ___ⓐ___ giving up, he thought about his grandfather's safety. After much trial and ___ⓑ___, he finally succeeded in making his device. When it first ⓒworked, he was so happy that he jumped for joy. He could not believe that his invention actually worked. For his grandfather, Kenneth is the best inventor in the world. For Kenneth, his grandfather is still his best friend.

28 출제율 90%
위 글의 빈칸 ⓐ에 알맞은 말을 쓰시오.

➡ _____

29 출제율 95%
위 글의 빈칸 ⓑ에 알맞은 것은?

① error   ② fault
③ lie   ④ blame
⑤ mistake

30 출제율 100%
위 글의 밑줄 친 ⓒ와 같은 의미로 쓰인 것은?

① I can't work if it is cold.
② Mary worked at mathematics last night.
③ Can you work this computer?
④ Mr. Jackson worked for an oil company.
⑤ The brakes on this car don't work.

31 출제율 90%
Why was Kenneth happy? Answer in English.

➡ _____

[01~03] 다음 글을 읽고, 물음에 답하시오.

> A: Can you ___ⓐ___ me a favor?
> B: Sure. What is it?
> A: Can you move this table with me? It's too ___ⓑ___ .
> B: Sure. No problem.
> A: Thank you for ⓒ<u>help</u> me.

01 위 대화의 빈칸 ⓐ에 알맞은 말을 쓰시오.

➡ _____

02 위 대화의 빈칸 ⓑ에 다음 정의에 해당하는 말을 쓰시오.

weighing a lot

➡ _____

03 위 대화의 밑줄 친 ⓒ를 알맞은 형으로 고치시오.

➡ _____

04 다음 대화의 순서를 바르게 배열하시오.

> (A) Yes, I can.
> (B) Sure. What is it?
> (C) Mark, can you do me a favor?
> (D) My family is going on vacation for a week. Can you come to our house and water the plants?

➡ _____

05 다음 괄호 안에 주어진 단어를 배열하여 문장을 완성하시오.

(1) Mr. Brown is a teacher (everyone, class, my, whom, in) respects.
   ➡ Mr. Brown is a teacher _____
      _____ respects.

(2) The movie (I, to, watch, want, which) is *Shrek*.
   ➡ The movie _____ is
      Shrek.

06 다음 〈조건〉에 맞게 괄호 안의 단어를 이용하여 우리말을 영어로 옮기시오.

> ┤ 조건 ├
> 1. 주어진 단어를 모두 이용할 것.
> 2. 필요시 관사를 붙이거나 단어를 추가하고 동사의 어형 변화를 할 것.
> 3. 대·소문자 및 구두점에 유의할 것.

(1) 음식이 너무 매워서 Chris는 많이 먹을 수 없었다. (spicy, that, can, eat, much)
   ➡ _____
      _____

(2) 날씨가 너무 추워서 우리는 소풍을 갈 수가 없었다. (it, too, for, go, picnic)
   ➡ _____

(3) 그는 저 자동차를 살 수 있을 만큼 부자이다. (rich, enough, buy)
   ➡ _____

07 다음 문장에서 어법상 <u>어색한</u> 부분을 찾아 바르게 고쳐 쓰시오.

I have a pen what my father gave me.

_____ ➡ _____

12 Why was everyone in Kenneth's family in shock? Answer in English.

➡ _____

_____

[13~16] 다음 글을 읽고, 물음에 답하시오.

[08~12] 다음 글을 읽고, 물음에 답하시오.

When Kenneth was four, his grandfather went out for a walk one day and ⓐgot lost. He had Alzheimer's disease. Everyone in Kenneth's family was in shock. His condition became ⓑbad over the next 10 years. He wandered off at night so often _____ⓒ_____ someone had to keep an eye on him all night long. One night, Kenneth's grandfather got out of bed, and Kenneth saw it. At that moment, he said to ⓓ(him, himself), "Why don't I put pressure sensors on the heels of his socks?"

There were many things ⓐthat Kenneth had to do. He first had to _____ⓑ_____ a pressure sensor and then find a way to send a signal to his smart phone. Kenneth also tried many different materials ⓒmake comfortable socks for his elderly grandfather.

08 위 글의 밑줄 친 ⓐ를 우리말로 옮기시오.

➡ _____

13 위 글의 밑줄 친 ⓐ와 바꿔 쓸 수 있는 것을 쓰시오.

➡ _____

14 위 글의 빈칸 ⓑ에 다음 정의에 해당하는 단어를 주어진 철자로 시작하여 쓰시오.

to cause something to happen or exist

➡ c_____

09 위 글의 밑줄 친 ⓑ를 알맞은 어형으로 고치시오.

➡ _____

★ 중요
15 위 글의 밑줄 친 ⓒ를 알맞은 형으로 고치시오.

➡ _____

★ 중요
10 위 글의 빈칸 ⓒ에 알맞은 말을 쓰시오.

➡ _____

16 위 글에서 Kenneth가 할아버지를 위해 한 일을 우리말로 쓰시오.

➡ _____

_____

11 위 글의 괄호 ⓓ에서 알맞은 것을 고르시오.

➡ _____

01 다음 주어진 어구를 이용하여 예시와 같이 쓰시오.

Teacher	teach, students, school	ex) A teacher is someone who teaches students at a school.
Waiter	serve, food, restaurant	(1)
Zookeeper	look after, animals, zoo	(2)
Dessert	sweet food, serve, after meal	(3)

the woman	I, met	ex) She is the woman whom I met in the park yesterday.
the sport	Ann, play, table tennis	(4)
the camera	you, got	(5)
the woman	I, talk about	(6)

(1) _____

(2) _____

(3) _____

(4) _____

(5) _____

(6) _____

02 다음 어구를 이용하여 〈보기〉와 같이 여러분의 상황에 맞게 영어 문장을 쓰시오. (3개 이상)

enough ... to   too ... to   so ... that
last year   last month   this year   yesterday   now
old   young   tall   short   strong   weak   early   late   noisy   quiet   light   heavy   busy

보기

Last year, I was too short to play basketball, but now I'm tall enough to play it.

(1) _____

(2) _____

(3) _____

단원별 모의고사

01 다음 중 우리말 뜻이 <u>잘못된</u> 것은?

① wander off: 여기저기 쏘다니다
② feel like -ing: ~하고 싶은 기분이다
③ at first: 마침내
④ for joy: 기뻐서
⑤ take care of: ~을 돌보다

02 다음 영영풀이에 해당하는 단어로 알맞은 것은?

an illness which affects people, animals, or plants, for example one which is caused by bacteria or infection

① disease
② death
③ treat
④ health
⑤ hospital

03 다음 빈칸에 알맞은 말이 바르게 짝지어진 것은?

• Will you do me a _____?
• The car won't start, can you _____ it?

① favor – fix
② pardon – mend
③ excuse – fix
④ service – mend
⑤ favor – attend

04 다음 짝지어진 두 단어의 관계가 같도록 빈칸에 알맞은 말을 쓰시오.

rain : rainy = luck : _____

05 다음 빈칸에 공통으로 들어갈 말을 쓰시오.

• I want to become a minister when I grow _____.
• They gave _____ without a fight.

06 다음 대화를 의미가 통하도록 알맞게 배열한 것은?

(A) Great! I'm having a birthday party this weekend. Can you come?
(B) Sure. Thank you for inviting me.
(C) Nothing special. I'll just stay home and watch TV.
(D) What are you doing this weekend, Eric?

① (A) – (D) – (B) – (C)
② (B) – (C) – (A) – (D)
③ (C) – (D) – (B) – (A)
④ (D) – (B) – (C) – (A)
⑤ (D) – (C) – (A) – (B)

07 다음 중 짝지어진 대화가 <u>어색한</u> 것은?

① A: May I ask you a favor?
　 B: No problem. What is it?
② A: Can you bring me a cup of coffee?
　 B: You're welcome.
③ A: Can you help me find my key?
　 B: Sorry, I can't. I have to go out now.
④ A: Thank you for taking care of my dog.
　 B: My pleasure.
⑤ A: Can you help me with something?
　 B: Sure. What's up?

08 다음 대화에서 밑줄 친 부분의 의도로 알맞은 것은?

> A: <u>Can you do me a favor?</u>
> B: Sure. What is it?
> A: Can you help me clean the board?
> B: No problem.

① 충고하기　　　② 초대하기
③ 위치 확인하기　　④ 도움 요청하기
⑤ 음식 주문하기

[09~13] 다음 대화를 읽고, 물음에 답하시오.

> Jaden: Can you do me a favor, Yuri?
> Yuri: Sure. What is it, Jaden? (①)
> Jaden: Can we go shopping together ___ⓐ___ a baseball cap for a girl? (②)
> Yuri: Yes, of course. (③)
> Jaden: It's for my little sister Kate. (④)
> Yuri: ⓑOh, are you getting her a birthday gift? (⑤)
> Jaden: No, her birthday isn't until October.
> Yuri: Then, why are you getting a baseball cap ___ⓒ___ her?
> Jaden: She broke her leg while she was riding her bike last week. I just want to cheer her up.
> Yuri: Oh, I see. I can go this Friday afternoon.
> Jaden: That sounds perfect. Thank you.

09 위 대화의 ①~⑤ 중 다음 주어진 문장이 들어갈 알맞은 곳은?

> Who is it for?

①　　②　　③　　④　　⑤

10 위 대화의 빈칸 ⓐ에 알맞은 전치사를 쓰시오.

➡ _____

11 위 대화의 밑줄 친 ⓑ를 우리말로 옮기시오.

➡ _____

12 위 대화의 빈칸 ⓒ에 알맞은 것은?

① to　　　　② for
③ in　　　　④ of
⑤ with

13 위 대화의 내용과 일치하지 <u>않는</u> 것은?

① Jaden wants to go shopping with Yuri.
② Jaden will buy a baseball cap for Yuri.
③ Jaden's little sister's name is Kathy.
④ Kathy broke her leg last week.
⑤ Yuri will go shopping with Jaden this Friday afternoon.

14 다음 빈칸에 공통으로 알맞은 것은?

> • My dad bought me a bag _____ was black.
> • I know the man _____ you are looking for.

① how　　　　② who
③ that　　　　④ whom
⑤ which

15 다음 두 문장의 의미가 같도록 할 때 빈칸에 알맞은 것은?

> The bags are so heavy that I can't carry them.
> = The bags are _____ heavy _____ carry.

① so – as　　　　② too – to
③ as – that　　　　④ very – to
⑤ such – that

16 다음 밑줄 친 that의 쓰임이 나머지와 다른 하나는?

① He is the man that I can trust.
② That is the dog that I really love.
③ I know the man that is singing a song.
④ I like the car that you bought yesterday.
⑤ She is wearing a sweater that she bought yesterday.

17 다음 문장 중 어법상 어색한 것은? (2개)

① You are too young to go swimming alone.
② Kate didn't have enough money to buy the smart phone.
③ She was enough kind to help the old woman.
④ This puzzle is so difficult that I can't solve.
⑤ Dad walked too fast for me to catch up with.

18 다음 문장의 빈칸에 알맞은 것은? (2개)

> Javlon's father got a new job in Korea, so his family moved to Seoul three months ago. Let's look at the writings _____ Javlon posted on his blog.

① who   ② whom
③ what   ④ that
⑤ which

19 다음 두 문장이 같은 의미가 되도록 빈칸에 알맞은 말을 쓰시오.

> The chair is so small that I can't sit on it.
> = The chair is _____ small for me _____ sit on.

20 다음 밑줄 친 부분 중 생략할 수 있는 것은?

① I know a boy whose name is Mark.
② He bought me a bag which was red.
③ I don't like the boy who makes a noise.
④ The cake that he baked was very nice.
⑤ Do you know the man who is playing with a ball?

[21~26] 다음 글을 읽고, 물음에 답하시오.

> Hello, I am Kim Doha, and I would like to ____ⓐ____ your volunteer project. One day, I saw some poor dogs ____ⓑ____ TV. They looked so sad ⓒthat I wanted to help them. ⓓI like dogs, and there are many things I can do for them. I can walk the dogs, give them a bath, and play with them. I am the person ⓔwho you are looking for!

21 위 글의 빈칸 ⓐ에 알맞은 것은?

① agree   ② pass
③ join   ④ belong
⑤ share

22 위 글의 빈칸 ⓑ에 알맞은 것은?

① on   ② in
③ at   ④ with
⑤ from

23 위 글의 밑줄 친 ⓒ와 용법이 같은 것은?

① It is strange that she doesn't come.
② It was such a big noise that we were awakened.
③ Look at the trees that stand on the hill.
④ It was here that she first met Mike.
⑤ This is the doll that my mother made for me.

24 위 글의 밑줄 친 ⓓ를 생략된 관계대명사를 보충하여 다시 쓰시오.

➡ _____

_____

25 위 글의 밑줄 친 ⓔ와 바꿔 쓸 수 있는 것은? (2개)

① that   ② what
③ whose   ④ whom
⑤ which

26 위 글의 내용과 일치하지 않는 것은?

① 김도하는 자원봉사 프로젝트에 가입하기를 원한다.
② 김도하는 텔레비전에서 불쌍한 개들을 보았다.
③ 김도하는 개를 좋아한다.
④ 김도하는 개를 목욕시킬 수 있다.
⑤ 김도하는 자원봉사 프로젝트에 적합하지 않다.

[27~30] 다음 글을 읽고, 물음에 답하시오.

_____ ⓐ _____ he felt like giving up, he thought about his grandfather's safety. (①) After much trial and error, he finally succeeded in making his device. (②) When it first worked, he was so happy _____ ⓑ _____ he jumped for joy. (③) He could not believe _____ ⓒ _____ his invention ⓓactual worked. (④) For Kenneth, his grandfather is still his best friend. (⑤)

27 위 글의 ①~⑤ 중 다음 주어진 문장이 들어갈 알맞은 곳은?

For his grandfather, Kenneth is the best inventor in the world.

①   ②   ③   ④   ⑤

28 위 글의 빈칸 ⓐ에 알맞은 것은? (2개)

① If   ② As
③ When   ④ Though
⑤ Because

29 위 글의 빈칸 ⓑ와 ⓒ에 공통으로 알맞은 것은?

① what   ② whether
③ that   ④ which
⑤ though

30 위 글의 밑줄 친 ⓓ를 알맞은 어형으로 고치시오.

➡ _____

1학기 전과정

적중100 plus

영어 기출문제집

영어 중 2

미래 | 최연희

Best Collection

내용문의 중등영어발전소 적중100 편집부 TEL 070-7707-0457

INSIGHT
on the textbook

교과서 파헤치기

영어 기출 문제집

적중100 plus
1학기 전과정

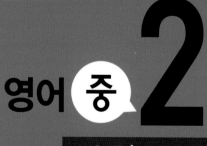

영어 중 2

미래 | 최연희

INSIGHT
on the textbook

교과서 파헤치기

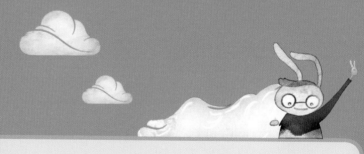

※ 다음 영어를 우리말로 쓰시오.

01 real	22 someone
02 tooth	23 practice
03 unique	24 ranger
04 vote	25 cloudy
05 wrong	26 activity
06 president	27 coworker
07 cartoonist	28 adventurous
08 recycle	29 decide
09 danger	30 awesome
10 push-up	31 skill
11 funny	32 skip stones
12 husband	33 cheerfully
13 janitor	34 speech
14 joke	35 be good at
15 jump rope	36 make one's day
16 listener	37 do a good job
17 nervous	38 fall asleep
18 once	39 give away
19 character	40 be good for
20 become	41 say hello to
21 superhero	42 such as
	43 be afraid of

※ 다음 우리말을 영어로 쓰시오.

01 기량, 기술 _____

02 실제로 _____

03 진정한, 진짜의 _____

04 이, 이빨 _____

05 여행하다 _____

06 독특한 _____

07 슈퍼히어로 _____

08 대통령, 회장 _____

09 물수제비뜨다 _____

10 투표하다 _____

11 연설, 담화 _____

12 틀린, 잘못된 _____

13 연습하다 _____

14 위험 _____

15 ～할 만큼 (충분히) _____

16 소설 _____

17 모험성이 강한 _____

18 문지기, 수위 _____

19 결정하다 _____

20 우스운 _____

21 만화가 _____

22 재활용[재생]하다 _____

23 남편 _____

24 대단한, 굉장히 좋은 _____

25 줄넘기를 하다 _____

26 기분 좋게 _____

27 불안해[초조해] 하는 _____

28 그림, 데생 _____

29 농담 _____

30 밖에(서) _____

31 각[매], ～당[마다] _____

32 공원[삼림] 관리원 _____

33 요리책 _____

34 동료 _____

35 ～와 같은 _____

36 ～에 좋다 _____

37 있잖아, 알겠니? _____

38 ～을 잘하다 _____

39 ～을 두려워하다 _____

40 잠들다 _____

41 마침내, 드디어 _____

42 ～을 보다 _____

43 조심하다 _____

※ 다음 영영풀이에 알맞은 단어를 <보기>에서 골라 쓴 후, 우리말 뜻을 쓰시오.

1 _____ : something that is said or done to make you laugh, for example a funny story: _____

2 _____ : the possibility that you will be hurt or killed: _____

3 _____ : a person who is making a speech or giving a talk: _____

4 _____ : a person whose job is to look after a building: _____

5 _____ : to be present at a meeting or event: _____

6 _____ : the hard white object in your mouth, which you use for biting and chewing: _____

7 _____ : a person whose job is to draw cartoons for newspapers and magazines: _____

8 _____ : a short period when you stop doing something before continuing: _____

9 _____ : the ability to speak or the act of speaking: _____

10 _____ : frightened or worried about something that is happening or might happen: _____

11 _____ : a long written story about imaginary people and events: _____

12 _____ : a small light motorcycle which has a low seat: _____

13 _____ : one of the sixty parts that a minute is divided into: _____

14 _____ : a restaurant where you choose your food from a counter and take it to your table after paying for it: _____

15 _____ : the people you work with, especially people on the same job or project as you: _____

16 _____ : to process things that have already been used, such as bottles or sheets of paper so that they can be used again: _____

보기			
scooter	cartoonist	attend	joke
cafeteria	danger	recycle	speaker
coworker	novel	speech	janitor
tooth	second	pause	nervous

※ 다음 우리말과 일치하도록 빈칸에 알맞은 말을 쓰시오.

해석

Listen & Speak 1 A. Listen and Check

1. B: What _____ you _____, Nami?

   G: I'm _____ a smart phone case _____ _____ my old jeans.

   B: Wow! You're _____ _____ _____ old things.

   G: Thanks. I _____ _____. It's fun, and it's also _____ _____ our Earth.

2. B: Hello, everyone. I'm Kim Yujin. I want _____ _____ your _____ president. I'm a good _____ and always _____ _____ _____ others. I'm also _____ _____ _____ fun school activities. I'll _____ _____ for our class, so please _____ _____ me. Thank you _____ _____!

Listen & Speak 2 A. Listen and Check

1. B: Hi, Cindy. _____ something _____?

   G: I _____ _____ give a speech _____ _____ _____ the whole school. I'm so _____.

   B: _____ worry. You're a very _____ _____. I'm _____ you'll _____ _____ _____ _____.

   G: Thanks, Minho. I _____ _____ _____ _____ now.

2. G: Tomorrow is _____ _____ birthday. What _____ I do _____ her?

   B: _____ _____ _____ bake a cake for her? You're _____ _____ _____.

   G: That's a good _____. I hope my mom _____ _____ my cake.

   B: _____ _____ your mom _____ _____ it.

1. B: 나미야, 뭐 하고 있니?
   G: 오래된 청바지로 스마트폰 케이스를 만들고 있어.
   B: 와! 너 오래된 것들을 재활용하는 것을 잘하는구나.
   G: 고마워. 나는 재활용하는 것을 좋아해. 그것은 재미있고, 우리의 지구에도 좋아.

2. B: 여러분, 안녕하세요. 저는 김유진입니다. 저는 여러분의 반 학급회장이 되고 싶습니다. 저는 남의 말을 잘 경청하고 항상 다른 사람들을 도우려고 노력합니다. 저는 재미있는 학교 활동 계획도 잘합니다. 저는 우리 반을 위해 열심히 일하겠으니 저에게 투표해 주세요. 들어주셔서 감사합니다!

1. B: 안녕, Cindy. 무슨 일 있니?
   G: 난 학교 전체 학생 앞에서 연설을 해야 해. 아주 긴장이 돼.
   B: 걱정하지 마. 너는 말을 아주 잘하잖아. 분명히 잘할 거야.
   G: 고마워, 민호야. 이제 기분이 훨씬 좋아졌어.

2. G: 내일은 우리 엄마의 생일이야. 내가 엄마를 위해 무엇을 해야 할까?
   B: 너의 엄마를 위해 케이크를 굽는 건 어때? 넌 빵을 잘 굽잖아.
   G: 좋은 생각이야. 엄마가 내 케이크를 좋아하셨으면 좋겠다.
   B: 너의 엄마는 분명히 아주 좋아하실 거야.

Communicate A. Listen and Answer

1. **Yuri:** What _____ you _____, Jaden?

   Jaden: I'm _____ _____.

   Yuri: Really? _____ I _____ a look _____ them?

   Jaden: No, _____ _____.

   Yuri: Why _____? You can show me a few, _____ _____?

   Jaden: Well, I _____ so.

   Yuri: (*pause*) Ha, ha, ha! _____! I like your cartoons. You're really _____ _____ _____.

   Jaden: Do you _____ _____? I want _____ _____ a cartoonist, but I don't think my _____ _____ are good _____.

   Yuri: Your cartoons are really _____, and you have _____ _____. I'm _____ you'll be a great _____.

   Jaden: Thank you, Yuri. You just _____ my day.

2. **A:** Why _____ you join our musical theater club? You're _____ _____ singing.

   B: Well, I'd _____ _____, but I don't think I'm good at _____ or _____.

   A: _____ worry. We can _____ _____. I'm sure you'll learn _____. Just _____ _____.

   B: O.K. I'll _____ _____ it.

Progress Check

1. **B:** _____ are you _____?

   G: I'm _____ _____ for dinner.

   B: Wow! You're really _____ _____ cooking!

   G: Thanks.

2. **B:** _____ something _____?

   G: I have to _____ _____ _____ in English. I'm so _____.

   B: Don't _____. Practice your speech _____ your family. I'm sure you'll do a _____ _____.

   G: Thank you. I'll _____.

3. **W:** Everybody _____ _____ _____ something. _____ people are good at drawing. _____ people are good at singing. What _____ you _____?

1. 유리: 너 뭐 하고 있니, Jaden?
   Jaden: 만화를 그리고 있어.
   유리: 정말? 내가 그것들을 봐도 되니?
   Jaden: 아니, 아직은 아니야.
   유리: 왜 안 되는데? 몇 개 보여줄 수 있지, 안 그래?
   Jaden: 음, 그럴 수 있지.
   유리: (멈춤) 하, 하, 하! 대단해! 너의 만화가 마음에 들어. 넌 그림을 정말 잘 그리는구나.
   Jaden: 그렇게 생각하니? 나는 만화가가 되고 싶지만, 내 그림 그리는 기술이 충분히 능숙하지 않다고 생각해.
   유리: 네 만화들은 정말 재미있고, 독특한 캐릭터를 가지고 있어. 나는 네가 훌륭한 만화가가 될 거라고 확신해.
   Jaden: 고마워, 유리야. 넌 날 행복하게 해줬어.

2. A: 우리 뮤지컬 연극 동아리에 가입하는 게 어때? 노래를 잘하는구나.
   B: 음, 그러고 싶지만, 연기나 춤을 잘 못해.
   A: 걱정하지 마. 우리가 가르쳐 줄 수 있어. 나는 네가 빨리 배울 거라고 확신해. 그냥 우리와 함께 해.
   B: 좋아. 생각해 볼게.

1. B: 너 뭐 하고 있니?
   G: 저녁으로 피자를 만들고 있어.
   B: 와! 넌 요리를 정말 잘하는구나!
   G: 고마워.

2. B: 무슨 문제 있어?
   G: 영어로 연설을 해야 해. 아주 긴장이 돼.
   B: 걱정하지 마. 가족 앞에서 연설을 연습해 봐. 넌 분명히 잘할 거야.
   G: 고마워. 그렇게 해볼게.

3. W: 모든 사람은 잘하는 것이 있습니다. 어떤 사람들은 그림을 잘 그립니다. 또 어떤 사람들은 노래를 잘 부릅니다. 당신은 무엇을 잘합니까?

※ 다음 우리말에 맞도록 대화를 영어로 쓰시오.

Listen & Speak 1 A. Listen and Check

1. B: _____

   G: _____

   B: _____

   G: _____

2. B: _____

   _____

   _____

   _____

Listen & Speak 2 A. Listen and Check

1. B: _____

   G: _____

   B: _____

   G: _____

2. G: _____

   B: _____

   G: _____

   B: _____

해석

1. B: 나미야, 뭐 하고 있니?
   G: 오래된 청바지로 스마트폰 케이스를 만들고 있어.
   B: 와! 너 오래된 것들을 재활용하는 것을 잘하는구나.
   G: 고마워. 나는 재활용하는 것을 좋아해. 그것은 재미있고, 우리의 지구에도 좋아.

2. B: 여러분, 안녕하세요. 저는 김유진입니다. 저는 여러분의 반 학급회장이 되고 싶습니다. 저는 남의 말을 잘 경청하고 항상 다른 사람들을 도우려고 노력합니다. 저는 재미있는 학교 활동 계획도 잘합니다. 저는 우리 반을 위해 열심히 일하겠으니 저에게 투표해 주세요. 들어주셔서 감사합니다!

1. B: 안녕, Cindy. 무슨 일 있니?
   G: 난 학교 전체 학생 앞에서 연설을 해야 해. 아주 긴장이 돼.
   B: 걱정하지 마. 너는 말을 아주 잘하잖아. 분명히 잘할 거야.
   G: 고마워, 민호야. 이제 기분이 훨씬 좋아졌어.

2. G: 내일은 우리 엄마의 생일이야. 내가 엄마를 위해 무엇을 해야 할까?
   B: 너의 엄마를 위해 케이크를 굽는 건 어때? 넌 빵을 잘 굽잖아.
   G: 좋은 생각이야. 엄마가 내 케이크를 좋아하셨으면 좋겠다.
   B: 너의 엄마는 분명히 아주 좋아하실 거야.

Communicate A. Listen and Answer

1. Yuri: _____

   Jaden: _____

   Yuri: _____

   Jaden: _____

   Yuri: _____

   Jaden: _____

   Yuri: _____

   _____

   Jaden: _____

   _____

   Yuri: _____

   _____

   Jaden: _____

2. A: _____

   B: _____

   A: _____

   B: _____

Progress Check

1. B: _____

   G: _____

   B: _____

   G: _____

2. B: _____

   G: _____

   B: _____

   _____

   G: _____

3. W: _____

   _____

1. 유리: 너 뭐 하고 있니, Jaden?
   Jaden: 만화를 그리고 있어.
   유리: 정말? 내가 그것들을 봐도 되니?
   Jaden: 아니, 아직은 아니야.
   유리: 왜 안 되는데? 몇 개 보여줄 수 있지, 안 그래?
   Jaden: 음, 그럴 수 있지.
   유리: (멈춤) 하, 하, 하! 대단해! 너의 만화가 마음에 들어. 넌 그림을 정말 잘 그리는구나.
   Jaden: 그렇게 생각하니? 나는 만화가가 되고 싶지만, 내 그림 그리는 기술이 충분히 능숙하지 않다고 생각해.
   유리: 네 만화들은 정말 재미있고, 독특한 캐릭터를 가지고 있어. 나는 네가 훌륭한 만화가가 될 거라고 확신해.
   Jaden: 고마워, 유리야. 넌 날 행복하게 해줬어.

2. A: 우리 뮤지컬 연극 동아리에 가입하는 게 어때? 노래를 잘하는구나.
   B: 음, 그러고 싶지만, 연기나 춤을 잘 못해.
   A: 걱정하지 마. 우리가 가르쳐 줄 수 있어. 나는 네가 빨리 배울 거라고 확신해. 그냥 우리와 함께 해.
   B: 좋아. 생각해 볼게.

1. B: 너 뭐 하고 있니?
   G: 저녁으로 피자를 만들고 있어.
   B: 와! 넌 요리를 정말 잘하는구나!
   G: 고마워.

2. B: 무슨 문제 있어?
   G: 영어로 연설을 해야 해. 아주 긴장이 돼.
   B: 걱정하지 마. 가족 앞에서 연설을 연습해 봐. 넌 분명히 잘할 거야.
   G: 고마워. 그렇게 해볼게.

3. W: 모든 사람은 잘하는 것이 있습니다. 어떤 사람들은 그림을 잘 그립니다. 또 어떤 사람들은 노래를 잘 부릅니다. 당신은 무엇을 잘합니까?

※ 다음 우리말과 일치하도록 빈칸에 알맞은 것을 골라 쓰시오.

1 _____ name is Hojin, and I _____ to make graphic _____.
A. novels　　　　B. like　　　　C. my

2 _____ I was _____ home from school last week, I _____ a woman _____ a scooter.
A. saw　　　B. on　　　C. walking　　　D. while

3 She _____ really _____, and her scooter was very _____.
A. unique　　　B. cool　　　C. looked

4 "Are you _____ home, Hojin?" she _____ to me _____.
A. suddenly　　　B. said　　　C. going

5 "Yes, _____ do I know you?" I _____.
A. asked　　　B. but

6 "Of _____," she _____.
A. answered　　　　B. course

7 "I _____ you at the school _____ _____ day."
A. cafeteria　　　B. every　　　C. see

8 _____, she was one _____ the cafeteria _____ at school.
A. workers　　　B. of　　　C. surprisingly

9 "Amazing! She looks so _____ _____ the school," I _____.
A. outside　　　B. thought　　　C. different

10 "I _____ write a _____ novel about _____."
A. her　　　B. graphic　　　C. should

11 _____ I _____ home, I _____ to write a new graphic novel, *Lunch Lady Begins*.
A. began　　　B. got　　　C. after

12 _____ it, Lunch Lady is a _____.
A. superhero　　　B. in

13 She _____ a _____ scooter _____ can fly.
A. that　　　B. super　　　C. rides

14 She _____ people from _____ _____ the world.
A. danger　　　B. saves　　　C. around

15 She also makes 100 cookies _____ _____ and gives them _____ to hungry children.
A. away　　　B. second　　　C. per

---

1 내 이름은 호진이고, 만화 소설 쓰는 것을 좋아한다.

2 지난주에 나는 학교에서 집으로 걸어가던 중에 스쿠터에 탄 여자를 보았다.

3 그녀는 정말 멋져 보였고 그녀의 스쿠터는 매우 독특했다.

4 "호진아, 너 집에 가는 중이니?" 그녀가 갑자기 나에게 말했다.

5 "네, 그런데 저를 아시나요?" 나는 물었다.

6 "물론이지."라고 그녀가 대답했다.

7 "난 매일 학교 식당에서 너를 본단다."

8 놀랍게도, 그녀는 학교 식당 직원 중 한 명이었다.

9 "놀라워! 그녀는 학교 밖에서는 아주 달라 보여."라고 나는 생각했다.

10 "그녀에 대한 만화 소설을 써야 겠다."

11 집에 도착한 후, 나는 〈런치 레이디 탄생하다〉라는 새로운 만화 소설을 쓰기 시작했다.

12 그 소설에서 런치 레이디는 슈퍼히어로이다.

13 그녀는 날 수 있는 슈퍼 스쿠터를 탄다.

14 그녀는 전 세계의 위험에 빠진 사람들을 구한다.

15 그녀는 또한 1초에 100개의 쿠키를 만들어 배고픈 아이들에게 나누어 준다.

16 A _____ days _____, I showed my _____ novel to my friends.

    A. graphic   B. later   C. few

17 "_____! I love this _____. She's so _____," said all my friends.

    A. cool   B. superhero   C. awesome

18 "_____ what? I modeled her _____ Ms. Lee, one of our cafeteria _____," I told them.

    A. on   B. guess   C. workers

19 I showed _____ book _____ Ms. Lee.

    A. to   B. my

20 She _____ it, _____.

    A. too   B. loved

21 She _____ told me about her _____ who had special _____.

    A. talents   B. coworkers   C. also

22 Ms. Park, _____ cafeteria worker, _____ a _____ contest.

    A. dancing   B. won   C. another

23 Mr. Kim, the _____ at our school, was once an _____ park _____.

    A. ranger   B. adventurous   C. janitor

24 "I'd _____ to write _____ stories about them. Do you _____ they'll like that?" I _____ Ms. Lee.

    A. think   B. superhero   C. asked   D. like

25 "Of _____ they will," she said _____.

    A. cheerfully   B. course

26 "Let's _____ and say _____ to _____ new superhero friends."

    A. our   B. hello   C. go

16 며칠 후에 나는 나의 만화 소설을 친구들에게 보여 주었다.

17 "멋져! 나는 이 슈퍼히어로가 너무 좋아. 그녀는 아주 멋져."라고 내 모든 친구들이 말했다.

18 "있잖아. 나는 그녀를 우리 식당 직원 중 한 명인 이 여사를 모델로 했어."라고 나는 친구들에게 말했다.

19 나는 이 여사에게 내 책을 보여 주었다.

20 그녀도 그것을 아주 좋아했다.

21 그녀는 또한 나에게 특별한 재능을 가진 그녀의 동료들에 대해 말해 주었다.

22 또 다른 식당 직원인 박 여사는 댄스 경연대회에서 우승했다.

23 우리 학교의 관리인인 김 선생님은 한때 모험적인 공원 관리원이었다.

24 "저는 그들에 대한 슈퍼히어로 이야기를 쓰고 싶어요. 그분들이 그걸 좋아할 것 같아요?" 나는 이 여사한테 물어보았다.

25 "물론 그럴 거야."라고 그녀가 기분 좋게 말했다.

26 "가서 우리의 새 슈퍼히어로 친구들에게 인사하자."

※ 다음 우리말과 일치하도록 빈칸에 알맞은 말을 쓰시오.

1 _____ _____ is Hojin, and I like to make _____ _____.

2 _____ I was _____ _____ from school last week, I _____ a woman _____ a scooter.

3 She _____ really _____, and her scooter was very _____.

4 "Are you _____ _____, Hojin?" she _____ to me _____.

5 "Yes, _____ do I know you?" I _____.

6 "Of _____," she _____.

7 "I see you _____ the school cafeteria _____ _____."

8 _____, she was _____ _____ the cafeteria _____ at school.

9 "Amazing! She _____ so _____ outside the school," I _____.

10 "I _____ _____ a graphic novel about her."

11 _____ I _____ _____, I began to write a new _____ _____, *Lunch Lady Begins*.

12 _____ it, Lunch Lady is a _____.

13 She _____ a super scooter that _____ _____.

14 She _____ people from danger _____ _____ _____.

15 She also makes 100 cookies _____ _____ and _____ them _____ to hungry children.

1 내 이름은 호진이고, 만화 소설 쓰는 것을 좋아한다.

2 지난주에 나는 학교에서 집으로 걸어가던 중에 스쿠터에 탄 여자를 보았다.

3 그녀는 정말 멋져 보였고 그녀의 스쿠터는 매우 독특했다.

4 "호진아, 너 집에 가는 중이니?" 그녀가 갑자기 나에게 말했다.

5 "네, 그런데 저를 아시나요?" 나는 물었다.

6 "물론이지."라고 그녀가 대답했다.

7 "난 매일 학교 식당에서 너를 본단다."

8 놀랍게도, 그녀는 학교 식당 직원 중 한 명이었다.

9 "놀라워! 그녀는 학교 밖에서는 아주 달라 보여."라고 나는 생각했다.

10 "그녀에 대한 만화 소설을 써야겠다."

11 집에 도착한 후, 나는 〈런치 레이디 탄생하다〉라는 새로운 만화 소설을 쓰기 시작했다.

12 그 소설에서 런치 레이디는 슈퍼히어로이다.

13 그녀는 날 수 있는 슈퍼 스쿠터를 탄다.

14 그녀는 전 세계의 위험에 빠진 사람들을 구한다.

15 그녀는 또한 1초에 100개의 쿠키를 만들어 배고픈 아이들에게 나누어 준다.

16 A _____ _____ _____, I _____ my graphic novel _____ my friends.

17 "_____! I love this superhero. She's so _____," said _____ _____ friends.

18 "_____ what? I _____ her _____ Ms. Lee, _____ _____ our cafeteria _____," I told them.

19 I _____ my book _____ Ms. Lee.

20 She _____ it, _____.

21 She _____ told me about her _____ who had _____ _____.

22 Ms. Park, _____ cafeteria _____, _____ a dancing contest.

23 Mr. Kim, the _____ at our school, was _____ an _____ park _____.

24 "I'd _____ _____ _____ superhero stories about them. Do you _____ they'll like that?" I _____ Ms. Lee.

25 "_____ _____ they will," she said _____.

26 "_____ go and _____ _____ _____ our new superhero friends."

16 며칠 후에 나는 나의 만화 소설을 친구들에게 보여 주었다.

17 "멋져! 나는 이 슈퍼히어로가 너무 좋아. 그녀는 아주 멋져."라고 내 모든 친구들이 말했다.

18 "있잖아. 나는 그녀를 우리 식당 직원 중 한 명인 이 여사를 모델로 했어."라고 나는 친구들에게 말했다.

19 나는 이 여사에게 내 책을 보여 주었다.

20 그녀도 그것을 아주 좋아했다.

21 그녀는 또한 나에게 특별한 재능을 가진 그녀의 동료들에 대해 말해 주었다.

22 또 다른 식당 직원인 박 여사는 댄스 경연대회에서 우승했다.

23 우리 학교의 관리인인 김 선생님은 한때 모험적인 공원 관리원이었다.

24 "저는 그들에 대한 슈퍼히어로 이야기를 쓰고 싶어요. 그분들이 그걸 좋아할 것 같아요?" 나는 이 여사한테 물어보았다.

25 "물론 그럴 거야."라고 그녀가 기분 좋게 말했다.

26 "가서 우리의 새 슈퍼히어로 친구들에게 인사하자."

※ 다음 문장을 우리말로 쓰시오.

1 My name is Hojin, and I like to make graphic novels.

➡ _____

2 While I was walking home from school last week, I saw a woman on a scooter.

➡ _____

3 She looked really cool, and her scooter was very unique.

➡ _____

4 "Are you going home, Hojin?" she said to me suddenly.

➡ _____

5 "Yes, but do I know you?" I asked.

➡ _____

6 "Of course," she answered.

➡ _____

7 "I see you at the school cafeteria every day."

➡ _____

8 Surprisingly, she was one of the cafeteria workers at school.

➡ _____

9 "Amazing! She looks so different outside the school," I thought.

➡ _____

10 "I should write a graphic novel about her."

➡ _____

11 After I got home, I began to write a new graphic novel, *Lunch Lady Begins*.

➡ _____

12 In it, Lunch Lady is a superhero.

➡ _____

13 She rides a super scooter that can fly.

➡ _____

14 She saves people from danger around the world.

➡ _____

15 She also makes 100 cookies per second and gives them away to hungry children.

➡ _____

16 A few days later, I showed my graphic novel to my friends.

➡ _____

17 "Awesome! I love this superhero. She's so cool," said all my friends.

➡ _____

18 "Guess what? I modeled her on Ms. Lee, one of our cafeteria workers," I told them.

➡ _____

19 I showed my book to Ms. Lee.

➡ _____

20 She loved it, too.

➡ _____

21 She also told me about her coworkers who had special talents.

➡ _____

22 Ms. Park, another cafeteria worker, won a dancing contest.

➡ _____

23 Mr. Kim, the janitor at our school, was once an adventurous park ranger.

➡ _____

24 "I'd like to write superhero stories about them. Do you think they'll like that?" I asked Ms. Lee.

➡ _____

25 "Of course they will," she said cheerfully.

➡ _____

26 "Let's go and say hello to our new superhero friends."

➡ _____

※ 다음 괄호 안의 단어들을 우리말에 맞도록 바르게 배열하시오.

1 (name / Hojin, / my / is / and / to / graphic / I / make / novels. / like)
➡ _____

2 (was / home / I / while / walking / last / school / from / week, / a / saw / I / on / scooter / a / woman)
➡ _____
_____

3 (really / she / cool, / looked / and / scooter / very / her / unique. / was)
➡ _____

4 (going / "are / Hojin?" / you / home, / to / she / suddenly. / said / me)
➡ _____

5 (but / know / "yes, / I / do / you?" / asked. / I)
➡ _____

6 (answered. / "of / she / course,")
➡ _____

7 (you / see / the / I / at / school / day." / cafeteria / every)
➡ _____

8 (she / surprisingly, / of / was / one / workers / the / school. / at / cafeteria)
➡ _____

9 (she / "amazing! / so / different / looks / the / outside / school," / thought. / I)
➡ _____

10 (write / I / a / novel / write / graphic / should / her. / about)
➡ _____

11 (got / I / after / home, / began / I / write / to / novel, / a / graphic / new / Begins. / Lady / Lunch)
➡ _____

12 (it, / Lady / in / is / superhero. / Lunch / a)
➡ _____

13 (rides / scooter / she / super / a / fly. / can / that)
➡ _____

14 (people / she / danger / from / saves / world. / the / around)
➡ _____

15 (also / she / cookies / makes / second / per / 100 / and / to / them / away / children. / give / hungry)
➡ _____
_____

1 　내 이름은 호진이고, 만화 소설 쓰는 것을 좋아한다.

2 　지난주에 나는 학교에서 집으로 걸어가던 중에 스쿠터에 탄 여자를 보았다.

3 　그녀는 정말 멋져 보였고 그녀의 스쿠터는 매우 독특했다.

4 　"호진아, 너 집에 가는 중이니?" 그녀가 갑자기 나에게 말했다.

5 　"네, 그런데 저를 아시나요?" 나는 물었다.

6 　"물론이지."라고 그녀가 대답했다.

7 　"난 매일 학교 식당에서 너를 본단다."

8 　놀랍게도, 그녀는 학교 식당 직원 중 한 명이었다.

9 　"놀라워! 그녀는 학교 밖에서는 아주 달라 보여."라고 나는 생각했다.

10 　"그녀에 대한 만화 소설을 써야겠다."

11 　집에 도착한 후, 나는 〈런치 레이디 탄생하다〉라는 새로운 만화 소설을 쓰기 시작했다.

12 　그 소설에서 런치 레이디는 슈퍼히어로이다.

13 　그녀는 날 수 있는 슈퍼 스쿠터를 탄다.

14 　그녀는 전 세계의 위험에 빠진 사람들을 구한다.

15 　그녀는 또한 1초에 100개의 쿠키를 만들어 배고픈 아이들에게 나누어 준다.

16 (later, / days / few / a / my / graphic / I / novel / showed / friends. / to / my)

➡ _____

17 (love / I / this / "awesome! / superhero. / so / she's / cool," / friends. / my / all / said)

➡ _____

18 (what? / "guess / her / modeled / I / Ms. / Lee, / on / workers," / of / cafeteria / one / our / them. / I / told)

➡ _____

19 (I / my / showed / Ms. / to / Lee. / book)

➡ _____

20 (too. / she / it, / loved)

➡ _____

21 (also / she / told / about / me / who / coworkers / her / talents. / had / special)

➡ _____

22 (Park, / another / Ms. / worker, / cafeteria / contest. / won / a / dancing)

➡ _____

23 (the / Mr. / Kim, / at / janitor / school, / our / once / was / ranger. / an / park / adventurous)

➡ _____

24 (like / I'd / superhero / write / stories / to / them. / about / think / like / they'll / do / you / that?" / I / Lee. / asked / Ms.)

➡ _____
_____

25 (they / "of / will, / course / cheerfully. / said / she)

➡ _____

26 (go / "let's / say / and / to / our / hello / friends." / superhero / new)

➡ _____

16 며칠 후에 나는 나의 만화 소설을 친구들에게 보여 주었다.

17 "멋져! 나는 이 슈퍼히어로가 너무 좋아. 그녀는 아주 멋져."라고 내 모든 친구들이 말했다.

18 "있잖아. 나는 그녀를 우리 식당 직원 중 한 명인 이 여사를 모델로 했어."라고 나는 친구들에게 말했다.

19 나는 이 여사에게 내 책을 보여 주었다.

20 그녀도 그것을 아주 좋아했다.

21 그녀는 또한 나에게 특별한 재능을 가진 그녀의 동료들에 대해 말해 주었다.

22 또 다른 식당 직원인 박 여사는 댄스 경연대회에서 우승했다.

23 우리 학교의 관리인인 김 선생님은 한때 모험적인 공원 관리원이었다.

24 "저는 그들에 대한 슈퍼히어로 이야기를 쓰고 싶어요. 그분들이 그걸 좋아할 것 같아요?" 나는 이 여사한테 물어보았다.

25 "물론 그럴 거야."라고 그녀가 기분 좋게 말했다.

26 "가서 우리의 새 슈퍼히어로로 친구들에게 인사하자."

※ 다음 우리말을 영어로 쓰시오.

1 내 이름은 호진이고, 만화 소설 쓰는 것을 좋아한다.

➡ _____

2 지난주에 학교에서 집으로 걸어가던 중에 스쿠터에 탄 여자를 보았다.

➡ _____

3 그녀는 정말 멋져 보였고 그녀의 스쿠터는 매우 독특했다.

➡ _____

4 "호진아, 너 집에 가는 중이니?" 그녀가 갑자기 나에게 말했다.

➡ _____

5 "네, 그런데 저를 아시나요?" 나는 물었다.

➡ _____

6 "물론이지," 그녀가 대답했다.

➡ _____

7 "난 매일 학교 식당에서 너를 본단다."

➡ _____

8 놀랍게도, 그녀는 학교 식당 직원 중 한 명이었다.

➡ _____

9 "놀라워! 그녀는 학교 밖에서는 아주 달라 보여."라고 나는 생각했다.

➡ _____

10 "그녀에 대한 만화 소설을 써야겠다."

➡ _____

11 집에 도착한 후, 나는 〈런치 레이디 탄생하다〉라는 새로운 만화 소설을 쓰기 시작했다.

➡ _____

12 그 소설에서 런치 레이디는 슈퍼히어로이다.

➡ _____

13 그녀는 날 수 있는 슈퍼 스쿠터를 탄다.

➡ _____

14 그녀는 전 세계의 위험에 빠진 사람들을 구한다.

➡ _____

15 그녀는 또한 1초에 100개의 쿠키를 만들어 배고픈 아이들에게 나누어 준다.

➡ _____

16 며칠 후에 나는 나의 만화 소설을 친구들에게 보여 주었다.

➡ _____

17 "멋져! 나는 이 슈퍼히어로가 너무 좋아. 그녀는 아주 멋져."라고 내 모든 친구들이 말했다.

➡ _____

18 "있잖아, 나는 그녀를 우리 식당 직원 중 한 명인 이 여사를 모델로 했어."라고 나는 친구들에게 말했다.

➡ _____

19 나는 이 여사에게 내 책을 보여 주었다.

➡ _____

20 그녀도 그것을 아주 좋아했다.

➡ _____

21 그녀는 또한 나에게 특별한 재능을 가진 그녀의 동료들에 대해 말해 주었다.

➡ _____

22 또 다른 식당 직원인 박 여사는 댄스 경연대회에서 우승했다.

➡ _____

23 우리 학교의 관리인인 김 선생님은 한때 모험적인 공원 관리원이었다.

➡ _____

24 "저는 그들에 대한 슈퍼히어로 이야기를 쓰고 싶어요. 그분들이 그걸 좋아할 것 같아요?"
나는 이 여사한테 물어보았다.

➡ _____

25 "물론 그럴 거야."라고 그녀가 기분 좋게 말했다.

➡ _____

26 "가서 우리의 새 슈퍼히어로로 친구들에게 인사하자."

➡ _____

※ 다음 우리말과 일치하도록 빈칸에 알맞은 말을 쓰시오.

Language Arts

1. Two boys are _____ in a _____.

2. There _____ a _____.

3. The boys _____ get _____.

4. Lunch Lady _____ on her scooter and _____ them.

1. 두 소년이 도서관에서 공부하고 있다.
2. 불이 났다.
3. 그 소년들은 나갈 수 없다.
4. Lunch Lady는 스쿠터를 타고 날아와
   서 그들을 구한다.

Write

1. My _____ is my _____ model.

2. She is _____, strong, and _____.

3. _____ her 30s, she _____ to 70 _____ countries.

4. _____ she was _____, she made friends from all _____ the world.

5. I want to _____ someone who is not _____ of _____ new things just _____ her.

1. 나의 이모는 내 롤 모델이다.
2. 그녀는 똑똑하고, 강하고, 모험심이 강
   하다.
3. 30대 때, 그녀는 70개국을 여행했다.
4. 여행을 하는 동안, 그녀는 전 세계의
   친구들을 사귀었다.
5. 나는 그녀처럼 새로운 것을 시도하는 것
   을 두려워하지 않는 사람이 되고 싶다.

Culture Project - Share

1. Julia Child was a person _____ found her _____ talent _____ her 30s.

2. _____ age 36, she _____ _____ Paris with her _____.

3. She _____ a _____ cooking school there.

4. _____ she was studying, she _____ _____ write a cookbook.

5. That book _____ a big _____.

1. Julia Child는 30대에 그녀의 진정한
   재능을 발견한 사람이었다.
2. 36살 때, 그녀는 남편과 함께 파리로
   이사를 했다.
3. 그녀는 그곳에서 유명한 요리 학교에
   다닌다.
4. 그녀는 공부하는 동안 요리책을 쓰기
   로 결심했다.
5. 그 책은 큰 인기를 끌었다.

※ 다음 우리말을 영어로 쓰시오.

Language Arts

1. 두 소년이 도서관에서 공부하고 있다.

   ➡ _____

2. 불이 났다.

   ➡ _____

3. 그 소년들은 나갈 수 없다.

   ➡ _____

4. Lunch Lady는 스쿠터를 타고 날아와서 그들을 구한다.

   ➡ _____

Write

1. 나의 이모는 내 롤 모델이다.

   ➡ _____

2. 그녀는 똑똑하고, 강하고, 모험심이 강하다.

   ➡ _____

3. 30대 때, 그녀는 70개국을 여행했다.

   ➡ _____

4. 여행을 하는 동안, 그녀는 전 세계의 친구들을 사귀었다.

   ➡ _____

5. 나는 그녀처럼 새로운 것을 시도하는 것을 두려워하지 않는 사람이 되고 싶다.

   ➡ _____

Culture Project - Share

1. Julia Child는 30대에 그녀의 진정한 재능을 발견한 사람이었다.

   ➡ _____

2. 36살 때, 그녀는 남편과 함께 파리로 이사를 했다.

   ➡ _____

3. 그녀는 그곳에서 유명한 요리 학교에 다닌다.

   ➡ _____

4. 그녀는 공부하는 동안 요리책을 쓰기로 결심했다.

   ➡ _____

5. 그 책은 큰 인기를 끌었다.

   ➡ _____

※ 다음 영어를 우리말로 쓰시오.

01 wind

02 fine dust

03 sometimes

04 build

05 goat

06 decide

07 since

08 else

09 southern

10 entrance

11 forest

12 cave

13 fresh

14 airplane-shaped

15 become

16 gate

17 century

18 practice

19 stone

20 harmony

21 cone

22 information

23 meal

24 kind

25 lovely

26 tour

27 enemy

28 storage

29 low

30 wooden

31 piano-shaped

32 mall

33 dining room

34 ocean

35 look for

36 be afraid of

37 watch out for

38 give it a try

39 upside down

40 in harmony with

41 pile up

42 take down

43 be good at

※ 다음 우리말을 영어로 쓰시오.

01 구내식당	22 세금
02 씌우다, 덮다	23 유일무이한, 독특한
03 디자인, 설계	24 풀, 잔디
04 자연	25 마을
05 다섯 번째의	26 미세먼지
06 마루, 바닥	27 때때로
07 환영하다	28 염소
08 방지하다, 피하다	29 숲, 삼림
09 대양, 바다	30 동굴
10 1,000, 천	31 입구, 문
11 ~ 없이	32 저장, 보관
12 적	33 나무로 된
13 지불하다	34 조화, 화합
14 징수원	35 ~을 보다
15 식물	36 ~ 옆에
16 경관, 전망	37 ~을 조심하다
17 게스트하우스	38 ~와 조화를 이루어
18 보호하다	39 ~을 잘하다
19 화장실, 세면실	40 쌓아 올리다
20 둥근, 동그란	41 거꾸로, 뒤집혀
21 ~의 모양[형태]의	42 (구조물을 해체하여) 치우다
	43 한번 해 보다

※ 다음 영영풀이에 알맞은 단어를 <보기>에서 골라 쓴 후, 우리말 뜻을 쓰시오.

1 _____ : the number 1,000: _____

2 _____ : made of wood: _____

3 _____ : someone who hates you or wants to harm you: _____

4 _____ : a large hole in the side of a cliff or hill, or one that is under the ground:
_____

5 _____ : facts about someone or something: _____

6 _____ : a period of a hundred years that is used when stating a date: _____

7 _____ : someone whose job is to collect taxes or debts etc.: _____

8 _____ : a large area where trees grow close together: _____

9 _____ : a current of air that is moving across the earth's surface: _____

10 _____ : a restaurant where you choose your food from a counter and take it to
your table after paying for it: _____

11 _____ : to prevent someone or something from being harmed or damaged:
_____

12 _____ : a room with a toilet for customers to use: _____

13 _____ : an amount of money that you have to pay to the government so that you
can use public services: _____

14 _____ : to take action in order to prevent something unpleasant from happening:
_____

15 _____ : a private home or boarding house offering accommodation to travellers:
_____

16 _____ : a living thing that grows in the earth and has a stem, leaves, and roots,
especially one that is smaller than a tree or bush: _____

※ 다음 우리말과 일치하도록 빈칸에 알맞은 말을 쓰시오.

Listen & Speak 1 A. Listen and Check

1. **B:** Hey, _____ _____ this house in the picture. It _____ _____ a big shoe!

   G: Oh, it's very _____, but I don't want _____ _____ _____ a shoe.

   B: _____ _____ of house do you want to _____ _____?

   G: Well, I _____ _____ live in an _____ house.

2. **M:** _____ me, is _____ a restaurant in this mall?

   W: Yes. What _____ of food _____ you _____?

   M: I'd _____ _____ food.

   W: _____ is a great restaurant _____ the _____ _____.

   M: Thank you.

Listen & Speak 2 A. Listen and Write

1. **W:** _____ me, _____ can I _____ women's shoes?

   M: You can find them on the _____ _____. They're _____ _____ the elevator.

   W: _____ you.

   M: You're _____.

2. **W:** _____ I _____ you?

   M: I'm _____ _____ watches. Where _____ _____ _____ them?

   W: They're _____ the _____ floor, _____ _____ the restroom.

   M: Thank _____.

Communicate A. Listen and Answer

Woman: _____ _____ Jeonju Hanok Guesthouse. _____ _____ _____ you?

Man: Yes, I'd _____ a room _____ two nights.

Woman: Well, what _____ _____ room would you _____?

Man: Do you have a room _____ a garden _____? You have a _____ garden.

Woman: Yes, we do. _____ room in our house _____ a garden _____, but there _____ _____ beds in the rooms.

Man: Do I _____ _____ sleep on the _____?

Woman: Yes, you _____.

Man: O.K. I'll _____ it a _____. Where can I _____ _____?

Woman: You _____ have breakfast in the _____ _____, _____ _____ the kitchen.

Man: I _____.

Woman: O.K. You're _____ the Nabi room. _____ your _____.

Man: _____ you.

W: 네, 그렇습니다.
M: 알았습니다. 한번 시도해 볼게요. 아침 식사는 어디서 해요?
W: 아침 식사는 부엌 옆에 있는 식당에서 할 수 있어요.
M: 알겠습니다.
W: 좋아요, 나비 방에 들어가세요. 여기 당신의 열쇠가 있습니다.
M: 고맙습니다.

Progress Check

1. **B:** Hey, look at this _____ house in the picture. It's _____ _____.

   G: Oh, it _____ _____, but I think it's _____ of _____.

   B: _____ _____ _____ house do you want to _____ _____?

   G: I like music, _____ I want to live _____ a _____ house.

2. **W:** _____ me, where can I find _____ _____?

   M: You _____ _____ them on the _____ _____. They're _____ _____ the elevator.

   W: _____ you.

   M: You're _____.

3. **M:** Excuse me, _____ can I _____ men's hats?

   W: You can find them _____ _____ _____. They're _____ _____ the elevator.

   M: _____ you.

   W: You're _____.

1. B: 이봐, 사진 속의 이 독특한 집을 봐. 집이 거꾸로 있어.
   G: 아, 재미있어 보이지만, 좀 이상한 것 같아.
   B: 넌 어떤 집에서 살고 싶니?
   G: 나는 음악을 좋아해서 피아노 모양의 집에서 살고 싶어.
2. W: 실례합니다. 여자 청바지는 어디에 있나요?
   M: 2층에서 찾을 수 있어요. 엘리베이터 옆에 있어요.
   W: 감사합니다.
   M: 천만에요.
3. M: 실례합니다. 남성용 모자는 어디에 있나요?
   W: 2층에서 찾을 수 있어요. 엘리베이터 옆에 있어요.
   M: 감사합니다.
   W: 천만에요.

Work -Act

A: _____ _____ of house do you want _____ _____?

B: I want to build a _____ house that _____ _____ a boat.

A: _____ is the _____?

B: It's _____ _____ _____ _____.

A: 넌 어떤 집을 짓고 싶어?
B: 보트처럼 생긴 2층짜리 집을 짓고 싶어.
A: 부엌이 어디 있어?
B: 2층에 있어.

※ 다음 우리말에 맞도록 대화를 영어로 쓰시오.

Listen & Speak 1 A. Listen and Check

1. B: _____

   G: _____

   B: _____

   G: _____

2. M: _____

   W: _____

   M: _____

   W: _____

   M: _____

Listen & Speak 2 A. Listen and Write

1. W: _____

   M: _____

   W: _____

   M: _____

2. W: _____

   M: _____

   W: _____

   M: _____

Communicate A. Listen and Answer

Woman: _____

Man: _____

Woman: _____

Man: _____

Woman: _____

Man: _____

해석

1. B: 어이, 이 사진 속의 집을 봐. 그것은 큰 신발처럼 보여!
   G: 오, 아주 독특하긴 하지만, 난 신발 속에서 살고 싶지 않아.
   B: 넌 어떤 종류의 집에서 살고 싶니?
   G: 음, 나는 비행기 모양의 집에서 살고 싶어.

2. M: 실례합니다, 이 쇼핑몰에 식당이 있나요?
   W: 네. 어떤 음식을 드시겠어요?
   M: 중국 음식을 먹고 싶어요.
   W: 5층에 멋진 식당이 있어요.
   M: 감사합니다.

1. W: 실례합니다, 여자 신발은 어디에 있어요?
   M: 2층에서 찾을 수 있어요. 엘리베이터 옆에 있어요.
   W: 감사합니다.
   M: 천만에요.

2. W: 뭘 도와드릴까요?
   M: 시계를 찾고 있어요. 어디에서 찾을 수 있습니까?
   W: 3층에, 화장실 옆에 있어요.
   M: 감사합니다.

W: 전주 한옥 게스트하우스에 오신 걸 환영합니다. 무엇을 도와드릴까요?
M: 네, 이틀 밤 묵을 방을 원해요.
W: 음, 어떤 방을 원하세요?
M: 정원이 보이는 방이 있어요? 정원이 아름답군요.
W: 네, 그렇습니다. 우리 집 모든 방에서는 정원이 보입니다. 하지만 방에는 침대가 없어요.
M: 바닥에서 자야 합니까?

Woman: _____

Man: _____

Woman: _____

Man: _____

Woman: _____

Man: _____

W: 네, 그렇습니다.

M: 알았습니다. 한번 시도해 볼게요. 아침 식사는 어디서 해요?

W: 아침 식사는 부엌 옆에 있는 식당에서 할 수 있어요.

M: 알겠습니다.

W: 좋아요, 나비 방에 들어가세요. 여기 당신의 열쇠가 있습니다.

M: 고맙습니다.

Progress Check

1. B: _____

   G: _____

   B: _____

   G: _____

2. W: _____

   M: _____

   W: _____

   M: _____

3. M: _____

   W: _____

   M: _____

   W: _____

1. B: 이봐, 사진 속의 이 독특한 집을 봐. 집이 거꾸로 있어.

   G: 아, 재미있어 보이지만, 좀 이상한 것 같아.

   B: 넌 어떤 집에서 살고 싶니?

   G: 나는 음악을 좋아해서 피아노 모양의 집에서 살고 싶어.

2. W: 실례합니다. 여자 청바지는 어디에 있나요?

   M: 2층에서 찾을 수 있어요. 엘리베이터 옆에 있어요.

   W: 감사합니다.

   M: 천만에요.

3. M: 실례합니다. 남성용 모자는 어디에 있나요?

   W: 2층에서 찾을 수 있어요. 엘리베이터 옆에 있어요.

   M: 감사합니다.

   W: 천만에요.

Work -Act

A: _____

B: _____

A: _____

B: _____

A: 넌 어떤 집을 짓고 싶어?

B: 보트처럼 생긴 2층짜리 집을 짓고 싶어.

A: 부엌이 어디 있어?

B: 2층에 있어.

※ 다음 우리말과 일치하도록 빈칸에 알맞은 것을 골라 쓰시오.

1 _____ you ever _____ a goat on the _____ of a house?
    A. roof   B. seen   C. have

2 _____ Norway, we can _____ animals _____ roofs.
    A. on   B. see   C. in

3 Norway has _____ _____.
    A. forests   B. large

4 In _____ with _____, people have built _____ houses for a long time.
    A. wooden   B. harmony   C. nature

5 To _____ strong and warm houses, they _____ their roofs _____ grass.
    A. with   B. cover   C. build

6 The grass roofs _____ them _____ the long cold winters and strong _____.
    A. winds   B. from   C. protect

7 _____, trees or plants grow _____ of the grass _____, and some animals enjoy their _____ there.
    A. roofs   B. meals   C. out   D. sometimes

8 A roof is an _____ part of a house, but long _____ some people _____ roofs only to take them _____ easily.
    A. ago   B. down   C. built   D. essential

9 _____ ago in _____ Italy, people who had a house _____ a roof _____ lower taxes.
    A. paid   B. southern   C. without   D. centuries

10 To _____ high _____ on their houses, some people built _____ roofs by _____ up stones.
    A. piling   B. taxes   C. cone-shaped   D. avoid

1 여러분은 집의 지붕 위에 있는 염소를 본 적이 있는가?

2 노르웨이에서, 우리는 지붕 위에 있는 동물들을 볼 수 있다.

3 노르웨이는 큰 숲을 가지고 있다.

4 자연과 조화를 이루면서, 사람들은 오랫동안 나무로 집을 지었다.

5 강하고 따뜻한 집을 만들기 위해, 그들은 지붕을 잔디로 덮는다.

6 잔디 지붕은 길고 추운 겨울과 강한 바람으로부터 그들을 보호한다.

7 때때로, 나무나 식물들이 잔디 지붕에서 자라며, 어떤 동물들은 거기서 식사를 즐긴다.

8 지붕은 집의 필수적인 부분이지만, 오래 전에 어떤 사람들은 오직 지붕을 쉽게 철거하기 위해 지었다.

9 수세기 전 남부 이탈리아에서는 지붕 없는 집을 가진 사람들이 더 적은 세금을 냈다.

10 그들의 집에 부과되는 높은 세금을 피하기 위해, 어떤 사람들은 돌을 쌓아 올려 원뿔 모양의 지붕을 만들었다.

11 _____ tax _____ came to the town, people _____ their roofs _____ quickly.

A. down   B. when   C. took   D. collectors

12 After the _____ collectors _____, they _____ up the stones again.

A. piled   B. left   C. tax

13 _____ the sky in a _____ of _____ China, you can see round roofs that look _____ big doughnuts.

A. like   B. from   C. southern   D. part

14 They are the _____ of the big _____ houses of the Hakka _____.

A. people   B. round   C. roofs

15 They _____ lived in houses _____ these for _____ a thousand years to protect _____ from enemies.

A. like   B. themselves   C. about   D. have

16 The houses have _____ one gate _____ any windows _____ the first floor.

A. on   B. without   C. only

17 _____ house is big _____ for a _____ village.

A. whole   B. enough   C. each

18 It _____ has four _____.

A. stories   B. usually

19 It has kitchens on the first floor, _____ rooms on the _____ floor, and _____ rooms and bedrooms on the third and _____ floors.

A. fourth   B. second   C. living   D. storage

11 세금 징수원들이 마을에 오면, 사람들은 재빨리 지붕을 철거했다.

12 세금 징수원들이 떠난 후 그들은 다시 돌을 쌓아 올렸다.

13 중국 남부의 일부 지역의 하늘에서 보면, 여러분은 큰 도넛처럼 생긴 둥근 지붕들을 볼 수 있다.

14 그것들은 하카족의 크고 둥근 집들의 지붕이다.

15 그들은 적으로부터 스스로를 보호하기 위해 약 천 년 동안 이런 집에서 살아왔다.

16 그 집들에는 1층에 창문이 하나도 없고 문이 하나만 있다.

17 각각의 집은 전체 마을이 들어갈 만큼 크다.

18 그 집은 보통 4개의 층을 가지고 있다.

19 1층에는 주방, 2층에는 창고, 3층과 4층에는 거실과 침실이 있다.

※ 다음 우리말과 일치하도록 빈칸에 알맞은 말을 쓰시오.

1 _____ you ever _____ a goat _____ _____ _____ of a house?

2 _____ Norway, we _____ see animals _____ _____ .

3 Norway _____ large _____ .

4 _____ _____ _____ nature, people _____ _____ wooden houses _____ a long time.

5 _____ _____ strong and warm houses, they _____ their roofs _____ grass.

6 The grass roofs _____ them _____ the long _____ winters and _____ winds.

7 Sometimes, trees or plants _____ _____ _____ the grass roofs, and some animals _____ their _____ there.

8 A roof is an _____ _____ of a house, but _____ _____ some people built roofs only to _____ them _____ easily.

9 _____ _____ in southern Italy, people _____ had a house without a roof _____ lower _____ .

10 _____ _____ high taxes on their houses, some people _____ cone-shaped roofs by _____ _____ stones.

1 여러분은 집의 지붕 위에 있는 염소를 본 적이 있는가?

2 노르웨이에서, 우리는 지붕 위에 있는 동물들을 볼 수 있다.

3 노르웨이는 큰 숲을 가지고 있다.

4 자연과 조화를 이루면서, 사람들은 오랫동안 나무로 집을 지었다.

5 강하고 따뜻한 집을 만들기 위해, 그들은 지붕을 잔디로 덮는다.

6 잔디 지붕은 길고 추운 겨울과 강한 바람으로부터 그들을 보호한다.

7 때때로, 나무나 식물들이 잔디 지붕에서 자라며, 어떤 동물들은 거기서 식사를 즐긴다.

8 지붕은 집의 필수적인 부분이지만, 오래 전에 어떤 사람들은 오직 지붕을 쉽게 철거하기 위해 지었다.

9 수세기 전 남부 이탈리아에서는 지붕 없는 집을 가진 사람들이 더 적은 세금을 냈다.

10 그들의 집에 부과되는 높은 세금을 피하기 위해, 어떤 사람들은 돌을 쌓아 올려 원뿔 모양의 지붕을 만들었다.

11 When _____ _____ came to the town, people _____ their roofs _____ quickly.

12 _____ the tax collectors _____, they _____ _____ the stones again.

13 _____ the sky in a part of _____ China, you can see _____ _____ that _____ _____ big doughnuts.

14 They are the _____ of the _____ _____ _____ of the Hakka people.

15 They _____ _____ in houses like these for about a _____ _____ to _____ themselves _____ enemies.

16 The houses have _____ one gate _____ any windows on the _____ _____.

17 _____ house is _____ _____ for a _____ _____.

18 It _____ has _____ _____.

19 It has kitchens on the _____ floor, _____ rooms on the _____ floor, and _____ _____ and bedrooms on the _____ and _____ floors.

11 세금 징수원들이 마을에 오면, 사람들은 재빨리 지붕을 철거했다.

12 세금 징수원들이 떠난 후 그들은 다시 돌을 쌓아 올렸다.

13 중국 남부의 일부 지역의 하늘에서 보면, 여러분은 큰 도넛처럼 생긴 둥근 지붕들을 볼 수 있다.

14 그것들은 하카족의 크고 둥근 집들의 지붕이다.

15 그들은 적으로부터 스스로를 보호하기 위해 약 천 년 동안 이런 집에서 살아왔다.

16 그 집들에는 1층에 창문이 하나도 없고 문이 하나만 있다.

17 각각의 집은 전체 마을이 들어갈 만큼 크다.

18 그 집은 보통 4개의 층을 가지고 있다.

19 1층에는 주방, 2층에는 창고, 3층과 4층에는 거실과 침실이 있다.

※ 다음 문장을 우리말로 쓰시오.

1 Have you ever seen a goat on the roof of a house?

➡ _____

2 In Norway, we can see animals on roofs.

➡ _____

3 Norway has large forests.

➡ _____

4 In harmony with nature, people have built wooden houses for a long time.

➡ _____

5 To build strong and warm houses, they cover their roofs with grass.

➡ _____

6 The grass roofs protect them from the long cold winters and strong winds.

➡ _____

7 Sometimes, trees or plants grow out of the grass roofs, and some animals enjoy their meals there.

➡ _____

8 A roof is an essential part of a house, but long ago some people built roofs only to take them down easily.

➡ _____

9 Centuries ago in southern Italy, people who had a house without a roof paid lower taxes.

➡ _____

10 To avoid high taxes on their houses, some people built cone-shaped roofs by piling up stones.

➡ _____

11 When tax collectors came to the town, people took their roofs down quickly

➡ _____

12 After the tax collectors left, they piled up the stones again.

➡ _____

13 From the sky in a part of southern China, you can see round roofs that look like big doughnuts.

➡ _____

14 They are the roofs of the big round houses of the Hakka people.

➡ _____

15 They have lived in houses like these for about a thousand years to protect themselves from enemies.

➡ _____

16 The houses have only one gate without any windows on the first floor.

➡ _____

17 Each house is big enough for a whole village.

➡ _____

18 It usually has four stories.

➡ _____

19 It has kitchens on the first floor, storage rooms on the second floor, and living rooms and bedrooms on the third and fourth floors.

➡ _____

※ 다음 괄호 안의 단어들을 우리말에 맞도록 바르게 배열하시오.

1 (you / seen / ever / have / on / goat / a / house? / the / of / roof / a)

➡ _____

2 (Norway, / we / in / see / can / roofs. / on / animals)

➡ _____

3 (has / forests. / Norway / large)

➡ _____

4 (with / harmony / nature, / in / people / wooden / built / have / for / houses / time. / long / a)

➡ _____

5 (warm / to / and / build / houses, / strong / they / roofs / grass. / with / their / cover)

➡ _____

6 (roofs / the / protect / grass / from / long / them / cold / the / winters / winds. / and / strong)

➡ _____

7 (trees / sometimes, / or / grow / plants / of / grass / out / the / roofs, / and / enjoy / there. / animals / some / meals / their)

➡ _____
_____

8 (is / an / roof / part / a / essential / house, / a / of / but / ago / long / roofs / people / only / some / to / built / them / easily. / down / take)

➡ _____
_____

9 (ago / Italy, / centuries / in / southern / who / people / house / a / had / taxes. / without / paid / a / lower / roof)

➡ _____
_____

10 (taxes / to / their / avoid / on / high / houses, / people / some / cone-shaped / by / built / piling / stones. / roofs / by / up)

➡ _____
_____

1 여러분은 집의 지붕 위에 있는 염소를 본 적이 있는가?

2 노르웨이에서, 우리는 지붕 위에 있는 동물들을 볼 수 있다.

3 노르웨이는 큰 숲을 가지고 있다.

4 자연과 조화를 이루면서, 사람들은 오랫동안 나무로 집을 지었다.

5 강하고 따뜻한 집을 만들기 위해, 그들은 지붕을 잔디로 덮는다.

6 잔디 지붕은 길고 추운 겨울과 강한 바람으로부터 그들을 보호한다.

7 때때로, 나무나 식물들이 잔디 지붕에서 자라며, 어떤 동물들은 거기서 식사를 즐긴다.

8 지붕은 집의 필수적인 부분이지만, 오래 전에 어떤 사람들은 오직 지붕을 쉽게 철거하기 위해 지었다.

9 수세기 전 남부 이탈리아에서는 지붕 없는 집을 가진 사람들이 더 적은 세금을 냈다.

10 그들의 집에 부과되는 높은 세금을 피하기 위해, 어떤 사람들은 돌을 쌓아 올려 원뿔 모양의 지붕을 만들었다.

11 (tax / came / when / the / collectors / down, / to / people / quickly. / roofs / took / their / down)

➡ _____

_____

12 (the / collectors / after / tax / left, / piled / they / stones / again. / the / up)

➡ _____

13 (the / from / sky / part / in / a / of / China, / southern / can / you / round / see / look / that / roofs / doughnuts. / big / like)

➡ _____

_____

14 (the / are / roofs / they / the / of / round / big / Hakka / the / people. / of / houses)

➡ _____

15 (lived / they / houses / in / have / these / like / about / a / for / years / thousand / to / enemies. / from / themselves / protect)

➡ _____

_____

16 (houses / the / only / gate / one / have / without / the / floor. / windows / any / on / first)

➡ _____

17 (house / each / enough / big / is / village. / whole / a / for)

➡ _____

18 (has / usually / stories. / it / four)

➡ _____

19 (has / kitchens / first / it / on / the / floor, / rooms / storage / the / floor, / second / on / and / rooms / living / bedrooms / on / and / fourth / the / floors. / and / third)

➡ _____

_____

11 세금 징수원들이 마을에 오면, 사람들은 재빨리 지붕을 철거했다.

12 세금 징수원들이 떠난 후 그들은 다시 돌을 쌓아 올렸다.

13 중국 남부의 일부 지역의 하늘에서 보면, 여러분은 큰 도넛처럼 생긴 둥근 지붕들을 볼 수 있다.

14 그것들은 하카족의 크고 둥근 집들의 지붕이다.

15 그들은 적으로부터 스스로를 보호하기 위해 약 천 년 동안 이런 집에서 살아왔다.

16 그 집들에는 1층에 창문이 하나도 없고 문이 하나만 있다.

17 각각의 집은 전체 마을이 들어갈 만큼 크다.

18 그 집은 보통 4개의 층을 가지고 있다.

19 1층에는 주방, 2층에는 창고, 3층과 4층에는 거실과 침실이 있다.

※ 다음 우리말을 영어로 쓰시오.

1 여러분은 집의 지붕 위에 있는 염소를 본 적이 있는가?

➡ _____

2 노르웨이에서, 우리는 지붕 위에 있는 동물들을 볼 수 있다.

➡ _____

3 노르웨이는 큰 숲을 가지고 있다.

➡ _____

4 자연과 조화를 이루면서, 사람들은 오랫동안 나무로 집을 지었다.

➡ _____

5 강하고 따뜻한 집을 만들기 위해, 그들은 지붕을 잔디로 덮는다.

➡ _____

6 잔디 지붕은 길고 추운 겨울과 강한 바람으로부터 그들을 보호한다.

➡ _____

7 때때로, 나무나 식물들이 잔디 지붕에서 자라며, 어떤 동물들은 거기서 식사를 즐긴다.

➡ _____

8 지붕은 집의 필수적인 부분이지만, 오래 전에 어떤 사람들은 오직 지붕을 쉽게 철거하기 위해 지었다.

➡ _____

9 수세기 전 남부 이탈리아에서는 지붕 없는 집을 가진 사람들이 더 적은 세금을 냈다.

➡ _____

10 그들의 집에 부과되는 높은 세금을 피하기 위해, 어떤 사람들은 돌을 쌓아 올려 원뿔 모양의 지붕을 만들었다.

➡ _____

11 세금 징수원들이 마을에 오면, 사람들은 재빨리 지붕을 철거했다.

　➡ _____

12 세금 징수원들이 떠난 후 그들은 다시 돌을 쌓아 올렸다.

　➡ _____

13 중국 남부의 일부 지역의 하늘에서 보면, 여러분은 큰 도넛처럼 생긴 둥근 지붕들을 볼 수 있다.

　➡ _____

14 그것들은 하카족의 크고 둥근 집들의 지붕이다.

　➡ _____

15 그들은 적으로부터 스스로를 보호하기 위해 약 천 년 동안 이런 집에서 살아왔다.

　➡ _____

16 그 집들에는 1층에 창문이 하나도 없고 문이 하나만 있다.

　➡ _____

17 각각의 집은 전체 마을이 들어갈 만큼 크다.

　➡ _____

18 그 집은 보통 4개의 층을 가지고 있다.

　➡ _____

19 1층에는 주방, 2층에는 창고, 3층과 4층에는 거실과 침실이 있다.

　➡ _____

　_____

※ 다음 우리말과 일치하도록 빈칸에 알맞은 말을 쓰시오.

Link

1. I can't open windows _____ _____ the fine dust _____ _____.

2. How _____ _____ a small garden on the _____?

3. _____ _____ has _____ a big problem in the spring.

4. We _____ a roof _____ has a small garden _____ trees and many _____ plants.

5. This garden will _____ us _____ air.

1. 나는 요즘 미세먼지 때문에 창문을 열 수가 없어요.
2. 지붕에 작은 정원을 만드는 것은 어떨까요?
3. 봄에는 미세먼지가 큰 문제가 되어 왔다.
4. 우리는 나무와 다른 많은 식물들이 있는 작은 정원을 가진 지붕을 설계했다.
5. 이 정원은 우리에게 신선한 공기를 줄 것이다.

Write

1. Sejong _____ Library is _____ Sejong, Korea.

2. It is a _____ building that _____ _____ an open book.

3. It has _____ 400 thousand books on the first and _____ _____ and a large cafeteria on the _____ floor.

4. It _____ _____ 2013.

5. _____ then, many people have _____ this _____ building.

1. 국립 세종 도서관은 한국의 세종시에 있다.
2. 그것은 펴놓은 책처럼 보이는 4층 건물이다.
3. 1층과 2층에는 약 40만 권의 책이 있고, 맨 위층에는 큰 구내식당이 있다.
4. 그것은 2013년에 문을 열었다.
5. 그 이후로, 많은 사람들이 이 독특한 건물을 방문했다.

Culture Project

1. _____ Granada, Spain, some people have _____ in cave houses _____ a long time.

2. The _____ in this place is very _____ in the summer and _____ in the winter.

3. It's not _____ cold or hot in _____ houses.

1. 스페인의 그라나다에서는, 몇몇 사람들이 오랫동안 동굴 집에서 살아왔다.
2. 이곳의 날씨는 여름에는 매우 덥고 겨울에는 춥다.
3. 동굴 집은 너무 춥거나 덥지도 않다.

※ 다음 우리말을 영어로 쓰시오.

Link

1. 나는 요즘 미세먼지 때문에 창문을 열 수가 없어요.

➡ _____

2. 지붕에 작은 정원을 만드는 것은 어떨까요?

➡ _____

3. 봄에는 미세먼지가 큰 문제가 되어 왔다.

➡ _____

4. 우리는 나무와 다른 많은 식물들이 있는 작은 정원을 가진 지붕을 설계했다.

➡ _____

5. 이 정원은 우리에게 신선한 공기를 줄 것이다.

➡ _____

Write

1. 국립 세종 도서관은 한국의 세종시에 있다.

➡ _____

2. 그것은 펴놓은 책처럼 보이는 4층 건물이다.

➡ _____

3. 1층과 2층에는 약 40만 권의 책이 있고, 맨 위층에는 큰 구내식당이 있다.

➡ _____

4. 그것은 2013년에 문을 열었다.

➡ _____

5. 그 이후로, 많은 사람들이 이 독특한 건물을 방문했다.

➡ _____

Culture Project

1. 스페인의 그라나다에서는, 몇몇 사람들이 오랫동안 동굴 집에서 살아왔다.

➡ _____

2. 이곳의 날씨는 여름에는 매우 덥고 겨울에는 춥다.

➡ _____

3. 동굴 집은 너무 춥거나 덥지도 않다.

➡ _____

※ 다음 영어를 우리말로 쓰시오.

01	perfect	
02	amazing	
03	become	
04	capture	
05	seafood	
06	travel	
07	simple	
08	bungee jumping	
09	forecast	
10	earth	
11	else	
12	famous	
13	portrait	
14	finally	
15	food	
16	graduate	
17	chance	
18	island	
19	remain	
20	weather	
21	guess	

22	market	
23	foreign	
24	mystery	
25	freezing	
26	actually	
27	expect	
28	journal	
29	scary	
30	indoors	
31	create	
32	university	
33	vacation	
34	appear	
35	get to	
36	be full of	
37	get into	
38	right now	
39	a lot of	
40	such as	
41	set foot at[in]	
42	a little	
43	show up	

※ 다음 우리말을 영어로 쓰시오.

01 만지다 _____

02 접시, 그릇 _____

03 살피다, 점검하다 _____

04 흐린 _____

05 (짐을) 싸다 _____

06 결정하다 _____

07 ~ 동안[내내] _____

08 외국의 _____

09 ~ 둘레에, ~ 주위에 _____

10 (차량을) 몰다 _____

11 바람이 많이 부는 _____

12 초대하다 _____

13 큰, 거대한 _____

14 화신 _____

15 현장 학습 _____

16 물건, 물체 _____

17 전문학교 _____

18 날씨 _____

19 잠깐, 잠시 _____

20 휴식을 취하다 _____

21 그림, 소묘 _____

22 여행 _____

23 거북 _____

24 시장 _____

25 존경하다, 감탄하며 바라보다 _____

26 수첩, 일기 _____

27 완전한 _____

28 예상[기대]하다 _____

29 포착하다, 담아내다 _____

30 졸업하다 _____

31 꽁꽁 얼게[너무나] 추운 _____

32 무서운, 겁나는 _____

33 간단한 _____

34 섬 _____

35 소수의, 약간의 _____

36 지금, 당장 _____

37 ~에 도착하다 _____

38 ~으로 가득 차다 _____

39 마침내 _____

40 나타나다 _____

41 ~에 발을 들여놓다 _____

42 ~에 들어가다, ~에 타다 _____

43 ~와 같은 _____

※ 다음 영영풀이에 알맞은 단어를 <보기>에서 골라 쓴 후, 우리말 뜻을 쓰시오.

1 _____ : what people and animals eat: _____

2 _____ : the possibility that something will happen: _____

3 _____ : a piece of land that is completely surrounded by water: _____

4 _____ : a place where goods are bought and sold, usually outdoors: _____

5 _____ : to like and respect someone or something very much: _____

6 _____ : a picture made with a pencil or pen: _____

7 _____ : very surprising and making you feel pleasure, approval, or wonder:
    _____

8 _____ : an area of sand or stones beside the sea: _____

9 _____ : to cause something to happen or exist: _____

10 _____ : to ask someone to come to something such as a party: _____

11 _____ : something that is not understood or known about: _____

12 _____ : unusual or unexpected, and making you feel slightly nervous or afraid:
    _____

13 _____ : to go from one place to another, often to a place that is far away:
    _____

14 _____ : to choose to do something, usually after you have thought carefully
    about the other possibilities: _____

15 _____ : to spend time resting or doing something enjoyable especially after you
    have been doing work: _____

16 _____ : to put clothes and other things into a bag, because you are leaving a
    place: _____

보기	create	chance	mystery	market
	admire	invite	travel	pack
	island	decide	food	drawing
	amazing	strange	relax	beach

※ 다음 우리말과 일치하도록 빈칸에 알맞은 말을 쓰시오.

Listen & Speak 1 A. Listen and Check

1. **G:** _____ you ever _____ Indian food?

   B: Yes, I _____, but I've _____ _____ Indian curry.

   G: _____ was _____?

   B: It was really _____, _____ I loved it.

2. **G:** Bill, _____ you ever _____ bungee jumping?

   B: _____, I _____. _____ _____ you, Katie?

   G: _____ I _____ New Zealand, I _____ bungee jumping

   _____.

   B: _____ it _____?

   G: No, I liked it. I _____ _____ do it _____.

Listen & Speak 2 A. Listen and Answer

1. **B:** Mom, _____ the _____ today? Do I _____ an umbrella?

   W: It's quite _____ _____. I'll _____ the weather _____.

   B: _____ you, Mom.

   W: Well, it's not _____ _____ _____ today.

   B: Good! Then, I _____ _____ an umbrella today.

2. **W:** Good morning, and _____ _____ the weather forecast.
   It's _____ _____, but we're _____ some rain in the
   afternoon. _____ _____ home _____ your umbrella.
   That's the _____ _____ for today. _____ a nice day.

해석

1. **G:** 너 인도 음식을 먹어 본 적이 있니?
   B: 응, 있어, 하지만 인도 카레만 먹어 봤어.
   G: 어땠어?
   B: 정말 매웠지만, 아주 좋았어.

2. **G:** Bill, 번지 점프하러 가 본 적 있니?
   B: 아니, 없어. Katie, 넌 어때?
   G: 뉴질랜드를 방문했을 때, 번지 점프를 한 번 해봤어.
   B: 무섭지 않았어?
   G: 아니, 좋았어. 또 하고 싶어.

1. **B:** 엄마, 오늘 날씨 어때요? 우산이 필요한가요?
   W: 바깥 날씨가 아주 흐려. 일기예보를 확인해 볼게.
   B: 고마워요, 엄마.
   W: 음, 오늘은 비가 안 올 거야.
   B: 좋아요! 그럼, 오늘은 우산이 필요 없어요.

2. **W:** 좋은 아침입니다, 일기예보에 오신 것을 환영합니다. 밖은 화창하지만 오후에는 약간의 비가 예상됩니다. 우산 없이 집을 나서지 마세요. 오늘의 일기예보입니다. 좋은 하루 되세요.

Communicate A~B

A. **Suho** Anna, _____ you _____ _____ Australia before?

    Anna: Yes, I _____. Actually, I _____ in Sydney _____ a year.

    Suho: Great! _____ the weather _____ in April? I'm _____ _____ visit Sydney _____ _____ next week.

    Anna: April is a great time _____ _____ Sydney. In April, it's _____ in Australia.

    Suho: Good. I'm _____ _____ _____ some time on the beach and _____ in the sun.

    Anna: Well, it _____ _____ in April, but you _____ have some _____ _____.

    Suho: I'll _____ my hat and _____ an umbrella, _____.

    Anna: That's a _____ _____. _____ a great time.

B. **A:** _____ you _____ _____ any special _____ in Korea?

    B: Yes, I _____. I _____ _____ Ulleungdo _____ summer _____ my family.

    A: _____ was the _____ there?

    B: It was _____ _____, but the weather _____ often.

Progress Check

1. **G:** _____ you ever _____ a horse?

    B: Yes, I _____. _____ _____ you?

    G: No, I _____. _____ was it?

    B: It was _____, but it was _____ _____ scary, _____.

2. **B:** Mom, how's the _____ today?

    W: It's quite _____ _____. I'll _____ the weather _____.

    B: Thanks, Mom.

    W: Well, it's _____ _____ _____ in the afternoon.

3. **M:** Good evening, and _____ _____ the weather forecast. It's _____ _____ _____, but we're _____ a sunny day tomorrow. Don't _____ home tomorrow _____ your hat.

A. 수호: Anna, 너 전에 호주에 가본 적 있어?

    Anna: 응, 있어. 사실, 나는 시드니에서 1년 동안 살았어.

    수호: 멋지다! 그곳의 4월 날씨는 어때? 난 다음 주 방학 때 시드니에 갈 거야.

    Anna: 4월은 시드니를 방문하기에 좋은 시기야. 4월에, 호주는 가을이야.

    수호: 좋아. 나는 해변에서 시간을 좀 보내고 햇빛을 쐬며 휴식을 취할 계획이야.

    Anna: 음, 4월에는 종종 비가 오지만, 맑은 날도 좀 있을 거야.

    수호: 나도 모자를 가져가고 우산도 챙길 거야.

    Anna: 좋은 생각이야. 좋은 시간 보내.

B. A: 넌 한국의 어느 특별한 장소들을 가본 적이 있니?

    B: 응, 있어. 나는 작년 여름에 가족과 울릉도에 갔어.

    A: 거기 날씨는 어땠어?

    B: 대체로 맑았지만, 날씨가 자주 바뀌었어.

1. G: 너 말을 타본 적 있니?

    B: 응, 있어. 너는 어때?

    G: 아니, 난 없어. 말 타는 거 어땠어?

    B: 재미있었지만, 조금 무섭기도 했어.

2. B: 엄마, 오늘 날씨 어때요?

    W: 바깥 날씨가 꽤 흐려. 일기예보를 확인해 볼게.

    B: 고마워요, 엄마.

    W: 음, 오후에 비가 올 거야.

3. M: 안녕하세요, 일기예보에 오신 것을 환영합니다. 지금은 비가 오지만 내일은 화창한 날씨가 예상됩니다. 내일 모자를 쓰지 않고 집을 나서지 마세요.

※ 다음 우리말에 맞도록 대화를 영어로 쓰시오.

해석

Listen & Speak 1 A. Listen and Check

1. G: _____
   B: _____
   G: _____
   B: _____

1. G: 너 인도 음식을 먹어 본 적이 있니?
   B: 응, 있어, 하지만 인도 카레만 먹어봤어.
   G: 어땠어?
   B: 정말 매웠지만, 아주 좋았어.

2. G: _____
   B: _____
   G: _____
   B: _____
   G: _____

2. G: Bill, 번지 점프하러 가 본 적 있니?
   B: 아니, 없어. Katie, 넌 어때?
   G: 뉴질랜드를 방문했을 때, 번지 점프를 한 번 해봤어.
   B: 무섭지 않았어?
   G: 아니, 좋았어. 또 하고 싶어.

Listen & Speak 2 A. Listen and Answer

1. B: _____
   W: _____
   B: _____
   W: _____
   B: _____

1. B: 엄마, 오늘 날씨 어때요? 우산이 필요한가요?
   W: 바깥 날씨가 아주 흐려. 일기예보를 확인해 볼게.
   B: 고마워요, 엄마.
   W: 음, 오늘은 비가 안 올 거야.
   B: 좋아요! 그럼, 오늘은 우산이 필요 없어요.

2. W: _____

2. W: 좋은 아침입니다, 일기예보에 오신 것을 환영합니다. 밖은 화창하지만 오후에는 약간의 비가 예상됩니다. 우산 없이 집을 나서지 마세요. 오늘의 일기예보입니다. 좋은 하루 되세요.

Communicate A~B

A. **Suho** _____

   Anna: _____

   Suho: _____

   _____

   Anna: _____

   Suho: _____

   Anna: _____

   Suho: _____

   Anna: _____

B. **A:** _____

   B: _____

   A: _____

   B: _____

Progress Check

1. **G:** _____

   B: _____

   G: _____

   B: _____

2. **B:** _____

   W: _____

   B: _____

   W: _____

3. **M:** _____

   _____

A. 수호: Anna, 너 전에 호주에 가본 적 있어?
   Anna: 응, 있어. 사실, 나는 시드니에서 1년 동안 살았어.
   수호: 멋지다! 그곳의 4월 날씨는 어때? 난 다음 주 방학 때 시드니에 갈 거야.
   Anna: 4월은 시드니를 방문하기에 좋은 시기야. 4월에, 호주는 가을이야.
   수호: 좋아. 나는 해변에서 시간을 좀 보내고 햇빛을 쐬며 휴식을 취할 계획이야.
   Anna: 음, 4월에는 종종 비가 오지만, 맑은 날도 좀 있을 거야.
   수호: 나도 모자를 가져가고 우산도 챙길 거야.
   Anna: 좋은 생각이야. 좋은 시간 보내.

B. A: 넌 한국의 어느 특별한 장소들을 가본 적이 있니?
   B: 응, 있어. 나는 작년 여름에 가족과 울릉도에 갔어.
   A: 거기 날씨는 어땠어?
   B: 대체로 맑았지만, 날씨가 자주 바뀌었어.

1. G: 너 말을 타본 적 있니?
   B: 응, 있어. 너는 어때?
   G: 아니, 난 없어. 말 타는 거 어땠어?
   B: 재미있었지만, 조금 무섭기도 했어.

2. B: 엄마, 오늘 날씨 어때요?
   W: 바깥 날씨가 꽤 흐려. 일기예보를 확인해 볼게.
   B: 고마워요, 엄마.
   W: 음, 오후에 비가 올 거야.

3. M: 안녕하세요, 일기예보에 오신 것을 환영합니다. 지금은 비가 오지만 내일은 화창한 날씨가 예상됩니다. 내일 모자를 쓰지 않고 집을 나서지 마세요.

※ 다음 우리말과 일치하도록 빈칸에 알맞은 것을 골라 쓰시오.

1 Hi, I _____ Lucy Hunter, and I _____ _____ London.
A. in　　　　　B. am　　　　　C. live

2 _____ week, my family went _____ a vacation _____ three days.
A. for　　　　　B. last　　　　　C. on

3 _____ our trip, I made _____ drawings in my _____.
A. journal　　　B. simple　　　C. during

4 That was a great _____ to _____ all the _____ moments.
A. special　　　B. capture　　　C. way

5 At _____, we _____ foot at Stonehenge, one of the most _____ places on Earth.
A. mysterious　B. set　　　　　C. last

6 _____ a two-hour _____ from our home in London, we _____ got to Stonehenge.
A. finally　　　B. drive　　　　C. after

7 It was just _____ to see the _____ of _____ stones.
A. huge　　　　B. ring　　　　　C. amazing

8 How did those huge _____ get there _____ of years _____?
A. ago　　　　　B. thousands　　C. stones

9 _____ were they _____?
A. for　　　　　B. what

10 I _____ Stonehenge will _____ a _____ for a long time.
A. remain　　　B. guess　　　　C. mystery

11 Don't _____ to make a _____ drawing.
A. perfect　　　B. try

12 A _____ colors will be _____.
A. enough　　　B. few

13 _____ the morning, we walked _____ the Cotswolds.
A. around　　　B. in

14 It _____ to rain in the afternoon, _____ we _____ to stay indoors at our B&B.
A. decided　　　B. started　　　C. so

15 A B&B is a _____ place to _____ in England.
A. stay　　　　　B. popular

1 안녕, 나는 Lucy Hunter이고 런던에 살아요.

2 지난주에 우리 가족은 3일 동안 휴가를 갔습니다.

3 여행 중에 나는 일기에 간단한 그림을 그렸어요.

4 그것은 모든 특별한 순간을 포착하는 훌륭한 방법이었어요.

5 마침내, 우리는 지구에서 가장 불가사의한 장소 중 하나인 스톤헨지에 발을 디뎠다.

6 런던에 있는 집에서 차로 두 시간을 달려서 우리는 마침내 스톤헨지에 도착했다.

7 원형으로 둘러서 있는 거대한 돌들을 보는 것은 정말 놀라웠다.

8 어떻게 그 거대한 돌들이 수천 년 전에 그곳에 도착했을까?

9 그것들은 무엇을 위한 것이었을까?

10 스톤헨지는 오랫동안 미스터리로 남을 것 같다.

11 완벽한 그림을 그리려고 하지 마세요.

12 몇 가지 색깔이면 충분할 것입니다.

13 아침에 우리는 코츠월드 언덕을 돌아다녔다.

14 오후에 비가 오기 시작해서, 우리는 B&B의 실내에서 머물기로 결정했다.

15 B&B는 영국에서 체류하는 곳으로 인기가 있다.

16 It feels more _____ a home _____ a hotel.

    A. than   B. like

17 The owner _____ us _____ afternoon tea today.

    A. for   B. invited

18 The _____ table was _____ of cookies, cake, bread, _____ cheese.

    A. and   B. full   C. dining

19 While I was _____ eating, Mom was _____ the beautiful cups and _____.

    A. plates   B. admiring   C. busy

20 I ate too _____, so I couldn't eat _____ for dinner.

    A. anything   B. much

21 It is O.K. to _____ everyday objects _____ cups and plates in your _____.

    A. journal   B. like   C. draw

22 _____ last _____ was Oxford.

    A. stop   B. our

23 We first _____ Christ Church _____.

    A. College   B. visited

24 It has _____ a world famous place to visit _____ it _____ in the *Harry Potter* movies.

    A. appeared   B. since   C. become

25 In the _____, Harry and everyone _____ eat _____ at the Hall of Christ Church.

    A. dinner   B. else   C. movies

26 We _____ saw _____ of famous people who _____ from the college.

    A. graduated   B. portraits   C. also

27 When we were _____ the building, I _____ to the famous olive tree and _____ it.

    A. touched   B. outside   C. walked

28 "_____ I _____ this tree," I said, "I will _____ into Oxford University!"

    A. get   B. touched   C. because

29 Then, my brother _____ to me with a _____, "I can't _____ to see your portrait on the wall."

    A. wait   B. smile   C. said

30 _____ your _____ avatar.

    A. own   B. create

31 Your _____ journal will become _____ more _____.

    A. interesting   B. much   C. drawing

---

16 그것은 호텔이라기보다는 집처럼 느껴진다.

17 주인은 오늘 오후의 다과회에 우리를 초대했다.

18 식탁에는 쿠키, 케이크, 빵, 그리고 치즈가 가득했다.

19 내가 먹느라고 바쁠 때, 엄마는 아름다운 컵과 접시를 감탄하며 바라보고 계셨다.

20 나는 너무 많이 먹어서 저녁으로 아무것도 먹을 수 없었다.

21 당신의 일기에 컵과 접시 같은 일상적인 물건들을 그려도 괜찮습니다.

22 우리가 마지막으로 머문 곳은 옥스퍼드였다.

23 우리는 먼저 Christ Church College를 방문했다.

24 이곳은 해리포터 영화에 등장한 이후 방문해야 할 세계적으로 유명한 장소가 되었다.

25 영화에서 Harry와 다른 모든 사람들이 Christ Church의 회관에서 저녁을 먹는다.

26 우리는 또한 그 대학을 졸업한 유명한 사람들의 초상화를 보았다.

27 우리가 건물 밖으로 나왔을 때, 나는 유명한 올리브 나무로 걸어가서 그것을 만졌다.

28 "이 나무를 만졌기 때문에, 난 옥스퍼드 대학교에 들어갈 거야!"라고 말했다.

29 그러자 오빠가 웃으면서 "벽에 걸린 네 초상화가 빨리 보고 싶어."라고 내게 말했다.

30 여러분 자신의 아바타를 만드세요.

31 그림일기가 훨씬 더 재미있을 거예요.

※ 다음 우리말과 일치하도록 빈칸에 알맞은 말을 쓰시오.

1 Hi, I _____ Lucy Hunter, and I _____ London.

2 _____ _____, my family _____ _____ a vacation _____ three days.

3 _____ our trip, I made simple _____ in my _____.

4 That was a great way _____ _____ all the _____ _____.

5 At last, we _____ _____ _____ Stonehenge, _____ _____ the most mysterious _____ on Earth.

6 _____ a two-hour _____ _____ our home in London, we finally _____ _____ Stonehenge.

7 It was just _____ to see the _____ of huge stones.

8 How did those _____ _____ get there _____ of years _____?

9 _____ were they _____?

10 I _____ Stonehenge will _____ a mystery _____ a long time.

11 _____ _____ to make a _____ drawing.

12 _____ _____ colors will be _____.

13 _____ the morning, we _____ _____ the Cotswolds.

14 It started _____ _____ in the afternoon, so we _____ _____ indoors at our B&B.

15 A B&B is a _____ place to _____ _____ England.

1 안녕, 나는 Lucy Hunter이고 런던에 살아요.

2 지난주에 우리 가족은 3일 동안 휴가를 갔습니다.

3 여행 중에 나는 일기에 간단한 그림을 그렸어요.

4 그것은 모든 특별한 순간을 포착하는 훌륭한 방법이었어요.

5 마침내, 우리는 지구에서 가장 불가사의한 장소 중 하나인 스톤헨지에 발을 디뎠다.

6 런던에 있는 집에서 차로 두 시간을 달려서 우리는 마침내 스톤헨지에 도착했다.

7 원형으로 둘러서 있는 거대한 돌들을 보는 것은 정말 놀라웠다.

8 어떻게 그 거대한 돌들이 수천 년 전에 그곳에 도착했을까?

9 그것들은 무엇을 위한 것이었을까?

10 스톤헨지는 오랫동안 미스터리로 남을 것 같다.

11 완벽한 그림을 그리려고 하지 마세요.

12 몇 가지 색깔이면 충분할 것입니다.

13 아침에 우리는 코츠월드 언덕을 돌아다녔다.

14 오후에 비가 오기 시작해서, 우리는 B&B의 실내에서 머물기로 결정했다.

15 B&B는 영국에서 체류하는 곳으로 인기가 있다.

16 It _____ more _____ a home _____ a hotel.

17 The _____ _____ us for afternoon tea today.

18 The _____ table _____ _____ _____ cookies, cake, bread, and cheese.

19 While I was _____ _____, Mom was _____ the beautiful cups and _____.

20 I _____ too much, _____ I _____ _____ anything for dinner.

21 It is O.K. _____ _____ everyday objects _____ cups and plates in your _____.

22 Our _____ _____ was Oxford.

23 We _____ _____ Christ Church College.

24 It _____ _____ a world _____ _____ to visit _____ it appeared in the *Harry Potter* movies.

25 In the movies, Harry and _____ else _____ _____ at the Hall of Christ Church.

26 We also _____ _____ of famous people who _____ _____ the college.

27 _____ we were _____ the building, I _____ _____ the famous olive tree and _____ it.

28 "_____ I _____ this tree," I said, "I will _____ _____ Oxford University!"

29 Then, my brother said to me _____ _____ _____, "I _____ _____ _____ see your portrait on the wall."

30 _____ your own _____.

31 Your _____ _____ will become _____ _____ interesting.

16 그것은 호텔이라기보다는 집처럼 느껴진다.

17 주인은 오늘 오후의 다과회에 우리를 초대했다.

18 식탁에는 쿠키, 케이크, 빵, 그리고 치즈가 가득했다.

19 내가 먹느라고 바쁠 때, 엄마는 아름다운 컵과 접시를 감탄하며 바라보고 계셨다.

20 나는 너무 많이 먹어서 저녁으로 아무것도 먹을 수 없었다.

21 당신의 일기에 컵과 접시 같은 일상적인 물건들을 그려도 괜찮습니다.

22 우리가 마지막으로 머문 곳은 옥스퍼드였다.

23 우리는 먼저 Christ Church College를 방문했다.

24 이곳은 해리포터 영화에 등장한 이후 방문해야 할 세계적으로 유명한 장소가 되었다.

25 영화에서 Harry와 다른 모든 사람들이 Christ Church의 회관에서 저녁을 먹는다.

26 우리는 또한 그 대학을 졸업한 유명한 사람들의 초상화를 보았다.

27 우리가 건물 밖으로 나왔을 때, 나는 유명한 올리브 나무로 걸어가서 그것을 만졌다.

28 "이 나무를 만졌기 때문에, 난 옥스퍼드 대학교에 들어갈 거야!"라고 말했다.

29 그러자 오빠가 웃으면서 "벽에 걸린 네 초상화가 빨리 보고 싶어."라고 내게 말했다.

30 여러분 자신의 아바타를 만드세요.

31 그림일기가 훨씬 더 재미있을 거예요.

※ 다음 문장을 우리말로 쓰시오.

1 ▶ Hi, I am Lucy Hunter, and I live in London.

➡ _____

2 ▶ Last week, my family went on a vacation for three days.

➡ _____

3 ▶ During our trip, I made simple drawings in my journal.

➡ _____

4 ▶ That was a great way to capture all the special moments.

➡ _____

5 ▶ At last, we set foot at Stonehenge, one of the most mysterious places on Earth.

➡ _____

6 ▶ After a two-hour drive from our home in London, we finally got to Stonehenge.

➡ _____

7 ▶ It was just amazing to see the ring of huge stones.

➡ _____

8 ▶ How did those huge stones get there thousands of years ago?

➡ _____

9 ▶ What were they for?

➡ _____

10 ▶ Don't try to make a perfect drawing.

➡ _____

11 ▶ A few colors will be enough.

➡ _____

12 ▶ I guess Stonehenge will remain a mystery for a long time.

➡ _____

13 ▶ In the morning, we walked around the Cotswolds.

➡ _____

14 ▶ It started to rain in the afternoon, so we decided to stay indoors at our B&B.

➡ _____

15 ▶ A B&B is a popular place to stay in England.

➡ _____

16 ⮞ It feels more like a home than a hotel.

➡ _____

17 ⮞ The owner invited us for afternoon tea today.

➡ _____

18 ⮞ The dining table was full of cookies, cake, bread, and cheese.

➡ _____

19 ⮞ While I was busy eating, Mom was admiring the beautiful cups and plates.

➡ _____

20 ⮞ I ate too much, so I couldn't eat anything for dinner.

➡ _____

21 ⮞ It is O.K. to draw everyday objects like cups and plates in your journal.

➡ _____

22 ⮞ Our last stop was Oxford.

➡ _____

23 ⮞ We first visited Christ Church College.

➡ _____

24 ⮞ It has become a world famous place to visit since it appeared in the *Harry Potter* movies.

➡ _____

25 ⮞ In the movies, Harry and everyone else eat dinner at the Hall of Christ Church.

➡ _____

26 ⮞ We also saw portraits of famous people who graduated from the college.

➡ _____

27 ⮞ When we were outside the building, I walked to the famous olive tree and touched it.

➡ _____

28 ⮞ "Because I touched this tree," I said, "I will get into Oxford University!"

➡ _____

29 ⮞ Then, my brother said to me with a smile, "I can't wait to see your portrait on the wall."

➡ _____

30 ⮞ Create your own avatar.

➡ _____

31 ⮞ Your drawing journal will become much more interesting.

➡ _____

※ 다음 괄호 안의 단어들을 우리말에 맞도록 바르게 배열하시오.

1 (am / hi, / Hunter, / I / Lucy / and / London. / live / I / in)
➡ _____

2 (week, / last / went / family / my / a / on / days. / three / for / vacation)
➡ _____

3 (our / during / trip, / made / I / drawings / in / journal. / simple / my)
➡ _____

4 (was / a / that / great / way / capture / to / moments. / the / all / special)
➡ _____

5 (last, / at / foot / set / we / Stonehenge, / at / of / one / places / Earth. / most / the / on / mysterious)
➡ _____

6 (a / drive / after / two-hour / our / from / home / London, / in / we / Stonehenge. / to / finally / got)
➡ _____

7 (just / it / amazing / was / see / to / the / stones. / of / huge / ring)
➡ _____

8 (did / how / stones / huge / those / there / get / ago? / years / of / thousands)
➡ _____

9 (were / they / for? / what)
➡ _____

10 (try / don't / make / to / drawing. / perfect / a)
➡ _____

11 (few / a / colors / enough. / be / will)
➡ _____

12 (guess / I / Stonehenge / remain / will / a / time. / a / mystery / long / for)
➡ _____

13 (the / morning, / in / walked / the / we / Cotswolds. / around)
➡ _____

14 (to / started / rain / the / it / in / afternoon, / so / decided / we / to / at / indoors / B&B. / stay / our)
➡ _____

15 (a / is / B&B / place / popular / a / stay / England. / to / in)
➡ _____

1 안녕, 나는 Lucy Hunter이고 런던에 살아요.

2 지난주에 우리 가족은 3일 동안 휴가를 갔습니다.

3 여행 중에 나는 일기에 간단한 그림을 그렸어요.

4 그것은 모든 특별한 순간을 포착하는 훌륭한 방법이었어요.

5 마침내, 우리는 지구에서 가장 불가사의한 장소 중 하나인 스톤헨지에 발을 디뎠다.

6 런던에 있는 집에서 차로 두 시간을 달려서 우리는 마침내 스톤헨지에 도착했다.

7 원형으로 둘러서 있는 거대한 돌들을 보는 것은 정말 놀라웠다.

8 어떻게 그 거대한 돌들이 수천 년 전에 그곳에 도착했을까?

9 그것들은 무엇을 위한 것이었을까?

10 스톤헨지는 오랫동안 미스터리로 남을 것 같다.

11 완벽한 그림을 그리려고 하지 마세요.

12 몇 가지 색깔이면 충분할 것입니다.

13 아침에 우리는 코츠월드 언덕을 돌아다녔다.

14 오후에 비가 오기 시작해서, 우리는 B&B의 실내에서 머물기로 결정했다.

15 B&B는 영국에서 체류하는 곳으로 인기가 있다.

16 (feels / it / like / a / more / hotel. / than / home / a)
➡ _____

17 (owner / the / us / invited / today. / for / tea / afternoon)
➡ _____

18 (dining / the / table / of / was / full / cookies, / bread, / and / cheese. / cake,)
➡ _____

19 (was / eating, / while / I / busy / was / Mom / admiring / the / plates. / cups / and / beautiful)
➡ _____

20 (ate / much, / I / too / so / I / eat / anything / couldn't / dinner. / for)
➡ _____

21 (is / to / O.K. / it / draw / objects / eveyday / cups / like / in / and / journal. / your / plates)
➡ _____

22 (last / our / was / Oxford. / stop)
➡ _____

23 (first / we / visited / College. / Church / Christ)
➡ _____

24 (it / become / has / a / place / famous / world / visit / to / in / since / appeared / it / movies. / the / Potter / Harry)
➡ _____

25 (the / in / movies, / and / everyone / Harry / eat / else / dinner / Church. / of / Hall / at / the / Christ)
➡ _____

26 (also / saw / we / portraits / people / of / famous / who / college. / the / from / graduated)
➡ _____

27 (were / we / when / the / building, / the / outside / I / walked / tree / the / olive / to / famous / and / it. / touched)
➡ _____

28 (I / tree," / touched / "because / this / I / said, / will / "I / into / University!" / get / Oxford)
➡ _____

29 (then, / brother / my / said / me / to / smile, / a / with / "I / wait / see / can't / to / on / wall." / the / portrait / your)
➡ _____

30 (your / avatar. / own / create)
➡ _____

31 (drawing / your / journal / become / will / more / interesting. / much)
➡ _____

16 그것은 호텔이라기보다는 집처럼 느껴진다.
17 주인은 오늘 오후의 다과회에 우리를 초대했다.
18 식탁에는 쿠키, 케이크, 빵, 그리고 치즈가 가득했다.
19 내가 먹느라고 바쁠 때, 엄마는 아름다운 컵과 접시를 감탄하며 바라보고 계셨다.
20 나는 너무 많이 먹어서 저녁으로 아무것도 먹을 수 없었다.
21 당신의 일기에 컵과 접시 같은 일상적인 물건들을 그려도 괜찮습니다.
22 우리가 마지막으로 머문 곳은 옥스퍼드였다.
23 우리는 먼저 Christ Church College를 방문했다.
24 이곳은 해리포터 영화에 등장한 이후 방문해야 할 세계적으로 유명한 장소가 되었다.
25 영화에서 Harry와 다른 모든 사람들이 Christ Church의 회관에서 저녁을 먹는다.
26 우리는 또한 그 대학을 졸업한 유명한 사람들의 초상화를 보았다.
27 우리가 건물 밖으로 나왔을 때, 나는 유명한 올리브 나무로 걸어가서 그것을 만졌다.
28 "이 나무를 만졌기 때문에, 난 옥스퍼드 대학교에 들어갈 거야"라고 말했다.
29 그러자 오빠가 웃으면서 "벽에 걸린 네 초상화가 빨리 보고 싶어."라고 내게 말했다.
30 여러분 자신의 아바타를 만드세요.
31 그림일기가 훨씬 더 재미있을 거예요.

※ **다음 우리말을 영어로 쓰시오.**

1 안녕, 나는 Lucy Hunter이고 런던에 살아요.

➡ _____

2 지난주에 우리 가족은 3일 동안 휴가를 갔습니다.

➡ _____

3 여행 중에 나는 일기에 간단한 그림을 그렸어요.

➡ _____

4 그것은 모든 특별한 순간을 포착하는 훌륭한 방법이었어요.

➡ _____

5 마침내, 우리는 지구에서 가장 불가사의한 장소 중 하나인 스톤헨지에 발을 디뎠다.

➡ _____

6 런던에 있는 집에서 차로 두 시간을 달려서 우리는 마침내 스톤헨지에 도착했다.

➡ _____

7 원형으로 둘러서 있는 거대한 돌들을 보는 것은 정말 놀라웠다.

➡ _____

8 어떻게 그 거대한 돌들이 수천 년 전에 그곳에 도착했을까?

➡ _____

9 그것들은 무엇을 위한 것이었을까?

➡ _____

10 완벽한 그림을 그리려고 하지 마세요.

➡ _____

11 몇 가지 색깔이면 충분할 것입니다.

➡ _____

12 스톤헨지는 오랫동안 미스터리로 남을 것 같다.

➡ _____

13 아침에 우리는 코츠월드 언덕을 돌아다녔다.

➡ _____

14 오후에 비가 오기 시작해서, 우리는 B&B의 실내에서 머물기로 결정했다.

➡ _____

15 B&B는 영국에서 체류하는 곳으로 인기가 있다.

➡ _____

16 그것은 호텔이라기보다는 집처럼 느껴진다.

➡ _____

17 주인은 오늘 오후의 다과회에 우리를 초대했다.

➡ _____

18 식탁에는 쿠키, 케이크, 빵, 그리고 치즈가 가득했다.

➡ _____

19 내가 먹느라 바쁠 때, 엄마는 아름다운 컵과 접시를 감탄하며 바라보고 계셨다.

➡ _____

20 나는 너무 많이 먹어서 저녁으로 아무것도 먹을 수 없었다.

➡ _____

21 당신의 일기에 컵과 접시 같은 일상적인 물건들을 그려도 괜찮습니다.

➡ _____

22 우리가 마지막으로 머문 곳은 옥스퍼드였다.

➡ _____

23 우리는 먼저 Christ Church College를 방문했다.

➡ _____

24 이곳은 해리포터 영화에 등장한 이후 방문해야 할 세계적으로 유명한 장소가 되었다.

➡ _____

25 영화에서 Harry와 다른 모든 사람들이 Christ Church의 회관에서 저녁을 먹는다.

➡ _____

26 우리는 또한 그 대학을 졸업한 유명한 사람들의 초상화를 보았다.

➡ _____

27 우리가 건물 밖으로 나왔을 때, 나는 유명한 올리브 나무로 걸어가서 그것을 만졌다.

➡ _____

28 "이 나무를 만졌기 때문에, 난 옥스퍼드 대학교에 들어갈 거야!"라고 말했다.

➡ _____

29 그러자 오빠가 웃으면서 "벽에 걸린 네 초상화가 빨리 보고 싶어."라고 말했다.

➡ _____

30 여러분 자신의 아바타를 만드세요.

➡ _____

31 그림일기가 훨씬 더 재미있을 거예요.

➡ _____

※ 다음 우리말과 일치하도록 빈칸에 알맞은 말을 쓰시오.

Link - Share

1. We _____ _____ a field trip to Namhae _____ month.

2. _____ was just _____ to see so many beautiful _____.

3. We _____ _____ Namhae German _____.

4. We'll _____ _____ that trip.

1. 우리는 지난달에 남해로 현장 학습을 갔다.
2. 그토록 아름다운 많은 섬들을 보는 것은 아주 놀라웠다.
3. 우리는 남해 독일 마을도 방문했다.
4. 우리는 그 여행을 절대 잊지 못할 것이다.

Write

1. _____ _____, I _____ to Laos _____ my family.

2. We visited a _____ of beautiful _____ and went to the night _____ in Vientiane.

3. Then, we _____ _____ Vang Vieng and _____ river tubing.

4. We also _____ their _____ food.

5. It was a _____ _____ fun _____ _____ new things in a _____ country.

6. I hope I will have a _____ _____ _____ Laos again.

1. 지난 겨울, 나는 가족과 함께 라오스에 갔다.
2. 우리는 아름다운 절들을 많이 방문했고 Vientiane의 야시장에 갔다.
3. 그러고 나서, 우리는 Vang Vieng으로 옮겨서 강에 튜브를 타러 갔다.
4. 우리는 또한 그들의 전통 음식을 즐겼다.
5. 외국에서 새로운 것을 시도하는 것은 매우 재미있었다.
6. 나는 라오스를 다시 방문할 기회가 있기를 바란다.

Culture Project

1. _____ 15, 1835

2. We finally _____ _____ this island.

3. There _____ many animals _____ _____ here.

4. Today, I _____ some _____ turtles.

5. It was _____ to _____ them.

1. 1835년 9월 15일
2. 우리는 마침내 이 섬에 도착했다.
3. 여기는 조사할 동물들이 많다.
4. 오늘, 나는 몇몇 이상한 거북들을 보았다.
5. 그들을 보는 것은 놀라웠다.

※ 다음 우리말을 영어로 쓰시오.

Link - Share

1. 우리는 지난달에 남해로 현장 학습을 갔다.

   ➡ _____

2. 그토록 아름다운 많은 섬들을 보는 것은 아주 놀라웠다.

   ➡ _____

3. 우리는 남해 독일 마을도 방문했다.

   ➡ _____

4. 우리는 그 여행을 절대 잊지 못할 것이다.

   ➡ _____

Write

1. 지난 겨울, 나는 가족과 함께 라오스에 갔다.

   ➡ _____

2. 우리는 아름다운 절들을 많이 방문했고 Vientiane의 야시장에 갔다.

   ➡ _____

3. 그러고 나서, 우리는 Vang Vieng으로 옮겨서 강에 튜브를 타러 갔다.

   ➡ _____

4. 우리는 또한 그들의 전통 음식을 즐겼다.

   ➡ _____

5. 외국에서 새로운 것을 시도하는 것은 매우 재미있었다.

   ➡ _____

6. 나는 라오스를 다시 방문할 기회가 있기를 바란다.

   ➡ _____

Culture Project

1. 1835년 9월 15일

   ➡ _____

2. 우리는 마침내 이 섬에 도착했다.

   ➡ _____

3. 여기는 조사할 동물들이 많다.

   ➡ _____

4. 오늘, 나는 몇몇 이상한 거북들을 보았다.

   ➡ _____

5. 그들을 보는 것은 놀라웠다.

   ➡ _____

※ 다음 영어를 우리말로 쓰시오.

01 inventor _____

02 pressure _____

03 activity _____

04 support _____

05 bath _____

06 shopping _____

07 childhood _____

08 purpose _____

09 trial _____

10 truly _____

11 driver _____

12 shock _____

13 project _____

14 favor _____

15 fix _____

16 gift _____

17 close _____

18 homeless _____

19 invention _____

20 joy _____

21 local _____

22 comfortable _____

23 perfect _____

24 still _____

25 board _____

26 person _____

27 plant _____

28 succeed _____

29 lucky _____

30 safety _____

31 always _____

32 sensor _____

33 condition _____

34 understand _____

35 give up _____

36 grow up _____

37 be thankful for _____

38 feel like -ing _____

39 for[with] joy _____

40 wander off _____

41 come up with _____

42 come over to _____

43 take care of _____

※ 다음 우리말을 영어로 쓰시오.

01 걱정하다

02 믿다

03 딸

04 질병

05 자랑스러워하는

06 오류

07 함께 쓰다, 공유하다

08 깨끗한; 청소하다

09 세대

10 행복

11 더 나쁜; 더 심하게

12 기쁨, 즐거움

13 그저, 단지

14 (물건의) 재료

15 발뒤꿈치

16 신호

17 이해하다

18 거닐다, 돌아다니다

19 목욕, 욕조

20 존경하다; 존경

21 실제로

22 무거운

23 신뢰할 수 있는

24 상태

25 ~할 때까지

26 자원 봉사자

27 안전

28 노숙자의

29 성공하다

30 지지하다

31 편안한

32 압력, 압박

33 발명, 발명품

34 기쁨, 환희

35 ~을 돌보다

36 ~에 오다

37 ~을 찾다

38 A에게 B에 대해 감사하다

39 (해답 등을) 찾아내다

40 처음에는

41 여기저기 쏘다니다

42 ~을 격려하다

43 ~을 계속 지켜보다

※ 다음 영영풀이에 알맞은 단어를 <보기>에서 골라 쓴 후, 우리말 뜻을 쓰시오.

1 _____ : weighing a lot: _____

2 _____ : at all times: _____

3 _____ : a feeling of great happiness: _____

4 _____ : the back part of your foot, just below your ankle: _____

5 _____ : cause something to happen or exist: _____

6 _____ : the person who is driving a vehicle: _____

7 _____ : as good as something could possibly be: _____

8 _____ : to accept or regard something as true: _____

9 _____ : something that you give someone as a present: _____

10 _____ : force that you produce when you press hard on something: _____

11 _____ : the state of being safe from harm or danger: _____

12 _____ : the period of a person's life when they are a child: _____

13 _____ : a person who has invented something, or whose job is to invent things: _____

14 _____ : making you feel physically relaxed when you use something: _____

15 _____ : to agree with someone, and perhaps help them because you want them to succeed: _____

16 _____ : to keep thinking about problems that you have or about unpleasant things that might happen _____

보기			
create	perfect	worry	inventor
heavy	joy	believe	heel
pressure	comfortable	gift	childhood
support	driver	safety	always

※ 다음 우리말과 일치하도록 빈칸에 알맞은 말을 쓰시오.

 해석

Listen & Speak 1 A. Listen and Check

1. G: Mark, can you _____ _____ _____ _____?

   B: Sure. _____ is it?

   G: My _____ is _____ _____ _____ for a week. Can you _____ to our house and _____ the plants?

   B: Yes, I _____.

2. G: Kevin, _____ you do me a _____?

   B: O.K. What is _____?

   G: Can you _____ _____ _____ my science _____ this afternoon?

   B: _____, but I _____. I _____ _____ _____ my grandma _____ my mom.

Listen & Speak 2 A. Listen and Check

1. G: _____, Mom! Hi, Dad! _____ _____ _____, today is my 15th _____. I _____ _____ a chance _____ thank you for _____ my parents. You've truly _____ my friends _____ my teachers. Thank you _____ _____ me and always _____ to understand me. I'm really _____ to be your _____.

2. G: What _____ you _____ this _____, Eric?

   B: _____ _____. I'll just _____ home and _____ TV.

   G: Great! I'm _____ a birthday _____ this weekend. Can you come?

   B: Sure. Thank you _____ _____ me.

Listen & Speak 1-B

A: _____ you _____ me a _____?

B: Sure. _____ is it?

A: Can you _____ this table _____ me? It's too _____.

B: Sure. _____ _____.

A: _____ you _____ _____ me.

1. G: Mark, 부탁 하나 들어줄래?
   B: 물론이지. 부탁할게 무엇이지?
   G: 우리 가족은 일주일 동안 휴가를 갈 거야. 우리 집에 와서 식물들에게 물을 줄 수 있니?
   B: 응, 할 수 있어.

2. G: Kevin, 부탁 하나 들어줄래?
   B: 좋아. 뭔데?
   G: 오늘 오후에 내 과학 프로젝트 좀 도와줄래?
   B: 미안하지만 안 돼. 엄마랑 할머니 댁에 가야 해.

1. G: 안녕, 엄마! 안녕, 아빠! 엄마, 아빠도 아시다시피, 오늘은 제 15번째 생일이에요. 제 부모님이 되어주신 것에 대해 감사할 기회가 없었어요. 두 분께서는 정말 제 친구이자 선생님이셨어요. 저를 지지해 주시고 항상 저를 이해하려고 노력해 주셔서 감사해요. 저는 두 분의 딸이 되어서 정말 자랑스러워요.

2. G: Eric, 이번 주말에 뭐 할 거니?
   B: 특별한 건 없어. 그냥 집에 있으면서 TV를 볼 거야.
   G: 좋아! 이번 주말에 생일 파티를 할 거야. 올 수 있니?
   B: 물론이지. 초대해 줘서 고마워.

A: 부탁 하나 들어줄래?
B: 그래. 뭔데?
A: 이 테이블 좀 옮겨줄래? 너무 무거워.
B: 물론이지. 문제없어.
A: 도와줘서 고마워.

Communicate A. Listen and Answer

Jaden: _____ you _____ _____ _____ _____, Yuri?

Yuri: Sure. _____ is it, Jaden?

Jaden: Can we _____ _____ together _____ a baseball cap for a girl?

Yuri: Yes, _____ _____. _____ is it _____?

Jaden: It's _____ _____ _____ _____ Kate.

Yuri: Oh, are you _____ her _____ _____ _____?

Jaden: No, her birthday _____ _____ _____.

Yuri: Then, _____ _____ you _____ a baseball _____ for her?

Jaden: She _____ her leg _____ _____ _____ _____ her bike _____ week. I _____ want to _____ _____ _____.

Yuri: Oh, I _____. I _____ _____ this Friday afternoon.

Jaden: That _____ _____. Thank you.

Jaden: 유리야, 부탁 하나 들어줄래?
유리: 물론이지. 뭔데, Jaden?
Jaden: 우리 같이 여자용 야구 모자 사러 쇼핑갈 수 있을까?
유리: 응, 물론이지. 누구 주려고?
Jaden: 내 여동생 Kate에게 줄 거야.
유리: 아, 너 그 애에게 생일 선물을 사 주려고 하는 거야?
Jaden: 아니, 그 애의 생일은 10월이 되어야 해.
유리: 그렇다면, 왜 야구 모자를 사 주려고 하는 거야?
Jaden: 그 애는 지난주에 자전거를 타다가 다리가 부러졌어. 난 그저 그 애를 격려하고 싶어
유리: 아, 그렇구나. 이번 주 금요일 오후에 갈 수 있어.
Jaden: 그거 아주 좋아. 고마워.

Progress Check

1. **G:** Andrew, _____ _____ _____ me a _____?

   B: O.K. _____ is _____?

   G: My family is _____ _____ _____ to Jejudo _____ _____. Can you _____ _____ _____ my cat _____ the weekend?

   B: Sure. Don't _____ about her. And _____ your trip.

2. **G:** _____, Mr. Smith. We _____ had _____ _____ _____ you _____ _____ our teacher. _____ morning, you _____ us in the classroom. You _____ _____ us important and interesting _____. We're _____ _____ _____ you, and we're _____ _____ _____ your _____.

3. **G:** Do you have _____ _____ _____ this weekend?

   B: No, I'm _____ _____ _____ home.

   G: Oh, _____ can you _____ _____ to my house _____ _____?

1. G: Andrew, 부탁 하나 들어줄래?
   B: 좋아. 뭔데?
   G: 우리 가족은 이번 주말에 제주도에 갈 거야. 주말에 내 고양이 좀 봐줄래?
   B: 물론이지. 고양이 걱정은 하지 말고, 여행을 즐겨.

2. G: 안녕하세요, Smith 선생님. 우리의 선생님이 되어주신 것에 대해 감사할 기회가 없었습니다. 매일 아침, 선생님은 교실에서 우리를 맞이하십니다. 선생님은 항상 우리에게 중요하고 흥미로운 것들을 가르쳐주십니다. 우리는 선생님이 계셔서 행운이고, 선생님의 학생이라는 것이 자랑스럽습니다.

3. G: 이번 주말에 무슨 특별한 계획 있니?
   B: 아니, 그냥 집에 있을 거야.
   G: 아, 그럼 우리 집에 저녁 먹으러 올 수 있어?

대화문 Test

※ 다음 우리말에 맞도록 대화를 영어로 쓰시오.

Listen & Speak 1 A. Listen and Check

1. G: _____

   B: _____

   G: _____

   _____

   B: _____

2. G: _____

   B: _____

   G: _____

   B: _____

Listen & Speak 2 A. Listen and Check

1. G: _____

   _____

   _____

   _____

2. G: _____

   B: _____

   G: _____

   B: _____

Listen & Speak 1-B

A: _____

B: _____

A: _____

B: _____

A: _____

해석

1. G: Mark, 부탁 하나 들어줄래?
   B: 물론이지. 부탁할게 무엇이지?
   G: 우리 가족은 일주일 동안 휴가를 갈 거야. 우리 집에 와서 식물들에게 물을 줄 수 있니?
   B: 응, 할 수 있어.

2. G: Kevin, 부탁 하나 들어줄래?
   B: 좋아. 뭔데?
   G: 오늘 오후에 내 과학 프로젝트 좀 도와줄래?
   B: 미안하지만 안 돼. 엄마랑 할머니 댁에 가야 해.

1. G: 안녕, 엄마! 안녕, 아빠! 엄마, 아빠도 아시다시피, 오늘은 제 15번째 생일이에요. 제 부모님이 되어주신 것에 대해 감사할 기회가 없었어요. 두 분께서는 정말 제 친구이자 선생님이셨어요. 저를 지지해 주시고 항상 저를 이해하려고 노력해 주셔서 감사해요. 저는 두 분의 딸이 되어서 정말 자랑스러워요.

2. G: Eric, 이번 주말에 뭐 할 거니?
   B: 특별한 건 없어. 그냥 집에 있으면서 TV를 볼 거야.
   G: 좋아! 이번 주말에 생일 파티를 할 거야. 올 수 있니?
   B: 물론이지. 초대해 줘서 고마워.

A: 부탁 하나 들어줄래?
B: 그래. 뭔데?
A: 이 테이블 좀 옮겨줄래? 너무 무거워.
B: 물론이지. 문제없어.
A: 도와줘서 고마워.

Communicate A. Listen and Answer

Jaden: _____

Yuri: _____

Jaden: _____

Yuri: _____

Jaden: _____

Yuri: _____

Jaden: _____

Yuri: _____

Jaden: _____
_____

Yuri: _____

Jaden: _____

Progress Check

1. G: _____
   B: _____
   G: _____
   _____
   B: _____

2. G: _____
   _____
   _____

3. G: _____
   B: _____
   G: _____

Jaden: 유리야, 부탁 하나 들어줄래?
유리: 물론이지. 뭐야, Jaden?
Jaden: 우리 같이 여자용 야구 모자 사러 쇼핑갈 수 있을까?
유리: 응, 물론이지. 누구 주려고?
Jaden: 내 여동생 Kate에게 줄 거야.
유리: 아, 너 그 애에게 생일 선물을 사 주려고 하는 거야?
Jaden: 아니, 그 애의 생일은 10월이 되어야 해.
유리: 그렇다면, 왜 야구 모자를 사 주려고 하는 거야?
Jaden: 그 애는 지난주에 자전거를 타다가 다리가 부러졌어. 난 그저 그 애를 격려하고 싶어
유리: 아, 그렇구나. 이번 주 금요일 오후에 갈 수 있어.
Jaden: 그거 아주 좋아. 고마워.

1. G: Andrew, 부탁 하나 들어줄래?
   B: 좋아. 뭔데?
   G: 우리 가족은 이번 주말에 제주도에 갈 거야. 주말에 내 고양이 좀 봐줄래?
   B: 물론이지. 고양이 걱정은 하지 말고, 여행을 즐겨.

2. G: 안녕하세요, Smith 선생님. 우리의 선생님이 되어주신 것에 대해 감사할 기회가 없었습니다. 매일 아침, 선생님은 교실에서 우리를 맞이하십니다. 선생님은 항상 우리에게 중요하고 흥미로운 것들을 가르쳐주십니다. 우리는 선생님이 계셔서 행운이고, 선생님의 학생이라는 것이 자랑스럽습니다.

3. G: 이번 주말에 무슨 특별한 계획 있니?
   B: 아니, 그냥 집에 있을 거야.
   G: 아, 그럼 우리 집에 저녁 먹으러 올 수 있어?

※ 다음 우리말과 일치하도록 빈칸에 알맞은 것을 골라 쓰시오.

1 Kenneth Shinozuka grew _____ in a big happy _____ of three _____.
A. generations   B. family   C. up

2 Since he was _____, he has always _____ very _____ to his grandfather.
A. close   B. been   C. little

3 He was Kenneth's _____ friend, his _____ driver, and his _____.
A. cook   B. first   C. trusty

4 He also _____ him many life _____.
A. lessons   B. taught

5 He was the _____ who Kenneth _____ the _____ in the world.
A. most   B. respected   C. person

6 When Kenneth was four, his grandfather _____ out _____ a walk one day and _____ lost.
A. got   B. for   C. went

7 He _____ Alzheimer's _____.
A. disease   B. had

8 _____ in Kenneth's family _____ in _____.
A. was   B. everyone   C. shock

9 His condition _____ worse _____ the next 10 years.
A. became   B. over

10 He _____ _____ at night so often that someone had to _____ an eye on him _____ night long.
A. keep   B. off   C. all   D. wandered

11 _____ night, Kenneth's grandfather _____ out of bed, and Kenneth _____ it.
A. saw   B. got   C. one

12 At that _____, he said to _____, "Why _____ I put pressure sensors on the _____ of his socks?"
A. heels   B. himself   C. don't   D. moment

---

1 Kenneth Shinozuka는 3대의 행복한 대가족에서 자랐다.

2 그는 어렸을 때부터 항상 할아버지와 매우 친했다.

3 그는 Kenneth의 첫 친구이자, 신뢰할 수 있는 운전기사이자, 요리사였다.

4 그는 또한 그에게 많은 인생 교훈을 가르쳐 주었다.

5 그는 Kenneth가 세상에서 가장 존경하는 사람이었다.

6 Kenneth가 네 살이었을 때, 그의 할아버지는 어느 날 산책을 나갔다가 길을 잃었다.

7 그는 알츠하이머병에 걸렸다.

8 Kenneth의 가족 모두는 충격에 빠졌다.

9 그의 상태는 10년 동안 더 악화되었다.

10 그는 자주 밤에 여기저기 돌아다니기 때문에 누군가가 그를 밤새 감시해야 했다.

11 어느 날 밤, Kenneth의 할아버지가 침대에서 일어났는데, Kenneth가 그것을 보았다.

12 그 순간, 그는 혼잣말을 했다. "내가 할아버지의 양말 뒤꿈치에 압력 감지기를 설치하는 게 어떨까?"

13 There _____ many things _____ Kenneth had to _____.

    A. do   B. that   C. were

14 He first had to create a pressure _____ and then find a _____ to send a _____ to his smart phone.

    A. signal   B. sensor   C. way

15 Kenneth also _____ many different _____ to make _____ socks for his _____ grandfather.

    A. comfortable   B. tried   C. elderly   D. materials

16 When he felt _____ giving _____, he thought about his grandfather's _____.

    A. safety   B. up   C. like

17 After much _____ and _____, he finally _____ in making his device.

    A. succeeded   B. error   C. trial

18 When it first _____, he was _____ happy _____ he jumped for joy.

    A. that   B. so   C. worked

19 He could not _____ that his _____ actually _____.

    A. worked   B. invention   C. believe

20 _____ his grandfather, Kenneth is the best _____ in the _____.

    A. world   B. for   C. inventor

21 For Kenneth, _____ grandfather is _____ his _____ friend.

    A. best   B. his   C. still

---

13 Kenneth가 해야 할 많은 일들이 있었다.

14 그는 처음에 압력 감지기를 만들고 나서 그의 스마트폰으로 신호를 보낼 방법을 찾아야 했다.

15 Kenneth는 또한 그의 연로한 할아버지에게 편안한 양말을 만들어 주기 위해 많은 다양한 재료들을 가지고 만들어 보았다.

16 그는 포기하고 싶은 생각이 들 때 할아버지의 안전에 대해 생각했다.

17 많은 시행착오 끝에 그는 마침내 자신의 장치를 만드는 데 성공했다.

18 그것이 처음 작동했을 때, 그는 너무 행복해 기뻐서 펄쩍 뛰었다.

19 그는 자신의 발명품이 실제로 작동했다는 것을 믿을 수 없었다.

20 그의 할아버지에게 Kenneth는 세계 최고의 발명가이다.

21 Kenneth에게 그의 할아버지는 여전히 그의 가장 친한 친구이다.

※ 다음 우리말과 일치하도록 빈칸에 알맞은 말을 쓰시오.

1 Kenneth Shinozuka _____ _____ in a big happy _____ of _____ _____.

2 _____ he _____ _____, he has always _____ very _____ _____ his grandfather.

3 He was Kenneth's _____ _____, his _____ _____, and his _____.

4 He _____ _____ him many _____ _____.

5 He was the person _____ Kenneth _____ _____ _____ in the world.

6 _____ Kenneth was four, his grandfather _____ _____ _____ _____ _____ one day and _____ _____.

7 He _____ Alzheimer's _____.

8 _____ in Kenneth's family _____ _____ _____ _____.

9 His condition _____ _____ _____ the next 10 years.

10 He _____ _____ at night _____ often _____ someone had to _____ _____ _____ on him _____ night long.

11 One night, Kenneth's grandfather _____ _____ _____ bed, and Kenneth _____ it.

12 At that _____, he _____ _____ _____, "Why _____ I put pressure sensors on the _____ of his socks?"

---

1 Kenneth Shinozuka는 3대의 행복한 대가족에서 자랐다.

2 그는 어렸을 때부터 항상 할아버지와 매우 친했다.

3 그는 Kenneth의 첫 친구이자, 신뢰할 수 있는 운전기사이자, 요리사였다.

4 그는 또한 그에게 많은 인생 교훈을 가르쳐 주었다.

5 그는 Kenneth가 세상에서 가장 존경하는 사람이었다.

6 Kenneth가 네 살이었을 때, 그의 할아버지는 어느 날 산책을 나갔다가 길을 잃었다.

7 그는 알츠하이머병에 걸렸다.

8 Kenneth의 가족 모두는 충격에 빠졌다.

9 그의 상태는 10년 동안 더 악화되었다.

10 그는 자주 밤에 여기저기 돌아다니기 때문에 누군가가 그를 밤새 감시해야 했다.

11 어느 날 밤, Kenneth의 할아버지가 침대에서 일어났는데, Kenneth가 그것을 보았다.

12 그 순간, 그는 혼잣말을 했다. "내가 할아버지의 양말 뒤꿈치에 압력 감지기를 설치하는 게 어떨까?"

13 There _____ many things _____ Kenneth _____

_____ _____ .

13 Kenneth가 해야 할 많은 일들
이 있었다.

14 He first _____ _____ _____ a pressure sensor and

_____ find _____ _____ _____ _____ a _____

to his smart phone.

14 그는 처음에 압력 감지기를 만들
고 나서 그의 스마트폰으로 신호
를 보낼 방법을 찾아야 했다.

15 Kenneth also _____ many different _____ to make

comfortable _____ for his elderly grandfather.

15 Kenneth는 또한 그의 연로한
할아버지에게 편안한 양말을 만
들어 주기 위해 많은 다양한 재
료들을 가지고 만들어 보았다.

16 When he _____ _____ _____ _____ , he thought about

his grandfather's _____ .

16 그는 포기하고 싶은 생각이 들
때 할아버지의 안전에 대해 생
각했다.

17 _____ much _____ and _____ , he finally _____

_____ _____ his device.

17 많은 시행착오 끝에 그는 마침
내 자신의 장치를 만드는 데 성
공했다.

18 When it first _____ , he was so happy _____ he _____

_____ _____ .

18 그것이 처음 작동했을 때, 그는
너무 행복해 기뻐서 펄쩍 뛰었다.

19 He _____ _____ _____ that his invention _____ _____ .

19 그는 자신의 발명품이 실제로 작
동했다는 것을 믿을 수 없었다.

20 _____ his grandfather, Kenneth is _____ _____

in the world.

20 그의 할아버지에게 Kenneth는
세계 최고의 발명가이다.

21 For Kenneth, his grandfather _____ _____ his _____

_____ .

21 Kenneth에게 그의 할아버지는
여전히 그의 가장 친한 친구이다.

※ 다음 문장을 우리말로 쓰시오.

1 Kenneth Shinozuka grew up in a big happy family of three generations.

➡ _____

2 Since he was little, he has always been very close to his grandfather.

➡ _____

3 He was Kenneth's first friend, his trusty driver, and his cook.

➡ _____

4 He also taught him many life lessons.

➡ _____

5 He was the person who Kenneth respected the most in the world.

➡ _____

6 When Kenneth was four, his grandfather went out for a walk one day and got lost.

➡ _____

7 He had Alzheimer's disease.

➡ _____

8 Everyone in Kenneth's family was in shock.

➡ _____

9 His condition became worse over the next 10 years.

➡ _____

10 He wandered off at night so often that someone had to keep an eye on him all night long.

➡ _____

11 One night, Kenneth's grandfather got out of bed, and Kenneth saw it.

➡ _____

12 At that moment, he said to himself, "Why don't I put pressure sensors on the heels of his socks?"

➡ _____

13 There were many things that Kenneth had to do.

➡ _____

14 He first had to create a pressure sensor and then find a way to send a signal to his smart phone.

➡ _____

15 Kenneth also tried many different materials to make comfortable socks for his elderly grandfather.

➡ _____

16 When he felt like giving up, he thought about his grandfather's safety.

➡ _____

17 After much trial and error, he finally succeeded in making his device.

➡ _____

18 When it first worked, he was so happy that he jumped for joy.

➡ _____

19 He could not believe that his invention actually worked.

➡ _____

20 For his grandfather, Kenneth is the best inventor in the world.

➡ _____

21 For Kenneth, his grandfather is still his best friend.

➡ _____

※ 다음 괄호 안의 단어들을 우리말에 맞도록 바르게 배열하시오.

1 (Shinozuka / Kenneth / up / grew / in / happy / a / family / big / generations. / three / of)

➡ _____

2 (he / little, / since / was / has / he / been / always / to / grandfather. / close / very / his)

➡ _____

3 (was / he / friend, / Kenneth's / first / his / driver, / and / trusty / cook. / his)

➡ _____

4 (also / he / taught / many / him / lessons. / life)

➡ _____

5 (was / the / he / person / Kenneth / who / the / respected / in / world. / the / most)

➡ _____

6 (Kenneth / when / four, / was / grandfather / his / for / went / out / one / a / day / walk / lost. / and / got)

➡ _____

7 (had / disease. / he / Alzheimer's)

➡ _____

8 (Kenneth's / in / family / everyone / shock. / in / was)

➡ _____

9 (condition / his / worse / became / the / years. / over / 10 / next)

➡ _____

10 (wondered / he / off / night / at / often / that / so / someone / to / had / keep / night / an / long. / all / eye / him / on)

➡ _____

11 (night, / one / grandfather / Kenneth's / out / bed, / got / of / and / it. / saw / Kenneth)

➡ _____

12 (moment, / that / at / he / to / said / himself, / "why / put / I / don't / sensors / pressure / socks?" / of / on / heels / the / his)

➡ _____

1 Kenneth Shinozuka는 3대의 행복한 대가족에서 자랐다.

2 그는 어렸을 때부터 항상 할아 버지와 매우 친했다.

3 그는 Kenneth의 첫 친구이자, 신뢰할 수 있는 운전기사이자, 요리사였다.

4 그는 또한 그에게 많은 인생 교 훈을 가르쳐 주었다.

5 그는 Kenneth가 세상에서 가장 존경하는 사람이었다.

6 Kenneth가 네 살이었을 때, 그 의 할아버지는 어느 날 산책을 나갔다가 길을 잃었다.

7 그는 알츠하이머병에 걸렸다.

8 Kenneth의 가족 모두는 충격에 빠졌다.

9 그의 상태는 10년 동안 더 악화 되었다.

10 그는 자주 밤에 여기저기 돌아 다니기 때문에 누군가가 그를 밤새 감시해야 했다.

11 어느 날 밤, Kenneth의 할아 버지가 침대에서 일어났는데, Kenneth가 그것을 보았다.

12 그 순간, 그는 혼잣말을 했다. "내가 할아버지의 양말 뒤꿈치 에 압력 감지기를 설치하는 게 어떨까?"

13 (were / things / there / many / that / do. / Kenneth / to / had)

➡ _____

14 (first / he / to / had / create / sensor / pressure / a / and / then / a / find / way / send / to / his / signal / to / a / phone. / smart)

➡ _____
_____

15 (also / Kenneth / many / tried / materials / different / socks / to / comfortable / make / grandfather. / his / for / elderly)

➡ _____
_____

16 (he / like / when / up, / felt / giving / he / about / thought / safety. / grandfather's / his)

➡ _____

17 (error, / much / and / after / trial / he / succeeded / finally / device. / his / making / in)

➡ _____

18 (first / it / worked, / when / he / so / was / happy / that / joy. / he / for / jumped)

➡ _____

19 (could / he / believe / not / that / worked. / his / invention / actually)

➡ _____

20 (his / for / grandfather, / is / Kenneth / inventor / best / the / world. / the / in)

➡ _____

21 (Kenneth, / for / grandfather / his / still / his / is / friend. / best)

➡ _____

13 Kenneth가 해야 할 많은 일들이 있었다.

14 그는 처음에 압력 감지기를 만들고 나서 그의 스마트폰으로 신호를 보낼 방법을 찾아야 했다.

15 Kenneth는 또한 그의 연로한 할아버지에게 편안한 양말을 만들어 주기 위해 많은 다양한 재료들을 가지고 만들어 보았다.

16 그는 포기하고 싶은 생각이 들 때 할아버지의 안전에 대해 생각했다.

17 많은 시행착오 끝에 그는 마침내 자신의 장치를 만드는 데 성공했다.

18 그것이 처음 작동했을 때, 그는 너무 행복해 기뻐서 펄쩍 뛰었다.

19 그는 자신의 발명품이 실제로 작동했다는 것을 믿을 수 없었다.

20 그의 할아버지에게 Kenneth는 세계 최고의 발명가이다.

21 Kenneth에게 그의 할아버지는 여전히 그의 가장 친한 친구이다.

※ 다음 우리말을 영어로 쓰시오.

1   Kenneth Shinozuka는 3대의 행복한 대가족에서 자랐다.

➡ _____

2   그는 어렸을 때부터 항상 할아버지와 매우 친했다.

➡ _____

3   그는 Kenneth의 첫 친구이자, 신뢰할 수 있는 운전기사이자, 요리사였다.

➡ _____

4   그는 또한 그에게 많은 인생 교훈을 가르쳐 주었다.

➡ _____

5   그는 Kenneth가 세상에서 가장 존경하는 사람이었다.

➡ _____

6   Kenneth가 네 살이었을 때, 그의 할아버지는 어느 날 산책을 나갔다가 길을 잃었다.

➡ _____

7   그는 알츠하이머병에 걸렸다.

➡ _____

8   Kenneth의 가족 모두는 충격에 빠졌다.

➡ _____

9   그의 상태는 10년 동안 더 악화되었다.

➡ _____

10   그는 자주 밤에 여기저기 돌아다니기 때문에 누군가가 그를 밤새 감시해야 했다.

➡ _____

11   어느 날 밤, Kenneth의 할아버지가 침대에서 일어났는데, Kenneth가 그것을 보았다.

➡ _____

12   그 순간, 그는 혼잣말을 했다. "내가 할아버지의 양말 뒤꿈치에 압력 감지기를 설치하는 게 어떨까?"

➡ _____

13 Kenneth가 해야 할 많은 일들이 있었다.

➡ _____

14 그는 처음에 압력 감지기를 만들고 나서 그의 스마트폰으로 신호를 보낼 방법을 찾아야 했다.

➡ _____

15 Kenneth는 또한 그의 연로한 할아버지에게 편안한 양말을 만들어 주기 위해 많은 다양한 재료들을 가지고 만들어 보았다.

➡ _____

16 그는 포기하고 싶은 생각이 들 때 할아버지의 안전에 대해 생각했다.

➡ _____

17 많은 시행착오 끝에 그는 마침내 자신의 장치를 만드는 데 성공했다.

➡ _____

18 그것이 처음 작동했을 때, 그는 너무 행복해 기뻐서 펄쩍 뛰었다.

➡ _____

19 그는 자신의 발명품이 실제로 작동했다는 것을 믿을 수 없었다.

➡ _____

20 그의 할아버지에게 Kenneth는 세계 최고의 발명가이다.

➡ _____

21 Kenneth에게 그의 할아버지는 여전히 그의 가장 친한 친구이다.

➡ _____

※ 다음 우리말과 일치하도록 빈칸에 알맞은 말을 쓰시오.

Link - Share

1. I'd like to talk about the _____ _____ that we're _____ to do for the _____ people in our city.

2. We _____ _____ _____ three activities.

3. _____ _____ them is to make *patbingsu* _____ them and eat it together.

1. 나는 우리가 우리 도시의 노인들을 위해 계획하고 있는 자원봉사에 대해 이야기하고 싶다.
2. 우리는 세 가지 활동을 생각해 냈다.
3. 그 중 하나는 그들을 위해 팥빙수를 만들어 함께 먹는 것이다.

Write - Write

1. Hello, I am Kim Doha, and I _____ _____ to join your _____ project.

2. _____ day, I saw some poor dogs _____ TV.

3. They looked _____ sad _____ I wanted _____ _____ them.

4. I like dogs, and _____ _____ many things _____ I can do for them.

5. I can _____ the dogs, give them a _____, and play _____ them.

6. I am the person _____ you are _____ _____!

1. 안녕, 나는 김도하야, 그리고 나는 너의 자원봉사 프로젝트에 참가하고 싶어.
2. 어느 날, 나는 TV에서 몇 마리의 불쌍한 개들을 보았어.
3. 그들은 너무 슬퍼 보여서 나는 그들을 돕고 싶었어.
4. 나는 개를 좋아하고, 그들을 위해 내가 할 수 있는 많은 것들이 있어.
5. 나는 개들을 산책시키고, 목욕시키고 그들과 함께 놀 수 있어.
6. 네가 찾는 사람이 바로 나야!

Culture Project

1. Do you want _____ _____ children?

2. _____ our Child _____ Project in Laos.

3. You'll teach _____ children.

4. You'll also _____ a school _____ them.

5. The work is _____ hard _____ you'll want to go home _____ first, but you'll find _____ in _____ these children.

1. 여러분은 아이들을 돕고 싶나요?
2. 라오스에 있는 우리의 아동 보호 프로젝트에 참여하십시오.
3. 여러분은 지역 아이들을 가르칠 겁니다.
4. 여러분은 또한 그들을 위해 학교를 지을 겁니다.
5. 일이 너무 힘들어 처음에는 집에 가고 싶지만, 이 아이들을 돕는 데서 행복을 찾을 수 있을 겁니다.

※ 다음 우리말을 영어로 쓰시오.

Link - Share

1. 나는 우리가 우리 도시의 노인들을 위해 계획하고 있는 자원봉사에 대해 이야기하고 싶다.

   ➡ _____

2. 우리는 세 가지 활동을 생각해 냈다.

   ➡ _____

3. 그 중 하나는 그들을 위해 팥빙수를 만들어 함께 먹는 것이다.

   ➡ _____

Write - Write

1. 안녕, 나는 김도하야, 그리고 나는 너의 자원봉사 프로젝트에 참가하고 싶어.

   ➡ _____

2. 어느 날, 나는 TV에서 몇 마리의 불쌍한 개들을 보았어.

   ➡ _____

3. 그들은 너무 슬퍼 보여서 나는 그들을 돕고 싶었어.

   ➡ _____

4. 나는 개를 좋아하고, 그들을 위해 내가 할 수 있는 많은 것들이 있어.

   ➡ _____

5. 나는 개들을 산책시키고, 목욕시키고 그들과 함께 놀 수 있어.

   ➡ _____

6. 네가 찾는 사람이 바로 나야!

   ➡ _____

Culture Project

1. 여러분은 아이들을 돕고 싶나요?

   ➡ _____

2. 라오스에 있는 우리의 아동 보호 프로젝트에 참여하십시오.

   ➡ _____

3. 여러분은 지역 아이들을 가르칠 겁니다.

   ➡ _____

4. 여러분은 또한 그들을 위해 학교를 지을 겁니다.

   ➡ _____

5. 일이 너무 힘들어 처음에는 집에 가고 싶지만, 이 아이들을 돕는 데서 행복을 찾을 수 있을 겁니다.

   ➡ _____

MEMO

MEMO

MEMO

1학기 전과정

plus

적중 100

영어 기출 문제집

영어 기출 문제집

적중 100 plus

1학기

정답 및 해설

미래 | 최연희

중 2

영어 기출 문제집

적중"100

1학기

정답 및 해설

미래 | 최연희

중 2

적중"100

Great Things about Yourself

시험대비 실력평가   p.08

01 ②	02 ②	03 ④	04 wife
05 ①	06 danger	07 decide	08 ②

01 ①, ③, ④, ⑤의 -er은 동사의 행위자를 나타내는 말이고, ②는 '스쿠터'

02 in front of: ~ 앞에 / be good for: ~에 좋다

03 한 장소에서 다른 장소로, 종종 멀리 떨어진 장소로 가다: 여 행하다(travel)

04 남성명사-여성명사의 관계이다. 소년 : 소녀 = 남편 : 아내

05 say hello to: ~에게 인사하다

06 누군가 다치거나 죽을지도 모를 가능성: danger(위험)

07 decide: 결정하다

08 be afraid of: ~을 무서워하다 / a lot of: 많은

핵심 Check   p.10~11

1 (1) good at
  (2) how to / poor at
  (3) how to swim
2 (1) am sure
  (2) Are, sure

교과서 대화문 익히기

Check(√) True or False   p.12

1 F   2 T   3 F   4 T   5 T   6 F

서술형 시험대비   p.09

01 (1) actor   (2) cartoonist   (3) inventor
02 (1) such as   (2) do a good job   (3) a look at
03 (1) fun   (2) give   (3) per   (4) unique
04 (1) cloudy   (2) nervous   (3) dangerous
05 (1) good at   (2) good for
   (3) give away   (4) fall asleep
06 (1) (h)unsband   (2) (d)ecide

01 (1), (3)은 '동사 : 행위자' 관계이고, (2)는 '명사 - 행위자' 관계이다.

02 (1) such as: ~과 같은 (2) do a good job: 잘하다 (3) take a look at: ~을 보다

03 (1) fun: 재미 (2) give a speech: 연설하다 (3) per: ~당[마다] (4) unique: 유일무이한, 독특한

04 (1) cloudy: 흐린 (2) nervous: 불안해[초조해] 하는 (3) dangerous: 위험한

05 (1) be good at: ~을 잘하다 (2) be good for: ~에 좋다 (3) give away: 나누어 주다 (4) fall asleep: 잠들다

06 (1) husband: 남편 (2) decide: 결정하다, 결심하다

교과서 확인학습   p.14~15

Listen & Speak 1 A. Listen and Check
1 What, doing / making, out / good, recycling / recycling, fun, good
2 everyone, be, president, listener, try, good, fun, work, class, vote, listening

Listen & Speak 2 A. Listen and Check
1 Hi, wrong / have, front, nervous / worry, speaker, sure, job / Thanks, better
2 birthday, should / don't, for, good / idea, hope, like / sure, love

Communicate A. Listen and Answer
1 What, doing / cartoons / Can, look / yet / not, show, can't / guess / cartoons, good, drawing / so, be, think, enough / funny, unique, sure, cartoonist / Thank, day
2 don't, musical, singing / like, think, good / worry, teach, sure, join / think

Progress Check
1 doing / making / really, at
2 wrong / give, in, nervous / worry, Practice, front, sure, job / try
3 something, Some, at, Other, good, What

01 ②　　02 ①　　03 ③　　04 ①, ③

01 be good at: ~을 잘하다

02 I'm sure that ~, Surely, ~. 등은 확신을 말할 때 사용하는 표현이다.

03 능력을 나타낼 때는 조동사 can이나 be good at을 써서 표현할 수 있다.

04 B가 마지막 말에서 I'm sure ~.라고 했으므로 '확신하니?'라는 표현이 들어가야 한다.

01 ②　　02 ③　　03 sure[certain]
04 I am not good at playing the guitar.　　05 ④
06 ④　　07 ④　　08 listen, well　09 ②
10 listening　　11 ④　　12 matter with
13 ③, ⑤　　14 나는 네가 잘할 것이라고 확신해.

01 나미야, 뭐 해? - 오래된 청바지로 스마트폰 케이스를 만들고 있어 - 와! 너 오래된 것들을 재활용하는 것을 잘하는구나. - 고마워. 나는 재활용하는 것을 좋아해. 그것은 재미있고, 우리의 지구에도 좋아.

02 '~할 줄 아는지' 능력을 묻는 표현이다.

03 Are you sure[certain] (that)+주어+동사 ~?는 확신 여부를 묻는 표현이다.

04 능력을 부인하는 표현으로 I'm not good at을 사용할 수 있다.

05 I'm sure that ~.은 It's certain that ~. 표현과 같은 의미이다.

06 ④ A가 '너는 바이올린을 정말 아름답게 연주하는구나.'라고 칭찬을 했는데 B가 '나는 바이올린 연주하는 법을 몰라.'라고 대답하는 것은 어색하다.

07 ⓐ, ④ 명사적 용법 ①,③ 형용사적 용법 ②,⑤ 부사적 용법

08 '형용사+명사' 구문은 '동사+부사' 구문으로 바꿔 쓸 수 있다.

09 be good at: ~을 잘하다

10 전치사의 목적어로는 동명사가 와야 한다.

11 김유진이 공부를 열심히 하는지는 위 담화문을 통해 알 수 없다.

12 Is something wrong?=What's the matter with you?: 무슨 좋지 않은 일이 있니?

13 give[make, deliver] a speech: 연설을 하다

14 do a good job: 잘하다

01 (1) He is good at Chinese.
　　(2) I'm sure (that) there are two boys in the room.

　　(3) Do you know how to make cookies?

02 I am not good at cooking. / I can't cook well.

03 (B) – (D) – (C) – (A)

04 I'm sure that he'll pass the exam.

05 about baking

06 at

07 소녀의 어머니를 위해 케이크를 굽는 것

01 (1) be good at: ~을 잘하다 (2) 「I'm sure that+주어+동사 ~」: 나는 ~을 확신한다. (3) how to ~: ~하는 방법

02 어떤 일을 할 능력이 없는 것을 나타낼 때 사용하는 표현을 쓴다.

03 너 뭐 하고 있니? - 저녁으로 피자를 만들고 있어. - 와! 넌 요리를 정말 잘하는구나! - 고마워.

04 I'm sure that+주어+동사 ~.: 나는 ~을 확신한다.

05 Why don't you ~?는 제안하는 표현으로 How[What] about -ing ~?로 바꿔 쓸 수 있다.

06 be good at: ~을 잘하다

07 that은 지시대명사로 앞에 나온 문장을 받는다.

핵심 Check　　　p.20~21

1 (1) who　(2) which　(3) who　(4) which　(5) who
2 (1) while　(2) after　(3) Before

01 (1) who　(2) which　(3) which　(4) who　(5) which
02 (1) while　(2) when　(3) after　(4) before
03 (1) who　(2) which　(3) who　(4) that　(5) which

01 주격 관계대명사는 선행사가 사람일 경우 who, 사물일 경우 which를 쓴다.

02 (1) while: ~하는 동안 (2) when: ~할 때 (3) after: ~한 후에 (4) before: ~하기 전에

03 (1) 선행사가 사람(the girl)이므로 who를 쓴다. (2) 선행사가 사물(the dolls)이므로 which를 쓴다. (3) 선행사가 사람(a friend)이므로 who를 쓴다. (4) 선행사가 사람(the girl)이므로 that 을 쓴다. (5) 선행사가 사물(the river)이므로 which를 쓴다.

01 ⑤　　　02 ①　　　03 ⑤
04 (1) who[that]　(2) that　05 ⑤　　　06 ②
07 ④　　　08 ⑤　　　09 ①　　　10 ①
11 ⑤　　　12 ②, ④　　　13 ⑤
14 which → that　　　15 ②　　　16 ④
17 I will ask him about it when he comes home.
18 ②　　　19 ①　　　20 ①, ③

01 첫 번째 문장은 이유, 두 번째 문장은 때를 나타낸다.
02 ⓐ 선행사가 사람이고 주격이므로 who를 쓴다. ⓑ is의 보어이
　므로 동명사나 to부정사가 올 수 있다.
03 A before B(B를 하기 전에 A를 하다) = B after A(A를 하
　고 나서 B를 하다)
04 (1) 선행사가 사람(the boy)이므로 which 대신 who나 that
　을 써야 한다. (2) 선행사 앞에 최상급이 왔으므로 관계대명사
　that을 쓴다.
05 before가 이끄는 때를 나타내는 부사절은 미래의 의미이더라도
　현재시제로 써야 한다. will get → gets
06 선행사가 사람이고 주격이므로 관계대명사 who가 들어가야 알맞
　다.
07 선행사 the building이 사물이고 주격이므로 관계대명사
　which가 들어가야 알맞다.
08 ①은 After, ②는 when, ③은 If, ④는 Though[Although]
　를 쓸 수 있다.
09 첫 문장은 선행사가 사람이고 주격이므로 관계대명사 who가 들
　어가야 알맞다. 두 번째 문장은 선행사가 사물이고 주격이므로
　관계대명사 which가 들어가야 알맞다.
10 ①은 '~인데 반해'의 뜻이고, 나머지는 '~하는 동안에'라는 뜻을
　지닌 접속사이다.
11 선행사가 사물이고, 주격이므로 관계대명사 which가 알맞다.
12 선행사가 사물이고, 관계사절에서 The bus는 주격이므로 관계
　대명사 which나 that이 알맞다.
13 while: ~하는 동안 / put on: ~을 입다
14 선행사가 사람과 동물 둘 다 있을 때는 that을 사용한다.
15 while은 '~하는 동안'과 '~인 반면에'의 두 가지 뜻이 있다.
16 <보기>와 ④는 관계대명사, ①은 지시부사(그렇게), ②는 접속
　사, ③은 지시대명사, ⑤는 지시형용사로 쓰였다.
17 when이 이끄는 때를 나타내는 부사절은 미래의 일이라도 현재
　시제를 쓴다.
18 나머지는 after가 접속사로 쓰여, 뒤에 「주어+동사」로 구성된
　절이 왔지만, ②는 전치사로 쓰였다.
19 ① 선행사가 사람이므로 which를 쓸 수 없다.
20 <보기> 접속사 ① 의문부사 ② 접속사 ③ 관계부사 ④ 접속사
　⑤ 접속사

01 that[which]
02 (1) I went shopping　(2) I had dinner
　(3) it started to rain.　(4) he looks around.
03 that
04 I will call you when I arrive.
05 (1) The young lady who is sitting on the bench is
　our music teacher.
　(2) We found a dog which was running toward us.
　(3) This is the firefighter that saved the baby from
　the burning building.
　(4) This is the only story that is interesting to read.
06 (1) before　(2) when　(3) after　(4) while
07 (1) I know the woman who[that] is standing by
　the car.
　(2) Did you see the car which[that] has only two
　doors?
　(3) This is a restaurant which[that] is famous for
　its spaghetti.
　(4) The lady who[that] lives next door is my English
　teacher.
08 While we are having dinner
09 which[that], was
10 Before they washed the dishes, they finished
　dinner. / They finished dinner before they
　washed the dishes.
11 before → while
12 I know the[a] doctor who[that] likes baseball.
13 They had a party after she arrived there. /
　After she arrived there, they had a party.

01 선행사가 동물(the cat)이므로 which 또는 that을 관계대명사
　로 쓴다.
02 after: ~한 후에 / before: ~하기 전에
03 선행사가 사람일 때와 사물일 때 모두 쓸 수 있는 관계대명사는
　that이다.
04 때를 나타내는 부사절에서는 미래의 일을 현재시제로 나타 낸다.
05 (1) The young lady를 선행사로 한다. (2) a dog를 선행사
　로 한다. (3) the firefighter를 선행사로 한다. (4) the only
　story를 선행사로 한다.
06 before: ~하기 전에 / when: ~할 때 / after: ~한 후에 / while:
　~하는 동안
07 (1) 선행사가 the woman이므로 주격 관계대명사 who 또는
　that으로 연결한다. (2) 선행사가 the car이므로 주격 관계대명
　사 which 또는 that으로 연결한다. (3) 선행사가 a restaurant
　이므로 주격 관계대명사 which 또는 that으로 연결한다. (3)
　선행사가 The lady이므로 주격 관계대명사 who 또는 that으

로 연결한다.

08 while은 '~하는 동안'의 의미를 지닌다.

09 선행사가 The traffic accident이므로 관계대명사는 which 또는 that이다. 또, 단수이므로 was가 알맞다.

11 엄마가 신을 벗을 동안 전화를 끊지 않고 기다려 주겠니? / hold the line: (전화를) 끊지 않고 기다리다

12 선행사가 사람이고 주격이므로 who나 that을 쓴다.

13 after가 이끄는 절은 주절의 앞이나 뒤에 위치할 수 있다.

교과서 Reading

확인문제   p.28

1 F 2 F 3 F 4 T 5 T

확인문제   p.29

1 T 2 F 3 F 4 T 5 T 6 F

교과서 확인학습 A   p.30~31

01 name, like, novels
02 While, home, woman
03 lookesd, unique
04 going, suddenly   05 but, asked
06 course   07 see, every
08 Surprisingly, workers
09 different, thought   10 should, about
11 After, began   12 superhero   13 rides, that
14 saves, danger 15 also, per, hungry
16 later, graphic 17 superhero, cool
18 what, on, worker   19 showed, to
20 loved   21 also, who, talents
22 another, dancing
23 janitor, once, ranger
24 like, stories, think, asked
25 course, cheerfully
26 go, hello, superhero

교과서 확인학습 B   p.32~33

1 My name is Hojin, and I like to make graphic novels.

2 While I was walking home from school last week, I saw a woman on a scooter.

3 She looked really cool, and her scooter was very unique.

4 "Are you going home, Hojin?" she said to me suddenly.

5 "Yes, but do I know you?" I asked.

6 "Of course," she answered.

7 "I see you at the school cafeteria every day."

8 Surprisingly, she was one of the cafeteria workers at school.

9 "Amazing! She looks so different outside the school," I thought.

10 "I should write a graphic novel about her."

11 After I got home, I began to write a new graphic novel, Lunch Lady Begins .

12 In it, Lunch Lady is a superhero.

13 She rides a super scooter that can fly

14 She saves people from danger around the world.

15 She also makes 100 cookies per second and gives them away to hungry children.

16 A few days later, I showed my graphic novel to my friends.

17 "Awesome! I love this superhero. She's so cool," said all my friends.

18 "Guess what? I modeled her on Ms. Lee, one of our cafeteria workers," I told them.

19 I showed my book to Ms. Lee.

20 She loved it, too.

21 She also told me about her coworkers who had special talents.

22 Ms. Park, another cafeteria worker, won a dancing contest.

23 Mr. Kim, the janitor at our school, was once an adventurous park ranger.

24 "I'd like to write superhero stories about them. Do you think they'll like that?" I asked Ms. Lee.

25 "Of course they will," she said cheerfully.

26 "Let's go and say hello to our new superhero friends."

시험대비 실력평가   p.34~37

01 ②   02 ③   03 suddenly   04 난 매일
학교 식당에서 너를 본단다.   05 ③   06 ④

07 ⑤	08 (d)anger	09 ①	10 ②
11 later	12 ③	13 ④	14 He modeled her on Ms. Lee, one of his cafeteria workers.
		15 ③	16 ④
17 adventurous		18 그들에 대한 슈퍼히어로 이야기를 쓰는 것	19 ④ 20 (r)ole (m)odel
21 ⑤	22 that	23 ②	
24 ①, ③	25 (t)alent	26 ④	27 ②
28 ③	29 ②	30 but	31 ⑤

01 스쿠터를 타고 있는 여인에 대한 문장 다음인 ②에 와야 한다.

02 while: ~하는 동안에

03 sudden+-ly=suddenly

04 every day: 매일

05 ③ 호진이가 어디 사는지는 알 수 없다.

06 문맥상 '다른'이 알맞다.

07 문맥상 '집에 온 후'가 알맞다.

08 누군가를 다치게 하거나 해를 입히거나 죽일 수 있는 어떤 일이 일어날 가능성

09 per와 a는 '~당[마다]'의 뜻으로 쓰인다.

10 ② 호진은 그 여인을 구내식당에서 본 적이 있지만, 밖에서 보니까 다른 여인 같았다고 진술하고 있다.

11 a few days later: 며칠 후에

12 show는 간접목적어를 직접목적어 뒤로 보낼 때 전치사 to를 붙인다.

13 Guess what: 있잖아, 알겠니?, 맞혀 봐!

14 호진이는 그녀를 학교 식당 직원의 한 명인 이 씨를 모델로 했다.

15 주격 관계대명사 who 대신 that을 쓸 수 있다.

16 another+단수명사: 또 다른 ~

17 adventure의 형용사형이 알맞다.

18 that은 지시대명사로 앞에 나온 내용을 받는다.

19 ④ 박 여사가 언제 춤 경연 대회에서 우승했는지는 언급되지 않았다.

20 당신이 숭배하고 닮기를 원하는 사람: role model(역할 모델)

21 while: ~하는 동안

22 주격 관계대명사 who 대신 that을 쓸 수 있다.

23 ⓓ와 ②는 전치사로 쓰였고, 나머지는 모두 동사로 쓰였다.

24 선행사가 사람이고 주격이므로 관계대명사 who나 that을 쓸 수 있다.

25 어떤 것을 잘 할 수 있는 타고난 능력: talent(재능)

26 attend: ~에 다니다

27 ⓓ, ② 명사적 용법 ①, ⑤ 형용사적 용법 ③, ④ 부사적 용법

28 liked의 보어로 형용사가 와야 한다. coolly → cool

29 '~을 타고'를 나타낼 때는 전치사 on을 쓴다.

30 문맥상 '그러나, 하지만'의 뜻이 알맞다.

31 ⑤ 그 여인이 식당에서 일하고 있는지는 위 글에서 알 수 없다.

01 Surprisingly	02 different	03 which
04 from	05 100 cookies	06 Lunch Lady는 초당 100개의 쿠키를 만든다.
		07 to
08 (s)uperhero	09 나는 그녀를 우리 식당 직원 중 한 명인 이 여사를 모델로 했어.	10 to 11 that
12 other → another	13 특수한 재능을 가진 이 여사의 동료들 14 cheerfully	15 Yes, she was.
16 adventurous	17 a friend → friends	
18 who[that] 19 of		

01 surprising: 놀라운 / surprisingly: 놀랍게도

02 same: 같은 / different: 다른

03 선행사가 사물이고 주격이므로 which나 that을 쓸 수 있다.

04 save A from B: B로부터 A를 구하다

05 them은 인칭대명사로 앞에 나온 복수명사를 받는다.

07 show+직접목적어+to+간접목적어

08 만화나 영화에 나오는 특별한 힘을 가지고 악에 대항해 싸우는 등장인물: superhero(슈퍼영웅)

09 model: 모델로 하다

10 4형식의 문장을 3형식의 문장으로 바꿔 쓴다.

11 선행사가 사람이고 주격이므로 who나 that을 쓸 수 있다.

12 other 뒤에는 복수명사, another 뒤에는 단수명사가 온다.

14 동사 said를 수식하므로 cheerful의 부사형이 되어야 한다.

15 박 여사는 댄싱 대회에서 우승한 적이 있다고 했다.

16 adventure의 형용사형을 쓴다.

17 make friends: 친구를 사귀다

18 선행사가 사람이고 주격이므로 who나 that을 쓸 수 있다.

19 be afraid of: ~을 두려워하다

01 ④	02 ③	03 (w)rong	04 ③
05 ⑤	06 ①	07 enough	08 ②
09 No, you can't take a look at them yet.			10 ①
11 ③	12 ④	13 It, certain	14 ②
15 ④	16 sure[certain]		17 ①
18 ④	19 ②	20 He brushed his teeth after he finished his dinner.	21 ⑤
			22 ③
23 ②	24 ①	25 ⑤	26 What is the name of the tallest boy that[who] just came in?
27 will see → sees		28 ②	29 Lunch Lady Begins 30 She saves people from danger around the world.
			31 ⑤ 32 ④
33 ③	34 workers	35 who	36 ranger
37 to	38 out	39 ④	

01 동사에 -er이 붙어 행위자를 나타내는 경우인데, ④의 cooker 는 행위자의 뜻이 아니다.

02 • 그는 결혼식에 참석하려고 한다. • 날씨가 흐리고 가끔씩 소나 기가 온다. • 그 여자는 결혼식 날에 초조했다. • 알루미늄 캔들 은 재활용하기가 매우 쉽다.

03 반의어 관계이다. 싼 : 비싼 = 옳은 : 틀린

04 be afraid of: ~을 두려워하다 / be good for: ~에 좋다

05 어떤 모임이나 행사에 참석하다: attend(참석하다)

06 take a look at: ~을 보다

07 enough: ~에 필요한 만큼의, ~할 만큼 (충분히)

08 A가 '너는 높이 점프할 수 있니?'라고 물었는데 B가 할 수 있다 고 대답했으므로 빈칸에는 '~을 잘하다'라는 의미의 good이 알 맞다.

09 No, not yet.: 아니, 아직 아니야.

10 Why not?: 왜 안 되지?

11 be good at: ~을 잘하다

12 상반되는 내용의 두 개의 절을 연결하므로 but이 알맞다.

13 It is certain that ~: ~은 확실하다 / It is sure that ~도 쓰이 지만, It is certain that ~을 더 많이 쓴다.

14 ② 유리가 왜 Jaden의 만화를 보고 싶어 하는지는 알 수 없다.

15 '~하는 방법을 알고 있다'의 뜻으로 능력을 표현한다.

16 Are you sure[certain] (that)+주어+동사 ~?는 확신 여부 를 묻는 표현이다.

17 선행사가 사람(the girl)이고 주격이므로 who가 적절하다.

18 접속사 while은 '~하는 동안에'라는 의미를 지닌다.

19 선행사가 동물일 경우에는 관계대명사 which나 that 둘 다 쓸 수 있는데, 둘 중 어느 것을 더 좋아하냐고 물을 때는 의문사 which로 시작해야 하므로 ②가 정답이다.

20 after가 이끄는 절이 주절 앞에 올 수 있으므로 After he finished his dinner, he brushed his teeth.도 가능하다.

21 ⑤ 선행사 The men이 복수이므로 who 다음의 동사도 복수형 are로 바꾼다.

22 나머지는 before가 접속사로 쓰여, 뒤에 「주어+동사」가 오지만, ③은 전치사로 쓰였다.

23 나머지는 앞에 있는 명사를 수식하는 형용사절을 이끄는 주격 관계대명사인데, ②는 명사절을 이끄는 접속사이다.

24 관계대명사 that 다음에 be동사 were가 왔으므로 선행사로 복 수명사가 와야 한다.

25 ⑤ 주절의 동사 arrived가 과거시제이므로, 종속절의 동사도 현 재가 아닌 과거로 시제를 맞춘다. leaves → left

26 선행사가 사람이고 주격이므로 관계대명사 that이나 who를 써 서 한 문장으로 만든다.

27 때를 나타내는 부사절(before ~)에서는 미래시제 대신 현재시 제를 사용한다.

28 문맥상 '~한 후에'가 알맞다.

29 it은 인칭대명사로 앞에 나오는 단수명사를 받는다.

30 save A from B: A를 B에서 구하다 / around the world: 전 세계에서

31 give away: 거저 주다

32 a few days later: 며칠 후에

33 Guess what?: (대화를 시작할 때) 있잖아, 이봐

34 work: 일하다 / worker: 근로자, 일하는 사람

35 선행사가 사람이고 주격이므로 관계대명사 that이나 who를 쓸 수 있다.

36 하는 일이 숲이나 큰 공원을 돌보는 사람: ranger(공원[삼림/자 연] 관리원)

37 say hello to: ~에게 인사를 하다

38 break out: (화재가) 발생하다

39 get out: 나오다

단원별 예상문제   p.46~49

01 ④	02 ②	03 rainy	04 ⑤
05 away	06 ④	07 ⑤	08 ④

09 Why can't I take a look at them?   10 (that)
I'm really good at drawing   11 너는 방금 나를 행복하게
했어.   12 ①   13 ③   14 is →
was   15 before   16 ②   17 ①
18 ②   19 ⑤   20 ②   21 ③
22 try → trying   23 am → was 24 ①
25 (s)uddenly 26 Amazing   27 ③   28 ④
29 ⑤

01 ④는 유의어 관계이고, 나머지는 반의어 관계이다.

02 out of: ~으로 / in front of: ~ 앞에

03 자연 현상을 나타내는 명사에 -y를 붙이면 형용사가 된다.

04 ⑤는 novel(소설)의 영영풀이이다.

05 give away: 거저 주다, 나누어 주다

06 Are you sure?는 상대방이 확신하고 있는지의 여부를 물 을 때 사용하는 표현이다.

07 문을 잠갔다고 하고 나서 가서 확인해 보겠다고 말하는 것은 어 색하다.

08 take[have] a look at: ~을 보다

09 not은 앞에 언급된 부정의 문장을 받을 수 있다.

10 so는 앞에 언급된 긍정의 문장을 받을 수 있다.

11 make one's day: ~을 행복하게 하다

12 선행사가 사람(a girl)이고 주격이므로 관계대명사 who가 들어 가야 알맞다.

13 문맥상 '~하는 동안에'라는 의미를 지닌 시간을 나타내는 접속사 while이 적절하다.

14 주절의 동사가 과거이므로 관계사절의 동사도 과거가 되어야 한

15 B after A = A before B

16 선행사가 사물일 때는 주격 관계대명사 which[that]를, 사람일 때는 주격 관계대명사 who[that]를 쓴다.

17 ①은 의문대명사이고, 나머지는 사물을 선행사로 하는 관계대명사 주격이다.

18 ②는 '~인 반면에'의 의미이고 나머지는 '~하는 동안'의 의미이다.

19 ⑤ a man이 선행사이고 관계사절에서 주어 역할을 하므로 who가 알맞다. whom → who

20 주어진 문장의 She는 My aunt를 받는다.

21 make friends: 친구를 사귀다

22 전치사 of의 목적어이므로 동명사로 고쳐야 한다.

23 전체 문장이 과거시제이므로 과거진행형으로 고쳐야 한다.

24 ⓑ, ① 2문형 ② 5문형 ③ 1문형 ④ 4문형 ⑤ 3문형

25 빨리 그리고 예기치 않게: suddenly(갑자기)

26 사람을 놀라게 하는 것이므로 현재분사형의 형용사로 고쳐야 한다.

27 ③ 호진이는 처음에 그 여인을 알아보지 못했다.

28 연령 앞에는 전치사 at을 쓴다.

29 become a hit: 히트를 치다, 성공하다

서술형 실전문제
p.50~51

01 |모범답안| What's the matter (with you)? / What's wrong (with you)? / Is (there) something wrong with you?

02 nervous   03 나는 네가 잘할 것이라고 확신해.

04 (B)-(C)-(D)-(A)

05 (1) Dad cooks me a fried egg which[that] is my favorite.

(2) I have an uncle who[that] is a math teacher.

(3) She has a bird which[that] speaks English.

06 (1) Kathy went to bed after she took a bath.

(2) Mr. Smith came to see you while you were out.

(3) You should come back before it gets dark.

07 (1) is → are

(2) who → which[that]

(3) who → that

08 strong   09 (d)ifferent

10 나는 나의 이모처럼 새로운 것들을 시도하기를 두려워하지 않는 사람이 되고 싶다.

11 who[that]   12 age

13 She attended a famous cooking school there.

14 to write

01 상대방에게 좋지 않은 일이 있는지 물을 때 사용하는 표현에는 What's wrong with you? / What's the matter with you? / Is (there) something wrong with you? 등이 있다.

02 nerve의 형용사형 nervous가 알맞다.

03 do a good job: 잘하다

04 (B) 내일은 우리 엄마 생일이야. 내가 엄마를 위해 무엇을 해야 할까? - (C) 너의 엄마를 위해 케이크를 굽는 건 어때? 넌 빵을 잘 굽잖아. - (D) 좋은 생각이야. 엄마가 내 케이크를 좋아하셨으면 좋겠다. - (A) 너의 엄마는 분명히 좋아하실 거야.

05 (1) 선행사가 사물(a fried egg)이므로 which나 that을 쓴다. (2) 선행사가 사람이므로 who나 that을 쓴다. (3) 선행사가 동물(a bird)이므로 which나 that을 쓴다.

06 after: ~한 후에 / while: ~하는 동안 / before: ~하기 전에

07 (1) The animals가 복수이다. (2) 선행사가 the letter이 므로 관계대명사는 which 또는 that을 쓴다. (3) 선행사가 사람과 동물이므로 관계대명사는 that을 쓴다.

08 weak: 약한 / strong: 강한

09 한 가지 또는 그 이상의 점에서 서로 같지 않은: different(다른)

10 someone: 어떤 사람 / like: ~처럼

11 선행사가 사람이고 주격이므로 who나 that을 쓸 수 있다.

12 당신이 살아온 해들의 수: age(나이, 연령)

13 attend는 타동사이므로 전치사 없이 목적어를 취한다.

14 decide는 to부정사를 목적어로 취한다.

창의사고력 서술형 문제
p.52

|모범답안|

01 (1) A waiter is someone who serves food in a restaurant.

(2) A zookeeper is someone who looks after animals in the zoo.

(3) Dessert is sweet food which is served after a meal.

02 (1) Before I leave this town, I'm going to visit my friend. / I'm going to visit my friend before I leave this town.

(2) After I saw the advertisement on TV, I bought the PS4. / I bought the PS4 after I saw the advertisement on TV.

(3) Before you go out, the rain will stop. / The rain will stop before you go out.

(4) While I put on my coat, hold my bag, please. / Please hold my bag while I put on my coat.

(5) After we eat something, we're going to see a movie. / We're going to see a movie after we eat something.

(6) When I came home, my sister was watching TV. /

My sister was watching TV when I came home.
(7) Before you go out, you have to finish this. /
You have to finish this before you go out.

---

01 ①	02 ④	03 ④
04 cartoonist	05 at	06 Everybody is good at something.
07 ②	08 matter	09 ③
10 speak, well	11 ③, ⑤	12 ①	13 tells → tell
14 ④	15 ①	16 before
17 ②	18 ⑤	19 Before	20 ③
21 hairs → hair	22 ②	23 second
24 ④	25 ③	26 ⑤	27 He is the janitor at the writer's school.	28 ⑤

29 그녀는 정말 멋져 보였고, 그녀의 스쿠터는 아주 독특했다.

30 ⑤

01 보통 다른 가능성들에 대해 주의 깊게 생각한 후에 어떤 것을 하기로 선택하다: 결정하다(decide)

02 be good for: ~에 좋다

03 once: 한 번 / per: ~에 대하여, ~당

04 '명사 : 행위자' 관계이다. 예술, 미술 : 예술가, 미술가 / 만화 : 만화가

05 take a look at: ~을 보다 / be good at: ~을 잘하다

06 everybody는 단수동사로 받는다.

07 some ~, other ...: 어떤 사람들은 ~하고, 또 어떤 사람들은 … 하다

08 Is something wrong?=What's the matter with you?: 무슨 일 있니?

09 많은 학생들 앞에서 연설을 해야 하므로 긴장될 것이다.

10 '형용사+명사' 구문은 '동사+부사' 구문으로 바꿔 쓸 수 있다.

11 확신을 나타낼 때는 I'm sure[certain] ~를 쓴다.

12 앞 문장의 빈칸에는 the famous singer를 선행사로 하는 주격 관계대명사 who가, 뒤 문장에는 a chair를 선행사로 하는 주격 관계대명사 which가 들어가야 알맞다.

13 선행사 three books가 복수이므로 that절의 동사는 복수 동사 tell이 되어야 한다.

14 '네가 조깅하는 동안에 ~'의 뒤에 어울리는 말을 찾아보자.

15 who는 관계대명사로 쓰일 수도 있지만 의문대명사로 쓰여 '누구'의 의미를 나타낸다. ①은 의문대명사로 쓰고, 나머지는 관계대명사로 쓴다.

16 첫 번째 문장에서는 부사로, 두 번째 문장에서는 접속사로 쓰인다.

17 빈칸에는 a boy를 선행사로 하는 주격 관계대명사 who가 들어

18 ⑤ 문장의 주어는 The man이고 who is sitting on the box는 The man을 수식하는 관계대명사절이다. 따라서 동사는 have가 아니라 단수형인 has가 알맞다.

19 B after A(A를 하고 나서 B를 하다) =A before B(B를 하기 전에 A를 하다)

20 be good at: ~에 능숙하다

21 hair는 머리카락 전체를 나타낼 때는 단수형을 취한다.

22 주어진 문장의 it은 Lunch Lady Begins를 받는다.

23 1분이 나뉘어지는 60개의 부분들 중의 하나: second(초)

24 ④ Lunch Lady가 어떻게 사람들을 위험으로부터 구하는 지는 알 수 없다.

25 ③ 뒤에 단수명사가 오므로 other를 another로 고쳐야 한다.

26 ④, ⑤ 3문형 ① 4문형 ② 2문형 ③ 1문형 ④ 5문형

27 김 씨의 직업은 무엇인가? - 그는 글쓴이의 학교 수위이다

28 while: ~하는 동안

29 cool: 멋진 / unique: 독특한

30 ⑤ 호진이는 그 여인을 만난 기억이 없다.

9

Where Do People Live?

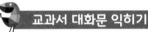

Conversation

핵심 Check p.62~63

1 (1) kind, want / to live (2) What, be, want to
2 (1) Where, find / next (2) Where / behind
  (3) Where / in (4) tell, where / front

시험대비 실력평가 p.60

01 ②	02 ②	03 ④	04 high
05 ③	06 jeans	07 grass	08 ②

01 ①, ③, ④, ⑤는 모두 animal(동물)에 속한다.

02 kind of: 약간, 어느 정도 / look for: ~을 찾다

03 예를 들면 문이나 정문처럼 어떤 곳에 들어가는 길: entrances(입구, 문)

04 반의어의 관계이다. 싼 : 비싼 = 낮은 : 높은

05 upside down: 거꾸로

06 보통 데님이라고 불리는 질긴 파란색 면직물로 만들어진 캐주얼 바지: jeans(바지, 청바지)

07 grass: 풀, 잔디

08 out of: ~에서 / a lot of: 많은

교과서 대화문 익히기

Check(√) True or False p.64

1 T 2 F 3 F 4 T 5 T 6 F

서술형 시험대비 p.61

01 (1) second (2) fifth (3) ninth
02 (1) in harmony with (2) next to (3) look at
03 (1) avoid (2) build (3) protect (4) entrance
04 (1) lovely (2) southern (3) wooden
05 (1) good at (2) take down (3) look for (4) pile up
06 (1) (c)ollector (2) (e)nemy

01 fifth, ninth는 기수에 th를 붙일 때 철자가 변한다.

02 (1) in harmony with: ~와 조화를 이루어 (2) next to: ~ 옆에 (3) look at: ~을 보다

03 (1) avoid: 피하다 (2) build: 짓다 (3) protect: 보호하다 (4) entrance: 입구, 문

04 (1) lovely: 사랑스러운 (2) southern: 남쪽의, 남부의 (3) wooden: 목제의

05 (1) be good at: ~을 잘하다 (2) take down: (구조물을 해체하여) 치우다 (3) look for: ~을 찾다 (4) pile up: (양이) 많아지다

06 (1) collector: 징수원 (2) enemy: 적

교과서 확인학습 p.66~67

Listen & Speak 1 A. Listen and Check

1 look, in, like / unique, want to / kind, live / to house
2 Excuse, there, mall / kind, would / like / There, on / Thank

Listen & Speak 2 A. Listen and Check

1 Excuse, find, can, second, next / you / welcome
2 help, for, can, on, next

Communicate A. Listen and Answer

Welcome, May / like, for / kind, like / with, view, garden / do, room, view, no / have, floor / do / give, try, Where, have / can, dining, to / see / in, Here's / Thank

Progress Check

1 at, in, down / look, but, kind / kind, want / so, live
2 Excuse, find / find, second, next / Thank / welcome
3 where, hats / can, floor, to / you / welcome

Work-Act

What, build / to, that, like / Where / second

시험대비 기본평가 p.68

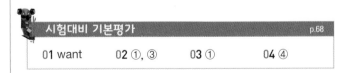

01 want	02 ①, ③	03 ①	04 ④

01 want to: ~하기를 원하다

02 사고 싶은 물건이 있는 장소를 물을 때는 Where can I

find[buy] ~?나 Where is[are] ~?의 표현을 쓴다.

03 want to: ~하기를 원하다

04 A가 여성복 매장의 위치를 물었으므로 ④와 같이 답한다. ③은 주어가 단수이므로 옳지 않다.

01 ②	**02** ④	**03** Where	**04** do
05 ③	**06** ⑤	**07** What can	**08** ②
09 give	**10** 알겠습니다.	**11** ④	**12** at
13 ①			

01 어이, 이 사진 속의 집을 봐. 그것은 큰 신발처럼 보여! - 아, 아주 독특하긴 하지만, 난 신발 속에서 살고 싶지 않아. - 넌 어떤 종류의 집에서 살고 싶니? - 음, 나는 비행기 모양의 집에서 살고 싶어.

02 ④는 도움을 제안하는 표현이고, 나머지는 길이나 위치를 묻는 표현이다.

03 B가 2층에 있다고 말했으므로 남성복이 있는 위치(where)를 물었을 것이다.

04 I do. = I want to go on a picnic.

05 대화 내용상 찾고자 하는 물건의 위치를 확인하는 것이다.

06 ⑤의 Do you know where ~?에 대한 응답으로 Yes, that's right.는 어색하다.

07 May I help you?는 상점 등에서 점원이 손님에게 도와주겠다는 표현으로 What can I do for you?라고 할 때도 있다.

08 ⓑ와 ②는 '~을 가진, ~이 있는'의 뜻으로 소유를 나타낸다. ① ~와 함께 ③ ~으로 ④ ~에게 ⑤ ~에, ~에 관하여

09 give it a try: 시도해 보다

10 I see.: 알겠습니다.

11 ④ 남자는 침대가 없는 방에서 자 보기로 했다.

12 look at: ~을 보다

13 상반의 접속사 but이 알맞다.

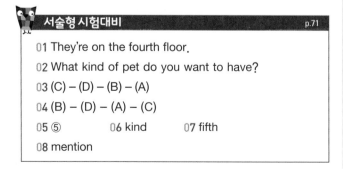

01 They're on the fourth floor.
02 What kind of pet do you want to have?
03 (C) – (D) – (B) – (A)
04 (B) – (D) – (A) – (C)
05 ⑤   **06** kind   **07** fifth
08 mention

01 be on the fourth floor: 4층에 있다

02 What kind of ~?: 어떤 종류의 ~?

03 실례합니다, 여자 신발은 어디에 있어요? - 2층에서 찾을 수 있어

요. 엘리베이터 옆에 있어요. - 감사합니다. - 천만에요.

04 (B) 넌 어떤 집을 짓고 싶어? - (D) 보트처럼 생긴 2층짜리 집을 짓고 싶어. - (A) 부엌이 어디 있어? - (C) 2층에 있어.

05 모르는 사람에게 말을 걸 때 관용적으로 쓰는 표현은 Excuse me.이다.

06 What kind of ~?: 어떤 종류의 ~?

07 five에 -th를 붙여 서수를 만들 때는 철자의 변화에 유의해야 한다.

08 You're welcome.=Don't mention it.: 천만에요.

교과서
Grammar

1 (1) done   (2) have, eaten   (3) has lived   (4) for
2 (1) has   (2) is   (3) each   (4) day   (5) are

01 (1) has been   (2) been   (3) finished
    (4) has just finished   (5) arrived   (6) did you reach
02 (1) does   (2) has   (3) side
    (4) students   (5) boy   (6) are
03 (1) He has been sick in bed since last Friday.
    (2) How long have you known Miss Smith?
    (3) Have you ever read Christmas Carol?
    (4) My father hasn't read the newspaper yet.

01 (1) 부사구 since ~가 있으므로 현재완료가 맞다. (2) '~에 다녀오다'=have been to (3) two hours ago와 같이 명백한 과거 시점을 나타내는 부사구가 있으므로 현재완료가 아닌 과거시제로 써야 한다. (4) just와 함께 '이제 막 마쳤다'라는 의미이므로 현재완료가 맞다. (5) yesterday 와 같이 명백한 과거시점을 나타내는 부사가 있으므로 현재완료가 아닌 과거시제로 써야 한다. (6) 의문사 when은 특정 시점에 대해 묻는 의문사이므로 현재완료와 함께 쓸 수 없다.

02 (1), (2) each가 주어일 때는 단수 동사로 받는다. (3) each가 형용사로 쓰일 때는 뒤에 단수 명사가 온다. (4) each가 대명사로 쓰일 때 each of 뒤에는 복수 명사가 온다. (5) every 뒤에는 단수 명사가 온다. (6) 주어에 both가 있을 때는 복수 동사로 받는다.

03 (1) 계속 용법의 현재완료이다. (2) 계속 용법의 현재완료이다. (3) 경험 용법의 현재완료이다. (4) 완료 용법의 현재완료이다.

01 ⑤	02 ③	03 ④	04 Each
05 have	06 ①	07 ④	08 ④
09 ④	10 ④	11 not	12 ②
13 since	14 ④	15 ②	16 Each
student, speaks		17 ②	18 ④
19 ③		20 has been absent	21 yet
22 ③		23 ④	

01 계속을 나타내는 현재완료이다.

02 'each of+복수 명사'는 단수로 취급한다.

03 계속을 나타내는 현재완료이다.

04 each+단수 명사: 각각의 ~ /
each of+복수 명사: ~의 각각

05 「have+p.p.」로 현재완료 시제로 쓰인 문장이다.

06 ①은 '각자'라는 뜻의 부사이다. 나머지는 '각각의 ~'라는 뜻의
형용사이다.

07 현재완료의 경험 용법이 사용된 문장에서 빈도부사 never는
have와 been 사이에 위치해야 한다.

08 each other: 서로

09 계속을 나타내는 현재완료이다.

10 every minute / Both the brothers / All the eggs / each of
them

11 앞 문장이 현재완료 결과의 문장이므로 '나의 엄마는 쇼핑하러
가서 여기 없다.'의 뜻이 되어야 한다.

12 뒤에 단수 명사 boy가 온 것으로 보아 '각각의'라는 뜻의 each
가 적절하다.

13 '~한 이래로'는 since로 나타낸다.

14 ⓐ는 단수 명사가 이어지므로 each 또는 every가 적절하고, ⓑ
는 복수 명사가 이어지므로 all 또는 each of가 적절하다.

15 현재완료형으로 물었으므로 현재완료형으로 대답해야 한다.

16 '각 학생'은 'each+단수 명사'로 나타내고 동사는 3인칭 단수형
으로 쓴다.

17 ②는 대명사이고, 나머지는 모두 형용사이다.

18 ④와 같이 when ~이 명백한 과거의 시점을 나타낼 때는 현재
완료 시제는 쓸 수 없다. (has been → was)

19 ③에서 'each of+복수명사'는 단수로 취급한다. (have their
→ has its)

20 얼마나 오랫동안 결석했는지 물었으므로 현재완료(have+p.p.)
로 쓴다.

21 yet: 1. 이미, 벌써(의문문) 2. 아직(부정문)

22 ③에서 'each of+복수 대명사'는 단수 취급하므로 have를 has
로 고쳐야 한다.

23 ④의 has gone은 '~에 가고 없다'는 의미의 현재완료 결과 용
법이다. 나머지는 모두 현재완료 경험의 용법으로 쓰였다.

01 (1) have, started　(2) has not returned
(3) has gone to

02 (1) each　(2) Both　(3) All　(4) each　(5) every

03 (1) has gone → went
(2) already → yet

04 Each / each

05 (1) didn't see → have not[haven't] seen
(2) is → has been

06 (1) He has been to Italy many times.
(2) I have been very busy these days.
(3) I have never visited Paris before.

07 (1) all　(2) every　(3) any
(4) each　(5) some　(6) both

08 (1) I went to London four years ago.
(2) When did you see a white lion?
(3) I often played with her when I was a child.
(4) He was ill in bed last month.

09 (1) Each of us has to finish our project.
(2) There were four books on the table. Each
book was in a different color.
(3) Every driver should be careful.

10 (1) He has lived in New York since 1970.
(2) Have you finished reading this story yet?
(3) I have seen the movie once.

11 Each, has

01 (1) 현재완료 완료 용법 (2) yet은 과거에서 현재까지 아직 완료
되지 않은 상태를 말한다. (3) 현재완료 결과 용법

02 (1) '각각'이라는 의미를 나타내는 부사는 each이다. (2) both:
둘 다 (3) all: 모든 (4) each of+복수 명사: ~의 각각 (5) '모든
학생이 시험에 합격한 것은 아니었다.'의 뜻으로 부분부정이다.

03 (1) 과거를 나타내는 부사구가 있으므로 현재완료 시제가 아니라
과거시제를 써야 한다. (2) 부정문에서 '아직'의 뜻으로는 yet을
쓴다.

04 Each student: 각각의 학생 / each other: 서로

05 since는 현재완료 시제와 함께 쓰이므로 didn't see는 have
not[haven't] seen이 되어야 한다.

06 (1) 현재완료 경험 용법 (2) 일정한 기간을 나타내는 부사구
(these days)는 현재완료와 함께 쓰일 수 있다. (3) 현재완료 경
험 용법

07 (1) all+소유격+단수 명사 (2) every+단수 명사 (3) not ~
any: 조금도 ~ 않다 (4) each+of+복수 대명사 (5) some: (긍
정문에서) 약간의 (6) both+복수 명사

08 (1) 과거 시점을 나타내는 four years ago가 있으므로 과거시
제로 쓴다. (2) when은 과거의 특정 시점을 묻는 표현이므로

과거시제로 써야 한다. (3) when 이하의 절이 과거의 특정 시점을 나타내므로 과거시제로 쓴다. (4) '지난달 (last month)'이라는 명백한 과거 시점이 있으므로 과거시제로 나타낸다.

09 (1) 'each of+복수 대명사+단수 동사'(have → has) (2) 'There are+복수 명사'(book → books) (3) 'every+단수명사'로 사용 (drivers → driver)

10 (1) 현재완료 계속 용법 (2) 현재완료 완료 용법 (3) 현재완료 경험 용법

11 '각각의 학생'은 each+단수명사(student)로 나타낸다.

Reading

확인문제 p.80

1 T 2 F 3 T 4 T 5 F

확인문제 p.81

1 T 2 F 3 T 4 F 5 T

교과서 확인학습 A p.82~83

01 Have, seen, roof　　02 see, on
03 forests　　04 harmony, built, for
05 build, cover, with
06 protect, from, strong
07 grow, some, meals　　08 part, ago, only
09 Centuries, who, paid
10 avoid, some, piling
11 When, town, took, down
12 After, piled, stone
13 stay, southern, round, like　　14 roofs, people
15 have, about, themselves　　16 only, without
17 is, whole　　18 usually
19 first, second, living, fourth

교과서 확인학습 B p.84~85

1 Have you ever seen a goat on the roof of a house?
2 In Norway, we can see animals on roofs.
3 Norway has large forests.
4 In harmony with nature, people have built wooden houses for a long time.

5 To build strong and warm houses, they cover their roofs with grass.
6 The grass roofs protect them from the long cold winters and strong winds.
7 Sometimes, trees or plants grow out of the grass roofs, and some animals enjoy their meals there.
8 A roof is an essential part of a house, but long ago some people built roofs only to take them down easily.
9 Centuries ago in southern Italy, people who had a house without a roof paid lower taxes.
10 To avoid high taxes on their houses, some people built cone-shaped roofs by piling up stones.
11 When tax collectors came to the town, people took their roofs down quickly.
12 After the tax collectors left, they piled up the stones again.
13 From the sky in a part of southern China, you can see round roofs that look like big doughnuts.
14 They are the roofs of the big round houses of the Hakka people.
15 They have lived in houses like these for about a thousand years to protect themselves from enemies.
16 The houses have only one gate without any windows on the first floor.
17 Each house is big enough for a whole village.
18 It usually has four stories.
19 It has kitchens on the first floor, storage rooms on the second floor, and living rooms and bedrooms on the third and fourth floors.

시험대비 실력평가 p.86~89

01 ②　　02 ③　　03 wooden　　04 ④
05 ①　　06 ④　　07 잔디 지붕 위에서
08 ⑤　　09 ④　　10 southern　　11 ②
12 paid　　13 ①　　14 piling　　15 ④
16 ③　　17 원뿔 모양의 지붕을 만들었다, 속히 지붕을
철거했다　　18 sky　　19 which　　20 ①
21 ②　　22 are → is　　23 kitchens　　24 ⑤
25 ⑤　　26 seen　　27 ①, ④　　28 with
29 ⑤　　30 ④　　31 southern　　32 ①, ④

01 지붕 위에 있는 염소를 본 적이 있느냐는 문장 다음인 ②에 와야 한다.

02 'in harmony with: ~와 조화롭게 / cover A with B: B로 A

13

를 덮다

03 wood(나무, 목재)+-en(형용사 어미)=wooden(목재의)

04 ⓒ, ④ 부사적 용법 ①, ⑤ 형용사적 용법 ②, ③ 명사적 용법

05 ① 노르웨이의 집들의 지붕 위에 염소가 올라가는지는 알 수 없다.

06 protect A from B: B로부터 A를 보호하다

07 there는 장소를 가리키는 부사이다.

08 상반의 접속사 but이 알맞다.

09 take down: 분해하다, 철거하다

10 south(남부)+-ern(형용사 어미)=southern(남부의)

11 선행사가 사람이고 주격이므로 who나 that을 쓸 수 있다.

12 pay의 과거형 paid를 써야 한다.

13 문맥상 '높은 세금을 피하기 위하여'가 알맞다.

14 'by+동명사' 구문이 알맞다.

15 '~할 때'의 뜻을 나타내는 접속사 when이 알맞다.

16 '~한 후에'의 뜻을 나타내는 접속사 after가 알맞다.

18 밖에 서서 위를 바라볼 때 볼 수 있는 지구 주위의 공간: sky(하늘)

19 선행사가 사물이고 주격이므로 which나 that을 쓸 수 있다.

20 ⓒ, ① 현재완료로 계속을 나타낸다. ②, ④ 경험 ③ 완료 ⑤ 결과

21 without any ~: ~이 하나도 없는

22 주어에 each가 있을 때는 단수 동사로 받는다.

23 요리와 식기를 씻는 것과 같은 집안일을 하기 위해 사용되는 방: kitchen(부엌)

24 ⑤ 4층에 얼마나 많은 침실이 있는지는 알 수 없다.

25 강하고 따뜻한 집을 짓기 위해 잔디로 지붕을 덮는다는 문장 다음에 와야 한다.

26 현재완료형이 되어야 하므로 과거분사 seen이 알맞다.

27 ⓑ, ①, ④ 계속 ② 경험 ③ 완료 ⑤ 결과

28 cover A with B: B로 A를 덮다

29 ⑤ 동물들이 지붕 위에서 산다는 말은 언급되지 않았다.

30 Centuries before → Centuries ago

31 south: 남쪽, 남부 southern: 남쪽의, 남부의

32 without : ~이 없는

서술형 시험대비　　　　　　　　　p.90~91

01 To avoid　02 by　　03 As　　04 down

05 세금 징수원들이 떠나간 후에 그들은 다시 돌을 쌓아올렸다.

06 which　07 doughnuts　　08 have lived　09 themselves　　10 1층에는 창문이 하나도 없이　　11 for　　12 Each house　13 third　14 They are on the second floor.　15 in　16 four-stories → four-story　17 Since　18 There are about 400 thousand books.　19 It opened in 2013.

---

01 문맥상 목적을 나타내는 부사적 용법의 to부정사가 되어야 한다.

02 by -ing: ~함으로써

03 when과 as는 '~할 때'의 뜻으로 때를 나타내는 접속사의 용법이 있다.

04 take down: ~을 철거하다

05 after: ~한 후에 / pile up: ~을 쌓아올리다

06 선행사가 사물이고 주격이므로 that이나 which를 쓸 수 있다.

07 뜨거운 기름으로 튀긴 달콤한 밀가루 반죽으로 만들어진 빵과 같은 케이크: doughnut(도넛)

08 과거에서 현재까지 계속된 일이므로 현재완료형을 써야 한다.

09 동사의 목적어가 주어 자신이므로 재귀대명사를 써야 한다.

10 without ~ 이하는 부대상황을 나타내는 부사구로 집의 상태를 나타낸다.

11 big enough for ~: ~에게 충분할 만큼 큰

12 It은 인칭대명사로 앞에 나온 단수 명사를 받는다.

13 three의 서수는 third이다.

14 저장실은 2층에 있다.

15 도시 앞에는 전치사 in을 쓴다.

16 '4층 건물'의 뜻으로 four-story가 building을 수식하므로 복수형인 stories는 틀린다.

17 '~부터'의 뜻이므로 since가 알맞다.

18 국립 세종 도서관에는 약 40만 권의 책이 있다고 언급되었다.

19 국립 세종 도서관은 2013년에 문을 열었다고 언급되었다.

영역별 핵심문제　　　　　　　　　p.93~97

01 ②, ④	02 ③	03 low	04 ④
05 ⑤	06 kind	07 give, a try	08 Where
09 to	10 ①, ④	11 lovely	12 have → has
13 ④		14 한번 시도해 보겠습니다.	
15 ④	16 ①	17 ③	18 ④
19 ④	20 each other	21 ③	22 ⑤
23 ④	24 ②	25 ③	26 ①
27 Each of their opinions are	28 ②	29 There	
30 ④	31 protect	32 ⑤	
33 ④	34 이곳의 날씨는 여름에는 아주 덥고 겨울에는 춥다. 35 ①	36 동굴 집은 너무 춥지도 덥지도 않기 때문이다.	37 like	38 ②

01 ②, ④는 명사에 -ly가 붙어 형용사가 된 것이고, 나머지는 형용사에 -ly가 붙어 부사가 된 것이다.

02 • 전망이 좋은 방을 주시면 좋겠군요.
   • 그는 우리를 맞이하기 위해 문에 나와 있었다.
   • 그는 그 장소를 어려움 없이 찾았다.
   • 그가 또 다른 말은 뭐라고 했나요?

03 반의어 관계이다. 따뜻한 : 서늘한 = 높은 : 낮은

04 be good for: ~에 좋다

05 나무들이 함께 가까이 자라는 넓은 지역: forest(삼림, 숲)

06 당신은 어떤 영화를 좋아하나요? / 그것 때문에 나는 약간 바보 같은 기분이 들었다.

07 give it a try: 시도하다, 한번 해 보다

08 B가 2층에 있다고 말했으므로 남성용 셔츠가 있는 위치 (where)를 물었을 것이다.

09 Welcome to ~.: ~에 오신 것을 환영합니다.

10 Can[May] I help you?: 도와드릴까요?

11 love에 -ly를 붙이면 형용사형이 된다.

12 'every+단수명사'가 주어이면 단수동사로 받는다.

13 상반되는 내용의 두 개의 절을 연결하므로 but이 알맞다.

14 give it a try: 한번 시도해 보다

15 ④ 방에 왜 침대가 없는지는 알 수 없다.

16 B가 스마트폰을 찾고 있다고 대답했으므로 도움을 제안하는 표현이 자연스럽다.

17 과거에서 지금까지의 경험을 나타내는 문장이므로 현재완료 (have+p.p.) 시제로 써야 한다.

18 each는 단수 동사로 받는다. some of+복수 명사는 복수 동사로 받는다.

19 계속을 나타내는 현재완료이다.

20 '서로'를 뜻하는 each other는 복수형을 쓰지 않는다.

21 ③ last week라는 특정 과거 시점이 있으므로 현재완료가 아니라 과거시제로 써야 한다. (have climbed → climbed)

22 ⑤는 앞에 almost가 있으므로 전체의 의미를 강조하는 every 가 들어가야 한다. each는 개별성을 강조하므로 almost가 있는 문장에 쓸 수 없다.

23 have[has] gone to ~: ~에 갔다(그래서 여기 없다) / 결과를 나타내는 현재완료이다.

24 보기, ② 경험 ①, ④ 계속 ③ 완료 ⑤ 결과

25 ③ each 뒤에는 관사나 대명사의 소유격이 올 수 없다. Each of the students나 Each student로 고쳐야 한다.

26 ① ~ ago라는 과거 시점이 있으므로 과거시제 went가 맞다.

27 each 다음에는 복수 명사나 대명사가 올 수 없다.

28 ⓐ, ② 경험 ①, ④ 계속 ③ 완료 ⑤ 결과

29 have[has]가 있는 문장을 there is[are]를 쓴 문장과 바꿔 쓸 수 있다.

30 cover A with B: B로 A를 덮다

31 누군가 또는 무언가가 다치거나 손상되지 않도록 막다: protect(보호하다)

32 ⑤ 동물들이 보통 집 지붕 위에서 사료를 먹는다는 말은 언급되지 않는다.

33 for a long time: 오랫동안

34 in this place(이곳의)는 weather를 수식하는 형용사구이다.

35 not A or B: A도 B도 아닌

37 look like+명사: ~처럼 보이다

38 ⓐ, ② 대략, 약(부사) ①, ④ ~에 관하여(전치사) ③ ~의 여기 저기에(전치사) ⑤ 여기저기(부사)

단원별 예상문제   p.98~101

01 ④	02 ②	03 third	04 ④
05 upside down		06 ④	07 ②
08 ④	09 ③	10 ③	11 ②, ③
12 ③	13 ⑤	14 has lived	15 before
16 ④	17 ④	18 ③	19 ③
20 ①	21 easily	22 ③	23 ②
24 (1) 지붕을 재빨리 철거했다		(2) 돌을 다시 쌓아올려 지붕을	
만들었다.	25 ③	26 ④, ⑤	27 둥근
지붕들	28 ④	29 themselves	

01 ④는 유의어 관계이고 나머지는 반의어 관계이다.

02 be fond of: ~을 좋아하다 / out of: ~ 밖으로

03 서수 first, second, third는 기수와 형태가 달라진다.

04 ④는 jeans(바지, 청바지)의 영영풀이다.

05 upside down: 거꾸로

06 대화 내용상 찾고자 하는 물건의 위치를 확인하는 것이다.

07 미래에 뭐가 되고 싶은지를 물었는데 ② '나는 차를 마실 거야.' 라고 대답하는 것은 어색하다.

08 ④ What으로 물었으므로 yes나 no로 대답할 수 없다.

09 대화의 흐름상 '~을 찾고 있다'는 의미인 'I'm looking for ~.' 가 알맞다.

10 '그것은 2층에 있다.'는 'It's on the second floor.'로 표현한다.

11 ② You're right.: 네 말이 옳아. ③ That's fine with me.: 나는 좋아.

12 현재완료의 경험 용법이 사용된 문장에서 빈도부사 never는 has와 been 사이에 위치해야 한다.

13 each는 단수 동사로 받는다. all of+복수 명사는 복수 동사로 받는다.

14 since 이하가 과거에서 현재에 이르는 기간을 말하므로 현재완료의 계속 용법이 필요하다.

15 B after A = A before B

16 each hand / Both of us / All of the milk / Every word

17 '시계를 잃어버려 현재 가지고 있지 않다는 것을 나타낸다. 결과를 나타내는 현재완료이다.

18 ③ both는 복수 동사로 받는다. looks → look

19 ③의 has gone은 '~에 가고 없다'는 의미의 현재완료 결과 용법이다. 나머지는 모두 현재완료 경험 용법으로 쓰였다.

20 문맥상 상반의 접속사 but이 알맞다.

21 동사를 수식하므로 부사형이 되어야 한다.

22 문맥상 '더 낮은 세금'이 되어야 알맞다.

23 by -ing: ~함으로써(이때의 by는 수단을 나타냄)

15

25 from the sky: 하늘에서(이때의 from은 기점을 나타냄)
26 선행사가 사물이고 주격이므로 that이나 which가 알맞다.
27 They는 인칭대명사로 앞에 나온 복수 명사를 받는다.
28 과거에서 현재까지 계속된 일이므로 현재완료를 쓴다.
29 목적어가 주어 자신이므로 재귀대명사를 써야 한다.

서술형 실전문제
p.102~103

01 Excuse   02 What   03 problem
04 (C)-(D)-(A)-(B)
05 (1) Peter has lived in Peking since 2010.
   (2) Tom has been in hospital for a week.
   (3) My mother has gone shopping.
06 (1) I ate breakfast each day during my stay in London.
   (2) There is a tree on both sides of the gate.
   (3) Every day seems the same to him.
07 (1) has been → went
   (2) have you seen → did you see
   (3) have often played → often played
08 gate   09 houses → house
10 fourth   11 They are on the first floor.
12 in   13 which[that]
14 cafeteria   15 visited → have visited

|모범답안|

01 (1) I want to see a movie.
   (2) Yes, I do.
02 Where can I buy them? / Where can I get them? 등
03 (1) Each of the films was very wonderful.
   (2) Every student has passed the exam.
   (3) Each room has a TV.
   (4) All friends of mine are very kind.

단원별 모의고사
p.105~108

01 ④   02 ②   03 ④
04 collector   05 up   06 ⑤   07 ⑤
08 find / get / buy   09 ②, ③   10 정원이
보이는 방이 있습니까?   11 have no   12 ①
13 ④   14 ④   15 ②, ⑤   16 ①
17 ③   18 have lost   19 Everyone in the boat
has to work together as a team.   20 ③
21 ③   22 ②   23 to   24 ④
25 have built → built   26 without   27 ①
28 ③   29 have built   30 on the grass roofs

01 Excuse me.: (모르는 사람에게 말을 걸 때) 죄송합니다, 실례합니다.
02 What kind of ~?: 어떤 종류의 ~?
03 No problem.: 괜찮아요.
04 실례합니다. 여자 청바지는 어디에 있나요? - 2층에서 찾을 수 있어요. 엘리베이터 옆에 있어요. - 감사합니다. - 천만에요.
05 현재완료(have+p.p.)를 이용해 문장을 완성한다. (1) 현재완료의 계속 용법 (2) 현재완료의 계속 용법 (3) 현재완료의 결과 용법
07 (1) 과거 시점을 나타내는 last year가 있으므로 과거시제로 쓴다. (2) 의문사 when으로 시작하므로 과거시제로 쓴다. (3) when 이하의 절이 과거의 특정 시점을 나타내므로 과거시제로 쓴다.
08 들판, 정원 또는 건물의 구내에 들어가는 입구로 사용되는 문과 같은 구조물: gate(대문, 정문)
09 each 다음에는 단수 명사가 온다.
10 four의 서수는 fourth이다.
11 주방은 1층에 있다고 언급되었다.
12 '~에'의 뜻으로 도시 앞에는 전치사 in을 쓴다.
13 선행사가 사물이고 주격이므로 which나 that을 쓸 수 있다.
14 당신이 카운터에서 음식을 선택하고 그것을 지불한 후에 테이블로 가져가는 레스토랑: cafeteria(구내식당)
15 과거의 일정한 때부터 지금까지 계속된 일이므로 현재완료형을 써야 한다.

01 take down: (구조물을 해체하여) 치우다
02 땅에서 자라며 줄기, 잎, 그리고 뿌리를 가지고 있는 살아 있는 것: 식물, 초목(plant)
03 floor: (건물의) 층 / else 또[그 밖의] 다른, 다른
04 '동사 : 행위자' 관계이다. 그리다 : 화가 / 수집하다 : 수집가
05 pile up: ~을 층층이 쌓다 / walk up: 걸어 올라가다
06 이봐, 사진 속의 이 독특한 집을 봐. 집이 거꾸로 있어.- 아, 재미있어 보이지만, 좀 이상한 것 같아. - 넌 어떤 집에서 살고 싶니? - 나는 음악을 좋아해서 피아노 모양의 집에서 살고 싶어.
07 ⑤에서 여성화를 찾고 있다는 말에 어떻게 거기에 가야 하느냐고 묻는 것은 어색하다.
08 Where can I find ~?는 상점의 위치를 묻는 표현으로 find 대신 get이나 buy를 쓸 수 있다.
09 상점 등에서 점원이 손님에게 하는 말은 관용적으로 정해져 있다.
10 view: 경관, 전망
11 'There is[are] ~' 구문은 have 동사를 써서 바꿔 쓸 수 있다.
12 next to: ~ 옆에
13 ④ 남자는 바닥 위에서 한번 자 보겠다고 말했다.
14 완료를 나타내는 현재완료의 부정문이다.
15 뒤에 단수 명사 student가 온 것으로 보아 '각각의'라는 뜻의 each와 '모든'이라는 뜻의 every가 적절하다.
16 ① ~ ago라는 과거 시점이 있으므로 과거시제 went가 맞다.

17 ③에서 'each of+복수 대명사'는 단수 취급하므로 have를 has 로 고쳐야 한다.

18 시계를 잃어버린 결과가 현재까지 영향을 미치므로 현재완료의 <결과> 용법으로 나타낸다.

19 주어는 everyone, 술어동사는 has to work이다. in the boat / together / as a team 등의 수식어구는 각각 주어, 동사에 연관시켜 배열한다.

20 과거에서 지금까지의 경험을 나타내는 문장이므로 현재완료 (have+p.p.) 시제로 써야 한다.

21 계절 앞에는 전치사 in을 쓴다.

22 ⓑ, ② ~을 가진, ~이 있는(소유) ① ~에 ③ ~으로(수단). ④ ~와 함께(동반) ⑤ ~으로(원인)

23 give는 수여동사로 간접목적어를 직접목적어 뒤로 보낼 때 전 치사 to를 붙인다.

24 세금 징수원들이 마을에 왔을 때 일어난 일이므로 세금 징수원 들이 떠난 후의 일을 서술하는 문장 앞에 와야 한다.

25 부사구 long ago가 있으므로 현재완료를 쓸 수 없다.

26 문맥상 '지붕이 없는 집'이 되어야 한다.

27 문맥상 '높은 세금을 피하기 위해'가 알맞다.

28 ⓐ in harmony with: ~와 조화를 이루어 ⓒ cover A with B: B로 A를 덮다

29 현재완료의 계속적 용법이다. build - built - built

30 장소 부사 there는 on the grass roofs를 가리킨다.

My Travel, My Way

시험대비 실력평가
p.112

01 ②	02 ②	03 ④	04 decision
05 ③	06 (c)hance	07 check	08 ②

01 ①, ③, ④, ⑤는 날씨와 관련된 단어이고, ②는 날씨와 관련이 없다.

02 a lot of: 많은 / get into: ~에 들어가다, ~을 타다

03 보통 옥외에서 물건을 사고파는 장소: 시장(market)

04 동사-명사의 관계이다. 충고하다 : 충고 = 결정하다 : 결정

05 a few: 소수의, 약간의

06 어떤 것이 일어날 가능성: chance(가능성)

07 check: 살피다, 점검하다

08 be full of: ~으로 가득 차다 / think of: ~을 생각하다

서술형 시험대비
p.113

01 (1) snowy (2) cool (3) creator
02 (1) at last (2) a little (3) stay indoors
03 (1) anything (2) mostly (3) pack (4) different
04 (1) actually (2) amazing (3) mysterious
05 (1) right now (2) get to
   (3) is full of (4) catch a cold
06 (1) (a)dmire (2) (d)rawing (3) (f)ood

01 (1) 명사 - 형용사 (2) 반의어 관계 (3) 동사 - 행위자 관계

02 (1) at last: 마침내 (2) a little: 조금 (3) stay indoors: 집안 에 머물러 있다

03 (1) anything: 무엇, 아무것, 무엇이든 (2) mostly: 주로, 일반적 으로 (3) pack: 짐을 싸다, 챙기다 (4) different: 각각 다른, (각 양) 각색의

04 (1) actually: 사실, 실제로, 정말로 (2) amazing: 놀라운 (3) mysterious: 신비한

05 (1) right now: 지금, 당장 (2) get to: ~에 도착하다 (3) be full of: ~으로 가득하다 (4) catch a cold: 감기에 걸리다

06 (1) admire: 존경하다 (2) drawing: 그림, 데생 (3) food: 음 식, 식량

Conversation

핵심 Check
p.114~115

1 (1) Have, read / have   (2) Have, eaten / haven't
2 (1) How, weather / snowy   (2) What's, like / hot
  (3) How's / raining

교과서 대화문 익히기

Check(√) True or False
p.116

1 F 2 T 3 F 4 T 5 T 6 F

교과서 확인학습
p.118~119

Listen & Speak 1 A. Listen and Check

1 Have, tired / have, tried / How / but
2 ever, jumping / haven't, about / When, tried / Wasn't / liked, want

Listen & Speak 2 A. Listen and Answer

1 weather, need / outside, check / going / don't
2 Good, welcome, forecast, sunny, but, rain, home, forecast, Have

Communicate A~B

A been, before / have, lived, for / weather, going, vacation / time, visit, autumn / planning, relax / often, may / take, pack / idea, great
B been, places / have, last / How, weather / mostly, changed

Progress Check

1 ridden / have, about / haven't, was / fun, little
2 weather / quite, check / Thanks / going
3 Good, welcome, raining, but, sunny, leave, without

시험대비 기본평가
p.120

01 What's, like
02 ③   03 ④   04 ③

01 날씨를 물을 때는 How is[How's] the weather?나 What is[What's] the weather like?의 표현을 쓴다.
02 '~에 가 본 적 있니?'라고 경험을 물을 때는 Have you been ~?

표현을 사용한다. '전에'는 before로 쓴다.
03 현재의 바깥 날씨를 묻는데 미래 시제로 답하는 것은 적절하지 않다.
04 현재완료로 경험을 묻는 말에 부정으로 답할 때는 No, I haven't.라고 한다.

시험대비 실력평가
p.121~122

01 ②   02 Have, ever / have   03 ③
04 ④   05 ①   06 ⑤   07 ②, ⑤
08 나는 뉴질랜드를 방문했을 때 번지 점프를 한 번 해 보았어.
09 bungee jumping
10 ④   11 Actually   12 What's, like
13 relax   14 ①

01 What's the weather like outside?(바깥 날씨 어떤가요?)처럼 날씨가 어떤지 물을 때는 비인칭 주어 it을 사용하여 「It's+날씨.」의 형태를 써서 답한다.
02 경험을 묻는 현재완료를 쓴다.
03 엄마, 오늘 날씨 어때요? - 바깥 날씨가 꽤 흐려. 일기예보를 확인해 볼게. - 고마워요, 엄마. - 음, 오후에 비가 올 거야.
04 영화를 본 경험이 있는지 묻는 말에 본 적이 없다고 답하며 '너는 봤니?'라고 상대방에게 되묻는 표현이다. 대화의 흐름상 현재완료형으로 물어야 하므로 Have you (seen it)?의 ④가 적절하다.
05 A가 선글라스를 써야겠다고 했으므로 빈칸에는 날씨가 화창하다는 대답이 와야 한다. ⑤는 특정 지역의 가을 날씨를 묻는 질문에 적절한 대답이다.
06 경험을 묻는 현재완료이므로 'have+과거분사'의 형태가 알맞다.
07 How[What] about you?: 너는 어때?
08 try: 시도해 보다 / once: 한 번
09 it은 인칭대명사로 앞에 나온 단수 명사를 받을 수 있다.
10 have been to: ~에 다녀오다, ~에 가 본 적이 있다 / have gone to: ~에 갔다(그래서 지금 여기 없다)
11 문장 전체를 수식하는 부사가 되어야 한다.
12 날씨를 나타낼 때는 How's the weather?나 What's the weather like?의 표현을 쓴다.
13 특히 일이 끝난 후 쉬거나 즐거운 일을 하면서 시간을 보내다
14 ① Ann이 언제 호주에 갔는지는 위 대화를 통해 알 수 없다.

서술형 시험대비
p.123

01 like, It   02 Have, haven't
03 (B) - (C) - (D) - (A)   04 weather
05 cloudy   06 forecast   07 welcome
08 sunny   09 비가 좀 내릴 것으로 예상된다.

18 정답 및 해설

01 It은 날씨를 나타내는 비인칭 용법이다.

02 경험을 나타내는 현재완료 문장이다.

03 너 인도 음식을 먹어 본 적이 있니? - 응, 있어, 하지만 인도 카레만 먹어 봤어. - 어땠어? - 정말 매웠지만, 아주 좋았어.

04 날씨를 묻는 표현이다.

05 cloud의 형용사형이 와야 한다.

06 특히 특별한 사건이나 상황에 관련하여 미래에 일어날 것으로 기대되는 것에 대한 언급: forecast(예측, 예보)

07 welcome to: ~에 오신 것을 환영합니다

08 sun의 형용사형이 와야 한다.

교과서
Grammar

핵심 Check   p.124~125

1 (1) to go   (2) to help   (3) to write with
  (4) cold to drink
2 (1) to understand   (2) It   (3) to exercise   (4) of   (5) for

시험대비 기본평가   p.126

01 (1) to visit   (2) to do   (3) It   (4) of   (5) for
02 (1) to exercise   (2) to finish   (3) It   (4) of   (5) for
03 (1) to change   (2) to visit   (3) to read

01 (1), (2) 형용사적 용법의 to부정사가 필요하다. (3) 가주어 It이 필요하다. (4) 형용사가 kind이므로 의미상의 주어는 'of+목적격'을 쓴다. (5) 형용사가 hard이므로 의미상의 주어는 'for+목적격'을 쓴다.

02 (1), (2) 가주어 It이 있는 구문이므로 밑줄 친 부분을 to부정사로 바꾼다. (3) 가주어는 It으로 나타낸다. (4) 형용사가 brave이므로 의미상의 주어는 'of+목적격'을 쓴다. (5) 형용사가 easy이므로 의미상의 주어는 'for+목적격'을 쓴다.

시험대비 실력평가   p.127~129

01 ③   02 ④   03 ③   04 to write
05 It, to   06 ①   07 ①   08 Do you
want anything to eat? [Do you want to eat anything?]
09 ④   10 ④   11 It is difficult to fix the
machine.   12 ②   13 ①   14 to
15 ①   16 ⑤   17 sit → sit on[in]
18 ③   19 ①   20 ③   21 It is

pleasant to listen to music. 22 ⑤   23 going
→ to go

01 가주어 It의 진주어로 to부정사가 필요하다.

02 부정대명사 anything을 수식하는 형용사적 용법의 to부정사가 와야 한다.

03 ③은 부사적 용법의 to부정사이다. '~하기 위해'로 해석한다. 나머지는 모두 형용사적 용법이다.

04 '써야 할 편지들'이라는 뜻으로 명사 letters를 수식하는 to부정사의 형용사적 용법이다.

05 주어로 쓰인 to부정사가 긴 경우, 이를 뒤로 보내고 그 자리에 가주어 it을 쓴다.

06 가주어 – 진주어 구문으로 「It is+형용사+to부정사」 형태가 적절하다.

07 <보기>의 to read는 앞에 나온 명사 books를 수식하는 형용사적 용법의 to부정사이다. ① 형용사적 용법 ② 명사적 용법 ③ 부사적 용법 ④ 명사적 용법 ⑤ 부사적 용법

08 부정대명사를 수식하는 to부정사의 형용사적 용법을 쓴다.

09 ④ to going 대신 time을 수식하는 형용사적 용법의 to부정사가 필요하다.

10 ④의 it은 인칭대명사이고 나머지는 가주어 it[It]이다.

11 '그 기계를 고치는 것은' to fix the machine으로 나타낸다.

12 첫 문장은 형용사가 kind이므로 의미상의 주어는 'of+목적격'을 쓴다. 두 번째 문장은 형용사가 natural이므로 의미상의 주어는 'for+목적격'을 쓴다.

13 honest와 wise는 의미상의 주어로 'of+목적격'을 쓴다.

14 don't have to: ~할 필요가 없다 / reason to be angry at: ~에게 화낸 이유

15 It이 가주어이므로 진주어인 to부정사가 와야 한다.

16 ①, ④ 진주어로 쓰인 to부정사 ② hopes는 to부정사를 목적어로 취한다. ③ enough to+동사원형: ~하기에 충분히 …한 ⑤ 사역동사의 목적격보어는 동사원형이 와야 한다.

17 to부정사의 수식을 받는 명사가 전치사의 목적어일 경우 뒤에 전치사가 온다.

18 to부정사의 수식을 받는 명사가 전치사의 목적어일 경우 to부정사 뒤에 전치사를 쓴다. ③은 to talk with라고 해야 옳다.

19 ①은 '때'를 나타내는 비인칭 주어이다. 나머지는 가주어 it으로 쓰였다.

20 ③은 앞의 명사 house를 꾸며주는 형용사적 용법의 to부정사이고, 나머지는 모두 명사적 용법으로 쓰였다.

21 to부정사로 쓰인 주어가 길거나 의미를 강조하고 싶을 때 가주어 it을 주어 자리에 쓰고 진주어인 to부정사를 문장 뒤로 보낸다.

22 time을 수식하는 to부정사와 「don't have to+동사원형」의 형태가 필요하다.

23 진주어로 to부정사가 와야 한다.

01 It, to   02 to

03 (1) It is easy to bake cookies.

(2) He bought a magazine to read on the train.

04 to receive

05 (1) It wasn't easy to visit him every weekend.

(2) It is an exciting experience to live in another country.

06 (1) She has a strong desire to be a singer.

(2) I will make every effort to solve this problem.

(3) We had something to talk about.

(4) I want a sheet[piece] of papeer to write on.

(5) Please give me something hot to drink.

07 (1) It (2) on (3) with (4) to

08 (1) play → to play

(2) of → for

09 to visit   10 for you   11 It, to learn 12 to

13 (1) for → of

(2) of → for

14 It's a place to sell many things for 24 hours.

01 가주어 it을 문장 앞에 두고 진주어 to부정사구를 뒤로 보낸다.

02 앞의 명사를 수식하는 형용사적 용법의 to부정사가 필요하다.

03 (1) 가주어-진주어 구문으로 「It is + 형용사 + to부정사」 어순이 되어야 한다. (2) '읽을 잡지'이므로 to부정사의 형용사적 용법을 쓴다.

04 가주어인 It의 진주어에 해당하는 to부정사구가 되어야 하므로 to receive로 쓴다.

05 (1) '주말마다 그를 방문하는 것은'는 to visit him every weekend로 나타낸다. (2) '다른 나라에서 사는 것은'는 to live in another country로 나타낸다.

06 (1), (2), (3) to부정사의 형용사적 용법을 이용해 「명사+to부 정사」의 형태로 쓴다. (4) to부정사의 목적어가 있고 to부정사의 동사가 자동사일 때는 전치사가 필요하다. (5) -thing으로 끝나는 부정대명사는 「-thing+형용사+to부정사」의 어순을 따른다.

07 (1) 가주어 it이 필요하다. (2) '~ 위에' 쓰는 것이므로 전치사 on이 필요하다. (3) '칼을 가지고 로프를 자르는' 것이므로 전치사 with가 필요하다. (4) 형용사적 용법의 to부정사가 온다.

08 (1) time을 수식하는 to부정사로 바꾼다. (2) important는 의미상의 주어로 'for+목적격'을 쓴다.

09 명사 places를 수식하는 to부정사의 형용사적 용법이다.

10 important는 의미상 주어로 「for+목적격」을 쓴다.

11 to learn to ride a bike가 주어인 문장으로, 가주어 it이 앞에 온다. to ride는 learn의 목적어로 쓰인 to부정사이다.

12 가주어인 It의 진주어에 해당하는 to부정사와 「don't have to+동사원형」의 형태가 필요하다.

13 (1) 형용사가 stupid이므로 의미상의 주어는 'of+목적격'을 쓴다. (2) 형용사가 necessary이므로 의미상의 주어는 'for+목적격'을 쓴다.

14 to부정사의 형용사적 용법(a place to sell ~)을 이용한다.

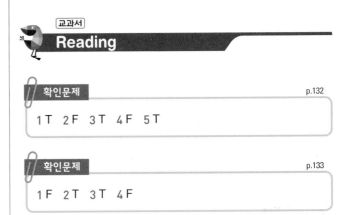

🐦 교과서 Reading

확인문제   p.132

1 T 2 F 3 T 4 F 5 T

확인문제   p.133

1 F 2 T 3 T 4 F

🦔 교과서 확인학습 A   p.134~135

01 live   02 week, vacation

03 trip, journal   04 way, special

05 set, mysterious, Earth   06 drive, finally

07 amazing, ring 08 stones, thousands

09 for   10 guess, mystery

11 perfect   12 colors   13 In, around

14 started, so   15 popular, stay 16 like

17 invited   18 full, and

19 busy, admiring

20 much, anything   21 draw, like

22 stop   23 visited   24 become, since

25 movies, else, dinner   26 also, who

27 When, outside, walked   28 touched, get

29 said, smile, portrait   30 Create

31 journal, much

교과서 확인학습 B   p.136~137

1 Hi, I am Lucy Hunter, and I live in London.

2 Last week, my family went on a vacation for three days.

3 During our trip, I made simple drawings in my journal.

4 That was a great way to capture all the special moments.

5 At last, we set foot at Stonehenge, one of the

most mysterious places on Earth.

6 After a two-hour drive from our home in London, we finally got to Stonehenge.

7 It was just amazing to see the ring of huge stones.

8 How did those huge stones get there thousands of years ago?

9 What were they for?

10 Don't try to make a perfect drawing.

11 A few colors will be enough.

12 I guess Stonehenge will remain a mystery for a long time.

13 In the morning, we walked around the Cotswolds.

14 It started to rain in the afternoon, so we decided to stay indoors at our B&B.

15 A B&B is a popular place to stay in England.

16 It feels more like a home than a hotel.

17 The owner invited us for afternoon tea today.

18 The dining table was full of cookies, cake, bread, and cheese.

19 While I was busy eating, Mom was admiring the beautiful cups and plates.

20 I ate too much, so I couldn't eat anything for dinner.

21 It is O.K. to draw everyday objects like cups and plates in your journal.

22 Our last stop was Oxford.

23 We first visited Christ Church College.

24 It has become a world famous place to visit since it appeared in the Harry Potter movies.

25 In the movies, Harry and everyone else eat dinner at the Hall of Christ Church.

26 We also saw portraits of famous people who graduated from the college.

27 When we were outside the building, I walked to the famous olive tree and touched it.

28 "Because I touched this tree," I said, "I will get into Oxford University!"

29 Then, my brother said to me with a smile, "I can't wait to see your portrait on the wall."

30 Create your own avatar.

31 Your drawing journal will become much more interesting.

시험대비 실력평가
p.138~141

01 ①   02 ④   03 일기에 간단한 그림을 그리는 것   04 특별한 순간을 모두 포착할 수 있다.

05 ③   06 ②   07 (m)ystery   08 ②

09 ④   10 ③   11 ⑤   12 ②

13 ④   14 because[as]   15 ④

16 ④   17 Christ Church College   18 ⑤

19 We also saw portraits of famous people who graduated from the college.

20 ③   21 ①   22 famous   23 ①, ③

24 ④   25 ②   26 ②   27 market

28 traditional   29 외국에서 새로운 일들을 해 보는 것

30 ②

01 go on a vacation: 휴가를 가다

02 for+수사가 붙은 기간을 나타내는 명사 / during+특정 기간을 나타내는 명사

03 That은 지시대명사로 앞에 나온 문장을 받는다.

05 What were they for?의 they는 those huge stones를 받으므로 이 문장 앞에 와야 한다.

06 get to: ~에 도착하다

07 이해되거나 알려지지 않은 어떤 것

08 colors가 복수형이고 문맥상 '약간의, 몇 개의'라는 뜻이 필요하므로 A few가 알맞다.

09 거대한 돌의 고리가 무슨 용도로 쓰였는지는 알 수 없다.

10 주어진 문장의 It은 A B&B를 받으므로 B&B를 설명하는 문장 다음에 와야 한다.

11 ⑤는 '그것'의 뜻으로 특정한 명사를 받는 인칭대명사이고 나머지는 모두 비인칭 용법으로 쓰였다.

12 be full of: ~으로 가득 차다

13 while: ~하는 동안

14 이유를 나타내는 접속사가 와야 하므로 because 외에 as나 since도 올 수 있다.

15 ④ 주인이 왜 그들을 초대했는지는 언급되지 않았다.

16 그 장소가 Harry Potter 영화에 등장해서 유명해졌다는 문장 다음에 와야 한다.

17 It은 인칭대명사로 앞에 나온 단수 명사를 받는다.

18 '~한 이래로'의 뜻으로 현재완료에 쓰이는 접속사는 since이다.

19 graduate는 자동사이기 때문에 목적어 앞에 전치사 from이 필요하다.

20 ③ Christ Church College가 영국에서 가장 인기 있는 관광지 중의 하나인지는 언급되지 않았다.

21 '~했을 때'의 뜻으로 때를 나타내는 접속사 when이 알맞다.

22 아주 잘 알려져 있는: famous(유명한)

23 비교급을 강조할 때는 much, far, even, a lot 등을 쓸 수 있다.

24 ④ Lucy의 초상화는 벽에 걸려 있지 않다.

25 Then이 있으므로 야시장에 갔다는 문장 다음에 와야 한다.

26 temples가 복수 명사이므로 much는 쓸 수 없다.

27 대개는 옥외에서 물건을 사고파는 장소: market(시장)

28 명사 food을 수식하므로 형용사형으로 고쳐야 한다.

29 It은 가주어로 진주어인 to try 이하를 받는다.

30 민수가 왜 절을 방문했는지는 언급되지 않았다.

서술형 시험대비
p.142~143

01 foot 02 After 03 amazing 04 at Stonehenge 05 완벽한 그림을 그리기 위해 노력하지 말라는 것이다. 06 on 07 During 08 That was a great way to capture all the special moments. 09 to stay 10 like 11 owner 12 with 13 nothing → anything 14 당신의 일기에 컵과 접시 같은 일상적인 물건들을 그려도 괜찮습니다. 15 She was admiring the beautiful cups and plates. 16 to 17 그토록 많은 아름다운 섬들을 보는 것 18 forget

01 사람이 그 위에 서 있거나 다리 끝에 있는 신체 부분: foot(발)

02 after a two-hour drive from ~: ~에서 두 시간 동안 운전한 후에

03 사물이 사람을 놀라게 하는 것이므로 현재분사형의 형용사를 쓴다.

04 there는 앞에 언급된 장소를 가리키는 부사이다.

06 go on a vacation: 휴가를 가다

07 for+수사가 붙은 일정한 기간 / during+특정한 기간

08 'all the+복수 명사'의 어순을 취한다.

09 decide는 to부정사를 목적어로 취한다.

10 feel like+명사: ~처럼 느껴지다

11 own: 소유하다 / owner: 소유자, 주인

12 be full of = be filled with: ~으로 가득 차다

13 앞에 not이 있기 때문에 nothing을 쓸 수 없다.

14 like: ~와 같은

16 go on a field trip to: ~으로 현장 학습을 가다

17 It은 가주어로 진주어인 to see ~의 내용을 나타낸다.

18 문맥상 '잊지 않을 것이다'가 되어야 한다.

영역별 핵심문제
p.145~149

01 ④	02 ③	03 different	04 ③
05 ⑤	06 ②	07 guess	08 ③
09 ③	10 ②	11 (B)-(C)-(A)-(D)	
12 ④	13 ②	14 ④	15 won't
16 No, he doesn't.		17 ①	18 ④
19 ②	20 it is	21 ③	22 ②
23 ②	24 write → write with		25 ⑤
26 anything to make myself look slimmer			27 It, to
28 ④	29 ①, ⑤	30 to visit	31 ③
32 ④	33 have	34 ②, ③	35 ①
36 ②, ④	37 ③	38 finally	
39 이상한 거북들을 보는 것			

01 ④는 '명사 - 형용사' 관계인데, 나머지는 '형용사 - 부사'의 관계이다.

02 • 저런 걸 들은 적이 있어요? • 제가 들어갈 만한 충분한 공간이 있나요? • 그가 또 다른 말은 뭐라고 했어요? • 넌 정말 내가 너를 믿으리라고 기대하니?

03 반의어 관계이다. 추운 : 더운 = 같은 : 다른

04 get into: ~에 들어가다 / watch out: 조심하다

05 육지에 완전히 둘러싸인 땅: island(섬)

06 at last: 마침내(=finally)

07 guess: 추측하다

08 ③은 '집에 갔니?'라고 결과를 묻는 표현이고, 나머지는 경험을 묻는 표현이다.

09 B가 비가 오고 있다고 말하고 있고, Yes나 No로 답하지 않았으므로 의문사를 이용한 날씨를 묻는 질문이 와야 알맞다.

10 It was very tasty.(그것은 매우 맛있었어.)라는 말로 보아 긍정의 대답이 들어가야 한다. Have you ever ~?의 긍정의 대답은 Yes, I have.이다.

11 너 말을 타본 적 있니? - 응, 있어. 너는 어때? - 아니, 난 없어. 말 타는 거 어땠어? - 재미있었지만, 조금 무섭기도 했어.

12 How about Seoul?은 서울의 날씨는 어떠냐는 의미이다. ④는 날씨를 묻는 말에 대한 응답으로 적절하지 않다.

13 주어진 문장은 일기예보를 확인해 보겠다는 문장이므로 우산이 필요하냐고 묻는 문장 다음에 와야 한다.

14 날씨를 묻는 표현은 How is the weather?와 What is the weather like?가 있다.

15 be going to는 will을 써서 바꿔 쓸 수 있다.

17 가주어 It을 설명하는 진주어 to부정사가 필요하다.

18 -thing으로 끝나는 부정대명사를 수식하는 to부정사가 필요하다.

19 형용사가 stupid와 clever이므로 의미상의 주어는 'of+목적격'을 쓴다.

20 뒤에 진주어인 to부정사구가 왔으므로 빈칸에는 가주어인 it과 be동사가 와야 한다.

21 -thing으로 끝나는 부정대명사는 「-thing+형용사+to부정사」의 어순을 취한다.

22 <보기>와 나머지는 모두 형용사적 용법이고 ②는 부사적 용법이다.

23 ②는 날씨를 나타내는 비인칭 주어 it이고, 나머지는 to부정사구를 진주어로 하는 가주어 it이다.

24 to부정사의 수식을 받는 명사가 전치사의 목적어일 경우 뒤에 전치사가 온다.

25 형용사적 용법의 to부정사는 명사나 대명사를 뒤에서 수식하여 형용사처럼 쓰인다. 또한, food는 보통 단수로 쓰인다.

26 anything: 어떤 것이든

27 To finish this work이 주어인 문장으로, 가주어 it이 앞에 온다.

28 주어진 문장은 외국에서 새로운 일들을 시도하는 것이 즐거웠다는 뜻이므로 여러 가지 일들을 했다는 문장 다음에 와야 한다.

29 a lot of는 '많은'의 뜻인데 뒤에 복수명사가 오므로 much는 쓸 수 없다.

30 명사 a chance를 꾸며 주는 to부정사의 형용사적 용법이다

31 ③ 민수가 쇼핑을 했다는 말은 언급되지 않았다.

32 부사절 since ~가 있으므로 계속을 나타내는 현재완료가 온다.

33 eat[have] dinner: 저녁을 먹다

34 선행사가 사람이고 주격이므로 who나 that을 쓴다.

35 이유를 나타내는 접속사로 because나 as를 쓸 수 있다.

36 비교급을 강조하는 부사(구)는 much, even, far, a lot 등이다.

37 ③ Christ Church College를 누가 졸업했는지는 언급되지 않았다.

38 final의 부사형은 finally이다.

39 It은 가주어로 진주어인 to watch ~의 내용을 받는다.

단원별 예상문제   p.150~153

01 ④	02 ②	03 creation	04 else
05 ⑤	06 ①, ④	07 ④	08 been

09 나는 해변에서 시간을 좀 보내고 햇빛을 쬐며 휴식을 취할 계획이야.

10 ⑤	11 write → write on	
12 ②	13 ④	14 It, to 15 ⑤
16 ①	17 ⑤	18 ④ 19 ②
20 ②	21 ⑤	22 ②

23 thousand → thousands   24 ③   25 to make   26 ④, ⑤   27 그토록 아름다운 많은 섬들을 보는 것은 아주 놀라웠다. 28 They went there last month.

01 ④는 유의어 관계이고 나머지는 반의어 관계이다.

02 appear: 나타나다 / show up: 나타나다

03 동사 - 명사의 관계이다.

04 else: 또 다른, 다른

05 ⑤는 pack(짐을 싸다)의 영영풀이이다.

06 날씨를 묻는 표현에는 How's the weather today?, What's the weather like today? 등이 있다

07 No, I haven't.로 답했으므로 현재완료를 이용해서 경험을 묻는 질문이 와야 알맞다.

08 be의 과거분사는 been이다.

09 be planning to: ~할 계획이다

10 4월에는 비가 자주 온다고 언급되었다.

11 to부정사의 수식을 받는 명사가 전치사의 목적어일 경우 뒤에 전치사가 온다.

12 첫 문장은 형용사가 wise이므로 의미상의 주어는 'of+목적격'을 쓴다. 두 번째 문장은 형용사가 impossible이므로 의미상의 주어는 'for+목적격'을 쓴다.

13 It이 가주어이므로 진주어인 to부정사가 와야 한다.

14 To solve this puzzle이 주어인 문장으로, 가주어 it이 앞에 온다.

15 <보기>와 ⑤의 It은 가주어이다. ①, ④ 비인칭 주어, ②, ③ 인칭대명사

16 ①에서 sit은 자동사이므로 chair를 목적어로 취하기 위해서는 전치사 in이나 on이 필요하다.

17 many places to visit(방문할 많은 장소)에서 to visit은 형용사적 용법의 to부정사로 명사인 many places를 수식한다.

18 ④는 to부정사의 형용사적 용법이고, 나머지는 모두 '~하기 위해서'라는 목적을 나타내는 부사적 용법이다.

19 for+수사가 붙은 기간

20 ⓐ, ② 형용사적 용법 ①, ⑤ 명사적 용법 ③, ④ 부사적 용법

21 at last=in the long run: 결국, 마침내

22 get to=arrive at=reach: ~에 도착하다

23 thousand 뒤에 of가 와서 '수천의, 수많은'의 뜻을 나타낼 때는 복수형을 취한다.

24 remain: 계속[여전히] ~이다, 남아 있다

25 try+to부정사: ~하기 위해 애쓰다 / try+-ing: 시험 삼아 ~해 보다

27 It은 to see 이하를 받는 가주어이다.

28 지난달에 남해에 갔다고 언급되었다.

서술형 실전문제   p.154~155

01 gone → been   02 What, like

03 but   04 (A) – (C) – (B) – (D)

05 (1) It isn't easy to keep a diary every day.

(2) I like the photographs which my little[younger] brother takes.

06 (1) It is difficult for me to park a car.

(2) It is safe to ride a bike with a helmet.

(3) It is an exciting experience to live in another country.

07 (1) to go to school

(2) to have lunch

(3) to play on the playground

(4) to do my homework

08 because[as]   09 A B&B

10 of   11 anything

12 They walked around the Cotswolds.   13 many

14 나는 다시 라오스를 방문할 기회를 갖기를 바란다.

15 He or she went to Laos with his or her family.

01 have gone to: ~에 갔다(그래서 여기 없다) / have been to: ~에 가 본 적이 있다, ~에 다녀왔다

02 날씨를 묻는 표현에는 How's the weather today?, What's the weather like today? 등이 있다.

03 상반되는 내용을 연결하는 접속사 but이 알맞다.

04 (A) 엄마, 오늘 날씨 어때요? - (C) 바깥 날씨가 꽤 흐려. 일기예보를 확인해 볼게. - (B) 고마워요, 엄마. - (D) 음, 오후에 비가 올 거야

05 (1) 「It ~ to부정사」 구문을 이용하여 문장을 완성한다. (2) 관계대명사 which를 이용하여 선행사 the photographs를 수식하도록 한다.

06 to부정사가 이끄는 구가 주어로 오는 경우, to부정사 주어를 문장 뒤로 보내고 그 자리에 It을 쓴다.

07 to부정사의 형용사적 용법을 이용하여 문장을 완성한다.

08 결과의 접속사 so는 이유를 나타내는 접속사를 써서 바꿔 쓸 수 있다. because나 as 대신 since를 쓸 수도 있다.

09 It은 인칭대명사로 앞에 나온 단수 명사를 받는다.

10 be full of: ~으로 가득 차다

11 something은 긍정문, anything은 부정문에서 쓰인다.

12 그들은 코츠월드 언덕을 돌아다녔다고 언급되었다.

13 temples가 복수 명사이기 때문에 much는 쓸 수 없다.

14 to visit는 chance를 수식하는 형용사적 용법이다.

창의사고력 서술형 문제   p.156

[모범답안]

01 (1) I need something to drink

   (2) I need a chair to sit on[in].

   (3) He needs friends to talk with

02 (1) It is kind of her to help the poor.

   (2) It is difficult for us to win the game.

   (3) It is stupid of you to agree to the proposal.

   (4) It is possible for you to finish the work on time.

   (5) It is necessary for foreigners to learn Korean.

03 (1) a movie to watch

   (2) a baseball game to watch

   (3) a piano lesson to take

   (4) four comic books to read

01 앞의 명사를 꾸며주는 to부정사의 형용사적 용법을 이용한다.

02 「It is ~ for[of]+목적어+to부정사」의 가주어, 진주어 구문을 이용한다.

03 to부정사의 형용사적 용법을 이용하여 내용에 맞도록 빈칸을 채운다.

단원별 모의고사   p.157~160

01 ④	02 ③	03 ④	
04 decision	05 up	06 ②	07 ③
08 ⑤	09 ①, ③	10 ④	11 ④
12 ⑤	13 ③	14 to finish	15 ③
16 ⑤	17 ②	18 ⑤	19 ⓐ to find ⓑ to find
	20 ③	21 ④	
22 ①, ②	23 ④	24 ③	25 portrait
26 ①	27 그 올리브 나무에 손을 대면 옥스퍼드 대학에 들어가기 때문이다.	28 ②	29 many
30 ④			

01 어떤 것이 일어나거나 존재하게 하다: create(창조하다)

02 right now: 지금, 당장

03 be full of: ~으로 가득 차다 / be fond of: ~을 좋아하다

04 '동사 : 명사'의 관계이다.

05 show up: 나타나다 / clean up: ~을 청소하다

06 Have you ever+과거분사 ~?에 대한 응답은 Yes, I have. / No, I haven't.이다. 빈칸 다음의 말로 보아 부정의 대답이 와야 한다.

07 대답이 No, I haven't.이므로 경험을 묻는 표현인 ③ '넌 곰을 본 적이 있니?'가 알맞다.

08 A가 날씨를 물었으므로 춥고 때때로 눈이 많이 내린다는 응답이 가장 적절하다.

09 How[What] about you?: 너는 어때?

10 Bill이 두려워서 번지 점프를 하지 않는다는 말은 언급되지 않았다.

11 명사 things를 수식하는 형용사적 용법의 to부정사가 와야 한다.

12 문맥상 '함께 여행할 친구를 찾고 있다'는 흐름이 자연스러우므로, 빈칸에는 '~와 함께'에 해당하는 with가 알맞다.

13 기숙사에서 사는 것이므로 live 다음에 전치사 in이 필요하다.

14 it은 가주어이고, 진주어는 형용사 뒤에 to부정사 형태로 와야 한다.

15 <보기>의 to eat는 형용사적 용법의 to부정사이다. ①, ②, ⑤ 부사적 용법 ③ 형용사적 용법 ④ 명사적 용법

16 ⑤ -thing이나 -body로 끝나는 부정대명사의 경우 형용사와 to부정사의 수식을 동시에 받으면 「부정대명사+형용사+to부정사」의 순서로 써야 한다. something important to tell

17 ②의 경우, 두 개의 동사(is, skate)가 같이 쓰일 수는 없다. 가주어 it과 진주어 to부정사구(to skate ~)의 구문으로 만든다.

18 to부정사의 형용사적 용법이다.

19 가주어 It의 진주어로 to부정사 형태가 필요하다.

20 other → else

21 현재완료형에서 '~한 이후로'의 뜻으로 부사절을 이끄는 접속사는 since이다.

22 선행사가 사람이고 주격이므로 who나 that을 쓴다.

23 ④ Harry Potter가 Christ Church College의 학생이라는 말은 언급되지 않았다.

24 ⓐ에는 때를 나타내는 접속사, ⓑ에는 이유를 나타내는 접속 사가 와야 한다.

25 어떤 특정한 사람을 그린 그림이나 찍은 사진: portrait(초상화)

26 very는 비교급을 수식할 수 없다.

28 Then이 있으므로 Vientiane의 야시장에 갔다는 문장 다음에 와야 한다.

29 a lot of: 많은

30 ④ 그들의 전통 음식이 무엇인지는 언급되지 않았다.

Giving a Hand

Lesson 4

Conversation 교과서

시험대비 실력평가
p.164

01 ②	02 ④	03 ③	04 heavy
05 ②	06 create	07 until[till]	08 ③

01 ①, ③, ④, ⑤는 모두 plant(식물)에 속한다.

02 at first: 처음에 / be thankful for: ~에게 감사하다

03 어떤 특정한 방향으로 갈 생각 없이, 종종 아무렇게나 어떤 장소를 거닐다: wander(거닐다, 헤매다)

04 반의어의 관계이다. 낮은 : 높은 = 가벼운 : 무거운

05 look for: ~을 찾다

06 어떤 것이 발생하거나 존재하게 하다 : create(창조하다, 만들어 내다)

07 until: ~할 때까지(=till)

08 grow up: 성장하다 / give up; 포기하다

서술형 시험대비
p.165

01 (1) daughter (2) activity
02 (1) with[for] joy (2) come over to (3) thank, for
03 (1) still (2) build (3) understand
    (4) someone (5) share
04 (1) comfortable (2) happiness (3) create
05 (1) Af first (2) Cheer up (3) come up with
    (4) Keep an eye on
06 (1) (g)ift (2) (d)river

01 (1) 남성명사 : 여성명사의 관계이다. (2) 형용사 : 명사의 관계이다.

02 (1) with[for] joy: 기뻐서 (2) come over to: ~으로 오다
    (3) thank A for B: B에 대하여 A에게 감사하다

03 (1) still: 아직(도) (2) build: 짓다, 건설하다 (3) understand: 이해하다, 알아듣다 (4) someone: 어떤 사람 (5) share: 함께 쓰다

04 (1) comfortable: 편안한 (2) happiness: 행복 (3) create: 만들어 내다, 창조하다

05 (1) at first: 처음에는 (2) cheer up: 기운 내다 (3) come up with: ~을 생각해 내다 (4) keep an eye on: ~을 계속 지켜보다

06 (1) gift: 선물 (2) driver: 운전자, 운전기사

핵심 Check
p.166~167

1 (1) do, favor / What (2) help me / course
  (3) help me find / can't
2 (1) Thank / pleasure (2) grateful / at all
  (3) appreciate / problem

교과서 대화문 익히기

Check(√) True or False
p.168

1 T 2 F 3 F 4 T 5 T 6 F

교과서 확인학습
p.170~171

Listen & Speak 1 A. Listen and Check
1 do, favor / What / family, vacation, come, water / can
2 can, favor / it / help, with, project / Sorry, can't, have

Listen & Speak 2 A. Listen and Check
1 Hi, know, birthday, haven't, to, being, been, and, supporting, trying, proud, daughter
2 doing, weekend, special, stay, watch, having, party, inviting

Listen & Speak 1-B
favor / What / move, with, heavy / problem / Thank, helping

Communicate A. Listen and Answer
Can, do / What / shopping, for / course, for / for / getting, gift / until / why, cap / broke, while, last, just, cheer / see, go / perfect

Progress Check
1 do, favor / it / going, this, care, during / worry, enjoy
2 Hello, haven't, being, Every, welcome, teach, things, lucky, proud, students
3 any, plans / just, stay / then, over, dinner

시험대비 기본평가
p.172

01 ④	02 ②	03 ①	04 ①

01 ①, ②, ③, ⑤는 도움을 요청하는 반면, ④ What can I do for you?는 도움을 주겠다고 제안하는 표현이다.

02 감사 표현에 대한 응답은 My pleasure. / Not at all. / Don't mention it. 등을 이용하여 나타낸다.

03 Can you do me a favor?는 '부탁 좀 해도 될까?'의 의미로 상대방에게 도움을 요청할 때 사용하는 표현이다.

04 감사의 의미를 나타내는 말이다.

시험대비 실력평가　　　　　　　　　p.173~174

01 ②	02 ④	03 appreciate, problem
04 Thank, for	05 ④	06 ②	07 give,
hand	08 shopping	09 ①	10 ③
11 ②	12 Nothing	13 ④	14 welcome

01 Kevin, 부탁 하나 들어줄래? - 좋아. 뭔데? - 오늘 오후에 내 과학 프로젝트 좀 도와줄래? - 미안하지만 안돼. 엄마랑 할머니 댁에 가야 해.

02 ④ 고맙다는 말에 대한 응답이다.

03 appreciate: 고맙게 여기다 / No problem.: 천만에.

04 thank you for -ing: ~에 감사하다

05 Can you give me a hand?는 상대방에게 도움을 요청하는 표현이다.

06 ② TV 소리를 줄여달라는 요청에 '천만에요.'라고 응답하는 것은 어울리지 않는다.

07 Can you do me a favor?와 Can you give me a hand?는 남에게 도움을 요청할 때 쓰는 표현이다.

08 go shopping: 쇼핑하러 가다

09 문맥상 이유를 묻는 의문부사 why가 알맞다.

10 cheer up: ~을 격려하다

11 ② Jaden은 여동생의 생일 선물을 사는 것이 아니라고 했다.

12 Nothing special.: 특별히 할 일은 없다.

13 thank A for B: B에 대하여 A에게 감사하다

14 You're welcome.: 천만에.

서술형 시험대비　　　　　　　　　p.175

01 for helping	02 hand	03 do / ahead / for
04 (D)–(A)–(C)–(B)		05 haven't	06 chance
07 trying		08 저는 두 분의 딸인 것을 자랑스럽게 여깁니다.

01 thank you for -ing: ~에 감사하다 / help with: ~을 돕다

02 Can you give me a hand?: 나를 도와 줄 수 있니?

03 Go ahead.: 어서 그렇게 해라., 어서 말해라. / buy A for B: B에게 A를 사 주다

---

04 (D) 소라야, 이번 주 금요일에 뭐 할 거니? - (A) 특별한 계획은 없어. 왜? - (C) 나는 내 생일파티를 열 거야. 너도 올래? - (B) 물론이지. 초대해 줘서 고마워.

05 문맥상 현재완료 부정문이 와야 한다.

06 뭔가를 할 기회가 있는 적절한 시간 또는 상황: 기회 (chance)

07 supporting과 함께 전치사 for의 목적어이므로 동명사형이 되어야 한다.

08 be proud to ~: ~해서 자랑스럽게 여기다

교과서
Grammar

핵심 Check　　　　　　　　　p.176~177

1 (1) that　(2) that　(3) whom　(4) which　(5) which
2 (1) enough to　(2) so, that　(3) too, to　(4) so, that
(5) too, to

시험대비 기본평가　　　　　　　　　p.178

01 (1) so　(2) too　(3) whom　(4) which
02 (1) so, that, could　(2) so poor, can't　(3) too, to
03 (1) who　(2) whom　(3) which　(4) that

01 (1) so ~ that+S+can't ... 구문으로 '너무 ~해서 …할 수 없다'의 의미이다. (2) too ~ to부정사 구문으로 '너무 ~해서 …할 수 없다'의 의미이다. (3) 선행사가 사람이고 목적격이므로 관계대명사 whom으로 연결한다. (4) 선행사가 사물이고 목적격이므로 관계대명사 which로 연결한다.

02 (1) 형용사+enough to+동사원형 → so+형용사+that+주어+can+동사원형 (2) too+형용사+to부정사 → so+형용사+that+주어+can't+동사원형 (3) so+형용사+that+주어+cannot+동사원형 → too+형용사+to부정사

03 (1) 주격관계대명사 who가 필요하다. (2) 전치사 다음에는 that을 쓸 수 없다. (3) 사물이 선행사 (a knife)이므로 전치사의 목적어 역할을 하는 목적격 관계대명사 which가 와야 한다. (4) the only가 선행사를 수식하므로 목적격 관계대명사 that이 온다.

시험대비 실력평가　　　　　　　　　p.179~181

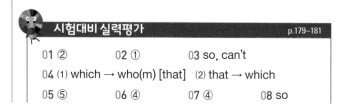

01 ②	02 ①	03 so, can't	
04 (1) which → who(m) [that]　(2) that → which			
05 ⑤	06 ④	07 ④	08 so

09 ⑤ 10 that 11 ① 12 The man gave me all the money that he had. 13 ⑤ 14 ④ 15 ③ 16 too, to carry 17 (1) which → who(m) [that] (2) were → was 18 ② 19 ③ 20 ① 21 ①, ⑤

01 선행사가 사람(the gentleman)이고 동사 met의 목적어 역할을 하므로 who(m)나 that이 와야 한다.

02 '상자가 너무 무거워서 나 혼자서 옮길 수 없었다.'고 하는 것이 자연스러우므로 so heavy that I couldn't move ~를 쓰는 것이 적절하다.

03 '걸어가기에 너무 멀다'는 '너무 멀어서 걸어갈 수 없다'는 의미와 같다.

04 (1) 선행사가 사람이므로 knows의 목적어 역할을 하는 who(m) 또는 that을 쓴다. (2) 관계대명사 that은 전치사 뒤에 올 수 없다.

05 '너무 바빠서 그녀를 기다릴 수 없다'는 의미가 자연스러우므로 too busy to wait를 쓴다.

06 ④에서 listen은 자동사이므로 목적어를 취할 때는 전치사 to가 필요하다. (which → to which)

07 ④ '아주 힘이 세서 상자들을 옮길 수 있었다'는 의미이므로 too 대신 so를 써야 한다.

08 so ~ that ... 구문은 '너무 ~해서 …할 수 없다'의 의미를 나타낸다.

09 목적격 관계대명사는 생략할 수 있다. that은 사물과 사람에 모두 쓸 수 있다.

10 선행사가 사람일 때와 사물일 때 모두 쓸 수 있는 관계대명사는 that이다.

11 so that ~ can: ~하기 위해서 / so ~ that ... can't: 너무 ~해서 …할 수 없다

12 선행사 all the money를 목적격 관계대명사 that이 이끄는 절이 수식한다.

13 '너무 ~해서 …할 수 없다'는 so ~ that ... can't로 나타낸다. 또한 too ~ to부정사로 나타낼 수도 있다. ②는 eat의 목적어가 되는 it이 필요하다.

14 ④ 전치사 다음에는 that을 쓸 수 없다.

15 'too+형용사+to부정사'는 'so+형용사+that+주어 +couldn't+동사원형'으로 바꿔 쓸 수 있다.

16 '너무 무거워 내가 옮길 수 없다'는 '내가 옮기기에는 너무 무겁다'로 바꿔 쓸 수 있다.

17 (1) 선행사가 사람이므로 목적격 관계대명사 who(m)이나 that이 와야 한다. (2) 문장의 주어(The knife)는 단수 명사이므로 be동사는 was가 되어야 한다.

18 목적격 관계대명사는 생략할 수 있다. ②의 who는 앞에 나온 The boy를 수식하는 주격 관계대명사이므로 생략할 수 없다.

19 ⓑ enough old → old enough ⓒ solve → solve it

20 ①의 that은 명사절을 이끄는 접속사로 쓰였고, 나머지는 관계대명사로 쓰였다.

21 시제는 과거이고, '너무 ~해서 …하지 못했다'는 「so ~ that+주어 +couldn't ~」 또는 too ~ to부정사 구문을 이용하여 나타낸다.

01 (1) I know the man who(m)[that] you are looking for.
(2) This is the bag which[that] I got from Nancy.
(3) He is the boy who(m)[that] I meet at the bus stop every morning.

02 (1) so (2) enough (3) too (4) that 03 that

04 (1) too → so (2) carry it → carry
(3) enough warm → warm enough (4) what → that

05 so, that

06 (1) I bought my sister a blouse (which[that] was) made in France.
(2) Do you know the boy whom I met on the street yesterday?
(3) This is the city that is famous for its beautiful buildings.

07 (1) so, that, can't (2) lucky enough to

08 (1) The question is so easy that everyone knows the answer.
(2) I am so tired that I can't do it right now.

09 (1) to / so, that, can't (2) enough / so, could blow
(3) so, couldn't / too, to

10 (1) The girl saw a man and his dog that looked very tired.
(2) John with whom I played tennis yesterday is the best player in this town.
(3) This bike which[that] my father bought (for) me last year is my treasure.
(4) My sister ate the only ice cream that my mother bought for me.
(5) The house in which we lived two years ago was in Incheon.

11 (1) who[m] (2) which[that]

01 목적격 관계대명사는 접속사와 대명사의 역할을 하며, 선행사가 사람일 경우 who(m)나 that, 사물일 경우 which나 that을 쓴다.

02 (1), (4) so ~ that ... 구문이다. (2) enough to부정사 구문이다. (3) too ~ to부정사 구문이다.

03 선행사가 사람일 때와 사물일 때 모두 쓸 수 있는 관계대명사는 that이다.

04 (1) that절이 있으므로 too 대신 so를 써야 한다. (2) 주어

The bag이 carry의 목적어이므로 it은 필요 없다. (3) 부사 enough는 형용사 뒤에 위치한다. (4) so ~ that 구문이다.

05 so+형용사+that+주어+동사: 너무 ~해서 …하다

06 (1) 선행사 a blouse가 사물이므로 관계대명사는 which나 that이 되어야 한다. 과거분사 앞에 있는 <주격 관계대명사+be 동사>는 생략할 수 있다. (2) whom은 생략할 수 있다. (3) that이 이끄는 절의 선행사가 단수명사이므로 동사는 is가 되어야 한다.

07 (1) so ~ that ... can't: 너무 ~해서 ...할 수 없다 (2) 형용사 + enough to + 동사원형: ~할 만큼 충분히 ...한

08 (1) so ~ that ...구문: 너무 ~해서 …하다 (2) so ~ that ... can't 구문: 너무 ~해서 …할 수 없다

09 (1), (3) 'too+형용사/부사+to부정사'는 'so+형용사/부사+that+주어+cannot+동사원형'의 형태로 바꿔 쓸 수 있다. (2) '형용사/부사+enough to+동사원형'은 'so+형용사/부사+that+ 주어+can+동사원형'의 형태로 바꿔 쓸 수 있다.

10 (1) 선행사가 사람과 동물(a man and his dog)이므로 관계대명사 that을 쓴다. (4) the only가 선행사를 수식할 때는 보통 관계대명사 that을 쓴다. (5) 선행사가 사물(the house)이므로, 전치사 in의 목적어 역할을 하는 목적격 관계대명사 which를 쓴다.

11 (1) 선행사가 사람이고 목적격이므로 관계대명사는 who, whom 또는 that을 쓸 수 있다. (2) 선행사가 사물이고 목적격이므로 관계대명사는 which나 that을 쓸 수 있다.

교과서 Reading

확인문제 p.184

1 F 2 T 3 T 4 F 5 T

확인문제 p.185

1 T 2 F 3 F 4 T 5 F

교과서 확인학습 A p.186~187

01 up, family   02 Since, been
03 friend, driver, cook
04 taught, lessons   05 who, most
06 When, went, got   07 disease
08 Everyone, shock
09 became, over 10 off, that, all
11 got, saw   12 moment, himself, don't, heels

13 that, do   14 create, then, signal
15 tried, materials, socks   16 like, safety
17 After, succeeded
18 worked, that, joy
19 believe, actually   20 For, inventor
21 friend

교과서 확인학습 B p.188~189

1 Kenneth Shinozuka grew up in a big happy family of three generations.

2 Since he was little, he has always been very close to his grandfather.

3 He was Kenneth's first friend, his trusty driver, and his cook.

4 He also taught him many life lessons.

5 He was the person who Kenneth respected the most in the world.

6 When Kenneth was four, his grandfather went out for a walk one day and got lost.

7 He had Alzheimer's disease.

8 Everyone in Kenneth's family was in shock.

9 His condition became worse over the next 10 years.

10 He wandered off at night so often that someone had to keep an eye on him all night long.

11 One night, Kenneth's grandfather got out of bed, and Kenneth saw it.

12 At that moment, he said to himself, "Why don't I put pressure sensors on the heels of his socks?"

13 There were many things that Kenneth had to do.

14 He first had to create a pressure sensor and then find a way to send a signal to his smart phone.

15 Kenneth also tried many different materials to make comfortable socks for his elderly grandfather.

16 When he felt like giving up, he thought about his grandfather's safety.

17 After much trial and error, he finally succeeded in making his device.

18 When it first worked, he was so happy that he jumped for joy.

19 He could not believe that his invention actually worked.

20 For his grandfather, Kenneth is the best inventor in the world.

21 For Kenneth, his grandfather is still his best friend.

01 ④	02 ③	03 driver	04 ①, ②, ⑤
05 ③	06 ⑤	07 lost	08 ②

09 Kenneth의 할아버지가 침대에서 나오는 것   10 ④

11 ⑤	12 ③	13 comfortable	14 ③
15 ①	16 trial	17 ④	18 할아버지

의 안전에 대해 생각했기 때문이다.   19 ②   20 been

21 그는 또한 그에게 많은 인생 교훈을 가르쳐 주었다.

22 ①, ②	23 ①	24 ③	25 disease

26 ①   27 어느 날 밤 Kenneth의 할아버지가 침대
에서 나왔는데, Kenneth가 그것을 보았다.   28 him →
himself   29 ②   30 ⑤   31 ②, ④
32 ⑤

01 주어진 문장은 할아버지가 추가적으로 해준 일을 나타내므로 할아버지가 Kenneth의 친구이자 운전기사이자 요리사였다는 문장 다음에 와야 한다.

02 since는 현재완료에서 '~한 이래로'의 뜻으로 쓰인다.

03 drive: 운전하다 / driver: 운전기사

04 선행사가 사람이고 목적격이므로 who, whom, that을 쓸 수 있다.

05 ③ Kenneth의 할아버지가 운전을 잘하는지는 알 수 없다.

06 ①, ②, ③, ④는 Kenneth의 할아버지를 가리키고, ⑤는 Kenneth를 가리킨다.

07 get lost: 길을 잃다

08 so ~ that ... 구문이다.

09 it은 인칭대명사로 앞 문장의 내용을 받는다.

10 ④ 할아버지를 지켜본 것은 Kenneth였다.

11 선행사가 사물이고 목적격이므로 that이나 which를 쓸 수 있다.

12 ⓑ, ③ 형용사적 용법 ①, ④ 명사적 용법 ②, ⑤ 부사적 용법

13 comfort: 편안함 / comfortable: 편안한

14 그의 장비가 처음 작동되었을 때 아주 기뻤다는 문장 다음에 와야 한다.

15 give up: 포기하다

16 try: 시도하다 / trial: 시도, 실험, 시험

17 for[with] joy: 기뻐서

19 grow up: 자라다, 성장하다

20 현재완료이므로 과거분사로 고쳐야 한다.

21 lesson은 여기서 '수업, 과'의 뜻이 아니라 '교훈'의 뜻으로 쓰였다.

22 선행사가 사람이고 목적격이므로 who, whom, that을 쓸 수 있다.

23 '~이었을 때'의 뜻으로 때를 나타내는 접속사가 와야 한다.

24 get lost: 길을 잃다

25 예를 들어 박테리아나 감염에 의해 생기는 것으로 사람, 동물, 식물에 걸리는 병: disease(병)

26 '~에'의 뜻으로 night이나 noon 앞에는 전치사 at이 붙는다.

27 get out of: ~에서 나오다

28 전치사 to의 목적어가 주어 자신이므로 재귀대명사를 써야 한다.

29 Why don't I ~?: ~하는 게 어떨까?

30 to → for

31 선행사가 사물이므로 that이나 which가 알맞다.

32 ⓑ, ⑤ 부사적 용법 ①, ③, ④ 명사적 용법 ② 형용사적 용법

01 giving	02 safety	03 in
04 because[as]		05 inventor

06 Because his device worked.   07 so

08 happiness   09 ① 지역 아이들을 가르친다.   ② 지역
아이들을 위한 학교를 세운다.   10 on   11 so

12 which	13 for	14 김도하는 개들을 산보

시키거나 목욕을 시킬 수 있다. 또 그는 개들과 놀 수 있다.

15 up   16 is → has   17 ① 차에 태우고 여기저기를
다녔다.   ② 음식을 요리해 주었다   18 to

19 He respected his grandfather the most in the world.

01 feel like+-ing(동명사): ~하고 싶은 생각이 들다

02 해로움이나 위험으로부터 안전한 상태: safety(안전)

03 succeed in -ing: ~하는 데 성공하다

04 so ~ that ... 구문은 because, as, since와 같은 이유를 나타내는 접속사를 써서 바꿔 쓸 수 있다.

05 invent: 발명하다 / inventor: 발명가

06 그가 만든 장비가 재대로 작동했기 때문이다.

07 so ~ that ... 구문이다.

08 happy: 행복한 / happiness: 행복

10 on TV: 텔레비전에서

11 so ~ that ... 구문은 결과를 나타내는 접속사 so를 써서 바꿔 쓸 수 있다.

12 선행사가 사물인 관계대명사의 목적격 that은 which로 바꿔 쓸 수 있다.

13 look for: ~을 찾다

15 grow up: 자라다, 성장하다

16 현재완료 구문이므로 has+과거분사형이 되어야 한다.

18 teach는 간접목적어가 직접목적어 뒤로 갈 때 전치사 to를 붙인다.

01 ④	02 ③	03 heavy	04 ②
05 ⑤	06 up	07 trial, error	08 ⑤
09 ④	10 ①	11 ⑤	12 to →
for	13 ⑤	14 ③	15 ④

16 ②	17 whom	18 ⑤	19 ④
20 ③	21 ④	22 ③	23 ③
24 ④	25 were → was		26 ②
27 ①	28 ⑤	29 ⑤	30 ④
31 ③	32 나이 드신 분들께 팥빙수를 만들어 드리고 함께 먹는 것이다.		33 ③
34 volunteer	35 so	36 ①, ④	37 ②

01 ④는 명사에 -ly가 붙어 형용사가 된 것이고, 나머지는 형용사에 -ly가 붙어 부사가 된 것이다.

02 • 비가 어느 때보다 더 심하게 내리고 있다. • 그들은 우리를 맞이하기 위해 문에 나와 있었다. • 나는 그가 무슨 말을 하는 건지 모르겠다. • 현지 시각은 오전 10시 50분입니다.

03 반의어 관계이다. 따뜻한 : 시원한 = 가벼운 : 무거운

04 keep an eye on: ~을 계속 지켜보다

05 어떤 사람과 의견이 일치하고 아마도 그들이 성공하기를 바라기 때문에 그들을 돕다: support(지지하다)

06 grow up: 자라다, 성장하다 / come up with: ~을 생각해 내다

07 trial and error: 시행착오

08 A는 상대방에게 도움을 요청하고 있다. 그러므로 상대방의 부탁에 대한 승낙이나 거절의 표현이 들어가야 한다.

09 주어진 문장은 그녀를 격려하고 싶다고 말하는 문장이므로 그녀가 다리가 부러졌다는 문장 다음에 와야 한다.

10 do me a favor: 나의 부탁을 들어주다

11 문맥상 '10월까지는 아니다'라는 뜻이 되어야 한다.

12 get은 직접목적어를 간접목적어 뒤로 보낼 때 전치사 for를 붙인다.

13 ⑤ Kate가 왜 다리가 부러졌는지는 알 수 없다.

14 No problem.은 '천만에요.'의 뜻으로 감사 표현에 답하는 말이다.

15 선행사 the ring이 사물이고 목적격이므로 관계대명사 which[that]가 들어가야 알맞다.

16 so ~ that ... 구문은 '너무 ~해서 …하다'의 의미를 나타낸다.

17 선행사가 사람(friend)이고 앞에 전치사 to가 있으므로 목적격 관계대명사 whom을 쓴다. look to: ~에게 기대하다[기대다]

18 '형용사+enough to+동사원형'은 'so+형용사+that+주어+can'으로 바꿔 쓸 수 있다.

19 ④ 동사 work는 자동사이므로 목적격 whom을 취하기 위해서는 '~와 함께'라는 의미의 전치사 with가 필요하다.

20 ③ enough fast → fast enough

21 <보기>와 나머지는 목적격 관계대명사로 쓰였고, ④는 명사절을 이끄는 접속사로 쓰였다.

22 '너무 ~해서 …할 수 없다'는 「so+형용사/부사+that ~ can't」 또는 「too+형용사/부사+to부정사」로 쓸 수 있다.

23 ③ 관계대명사 that은 전치사(in)의 목적어가 될 수 없다. (that → which)

24 go out for a walk: 산책하러 나가다

25 everyone은 단수동사로 받는다.

26 keep an eye on: ~을 계속 지켜보다

27 Why don't I ~?: 내가 ~하는 게 어떨까?

28 ⑤ Kenneth가 할아버지 양말 뒤꿈치에 압력 센서를 부착했다는 말은 언급되지 않았다.

29 선행사가 사물이고 목적격이므로 that이나 which를 쓸 수 있다.

30 come up with: ~을 제안하다, ~을 생각해 내다

31 make A for B: B에게 A를 만들어 주다

33 개를 위해 할 수 있는 일을 나타내는 문장 앞에 와야 한다.

34 일을 하기를 위해서 보수를 받지 않고 일하는 사람: volunteer(자원봉사자)

35 so: 그래서

36 선행사가 사람인 관계대명사 목적격은 who, whom, that을 쓸 수 있다.

37 ② 김도하의 취미가 무엇인지는 본문에서 언급되지 않았다.

단원별 예상문제　　　　　　　p.202~205

01 ④	02 ②	03 ③	04 queen
05 worse	06 ④	07 ②	08 ④
09 favor	10 weekend	11 ③	12 ⑤
13 ③	14 know them → know		15 too → so
16 This is the book which I borrowed from Paul.		17 ③	18 so, that	19 ⑤
20 ①	21 ③	22 helping	23 지역 아이들을 가르치고 그들을 위한 학교를 세우는 것이다.
24 There were many things that[which] Kenneth had to do.		25 ④	26 ③	27 여러 가지 재료를 써서 양말을 만들어 보았다.	28 like
29 ①	30 ⑤	31 Because his device worked.	

01 ④는 유의어 관계이고 나머지는 반의어 관계이다.

02 look for: ~을 찾다 / be thankful for: ~에 대해 감사히 여기다

03 ③은 support(지지하다)의 영영풀이이다.

04 남성명사 : 여성명사의 관계이다.

05 worse: 더 나쁜, 더 심한

06 Thank you for ~.는 감사를 나타내는 표현이다.

07 책을 대신 반납해 줄 수 있냐고 도움을 요청하는 말에 승낙이나 거절로 답한다.

08 ④ Thank you for ~.는 감사를 나타내는 표현이다.

09 do me a favor: 나의 부탁을 들어주다

10 토요일과 일요일: weekend(주말)

11 take care of=look after: ~을 돌보다

12 앞 문장에는 the doll을 선행사로 하는 목적격 관계대명사 which나 that이 들어가고, 뒤 문장에는 the man을 선행사로

하는 목적격 관계대명사 who(m)이나 that이 들어간다.

13 「so + 형용사/부사 + that ...」 구문으로 '너무 ~해서 …하다'의 의미를 나타낸다. 빈칸에 알맞은 말은 so와 that이다.

14 know의 목적어 them은 관계대명사로 바뀌고, 목적격 관계대명사이기 때문에 생략된 형태이다.

15 「so+형용사/부사+that ~」 구문으로, so 대신 too를 사용할 수 없다. that절이 있으므로 too를 so로 바꿔야 한다.

16 주절에서 무엇이 선행사인지 찾은 다음, 선행사를 꾸며주는 관계사절을 관계대명사로 연결한다.

17 ③ 선행사가 사람이고 목적격으로 쓰였으므로 관계대명사 who(m) 또는 that이 알맞다.

18 '너무 ~해서 …하다'는 so ~ that 구문을 이용하여 나타낸다.

19 관계대명사 목적격은 생략할 수 있다. ⑤의 who는 주격 관계대명사이므로 생략할 수 없다.

20 아이들을 돕기를 원한다면 Child Care Project에 가입하라는 흐름이 자연스럽다.

21 at first: 처음에는

22 전치사 뒤에는 동명사가 와야 한다.

24 목적격 관계대명사 that이나 which가 생략된 문장이다.

25 a way를 수식하는 형용사적 용법의 to부정사가 와야 한다.

26 make A for B: B에게 A를 만들어 주다

28 feel like -ing: ~하고 싶은 생각이 들다

29 trial and error: 시행착오

30 ⓒ, ⑤ 작동되다, 효과가 있다 ① 일하다 ② 공부하다 ③ 작동시키다 ④ 근무하다

서술형 실전문제 p.206~207

01 do　　02 heavy　　03 helping
04 (C)-(B)-(D)-(A)
05 (1) whom everyone in my class
　　(2) which I want to watch
06 (1) The food was so spicy that Chris couldn't eat it much.
　　(2) It was too cold for us to go on a picnic.
　　(3) He is rich enough to buy that car.
07 what → which[that]　　08 길을 잃었다
09 worse　　10 that　　11 himself
12 Because Kenneth's grandfather had Alzheimer's disease.
13 which　　14 (c)reate　　15 to make
16 압력 감지기를 만들어 그의 스마트폰으로 신호를 보낼 방법을 찾으려고 노력했다. 그는 또한 할아버지에게 편안한 양말을 만들어 주기 위해 많은 다양한 재료들을 가지고 만들어 보았다.

01 do me a favor: 나의 부탁을 들어주다

02 무게가 많이 나가는: heavy(무거운)

03 전치사 다음에는 동명사형이 온다.

04 Mark, 부탁 하나 들어줄래? - 물론이지. 부탁할게 무엇이지? - 우리 가족은 일주일 동안 휴가를 갈 거야. 우리 집에 와서 식물들에게 물을 줄 수 있니? - 응, 할 수 있어.

05 (1) 목적격 관계대명사 whom이 이끄는 절이 선행사 a teacher를 수식한다. (2) 목적격 관계대명사 which가 이끄는 절이 선행사 The movie를 수식한다.

06 (1) so ~ that ... 구문을 쓴다. (2) too ~ to ... 구문을 쓴다. (3) enough to ~ 구문을 쓴다.

07 a pen이 선행사이므로 관계대명사는 which나 that을 쓴다.

08 get lost: 길을 잃다

09 bad의 비교급이 와야 한다.

10 so ~ that ... 구문이다.

11 전치사 to의 목적어가 주어 자신이므로 재귀대명사가 와야 한다.

12 할아버지가 알츠하이머병에 걸렸기 때문에 가족 모두가 충격에 빠졌다고 언급되었다.

13 선행사가 사물이므로 that이나 which를 쓸 수 있다.

14 어떤 것이 일어나거나 존재하게 하다: create(창조하다, 만들어내다)

15 목적을 나타내는 to부정사의 부사적 용법이다.

창의사고력 서술형 문제 p.208

[모범답안]

01 (1) A waiter is someone who serves food in a restaurant.
　　(2) A zookeeper is someone who looks after animals in the zoo.
　　(3) Dessert is sweet food which is served after a meal.
　　(4) The sport (which[that]) Ann plays best is table tennis.
　　(5) Show me the camera (that[which]) you got last week.
　　(6) Do you remember the woman (whom, who, that]) I was talking about?

02 (1) Last year, my sister was too young to go to school, but now she is old enough to go to school.
　　(2) Yesterday, my dad was too busy to play with me, but today he is not so busy that he can play with me.
　　(3) Last month, my puppy was so light that I could pick it up, but now it is too heavy to pick up.

01 ③	02 ①	03 ①	04 lucky
05 up	06 ⑤	07 ②	08 ④
09 ③	10 for	11 아, 네 여동생에게 생일 선물을 사 줄 거니?	
		12 ②	13 ②
14 ③	15 ②	16 ③	17 ③, ④
18 ④, ⑤	19 too, to	20 ④	21 ③
22 ①	23 ②	24 I like dogs, and there are many things that[which] I can do for them.	
25 ①, ④	26 ⑤	27 ④	28 ②, ③
29 ③	30 actually		

01 at first: 처음에

02 예를 들어 박테리아나 감염에 의해 생기는 것으로 사람, 동물, 식물에게 걸리는 병: disease(병)

03 do A a favor: A의 부탁을 들어주다 / fix: 고치다, 수리하다

04 '명사 : 형용사'의 관계이다. 비 : 비오는 / 운 : 운이 좋은

05 grow up: 자라다, 성장하다 / give up: 포기하다

06 Eric, 이번 주말에 뭐 할 거니? - 특별한 건 없어. 그냥 집에 있으면서 TV를 볼 거야. - 좋아! 이번 주말에 생일 파티를 할 거야. 올 수 있니? - 물론이지. 초대해 줘서 고마워.

07 ② 커피 한 잔을 달라는 요청에 '천만에요.'라고 응답하는 것은 어울리지 않는다.

08 Can you do me a favor?는 상대방에게 도움을 요청할 때 사용하는 표현이다.

09 주어진 문장은 그것은 누구에게 줄 것이냐고 묻는 문장이므로 내 여동생에게 줄 것이라는 문장 앞에 와야 한다.

10 for: ~을 (얻기) 위해, ~을 사러

11 현재진행형의 의문문으로 이때의 현재진행형은 가까운 미래의 일을 나타내고 있다.

12 get+직접목적어+for+간접목적어의 어순을 취한다.

13 ② Jaden은 모자를 유리가 아니라 여동생에게 사 주려고 한다.

14 앞 문장은 선행사가 사물이고 주격이므로 which나 that이 알맞고, 뒤 문장은 선행사가 사람이고 목적격이므로 who(m)나 that이 알맞다.

15 so ~ that+S+can't ... 구문은 '너무 ~해서 …할 수 없다'의 의미로 too ~ to부정사 구문으로 바꿔 쓸 수 있다.

16 ③은 주격 관계대명사로 쓰인 that이고, 나머지는 모두 목적격 관계대명사로 쓰였다.

17 ③ enough kind → kind enough ④ solve → solve it

18 선행사가 the writings로 사물이므로 목적격 관계대명사 that 또는 which가 알맞다.

19 '너무 ~해서 …할 수 없다'는 so ~ that ... can't 구문을 이용하여 나타낸다.

20 ④ 관계대명사 목적격은 생략할 수 있다.

21 문맥상 '프로젝트에 합류하다'가 알맞다.

22 on TV: 텔레비전으로

23 ⓒ, ② so ~ that ...과 such ~ that ...은 '아주 ~해서 … 하다'의 뜻을 나타낸다. ① 명사절을 이끄는 접속사 ③, ⑤ 관계대명사 ④ It ... that 강조구문

24 선행사가 사물이고 목적격이므로 which나 that을 보충할 수 있다.

25 선행사가 사람이고 목적격이므로 who, whom, that을 쓸 수 있다.

26 ⑤ 김도하는 자신이 자원봉사 프로젝트에 적합하다고 생각한다.

27 글의 흐름상 Kenneth에게는 그의 할아버지가 여전히 가장 좋은 친구라는 문장 앞에 와야 한다.

28 '~할 때'의 뜻으로 때를 나타내는 접속사가 와야 한다.

29 ⓑ에는 so ~ that ... 구문의 that이, ⓒ에는 명사절을 이끄는 that이 와야 한다

30 actual의 부사형이 와야 한다.

34 coworker　　35 such as　　36 be good for

37 Guess what?　38 be good at　39 be afraid of

40 fall asleep　　41 at last　　42 take a look at

43 watch out

교과서 파헤치기

Lesson 1

단어 TEST Step 1　　　　　　　　p.02

01 진정한, 진짜의　02 이, 치아, 이빨　03 유일무이한, 독특한

04 투표하다　05 틀린, 잘못된　06 대통령, 회장

07 만화가　08 재활용[재생]하다　09 위험

10 엎드려 팔굽혀펴기　11 우스운, 웃기는

12 남편　13 문지기, 수위　14 우스개, 농담

15 줄넘기를 하다　16 듣는 사람, 청자

17 불안해[초초해/두려워] 하는　18 한 번, 언제가

19 성격, 등장인물　20 ~이 되다　21 슈퍼히어로로

22 어떤 사람, 누군가　23 연습하다

24 공원[삼림] 관리원

25 흐린, 구름이 잔뜩 낀　26 활동

27 함께 일하는 사람, 동료

28 모험심이 강한, 모험을 즐기는

29 결정하다, 결심하다

30 경탄할 만한, 엄청난　31 기량, 기술

32 물수제비뜨다　33 기분 좋게, 쾌활하게

34 연설, 담화　35 ~을 잘하다

36 ~를 행복하게 만들다　37 (~을) 잘하다

38 잠들다　39 거저 주다, 나누어 주다

40 ~에 좋다　41 ~에게 안부 전하다

42 ~와 같은　43 ~을 두려워하는

단어 TEST Step 2　　　　　　　　p.03

01 skill　02 actually　03 real

04 tooth　05 travel　06 unique

07 superhero　08 president　09 skip stones

10 vote　11 speech　12 wrong

13 practice　14 danger　15 enough

16 novel　17 adventurous　18 janitor

19 decide　20 funny　21 cartoonist

22 recycle　23 husband　24 super

25 jump rope　26 cheerfully　27 nervous

28 drawing　29 joke　30 outside

31 per　32 ranger　33 cookbook

단어 TEST Step 3　　　　　　　　p.04

1 joke, 농담, 우스개　2 danger, 위험

3 speaker, 연사, 말[이야기]하는 사람　4 janitor, 문지기, 수위

5 attend, 참석하다　6 tooth, 이, 이빨

7 cartoonist, 만화가　8 pause, (말이나 행동 등의) 멈춤

9 speech, 연설, 담화　10 nervous, 불안해[초조해] 하는

11 novel, 소설　12 scooter, 스쿠터(소형 오토바이)

13 second, (시간 단위인) 초　14 cafeteria, 카페테리아,

구내식당　15 coworker, 함께 일하는 사람, 동료

16 recycle, 재활용[재생]하다

대화문 TEST Step 1　　　　　　　p.05~06

Listen & Speak 1 A. Listen and Check

1 are, doing / making, out of / good at recycling / like recycling, good for

2 to be, class, listener, try to help, good at planning, work hard, vote for, for listening

Listen & Speak 2 A. Listen and Check

1 is, wrong / have to, in front of, nervous / Don't, good speaker, sure, do a good job / feel much better

2 my mom's, should, for / Why don't you, good at baking / idea, will like / I'm sure, will love

Communicate A. Listen and Answer

1 are, doing / drawing cartoons / Can, take, at / not yet / not, can't you / guess / Awesome, good at drawing / think so, to be, drawing skill, enough / funny, unique characters, sure, cartoonist / made

2 don't, good at / like to, acting, dancing / Don't, teach you, fast, join us / think about

Progress Check

1 What, doing / making pizza / good at

2 Is, wrong / give a speech, nervous / worry, in front of, good job, / try

3 is good at, Some, Other, are, good at

Listen & Speak 1 A. Listen and Check

1 B: What are you doing, Nami?

  G: I'm making a smart phone case out of my old jeans.

  B: Wow! You're good at recycling old things.

  G: Thanks. I like recycling. It's fun, and it's also good for our Earth.

2 B: Hello, everyone. I'm Kim Yujin. I want to be your class president. I'm a good listener and always try to help others. I'm also good at planning fun school activities. I'll work hard for our class, so please vote for me. Thank you for listening!

Listen & Speak 2 A. Listen and Check

1 B: Hi, Cindy. Is something wrong?

  G: I have to give a speech in front of the whole school. I'm so nervous.

  B: Don't worry. You're a very good speaker. I'm sure you'll do a good job.

  G: Thanks, Minho. I feel much better now.

2 G: Tomorrow is my mom's birthday. What should I do for her?

  B: Why don't you bake a cake for her? You're good at baking.

  G: That's a good idea. I hope my mom will like my cake.

  B: I'm sure your mom will love it.

Communicate A. Listen and Answer

1 Yuri: What are you doing, Jaden?

  Jaden: I'm drawing cartoons.

  Yuri: Really? Can I take a look at them?

  Jaden: No, not yet.

  Yuri: Why not? You can show me a few, can't you

  Jaden: Well, I guess so.

  Yuri: (pause) Ha, ha, ha! Awesome! I like your cartoons. You're really good at drawing.

  Jaden: Do you think so? I want to be a cartoonist, but I don't think my drawing skills are good enough.

  Yuri: Your cartoons are really funny, and you have unique characters. I'm sure you'll be a great cartoonist.

  Jaden: Thank you, Yuri. You just made my day.

2 A: Why don't you join our musical theater club? You're good at singing.

  B: Well, I'd like to, but I don't think I'm good at acting or dancing.

  A: Don't worry. We can teach you. I'm sure you'll learn fast. Just join us.

  B: O.K. I'll think about it.

Progress Check

1 B: What are you doing?

  G: I'm making pizza for dinner.

  B: Wow! You're really good at cooking!

  G: Thanks.

2 B: Is something wrong?

  G: I have to give a speech in English. I'm so nervous.

  B: Don't worry. Practice your speech in front of your family. I'm sure you'll do a good job.

  G: Thank you. I'll try.

3 W: Everybody is good at something. Some people are good at drawing. Other people are good at singing. What are you good at?

01 My, like, novels

02 While, walking, saw

03 looked, cool, unique

04 going, said, suddenly   05 but, asked

06 course, answered

07 see, cafeteria every

08 Suprisingly, of, workers

09 different outside, thought

10 should, graphic, her

11 After, got, began   12 In, superhero

13 rides, super, that

14 saves, danger around

15 per second, away

16 few, later, graphic

17 Awesome, superhero, cool

18 Guess, on, workers   19 my, to

20 loved, too

21 also, coworkers, talents

22 another, won dancing

23 janitor, adventurous, ranger

24 like, superhero, think, asked

25 course, cheerfully   26 go, hello, our

01 My name, graphic novels

02 While, walking home, saw, on

03 lookesd, cool, unique

04 going home, said, suddenly   05 but, asked

06 course, answered   07 at, every day

08 Surprisingly, one of, workers

09 looks, different, thought   10 should, write

11 After, got home, graphic novel   12 In, superhero

13 rides, can fly   14 saves, around the world

15 per second, gives, away

16 few days later, showed, to

17 Awesome, cool, all my

18 Guess, modeled, on, one of, workers

19 showed, to   20 loved, too

21 also, coworkers, special talents

22 another, worker, won

23 janitor, once, adventurous, ranger

24 like to write, think, asked

25 Of course, cheerfully

26 Let's, say hello to

1 내 이름은 호진이고, 만화 소설 쓰는 것을 좋아한다.

2 지난주에 학교에서 집으로 걸어가던 중에 스쿠터에 탄 여자를 보았다.

3 그녀는 정말 멋져 보였고 그녀의 스쿠터는 매우 독특했다.

4 "호진아, 너 집에 가는 중이니?" 그녀가 갑자기 나에게 말했다.

5 "네, 그런데 저를 아시나요?" 나는 물었다.

6 "물론이지," 그녀가 대답했다.

7 "난 매일 학교 식당에서 너를 본단다."

8 놀랍게도, 그녀는 학교 식당 직원 중 한 명이었다.

9 "놀라워! 그녀는 학교 밖에서는 아주 달라 보여."라고 나는 생각했다.

10 "그녀에 대한 만화 소설을 써야겠다."

11 집에 도착한 후, 나는 〈런치 레이디 탄생하다〉라는 새로운 만화 소설을 쓰기 시작했다.

12 그 소설에서 런치 레이디는 슈퍼히어로이다.

13 그녀는 날 수 있는 슈퍼 스쿠터를 탄다.

14 그녀는 전 세계의 위험에 빠진 사람들을 구한다.

15 그녀는 또한 1초에 100개의 쿠키를 만들어 배고픈 아이들에게 나누어 준다.

16 며칠 후에 나는 나의 만화 소설을 친구들에게 보여 주었다.

17 "멋져! 나는 이 슈퍼히어로가 너무 좋아. 그녀는 아주 멋져." 라고 내 모든 친구들이 말했다.

18 "있잖아, 나는 그녀를 우리 식당 직원 중 한 명인 이 여사를 모델로 했어."라고 나는 친구들에게 말했다.

19 나는 이 여사에게 내 책을 보여 주었다.

20 그녀도 그것을 아주 좋아했다.

21 그녀는 또한 나에게 특별한 재능을 가진 그녀의 동료들에 대해 말해 주었다.

22 또 다른 식당 직원인 박 여사는 댄스 경연대회에서 우승했다.

23 우리 학교의 관리인인 김 선생님은 한때 모험적인 공원 관리원이었다.

24 "저는 그들에 대한 슈퍼히어로 이야기를 쓰고 싶어요. 그분들이 그걸 좋아할 것 같아요?" 나는 이 여사한테 물어보았다.

25 "물론 그럴 거야."라고 그녀가 기분 좋게 말했다.

26 "가서 우리의 새 슈퍼히어로로 친구들에게 인사하자."

1 My name is Hojin, and I like to make graphic novels.

2 While I was walking home from school last week, I saw a woman on a scooter.

3 She looked really cool, and her scooter was very unique.

4 "Are you going home, Hojin?" she said to me suddenly.

5 "Yes, but do I know you?" I asked.

6 "Of course," she answered.

7 "I see you at the school cafeteria every day."

8 Surprisingly, she was one of the cafeteria workers at school.

9 "Amazing! She looks so different outside the school," I thought.

10 "I should write a graphic novel about her."

11 After I got home, I began to write a new graphic novel, Lunch Lady Begins .

12 In it, Lunch Lady is a superhero.

13 She rides a super scooter that can fly

14 She saves people from danger around the world.

15 She also makes 100 cookies per second and gives them away to hungry children.

16 A few days later, I showed my graphic novel to my friends.

17 "Awesome! I love this superhero. She's so cool," said all my friends.

18 "Guess what? I modeled her on Ms. Lee, one of our cafeteria workers," I told them.

19 I showed my book to Ms. Lee.

20 She loved it, too.

21 She also told me about her coworkers who had special talents.

22 Ms. Park, another cafeteria worker, won a dancing contest.

23 Mr. Kim, the janitor at our school, was once an

adventurous park ranger.

24 "I'd like to write superhero stories about them. Do you think they'll like that?" I asked Ms. Lee.

25 "Of course they will," she said cheerfully.

26 "Let's go and say hello to our new superhero friends."

구석구석지문 TEST Step 1 p.19

Language Arts
1. studying, library
2. is, fire
3. can't, out
4. flies, saves

Write
1. aunt, role
2. smart, adventurous
3. In, traveled, different
4. While, traveling, over
5. be, afraid, trying, like

Culture Project - Share
1. who, real, in
2. At, moved to, husband
3. attends, famous
4. While, decided to
5. became, hit

구석구석지문 TEST Step 2 p.20

Language Arts
1. Two boys are studying in a library.
2. There is a fire.
3. The boys can't get out.
4. Lunch Lady flies on her scooter and saves them.

Write
1. My aunt is my role model.
2. She is smart, strong, and adventurous.
3. In her 30s, she traveled to 70 different countries.
4. While she was traveling, she made friends from all over the world.
5. I want to be someone who is not afraid of trying new things just like her.

Culture Project - Share
1. Julia Child was a person who found her real talent in her 30s.
2. At age 36, she moved to Paris with her husband.
3. She attends a famous cooking school there.
4. While she was studying, she decided to write a cookbook.
5. That book became a big hit.

단어 TEST Step 1 p.21

01 바람	02 미세먼지	03 때때로, 가끔
04 짓다, 건설[건축]하다		05 염소
06 결정하다, 결심하다		07 ~부터[이후]
08 또[그 밖의] 다른, 다른		
09 남쪽[남부]에 위치한		10 입구, 문
11 숲, 삼림	12 동굴	13 신선한
14 비행기 모양의	15 ~이 되다	16 문, 정문
17 100년, 세기	18 연습하다	19 돌
20 조화, 화합	21 원뿔, 원뿔형 물체	22 정보
23 식사, 끼니	24 종류	
25 사랑스러운, 아름다운		26 여행, 관광
27 적	28 저장, 보관	29 낮은
30 나무로 된, 목재의	31 피아노 모양의	32 쇼핑몰, 쇼핑 센터
33 식당	34 대양, 바다	35 ~을 찾다
36 ~을 두려워하다	37 ~을 조심하다	
38 시도하다, 한번 해 보다		39 거꾸로, 뒤집혀
40 ~와 조화를 이루어		41 쌓아 올리다
42 (구조물을 해체하여) 치우다		43 ~을 잘하다

단어 TEST Step 2 p.22

01 cafeteria	02 cover	03 design
04 nature	05 fifth	06 floor
07 welcome	08 avoid	09 ocean
10 thousand	11 without	12 enemy
13 pay	14 collector	15 plant
16 view	17 guesthouse	18 protect
19 restroom	20 round	21 shaped
22 tax	23 unique	24 grass
25 village	26 fine dust	27 sometimes
28 goat	29 forest	30 cave
31 entrance	32 storage	33 wooden
34 harmony	35 look at	36 next to
37 watch out for	38 in harmony with	
39 be good at	40 pile up	41 upside down
42 take down	43 give it a try	

단어 TEST Step 3 p.23

1 thousand, 1,000, 천　2 wooden, 나무로 된, 목재의
3 enemy, 나무로 된, 목재의　4 cave, 동굴

37

5 information, 정보　6 century, 100년, 세기

7 collector, 징수원　8 forest, 숲, 삼림　9 wind, 바람

10 cafeteria, 카페테리아, 구내식당

11 protect, 보호하다, 지키다　12 restroom, 화장실, 세면실

13 tax, 세금　14 avoid, 방지하다, 피하다

15 guesthouse, 게스트하우스　16 plant, 식물, 초목

대화문 TEST Step 1

Listen & Speak 1 A. Listen and Check

1 look at, looks like / unique, to live in / What kind, live in, want to, airplane-shaped

2 Excuse, there / kind, would, like / like Chinese / There, on, fifth floor

Listen & Speak 2 A. Listen and Writ

1 Excuse, where, find / second floor, next to / Thank / welcome

2 Can, help / looking for, can I find / on, third, next to / you

Communicate A. Listen and Answer

Welcome to, May I help, like, for / kind of, like / with, view, lovely / Every, has, view, are no / have to, floor / do / give, try, have breakfast / can, dining room, next to / see / in, Here's, key / Thank

Progress Check

1 unique, upside, down / looks interesting, kind, strange / What kind of, live in / so, in, piano-shaped

2 Excuse, women's jeans / can find, second floor, next to / Thank / welcome

3 where, find / on the second floor / next to / Thank / welcome

Work -Act

What kind, to build / two-story, looks like / Where, kitchen / on the second floor

대화문 TEST Step 2

p.26~27

Listen & Speak 1 A. Listen and Check

1 B: Hey, look at this house in the picture. It looks like a big shoe!

G: Oh, it's very unique, but I don't want to live in a shoe.

B: What kind of house do you want to live in?

G: Well, I want to live in an airplane-shaped house.

2 M: Excuse me, is there a restaurant in this mall?

W: Yes. What kind of food would you like?

M: I'd like Chinese food.

W There is a great restaurant on the fifth floor.

M: Thank you.

Listen & Speak 2 A. Listen and Write

1 W: Excuse me, where can I find women's shoes?

M: You can find them on the second floor. They're next to the elevator.

W: Thank you.

M: You're welcome.

2 W: Can I help you?

M: I'm looking for watches. Where can I find them?

W: They're on the third floor, next to the restroom.

M: Thank you.

Communicate A. Listen and Answer

Woman: Welcome to Jeonju Hanok Guesthouse. May I help you?

Man: Yes, I'd like a room for two nights.

Woman: Well, what kind of room would you like?

Man: Do you have a room with a garden view? You have a lovely garden.

Woman: Yes, we do. Every room in our house has a garden view, but there are no beds in the rooms.

Man: Do I have to sleep on the floor?

Woman: Yes, you do.

Man: O.K. I'll give it a try. Where can I have breakfast?

Woman: You can have breakfast in the dining room, next to the kitchen.

Man: I see.

Woman: O.K. You're in the Nabi room. Here's your key.

Man: Thank you.

Progress Check

1 B: Hey, look at this unique house in the picture. It's upside down.

G: Oh, it looks interesting, but I think it's kind of strange.

B: What kind of house do you want to live in?

G: I like music, so I want to live in a piano-shaped house.

2 W: Excuse me, where can I find women's jeans?

M: You can find them on the second floor. They're next to the elevator.

W: Thank you.

M: You're welcome.

3 M: Excuse me, where can I find men's hats?

W: You can find them on the second floor. They're next to the elevator.

M: Thank you

W: You're welcome.

Work -Act

A: What kind of house do you want to build?

B: I want to build a two–story house that looks like a boat.

A: Where is the kitchen?

B: It's on the second floor.

01 Have, seen roof

02 In, see, on　　03 large forests

04 harmony, nature, wooden

05 build, cover, with

06 protect, from, winds

07 Somtimes, out, roofs, meals

08 essential, ago, built, down

09 Centuries, southern, without, paid

10 avoid, taxes, cone-shaped, pilling

11 When, collectors, took, down　　12 tax, left, piled

13 From, part, southern, like

14 roofs, round, people

15 have, like, about, themselves

16 only, without, on

17 Each, enough, whole

18 usually, stories

19 storage, second, living, fourth

01 Have, seen, on the roof

02 In, can, on roofs　　　　　　03 has,　forests

04 In harmony with, have built, for

05 To build, cover, with

06 protect, from, cold, strong

07 grow out of, enjoy, meals

08 Essential part, long ago, take, down

09 Centuries ago, who, paid, taxes

10 To avoid, some, built, piling up

11 tax collectors, took, down

12 After, left, piled up

13 From, southern, round roofs, look like

14 roofs, big round houses

15 have lived, thousand years, protect, from

16 only, without, first floor

17 Each, big enough, whole village

18 usually, four stories

19 first, storage, second, living rooms, third, fourth

1 여러분은 집의 지붕 위에 있는 염소를 본 적이 있는가?

2 노르웨이에서, 우리는 지붕 위에 있는 동물들을 볼 수 있다.

3 노르웨이는 큰 숲을 가지고 있다.

4 자연과 조화를 이루면서, 사람들은 오랫동안 나무로 집을 지었다.

5 강하고 따뜻한 집을 만들기 위해, 그들은 지붕을 잔디로 덮는다.

6 잔디 지붕은 길고 추운 겨울과 강한 바람으로부터 그들을 보호한다.

7 때때로, 나무나 식물들이 잔디 지붕에서 자라며, 어떤 동물들은 거기서 식사를 즐긴다.

8 지붕은 집의 필수적인 부분이지만, 오래 전에 어떤 사람들은 오직 지붕을 쉽게 철거하기 위해 지었다.

9 수세기 전 남부 이탈리아에서는 지붕 없는 집을 가진 사람들이 더 적은 세금을 냈다.

10 그들의 집에 부과되는 높은 세금을 피하기 위해, 어떤 사람들은 돌을 쌓아 올려 원뿔 모양의 지붕을 만들었다.

11 세금 징수원들이 마을에 오면, 사람들은 재빨리 지붕을 철거했다.

12 세금 징수원들이 떠난 후 그들은 다시 돌을 쌓아 올렸다.

13 중국 남부의 일부 지역의 하늘에서 보면, 여러분은 큰 도넛처럼 생긴 둥근 지붕들을 볼 수 있다.

14 그것들은 하카족의 크고 둥근 집들의 지붕이다.

15 그들은 적으로부터 스스로를 보호하기 위해 약 천 년 동안 이런 집에서 살아왔다.

16 그 집들에는 1층에 창문이 하나도 없고 문이 하나만 있다.

17 각각의 집은 전체 마을이 들어갈 만큼 크다.

18 그 집은 보통 4개의 층을 가지고 있다.

19 1층에는 주방, 2층에는 창고, 3층과 4층에는 거실과 침실이 있다.

1 Have you ever seen a goat on the roof of a house?

2 In Norway, we can see animals on roofs.

3 Norway has large forests.

4 In harmony with nature, people have built wooden houses for a long time.

5 To build strong and warm houses, they cover their roofs with grass.

6 The grass roofs protect them from the long cold winters and strong winds.

7 Sometimes, trees or plants grow out of the grass roofs, and some animals enjoy their meals there.

8 A roof is an essential part of a house, but long ago some people built roofs only to take them down easily.

9 Centuries ago in southern Italy, people who had a house without a roof paid lower taxes.

10 To avoid high taxes on their houses, some people built cone-shaped roofs by piling up stones.

11 When tax collectors came to the town, people took their roofs down quickly.

12 After the tax collectors left, they piled up the stones again.

13 From the sky in a part of southern China, you can see round roofs that look like big doughnuts.

14 They are the roofs of the big round houses of the Hakka people.

15 They have lived in houses like these for about a thousand years to protect themselves from enemies.

16 The houses have only one gate without any windows on the first floor.

17 Each house is big enough for a whole village.

18 It usually has four stories.

19 It has kitchens on the first floor, storage rooms on the second floor, and living rooms and bedrooms on the third and fourth floors.

Link

1. because of, these days
2. about making, roof
3. Find dust, been
4. designed, that, with, other
5. give, fresh

Write

1. National, in
2. four-story, looks like
3. about, second, floors, top
4. opened in
5. Since, visited, unique

Culture Project

1. In, lived, for
2. weather, hot, cold

3. too, cave

Link

1. I can't open windows because of the fine dust these days.
2. How about making a small garden on the roof?
3. Fine dust has been a big problem in the spring.
4. We designed a roof that has a small garden with trees and many other plants.
5. This garden will give us fresh air.

Write

1. Sejong National Library is in Sejong, Korea.
2. It is a four-story building that looks like an open book.
3. It has about 400 thousand books on the first and second floors and a large cafeteria on the top floor.
4. It opened un 2013.
5. Since then, many people have visited this unique building.

Culture Project

1. In Granada, Spain, some people have lived in cave houses for a long time.
2. The weather in this place is very hot in the summer and cold in the winter.
3. It's not too cold or hot in cave houses.

단어 TEST Step 1 p.40

01 완전한 02 놀라운
03 ~(해)지다, ~이 되다
04 잡다, 포착하다,담아내다 05 해산물
06 여행; 여행하다 07 간단한, 단순한 08 번지 점프
09 예측, 예보 10 지구, 땅 11 또 다른, 다른
12 유명한 13 초상화 14 마침내
15 식량, 음식 16 졸업하다 17 가능성, 기회
18 섬 19 남다, 남아 있다 20 날씨
21 추측하다, 짐작하다 22 시장
23 외국의 24 수수께끼, 미스터리
25 꽁꽁 얼게[너무나] 추운 26 실제로, 정말로
27 예상[기대]하다 28 일기 29 무서운, 겁나는
30 실내에, 집안에 31 창조[창작/창출]하다
32 대학교 33 방학, 휴가
34 나타나다, 출연하다 35 ~에 도착하다
36 ~으로 가득 차다 37 ~에 들어가다, ~에 타다
38 지금, 당장 39 많은 40 ~와 같은
41 ~에 발을 들여놓다 42 좀, 약간, 약간의
43 나타나다

단어 TEST Step 2 p.41

01 touch 02 plate 03 check
04 cloudy 05 pack 06 decide
07 during 08 foreign 09 around
10 drive 11 windy 12 invite
13 huge 14 avatar 15 field trip
16 object 17 college 18 weather
19 moment 20 relax 21 drawing
22 trip 23 turtle 24 market
25 admire 26 diary 27 perfect
28 expect 29 capture 30 graduate
31 freezing 32 scary 33 simple
34 island 35 a few 36 right now
37 get to 38 be full of 39 at last
40 show up 41 set foot at[in] 42 get into
43 such as

단어 TEST Step 3 p.42

1 food, 식량, 음식 2 chance, 가능성
3 island, 섬 4 market, 시장 5 admire, 존경하다
6 drawing, 그림, 소묘 7 amazing, 놀라운
8 beach, 해변, 바닷가 9 create, 창조[창작/창출]하다
10 invite, 초대하다 11 mystery, 수수께끼, 미스터리
12 strange, 이상한, 낯선 13 travel, 여행하다
14 decide, 결정하다 15 relax, 휴식을 취하다
16 pack, (짐을) 싸다

대화문 TEST Step 1 p.43~44

Listen & Speak 1 A. Listen and Check

1 Have, tried / have, only tried / How it / hot, but
2 have, gone / No, haven't, How about / When, visited, tried once / Wasn't, scary / want to, again

Listen & Speak 2 A. Listen and Answer

1 how's weather, need / cloudy outside, check, forecast / Thank / going to rain / don't need
2 welcome to, sunny outside, expectiong, Don't leave, without, weather forecast, Have

Communicate A~B

A have, been to / have, lived, for / How's, there, going to, on vacation / to visit, autumn / planning to spend, relax / often rains, may, sunny days / take, pack, too / good idea, Have
B Have, been to, places / have, went to, last, with / How, weather / mostly sunny, changed

Progress Check

1 Have, ridden / have, How about / haven't, How / fun, a little, too
2 weather / cloudy outside, check, forecast / going to rain
3 welcome to, raining right now, expecting, leave, without

대화문 TEST Step 2 p.45~46

Listen & Speak 1 A. Listen and Check

1 G: Have you ever tried Indian food?
  B: Yes, I have, but I've only tried Indian curry.
  G: How was it?
  B: It was really hot, but I loved it.
2 G: Bill, have you ever gone bungee jumping?
  B: No, I haven't. How about you, Katie?
  G: When I visited New Zealand, I tried bungee jumping

once.

B: Wasn't it scary?

G: No, I liked it. I want to do it again.

Listen & Speak 1 A. Listen and Answer

1 B: Mom, how's the weather today? Do I need an umbrella?

W: It's quite cloudy outside. I'll check the weather forecast.

B: Thank you, Mom.

W: Well, it's not going to rain today.

B: Good! Then, I don't need an umbrella today.

2 W: Good morning, and welcome to the weather forecast. It's sunny outside, but we're expecting some rain in the afternoon. Don't leave home without your umbrella. That's the weather forecast for today. Have a nice day.

Communicate A~B

A Suho: Anna, have you been to Australia before?

Anna: Yes, I have. Actually, I lived in Sydney for a year.

Suho: Great! How's the weather there in April? I'm going to visit Sydney on vacation next week.

Anna: April is a great time to visit Sydney. In April, it's autumn in Australia.

Suho: Good. I'm planning to spend some time on the beach and relax in the sun.

Anna: Well, it often rains in April, but you may have some sunny days.

Suho: I'll take my hat and pack an umbrella, too

Anna: That's a good idea. Have a great time.

B A: Have you been to any special places in Korea?

B: Yes, I have. I went to Ulleungdo last summer with my family.

A: How was the weather there?

B: It was mostly sunny, but the weather changed often.

Progress Check

1 G: Have you ever ridden a horse?

B: Yes, I have. How about you?

G: No, I haven't. How was it?

B: It was fun, but it was a little scary, too.

2 B: Mom, how's the weather today?

W: It's quite cloudy outside. I'll check the weather forecast.

B: Thanks, Mom.

W: Well, it's going to rain in the afternoon.

3 M: Good evening, and welcome to the weather forecast. It's raining right now, but we're

expecting a sunny day tomorrow. Don't leave home tomorrow without your hat.

본문 TEST Step 1　　　　　　　　　　　p.47~48

01 am, live in

02 Last, on, for

03 During, simple, journal

04 way, capture, special

05 last, set, mysterious

06 After, drive, finally

07 amazing, ring, huge

08 stones, thousands, ago　　　09 What, for

10 guess, remain, mystery　　　11 try, perfect

12 few, enough　　13 In, around

14 started, so, decided　　　15 popular, stay

16 like, than　　　17 invited, for

18 dining, full, and

19 busy, admiring, plates

20 much, anything

21 draw, like, journal　　　22 Our, stop

23 visited, College

24 become, since, appeared

25 movies, else, dinner

26 also, portraits, graduated

27 outside, walked, touched

28 Because, touched, get

29 said, smile, wait　　　30 Create, own

31 drawing, much, interesting

본문 TEST Step 2　　　　　　　　　　　p.49~50

01 am, live in　　　02 Last week, went on, for

03 During, drawings, journal

04 to capture, special moments

05 set foot at, one of, places

06 After, drive from, got to　　　07 amazing, ring

08 huge stones, thousands, ago　　　09 What, for

10 guess, remain, for

11 Don't try, perfect　　　12 A few, enough

13 In, walked around

14 to rain, decided to stay

15 popular, stay in

16 feels, like, than　　　17 owner, invited

18 dining, was full of

19 busy eating, admiring, plates

20 ate, so, couldn't eat

21 to draw, like, journal　　　　22 last stop

23 first visited

24 has become, famous place, since

25 everyone, eat dinner

26 saw portraits, graduated from

27 When, outside, walked to, touched

28 Because, touched, get into

29 with a smile, can't wait to　　　30 Create, avatar

31 drawing journal, much more

27 우리가 건물 밖으로 나왔을 때, 나는 유명한 올리브 나무로 걸어가서 그것을 만졌다.

28 "이 나무를 만졌기 때문에, 난 옥스퍼드 대학교에 들어갈 거야!"라고 말했다.

29 그러자 오빠가 웃으면서 "벽에 걸린 네 초상화가 빨리 보고 싶어."라고 말했다.

30 여러분 자신의 아바타를 만드세요.

31 그림일기가 훨씬 더 재미있을 거예요.

1 안녕, 나는 Lucy Hunter이고 런던에 살아요

2 지난주에 우리 가족은 3일 동안 휴가를 갔습니다.

3 여행 중에 나는 일기에 간단한 그림을 그렸어요.

4 그것은 모든 특별한 순간을 포착하는 훌륭한 방법이었어요.

5 마침내, 우리는 지구에서 가장 불가사의한 장소 중 하나인 스톤헨지에 발을 디뎠다.

6 런던에 있는 집에서 차로 두 시간을 달려서 우리는 마침내 스톤헨지에 도착했다.

7 원형으로 둘러서 있는 거대한 돌들을 보는 것은 정말 놀라웠다.

8 어떻게 그 거대한 돌들이 수천 년 전에 그곳에 도착했을까?

9 그것들은 무엇을 위한 것이었을까?

10 완벽한 그림을 그리려고 하지 마세요.

11 몇 가지 색깔이면 충분할 것입니다.

12 스톤헨지는 오랫동안 미스터리로 남을 것 같다.

13 아침에 우리는 코츠월드 언덕을 돌아다녔다.

14 오후에 비가 오기 시작해서, 우리는 B&B의 실내에서 머물기로 결정했다.

15 B&B는 영국에서 체류하는 곳으로 인기가 있다.

16 그것은 호텔이라기보다는 집처럼 느껴진다.

17 주인은 오늘 오후의 다과회에 우리를 초대했다

18 식탁에는 쿠키, 케이크, 빵, 그리고 치즈가 가득했다.

19 내가 먹느라 바쁠 때, 엄마는 아름다운 컵과 접시를 감탄하며 바라보고 계셨다.

20 나는 너무 많이 먹어서 저녁으로 아무것도 먹을 수 없었다.

21 당신의 일기에 컵과 접시 같은 일상적인 물건들을 그려도 괜찮습니다.

22 우리가 마지막으로 머문 곳은 옥스퍼드였다.

23 우리는 먼저 Christ Church College를 방문했다.

24 이곳은 해리포터 영화에 등장한 이후 방문해야 할 세계적으로 유명한 장소가 되었다.

25 영화에서 Harry와 다른 모든 사람들이 Christ Church의 회관에서 저녁을 먹는다.

26 우리는 또한 그 대학을 졸업한 유명한 사람들의 초상화

1 Hi, I am Lucy Hunter, and I live in London.

2 Last week, my family went on a vacation for three days.

3 During our trip, I made simple drawings in my journal.

4 That was a great way to capture all the special moments.

5 At last, we set foot at Stonehenge, one of the most mysterious places on Earth.

6 After a two-hour drive from our home in London, we finally got to Stonehenge.

7 It was just amazing to see the ring of huge stones.

8 How did those huge stones get there thousands of years ago?

9 What were they for?

10 Don't try to make a perfect drawing.

11 A few colors will be enough.

12 I guess Stonehenge will remain a mystery for a long time.

13 In the morning, we walked around the Cotswolds.

14 It started to rain in the afternoon, so we decided to stay indoors at our B&B.

15 A B&B is a popular place to stay in England.

16 It feels more like a home than a hotel.

17 The owner invited us for afternoon tea today.

18 The dining table was full of cookies, cake, bread, and cheese.

19 While I was busy eating, Mom was admiring the beautiful cups and plates.

20 I ate too much, so I couldn't eat anything for dinner.

21 It is O.K. to draw everyday objects like cups and plates in your journal.

22 Our last stop was Oxford.

23 We first visited Christ Church College.

24 It has become a world famous place to visit

since it appeared in the Harry Potter movies.

25 In the movies, Harry and everyone else eat dinner at the Hall of Christ Church.

26 We also saw portraits of famous people who graduated from the college.

27 When we were outside the building, I walked to the famous olive tree and touched it.

28 "Because I touched this tree," I said, "I will get into Oxford University!"

29 Then, my brother said to me with a smile, "I can't wait to see your portrait on the wall."

30 Create your own avatar.

31 Your drawing journal will become much more interesting.

2. We visited a lot of beautiful temples and went to the night market in Vientiane.

3. Then, we moved to Vang Vieng and went river tubing.

4. We also enjoyed their traditional food.

5. It was a lot of fun to try new things in a foreign country.

6. I hope I will have a chance to visit Laos again.

Culture Project

1. September 15, 1835

2. We finally arrived on this island.

3. There are many animals to study here.

4. Today, I saw some strange turtles.

5. It was amazing to watch them.

구석구석지문 TEST Step 1 p.57

Link - Share

1. went on, last

2. It, amazing, islands

3. also visitied, Village

4. never forget

Write

1. Last winter, went, with

2. lot, temples, market

3. moved to, went

4. enjoyed, traditional

5. lot of, to try, foreign

6. chance to visit

Culture Project

1. September

2. arrived on

3. are, to study

4. asw, strange

5. amazing, watch

구석구석지문 TEST Step 2 p.58

Link - Share

1. We went on a field trip to Namhae last month.

2. It was just amazing to see so many beautiful islands.

3. We also visited Namhae German Village.

4. We'll never forget that trip.

Write

1. Last winter, I went to Laos with my family.

8 believe, 믿다   9 gift, 선물   10 pressure, 압력, 압박

11 safety, 안전   12 childhood, 어린 시절

13 inventor, 발명가   14 comfortable, 편안한

15 support, 지지하다, 후원하다   16 worry, 걱정하다

단어 TEST Step 1   p.59

01 발명가, 창안자	02 압력, 압박	03 활동
04 지지하다, 지원하다		05 목욕, 욕조
06 쇼핑	07 어린 시절	08 목적
09 시험, 실험	10 정말로, 진심으로	11 운전자, 운전기사
12 충격; 쇼크[충격]를 주다		13 프로젝트, 과제
14 호의, 친절	15 고정시키다, 수리하다	
16 선물, 재능	17 가까운, 친한	18 노숙자의
19 발명, 발명품	20 기쁨, 환희	
21 (특정) 지역의, 현지의		22 편한, 편안한
23 완전한, 완벽한	24 아직(도), 여전히	25 판자, 널
26 사람, 개인	27 식물, 초목	28 성공하다
29 운이 좋은, 행운의	30 안전, 안전성	31 항상, 언제나
32 센서, 감지기	33 상태	34 이해하다
35 포기하다	36 성장하다, 자라다	
37 ~에 대해 감사히 여기다		38 ~하고 싶다
39 기뻐서	40 여기저기 쏘다니다	
41 (해답 등을) 찾아내다[내놓다]		42 ~에 오다
43 ~을 돌보다, 뒷바라지하다		

단어 TEST Step 2   p.60

01 worry	02 believe	03 daughter
04 disease	05 proud	06 error
07 share	08 clean	09 generation
10 happiness	11 worse	12 pleasure
13 just	14 material	15 heel
16 signal	17 understand	18 wander
19 bath	20 respect	21 actually
22 heavy	23 trusty	24 condition
25 until	26 volunteer	27 safety
28 homeless	29 succeed	30 support
31 comfortable	32 pressure	33 invention
34 joy	35 take care of	36 come over to
37 look for	38 thank A for B	39 come up with
40 at first	41 wander off	42 cheer up
43 keep an eye on		

단어 TEST Step 3   p.61

1 heavy, 무거운   2 always, 항상, 언제나   3 joy, 기쁨, 환희

4 heel, 발뒤꿈치   5 create, 창조하다

6 driver, 운전자, 운전기사   7 perfect, 완벽한, 완전한

대화문 TEST Step 1   p.62~63

Listen & Speak 1 A. Listen and Check

1 do me a favor / What / family, going on vacation, come, water / can

2 can, favor / it / help me with, project / Sorry, can't, have to visit, with

Listen & Speak 2 A. Listen and Check

1 Hi, As you know, birthday, haven't had, to, beging, been, and, for supporting, trying, proud, daughter

2 are, doing, weekend / Nothing special, stay, watch / having, party / for inviting

Listen & Speak 1-B

Can, do, favor / What / move, with, heavy / No problem / Thank, for helping

Communicate A. Listen and Answer

Can, do me a favor / What / go shopping, for / of course, Who, for / for my little sister / getting, a birthday gift / isn't until October / why are, getting, cap / broke, while she was riding, last, just, cheer her up / see, can go / sounds perfect

Progress Check

1 can you do, favor / What, it / going to go, this, weekend, take care of, during / worry, enjoy

2 Hello, haven't, a chance to thank, for being, Every, welcome, always teach, things, lucky to have, proud to be, students

3 any special plans, just going to stay, then, come over, for dinner

대화문 TEST Step 2   p.64~65

Listen & Speak 1 A. Listen and Check

1 G: Mark, can you do me a favor?

B: Sure. What is it?

G: My family is going on vacation for a week. Can you come to our house and water the plants?

B: Yes, I can.

2 G: Kevin, can you do me a favor?

B: O.K. What is it?

G: Can you help me with my science project this

45

afternoon?

B: Sorry , but I can't . I have to visit my grandma with my mom.

1 G: Hi, Mom! Hi, Dad! As you know, today is my 15th birthday. I haven't had a chance to thank you for being my parents. You've truly been my friends and my teachers. Thank you for supporting me and always trying to understand me. I'm really proud to be your daughter.

2 G: What are you doing this weekend, Eric?

B: Nothing special. I'll just stay home and watch TV.

G: Great! I'm having a birthday party this weekend. Can you come?

B: Sure. Thank you for inviting me.

A: Can you do me a favor?

B: Sure. What is it?

A: Can you move this table with me? It's too heavy.

B: Sure. No problem.

A: Thank you for helping me.

Jaden: Can you do me a favor, Yuri?

Yuri: Sure. What is it, Jaden?

Jaden: Can we go shopping together for a baseball cap for a girl?

Yuri: Yes, of course. Who is it for?

Jaden: It's for my little sister Kate.

Yuri: Oh, are you getting her a birthday gift?

Jaden: No, her birthday isn't until October.

Yuri: Then, why are you getting a baseball cap for her?

Jaden: She broke her leg while she was riding her bike last week. I just want to cheer her up.

Yuri: Oh, I see. I can go this Friday afternoon.

Jaden: That sounds perfect. Thank you.

1 G: Andrew, can you do me a favor?

B: O.K. What is it?

G: My family is going to go to Jejudo this weekend. Can you take care of my cat during the weekend?

B: Sure. Don't worry about her. And enjoy your trip.

2 G: Hello , Mr. Smith. We haven't had a chance to thank you for being our teacher. Every morning, you welcome us in the classroom. You always

teach us important and interesting things. We're lucky to have you, and we're proud to be your students.

3 G: Do you have any special plans this weekend?

B: No, I'm just going to stay home.

G: Oh, then can you come over to my house for dinner?

01 up, family, generations

02 little, been, close

03 first, trusty, cook

04 taught, lessons

05 person, respected, most   06 went, for, got

07 had, disease   08 Everyone, was, shock

09 became, over 10 wandered off, keep, all

11 One, got, saw 12 moment, himself, don't, heels

13 were, that, do 14 sensor, way, signal

15 tried, materials, comfortable, elderly

16 like, up, safety 17 trial, error, succeeded

18 worked, so, that

19 believe, invention, worked

20 For, inventor, world   21 his, still, best

01 grew up, family, three generations

02 Since, was little, been, close to

03 first friend, trusty driver, cook

04 also taught, life lessons

05 who, respected the most

06 When, went out for a walk, got lost

07 had, disease   08 Everyone, was in shock

09 became worse over

10 wandered off, so, that, keep an eye, all

11 got out of, saw

12 moment, said to himself, don't, heels

13 were, that, had to do

14 had to create, then, a way to send, signal

15 tried, materials, socks

16 felt like giving up, safety

17 After, trial, error, succeeded in making

18 worked, that, jumped for joy

19 could not believe, actually worked

20 For, the best inventor

21 is still, best friend

1 Kenneth Shinozuka는 3대의 행복한 대가족에서 자랐다.

2 그는 어렸을 때부터 항상 할아버지와 매우 친했다.

3 그는 Kenneth의 첫 친구이자, 신뢰할 수 있는 운전기사이자, 요리사였다.

4 그는 또한 그에게 많은 인생 교훈을 가르쳐 주었다.

5 그는 Kenneth가 세상에서 가장 존경하는 사람이었다.

6 Kenneth가 네 살이었을 때, 그의 할아버지는 어느 날 산책을 나갔다가 길을 잃었다.

7 그는 알츠하이머병에 걸렸다.

8 Kenneth의 가족 모두는 충격에 빠졌다.

9 그의 상태는 10년 동안 더 악화되었다.

10 그는 자주 밤에 여기저기 돌아다니기 때문에 누군가가 그를 밤새 감시해야 했다.

11 어느 날 밤, Kenneth의 할아버지가 침대에서 일어났는데, Kenneth가 그것을 보았다.

12 그 순간, 그는 혼잣말을 했다. "내가 할아버지의 양말 뒤꿈치에 압력 감지기를 설치하는 게 어떨까?"

13 Kenneth가 해야 할 많은 일들이 있었다.

14 그는 처음에 압력 감지기를 만들고 나서 그의 스마트폰으로 신호를 보낼 방법을 찾아야 했다.

15 Kenneth는 또한 그의 연로한 할아버지에게 편안한 양말을 만들어 주기 위해 많은 다양한 재료들을 가지고 만들어 보았다.

16 그는 포기하고 싶은 생각이 들 때 할아버지의 안전에 대해 생각했다.

17 많은 시행착오 끝에 그는 마침내 자신의 장치를 만드는 데 성공했다.

18 그것이 처음 작동했을 때, 그는 너무 행복해 기뻐서 펄쩍 뛰었다.

19 그는 자신의 발명품이 실제로 작동했다는 것을 믿을 수 없었다.

20 그의 할아버지에게 Kenneth는 세계 최고의 발명가이다.

21 Kenneth에게 그의 할아버지는 여전히 그의 가장 친한 친구이다.

1 Kenneth Shinozuka grew up in a big happy family of three generations.

2 Since he was little, he has always been very close to his grandfather.

3 He was Kenneth's first friend, his trusty driver, and his cook.

4 He also taught him many life lessons.

5 He was the person who Kenneth respected the most in the world.

6 When Kenneth was four, his grandfather went out for a walk one day and got lost.

7 He had Alzheimer's disease.

8 Everyone in Kenneth's family was in shock.

9 His condition became worse over the next 10 years.

10 He wandered off at night so often that someone had to keep an eye on him all night long.

11 One night, Kenneth's grandfather got out of bed, and Kenneth saw it.

12 At that moment, he said to himself, "Why don't I put pressure sensors on the heels of his socks?"

13 There were many things that Kenneth had to do.

14 He first had to create a pressure sensor and then find a way to send a signal to his smart phone.

15 Kenneth also tried many different materials to make comfortable socks for his elderly grandfather.

16 When he felt like giving up, he thought about his grandfather's safety.

17 After much trial and error, he finally succeeded in making his device.

18 When it first worked, he was so happy that he jumped for joy.

19 He could not believe that his invention actually worked.

20 For his grandfather, Kenneth is the best inventor in the world.

21 For Kenneth, his grandfather is still his best friend.

Link - Share

1. volunteer work, planning, elderly

2. came up with

3. One of, for

Write - Write

1. would like, volunteer

2. One, on

3. so, that, to help

4. there are, that

5. walk, bath, with

6. who, looking for

Culture Project

1. to help

2. John, Care

3. local

4. build, for

5. so, that, at, happiness, helping

Link - Share

1. I'd like to talk about the volunteer work that we're planning to do for the elderly people in our city.
2. We came up with three activities.
3. One of them is to make patbingsu for them and eat it together.

Write - Write

1. Hello, I am Kim Doha, and I would like to join your volunteer project.
2. One day, I saw some poor dogs on TV.
3. They looked so sad that I wanted to help them.
4. I like dogs, and there are many things that I can do for them.
5. I can walk the dogs, give them a bath , and play with them.
6. I am the person who you are looking for !

Culture Project

1. Do you want to help children?
2. Join our Child Care Project in Laos.
3. You'll teach local children.
4. You'll also build a school for them.
5. The work is so hard that you'll want to go home at first, but you'll find h`appiness in helping these children.

적중 100 + 특별부록

Plan B

우리학교
최신기출

미래 · 최연희 교과서를 배우는

학교 시험문제 분석 · 모음 · 해설집

전국단위 학교 시험문제 수집 및 분석
출제 빈도가 높은 문제 위주로 선별
문제 풀이에 필요한 상세한 해설

중2-1
영어

미래 · 최연희

◎ 선택형 문항의 답안은 컴퓨터용 수정 싸인펜을 사용하여 OMR 답안지에 바르게 표기하시오.
◎ 서술형 문제는 답을 답안지에 반드시 검정 볼펜으로 쓰시오.
◎ 총 29문항 100점 만점입니다. 문항별 배점은 각 문항에 표시되어 있습니다.

[전북 ○○중]

1. 문맥상 다음 빈칸에 들어갈 말로 가장 적절한 것은? (3점)

Julia Child was a person who found her real _____ in her 30s. At age 36, she moved to Paris with her husband. She attended a famous cooking school there. While she was studying, she decided to write a cookbook. That book became a big hit.

① cook   ② family   ③ talent
④ hometown   ⑤ cafeteria

[전북 ○○중]

2. 다음 〈보기〉와 같이 조건에 맞게 '나'에 대한 시를 쓰시오. (5점)

<보기>
I'm a person
who likes puppies
who wants to be a singer.

<조건>
• 주격 관계대명사를 사용할 것.
• 완전한 문장으로 쓸 것.
• I'm a person을 포함하여 3행시로 쓸 것.
• <보기>에 나온 puppies, a singer는 쓰지 말 것.

답: I'm a person
_____
_____

[전북 ○○중]

3. 다음 (A)~(D)를 자연스러운 대화가 되도록 바르게 배열한 것은? (3점)

(A) Well, I'd like to, but I don't think I'm good at acting or dancing.
(B) O.K. I'll think about it.
(C) Why don't you join our musical theater club? You're good at singing.
(D) Don't worry. We can teach you. I'm sure you'll learn fast. Just join us.

① (A)-(C)-(D)-(B)
② (A)-(D)-(C)-(B)
③ (C)-(A)-(D)-(B)
④ (C)-(D)-(A)-(B)
⑤ (A)-(D)-(B)-(C)

[전북 ○○중]

4. 다음 중 짝지어진 대화가 <u>어색한</u> 것은? (3점)

① A: What kind of music do you want to listen to?
　 B: I love listening to music.
② A: Tomorrow is my mom's birthday. What should I do for her?
　 B: Why don't you bake a cake for her?
③ A: What are you good at?
　 B: I can play badminton very well.
④ A: What are you doing, Nami?
　 B: I'm making a smart phone case out of my old jeans.
⑤ A: Excuse me, where can I find women's shoes?
　 B: You can find them on the second floor.

[5~6] 다음 대화를 읽고 물음에 답하시오.

G: What are you doing, Jaden?

B: I'm drawing cartoons.

G: Really? Can I take a look at them?

B: No, not yet.

G: Why not? ⓐYou can show me a few, can't you?

B: Well, I guess so.

G: (pause) Ha, ha, ha! Awesome! I like your cartoons. ⓑYou're really good at drawing.

B: Do you think so? I want to be a cartoonist, but ⓒI don't think my drawing skills are good enough.

G: ⓓYour cartoons are really funny, and you have unique characters. ⓔYou'll be a great cartoonist.

B: Thank you, Yuri. (A)You just made my day.

5. 위 대화의 ⓐ~ⓔ를 어색하게 해석한 것은? (3점)

① ⓐ: 내게 조금 보여줄 수 있잖아, 그렇지 않니?

② ⓑ: 너 정말 그림을 잘 그리는구나.

③ ⓒ: 나는 내 그리기 실력이 충분치 않다고 생각하지 않아.

④ ⓓ: 너의 만화들은 정말로 재미있어.

⑤ ⓔ: 너는 훌륭한 만화가가 될 거야.

6. 위 대화의 (A)와 바꾸어 쓰기에 가장 적절한 것은? (4점)

① You will be happy.

② You gave me a time.

③ You made me happy.

④ You drew me cartoons.

⑤ You like to draw cartoons.

7. 다음 대화의 빈칸 (A)에 가장 알맞은 것은? (3점)

B: Hi, Jennie. Is something wrong?

G: I have to give a speech in English tomorrow. I'm so nervous.

B: Don't worry. You're a very good speaker.

G: (A)_____

① Speech in English is so easy!

② My favorite subject is English.

③ I think my speech is very good.

④ I feel much better now. Thanks!

⑤ You will do a good job tomorrow.

[8~9] 다음 글을 읽고 물음에 답하시오.

I showed my book ⓐfor Ms. Lee. She loved it, too. She also told me about her coworkers ⓑthat had special talents. Ms. Park, another cafeteria worker, won a dancing contest. Mr. Kim, the janitor at our school, was once an adventurous park ranger. ⓒ"I'd like to write superhero stories about them. Do you think they'll like that?" I asked Ms. Lee. ⓓ"Of course they can," she said ⓔcheerfully. "Let's go and say hello to our new superhero friends."

8. 위 글의 ⓐ~ⓔ 중 바르게 쓰인 것의 개수는? (4점)

① 1개 ② 2개 ③ 3개 ④ 4개 ⑤ 5개

9. 위 글의 내용과 일치하지 않는 것은? (3점)

① I showed Ms. Lee my book.

② Mr. Kim works as a park ranger.

③ Ms. Park works at the school cafeteria.

④ Ms. Lee has coworkers who have special talents.

⑤ I want to write superhero stories about Ms. Lee's coworkers.

10. What is Nami good at? (3점)

> B: What are you doing, Nami?
> G: I'm making a smart phone case out of my old jeans.
> B: Wow! You're good at recycling old clothes.
> G: Thanks. I like recycling. It's fun, and it's also good for our Earth.

① She is good at making jeans.
② She is good at recycling old clothes.
③ She is good at making smart phones.
④ She is good at making funny clothes.
⑤ She is good at recycling smart phone cases.

[11~12] 다음 글을 읽고 물음에 답하시오.

> My name is Hojin, and I like ⓐmaking graphic novels. While I was walking home from school last week, I saw a woman on a scooter. (A)She looked really ⓑcool, and her scooter was very unique.
> "Are you going home, Hojin?" she said to me ⓒsuddenly.
> "Yes, but do I know you?" I asked.
> "Of course," she answered. "I see you at the school cafeteria every day."
> ⓓSurprisingly, she was one of the cafeteria ⓔworker at school.
> "Amazing! She looks so different outside the school," I thought. "I should write a graphic novel about her."

11. 위 글의 밑줄 친 ⓐ~ⓔ 중 어법상 잘못 쓰인 것은? (2점)

① ⓐ ② ⓑ ③ ⓒ ④ ⓓ ⑤ ⓔ

12. 위 글을 참고하여 다음 질문에 대한 답을 영어로 한 문장으로 쓰시오. (5점)

> Q: What did Hojin decide to write about?

답: _____.

13. 다음 대화문에서 주어진 문장이 들어갈 알맞은 곳은? (3점)

> I'm so nervous.

> B: Hi, Cindy. Is something wrong? (A)
> G: I have to give a speech in front of the whole school. (B)
> B: Don't worry. (C) You're a very good speaker. I'm sure you'll do a good job. (D)
> G: Thanks, Minho. I feel much better now. (E)

① (A) ② (B) ③ (C) ④ (D) ⑤ (E)

14. 다음 상자 속 문장들을 활용하여 주어진 우리말과 일치하도록 문장을 완성하시오. (5점)

> • I was eating lunch.
> • He watched a movie.
> • I listened to music.
> • He did his homework.

(1) 나는 점심을 먹는 동안 음악을 들었다.

_____ while _____.

(2) 그는 숙제를 한 후 영화를 보았다.

_____ after _____.

[15~16] 다음 글을 읽고 물음에 답하시오.

After I got home, I began to write a new graphic novel, *Lunch Lady Begins*. In it, Lunch Lady is a superhero. ⓐShe rides a super scooter who can fly. She saves people from danger around the world. ⓑShe also makes 100 cookies per seconds and gives them away to hungry children.
ⓒA few days later, I showed my graphic novel to my friends.
"Awesome! I love this superhero. She's so cool," said all my friends.
"Guess what? ⓓI modeled her on Ms. Lee, one of our cafeteria worker." I told them.
I showed my book to Ms. Lee. She loved it, too. She also told me about her coworkers who had special talents. Ms. Park, another cafeteria worker, won a dancing contest. Mr. Kim, the janitor at our school, was once an adventurous park ranger.
"I'd like to write superhero stories about them. Do you think they'll like that?" I asked Ms. Lee.
"Of course they will," ⓔshe said cheerful.
"Let's go and say hello to our new superhero friends."

15. 위 글의 내용과 일치하는 것은?　　(3점)

① There is only one cafeteria worker at school.

② I showed my graphic novel to my family.

③ Lunch Lady rides a super scooter that can make cookies.

④ Ms. Park, the janitor at our school, won a dancing contest.

⑤ Ms. Lee thought her coworkers would like the superhero stories.

16. 위 글의 밑줄 친 ⓐ~ⓔ 중 어법상 올바른 것은? (3점)
① ⓐ　② ⓑ　③ ⓒ　④ ⓓ　⑤ ⓔ

[17~19] 다음 글을 읽고 물음에 답하시오.

My name is 'Hojin', and I like to make graphic novels. While I was walking home from school last week, I saw a woman on a scooter. ⓐShe looked really cool, and her scooter was very unique.
"Are you going home, Hojin?" she said to me suddenly.
"Yes, but do I know ⓑyou?" I asked.
"Of course," she answered. "I see ⓒyou at the school cafeteria every day."
Surprisingly, she was one of the cafeteria workers at school.
"Amazing! ⓓShe looks so different outside the school," I thought. "I should write a graphic novel about ⓔher."

17. 위 글의 밑줄 친 ⓐ~ⓔ 중 가리키는 것이 <u>다른</u> 것은?　　(4점)
① ⓐ　② ⓑ　③ ⓒ　④ ⓓ　⑤ ⓔ

18. 위 글의 제목으로 가장 알맞은 것은?　(3점)
① What Is Hojin Good at?
② What Is the Graphic Novel?
③ What Will Hojin Write about?
④ What Does the Cafeteria Worker Do?
⑤ Why Does Hojin Like Graphic Novels?

19. 위 글의 밑줄 친 'Hojin'에 대한 설명이 <u>아닌</u> 것은?
　　(4점)
① knew the woman's name
② likes to make graphic novels
③ saw a woman on a scooter last week
④ thought a woman's scooter looked unique
⑤ will write a graphic novel about the woman on a scooter

20. 다음 중 어법상 올바른 문장은? (3점)

① I like the dogs which is white.

② He has an uncle who live in LA.

③ Bill is the boy that wear a red hat.

④ I like the house who has a lot of windows.

⑤ I know the woman who wrote *Harry Potter*.

[21~23] 다음 글을 읽고 물음에 답하시오.

She saves people from danger around the world. She also makes 100 cookies per second and gives them away to hungry children.
A few days later, I showed my graphic novel to my friends.
(A) "Awesome! I love this superhero. She's so cool," said all my friends.
(B) "Guess what? ⓐ<u>나는 우리 학교 식당 조리사님 중 한 분을 본떠서 그녀를 만들었어,</u>" I told them.
(C) She also told me about her coworkers ⓑ<u>who</u> had special talents. (D) Ms. Park, another cafeteria worker, won a dancing contest, and Mr. Kim, the janitor at our school, was once an adventurous park ranger.
(E) "I'd like to write superhero stories about them. Do you think they'll like that?" I asked Ms. Lee.
"Of course they will," she said cheerfully. "Let's go and say hello to our new superhero friends."

21. 위 글의 (A)~(E) 중 아래의 주어진 문장이 들어가기에 가장 적절한 위치는? (4점)

I showed my book to Ms. Lee. She loved it, too.

① (A) ② (B) ③ (C) ④ (D) ⑤ (E)

22. 위 글의 ⓐ를 바르게 영작한 것은? (4점)

① I modeled her on Ms. Lee, a cafeteria worker

② I modeled her on Ms. Lee, one of our cafeteria worker

③ I modeled her on Ms. Lee, one of our cafeteria workers

④ I modeled Ms. Lee, one of our cafeteria workers on her

⑤ I modeled her of Ms. Lee, one of our cafeteria workers

23. 위 글의 ⓑ<u>who</u>와 용법이 <u>다른</u> 것은? (3점)

① I have a dog <u>which</u> can jump high.

② Look at the tree <u>that</u> has many big leaves.

③ I know a famous cook <u>who</u> won a cooking contest.

④ The girl <u>who</u> is wearing sunglasses is my daughter.

⑤ The red bag <u>which</u> I want to buy is very expensive.

24. 다음 글의 목적으로 가장 알맞은 것은? (3점)

Dave: Hello, everyone. I'm Dave. I want to be your class president. I'm a good listener and always try to help others. I'm also good at planning fun school activities. I'll work hard for our class, so please vote for me. Thank you for listening.

① 나의 장점 말하기

② 나의 인생 요약하기

③ 자기 소개하기

④ 학급 실장을 위한 투표 요청하기

⑤ 학급 실장을 위한 친구 추천하기

25. 다음 (A)~(C)에 알맞은 말이 짝지어진 것은? (4점)

- I bought a car (A)[who / which] looked very nice.
- Look at the girl and her dog (B)[which / that] are running.
- She has a brother (C)[who / which] is a famous singer.

	(A)	(B)	(C)
①	who	which	which
②	which	that	who
③	which	which	who
④	who	that	who
⑤	which	which	which

[26~28] 다음 글을 읽고 물음에 답하시오.

My name is Hojin, and I like to make graphic novels. (A)_____ I was walking home from school last week, I saw a woman on a scooter. She looked really cool, and her scooter was very unique.

"Are you going home, Hojin?" she said to me suddenly.

"Yes, but do I know you?" I asked.

"Of course," she answered. "I see you at the school cafeteria every day."

Surprisingly, she was one of the cafeteria workers at school.

"Amazing! She looks so different outside the school," I thought. "I should write a graphic novel about her."

After I got home, I began to write a new graphic novel, *Lunch Lady Begins*. In it, Lunch Lady is a superhero. ⓐ그녀는 날 수 있는 슈퍼 스쿠터를 탄다.

26. 위 글의 빈칸 (A)에 가장 적절한 것은? (3점)

① Though   ② If   ③ Before
④ While   ⑤ During

27. 위 글의 내용과 일치하는 것은? (3점)

① The woman works at the school cafeteria.
② Hojin met the woman on the way to school.
③ The woman's scooter looks like other ordinary scooters.
④ Hojin wants to make a poster about the woman.
⑤ Hojin saw the woman on a scooter for the first time.

28. 위 글의 밑줄 친 ⓐ를 관계대명사를 사용하여 영어 문장으로 쓰시오. (단, that은 사용하지 말 것) (4점)

답: _____

29. 자연스러운 대화가 되도록 (A)~(D)를 바르게 배열한 것은? (3점)

(A) Wow! You're good at recycling old clothes.
(B) What are you doing, Nami?
(C) Thanks. I like recycling. It's fun, and it's also good for our Earth.
(D) I'm making a smart phone case out of my old jeans.

① (A)-(B)-(C)-(D)
② (B)-(D)-(A)-(C)
③ (A)-(D)-(C)-(B)
④ (B)-(C)-(A)-(D)
⑤ (C)-(A)-(B)-(D)

문항수 : 선택형(25문항) 서술형(6문항)   20 . . .

◎ 선택형 문항의 답안은 컴퓨터용 수정 싸인펜을 사용하여 OMR 답안지에 바르게 표기하시오.
◎ 서술형 문제는 답을 답안지에 반드시 검정 볼펜으로 쓰시오.
◎ 총 31문항 100점 만점입니다. 문항별 배점은 각 문항에 표시되어 있습니다.

[전북 ○○중]

1. 다음 글의 흐름상 빈칸에 가장 적절한 말은?   (2점)

Hello, everyone. I'm Kim Yujin. I want to be your _____. I'm a good listener and always try to help others. I'm also good at planning fun school activities. I'll work hard for our class, so please vote for me. Thank you for listening!

① class president
② superhero
③ cartoonist
④ cafeteria worker
⑤ role model

[전북 ○○중]

[2~3] 다음 대화를 읽고 물음에 답하시오.

Yuri: What are you doing, Jaden?
Jaden: I'm drawing cartoons.
Yuri: Really? Can I take a look at them?
Jaden: No, not yet.
Yuri: Why not? You can show me a few, can't you?
Jaden: Well, I guess so.
Yuri: Ha, ha, ha! Awesome! I like your cartoons. You draw really well.
Jaden: Do you think so? I want to be a cartoonist, but I don't think my drawing skills are good enough.
Yuri: Your cartoons are really funny, and you have unique characters. I think you'll be a great cartoonist.
Jaden: Thank you, Yuri. ⓐ네가 나를 정말 기쁘게 해 줬어.

2. 위 대화의 내용과 일치하지 않는 것은?   (3점)

① Jaden은 만화를 그리고 있다.
② Yuri는 Jaden이 그림을 잘 그린다고 생각한다.
③ Jaden은 만화가가 되고 싶다.
④ Jaden은 본인의 그림 실력에 만족한다.
⑤ Yuri는 Jaden이 멋진 만화가가 될 것이라고 생각한다.

3. 위 대화의 ⓐ의 우리말과 같도록 다음 단어들을 알맞게 배열하여 You로 시작하는 문장을 완성하시오.(4점)

my / day / just / made

답: You _____.

[대전 ○○중]

4. 다음 짝지어진 대화가 어색한 것은?   (3점)

① M: I think I will fail the test.
   W: I'm sure you can pass the test.
② M: What are you good at?
   W: I can sing a song very well.
③ M: I want to be a model in the future.
   W: I'm sure you can be a great model.
④ M: I'm good at math. How about you?
   W: Me too. Math is very hard for me.
⑤ M: What do you want to be?
   W: My dream is an English teacher because I'm good at English.

5. 다음 (a)~(d)를 대화의 흐름상 가장 알맞게 배열한
   것은? (3점)

(a) That's a good idea.
(b) I'm sure your mom will love it.
(c) Tomorrow is my mom's birthday.
(d) Why don't you bake a cake for her?

① (a) - (c) - (b) - (d)

② (a) - (d) - (b) - (c)

③ (c) - (a) - (b) - (d)

④ (c) - (a) - (d) - (b)

⑤ (c) - (d) - (a) - (b)

6. 다음 빈칸에 들어갈 알맞은 단어가 순서대로 짝지
   어진 것은? (2점)

• I have a bag _____ has many pockets.
• Do you know the girl _____ is cleaning the room?

① who – which

② who – that

③ which – who

④ that – which

⑤ who – who

7. 다음 빈칸에 공통으로 들어갈 말은? (2점)

• My brother is good _____ playing soccer.
• My mom and I ate _____ the Chinese restaurant last weekend.

① for ② at ③ in ④ with ⑤ on

[8~10] 다음 글을 읽고 물음에 답하시오.

I showed my book to Ms. Lee. She loved it. She also told me about her coworkers ⓐ who had special talents. Ms. Park, another cafeteria worker, won a dancing contest. Mr. Kim, the janitor at our school, ⓑwere once an adventurous park ranger. "I'd like ⓒwriting superhero stories about them. Do you think they'll like (A)that?" I asked Ms. Lee. "Of course they will," she said ⓓcheerfully. "Let's go and ⓔsay hello to our new superhero friends."

8. 위 글의 (A)that이 가리키는 것으로 적절한 것은? (4점)

① Working in a school with special talents.

② Writing superhero stories about people who have special talents.

③ Meeting with the people who are working in the school.

④ Showing the superhero stories to the people with special talents.

⑤ Writing about the life of an adventurous park ranger.

9. 위 글의 밑줄 친 ⓐ~ⓔ 중, 어법상 어색한 것을 두
   개 고르면? (3점)

① ⓐ ② ⓑ ③ ⓒ ④ ⓓ ⑤ ⓔ

10. 위 글을 읽고 알 수 없는 것은? (3점)

① Ms. Park의 현재 직업

② Mr. Kim의 현재 직업

③ Ms. Park의 특별한 재능

④ Ms. Lee의 특별한 재능

⑤ Mr. Kim의 과거 직업

[11~13] 다음 대화를 읽고 물음에 답하시오.

Yuri: What are you doing, Jaden?
Jaden: I'm drawing cartoons.
Yuri: Really? Can I take a look at them?
Jaden: No, not yet.
Yuri: Why not? You can show me a few, (A)_____?
Jaden: Well, I guess so.
Yuri: (pause) Ha, ha, ha! Awesome! I like your cartoons. (B)"넌 그림을 잘 그려."
Jaden: Do you think so? I want to be a cartoonist, but I don't think my drawing skills are good enough.
Yuri: Your cartoons are really funny, and you have unique characters.

11. 위 대화의 빈칸 (A)에 들어갈 부가의문문을 쓰시오. (3점)

→ _____

12. 위 대화에서 Yuri가 말하는 Jaden의 만화의 장점 두 가지를 우리말로 쓰시오. (3점)

→ _____

→ _____

13. 위 대화의 밑줄 친 (B)"넌 그림을 잘 그려."를 good 을 사용하여 영작하시오. (4점)

→ _____

[14~15] 다음 글을 읽고 물음에 답하시오.

My name is Hojin, and I like (A)[make / to make] graphic novels. (B)[While / After] I was walking home from school last week, ⓐI saw a woman on a scooter. She looked really cool, and her scooter was very unique. "Are ⓑyou going home, Hojin?" she said to me suddenly.
"Yes, but do I know ⓒyou?" I asked.
"Of course," she answered. "I see ⓓyou at the school cafeteria every day."
Surprisingly, she was one of the cafeteria (C)[worker / workers] at school.
"Amazing! She looks so different outside the school," I thought. "ⓔI should write a graphic novel about her."

14. 위 글의 (A), (B), (C) 괄호 안에서 알맞은 것끼리 짝지은 것은? (3점)

	(A)	(B)	(C)
①	make	While	worker
②	make	After	worker
③	to make	While	workers
④	to make	After	worker
⑤	to make	After	workers

15. 위 글의 밑줄 친 ⓐ~ⓔ 중 가리키는 대상이 다른 하나는? (4점)

① ⓐ　② ⓑ　③ ⓒ　④ ⓓ　⑤ ⓔ

16. 다음 빈칸 (A)에 가장 적절한 것은? (3점)

> G: Tomorrow is my mom's birthday. What should I do for her?
> B: Why don't you bake a cake for her? You're good at baking.
> G: That's a good idea. I hope my mom will like my cake.
> B: (A)_____

① I think you will love it.
② I guess she didn't like it.
③ I'm sure your mom will love it.
④ I'm sure that the cake is delicious.
⑤ I'm not sure your mom will enjoy it.

[17~19] 다음 글을 읽고 물음에 답하시오.

> ⓐAfter I got home, I began to write a new graphic novel, *Lunch Lady Begins*. In it, Lunch Lady is a superhero. (A)_____ She ⓑsaves people from danger around the world. She also makes 100 cookies per second and ⓒgive them away to hungry children.
> ⓓA few days later, I showed my graphic novel to my friends.
> "Awesome! I love this superhero. She's so cool," said all my friends.
> "Guess what? I modeled her ⓔon Ms. Lee, one of our cafeteria workers," I told them.

17. <보기>에서 알맞은 관계대명사를 골라, 다음 두 문장을 연결하여 위 글의 빈칸 (A)에 들어갈 알맞은 문장을 완성하시오. (4점)

> <보기>
> who / whom / which

> • She rides a super scooter.
> • It can fly.

→ _____

18. 위 글의 밑줄 친 ⓐ~ⓔ 중에서 어법상 어색한 것은? (3점)

① ⓐ ② ⓑ ③ ⓒ ④ ⓓ ⑤ ⓔ

19. 위 글의 만화 소설 속 Lunch Lady에 관한 내용과 일치하지 않는 것은? (3점)

① 1분에 100개의 쿠키를 만들어 배고픈 아이들에게 나눠준다.
② 전 세계의 위험에 빠진 사람들을 구한다.
③ 날아다니는 스쿠터를 탄다.
④ "I"가 쓴 소설의 주인공이다.
⑤ Ms. Lee를 모델로 만들어졌다.

[20~22] 다음 글을 읽고 물음에 답하시오.

> I showed my book to Ms. Lee. (A) She also told me about her coworkers who had special talents. (B) Ms. Park, another cafeteria worker, won a dancing contest. Mr. Kim, the janitor at our school, was once an adventurous park ranger. (C)
> "I'd like to write superhero stories about them. Do you think they'll like that?" (D) I asked Ms. Lee.
> "Of course they ⓐwill," she said cheerfully. "Let's go and say hello to our new superhero friends." (E)

20. 위 글에서 다음 문장이 들어가기에 가장 적절한 곳은? (3점)

> • She loved it, too.

① (A) ② (B) ③ (C) ④ (D) ⑤ (E)

21. 위 글의 Ms. Lee가 글쓴이에게 말한 직장 동료 두 명의 특별한 재능을 영어로 서술하시오. (5점)

→ _____

22. 위 글의 밑줄 친 ⓐwill 뒤에 생략된 문장으로 가장 적절한 것은? (3점)

① say hello to our new superhero friends
② tell me about her coworkers
③ write superhero stories
④ like that
⑤ win a dancing contest

23. 다음 글을 읽고 내용과 일치하지 <u>않는</u> 것은? (4점)

My aunt is my role model. She is smart, strong, and adventurous. In her 30s, she traveled to 70 different countries. While she was traveling, she made friends from all over the world. I want to be someone who is not afraid of trying new things just like her.

① 나의 숙모가 나의 롤 모델이다.
② 그녀는 모험심이 강하고 똑똑하다.
③ 나는 그녀와 같은 사람이 되고 싶다.
④ 그녀는 30세에 70개의 나라를 여행했다.
⑤ 그녀는 여행하는 동안에 많은 친구를 사귀었다.

24. 다음 중 어법상 가장 올바른 것은? (4점)

① I'll look after your dog while you away.
② I read a comic book while I was eating lunch.
③ You'll get ice cream after you'll clean your room.
④ I brushed my teeth after I meet the school nurse.
⑤ During she was traveling, she made friends from all over the world.

[25~27] 다음 글을 읽고 물음에 답하시오.

After I got home, I began to write a new graphic novel, *Lunch Lady Begins*. In it, Lunch Lady is a superhero. She ⓐride a super scooter (A)that can fly. She saves people from ⓑdangerous around the world. She also makes 100 cookies per second and gives them away ⓒfrom hungry children. ⓓA few days later, I showed my graphic novel ⓔmy friends.
"Awesome! I love this superhero. She's so cool," said all my friends.
"Guess what? (B)<u>나는 Ms. Lee를 본떠서 그녀를 만들었어</u>," I told them.

25. 위 글의 밑줄 친 (A)that과 쓰임이 <u>다른</u> 하나는? (3점)

① This is the boy <u>that</u> came from England.
② It is true <u>that</u> he won the piano contest.
③ Look at the boys <u>that</u> are running there.
④ I have a sister <u>that</u> is only five years old.
⑤ I know a great park <u>that</u> is good for taking a walk.

26. 위 글의 ⓐ~ⓔ 중 어법상 올바른 것은? (3점)

① ⓐ   ② ⓑ   ③ ⓒ   ④ ⓓ   ⑤ ⓔ

27. 다음 주어진 단어들을 이용하여 위 글의 밑줄 친 (B)를 영작할 때, 순서로 알맞은 것은? (4점)

on / her / Ms. Lee / modeled
I (　　) (　　) (　　) (　　).

① modeled, her, on, Ms. Lee
② Ms. Lee, modeled, on, her
③ Ms. Lee, on, modeled, her
④ modeled, on, her, Ms. Lee
⑤ modeled, Ms. Lee, on, her

[28~29] 다음 글을 읽고 물음에 답하시오.

My name is Hojin, and I like (A)[making / make] graphic novels. While I was walking home from school last week, I saw a woman on a scooter. She looked really cool, and her scooter was very unique.

"Are you going home, Hojin?" she said to me suddenly.

"Yes, but do I know you?" I asked.

"Of course," she answered. "I (B)[see / saw] you at the school cafeteria every day."

Surprisingly, she was one of the cafeteria workers at school.

"Amazing! She looks so (C)[different / differently] outside the school." I thought. "I should write a graphic novel about her."

28. 위 글의 내용과 일치하는 것은?   (3점)

① Hojin wants to become a writer.

② Hojin saw the woman at the cafeteria.

③ The woman was once a cafeteria worker.

④ The woman looks the same outside the school.

⑤ The woman thinks that she has never met Hojin before.

29. 위 글의 (A)~(C)에 알맞은 말이 바르게 짝지어진 것은?   (3점)

	(A)	(B)	(C)
①	making	see	differently
②	make	saw	differently
③	making	see	different
④	make	saw	different
⑤	making	see	differently

[30~31] 다음 글을 읽고 물음에 답하시오.

Ms. Lee also told me about her coworkers (A)who had special talents. Ms. Park, another cafeteria worker, won a dancing contest. Mr. Kim, the janitor at our school, was once an adventurous park rager.

"I'd like to write superhero stories about them. Do you think they'll like that?" I asked Ms. Lee.

"Of course they will," she said cheerfully.

"Let's go and say hello to our new superhero friends."   (I = Hojin)

30. 위 글의 내용과 가장 일치하는 것은?   (3점)

① Ms. Lee only has two friends.

② Mr. Kim was good at dancing.

③ Mr. Kim works at Hojin's school.

④ Hojin wrote superhero stories about Ms. Park.

⑤ Hojin modeled the main characters after his new friends.

31. 위 글의 밑줄 친 (A)who가 들어갈 수 없는 곳은?   (3점)

① I have a brother _____ likes to walk his dog.

② Look at the boy _____ is sleeping on the sofa.

③ David is the person _____ loves his students.

④ She is a famous cook _____ won the cooking contest.

⑤ I want to visit my friend's house _____ has a beautiful garden.

◎ 선택형 문항의 답안은 컴퓨터용 수정 싸인펜을
  사용하여 OMR 답안지에 바르게 표기하시오.
◎ 서술형 문제는 답을 답안지에 반드시 검정
  볼펜으로 쓰시오.
◎ 총 32문항 100점 만점입니다. 문항별 배점
  은 각 문항에 표시되어 있습니다.

[전북 ○○중]

1. 다음 짝지어진 단어의 관계가 나머지 넷과 <u>다른</u> 것은?
(3점)

① nature - grass
② meal - breakfast
③ clothes - skirt
④ school - blackboard
⑤ hundred – thousand

[전북 ○○중]

2. 다음 주어진 말 다음에 이어질 대화의 순서로 가장
알맞은 것은?   (2점)

A: Excuse me, is there a restaurant in this
   mall?

(A) Thank you.
(B) I'd like Italian food.
(C) Yes. What kind of food would you like?
(D) There is a great Italian restaurant on the
   fourth floor.

① (A)-(D)-(C)-(B)   ② (B)-(A)-(D)-(C)
③ (B)-(C)-(A)-(D)   ④ (C)-(D)-(B)-(A)
⑤ (C)-(B)-(D)-(A)

[종로구 ○○중]

3. 다음 문장에서 어법상 <u>어색한</u> 곳을 찾아 바르게 고
친 후, 전체 문장을 쓰시오. 단, 밑줄 친 부분은 고칠
수 없음.   (3점)

I <u>have done</u> volunteer work to help the poor
two years ago.

답: _____

[강동구 ○○중]

[4~5] 다음 대화를 읽고 물음에 답하시오.

A: Welcome to Jeonju Hanok Guesthouse.
   May I help you?
B: Yes, I'd like a room for two nights.
A: Well, what type of room would you like?
B: (A)_____
   You have a lovely garden.
A: Yes, we do. Every room in our house has
   a garden view, but there are no beds in
   the rooms.
B: Do I have to sleep on the floor?
A: Yes, you do.
B: O.K. I'll give it a try. Where can I have
   breakfast?
A: You can have breakfast in the dining
   room.
B: I see. Thank you.

4. 위 대화의 (A)에 가장 적절한 것은?   (3점)
① Where do you want to stay?
② How long will you stay here?
③ Do you have a room with a garden view?
④ Do you have a pretty garden with a fine
   view?
⑤ Where can I have breakfast tomorrow
   morning?

5. 위 대화의 내용과 일치하는 것은?   (2점)
① 식당에서 일어나는 대화이다.
② 손님은 하룻밤을 묵을 예정이다.
③ 침대가 없는 방에서는 정원을 볼 수 없다.
④ 손님은 바닥에서 자야 한다.
⑤ 아침 식사는 부엌에서 할 수 있다.

6. 다음 짝지어진 대화 중 <u>어색한</u> 것은? (2점)

① A: What kind of food would you like?

   B: I'd like Chinese food.

② A: Hey, look at this house in the picture. It looks like a big shoe!

   B: Oh, it's very unique, but I don't want to live in a shoe.

③ A: What kind of house do you want to live in?

   B: Well, I want to live in an airplane-shaped house.

④ A: What kind of music do you want to listen to?

   B: I want to have a pet dog.

⑤ A: Excuse me, where can I find women's shoes?

   B: You can find them on the second floor.

7. 다음 글을 읽고 <u>어색한</u> 문장의 개수는? (3점)

> People in Norway have built wooden houses for a long time. To build strong and warm houses, they cover their roofs with grass. The grass roofs protect them from the long cold winters and strong winds. Sometimes, trees or plants grow out of the grass roofs.

① 1개　　　　② 2개　　　　③ 3개

④ 4개　　　　⑤ 틀린 문장이 없음.

8. 다음 중 어법상 적절한 문장은? (4점)

① Each person has different strengths.

② Each boys are wearing sunglasses.

③ Each room were clean enough.

④ Each women has long hair.

⑤ Each of the house was different.

9. Based on the dialogue below, where can the speakers find watches? (3점)

> W: Excuse me, where can I find watches in this mall?
> M: You can find them on the second floor.
> W: Are they not on the first floor?
> M: No, they are between dresses and jeans.
> W: Thank you.
> M: No problem.

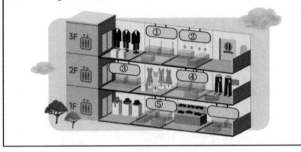

①　　　　②　　　　③　　　　④　　　　⑤

10. 다음 조건을 충족시키도록 세 문장을 영작하시오. (5점)

> - 주어는 I로 할 것.
> - 반드시 현재완료 구문을 넣을 것.
> - 각 문항에 주어진 단어들을 반드시 활용할 것.
> - 내용은 제약이 없음.

(1) _____

   (be / a fan of)

(2) _____

   (know / my best friend)

11. 다음 대화의 내용과 일치하지 <u>않는</u> 것은? (3점)

A: Welcome to Jeonju Hanok Guesthouse. May I help you?
B: Yes, I'd like a room for two nights.
A: Well, what kind of room would you like?
B: Do you have a room with a garden view? You have a lovely garden.
A: Yes, we do. Every room in our house has a garden view, but there are no beds in the rooms.
B: Do I have to sleep on the floor?
A: Yes, you do.
B: O.K. I'll give it a try. Where can I have breakfast?
A: You can have breakfast in the dining room, next to the kitchen.
B: I see.
A: O.K. You're in the Nabi room. Here's your key.
B: Thank you.

① B가 묵을 방은 침대가 없다.
② B가 묵을 방 이름은 나비방이다.
③ B는 한옥 게스트하우스에서 묵을 예정이다.
④ 게스트하우스의 아침식사는 주방 옆의 식당에서 먹는다.
⑤ 한옥 게스트하우스의 방에서는 정원이 보이지 않는다.

12. 다음 문장의 빈칸에 들어갈 단어로 알맞은 것은? (2점)

• He _____ Chinese for the last two years.

① studies
② studied
③ has studied
④ have studied
⑤ has been studied

[13~15] 다음 글을 읽고 물음에 답하시오.

Have you ever (A)_____ a goat on the roof of a house? In Norway, we can see animals on roofs. Norway has large forests. In harmony with nature, people (B)_____ wooden houses for a long time. To build strong and warm houses, they cover their roofs with grass. The grass roofs protect (C)them from the long cold winters and strong winds. Sometimes, trees or plants grow out of the grass roofs, and some animals enjoy their meals there.

13. 위 글의 (A), (B)에 들어갈 말이 차례대로 바르게 짝지어진 것은? (3점)

① saw — build
② seen — have built
③ seen — has built
④ saw — have built
⑤ seen — have build

14. 위 글의 (C)가 가리키는 것은? (3점)

① goats   ② houses   ③ plants
④ forests   ⑤ Norwegians

15. 위 글을 읽고 답할 수 <u>없는</u> 질문은? (4점)

① What can we see on roofs in Norway?
② What have people used to build houses in Norway?
③ Why do people in Norway cover their roofs with grass?
④ How long is the cold winter season in Norway?
⑤ What do some animals do on the grass roof?

[16~17] 다음 글을 읽고 물음에 답하시오.

From the sky in a part of southern China, you can see round roofs (A)_____ look like big doughnuts. They are the roofs of the big round houses of the Hakka people. They have lived in houses like these (B)_____ about a thousand years to protect (C)_____ from enemies. The houses have only one gate without any windows on the first floor. Each (D)_____ is big enough for a whole village. It usually has four stories.

16. 위 글의 빈칸에 들어갈 단어로 바르게 짝지어진
　　 것은?　　　　　　　　　　　　　　(4점)

	(A)	(B)	(C)	(D)
①	that	since	them	houses
②	which	since	them	house
③	that	for	themselves	houses
④	which	for	themselves	house
⑤	who	for	themselves	houses

17. 위 글의 내용과 일치하지 <u>않는</u> 것은?　　(3점)
① The roofs look like big doughnuts.
② The Hakka people have lived in
　　four-story houses.
③ The house doesn't have gates on the first
　　floor.
④ The house has protected Hakka people
　　from enemies.
⑤ The house is so big that a whole village
　　can live together in it.

[18~19] 다음 글을 읽고 물음에 답하시오.

Have you ever seen a goat on the roof of a house? In Norway, we can see animals on roofs. Norway has large forests. In harmony with nature, people have built wooden houses for a long time.
To build strong and warm houses, (A)they cover their roofs with grass. ⓐThey protect ⓑthem from the long cold winters and strong winds. Sometimes, trees or plants grow out of ⓒthem, and some animals enjoy ⓓtheir meals ⓔthere.

18. 위 글의 제목으로 가장 알맞은 것은?　　(3점)
① Grass Roofs in Norway
② Strong Winds in Norway
③ Large Forests in Norway
④ Wooden Houses in Norway
⑤ How to Cover Roofs with Grass

19. 위 글의 밑줄 친 ⓐ~ⓔ 중 (A)they가 가리키는
　　 대상과 같은 것은?　　　　　　　　(3점)
① ⓐ　　② ⓑ　　③ ⓒ　　④ ⓓ　　⑤ ⓔ

20. 다음 대화의 흐름에서 불필요한 문장은?　(3점)

A: Hey, ⓐlook at this house in the picture.
　　ⓑIt looks like a big shoe.
B: Oh, it's very unique, ⓒbut I don't want
　　to live in a shoe.
A: ⓓI don't like to wear shoes. Then, what
　　kind of house do you want to live in?
B: ⓔWell, I want to live in an airplane-shaped
　　house.

① ⓐ　　② ⓑ　　③ ⓒ　　④ ⓓ　　⑤ ⓔ

[21~24] 다음 글을 읽고 물음에 답하시오.

A roof is an essential part of a house, but long ago ⓐsome people built roofs only to (A)_____. Centuries ago in southern Italy, people who had a house without a roof paid lower taxes. To (B)_____ high taxes on ⓑtheir houses, some people built cone-shaped roofs by piling up stones. When ⓒtax collectors came to the town, people took ⓓtheir roofs down quickly. After the tax collectors left, ⓔthey piled up the stones again.

21. 위 글의 ⓐ~ⓔ 중 가리키는 대상이 다른 것은?
(3점)

① ⓐ   ② ⓑ   ③ ⓒ   ④ ⓓ   ⑤ ⓔ

22. 위 글의 (A)에 가장 적절한 것은? (3점)

① collect stones easily
② take them down quickly
③ pay higher taxes than others
④ look more beautiful and amazing
⑤ protect themselves from cold weather

23. 위 글의 (B)에 들어갈 단어의 영영사전 뜻으로 가장 알맞은 것은? (4점)

① to stay away from something
② to make something, especially a building
③ to put something over to hide or protect it
④ to put plants or seeds in the ground to grow
⑤ to get things of the same type and bring them together

24. 위 글의 제목으로 가장 적절한 것은? (4점)

① Cone-shaped Roofs
② History of Southern Italy
③ Houses with High Taxes
④ Roofs Around the World
⑤ An Essential Part of a House

[25~26] 다음 글을 읽고 물음에 답하시오.

(1)From the sky in a part of southern China, you can see round roofs ⓐthat look like big doughnuts. (2)They are the big round houses of the roofs of the Hakka people. They ⓑhave lived in houses like these for about a thousand years to protect ⓒthemselves from enemies. The houses have only one gate (3)without any windows on the first floor. ⓓEach house are big enough for a whole village. (4)It usually has four stories. It ⓔhas kitchens on the first floor, storage rooms on the second floor, (5)and living rooms and bedrooms on the third and fourth floors.

25. 위 글의 (1)~(5) 중 어색한 문장을 찾아 번호를 적고 바르게 고치시오. (3점)

답: (   ), _____

26. 위 글과 일치하지 않는 내용은? (3점)

① 중국 남부 일부 지역의 지붕의 모습은 도넛 모양이다.
② 하카족은 적들로부터 자신들을 보호하기 위해 특별한 모양의 집에서 살아왔다.
③ 집들은 오직 하나의 출입문만 있다.
④ 집들은 주로 4층 건물이다.
⑤ 집은 1층에는 창고가, 2층에는 부엌이 있다.

[27~30] 다음 글을 읽고 물음에 답하시오.

A roof is a(n) (A)_____ part of a house, but long ago some people built roofs only to ⓐtake down them easily. Centuries ago in southern Italy, people (B)지붕이 없는 집을 가진 ⓑpay lower taxes. To avoid high taxes on their houses, some people built cone-shaped roofs ⓒby pile up stones. When tax collectors came to the town, people ⓓtook their roofs down quickly. After the tax collectors left, they ⓔpile up the stones again.

27. 위 글의 ⓐ~ⓔ 중 문법적으로 올바른 것은? (3점)
① ⓐ   ② ⓑ   ③ ⓒ   ④ ⓓ   ⑤ ⓔ

28. 위 글의 빈칸 (A)에 들어갈 단어로 가장 적절한 것은? (2점)
① small   ② essential   ③ tiny
④ enough   ⑤ unnecessary

29. Why did people in southern Italy take their roofs down quickly? (3점)
① 높은 세금이 부과되는 것을 피하기 위해서
② 자연과의 조화를 이루기 위해서
③ 세금 징수원들이 높은 지붕을 싫어했기 때문에
④ 높은 지붕이 필요 없었기 때문에
⑤ 적들로부터 그들을 보호하기 위해서

30. 위 글의 (B) 문장은 관계대명사가 포함된 문장이다. 밑줄 친 (B)의 해석에 맞게 빈칸에 알맞은 영어 단어를 순서대로 쓰시오. (5점)

지붕이 없는 집을 가진 (과거형)

답: _____ _____ a _____ _____ a _____

31. 다음 문장이 들어갈 곳으로 알맞은 것은? (3점)

Since then, many people have visited this unique building.

(A) Sejong National Library is in Sejong, Korea. (B) It is a four-story building that looks like an open book. (C) It has about 400 thousand books on the first and second floors and a large cafeteria on the top floor. (D) It opened in 2013. (E)

① (A)   ② (B)   ③ (C)   ④ (D)   ⑤ (E)

32. 다음 글의 빈칸 (A)와 (B)에 알맞은 것끼리 바르게 연결한 것은? (3점)

A roof is an essential part of a house, but long ago some people built roofs only to take them down easily. Centuries ago in southern Italy, people who had a house without a roof paid lower taxes. To avoid high waxes on their houses, some people built cone-shaped roofs by (A)_____ up stones. When tax collectors came to the town, people took their roofs down quickly. After the tax collectors left, they (B)_____ up the stones again.

	(A)	(B)
①	piling	piles
②	piling	piled
③	piling	pile
④	piled	piling
⑤	piled	piled

◎ 선택형 문항의 답안은 컴퓨터용 수정 싸인펜을 사용하여 OMR 답안지에 바르게 표기하시오.
◎ 서술형 문제는 답을 답안지에 반드시 검정 볼펜으로 쓰시오.
◎ 총 30문항 100점 만점입니다. 문항별 배점은 각 문항에 표시되어 있습니다.

[경기 ○○중]

1. 다음 중 문맥상 단어의 쓰임이 적절한 것은?　(4점)

Have you ever seen a goat on the roof of a house? In Norway, we can see ①floors on roofs. Norway has large forests. In ②jump with nature, people have built wooden houses for a long time. To build strong and ③warm houses, they cover their roofs with grass. The grass roofs protect them from the long cold winters and ④fresh winds. Sometimes, trees or plants grow out of the grass roofs, and some animals enjoy their ⑤talent there.

[경북 ○○중]

2. 다음 중 동사의 3단 변화가 **틀린** 것은?　(2점)

① put - put - put
② ride - rode - riden
③ wear - wore - worn
④ find - found - found
⑤ swim - swam - swum

[전북 ○○중]

3. 다음 중 밑줄 친 부분의 쓰임이 <보기>와 같은 것은?
　(2점)

<보기> I <u>have seen</u> the movie before.

① He <u>has lost</u> his cell phone.
② The man <u>has gone</u> to London.
③ <u>Have</u> you ever <u>eaten</u> tacos?
④ She <u>has wanted</u> to be a singer.
⑤ They <u>haven't finished</u> the report yet.

[충북 ○○중]

4. What's the topic in the dialogue?　(3점)

Nayeong: Take a look at this special house in the picture. It's upside down.
Jaseon: Oh, it looks interesting, but I think it's strange.
Nayeong: What type of house do you want to live in?
Jaseon: I like big things, so I want to live in a big house.

① house
② life
③ nature
④ size
⑤ personality

[강북구 ○○중]

5. 다음 ○○백화점 안내도를 바탕으로, 대화의 (A)와 (B)에 들어갈 단어가 알맞게 짝지어진 것은?　(3점)

○○백화점		
3F	Women's shoes	Restroom
2F	Men's shoes	Bags
1F	Hats	Watches

Woman: Excuse me, where can I find women's shoes?
Man: You can find them on the (A)_____ floor.
Woman: Thank you. How about watches? Where can I find them?
Man: They're on the (B)_____ floor.

	(A)	(B)
①	second	first
②	second	second
③	second	third
④	third	first
⑤	third	second

[6～7] 다음 대화를 읽고 물음에 답하시오.

Woman: Welcome to Jeonju Hanok Guesthouse. May I help you?
Man: Yes, I'd like a room for two nights.
Woman: Well, what kind of room would you like?
Man: Do you have a room with a garden view? You have a lovely garden.
Woman: Yes, we do. Every room in our house has a garden view, but there are no beds in the rooms.
Man: Do I have to sleep on the floor?
Woman: Yes, you do.
Man: O.K. I'll give it a try. (A)_____
_____
Woman: You can have breakfast in the dining room, next to the kitchen.
Man: I see.
Woman: O.K. You're in the Nabi room. Here's your key.
Man: Thank you.

6. 위 대화의 빈칸 (A)에 들어갈 가장 알맞은 것은?

(3점)

① Where is the dining room?
② Where can I have breakfast?
③ When is the breakfast time?
④ Where is Jeonju Hanok Guesthouse?
⑤ What kind of food do you like for breakfast?

7. 위 대화의 내용과 일치하지 않는 것은? (3점)

① 남자는 바닥에서 자야만 한다.
② Guesthouse에는 정원이 있다.
③ 여자는 Guesthouse의 직원이다.
④ Nabi room에서만 정원을 볼 수 있다.
⑤ 남자는 Guesthouse에서 두 번 잘 것이다.

8. 다음 대화의 빈칸에 알맞은 문장을 주어진 조건에 맞게 영어로 쓰시오. (5점)

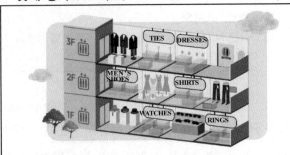

A: Excuse me, _____?
B: You can find them on the second floor. They're next to the elevator.
A: Thank you.

<조건>
1. 동사 find를 사용할 것.
2. 의문문으로 완성할 것.

답: _____

9. 다음 대화에 근거하여 일치하지 않는 내용은? (3점)

A: Excuse me, is there a restaurant in this mall?
B: Yes. What do you want to eat?
A: I want to eat Chinese food.
B: There is a great Chinese restaurant on the fifth floor. It is next to a newly opened Italian restaurant.
A: Thank you.

① A가 찾는 식당은 5층에 있다.
② A는 중국식 식당을 찾고 있다.
③ B는 A가 원하는 답을 알고 있다.
④ 쇼핑센터의 안내 데스크에서 발생한 대화이다.
⑤ 중국식 식당은 이탈리안 레스토랑 옆에 있다.

[10~12] 다음 글을 읽고 물음에 답하시오.

Have you ever ⓐsee a goat on the roof of a house? In Norway, we can see animals on roofs. Norway has large forests. In harmony (A)_____ nature, people have ⓑbuild wooden houses for a long time. To ⓒbuild strong and warm houses, they cover their roofs (A)_____ grass. The grass roofs protect them from the long cold winters and strong winds. Sometimes, trees or plants grow (B)_____ _____ the grass roofs, and some animals enjoy their meals there.

10. 위 글의 ⓐ~ⓒ에 들어갈 동사의 형태로 알맞은 것은? (4점)
   ① ⓐ: saw   ⓑ: building   ⓒ: build
   ② ⓐ: seen   ⓑ: built   ⓒ: build
   ③ ⓐ: seen   ⓑ: building   ⓒ: built
   ④ ⓐ: seen   ⓑ: build   ⓒ: build
   ⑤ ⓐ: saw   ⓑ: built   ⓒ: built

11. 위 글의 빈칸 (A)에 공통으로 들어갈 말로 가장 적절한 것은? (2점)
   ① to   ② for   ③ with
   ④ from   ⑤ on

12. 위 글의 빈칸 (B)에 들어갈 두 단어를 쓰세요. (4점)
   답: _____ _____

[13~14] 다음 글을 읽고 물음에 답하시오.

A roof is an essential part of a house, but long ago some people ⓐbuilt roofs only ⓑto take them down easily. Centuries ago in southern Italy, people ⓒwho had a house without a roof paid lower taxes. (A)_____, some people built cone-shaped roofs ⓓby pile up stones. When tax collectors came to the town, people ⓔtook their roofs down quickly. After the tax collectors left, they piled up the stones again.

13. 위 글의 ⓐ~ⓔ 중 어법상 어색한 것은? (3점)
   ① ⓐ   ② ⓑ   ③ ⓒ   ④ ⓓ   ⑤ ⓔ

14. 위 글의 빈칸 (A)에 가장 적절한 것은? (3점)
   ① To make their houses light
   ② To get high taxes on their houses
   ③ To put a lot of stones on the roof
   ④ To avoid high taxes on their houses
   ⑤ To protect themselves from their house

15. 다음 중 어법상 쓰임이 같은 것끼리 바르게 짝지어진 것은? (4점)

   ⓐ The bus has just arrived.
   ⓑ I have lost my pen.
   ⓒ She has drawn pictures since then.
   ⓓ I have visited Korea twice.
   ⓔ Dean and his friends have finished their project.
   ⓕ Amy has been in Seoul for three months.

   ① ⓐ, ⓒ   ② ⓑ, ⓔ
   ③ ⓒ, ⓕ   ④ ⓐ, ⓑ, ⓔ
   ⑤ ⓒ, ⓓ, ⓕ

16. 다음 글의 ⓐ에 문맥상 가장 알맞은 것은? (3점)

A roof is an essential part of a house, but long ago some people built roofs only to ⓐ_____. Centuries ago in southern Italy, people who had a house without a roof paid lower taxes.
To avoid high taxes on their houses, some people built cone-shaped roofs by piling up stones. When tax collectors came to the town, people took their roofs down quickly. After the tax collectors left, they piled up the stones again.

① pay higher taxes

② take them down easily

③ keep their houses warm

④ pile up the stones again

⑤ protect themselves from enemies

[17~18] 다음 글을 읽고 물음에 답하시오.

Have you ever seen a goat on the roof of a house? In Norway, we can see animals on roofs. Norway has large forests. In harmony with nature, people have built wooden houses for a long time. To build strong and warm houses, they cover their roofs with grass. The grass roofs protect ⓐthem from the long cold winters and strong winds. Sometimes, trees or plants grow out of the grass roofs, and some animals enjoy their meals there.

17. 위 글의 제목으로 가장 적절한 것은? (4점)

① Grass Roofs in Norway

② Cold Winters in Norway

③ Large Forests in Norway

④ Wild Animals in Norway

⑤ Beautiful Towns in Norway

18. 위 글의 밑줄 친 ⓐ가 가리키는 것은? (3점)

① people   ② plants   ③ winters

④ animals   ⑤ forests

[19~20] 다음 글을 읽고 물음에 답하시오.

From the sky in a part of southern China, you can see round roofs that look like big doughnuts. They are the roofs of the big round houses of the Hakka people. They have lived in houses like these for about a thousand years to protect themselves from enemies. The houses have only one gate without any windows on the first floor. Each house is big enough for a whole village. It usually has four stories. It has kitchens on the first floor, storage rooms on the second floor, and living rooms and bedrooms on the third and fourth floors.

19. 위 글의 제목으로 가장 적절한 것은? (3점)

① Village People

② Big Round Roofs

③ Big Window House

④ No Window House

⑤ Two Gates House

20. 위 글의 내용과 일치하는 것은? (4점)

① There is one gate on each floor.

② Few families live in the big round house.

③ There are a few windows on the first floor.

④ There is only one living room in the round house.

⑤ The Hakka people started to live in the big round house about a thousand years ago.

[21~23] 다음 글을 읽고 물음에 답하시오.

[A] From the sky in a part of southern China, you can see round roofs (A)_____ look like big doughnuts. They are the roofs of the big round houses of the Hakka people. ⓐThey have lived in houses like these for about a thousand years to protect themselves from enemies.

[B] The houses have only one gate without any windows on the first floor. Each house (be) big enough for a whole village. It usually has four stories. It has kitchens on the first floor, storage rooms on the second floor, and living rooms and bedrooms on the third and fourth floors.

21. 위 글의 설명 방식으로 볼 때 [A]와 [B]의 관계로 가장 알맞은 것은? (4점)

① 설명 - 원인　　　② 주장 - 반박
③ 예시 - 예시　　　④ 원인 - 결과
⑤ 주장 - 예시

22. 위 글의 [A]에서 빈칸 (A)에 들어갈 말과 ⓐThey 가 가리키는 말을 각각 쓰시오. (4점)

(A) _____

ⓐ They: _____

23. 위 글의 [B]에서 괄호 안의 (be)의 알맞은 말을 쓰시오. (3점)

답: _____

24. 주어진 글 다음에 이어질 글의 순서로 가장 적절한 것은? (4점)

A roof is an essential part of a house, but long ago some people built roofs only to take them down easily.

(A) To avoid high taxes on their houses, some people built cone-shaped roofs by piling up stones.
(B) Centuries ago in southern Italy, people who had a house without a roof paid lower taxes.
(C) After the tax collectors left, they piled up the stones again.
(D) When tax collectors came to the town, people took their roofs down quickly

① (A)-(C)-(D)-(B)
② (A)-(B)-(D)-(C)
③ (B)-(A)-(D)-(C)
④ (B)-(D)-(C)-(A)
⑤ (C)-(B)-(A)-(D)

25. 다음 대화의 의도로 알맞은 것은? (3점)

A: What kind of music do you want to listen to?
B: I want to listen to K-pop.

① 경험 묻고 대답하기
② 권유하기
③ 변명하기
④ 의향 묻고 답하기
⑤ 인물의 특징 말하기

[26~28] 다음 글을 읽고, 물음에 답하시오.

From the sky in a part of southern China, you can see round roofs that look like big doughnuts. They are the roofs of the big round houses of the Hakka people. ⓐThey built houses like these to protect themselves from enemies. The houses have only one gate without any windows on the first floor. These houses usually have four stories. They have kitchens on the first floor, storage rooms on the second floor, and living rooms and bedrooms on the third and fourth floors.

26. 위 글의 제목으로 알맞은 것은? (3점)

① Roofs in Italy
② How Grass Roofs are Made
③ Who are the Hakka People?
④ Houses with Big Round Roofs
⑤ The Weather in Southern China

27. 위 글의 내용과 일치하는 것은? (4점)

① 둥근 지붕은 중국의 동부 지역에서 볼 수 있다.
② 하카족은 직사각형 지붕을 사용하고 있다.
③ 하카족들의 집의 2층에는 창고가 있다.
④ 하카족들의 집은 대문이 둘 이상이다.
⑤ 하카족들의 집은 보통 3층 구조이다.

28. 위 글의 밑줄 친 문장 ⓐ를 다음과 같이 고칠 때, 빈칸에 들어갈 접속사로 가장 적절한 것은? (3점)

They built houses like these _____ they wanted to protect themselves from enemies.

① because ② but ③ so
④ before ⑤ or

[29~30] 다음 글을 읽고 물음에 답하시오.

From the sky in a part of southern China, you can see round roofs that look like big doughnuts. They are the roofs of the big round houses of the Hakka people. They have lived in houses like these for about a thousand years to protect themselves from enemies. The houses have only one gate without any windows on the first floor. ⓐ각각의 집은 전체 마을이 들어갈 정도로 충분히 크다. It usually has four stories. It has kitchens on the first floor, storage rooms on the second floor, and living rooms and bedrooms on the third and fourth floors.

29. 위 글의 'round roofs'에 관해 올바른 것은? (3점)

① They usually have three stories.
② They are in a part of southern Korea.
③ They protect the Hakka people from animals.
④ There are kitchens and storage rooms in them.
⑤ They have many windows on the first floor.

30. 위 글의 밑줄 친 ⓐ와 의미가 같은 문장은? (4점)

① Each houses is big enough for a whole village
② Each house are big enough for a whole village.
③ Each house is enough big for a whole village.
④ Each house is big enough for a whole village.
⑤ Each houses is enough big for a whole village.

2학년 영어 1학기 기말고사(3과) 1회

반		점수
이름		

문항수 : 선택형(29문항) 서술형(6문항)　　20 ． ． ．

◎ 선택형 문항의 답안은 컴퓨터용 수정 싸인펜을
　사용하여 OMR 답안지에 바르게 표기하시오.
◎ 서술형 문제는 답을 답안지에 반드시 검정
　볼펜으로 쓰시오.
◎ 총 35문항 100점 만점입니다. 문항별 배점
　은 각 문항에 표시되어 있습니다.

[충남 ㅇㅇ중]

1. 다음 설명하는 단어로 가장 알맞은 것은?　　(2점)

> a flat dish, from which food is served

① portrait　　② journal　　③ plate
④ object　　⑤ avatar

[부산 ㅇㅇ중]

2. 다음 글의 (a)와 (b)에 들어갈 말이 알맞게 짝지어
　진 것은?　　(3점)

> Good morning, and welcome to the weather
> (a)_____. It's sunny outside, but we're
> (b)_____ some rain in the afternoon.
> Don't leave home without your umbrella.
> That's the weather (a)_____ for today.
> Have a nice day!

	(a)	(b)
①	chart	changing
②	check	enjoying
③	report	starting
④	forecast	expecting
⑤	journal	stopping

[동작구 ㅇㅇ중]

3. 다음 대화의 흐름상 어울리지 않는 것은? (2개) (3점)

> A: Have you ever _____ Indian food?
> B: Yes, but only Indian curry.
> A: How was it?
> B: It was really hot. I didn't like it.

① tried　　　　② eaten
③ had　　　　④ drunk
⑤ taken

[전북 ㅇㅇ중]

[4~6] 다음 대화를 읽고 물음에 답하시오.

> Suho: Anna, have you been to Australia
> 　before?
> Anna: Yes. (A)_____, I lived in Sydney
> 　for a year.
> Suho: Great! How's the weather there in
> 　April? I'm going to visit Sydney on
> 　vacation next week.
> Anna: April is a great time to visit Sydney.
> 　In April, it's autumn in Australia.
> Suho: Good. <u>I'm planning to</u> spend some
> 　time on the beach and relax in the sun.
> Anna: Well, it often rains in April, but you
> 　may have some sunny days.
> Suho: I'll take my hat and pack an umbrella,
> 　too.
> Anna: That's a good idea. Have a great trip.

4. 위 대화의 빈칸 (A)에 'in fact'의 의미로 쓸 수 있는
　것은?　　(2점)

① Actually　　② So　　③ Because
④ When　　⑤ But

5. 위 대화의 밑줄 친 'I'm planning to'와 바꾸어 쓸
　수 있는 것은?　　(2점)

① I can　　　　② I must
③ I'm going to　　④ I have to
⑤ I don't know

6. 위 대화에서 다음의 의미를 가진 동사를 쓰시오. (3점)

> to put things into cases or bags for journey

→ _____

- 25 -

7. 다음 대화의 빈칸에 들어갈 가장 알맞은 것은? (2점)

A: Have you ever tried Indian food?
B: _____, but I've only tried Indian curry.
A: How was it?
B: It was really hot, but I loved it.

① Yes, I am
② No, I didn't
③ I'm afraid I can't
④ You're welcome
⑤ Yes, I have

8. 다음 문장을 문맥에 맞게 배열한 것은? (3점)

ⓐ How was the weather there?
ⓑ Yes, I have. I went to Ulleungdo last summer with my family.
ⓒ It was mostly sunny but the weather changed often.
ⓓ Have you been to any special places in Korea?

① ⓐ-ⓒ-ⓓ-ⓑ   ② ⓒ-ⓐ-ⓓ-ⓑ
③ ⓓ-ⓒ-ⓐ-ⓑ   ④ ⓐ-ⓑ-ⓓ-ⓒ
⑤ ⓓ-ⓑ-ⓐ-ⓒ

9. 다음 중 빈칸에 들어갈 말이 <u>다른</u> 것은? (2점)

① How can I learn to _____ kickboxing?
② I don't like to _____ computer games.
③ My mom wants me to _____ the piano.
④ Many people _____ badminton in the park.
⑤ How often do you _____ tennis on Sunday?

10. 대화를 읽고 질문에 가장 알맞은 답은? (2점)

B: Mom, how's the weather today? Do I need an umbrella?
W: It's quite cloudy outside. I'll check the weather forecast.
B: Thank you, Mom.
W: Well, it's not going to rain today.
B: Good! Then, I don't need an umbrella today.

Q: Why doesn't the boy take his umbrella?

① 집에 우산이 없어서
② 비가 예상되지 않아서
③ 학교에 놓고 와서
④ 일기예보를 확인하지 못해서
⑤ 날씨가 맑아져서

11. 다음 중 짝지어진 대화가 <u>어색한</u> 것은? (3점)

① A: What are you doing?
   B: I'm making a smart phone case out of my old jeans.
② A: Is something wrong?
   B: I have to give a speech in front of the whole school. I'm so nervous.
③ A: Well, it's not going to rain today.
   B: Good! Then, I need an umbrella today.
④ A: Tomorrow is my mom's birthday. What should I do for her?
   B: Why don't you bake a cake for her?
⑤ A: Hey, look at this house in the picture. It looks like a big shoe!
   B: Oh, it's very unique, but I don't want to live in a shoe.

[12~13] 다음 대화를 읽고 물음에 답하시오.

> Suho: Anna, have you been to Australia before?
>
> Anna: Yes, I have. Actually, I lived in Sydney for a year.
>
> Suho: Great! How's the weather there in April? I'm going to visit Sydney on vacation next week.
>
> Anna: April is a great time @to visit Sydney. In April, it's autumn in Australia.
>
> Suho: Good. I'm planning to spend some time on the beach and relax in the sun.
>
> Anna: Well, it often rains in April, but you may have some sunny days.
>
> Suho: I'll take my hat and pack an umbrella, too.
>
> Anna: That's a good idea. Have a great trip.

12. 위 대화의 내용과 일치하는 것은? (3점)

① Anna still lives in Sydney.

② Suho will buy an umbrella in Sydney.

③ Anna knows well about the weather of Sydney.

④ Suho is asking Anna about the foods in Sydney.

⑤ Suho is going to visit Sydney next week with Anna.

13. 위 대화의 밑줄 친 @와 쓰임이 같은 것은? (3점)

① Is there a place to visit near hear?

② It is great to visit the Hanok village.

③ He decided to visit his grandmother.

④ I will go to America to visit my friends.

⑤ It was kind of her to visit me when I was sick.

[14~15] 다음을 읽고 물음에 답하시오.

> August 5
>
> At last, we set foot at Stonehenge, one of the most mysterious places on Earth. @After a two-hour drive from our home in London, we finally got to Stonehenge. ⓑTo see the ring of huge stones was just amazing. ⓒDon't try to make a perfect drawing. ⓓHow did those huge stones get there thousands of years ago? ⓔWhat were they for? I guess Stonehenge (A)_____ for a long time.

14. 위 글에서 전체 흐름과 관계가 없는 문장은? (3점)

① @   ② ⓑ   ③ ⓒ   ④ ⓓ   ⑤ ⓔ

15. 위 글의 문맥상 (A)에 들어갈 가장 알맞은 표현을 아래 〈보기〉의 표현을 사용하여 재배열하시오. (3점)

> 〈보기〉
> a mystery / remain / will

정답: _____

16. 다음 글의 @~ⓔ 중 가리키는 대상이 <u>다른</u> 것은?

(3점)

> When we were outside Christ Church College, @I walked to the famous olive tree and touched it. "Because ⓑI touched this tree," I said, "I will get into Oxford University!" Then, my brother said to ⓒme with a smile, "ⓓI can't wait to see ⓔyour portrait on the wall."

① @   ② ⓑ   ③ ⓒ   ④ ⓓ   ⑤ ⓔ

- 27 -

[17~20] 다음 글을 읽고 물음에 답하시오.

August 6
In the morning, we walked around the Cotswolds. <u>It started to rain in the afternoon, so we decided staying indoors at our B&B.</u> A B&B is a popular place to stay in England. It feels more like a home than a hotel. The owner invited us for afternoon tea today. The dining table was full of cookies, cake, bread, and cheese. While I was busy (A)_____, Mom was admiring the beautiful cups and plates. I ate too much, (B)_____ I couldn't eat anything for dinner.

17. 위 글의 빈칸 (A)에 알맞은 것은?　　　(3점)
① to eat　　② eat　　③ eating
④ of eating　　⑤ by eating

18. 위 글의 빈칸 (B)에 알맞은 것은?　　　(2점)
① for　　② so　　③ when
④ or　　⑤ that

19. 위 글의 내용과 일치하지 않는 것은?　　(3점)
① 오후에는 비가 오기 시작했다.
② 글쓴이는 저녁을 아무것도 먹지 않았다.
③ 글쓴이의 가족은 오후에 실내에 머물렀다.
④ B&B는 영국에서 머물기에 인기 있는 곳이다.
⑤ 글쓴이는 오후에 코츠월드 주변을 걸어 다녔다.

20. 위 글의 밑줄 친 부분에서 어법상 <u>어색한</u> 것을 찾아 바르게 고쳐 쓰시오.　　(3점)

정답: _____ → _____

21. (A)를 어법에 맞게 영작한 문장은?　　(2점)

Last summer, I went to Laos with my family. We visited a lot of beautiful temples and went to the night market in Vientiane. Then, we moved to Vang Vieng and went river tubing. We also enjoyed their traditional food. (A)(a lot of fun / was / it / new things / to try) in a foreign country. I hope to visit there again.

① A lot of fun to try new things was it
② It was new things to try a lot of fun
③ It was a lot of fun to try new things
④ It was to fun a lot of new things try
⑤ Was it a lot of new things to fun to try

22. 다음 문장에서 틀린 부분을 찾아 바르게 고치시오. (고친 후 문장 전체를 다시 쓰시오.)　　(5점)
(1) It is dangerous for we to swim in the sea.
→ _____
(2) It was very nice for him to give us a gift.
→ _____
(3) It is fun to talking with you.
→ _____

23. 다음 〈A〉의 뜻이 되도록 주어진 단어를 배열할 때 5번째 오는 단어는?　　(3점)

〈A〉 공기 없이 사는 것은 불가능하다.
is / air / to / impossible / without / it / live

① is　　② it　　③ air
④ live　　⑤ impossible

[24~26] 다음 글을 읽고 물음에 답하시오.

> August 7
> Our last stop was Oxford. We first visited ⓐ <u>Christ Church College</u>. It has become a world famous place to visit (A)_____ ⓑ<u>it</u> appeared in the *Harry Potter* movies. In the movies, Harry and everyone else eat dinner at the Hall of Christ Church. We also saw portraits of famous people who graduated from ⓒ<u>the college</u>. (B)_____ we were outside ⓓ<u>the building</u>, I walked to the famous olive tree and touched it. "Because I touched ⓔ<u>this</u>." I said, "I will get into Oxford University!" Then, my brother said to me with a smile, "I can't wait to see your portrait on the wall."

24. 위 글의 종류로 가장 알맞은 것은? (3점)

① 시 　　　 ② 소설 　　　 ③ 동화
④ 설명문 　　 ⑤ 기행문

25. 위 글의 밑줄 친 ⓐ~ⓔ 중, 가리키는 대상이 나머지 넷과 <u>다른</u> 것은? (3점)

① Christ Church College ② it
③ the college ④ the building
⑤ this

26. 위 글의 빈칸 (A)와 (B)에 들어갈 말이 순서대로 짝지어진 것은? (3점)

① if － After 　　　 ② if － When
③ since － When 　　 ④ since － If
⑤ when － Because

27. 어법상 적절한 것을 고르시오. (2점)

① It is not easy to raising pets.
② It is useful to learn how to use a computer.
③ It is importantly for him to pass the exam.
④ It is true that Jin like Suji.
⑤ It is nice that going out with friends on weekend.

28. 다음 빈칸 (A)~(E) 중 어느 곳에도 쓸 수 <u>없는</u> 것은? (3점)

> • Have you ever (A)_____ a marathon?
> • Have you ever (B)_____ *Harry Potter*?
> • Have you ever (C)_____ a motorcycle?
> • Have you ever (D)_____ a famous star?
> • Have you ever (E)_____ tacos at home?

① eaten 　　 ② met 　　 ③ read
④ rode 　　 ⑤ run

29. 다음 우리말과 같도록 주어진 단어를 사용하여 문장을 완성하시오. [주의] 반드시 주어진 단어들을 이용하여 답할 것. 대·소문자에 유의할 것 (5점)

> (1) 패션 디자이너가 되는 것은 어렵다. (a fashion designer / it / difficult / to become / is)

> (2) 지금이 인도를 방문할 가장 좋은 계절이다. (this / to visit / is / the best season / India)

(1) 정답: _____

(2) 정답: _____

[30~34] 다음 글을 읽고 물음에 답하시오.

> I made simple drawings in my journal. ⓐ그건 모든 특별한 순간을 포착하는 데 좋은 방법이었어. August 5 – At last, we ⓑset foot at Stonehenge, one of the most mysterious places (A)_____ Earth. After a two-hour drive (B)_____ our home in London, we finally got (C)_____ Stonehenge. ⓒTo see the ring of huge stones was just amazing. How did those huge stones get there thousands of years ago? What were they (D)_____? I guess Stonehenge will remain a mystery for a long time.

30. 위 글의 ⓐ 문장은 to부정사가 포함된 문장이다. 위 ⓐ의 해석에 맞게 빈칸에 알맞은 영어 단어를 순서대로 쓰시오. (4점)

> - 그건 모든 특별한 순간을 포착하는 데 좋은 방법이었어. (과거형)
> → That _____ a great _____ _____ _____ all the special moments.

답: _____ _____ _____ _____

31. 위 글의 ⓑset foot의 해석으로 가장 적절한 것은? (2점)

① 발을 들여놓다　② 길을 돌리다

③ 헤매다　　　　④ 남아 있다

⑤ 시작하다

32. 위 글의 빈칸 (A)~(D) 안에는 각각 다른 전치사가 들어간다. 아래의 보기 중 빈칸 (A)~(D) 안에 들어갈 수 없는 전치사는? (4점)

① on　　　② by　　　③ for

④ to　　　⑤ from

33. 위 글의 ⓒ를 가주어 It으로 시작하는 문장으로 바꿀 때 옳은 문장은? (2점)

① It is to see the ring of huge stones was just amazing.

② It was just amazing that see the ring of huge stones.

③ It is just amazing that see the ring of huge stones.

④ It was just amazing to see the ring of huge stones.

⑤ It is just amazing to see the ring of huge stones.

34. 위 글과 일치하지 않는 내용은? (3점)

① 스톤헨지는 지구상에서 가장 불가사의한 장소 중 하나이다.

② 스톤헨지는 런던에서 거리가 차로 약 2시간 정도이다.

③ 글쓴이의 집은 런던에 있다.

④ 거대한 돌들이 어떻게 도달하였는지 글쓴이는 알아냈다.

⑤ 글쓴이는 스톤헨지가 미스터리로 남을 것으로 생각한다.

35. 다음 중 밑줄 친 부분의 쓰임이 같은 것끼리 묶인 것은? (3점)

> ⓐ I need a book to read on the train.
> ⓑ He went to China to learn Chinese.
> ⓒ They don't have anything to drink.
> ⓓ I wanted to go to England.

① ⓐ, ⓒ　　　② ⓑ, ⓒ　　　③ ⓑ, ⓓ

④ ⓐ, ⓑ, ⓒ　　　⑤ ⓑ, ⓒ, ⓓ

◎ 선택형 문항의 답안은 컴퓨터용 수정 싸인펜을 사용하여 OMR 답안지에 바르게 표기하시오.
◎ 서술형 문제는 답을 답안지에 반드시 검정 볼펜으로 쓰시오.
◎ 총 35문항 100점 만점입니다. 문항별 배점은 각 문항에 표시되어 있습니다.

[전북 ○○중]

1. 다음 글의 내용과 관련이 있는 직업은?　　(2점)

Good morning, and welcome to the weather forecast. It's sunny outside, but we're expecting some rain in the afternoon. Don't leave home without your umbrella. That's the weather forecast for today. Have a nice day!

① fire fighter
② policeman
③ weather reporter
④ salesperson
⑤ nurse

[전북 ○○중]

[2~3] 다음 대화를 읽고 물음에 답하시오.

Yura: Have you (A)_____ tried Indian food?
Kevin: Yes, I have, but I've only tried Indian curry.
Yura: How was it?
Kevin: (B)_____

2. 위 대화의 빈칸 (A)에 들어갈 말로 가장 적절한 것은?　　(2점)

① after
② ever
③ never
④ each
⑤ been

3. 위 대화의 빈칸 (B)에 들어갈 문장으로 가장 적절한 것은?　　(3점)

① I will love it.
② Actually, it was so scary.
③ It was quite hot, but I enjoyed it a lot.
④ I wanted to be like him.
⑤ I am fine. Thank you.

[경기 ○○중]

4. 다음 뜻풀이에 맞게 대화의 빈칸에 알맞은 단어를 쓰시오.　　(4점)

Brian: Mom, how's the weather today?
Mom: It's (1)q_____ cloudy outside. I'll check the weather (2)f_____.
Brian: Thanks, Mom.
Mom: Well, it's going to rain the afternoon.

(1) very, completely and really: _____

(2) a statement of future events you can expect: _____

[전북 ○○중]

5. 다음 대화의 (A)에 들어갈 가장 적절한 표현은?　　(2점)

Seho: Ann, have you ever gone bungee jumping before?
Ann: (A)_____
Seho: Wasn't it scary?
Ann: No, I liked it a lot. I want to do it again.

① Yes, I have.
② No, I don't.
③ No, I haven't.
④ Yes, I haven't.
⑤ Yes, I don't have it.

[동작구 ○○중]

6. 다음 대화의 흐름상 빈칸에 들어갈 단어는?　　(3점)

A: How's the weather today?
B: -15℃ in the afternoon! It's _____.
A: Then I need a very warm coat.

① sunny
② cloudy
③ rainy
④ freezing
⑤ hot

[7~11] 다음 대화를 읽고 물음에 답하시오.

Suho: Anna, have you been to Australia (A)_____?

Anna: Yes, I have. Actually, I lived in Sydney for a year.

Suho: Great! How's the weather there in April?

Anna: April is a great time to visit Sydney. In April, it's ⓐautumn in Australia.

Suho: Good. I'm planning (B)_____ some time on the beach and relax in the sun.

Anna: Well, it often rains in April, but you ⓑ~일지 모른다 have some sunny days.

Suho: I'll take my hat and pack an umbrella, too.

7. What are the speakers talking about? (2점)

① places to go in Sydney

② the weather in Sydney in April

③ tourist attractions in April

④ the four seasons in Australia

⑤ the reason why Anna has been to Australia

8. 위 대화의 빈칸 (A)에 들어갈 말로 적절한 것은? (3점)

① after　　② from　　③ before

④ for　　⑤ later

9. 위 대화의 빈칸 (B)에 들어갈 형태로 적절한 것은?

(2점)

① to spend　　② spend　　③ spent

④ spending　　⑤ spending

10. 위 대화의 ⓐautumn 대신에 쓸 수 있는 한 단어의 영어를 쓰시오. (2점)

→ autumn = _____

11. 위 대화의 밑줄 친 ⓑ'~일지 모른다'의 의미와 일치하는 단어는? (2점)

① may　　② must　　③ will

④ have to　　⑤ should

12. 다음 중 대화가 어색한 것은? (2점)

① A: How did you like the movie?
   B: It wasn't good, but I enjoyed it.

② A: What's it like outside?
   B: I'm sure it's going to rain soon.

③ A: Have you ever been to Paris?
   B: No, I didn't.

④ A: What are you doing this weekend, Eric?
   B: Nothing special.

⑤ A: How long does it take from the school to the station?
   B: It takes 30 minutes.

13. 다음 (A)~(D)를 대화의 흐름상 가장 알맞게 배열한 것은? (3점)

(A) Oh, it's not going to be rain.
(B) I'll check the weather forecast.
(C) Thank you.
(D) Mom, do I need an umbrella?

① (B)-(A)-(D)-(C)

② (B)-(C)-(D)-(A)

③ (B)-(D)-(A)-(C)

④ (D)-(A)-(C)-(B)

⑤ (D)-(B)-(C)-(A)

14. 다음 (A)에 들어갈 가장 알맞은 표현은? (3점)

Good morning, and welcome to the weather forecast. It's windy and rainy outside, but we're expecting (A)_____ in the afternoon. So, don't forget to take your hat and wear sunblock when you leave home. That's the weather forecast for today. Have a great day!

① to be cloudy

② to be snowy

③ to be smoggy

④ to be sunny

⑤ to be windy

16. 위 글의 밑줄 친 (A)got to와 바꿔 쓸 수 있는 것은? (3점)

① reached   ② started

③ entered   ④ appeared

⑤ captured

17. 위 글의 내용과 일치하지 않는 것은? (2점)

① Lucy는 여행 중에 그림을 그렸다.

② Lucy는 3일 동안 휴가를 떠났다.

③ 런던에서 스톤헨지까지는 한 시간이 걸렸다.

④ 글쓴이는 스톤헨지의 미스터리가 오랫동안 남아 있을 거라고 생각한다.

⑤ 스톤헨지는 지구상에서 가장 불가사의한 장소이다.

[15~17] 다음 글을 읽고 물음에 답하시오.

Hi, I am Lucy Hunter, and I live in London. Last week, my family ⓐwent on a vacation for three days. During our trip, I ⓑmade simple drawings in my journal. That was a great way ⓒto capture all the special moments.

August 5

At last, we ⓓset foot at Stonehenge, one of the most mysterious places on Earth. After a two-hour drive from our home in London, we finally (A)got to Stonehenge. It was just ⓔamazed to see the ring of huge stones. How did those huge stones get there thousands of years ago? What were they for? I guess Stonehenge will remain a mystery for a long time.

15. 위 글의 밑줄 친 ⓐ~ⓔ에서 어법상 어색한 것은? (3점)

① ⓐ   ② ⓑ   ③ ⓒ   ④ ⓓ   ⑤ ⓔ

18. 다음 글의 빈칸 (A)에 가장 알맞은 것은? (3점)

Good morning, and welcome to the weather forecast. It's sunny outside, but we're expecting some rain in the afternoon. (A)_____ That's the weather forecast for today.

① It means today is very hot all day.

② It will be wonderful to go on a picnic.

③ Please remember to take your umbrella.

④ Don't leave home without your sunglasses!

⑤ How about making a snowman in the afternoon?

19. 다음 문장을 가주어 it을 이용하여 다시 쓰시오. (3점)

• To find your dream is important.

→ _____

답: _____

[20~22] 다음을 읽고 물음에 답하시오.

August 6

In the morning, we walked around the Cotswolds. It ⓐstarted to rain in the afternoon, so we ⓑdecided to stay indoors at our B&B. A B&B is (A)머물기에 인기 있는 곳 in England. It feels more like a home than a hotel. The owner invited us for afternoon tea today. The dining table ⓒwas full of cookies, cake, bread, and cheese. While I ⓓwas busy eat, Mom was ⓔadmiring the beautiful cups and plates. I ate too much, so I couldn't eat anything for dinner.

20. 위 글의 내용과 일치하는 것은? (3점)

① 코츠월드 주변을 오후에 걸어다녔다.

② 나는 아름다운 컵과 접시에 감탄했다.

③ 하루 종일 비가 와서 숙소에 머물렀다.

④ 저녁을 너무 많이 먹어서 속이 좋지 않았다.

⑤ 비앤비는 호텔보다는 오히려 집처럼 더 느껴졌다.

21. 위 글의 밑줄 친 ⓐ~ⓔ 중, 어법상 어색한 것은? (2점)

① ⓐ   ② ⓑ   ③ ⓒ   ④ ⓓ   ⑤ ⓔ

22. 위 글의 (A)를 주어진 표현을 활용해 어법에 맞게 영작하시오. (3점)

<보기>
stay / place / popular
*밑줄 한 칸당 한 단어씩 쓰되, 필요시 단어를 추가해 쓰시오.

정답: a p_____ _____ _____ _____

[23~24] 다음 글을 읽고, 물음에 답하시오.

At last, we ⓐset foot at Stonehenge, one of the most mysterious places on Earth. After a two-hour drive from our home in London, we finally ⓑgot to Stonehenge. (A)원형으로 둘러서 있는 거대한 돌들을 보는 것은 정말 굉장했어 (huge stones, see, ring, amazing). How did those huge stones ⓒget there thousands of years ago? ⓓWhat were they for? I guess Stonehenge ⓔwill remain a mystery for a long time.

23. 위 글의 밑줄 친 ⓐ~ⓔ를 우리말로 <u>잘못</u> 해석한 것은? (3점)

① ⓐ: 들어섰다

② ⓑ: 도착했다

③ ⓒ: 도달하다

④ ⓓ: 그것들은 얼마 동안 있었을까?

⑤ ⓔ: 불가사의로 남을 것이다

24. 위 글의 밑줄 친 (A)를 괄호 안에 주어진 단어를 모두 활용하여 '가주어-진주어' 구문으로 영작하시오. (4점)

→ _____

25. 다음 문장을 괄호 안의 단어를 사용하여 완성하시오. (3점)

James는 이야기할 친구가 거의 없다. (talk)

→ James has few friends _____ _____

_____.

- 34 -

[26~28] 다음 글을 읽고 물음에 답하시오.

Hi, I am Lucy Hunter, and I live in London. Last week, my family (A)[went / have gone] on a vacation for three days. (B)[During / While] I was on the trip, I made simple drawings in my journal to capture all the special moments.

August 5

At last, we ⓐset foot at Stonehenge, one of the most mysterious places on Earth. After a two-hour drive from our home in London, we finally got to Stonehenge. It was just amazing (C)[to see / to have seen] the ring of huge stones. How did those huge stones get there thousands of years ago? What were they for? I guess Stonehenge will ⓑremain a mysterious place for a long time.

August 6

In the morning, we walked around the Cotswolds. It started to rain in the afternoon, so we decided to stay indoors at our ⓒB&B. A B&B is a popular place to stay in England. It feels more like a home than a hotel. The owner invited us for afternoon tea today. The dining table was full of cookies, cake, bread, and cheese. While I was busy eating, Mom was ⓓadmiring the beautiful cups and ⓔplates. I ate too much, so I couldn't eat anything for dinner.

26. 위 글의 (A)~(C)에 들어갈 말을 바르게 연결한 것은? (3점)

	(A)	(B)	(C)
①	have gone	While	to see
②	went	While	to see
③	went	While	to have seen
④	have gone	During	to have seen
⑤	went	During	to have seen

27. 위 글의 내용과 일치하는 것은? (3점)

① Lucy enjoyed afternoon tea that the owner offered.

② Lucy's family decided to stay in London for three days.

③ Lucy stayed indoors because it rained all day long on August 6.

④ Lucy thought B&B, a popular place in England, is like hotel than a home.

⑤ Lucy's family ate cookies, cake, bread, and cheese at the B&B for dinner.

28. 위 글의 ⓐ~ⓔ의 영어 뜻풀이가 가장 적절한 것은? (3점)

① ⓐset foot: to leave a place, especially to start a trip

② ⓑremain: to appear again and come into view after having hidden

③ ⓒB&B: a hotel for bread and bed

④ ⓓadmire: to look at something and think that it is attractive

⑤ ⓔplate: a style of cooking in a very expensive restaurant

29. 괄호 안의 단어를 사용하여 우리말을 영어로 옮기시오. (주어를 'It'으로 시작할 것.) (5점)

(1) 나를 도와주다니 그는 참 친절했다.
(very kind, help)

→ It _____.

(2) 규칙적으로 운동하는 것은 중요하다.
(important, exercise)

→ _____

[30~31] 다음 글을 읽고 물음에 답하시오.

August 7

Our last stop was Oxford. We first visited Christ Church College. It (A)[became / has become] a world famous place to visit since it appeared in the *Harry Potter* movies. In the movies, Harry and everyone else (B)[eat / eats] dinner at the Hall of Christ Church. We also saw portraits of famous people who graduated from the college. When we were outside the building, I walked to the famous olive tree and touched it. "Because I touched this tree," I said. "I will get into Oxford University!" Then, my brother said to me with a smile. "I (C)[can / can't] wait to see your portrait on the wall."

30. 위 글의 괄호 (A)~(C) 중 어법이나 문맥상 알맞은 것은? (3점)

	(A)	(B)	(C)
①	became	eat	can
②	became	eats	can't
③	has become	eat	can
④	has become	eats	can't
⑤	has become	eat	can't

31. 위 글의 내용으로 옳은 것은? (3점)

① 글쓴이는 *Harry Potter* 영화를 가장 좋아한다.

② Hall of Christ Church는 영화 속에서 식당으로 등장한다.

③ 글쓴이의 오빠는 Oxford University에 들어오고 싶어한다.

④ Hall of Christ Church 벽면에는 영화 속 등장인물의 사진이 붙어 있다.

⑤ Hall of Christ Church 건물 안쪽에는 유명한 올리브나무가 한 그루 있다.

[32~33] 괄호 안의 단어를 알맞게 바꾸어 문장 전체를 답안지에 옮겨 쓰시오.

32. Watching movies is a good way _____ English. (learn) (3점)

→ _____

33. It is easy _____ a cold in the winter. (catch) (3점)

→ _____

34. 다음 밑줄 친 ⓐ~ⓔ 중 어법상 어색한 것은? (3점)

Hi, I am Lucy Hunter, and I live ⓐin London. Last week, my family went on a vacation ⓑfor three days. ⓒDuring our trip, I ⓓmade simple drawings in my journal. That was a great way ⓔcapture all the special moments.

① ⓐ　　② ⓑ　　③ ⓒ　　④ ⓓ　　⑤ ⓔ

35. 다음 주어진 우리말에 맞도록 괄호 안의 단어들을 배열하여 문장을 완성할 때, 빈칸 (A)에 들어갈 단어는? (4점)

그것은 모든 특별한 순간을 포착하기에 좋은 방법이었다.

(all / a / the / great / moments / to / was / capture / special / way)

→ That _____ _____ _____ (A) _____ _____ _____ _____.

① a　　　　② to　　　　③ way

④ special　　⑤ capture

◎ 선택형 문항의 답안은 컴퓨터용 수정 싸인펜을 사용하여 OMR 답안지에 바르게 표기하시오.
◎ 서술형 문제는 답을 답안지에 반드시 검정 볼펜으로 쓰시오.
◎ 총 31문항 100점 만점입니다. 문항별 배점은 각 문항에 표시되어 있습니다.

[충북 ○○중]

1. 다음 글을 바탕으로 빈칸에 가장 알맞은 말을 고르면? (2점)

Hello, Mr. Smith. We haven't had a chance to thank you for taking good care of us. Every morning, you welcome us in the classroom. You always teach us important and interesting things. We're proud of you, and we're proud to be members of your class.

Q: Who is Mr. Smith?
A: He is _____.

① a parent   ② a teacher   ③ a janitor
④ a principal   ⑤ a classmate

[경북 ○○중]

2. 다음 설명에 해당하는 단어는? (3점)

someone who works without being paid for it because they want to do it

① helper   ② author   ③ inventor
④ volunteer   ⑤ representative

[경기 ○○중]

3. 빈칸에 공통으로 들어갈 말로 가장 알맞은 것은? (3점)

• We come _____ with some solutions.
• I was born in Seoul, but I grew _____ in Ansan.
• When he felt like giving _____, he thought about his grandfather's safety.

① in   ② up   ③ to   ④ on   ⑤ off

[송파구 ○○중]

4. 다음 중 짝지어진 대화가 <u>어색한</u> 것은? (2점)

① A: Thank you for coming.
   B: Don't mention it.
② A: Can you water the plants?
   B: Sorry, but I can't. I'm busy.
③ A: I really appreciate everything.
   B: My pleasure.
④ A: Could you take a picture of me?
   B: Sure. No problem.
⑤ A: Can you help me with my math report?
   B: Thank you for helping me.

[충북 ○○중]

5. 다음 빈칸 (A)에 들어가기에 <u>어색한</u> 것은? (3점)

G: Can you water the plants?
B: Sure.
G: (A)_____

① I am very grateful.
② Thank you so much.
③ I really appreciate it.
④ I can't thank you enough.
⑤ I know how to thank you enough.

[동작구 ○○중]

6. 다음 우리말과 뜻이 일치하는 영어 문장을 쓰시오. 주어진 단어를 이용할 것. (4점)

이 선물은 누구를 위한 것입니까? (who, present)

답: _____

[7~8] 다음 대화를 읽고 물음에 답하시오.

Jaden: Can you do me a favor, Yuri?

Yuri: Sure. What is it, Jaden?

Jaden: Can we go shopping together for a baseball cap for a girl?

Yuri: _____(A)_____ Who is it for?

Jaden: It's for my little sister Kate.

Yuri: Oh, are you getting her a birthday gift?

Jaden: No, her birthday isn't until October.

Yuri: Then, why are you getting a baseball cap for her?

Jaden: She broke her leg while she was riding her bike last week. I just want to cheer her up.

Yuri: Oh, I see. I can go this Friday afternoon.

Jaden: That sounds perfect. Thank you.

7. 위 대화의 빈칸 (A)에 들어갈 말로 가장 알맞은 것은? (2점)

① Nothing special.

② Sorry, but I can't.

③ Yes, of course.

④ I agree with you.

⑤ Well, I don't think so.

8. 위 대화를 읽고 알 수 있는 것은? (3점)

① Kate는 Yuri와 친구이다.

② Kate의 생일은 9월이다.

③ Jaden과 Yuri는 쇼핑을 함께 할 예정이다.

④ Jaden은 Kate의 생일 선물을 미리 사기를 원한다.

⑤ Yuri는 Kate에게 야구 모자를 선물하기 원한다.

9. Arrange the following sentences in correct order. (3점)

(A) Sure. Thank you for inviting me.

(B) Nothing special. I'll just stay home and watch TV.

(C) What are you doing this weekend, Eric?

(D) I'm having a birthday party this weekend. Can you come?

① (A) - (B) - (C) - (D)

② (B) - (C) - (D) - (A)

③ (B) - (D) - (A) - (C)

④ (C) - (B) - (D) - (A)

⑤ (C) - (D) - (A) - (B)

10. 다음 〈예시〉를 참고하여 주어진 상황에 맞게 요청하는 문장을 영어로 서술하시오. (5점)

〈예시〉

Q: You need a dictionary and your classmate has one. What can you say?

A: Do you mind lending me a dictionary? or Can you lend me a dictionary? (이외에도 다른 표현 사용 가능)

(1) Q: You want to go to the museum, but don't know where it is. What can you ask someone?

　　A: _____

(2) Q: You are studying in your best friend's room, but it is hot inside. What can you ask?

　　A: _____

(1) _____

(2) _____

11. 다음 중 어법상 어색한 문장을 <u>두 개</u> 고르면? (3점)

① She is the girl who I told you about.
② This is the cell phone that I bought yesterday.
③ She is the woman whom I met her last weekend.
④ This is the watch you gave me.
⑤ A student which spoke English well helped me.

13. 다음 중에서 어법상 옳은 것을 <u>모두</u> 고른 것은? (4점)

ⓐ I bought the new book what Mr. Kim wrote.
ⓑ This is the cake who I made.
ⓒ The dress you ordered was sold out.
ⓓ I have a science project to finishing by tomorrow.
ⓔ James has few friends to talk with.
ⓕ Chinese is a language that many people speak it.
ⓖ Your drawing journal will become very more interesting.

① ⓐ, ⓒ
② ⓑ, ⓓ
③ ⓒ, ⓔ
④ ⓒ, ⓔ, ⓕ
⑤ ⓑ, ⓓ, ⓖ

12. 다음 〈보기〉의 표현을 활용하여 그림을 묘사하는 문장을 완성하시오. (5점)

<보기>
so / nice / ride a bike / I

<조건>
1. 한 칸에 한 단어씩만 쓸 것.
2. 필요한 경우 주어진 단어를 변형할 수 있음.

The weather was _____ _____ _____ _____ _____ _____ _____ in the park.

14. 다음 빈칸에 알맞은 관계대명사가 순서대로 짝지어진 것은? (3점)

ⓐ There were many things _____ Kenneth had to do.
ⓑ He is the person _____ I have been waiting for.
ⓒ I have a friend _____ lives in Japan.

	ⓐ	ⓑ	ⓒ
①	that	which	who
②	which	that	which
③	which	who	whom
④	that	who	which
⑤	that	whom	who

15. 다음 (A), (B)를 한 문장으로 바르게 연결한 것은? (2점)

(A) The cake was delicious.
(B) I bought the cake.

① The cake was delicious which I bought.
② The cake was delicious whom I bought.
③ The cake which I bought was delicious.
④ The cake whom I bought was delicious.
⑤ The cake which I bought were delicious.

[16~17] 다음 글을 읽고 물음에 답하시오.

Hi, Mom! Hi, Dad! As you know, today is my 15th birthday. I haven't had a chance to thank you for being my parents. You've truly been my friends and my teachers. Thank you for (A)_____. I'm really proud to be your daughter.

16. 위 글의 의도로 가장 알맞은 것은? (2점)

① 감사　　　② 격려　　　③ 칭찬
④ 비난　　　⑤ 경고

17. 위 글의 빈칸 (A)에 가장 알맞지 않은 것은? (3점)

① lending me your textbook
② making me happy and healthy
③ cooking delicious foods every day
④ supporting and understanding me
⑤ taking care of me when I was sick

[18~20] 다음 글을 읽고 물음에 답하시오.

Kenneth Shinozuka grew up in a big happy family of three (가)_____. Since he was little, ⓐhe has always been very close to his grandfather. He was Kenneth's first friend. ⓑhis trusty driver, and his cook. ⓒHe also taught him many life lessons. He was ⓓthe person (A)[whom / which] Kenneth respected the most in the world.
When Kenneth was four, his grandfather went out for a walk one day and got lost. He had Alzheimer's disease. Everyone in Kenneth's family (B)[was / were] in shock. His condition became (C)[better / worse] over the next 10 years. He wandered off at night so often that someone had to keep an eye on ⓔhim all night long.

18. 위 글의 문맥상 빈칸 (가)에 알맞은 말을 다음 영영풀이를 참고하여 고르면? (3점)

영영풀이: all the people in a group or country who are of a similar age　　*similar: 비슷한

① houses　　② owners　　③ members
④ conditions　　⑤ generations

19. 위 글의 ⓐ~ⓔ 중 가리키는 인물이 다른 하나는? (3점)

① ⓐ　② ⓑ　③ ⓒ　④ ⓓ　⑤ ⓔ

20. 위 글의 (A)~(C)에 들어갈 말을 골라 바르게 짝지은 것은? (4점)

	(A)	(B)	(C)
①	whom	were	better
②	whom	was	better
③	whom	was	worse
④	which	was	worse
⑤	which	were	better

[21~24] 다음 글을 읽고, 물음에 답하시오.

(A) When Kenneth was four, his grandfather went out for a walk one day and got lost. (B) Everyone in Kenneth's family was in shock. (C) His condition became worse over the next 10 years. (D) He wandered off at night so often that someone had to keep an eye _____ him all night long. (E) One night, Kenneth's grandfather got out of bed, and Kenneth saw ⓐit. At that moment, he said to himself, "Why don't I put pressure sensors _____ the heels of his socks?"

21. 위 글의 빈칸에 공통으로 들어갈 단어는? (3점)

① on   ② in   ③ over
④ out   ⑤ with

22. 위 글의 (A)~(E) 중, 다음 문장이 들어갈 가장 알맞은 곳은? (3점)

He had Alzheimer's disease.

① (A)   ② (B)   ③ (C)
④ (D)   ⑤ (E)

23. 위 글의 밑줄 친 ⓐ가 가리키는 것은? (3점)

① Kenneth's grandfather became worse.
② Kenneth's grandfather got out of bed.
③ Someone had to watch him all night long.
④ Everyone in Kenneth's family was in shock.
⑤ Kenneth's grandfather wandered off at night.

24. 위 글의 다음에 전개될 내용으로 가장 알맞은 것은? (4점)

① His grandfather was proud of Kenneth.
② He went on a trip with his grandfather.
③ He bought his grandfather lots of socks.
④ He went to see a doctor with his grandfather.
⑤ He tried to invent the socks with pressure sensors.

[25~26] 다음 글을 읽고 물음에 답하시오.

(A) He first had to create a pressure sensor and then find a way to send a signal to his smart phone.
(B) There were many things ⓐthat Kenneth had to do.
(C) Kenneth also tried many different materials to make comfortable socks for his elderly grandfather.

25. 위 글의 순서로 가장 적절한 것은? (4점)

① (A)-(B)-(C)   ② (A)-(C)-(B)
③ (B)-(A)-(C)   ④ (B)-(C)-(A)
⑤ (C)-(A)-(B)

26. 위 글의 ⓐ와 어법상 쓰임이 같은 것은? (3점)

① She loves that dress you are wearing.
② I believe that a family is more important.
③ It was so noisy that I could not sleep well.
④ This is the bag that I have been looking for.
⑤ He exercises every day so that he can stay healthy.

[27~29] 다음 글을 읽고 물음에 답하시오.

There were many things that Kenneth had to do. (A) He first had to create a pressure sensor and then find a way to send a signal to his smart phone. (B) When he felt like giving up, he thought about his grandfather's safety. (C) After much trial and error, he finally succeeded in making his device. (D) When it first worked, he was so happy that he jumped for joy. (E) He could not believe that his invention actually worked. For his grandfather, Kenneth is the best inventor in the world. For Kenneth, his grandfather is still his best friend.

27. 위 글에서 〈보기〉의 문장이 들어가기에 가장 알맞은 곳은? (3점)

<보기>

Kenneth also tried many different materials to make comfortable socks for his elderly grandfather.

① (A)　② (B)　③ (C)　④ (D)　⑤ (E)

28. What did Kenneth think about when he felt like giving up? (3점)

① He just gave up.

② He tried to make comfortable socks.

③ He thought about his grandfather's safety.

④ He discussed his inventions with his parents.

⑤ He believed that his pressure sensor would be the best invention in the world.

29. 위 글의 내용과 일치하지 <u>않는</u> 것은? (4점)

① Kenneth는 발명가이다.

② 많은 시행착오가 있었다.

③ 신호 수신기는 양말에 붙였다.

④ 할아버지를 위해 압력 감지기를 만들었다.

⑤ Kenneth는 여전히 할아버지와 최고의 친구이다.

30. What is the purpose of the girl's talk? (3점)

Hi, Mom! Hi, Dad! As you know, today is my 15th birthday. I haven't had a chance to thank you for being my parents. You've truly been my friends and my teachers. Thank you for supporting me and always trying to understand me. I'm really proud to be your daughter.

① to help her teacher

② to thank her parents

③ to teach her brother English

④ to invite her friends to a party

⑤ to help them with their homework

31. 다음 전체 문장의 맥락에 맞게 밑줄 친 부분을 영어로 쓰시오. 단, 다음의 조건을 반드시 지키시오. (5점)

Since he was little, <u>그는 그의 할아버지와 언제나 매우 가깝게 지냈다.</u>

<조건>

단어 to, always, very, be를 사용하시오. 필요할 경우 이 단어의 형태를 변형할 수 있음.

답: ＿＿＿＿＿＿＿＿＿＿＿＿＿＿＿

2학년 영어 1학기 기말고사(4과) 2회

문항수 : 선택형(27문항) 서술형(4문항)   20 . . .

반	
이름	

점수

◎ 선택형 문항의 답안은 컴퓨터용 수정 싸인펜을 사용하여 OMR 답안지에 바르게 표기하시오.
◎ 서술형 문제는 답을 답안지에 반드시 검정 볼펜으로 쓰시오.
◎ 총 31문항 100점 만점입니다. 문항별 배점은 각 문항에 표시되어 있습니다.

1. 다음 문장에서 밑줄 친 단어의 우리말 뜻이 어색한 것은? (3점)

① Thomas Edison invented the light bulb after a lot of trial and error. (재판)
② I easily get lost when I go to strange places. (길을 잃은)
③ There is a hole in the heel of my sock. (발뒤꿈치)
④ Lifestyles change through generations. (세대)
⑤ Matthew is my trusty friend. (믿음직한)

2. 다음 문장의 빈칸에 알맞은 단어는? (3점)

A _____ is a gesture, sound, or action to the person who sees or heard it.

① heel   ② sensor   ③ support
④ guess   ⑤ signal

3. 다음 빈칸에 들어가기에 어색한 것은? (2점)

"Hey boys, I need someone to clean the room with me. _____"

① Who can help me?   ② It's too dirty.
③ Any volunteers?   ④ Cheer up.
⑤ Let's do it together.

4. 다음 대화의 내용을 읽고 알 수 있는 것은? (3점)

Jaden: Can you do me a favor, Yuri?
Yuri: Sure. What is it, Jaden?
Jaden: Can we go shopping together for a baseball cap for a girl?
Yuri: Yes, of course. Who is it for?
Jaden: It's for my little sister Kate.
Yuri: Oh, are you getting her a birthday gift?
Jaden: No, her birthday isn't until October.
Yuri: Then, why are you getting a baseball cap for her?
Jaden: She broke her leg while she was riding her bike last week. I just want to cheer her up.
Yuri: Oh, I see. I can go this Friday afternoon.
Jaden: That sounds perfect. Thank you.

① Yuri는 여동생이 있다.
② Kate의 생일은 10월이다.
③ Yuri는 야구 모자를 사기를 원한다.
④ Yuri는 Jaden의 부탁을 들어 줄 수 없다.
⑤ Jaden은 여동생의 생일선물을 살 예정이다.

5. 다음 대화의 순서를 가장 적절하게 배열한 것은? (3점)

(A) Can you help me with my science project this afternoon?
(B) Kevin, can I ask a favor of you?
(C) OK. How can I help you?
(D) Sorry, but I can't. I have to visit my grandma with my mom.

① (A)-(B)-(C)-(D)
② (A)-(C)-(B)-(D)
③ (B)-(A)-(C)-(D)
④ (B)-(C)-(A)-(D)
⑤ (B)-(C)-(D)-(A)

[6~7] 다음 대화를 읽고 물음에 답하시오.

Jaden: Yuri, (A)_____
Yuri: Sure. What is it, Jaden?
Jaden: Can we go shopping together for a baseball cap for a girl?
Yuri: Yes, of course. Who is it for?
Jaden: It's for my little sister Kate.
Yuri: Oh, are you getting her a birthday gift?
Jaden: No, her birthday isn't until October.
Yuri: Then, why are you getting a baseball cap for her?
Jaden: She broke her leg while she was riding her bike last week. I just want to cheer her up.
Yuri: Oh, I see. I can go this Friday afternoon.
Jaden: That sounds perfect. Thank you.

6. 위 대화의 빈칸 (A)에 들어올 수 없는 것은?   (3점)
① I need your help.
② Can you help me?
③ What can I do for you?
④ Can you do me a favor?
⑤ Can you give me a hand?

7. 위 대화의 내용과 일치하는 것은?   (3점)
① Kate broke her arm last week.
② Yuri's birthday isn't until October.
③ Jaden had a baseball game last week.
④ Yuri can help Jaden this Friday afternoon.
⑤ Jaden wants to buy a birthday gift for Kate.

8. 대화가 자연스럽지 않은 것은?   (3점)
① A: What are you doing this weekend?
   B: Nothing special.
② A: Can you do me a favor?
   B: Sure. What is it?
③ A: What can I do for you?
   B: I can't help you with the science project.
④ A: Can you take care of my cat?
   B: Sure. Don't worry about the cat.
⑤ A: Can you water the plants this afternoon?
   B: Sorry, but I can't. I have to visit my aunt.

9. 다음 대화의 흐름상 (A)에 들어갈 말로 가장 알맞은 것은?   (3점)

A: Steve, can you do me a favor?
B: Sure. What is it?
A: My family is going on vacation for a week. (A)_____
B: Yes, I can.

① Can you swim in a river?
② Can you open the window?
③ Can you move this table with me?
④ Can you help me with my science project tomorrow?
⑤ Can you come to our house and water the plants?

10. 다음 중 어법상 올바른 문장은? (3점)

① He is the man whom wants to help us.

② That is the car whom I want to buy.

③ The dress you ordered was sold out.

④ Ms. Lee is a teacher which I respect very much.

⑤ This is the airplane which the Wright Brothers made it.

11. 다음 밑줄 친 ⓐ~ⓔ 중 어법상 어색한 것은? (3점)

Happy teacher's day, Mr. Smith! ⓐWe don't know what to say to thank you. Every morning, ⓑyou welcome us in the classroom. ⓒYou always teach important and interesting things to us. ⓓWe're proud to you, and ⓔwe're proud to be your students.

① ⓐ ② ⓑ ③ ⓒ ④ ⓓ ⑤ ⓔ

12. 다음 중 그림의 물건을 소개하는 문장을 완성할 때, 사용할 수 없는 단어는? (3점)

This is _____.

① who ② that ③ invented

④ Steve Jobs ⑤ the smart phone

13. 다음을 'so ~ that' 구문을 활용하여 아래 우리말의 의미에 맞게 영어로 문장을 서술하시오. (4점)

<예시>

He wandered off at night so often that someone had to keep an eye on him all night long.

의미: 그는 너무 행복해서 나에게 돈을 주었다. (과거형)
→ _____

→ _____

14. 다음 밑줄 친 것 중 관계대명사의 용법이 나머지 넷과 다른 하나는? (3점)

① I'm the person who you are looking for.

② Max is a singer who many Asians love.

③ My mom is a scientist who studies plants.

④ He is the boy who I met on the bus yesterday.

⑤ This is the man who I respect the most in the world.

15. 다음 두 문장을 관계대명사를 사용하여 한 문장으로 만드시오. (관계대명사를 생략하지 말 것.) (4점)

These are the cookies.
My mom made the cookies.

→ _____

[16~18] 다음을 읽고 물음에 답하시오.

Kenneth Shinozuka grew up in a big happy family of three generations. (A)_____ ⓐhe was little, he has always been very close to ⓑhis grandfather. ⓒHe was Kenneth's first friend, his trusty driver, and ⓓhis cook. He also taught ⓔhim many life lessons. He was the person (B)who Kenneth respected the most in the world.

16. 위 글의 문맥상 (A)에 들어갈 접속사로 가장 적절한 것은? (3점)
① After
② Before
③ Because
④ For
⑤ Since

17. 위 글의 밑줄 친 ⓐ~ⓔ 중 가리키는 대상이 나머지 넷과 다른 것은? (3점)
① ⓐ
② ⓑ
③ ⓒ
④ ⓓ
⑤ ⓔ

18. 위 글의 (B)who와 용법이 다른 하나는? (3점)
① This is the man who I want to help.
② This is my friend who I told you about.
③ Mr. Kim is a teacher who I like very much.
④ The man who we met yesterday is a soccer player.
⑤ She told me about her friend who had three children.

[19~20] 다음 글을 읽고 물음에 답하시오.

There were many things that Kenneth had to do. He first had to create a pressure sensor and then find a way to send a signal to his smart phone. (A) Kenneth also tried many different materials to make comfortable socks for his elderly grandfather. (B) When he felt like giving up, he thought about his grandfather's safety. (C) When it first worked, he was very happy, and he jumped for joy. (D) He could not believe that his invention actually worked. (E) For his grandfather, Kenneth is the best inventor in the world. For Kenneth, his grandfather is still his best friend.

19. 위 글의 (A)~(E) 중 다음 문장이 들어갈 곳으로 가장 적절한 것은? (4점)

After much trial and error, he finally succeeded in making his device.

① (A)
② (B)
③ (C)
④ (D)
⑤ (E)

20. 위 글의 요지로 가장 적절한 것은? (4점)
① Trial and error is the mother of invention.
② There are many people who have special talents.
③ Due to the disease of Kenneth's grandfather, Kenneth could become a great inventor.
④ Kenneth family overcame their difficulties and hardships by an unknown inventor's idea.
⑤ Thanks to Kenneth's thoughtful invention, he could keep his grandfather's safety and friendship.

[21~23] 다음 글을 읽고 물음에 답하시오.

When Kenneth was four, his grandfather went out for a walk one day and ⓐgot lost. He had Alzheimer's disease. Everyone in Kenneth's family ⓑwere in shock. His condition ⓒbecame worse over the next 10 years. He (A)wandered off at night so often that someone had to keep an eye _____ him all night long. One night, Kenneth's grandfather ⓓgot out of bed, and Kenneth saw it. At that moment, he said to himself, "Why don't I put pressure sensors ⓔon the heels of his socks?"

21. 위 글의 밑줄 친 ⓐ~ⓔ에서 어법상 어색한 것은?
(3점)

① ⓐ   ② ⓑ   ③ ⓒ

④ ⓓ   ⑤ ⓔ

22. 위 글의 밑줄 친 (A)wandered off의 우리말 뜻이 알맞은 것은?
(3점)
① 소리를 질렀다
② 돌아다녔다
③ 충격을 받았다
④ 길을 잃었다
⑤ 궁금해 했다

23. 위 글의 빈칸에 알맞은 것은?
(3점)
① by   ② for
③ from   ④ about
⑤ on

[24~25] 다음을 읽고 물음에 답하시오.

Hello, I am Kim Doha, and I would like to ㉠[join / avoid] your volunteer project. (A) One day, I saw some poor dogs on TV. (B) I like dogs, and there are ㉡[few / many] things that I can do for them. (C) I can walk the dogs, give them a bath, and play with them. (D) I am the person who you are ㉢[looking for / afraid of]! (E)

24. 위 글의 (A)~(E) 중 문맥상 다음 문장이 들어가기에 가장 적절한 곳은?
(3점)

They looked so sad that I wanted to help them.

① (A)   ② (B)   ③ (C)   ④ (D)   ⑤ (E)

25. 위 글의 문맥상 ㉠, ㉡, ㉢에 들어갈 말로 알맞게 짝지어진 것은?
(4점)

	㉠	㉡	㉢
①	join	many	looking for
②	join	few	looking for
③	join	few	afraid of
④	avoid	many	afraid of
⑤	avoid	few	afraid of

26. 다음 두 문장을 관계대명사를 사용하여 한 문장으로 만드시오. (관계대명사를 생략하지 말 것.) (4점)

The markers were sold out.
You ordered the markers.

→ _____

[27~29] 다음 글을 읽고 물음에 답하시오.

Kenneth Shinozuka grew (A)_____ in a big happy family of three generations. Since he was little, he has always been very close to his grandfather. He was Kenneth's first friend, his trusty driver, and his cook. He also taught him many life lessons. He was the person (가)[who / which] Kenneth respected the most in the world.

When Kenneth was four, his grandfather went out for a walk one day and got lost. He had Alzheimer's disease. Everyone in Kenneth's family was in shock. His condition became worse over the next 10 years. He wandered (B)_____ at night (나)[so / such] often that someone had to keep an eye (C)_____ him all night long. One night, Kenneth's grandfather got out of bed, and Kenneth saw it. At that moment, he said to (다)[him / himself], "Why don't I put pressure sensors on the heels of his socks?"

27. 빈칸 (A)~(C)에 들어갈 알맞은 단어는? (3점)

	(A)	(B)	(C)
①	on	up	to
②	up	on	off
③	up	off	on
④	in	off	on
⑤	to	in	up

28. 괄호 (가)~(다)에 들어갈 알맞은 단어는? (4점)

	(가)	(나)	(다)
①	who	such	him
②	who	so	himself
③	who	so	him
④	which	so	him
⑤	which	such	himself

29. 위 글의 Kenneth의 할아버지에 대한 설명 중 내용과 일치하지 <u>않는</u> 것은? (3점)

① 밤에 돌아다녔다.

② 길을 잃은 적이 있다.

③ 대가족을 이루고 사셨다.

④ 온종일 Kenneth를 지켜야 했다.

⑤ 10년간 건강이 악화되었다.

30. What is the purpose of this email? (3점)

To: homelessdogcare@cheongun.com
Subject: I would like to join your volunteer project.

Hello, I am John, and I would like to join your volunteer project. One day, I saw some poor dogs on TV. They looked so sad that I wanted to help them. I like dogs, and there are many things that I can do for them. I can walk the dogs, give them a bath, and play with them. I am the person who you are looking for!

① To join an art project

② To help homeless people

③ To give dogs a helping hand

④ To invite people to a project

⑤ To take care of his friend's dogs

31. 다음 글의 밑줄 친 ⓐ~ⓕ 중 어법이 어색한 <u>두</u> 곳을 바르게 고치시오. (4점)

Hi, Mom! Hi, Dad! As you know, today is my 15th birthday. I ⓐ<u>have not have</u> a chance ⓑ<u>for thank you</u> ⓒ<u>for being my parents</u>. You ⓓ<u>have truly been</u> my friends and my teachers. Thank you ⓔ<u>for supporting me</u> and always ⓕ<u>trying to understand me</u>.

(1) _____ → _____, (2) _____ → _____

정답 및 해설

Lesson 1 (중간)

1회

01 ③
02 who likes animals
   who wants to be a vet.

   who hates smoking
   who is called a princess.
03 ③ 04 ① 05 ③ 06 ③ 07 ④ 08 ③ 09 ②
10 ② 11 ⑤
12 He decided to write a graphic novel about her.
13 ②
14 (1) I listened to music while I was eating lunch.
   (2) He watched a movie after he did his homework.
15 ⑤ 16 ③ 17 ③ 18 ③ 19 ① 20 ⑤ 21 ③
22 ③ 23 ⑤ 24 ④ 25 ② 26 ④ 27 ①
28 She rides a super scooter which can fly.
29 ②

01 각각 '① 요리사, ② 가족, ③ 재능, ④ 고향, ⑤ 식당'이라는 뜻이므로 ③번 '재능'이 적절하다.

02 a person이 선행사이므로 주격 관계대명사로 <보기>에 나와 있는 who를 이용한다.

03 (C)에서 동아리 가입을 권유하고, (A)에서 못하겠다며 이유를 밝히자 (D)에서 걱정하지 말라며 다시 권유하자 (B)에서 생각해 보겠다고 하는 순서가 자연스럽다.

04 어떤 종류의 음악을 듣고 싶은지 묻는 말에 음악 듣는 것을 좋아한다는 대답은 어색하다.

05 ⓒ의 해석은 '내 그림 실력이 충분히 좋은 것 같지가 않아.'로 'good enough'는 '충분히 좋은'으로 해석된다.

06 make my day = make me happy

07 긴장하고 있다고 하자 걱정하지 말라며 격려하는 말에 훨씬 나아졌다며 고마워하는 응답이 적절하다.

08 ⓐ to ⓓ "Of course they will,"이 적절하다.

09 Mr. Kim worked as a park ranger.

10 'You're good at recycling old clothes.'라고 했다.

11 'one of+복수명사'로 '~ 중 하나'라는 뜻을 나타낸다.

12 'I should write a graphic novel about her.'라고 했다.

13 주어진 문장은 '너무 긴장돼'라는 말로 '전교생 앞에서 연설해야 한다'는 말 다음에 들어가는 것이 자연스럽다.

14 접속사 while은 두 가지 동작을 함께 하는 것을, after는 어떤 것을 먼저 한 후에 다음 것을 하는 것을 나타낸다.

15 "Do you think they'll like that?"이라는 I의 질문에 Ms. Lee는 "Of course they will"이라고 답했다.

16 ⓐ who → which[that] ⓑ seconds → second
   ⓓ worker → workers ⓔ cheerful → cheerfully

17 ⓒ의 you는 호진을 가리키지만 나머지는 모두 a woman on a scooter를 가리킨다.

18 호진이 집에 가다가 스쿠터에 탄 한 여자를 보고 몰라봤다가 학교 밖에서는 달라보였기 때문에 그녀에 대한 만화 소설을 쓰겠다고 결심하는 내용이므로 ③번이 적절하다.

19 호진은 스쿠터에 탄 한 여자를 나중에 알아 봤지만 이름을 아는지는 나와 있지 않다.

20 ① is → are, ② live → lives, ③ wear → wears, ④ who → which[that]이 적절하다.

21 책을 이 조리사님께 보여드린 후 그녀도 그것을 좋아했다고 하는 것이 자연스럽다.

22 model … on ~: ~을 본떠서 …을 만들다, one of+복수명사: ~ 중 하나

23 ⑤번의 which는 목적격 관계대명사이지만 ⓑ의 who와 나머지는 모두 주격 관계대명사이다.

24 I'll work hard for our class, so please vote for me. 라고 했다.

25 (A) a car가 선행사이므로 which, (B) the girl and her dog이 선행사이므로 that, (C) a brother가 선행사이므로 who가 적절하다.

26 '~하는 동안'이라는 의미로, 두 가지 일이 동시에 일어나고 있을 때 사용하는 시간의 접속사 While이 적절하다.

27 'she was one of the cafeteria workers at school'이라고 했다.

28 a super scooter를 선행사로 하고 주격 관계대명사 which를 이용한다.

29 (B)에서 무엇을 하는지 묻자 (D)에서 답하고 (A)에서 칭찬하자 (C)에서 고맙다고 하는 순서가 자연스럽다.

Lesson 1 (중간)

> 01 ① 02 ④ 03 You just made my day. 04 ④
> 05 ⑤ 06 ③ 07 ② 08 ② 09 ②, ③ 10 ④
> 11 can't you
> 12 만화가 매우 재미있다. / 독특한 등장인물들을 가지고 있다.
> 13 You are good at drawing. 14 ③ 15 ③ 16 ③
> 17 She rides a super scooter which can fly.
> 18 ③ 19 ① 20 ①
> 21 Ms. Park won a dancing contest. Mr. Kim was once an adventurous park ranger.
> 22 ④ 23 ④ 24 ② 25 ② 26 ④ 27 ① 28 ②
> 29 ③ 30 ③ 31 ⑤

01 마지막 부분의 'I'll work hard for our class, so please vote for me.'로 보아 class president가 적절하다.

02 Jaden이 'I don't think my drawing skills are good enough.'라고 하는 것으로 보아 Jaden은 본인의 그림 실력에 만족하지 못한다.

03 make my day: 나를 기쁘게[행복하게] 해 주다

04 수학을 잘한다면서 '넌 어때?'라고 묻고 있는데, '나도.'라고 대답한 후에 '수학은 나한테 너무 어려워.'라고 하는 것은 어색하다.

05 (c)에서 내일이 나의 엄마의 생일이라고 언급하고 (d)에서 케이크를 구우라는 제안을 하자 (a)에서 좋은 생각이라고 대답하고 (b)에서 너의 엄마가 좋아하실 거라고 마무리하는 순서가 적절하다.

06 첫 번째 빈칸에는 a bag을 선행사로 하는 주격 관계대명사가 필요하므로 which나 that, 두 번째 빈칸에는 the girl을 선행사로 하는 주격 관계대명사가 필요하므로 who나 that이 적절하다.

07 첫 번째 빈칸에는 be good at(~을 잘하다)의 at, 두 번째 빈칸에는 장소를 나타내는 전치사 at이 적절하다.

08 (A)의 that은 박 조리사님이나 김 선생님 같은 분들에 관한 슈퍼히어로로 이야기를 쓰는 것을 가리킨다.

09 ⓑ는 Mr. Kim이 주어이므로 was, ⓒ는 would like 다음에는 to부정사가 나오므로 to write가 적절하다.

10 위 글에서 Ms. Lee의 특별한 재능에 관한 언급은 없다.

11 부가의문문은 앞이 긍정이면 부정으로 쓰고, 주어는 항상 대명사로 쓰며, 조동사가 있으면 그 조동사를 이용하여 축약형으로 써야 하므로 can't you가 적절하다.

12 Yuri는 'Your cartoons are really funny, and you have unique characters.(네 만화는 정말 재미있어. 독특한 등장인물들도 있고 말이야.)'라고 말하고 있다.

13 'be good at(~을 잘하다)'을 이용하여 영작하는 것이 적절하다.

14 (A) like의 목적어로 to make, (B) '~하는 동안'을 의미하는 While, (C) 'one of+복수 명사'이므로 workers가 적절하다.

15 ⓒ의 you는 a woman이지만 나머지는 모두 Hojin이다.

16 G가 'I hope my mom will like my cake.'라고 했으므로 확신을 표현하는 ③번이 적절하다.

17 a super scooter를 선행사로 해야 하므로 which를 이용하는 것이 적절하다.

18 ⓒ가 있는 문장의 주어는 She이며 앞에 makes가 나와 있으므로 병렬 관계로 연결하여 gives가 적절하다.

19 1분이 아니라 1초에 100개의 쿠키를 만든다.

20 주어진 문장의 She와 it이 가리키는 것이 (A) 앞에 나온 Ms. Lee와 my book이므로 (A)가 적절하다.

21 (B) 다음에 나오는 내용을 쓰는 것이 적절하다.

22 'Do you think they'll like that?'에 대한 답으로 반복되는 부분을 생략한 것이다.

23 In her 30s: 30대에

24 ① while you are away, ③ after you clean your room, ④ after I met, ⑤ While she was traveling

25 ②는 접속사이고, (A)와 나머지는 모두 관계대명사이다.

26 ⓐ rides ⓑ danger ⓒ to ⓔ to my friends

27 model+목적어+on[after, upon]: (~을) 따라 만들다, 본뜨다

28 "I see you at the school cafeteria every day."라고 했다.

29 (A) like의 목적어로 to부정사나 동명사, (B) every day로 보아 현재의 습관을 말하는 것으로 현재시제인 see, (C) looks의 보어로 형용사 different가 적절하다.

30 ① Ms. Lee의 친구가 몇 명인지는 나와 있지 않다. ② Ms. Park이 춤 경연 대회에서 우승했다. ④ Hojin은 Ms. Park에 관한 슈퍼히어로로 이야기를 쓰고 싶어 한다. ⑤ 본문에는 언급이 없다.

31 ⑤는 선행사가 my friend's house이므로 that이나 which가 적절하다.

Lesson 2 (중간)

01 ⑤ 02 ⑤
03 I have done volunteer work to help the poor for
   two years.
04 ③ 05 ④ 06 ④ 07 ⑤ 08 ① 09 ④
10 (1) I have been a big fan of Harry Potter since I was
   a child. (2) I have known my best friend Minji for
   three years.
11 ⑤ 12 ③ 13 ② 14 ⑤ 15 ④ 16 ④ 17 ③
18 ① 19 ② 20 ④ 21 ③ 22 ② 23 ① 24 ①
25 (2), They are the roofs of the big round houses of
   the Hakka people.
26 ⑤ 27 ④ 28 ② 29 ①
30 that[who] had a house without a roof
31 ⑤ 32 ②

01 ⑤번은 '100-1000'으로 둘 다 숫자를 나타내지만 나머지는 모두 앞의 단어가 뒤의 단어를 포함하는 관계이다.

02 식당이 있는지 묻는 주어진 말에 이어 '어떤 음식을 좋아하는지' 묻는 (C)가 나오고, (B) '이탈리아 음식을 좋아한다'고 답하자, (D) 4층에 있다고 하고, (A) 감사하는 순서가 적절하다.

03 ~ ago는 현재완료 시제와 함께 쓸 수 없으므로 'two years ago'를 'for two years'로 고치는 것이 적절하다.

04 '그렇다'고 하면서 '모든 방이 정원이 보인다'고 답하고 있으므로 '정원이 보이는 방이 있는지' 묻는 것이 적절하다.

05 ① 게스트 하우스에서 일어나는 대화이다. ② 손님은 이틀 밤을 묵을 예정이다. ③ 모든 방은 침대가 없고 정원을 볼 수 있다. ⑤ 아침 식사는 식당에서 할 수 있다.

06 '어떤 음악을 듣고 싶은지' 묻는 질문에 '애완견을 갖고 싶다'는 대답은 어색하다.

07 틀린 것이 없이 적절하게 쓰인 글이다.

08 'each+단수 명사+단수 동사', 'each of the+복수 명사'가 되어야 한다.

09 '2층에 있다'고 했고 '드레스와 청바지 사이에 있다'고 했으므로 ④번이 적절하다.

10 (1) 'be'가 주어졌으므로 'I have been'으로 시작하여 'a fan of'를 이용하여 쓴다. (2) 'know'가 주어졌으므로 'I have known'으로 시작하여 'my best friend'를 이용하여 쓴다.

11 '모든 방이 정원이 보인다'고 했다.

12 'for the last two years'가 있으므로 현재완료 시제가 적절하며 공부하는 것이므로 능동태여야 한다.

13 (A) 현재완료 시제이므로 seen, (B) 'for a long time'이 있으므로 현재완료 시제가 적절하다.

14 people을 가리키므로 Norwegians(노르웨이 사람들)가 적절하다.

15 추운 겨울이 얼마나 긴지는 알 수 없다.

16 (A) 선행사가 roofs이므로 that이나 which, (B) 'about a thousand years'라는 기간 명사구가 나오므로 for (C) 목적어가 주어와 같은 대상이므로 재귀대명사 themselves, (D) 'each+단수 명사'이므로 house가 적절하다.

17 The houses have only one gate without any windows on the first floor.라고 했다.

18 노르웨이의 잔디 지붕에 관한 글이다.

19 (A)의 they가 가리키는 것은 people이다. 각각 ⓐ roofs ⓑ people ⓒ roofs ⓓ animals ⓔ at the roofs를 가리킨다.

20 집 이야기를 하다가 갑자기 '신발을 신고 싶지 않다.'는 말은 어울리지 않는다.

21 ⓒ는 tax collectors이고 나머지는 모두 some people이다.

22 세금 징수원들이 마을에 오면, 사람들이 재빨리 지붕을 무너뜨렸다가 그들이 떠나면, 다시 돌을 쌓아 올렸으므로 '재빨리 지붕을 부수기'가 적절하다.

23 avoid: to stay away from something

24 높은 세금을 피하려고 어떤 사람들은 돌을 쌓아 올려 원뿔 모양의 지붕을 지었다는 것이므로 원뿔 모양의 지붕이 적절하다.

25 '지붕의 집'이 아니라 '집의 지붕'이라는 것이 적절하다.

26 1층에는 부엌이, 2층에는 창고가 있다.

27 각각 ⓐ take them down ⓑ paid ⓒ by piling ⓔ piled up이 적절하다.

28 지붕은 집의 필수적인 부분이라고 하는 것이 적절하다.

29 '수백 년 전 남부 이탈리아에서는, 지붕이 없는 집을 가진 사람들이 더 적은 세금을 냈다.'라고 했고 '세금 징수원들이 마을에 오면, 사람들은 재빨리 지붕을 무너뜨렸다. 세금 징수원들이 떠나면, 그들은 다시 돌을 쌓아 올렸다.'라고 했다.

30 people이 선행사이므로 that이나 who를 쓰고 '~이 없는'은 without을 이용한다.

31 주어진 문장의 then이 가리키는 것이 2013년이므로 (E)가 적절하다.

32 (A) 전치사 by의 목적어로 동명사 piling, (B) 과거 시제이므로 piled가 적절하다.

Lesson 2 (중간)

01 ③	02 ②	03 ③	04 ①	05 ④	06 ②	07 ④

08 where can I find men's shoes (store)?   09 ④

10 ②	11 ③	12 out of		13 ④	14 ④ 15 ③
16 ②	17 ①	18 ①	19 ②	20 ⑤	21 ④

22 (A) that[which] ⓐ They: the Hakka people

23 is	24 ③	25 ④	26 ④	27 ③	28 ①	29 ④
30 ④						

01 각각 ① animals ② harmony ④ strong ⑤ meals가 적절하다.

02 ride-rode-ridden이 적절하다.

03 <보기>와 ③번은 '경험' 용법이다. ① 결과 ② 결과 ④ 계속 ⑤ 완료

04 전체적으로 집에 관한 이야기를 하고 있다.

05 (A) women's shoes는 3층에 있으므로 third, (B) watches는 1층에 있으므로 first가 적절하다.

06 'You can have breakfast in the dining room, next to the kitchen.'이라는 답으로 보아 아침을 어디서 먹는지 묻는 질문이 적절하다.

07 'Every room in our house has a garden view'라고 했다.

08 '2층에 있고 엘리베이터 옆에 있다'고 답했으므로 '남성용 신발이 어디에 있는지' 묻는 질문이 적절하다.

09 안내 데스크에서 하는 대화인지는 알 수 없다.

10 ⓐ 현재완료 시제로 seen(경험), ⓑ 현재완료 시제로 built(계속), ⓒ to부정사로 build(~하기 위하여: 목적)가 적절하다.

11 in harmony with: ~와 조화를 이루어, cover A with B: A를 B로 덮다

12 out of: ~에서(= from)

13 전치사 by 다음에 by의 목적어로 동명사 piling이 적절하다.

14 세금 징수원들이 오면 무너뜨렸다가 떠나면 다시 쌓아 올렸다고 했으므로 '더 적은 세금을 내기 위해서'임을 알 수 있다.

15 ⓐ 완료, ⓑ 결과, ⓒ 계속, ⓓ 경험, ⓔ 완료, ⓕ 계속

16 세금 징수원들이 마을에 오면, 사람들이 재빨리 지붕을 무너뜨렸다가 그들이 떠나면, 다시 돌을 쌓아 올렸으므로 '쉽게 지붕을 부수기'가 적절하다.

17 노르웨이의 잔디 지붕에 관한 글이다.

18 잔디 지붕은 사람들을 보호하기 위한 것이다.

19 하늘에서 보면 하카족의 큰 도넛처럼 생긴 크고 둥근 집의 지붕에 관한 글이다.

20 '약 천 년간 이와 같은 집에 살아왔다.'라고 했다.

21 무슨 일이 어떻게 왜 일어났는지 설명하기 위해 원인과 결과의 관계를 논리적으로 풀어 쓴 글이다.

22 (A) 'round roofs'를 선행사로 하는 주격 관계대명사가 필요하므로 that이나 which가 적절하다. ⓐ의 They는 바로 앞 문장에 나오는 'the Hakka people'을 가리킨다.

23 each 다음에는 단수 명사와 단수 동사가 나온다.

24 '부수기 위한 지붕을 지었다'는 주어진 글에 이어 (B)에서 수백 년 전 지붕이 없는 집을 가진 사람들이 더 적은 세금을 내는 것을 설명하고 (A)에서 그 결과로 세금을 피하기 위한 원뿔 모양의 지붕을 짓고 (D)에서 세금 징수원들이 마을에 오면, 재빨리 지붕을 무너뜨렸다가 (C)에서 그들이 떠나면, 다시 돌을 쌓아 올렸다는 순서가 적절하다.

25 상대방의 '의향을 묻고' 그에 대해 '답하고' 있다.

26 중국 남부 일부 지역의 큰 도넛처럼 생긴 하카족의 크고 둥근 집의 지붕에 관한 글이다.

27 'storage rooms on the second floor'라고 했다.

28 '보호하기 위하여'를 '보호하기 원했기 때문에'로 쓸 수 있으므로 because가 적절하다.

29 ① 3 → 4 ② 한국 → 중국 ③ 동물 → 적 ⑤ 창문 → 없음

30 'each+단수 명사, 단수 동사', '형/부+enough'가 적절하다.

Lesson 3 (기말)

01 ③	02 ④	03 ④, ⑤	04 ①	05 ③

06 pack	07 ⑤	08 ⑤	09 ①	10 ②	11 ③
12 ③	13 ①	14 ③	15 will remain a mystery		
16 ④	17 ③	18 ②	19 ⑤	20 staying → to stay	
21 ③					

22 (1) we → us, It is dangerous for us to swim in the sea. (2) for → of, It was very nice of him to give us a gift. (3) talking → talk, It is fun to talk with you.

23 ④	24 ⑤	25 ⑤	26 ③	27 ②	28 ④

29 (1) It is difficult to become a fashion designer.
(2) This is the best season to visit India.

30 was, way, to, capture   31 ①   32 ②   33 ④

34 ④   35 ①

01 ① 초상, 초상화 ② 일지, 일기 ③ 접시 ④ 물건, 물체, 사물 ⑤ (힌두교·불교에서 신의) 화신, (컴퓨터의) 아바타

02 (a) weather forecast: 일기 예보 (b) expect: 예상하다

03 음식 중에는 '마실 수' 없는 것도 있으므로 ④는 어울리지 않는다. take도 어울리지 않는다. try와 have 모두 '먹다' 라는 뜻으로 쓰일 수 있다.

04 in fact = actually: 사실

05 be planning to = be going to: ~할 예정이다

06 '여행을 위해 상자나 가방에 물건을 넣다'라는 의미로 pack(싸다, 꾸리다)가 적절하다.

07 뒤에서 'I've only tried Indian curry'라고 했으므로 긍정의 답이 적절하며 현재완료 시제로 물었으므로 have 를 이용하여 답한다.

08 ⓓ에서 특별한 곳에 갔는지 경험을 묻고 ⓑ에서 긍정의 답을 하며 ⓐ에서 그곳의 날씨를 묻고 ⓒ에서 답하는 순서가 적절하다.

09 ①은 do가 들어가지만 나머지는 모두 play가 들어간다.

10 'it's not going to rain today'라고 했다.

11 비가 안 올 것이라고 했는데 우산이 필요하다는 것은 어색하다.

12 Anna는 Sydney에서 일 년간 살았다고 하면서 날씨에 대해 여러 가지를 알려주고 있다.

13 ⓐ와 ①: 형용사적 용법 ②, ⑤ 명사적 용법(진주어) ③ 명사적 용법(목적어) ④ 부사적 용법(목적)

14 스톤헨지 방문에 관한 내용에서 '완벽한 그림을 그리려고 하지 마.'라는 말은 전체 흐름과 관계 없다.

15 생략된 that절에서 주어로 Stonehenge가 나와 있으므로 동사 'will remain'을 쓰고 보어로 'a mystery'를 쓴다.

16 ⓓ는 글쓴이의 오빠(brother)이지만 나머지는 모두 글쓴이이다.

17 be busy ~ing: ~하느라 바쁘다

18 앞 문장의 '결과'가 이어지고 있으므로 결과를 이끄는 접속사가 적절하다.

19 아침에 코츠월드 주변을 걸어 다녔다.

20 decide는 to부정사를 목적어로 받는다.

21 가주어 It을 쓰고, 'a lot of fun'을 was의 보어로 쓴 후, 진주어로 'to try new things'를 쓴다.

22 (1) 의미상의 주어로 'for+목적격'을 쓴다. (2) 성격을 나타내는 형용사 nice가 나왔으므로 의미상의 주어로 'of+목적격'을 쓴다. (3) 진주어로 to부정사를 쓴다.

23 It is impossible to live without air.

24 여행을 기록한 글이다.

25 ⓔ의 this는 'the famous olive tree'를 가리키지만 나머지는 모두 'Christ Church College'를 가리킨다.

26 (A) 뒤에 '이유'를 나타내는 말이 나오므로 since가 적절하다. (B) 건물 밖으로 나와서 올리브 나무를 만진 것이므로 After나 When이 적절하다.

27 ① It is not easy to raise pets. ③ It is important for him to pass the exam. ④ It is true that Jin likes Suji. ⑤ It is nice to go out with friends on weekend.

28 현재완료는 'have+과거분사'이다. rode는 ride의 과거형이다.

29 (1) it을 가주어로 쓰고 'to become ~'을 진주어로 쓴다. (2) to visit이 the best season을 수식하도록 쓴다.

30 'to capture'가 'a great way'를 수식하도록 쓴다.

31 set foot: 들어서다, 발을 들여놓다

32 (A) on (B) from (C) to (D) for

33 가주어 It을 쓰고 'just amazing'을 was의 보어로 쓴 후 진주어 'to see the ring of huge stones'를 쓴다.

34 'How did those huge stones get there thousands of years ago?'라고 한 후 'I guess Stonehenge will remain a mystery for a long time.'라고 했으므로, 어떻게 도달하였는지 글쓴이는 '모른다.'

35 ⓐ, ⓒ 형용사적 용법 ⓑ 부사적 용법 ⓓ 명사적 용법

Lesson 3 (기말)

01 ③ **02** ② **03** ③ **04** (1) quite (2) forecast
05 ① **06** ④ **07** ② **08** ③ **09** ① **10** fall
11 ① **12** ③ **13** ⑤ **14** ④ **15** ⑤ **16** ① **17** ③
18 ③ **19** It is important to find your dream.
20 ⑤ **21** ④ **22** a popular place to stay **23** ④
24 It was just amazing to see the ring of huge stones.
25 to talk with **26** ② **27** ① **28** ④
29 (1) was very kind of him to help me
(2) It is important to exercise regularly.
30 ⑤ **31** ②
32 Watching movies is a good way to learn English.
33 It is easy to catch a cold in the winter.
34 ⑤ **35** ③

01 날씨에 관한 정보를 알려주고 있다.

02 뒤에서 'Yes'라고 했으므로 현재완료의 '경험'을 묻는 질문이므로 ever가 적절하다.

03 인도 음식이 어땠는지 묻는 질문에 대한 답으로 ③번이 적절하다.

04 (1) '매우, 완전히, 정말로'의 뜻을 갖는 quite, (2) '기대할 수 있는 미래의 일에 대한 언급'의 뜻을 갖는 forecast

가 적절하다.

05 'I liked it a lot,'이라고 했으므로 ①번이 적절하다.

06 영하 15도이므로 매우 추운 날씨라고 할 수 있다.

07 시드니의 4월 날씨에 대해 대화하고 있다.

08 '전에' 간 적이 있는지 묻고 있다.

09 plan은 to부정사와 쓰여 '~할 계획이다' 정도의 뜻으로 쓰인다.

10 autumn = fall: 가을

11 '약한 추측'을 나타내는 조동사는 may이다. must는 '~임에 틀림없다'라는 뜻으로 '강한 추측'의 의미이다.

12 'No, I haven't.'로 답해야 한다.

13 (D)에서 우산이 필요한지 묻고 (B)에서 일기 예보를 확인하겠다고 한 후 (C)에서 비가 안 올 거라고 답하고 (A)에서 감사하는 순서가 적절하다.

14 뒤에서 'don't forget to take your hat and wear sunblock when you leave home'라고 했으므로 'sunny'를 유추할 수 있다.

15 It(= Stonehenge)이 놀라게 하는 것이므로 ⓔamazing이 적절하다.

16 (A)의 got to는 '~에 도착했다'의 의미이다.

17 'After a two-hour drive'라고 했다.

18 '오후에 비가 예상된다'고 했으므로 '우산을 가져가라'고 하는 것이 적절하다.

19 'It'을 가주어로 하고 'to find ~'를 진주어로 하여 문장의 뒤쪽에 쓴다.

20 ① 오후 → 아침 ② 나 → 엄마 ③ 하루 종일 → 오후 ④ 너무 많이 먹어서 저녁 식사 때는 아무것도 먹을 수가 없었다.

21 be busy -ing: ~하느라 바쁘다

22 popular가 place를 앞에서 수식하도록 하고 to stay로 형용사적 용법으로 수식하도록 한다.

23 그것들은 무엇을 위한 것이었을까?

24 가주어 It을 쓰고 과거이므로 was를 쓴 다음에 보어로 'just amazing'을 쓴 후 진주어로 to부정사 'to see the ring of huge stones'를 쓴다.

25 'to talk'가 friends를 수식하도록 하고 함께 말하는 것이므로 전치사 with를 빠뜨리지 않도록 주의한다.

26 (A) Last week이 있으므로 went, (B) 절이 이어지므로 While, (C) '본 것'과 '놀란 것'이 같은 시점이므로 to see가 적절하다.

27 'The owner invited us for afternoon tea today.'라고 했다.

28 ① set foot: 들어서다, 발을 들여놓다 ② remain: 여전

히 ~이다, 남아 있다 ③ B&B: Bed and Breakfast ⑤ plate: 접시, 그릇

29 'It'을 가주어로 하고 to부정사를 진주어로 하여 쓴다.

30 (A) since 이하로 보아 현재완료 시제 has become, (B) 주어가 'Harry and everyone else'이므로 eat, (C) I can't wait: 빨리 ~하고 싶다

31 'Harry and everyone else eat dinner at the Hall of Christ Church.'라고 했다.

32 'to learn'이 'a good way'를 수식하도록 한다.

33 'to catch'로 하여 진주어가 되도록 쓴다.

34 'to capture'가 a great way를 수식하도록 해야 한다.

35 That was a great way to capture all the special moments.

Lesson 4 (기말) 1회

01 ② **02** ④ **03** ② **04** ⑤ **05** ⑤
06 Who is this present for? **07** ③ **08** ③ **09** ④
10 (1) Can you tell me how I can go to the museum?
(2) Do you mind if I turn on the fan[air conditioner]?
11 ③, ⑤ **12** so nice that I rode a bike **13** ③
14 ⑤ **15** ③ **16** ① **17** ① **18** ⑤ **19** ① **20** ③
21 ① **22** ② **23** ② **24** ⑤ **25** ③ **26** ④ **27** ②
28 ③ **29** ③ **30** ②
31 he has always been very close to his grandfather.

01 매일 교실에서 반갑게 맞아주며 중요한 것들을 가르쳐 주고 학급의 일원이 된 것을 자랑스럽게 여긴다고 했으므로 '선생님'이 적절하다.

02 하고 싶어서 대가 없이 일을 하는 사람은 '자원봉사자'이다.

03 • come up with: ~을 생각해 내다 • grow up: 자라다, 성장하다 • give up: 포기하다

04 도와달라는 말에 도와줘서 고맙다는 응답은 어색하다.

05 모두 감사를 나타내는 말인데 ⑤번은 감사하는 방법을 알고 있다는 말이다. 'I don't know how to thank you enough.'라면 감사하는 표현이 된다.

06 '~를 위한'으로 for를 쓰고 의문사 Who를 문두에 쓴다.

07 뒤에 나오는 내용으로 보아 요청을 수락하는 표현이 적절하다.

08 Yuri가 'I can go this Friday afternoon.'이라고 했으므로 Jaden과 Yuri가 함께 쇼핑을 할 것임을 알 수 있다.

09 (C)에서 주말에 무엇을 할지 묻고 (B)에서 집에서 TV를

볼 거라고 답하자 (D)에서 생일 파티에 초대하고 (A)에서 초대에 감사하는 순서가 적절하다.

10 (1) 박물관에 가고 싶은데 어디에 있는지 모르므로 어떻게 박물관에 갈 수 있는지 묻는 표현이 적절하다. (2) 방이 더 우우므로 선풍기나 에어컨을 켜도 되는지 묻는 표현이 적절하다.

11 ③ She is the woman whom I met last weekend. ⑤ A student who[that] spoke English well helped me.

12 'so+형용사/부사+that(너무 ~해서 …하다)' 구문을 이용하고 시제가 과거이므로 rode로 쓰는 것에 유의한다.

13 ⓐ I bought the new book that[which] Mr. Kim wrote. ⓑ This is the cake which[that] I made. ⓓ I have a science project to finish by tomorrow. ⓕ Chinese is a language that many people speak. ⓖ Your drawing journal will become much[far, even] more interesting.

14 ⓐ things가 선행사이므로 목적격 관계대명사로 which나 that이 적절하다. ⓑ the person이 선행사이므로 목적격 관계대명사로 who나 whom 또는 that이 적절하다. ⓒ a friend가 선행사이므로 주격 관계대명사로 who나 that이 적절하다.

15 The cake을 선행사로 하여 목적격 관계대명사 which나 that을 이용한다.

16 생일을 맞아 엄마와 아빠께 감사하다는 말을 하고 있는 내용이다.

17 부모님께 감사하는 내용이 나오는 것이 적절하다. ①번은 부모님께 감사하는 내용으로 적절하지 않다.

18 어떤 모임이나 나라에서 비슷한 나이의 모든 사람은 '세대'(generations)이다.

19 ⓐ의 he는 Kenneth를 가리킨다. 나머지는 모두 그의 할아버지를 가리킨다.

20 (A) 선행사가 사람이므로 whom (B) 주어가 Everyone이므로 was (C) 뒤의 내용에서 더 나빠졌으므로 worse가 적절하다.

21 keep an eye on ~: ~을 계속 지켜보다 put A on B: B 위에 A를 놓다[붙이다]

22 주어진 문장의 He가 (B) 앞에 나오는 his grandfather를 가리키므로 (B)가 가장 적절하다. (B) 이후부터 his grandfather를 계속해서 he나 his 또는 him으로 받고 있음에 유의한다.

23 ⓐ의 it은 Kenneth가 본 것으로 할아버지가 침대에서 나온 것을 본 것이다.

24 "그의 양말 뒤꿈치에 압력 감지기를 붙이는 건 어떨까"라고 혼잣말을 했다고 했으므로 압력 감지기가 있는 양말에 대한 이야기가 나오는 것이 적절하다.

25 (B)에서 할 일이 많다고 한 후에 (A)에서 할 일을 설명하고 (C)에서 also로 추가하는 순서가 적절하다.

26 ⓐ와 ④: 목적격 관계대명사 ① 지시형용사 ②, ③, ⑤ 접속사

27 주어진 문장의 also로 보아 앞에 비슷한 내용이 나왔음을 알 수 있다. (B) 앞에 비슷한 내용이 나왔으므로 (B)가 적절하다.

28 Kenneth는 포기하고 싶었을 때, 그의 할아버지의 안전에 대해 생각했다.

29 신호 수신기에 대한 언급은 본문에 나오지 않는다.

30 생일을 맞아 부모님께 감사의 말을 전하는 글이다.

31 Since(~이래로)가 나와 있으므로 완료 시제로 쓰는 것이 적절하다. 이때 always를 have 동사와 과거분사 사이에 쓰는 것이 일반적이다.

Lesson 4 (기말) 2회

```
01 ①   02 ⑤   03 ④   04 ②   05 ④   06 ③   07 ④
08 ③   09 ⑤   10 ③   11 ④   12 ①
13 He was so happy that he gave me money.   14 ③
15 These are the cookies which[that] my mom made.
16 ⑤   17 ⑧   18 ⑤   19 ③   20 ⑤   21 ②   22 ②
23 ⑤   24 ②   25 ①
26 The markers which[that] you ordered were sold out.
27 ③   28 ②   29 ④   30 ③
31 ⓐ have → had, ⓑ for → to
```

01 trial and error는 '시행착오'라는 뜻으로 여기서 trial은 '시도' 정도의 뜻이다.

02 '그것을 보거나 듣는 사람에게 보내는 몸짓, 소리 또는 행동'은 'signal(신호)'이다.

03 모두 청소하려는데 도움을 요청하면서 쓸 수 있으나 ④번은 '기운 내.'라는 뜻으로 어울리지 않는다.

04 'her birthday isn't until October'에서 10월임을 짐작할 수 있다.

05 (B)에서 부탁해도 되는지 묻고 (C)에서 좋다며 어떻게 도와줄지 묻고 (A)에서 오후에 과학 숙제를 도와달라고 하자 (D)에서 할머니를 뵈러 가야 한다고 거절하는 것이 자연스럽다.

06 모두 도움을 요청하는 말이지만 ③번은 도움을 주겠다는 말이므로 어색하다.

07 ① 팔이 아니라 다리가 부러졌다. ② Yuri가 아니라 Kate의 생일이다. ③ Jaden이 지난주에 야구를 했는지는 나와 있지 않다. ⑤ 생일 선물이 아니다.

08 '무엇을 도와드릴까요?'라고 묻는데 '나는 도와줄 수 없다.'라고 답하는 것은 어색하다.

09 일주일간 가족 휴가를 가면서 부탁하는 말로 ⑤번이 적절하다.

10 ① He is the man who wants to help us.
② That is the car which[that] I want to buy.
④ Ms. Lee is a teacher whom I respect very much.
⑤ This is the airplane which the Wright Brothers made.

11 be proud of: ~을 자랑으로 여기다

12 the smart phone that Steve Jobs invented

13 so와 that 사이에 happy를 쓰고 결과를 나타내는 he gave me money를 쓴다.

14 ③번은 주격 관계대명사이고 나머지는 모두 목적격 관계대명사이다.

15 cookies를 선행사로 하여 목적격 관계대명사 which나 that을 이용하여 한 문장으로 만든다.

16 이어지는 절에서 완료시제가 나오므로 Since가 적절하다.

17 ⓐ의 he가 Kenneth이므로 이후부터 Kenneth를 대입해서 읽어보면 ⓒ의 He는 Kenneth의 grandfather임을 알 수 있다.

18 (B)의 who는 목적격 관계대명사이다. ⑤번은 주격 관계대명사이며 나머지는 모두 목적격 관계대명사이다.

19 (C) 다음의 문장에 있는 it이 가리키는 것이 주어진 문장의 his device이므로 (C)에 들어가는 것이 적절하다.

20 Kenneth의 발명으로 인해 할아버지께서 안전하고 할아버지는 여전히 Kenneth의 가장 친한 친구라는 내용의 글이다.

21 주어가 Everyone이므로 단수 동사 was가 적절하다.

22 wander off: 돌아다니다, 헤매다

23 keep an eye on: ~을 계속 지켜보다

24 주어진 문장의 They가 (B) 앞 문장의 some poor dogs를 가리키므로 (B)가 적절하다.

25 ㉠에는 뒤에서 불쌍한 개들을 위해 본인이 할 수 있는 일들을 언급하고 있으므로 join이 적절하다. few는 '거의 없는'이라는 부정의 뜻이므로 ㉡에는 many가 적절하다. ㉢에는 사람을 두려워하는 것이 아니라 찾는 것이므로

looking for가 적절하다.

26 The markers를 선행사로 하여 목적격 관계대명사 which나 that을 이용한다.

27 (A) grow up: 자라다, 성장하다 (B) wander off: 돌아다니다, 헤매다 (C) keep an eye on ~: ~을 계속 지켜보다

28 (가) the person이 선행사이므로 who가 적절하다. (나) so+형/부+that: 너무 ~해서 …하다 (다) say to oneself: 혼잣말하다

29 누군가가 Kenneth의 할아버지를 밤새 지켜보아야 했다.

30 개들을 돕기 위해 자원봉사에 참여하고 싶다는 내용의 글이다. give a helping hand: ~를 도와주다

31 ⓐ 완료형은 'have+(not)+과거분사'이다. ⓑ to부정사로 앞의 명사 a chance를 수식하도록 해야 한다.